JOWETT'S

NATIONALISED RAILWAY ATLAS

of Great Britain and Ireland

JOWETT'S

NATIONALISED RAILWAY ATLAS

of Great Britain and Ireland

with the privatised situation as at the 31st December 1993

Alan Jowett

Atlantic Publishers, Trevithick House, West End, Penryn, Cornwall, TR10 8HE

First published 2000

ISBN : 0 906899 99 0

A catalogue record for this book is available from the British Library.

Reproduction and printing by The Amadeus Press Ltd, Cleckheaton, West Yorkshire.

CONTENTS

AUTHOR'S INTRODUCTION

Following the privatisation of the railway network of Great Britain, it appeared appropriate to compile a companion volume to my original atlas, Jowett's Railway Atlas. Whereas the first atlas concentrated on the pre-grouping period, this volume will focus on both the start and end of nationalisation.

It is well known that the vesting date for the nationalisation of Britain's railways was the 1st of January 1948, but the position in Ireland was very different. The start of public ownership in the Emerald Isle was dependent upon the domicile of the owning company in addition to its actual location. However it has been possible in dealing with Ireland to show both the position as at 1st. January 1948 and its subsequent nationalisation.

But selecting a terminal date has been more difficult. In Great Britain privatisation has been a process which is still continuing, whilst it has not started in any part of Ireland. After consideration the date selected has been the 31st December 1993. The temptation to utilise the end of 1997, making nationalisation a period of precisely fifty years had to be resisted.

Once again the map sources mainly utilised have been those of the Railway Clearing House, although these have needed to be up-dated. The more recent maps utilised have need careful checking as often a map will show passenger stations which had closed as long as twenty years earlier whilst often recently opened stations were not shown. However, in this respect, one needs to bear in mind that map use was in calculating goods rates, and most early passenger closures were not closures for goods. Also many later openings were for passenger purposes only, so this information, or the lack of it was not relevant to the users.

The primary objective of this atlas is to show clearly, the railway network of Great Britain and Ireland and its passenger stations during the period of public ownership. This period has been defined above, whilst the intricacies of Irish nationalisation are examined and explained opposite the appropriate map index sheet, page X.

By using different styles of station indication it has been possible to distinguish the London Underground, Glasgow Subway and the various modern Metro systems. However some of these latter, classed as trams or supertrams MAY be omitted. Private railways are also often shown together with re-opened sections of line which are usually referred to as preserved lines.

Lines which were closed during the grouping are shown, together with those lines which had been reduce to goods only within the grouping period but had previously carried a passenger service. Sometimes lines which lost passenger service or all services a little earlier are shown, but lines which have always carried goods only services are not usually distinguished. The reason for this treatment is so that, a glance at the map will show what has been lost during the grouping period. The atlas also shows, again in distinctive style, the planned future development showing new lines and stations and identifying previously closed stations scheduled to reopen.

Another landmark event profoundly affecting the industry on mainland Great Britain was the notorious Beeching Report. Every station scheduled for closure in the report has its gazetteer entry distinctly designated. In addition the stations proposed for closure before the report was formulated are distinguished. There was no precise parallel to Beeching in Ireland, but the strange situation of Irish nationalisation played an earlier but equivalent part in decimating the railways of the Emerald Isle. This was particularly the case when a railway was shared between North and South as will be evident from a study of MAP 1.

Another item covered on the facing pages gazetteers is opening and closing dates if within the period covered by the atlas. However this information has had to be restricted to the principal of such dates and does not include seasonal openings, occasional use after closure, or official closure occuring long after regular services ceased. In these cases a general indication of the situation may be given (see key to station types on page ix). The stations shown in the atlas are those to be found in Bradshaw, or the appropriate BR timetable for later years. However some stations had the service suspended according to Bradshaw and will not be included, whilst on the other hand there were many unofficial and untimetable halts or stopping places used by miners, workers, golfers and others. These stopping places are included in the atlas, even though some of them were illegal, provided they could be accurately located and there was clear evidence of useage within the terminal dates of the atlas.

Attention has also been given to name changes. The map shows the name as at the 31st December 1947, or later opening, whilst the gazetteer will show this name, and if appropriate, the name as at the end of 1993 or earlier closure. This does mean that any other changes may not be recorded. Irish stations can be treated differently. If a station has both an Irish and English name, the former will often have been used from the 1920's, although modern useage is to use both names indiscriminately. The atlas therefore uses the English name on the map, but the Irish name will be gazetteered. On some maps, where space permits both names may be on the map. Where just a portion of the title has been dropped, this can be shown in the gazetteer without the need of a second entry. Many station suffixes were never part of the official title but were used by Bradshaw to distinguish the station for the user. These suffixes are not used on the maps or gazetteers unless needed to distinguish stations on the same page. But these suffixes are used in the station index.

A final matter relative to names is the use of word 'Halt' as part of the title. In this connection there is a difference between a place being called a halt and actually being one, or there can be. Additionally there is a similar but not so usual suffix 'Platform'. A large number of 'Halts' were opened in the 20's and 30's and the purpose was to have a stopping place which was unstaffed, helping the railway to compete with road competition. 'Platforms' were the same but where a company had both halts and platforms, the latter tended to be distinguished by having a small staff. But in the wake of nationalisation and the need to economise on staffing costs, many small wayside station lost their staff. Initially nothing happened although in many cases the loss of staff was but a prelude to closure, but in other cases after a period as a halt, 'Halt' would become part of the station title. This policy continued until about 1962-3 after which with unstaffed stations or halts becoming more numerous, the policy of making unstaffed stations 'Halts' was discontinued with both new and existing stations. The final outcome of this process took place during the period 1969-70 when 'Halt' was officially deleted from all stopping places so named. These notes about 'Halts' does not apply in Ireland. The dates of name changes, including the 'Halt' situation, are included in the gazetteers, if known

The foregoing outline of the atlas indicates its scope relating to lines and passenger stations during the period of the nationalised railways. But where space permits some additional information is included. It should however be remembered that such additional information is only supplemental and is sometimes omitted due to both lack of space or lack of information. This additional information may include the following:

(1) Goods locations, particularly those which had been passenger stations but closed as passenger stations during the grouping period. Goods only locations tend to be concentrated in the map enlargement areas and even in these areas cover is not comprehensive.

(2) Engine Sheds as at 31·12·1947 and 31·12·93. There may be some omissions in Eastern England, but the cover for Great Britain is fairly comprehensive. There is no detailed information about Irish sheds.

(3) Tunnels are included on the following basis. If outside the central London area and still open are included if space permits. Closed tunnels: Inclusion depends on availability of information, which is governed, apart from the dictates of space, on official name being known or length.

(4) Bridges and Viaducts. There is a limited selection of these, being restricted to the well known scenic routes which remain open for passengers, for example those on the Settle - Carlisle line.

(5) Company Works. Only major locations considered for inclusion, and can be omitted due to lack of space.

(6) Junctions are only named if the name does not stem from a nearby station shown on the map. This policy has been adopted to avoid needless clutter.

(7) Summits: Inclusion depends on information available. Site is usually well known but summit heights are not always available.

Alan Jowett
Laycock
December 1997

THE FACING PAGE GAZETTEERS

Besides listing all stations and railway companies, these include many other features, some of which may be identified in code. Coded features are identified together with a note of the owning company and/or other information, eg - date closed, height of summit, length of tunnel.

In addition each feature is identified in its location on the map. The entire area covered by the maps has been divided into squares measuring 100km x 100km and allocated two letters based on the National Grid (a similar system has been assigned to Ireland). The edges of these squares are outlined in green and they are designated at their intersections on the maps. Sometimes additional green lines are drawn on the maps to make it easier to locate a feature within its square. Where the entire map is within one square the letters of the square are shown in the top left corner of the map.

Each of these large squares is then divided into 100 (10x10). In reading the reference, the eastwards figures are read first (bottom or top margin), followed by the northwards figures (side margin).

For example: DUNROBIN CASTLE Map 13 NC80

STEP 1	The map shows parts of four squares: NC, ND, NH, NJ. It is clear which part of the map is within NC
STEP 2	Go along the top (or bottom) margin to identify the eastward limits of squares 8 in NC
STEP 3	Go along the side margin to identify the limits of northward squares 0 in NC. Where the two coincide is 80 where you will find DUNROBIN CASTLE.

On some maps, at a larger scale, a further subdivision of squares may occur. If this were done with the example above - DUNROBIN CASTLE we should need to imagine one tenths along each margin of square NC80. In doing this both eastwards figures precede the northwards figures, thus NC8302. The larger figures show how the shorter reference fits into the longer one.

The indication of a grid reference on the maps is for identification purposes only. Due to differences in the projections and due to minor inaccuracies on source maps the reference will not always coincide precisely with the actual National Grid reference.

There are two further aspects concerning station entries in the gazetteers; these are colour of the entry and opening and closing dates. The grouped railways in Britain and their equivalent in Ireland are shown in black, with stations opened in 1948 or later being distinguished by red lettering. Capitals distinguish open stations, whilst those closing before the end of 1993 are in lower case style. Blue is utilised to distinguish London Underground, Glasgow Subway and various modern Metro systems, but it should be remembered that many of the origins of these systems were grouped railways. To cover this aspect station in black have blue underlining to emphasize the dual nature of the location. Minor railways, into which category preserved railways fall, are in green, whilst locations which were goods are shown purple. Projected stations are also shown in green.

The opening and closing dates show the year and here again colours are utilised to distinguish the various types of event. Black is for closing, red for opening or re-opening, whilst name changes where date is known are in blue. Occasionally a green date appears and this is where an opening proposed at the terminal date of the atlas, 31st December 1993 was known to have opened before the atlas was completed.

Stations which appeared in the Beeching Report have * against them in the gazetteer. Whilst those stations under consideration for closure before the Report was formulated are marked † in the gazetteer.

KEY TO SYMBOLS USED ON MAPS

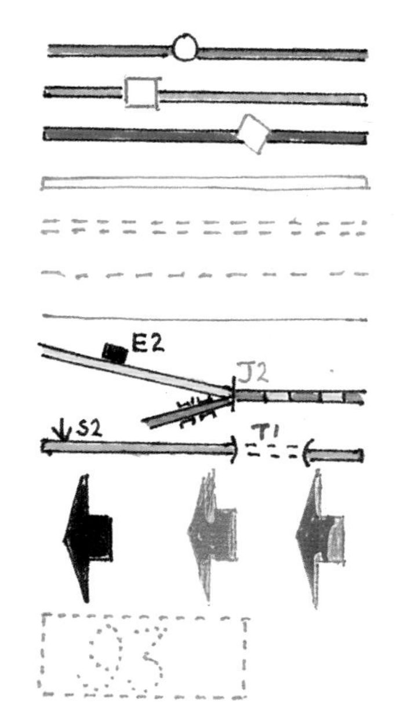

STATION. The uncoloured circle indicates open at 31·12·93. Closed station coloured.
METRO STATION OPEN. Closed would be coloured as before.
MINOR RAILWAY or PRESERVED STATION open. Closed indicated as above
NEW LINE opened after 1·1·48 BLUE or GREEN would show NEW METRO or NEW MINOR
PROPOSED NEW LINE not yet opened at 31·12·1993 BLUE or GREEN woulds show METRO or MINOR
Line closed to all traffic during the grouping period.
Line reduced from all traffic to goods only during the grouping period.
ENGINE SHED, on some smaller scale maps code letter and number only shown.
VIADUCT/BRIDGE if V followed by number see gazetteer: Junction, details see gazetteer.
SUMMIT, TUNNEL, Number refers to gazetteer where height in feet, or length in yards may be given
Page of continuation map: At the same scale, At a larger scale, at a smaller scale, the latter two only shown if there is not a continuation at the same scale.
Area surrounded by a fine dotted line in red and a dotted number in red shows there is an enlargement of the area on the map page indicated by the number.

KEY TO STATION TYPES SHOWN ON MAPS

BINGLEY	Open throughout the period
NEWCASTLE	Open throughout the period and METRO also
KEIGHLEY	Open throughout the period and now for PRESERVED railway also
WICK	Open throughout the period and still in use for GOODS at 31·12·1993
SALTAIRE	Open 1·1·1948 and at 31·12·1993 but closed for a period in between
BELLARENA	Open 1·1·1948 and at 31·12·1993 but at the latter date for excursions only
Tuam	as above but in this case the line is normally in use only for goods traffic
Great Horton	Open 1·1·1948 closed before 31·12·1993
CROSSFLATTS	Opened after 1·1·1948 and remained open beyond 31·12·93
Friary Halt	Opened after 1·1·1948 and closed before 31·12·93
Ballyboley	Reduced to goods only before 1·1·1948 and since closed
KINGSCOURT	Reduced to goods only before 1·1·1948 and still in use as goods beyond 31·12·1993
DONEGAL QUAY	Proposed New Station Alloa shows proposed to re-open
Charfield	Open 1·1·1948 closed before 31·12·1993 Proposed to re-open
Pallion	Open 1·1·1948 closed before 31·12·1993 Proposed to re-open as METRO
EPPING	Underground or Metro opened throughout the period METRO
COWCADDENS	Open 1·1·1948 and at 31·12·93 but closed for a period in between METRO
Benton Square	Open 1·1·1948 closed subsequently then re-opened as METRO with change of name METRO
(North Weald)	Opened after 1·1·1948 and closed before 31·12·1993 METRO
South Acton	Open 1·1·1948 but since closed METRO
(BANKFOOT)	Open goods only 1·1·1948 later became METRO
(HAYMARKET)	Opened after 1·1·1948 and remained open beyond 31·12·1993 METRO
ESKDALE GREEN	Open throughout the period MINOR/PRESERVED
Oakworth	Open 1·1·1948 and subsequently closed but re-opened as MINOR/PRESERVED
Marsden Cottage	Open 1·1·1948 closed before 31·12·93 MINOR/PRESERVED
(KELLING HEATH)	Opened after 1·1·1948 and remained open until after 31·12·1993 MINOR/PRESERVED
(Knightswood)	Opened after 1·1·1948 closed before 31·12·1993 MINOR/PRESERVED

Station names shown in a mixture of CAPITALS and lower case shows lower case portion dropped. Where a portion of name in red this shows a post 1·1·1948 addition, if it is a lower case addition in red it indicates the addition has been later dropped.

Other symbols used occasionally - explained on appropriate map or gazetteer.

(x)

IRELAND

MAP	AREA	REF	SIZE IN KMS
1	DONEGAL + COLLOONEY	RE7070	80x130
2	LONDONDERRY + STRABANE	SA5070	80x130
3	BELFAST	SB3070	80x130
	Belfast		
4	WESTPORT + CLAREMORRIS	RJ9050	80x130
5	ATHLONE + ATHENRY	RK7050	70x120
6	NAVAN, CLARA + MARYBOROUGH	SF4049	80x121
7	DUBLIN + DUNDALK	SG2050	80x120
	Dublin		
8	KILRUSH + TRALEE	RO5027	80x123
9	LIMERICK, LIMERICK JUNCTION + MALLOW	RP3030	80x120
	Limerick		
	Limerick Junction		
10	KILKENNY + WATERFORD	SL1020	80x130
	Waterford		
11	WICKLOW, WEXFORD + ROSSLARE	SL9030	80x120
12	CORK + BALTIMORE	RU1050	120x80
	Cork		

NOTES:

1. All main maps are a uniform scale of 7½ miles to the inch. The insets are at various scales.
2. Reference is South-West corner.
3. Size: Eastwards distance first.
4. No information on sheds and other information is restricted.

IRISH NATIONALISATION

As mentioned earlier this a complex situation. Eire nationalisation obviously had a different date and this was 1·6·1950. But effective nationalisation in the north depended on several different factors. Where a railway was owned by a British company such as the LONDON, MIDLAND + SCOTTISH it was subject to public ownership as in mainland Britain on 1·1·1948. There was one company operating in Northern Ireland exclusively, this was BELFAST + COUNTY DOWN, who were nationalised 1·10·1948. The remaining companies operated on both sides of the border and there was no agreement on how they should proceed. As a result all companies except the Irish Great Northern eventually ceased operating. This company then gave short notice that they too would close forcing the nationalised companies to take action. This was done by different parts of an existing board taking over the respective lines on each side of the border. But it would be 1958, a further five years before the finalisation of public ownership divided the GREAT NORTHERN between the two nationalised bodies (see chart below).

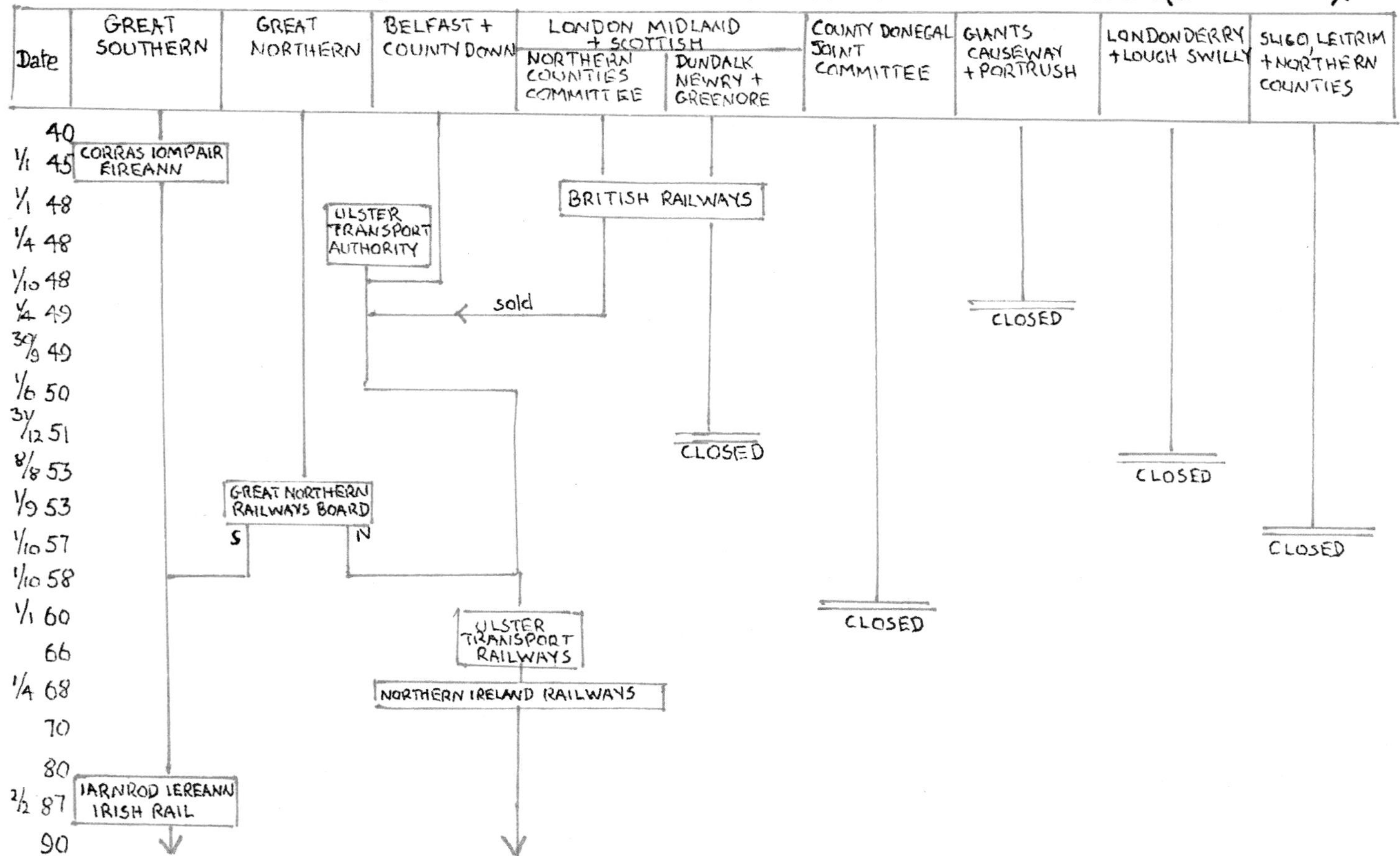

To distinguish stations which opened or closed on or after 1.1.1948 but before nationalisation in Ireland, these are shown in brackets on the facing page gazetteers.

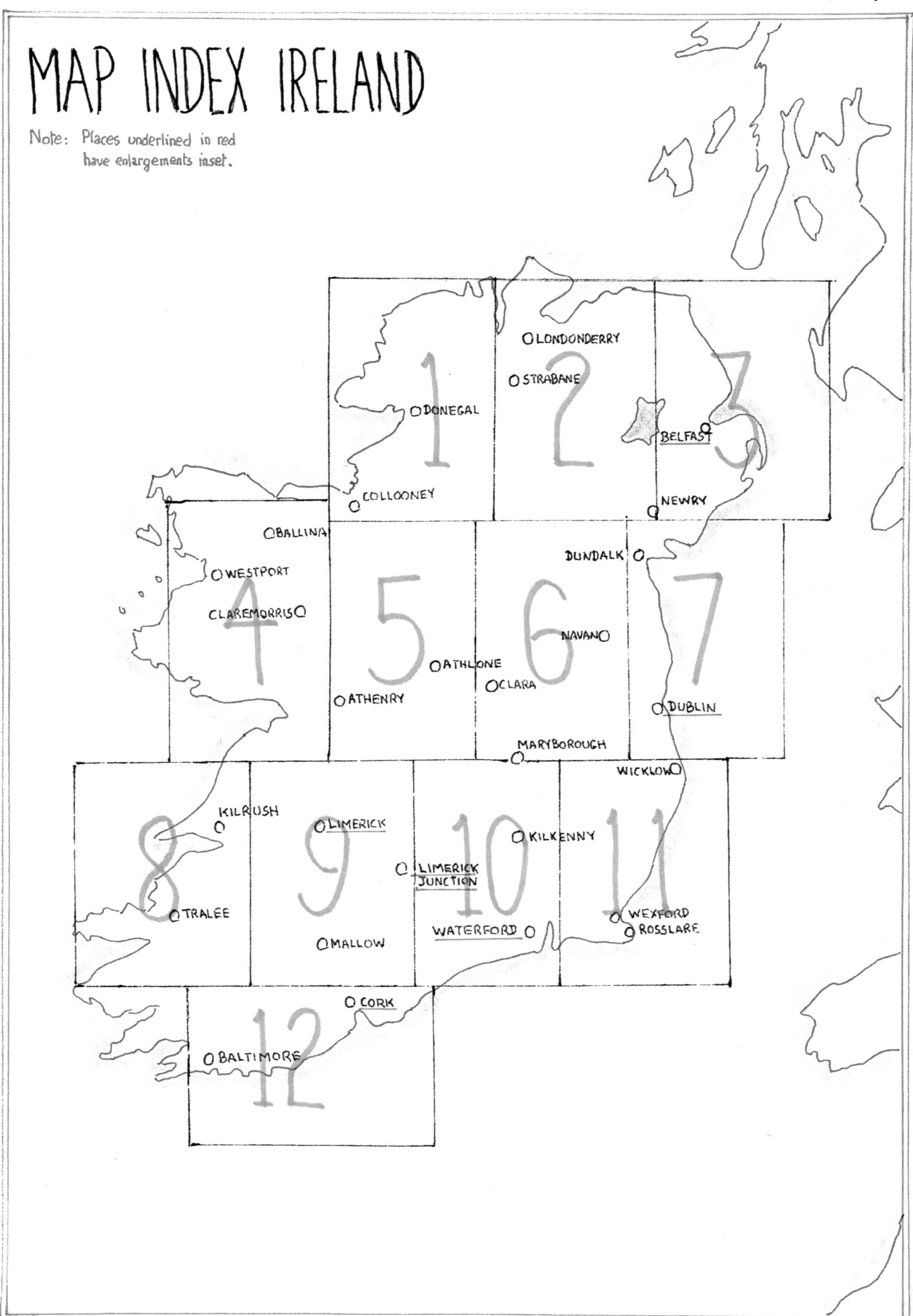
MAP INDEX IRELAND
Note: Places underlined in red have enlargements inset.
1
2
3
4
5
6
7
8
9
10
11
12
LONDONDERRY
STRABANE
DONEGAL
BELFAST
COLLOONEY
NEWRY
BALLINA
DUNDALK
WESTPORT
CLAREMORRIS
NAVAN
ATHLONE
CLARA
ATHENRY
DUBLIN
MARYBOROUGH
WICKLOW
KILRUSH
LIMERICK
KILKENNY
LIMERICK JUNCTION
TRALEE
WEXFORD
ROSSLARE
WATERFORD
MALLOW
CORK
BALTIMORE

NORTH BRITAIN

Map Page	Area	Scale	Ref.	Size
13	THURSO, WICK + DORNOCH	7½	NH5570	85x110
14	INVERNESS, KYLE OF LOCHALSH + MALLAIG	7½	NM6090	130x80
15	ABERDEEN	7½	NN9090	130x80
16	FORT WILLIAM, OBAN + CRIANLARICH	7½	NM6010	130x80
17	MONTROSE, DUNDEE + PERTH	7½	NN9010	130x80
	Dundee			
18	GREENOCK, GLASGOW + KILMARNOCK	5	NS1530	55x80
19	GLASGOW + PAISLEY	2	NS3855	32x20
20	GLASGOW	½	NS5563	8x5
21	STIRLING, DUNFERMLINE + MOTHERWELL	5	NS7030	50x80
22	AIRDRIE + MOTHERWELL	2	NS7040	20x32
23	EDINBURGH + GALASHIELS	5	NT2030	50x80
	Thornton Junction			
24	EDINBURGH	1	NT2071	13x8
25	BERWICK-UPON-TWEED + KELSO	5	NT7030	55x80
26	AYR, GIRVAN + STRANRAER	5	NW9540	55x90
	KINTYRE	5	NR5515	20x20
27	CUMNOCK + DUMFRIES	5	NX5050	50x80
28	CARLISLE + MOFFAT	5	NY0050	50x80
	Carlisle			
29	JEDBURGH + HEXHAM	5	NY5050	50x80
30	MORPETH NEWCASTLE + SUNDERLAND	5	NZ0049	50x83
31	NEWCASTLE, SOUTH SHIELDS + SUNDERLAND	2	NZ1550	35x22
	Newcastle			
32	THE LAKE COUNTIES	5	SC9565	55x85
33	PENRITH, KENDAL + KIRKBY STEPHEN	5	SD5067	50x83
34	DURHAM, MIDDLESBROUGH + NORTHALLERTON	5	SE0070	50x80
35	WHITBY + MALTON	5	SE5070	50x80
	SCARBOROUGH + FILEY	5	TA0070	30x30
36	ISLE OF MAN	4	SC1060	40x60
	St John's			
37	LANCASTER PRESTON + WIGAN	5	SD2500	55x70
	Southport			
	Preston			
38	BOLTON, BURY + WIGAN	2	SD5500	25x24
	Wigan			
39	SKIPTON, LEEDS + OLDHAM	5	SD8000	50x70
	Oldham + Greenfield			
40	BRADFORD + HUDDERSFIELD	2	SE0707	23x38
41	HARROGATE, YORK + DONCASTER	5	SE3000	50x70
	Leeds			
42	METHLEY, BARNSLEY + DONCASTER	2	SE3000	40x25
	Methley			
	South Doncaster			
43	HUMBERSIDE	5	SE8000	55x70

NOTES: Scale is miles to the inch and is approximate. Insets at various scales; if in capitals same scale as main map.
Reference is SW corner of map.
Size is in kms., the eastward distance is always given first.

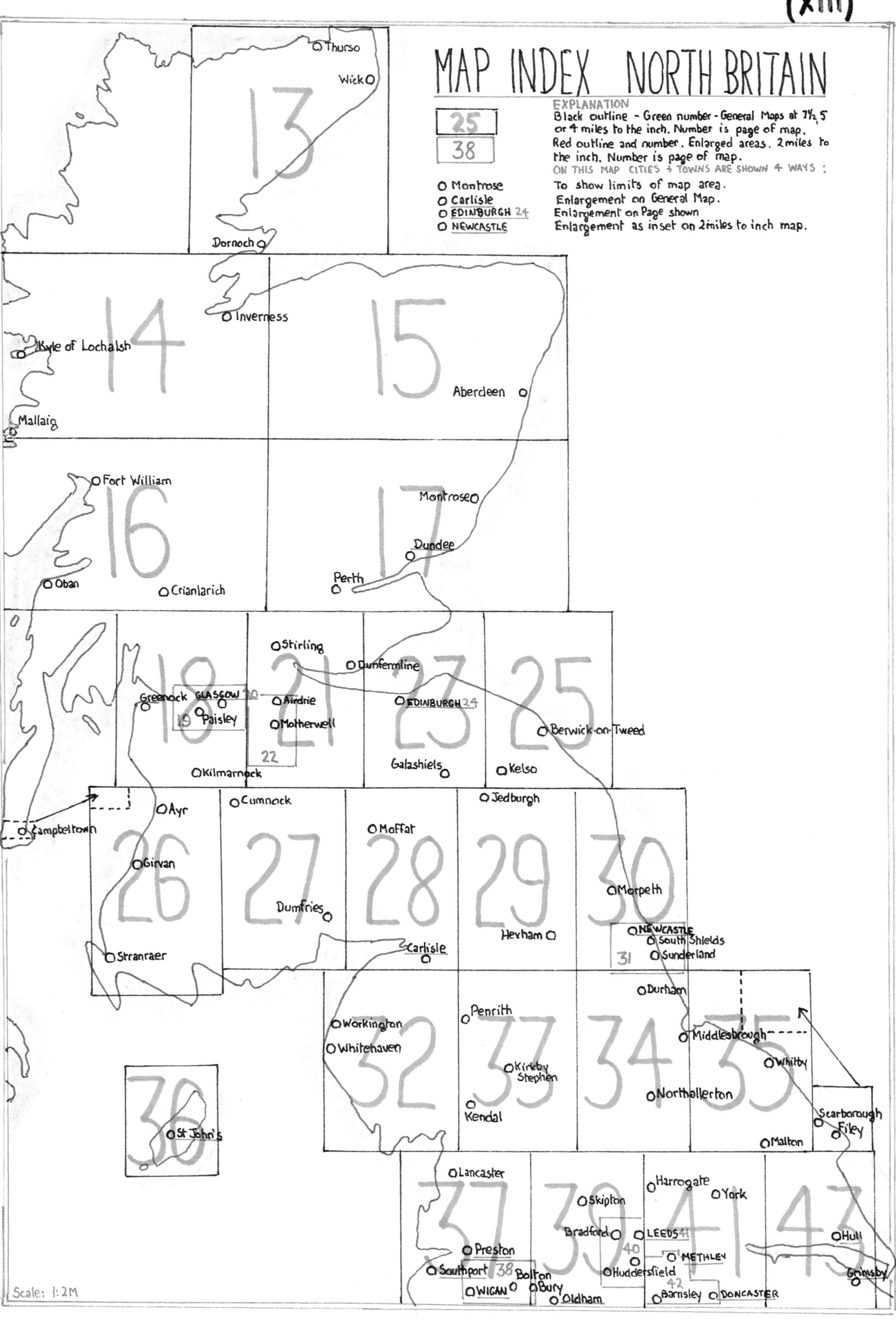

MAP INDEX NORTH BRITAIN
EXPLANATION
25
38
Black outline - Green number - General Maps at 7½, 5 or 4 miles to the inch. Number is page of map.
Red outline and number. Enlarged areas. 2 miles to the inch. Number is page of map.
ON THIS MAP CITIES + TOWNS ARE SHOWN 4 WAYS:
Montrose
To show limits of map area.
Carlisle
Enlargement on General Map.
EDINBURGH 24
Enlargement on Page shown
NEWCASTLE
Enlargement as inset on 2 miles to inch map.
Thurso
Wick
Dornoch
Inverness
Kyle of Lochalsh
Mallaig
Aberdeen
Fort William
Montrose
Dundee
Perth
Oban
Crianlarich
Stirling
Dunfermline
Greenock
GLASGOW 20
Paisley
Airdrie
Motherwell
EDINBURGH 24
Berwick-on-Tweed
Kilmarnock
Galashiels
Kelso
Jedburgh
Ayr
Cumnock
Campbeltown
Moffat
Girvan
Morpeth
Dumfries
Hexham
NEWCASTLE
South Shields
Sunderland
Stranraer
Carlisle
Durham
Penrith
Workington
Whitehaven
Middlesbrough
Whitby
Kirkby Stephen
Northallerton
Kendal
Scarborough
Filey
St John's
Malton
Lancaster
Harrogate
York
Skipton
Bradford
LEEDS 41
Hull
METHLEY
Preston
Southport
Bolton
Huddersfield
Grimsby
WIGAN
Bury
Oldham
Barnsley
DONCASTER
13
14
15
16
17
18
19
21
22
23
25
26
27
28
29
30
31
32
33
34
35
36
37
38
39
40
41
42
43
Scale: 1:2M

SOUTH BRITAIN

Map	Area	Scale	Ref	Size
44	ANGLESEY + SNOWDONIA	5	SH 1816	51 x 84
45	NORTH WALES	5	SH 7016	50 x 84
46	LIVERPOOL, WREXHAM + OSWESTRY	5	SJ 2016	50 x 84
47C	LIVERPOOL + BIRKENHEAD	2	SJ 2885	16 x 16
A	Birkenhead	1	SJ 2888	*
B	Liverpool	1	SJ 3587	6 x 12
48A	St Helens			
B	Widnes			
C	Warrington			
D	Chester			
E	Crewe			
49	MANCHESTER + STAFFORD	5	SJ 7020	50 x 80
50	MANCHESTER	1	SJ 8090	20 x 11
51	SHEFFIELD, DERBY + NOTTINGHAM	5	SK 2020	50 x 80
52A	Sheffield + Rotherham			
B	Retford			
C	Basford + Bulwell			
D	Trent			
E	Lincoln			
F	Nottingham			
53	LINCOLN, NEWARK + SLEAFORD	5	SK 7020	50 x 80
54	SKEGNESS, SPALDING + KINGS LYNN	5	SK 2018	50 x 82
55A	WELLS-NEXT-THE-SEA + FAKENHAM	5	TF 7020	50 x 40
B	CROMER + NORTH WALSHAM	5	TG 2020	50 x 40
56	FAIRBOURNE, ABERYSTWYTH + LLANDOVERY	5	SN 4530	52 x 86
57	SHREWSBURY, CAERSWS + BUILTH	5	SN 9730	53 x 86
58	TELFORD, WOLVERHAMPTON + WORCESTER	5	SO 5040	50 x 80
59	BIRMINGHAM + WOLVERHAMPTON	2	SO 8180	39 x 24
60	LICHFIELD, BIRMINGHAM + BANBURY	5	SP 0040	50 x 80
61	LEICESTER + NORTHAMPTON	5	SP 5040	50 x 80
62	PETERBOROUGH, BEDFORD + CAMBRIDGE	5	TL 0040	50 x 80
63	DEREHAM, ELY + NEWMARKET	5	TL 5040	55 x 80
64	NORWICH, LOWESTOFT + IPSWICH	5	TM 0540	55 x 80
65	FISHGUARD, CARMARTHEN + PEMBROKE	5	SR 8990	55 x 80

Map	Area	Scale	Ref	Size
66	LLANGADOCK + PANTYFFYNON	2	SN 4308	33 x 22
67	BRECON	2	SN 7610	33 x 22
68	RHYMNEY, EBBW VALE + PONTYPRIDD	2	ST 1097	20 x 33
69	PONTRILAS + ABERGAVENNY	2	ST 3097	20 x 33
70	LLANELLY + SWANSEA	2	SS 4286	34 x 22
71	ABERDARE, CYMMER, DOWLAIS, MERTHYR + PONTYPRIDD	2	SS 7589	34 x 21
72	PORT TALBOT, BRIDGEND, PETERSTON + ABERTHAW	2	SS 7766	33 x 24
73	HENCOED, CAERPHILLY, CARDIFF + BARRY	2	ST 1064	20 x 33
74	NEWPORT + WESTON-SUPER-MARE	2	ST 3066	20 x 34
75	CHELTENHAM, GLOUCESTER + BRISTOL	5	ST 5060	50 x 80 *
76	BANBURY, SWINDON + NEWBURY	5	SU 0060	50 x 80
77	VERNEY JUNCTION, DIDCOT + READING	5	SU 5060	50 x 80
78	HITCHIN, ST ALBANS + LONDON	5	TQ 0060	50 x 80
79	LONDON NORTH WEST	1	TQ 1576	12 x 19
80	LONDON NORTH CENTRAL	1	TQ 2776	12 x 19
81	LONDON NORTH EAST	1	TQ 3976	12 x 19
82A	LONDON SOUTH WEST	1	TQ 1567	12 x 9
82B	LONDON SOUTH CENTRAL	1	TQ 2767	12 x 9
83A	LONDON SOUTH EAST	1	TQ 3967	12 x 9
B	Clapham Junction			
84	LONDON UNDERGROUND (Diagramatic Map)			
85	CHELMSFORD + ROCHESTER	5	TQ 5060	55 x 80
86A	MANNINGTREE + HARWICH	5	TM 0510	50 x 30
B	MARGATE, ASHFORD + DOVER	5	TR 0015	50 x 57
87	LAUNCESTON, HALWILL + BIDEFORD	5	SX 0080	50 x 80
88	BARNSTAPLE + EXETER	5	SX 5080	50 x 80
89	HIGHBRIDGE, TAUNTON + EXMOUTH	5	SY 0080	50 x 80
90	WESTBURY + WEYMOUTH	5	SY 5070	50 x 90
91	ANDOVER + SOUTHAMPTON	5	SZ 0075	50 x 85
92	GUILDFORD + PORTSMOUTH	5	SZ 5075	50 x 85
93	DORKING + BRIGHTON	5	TV 0075	50 x 85
94	MAIDSTONE, TUNBRIDGE + HASTINGS	5	TV 5080	50 x 80
95	REDRUTH, TRURO + PENZANCE	5	SW 4700	53 x 87
96A	BODMIN + PLYMOUTH	5	SX 0040	50 x 40
B	TOTNES + NEWTON ABBOT	5	SX 5040	50 x 40

NOTES: Scale is miles to the inch and is approximate. Insets at various scales. Reference is SW corner of map. Size is in kms, the eastward distance is always given first. * Irregular shape

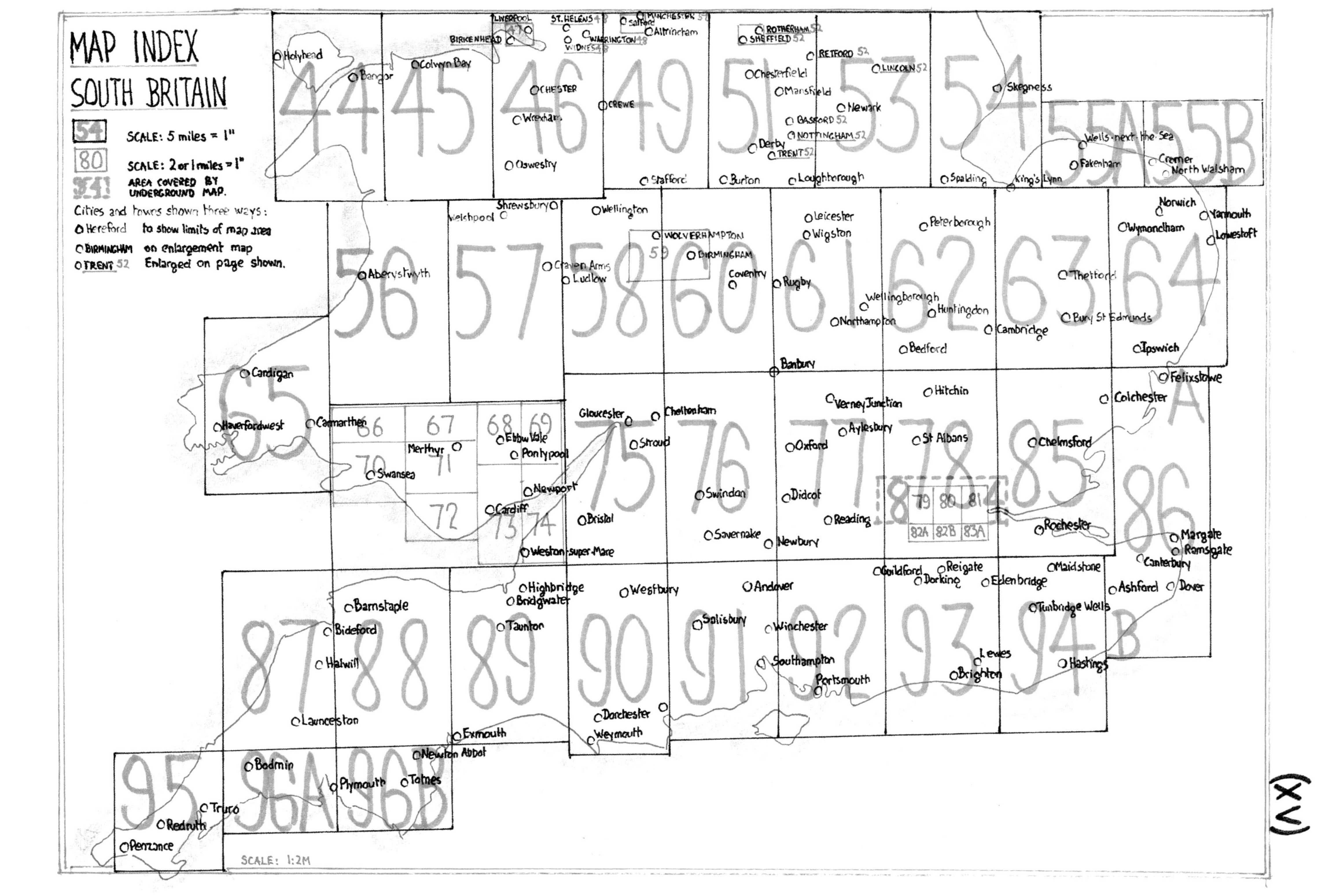
MAP INDEX
SOUTH BRITAIN
54 SCALE: 5 miles = 1"
80 SCALE: 2 or 1 miles = 1"
AREA COVERED BY UNDERGROUND MAP.
Cities and towns shown three ways:
Hereford to show limits of map area
BIRMINGHAM on enlargement map
TRENT 52 Enlarged on page shown.
SCALE: 1:2M
44 Holyhead Bangor
45 Colwyn Bay
46 LIVERPOOL 47 BIRKENHEAD ST. HELENS 48 WIDNES 48 CHESTER Wrexham Oswestry
49 MANCHESTER 50 Salford Altrincham WARRINGTON 48 CREWE Stafford
51 ROTHERHAM 52 SHEFFIELD 52 Chesterfield Mansfield BASFORD 52 NOTTINGHAM 52 Derby TRENT 52 Burton Loughborough
53 RETFORD 52 LINCOLN 52 Newark
54 Skegness Spalding King's Lynn
55A Wells-next-the-Sea Fakenham
55B Cromer North Walsham
56 Aberystwyth
57 Welshpool Shrewsbury
58 Wellington Craven Arms Ludlow
59 WOLVERHAMPTON
60 BIRMINGHAM Coventry
61 Leicester Wigston Rugby Northampton
62 Peterborough Wellingborough Huntingdon Bedford
63 Thetford Bury St Edmunds Cambridge
64 Norwich Wymondham Yarmouth Lowestoft Ipswich
65 Cardigan Haverfordwest Carmarthen
66 67 68 69 70 71 72 73 74
Merthyr Swansea Ebbw Vale Pontypool Newport Cardiff Weston-super-Mare
Banbury
75 Gloucester Cheltenham Stroud Bristol
76 Swindon Savernake
77 Verney Junction Aylesbury Oxford Didcot Reading Newbury
78 Hitchin St Albans
79 80 81 82A 82B 83A
84
85 Chelmsford Rochester
86A Felixstowe Colchester
86 Margate Ramsgate Canterbury Ashford Dover
87 Bideford Halwill Launceston
88 Barnstaple
89 Highbridge Bridgwater Taunton Exmouth
90 Westbury Dorchester Weymouth
91 Salisbury Andover
92 Winchester Southampton Portsmouth
93 Guildford Dorking Reigate Lewes Brighton
94 Maidstone Edenbridge Tunbridge Wells Hastings
94B
95 Truro Redruth Penzance
96A Bodmin Plymouth
96B Newton Abbot Totnes

1

DONEGAL + COLLOONEY

RAILWAYS

No	Company	Note	Gauge[3]
1	GREAT NORTHERN (IRELAND)		S
2	CORAS IOMPAIR EIREANN		S
3	COUNTY DONEGAL JOINT COMMITTEE	1	N
5	SLIGO LEITRIM + NORTHERN COUNTIES		S
6	LONDONDERRY + LOUGH SWILLY		N

STATIONS

Station	Note	Opened Closed	Ry	Ref
(Abohill)	H	57	5	SA39
(Ardara Road)	H	60	3	MZ93
(Ballinamallard)		57	1	NV40
(Ballintogher)	H	57	3	RE97
(Ballintra)		60	3	NV12
(Ballygawley Market Platform)	H	57	5	RE97
(Ballylucas Crossing)	H	57	1	SA49
(Ballyshannon)		57	1	NV01
(Ballyshannon)		60	3	NV01
(Ballysodare)		63	2	RE88
(Barnesmore)	H	60	3	NV23
(Belcoo)		57	5	SA39
(Beleek)		57	1	NV11
(Bridgetown)	H	60	3	NV12
(Bruckless)	H	60	3	MZ92
(Bundoran)		57	1	NV01
(Bundoran Junction		57	1	NV40
(Castlecaldwell)		57	1	NV21
(Castlefinn)		60	3	NV44
(Cavan)	H	60	3	NV34
(Clady)	H	60	3	NV44
(Clar Bridge)	H	60	3	NV13
COLLOONEY			2	RE87
(Collooney)		57	5	RE87
Collooney South		63	2	RE87
(Convoy)	H	60	3	NV45
(Coolaghy)	H	60	3	NV45
(Coolmore)	H	60	3	NV01
(Comagillagh)	H	60	3	NV45
(Creevy)	2 H	60	3	NV01
(Dergbridge)	H	60	3	NV24
(Donegal)		60	3	NV13
(Dooring Road)	4 H	60	3	NV02
(Dorrian's Bridge)	H	60	3	NV01
(Dromahair)		57	5	SA08
(Dromore)	H	56	3	NV02
(Drumbar Bridge Halt)	H	60	3	NV12
(Dunkineely)		60	3	MZ92
(Enniskillen)		57	1	SA49
(Florencecourt)		57	5	SA49
(Friary Halt)	H	53 60	3	NV01
(Glenfarne)		57	5	SA28
(Glenmaquin)		60	3	NV45
(Glenties)	G	52	3	NV04
(Gortaloughan)	H	57	1	SA49
(Hospital)	H	60	3	NV12
(Inver)		60	3	NV03
(Irvinestown)		57	1	NV40
(Kesh)		57	1	NV31
(Killybegs)		60	3	MZ92
(Killygordon)		60	3	NV44
(Killymard)	H	56	3	NV13
(Kilmakerra)	5 H	60	3	SA19
(Laghey)	H	60	3	NV12
(Letterkenny)		60	3	NV36
(Letterkenny)		53	6	NV36
Leyny		63	2	RE87
(Liscooly)	H	60	3	NV44
(Lisgorman)	H	57	5	SA08
(Lougheske)		60	3	NV23
(Manorcunningham)		53	6	NV46
(Manorhamilton)		57	3	SA19
(Meenglas)	H	60	3	NV34
(Mountcharles)		60	3	NV02
(Mullanboy)	H	60	3	NV03
(Newtoncunningham)		53	6	NV46
(Pettigo)		57	1	NV31
(Pluck)		53	6	NV46
(Port)	H	60	3	NV03
(Raphoe)		60	3	NV45
(Rossnowlagh)		60	3	NV01
(Sallybrook)		53	6	NV46
SLIGO			2	RE98
SLIGO QUAY	G		2	RE88
(Spamount)	H	60	3	MZ92
(Stranorlar)		60	3	NV34
(Town Bridge)	H	60	3	NV34
(Trillick)		57	1	NV40

NOTES:

1 Joint owners as at 31·12·47 were LONDON MIDLAND + SCOTTISH and GREAT NORTHERN (IRELAND)

2 Alternative spelling: Creevey

3 S = Standard gauge which is 5'3" in Ireland
N = Narrow gauge 3'0"

4 Alternative spellings Dooran Dooring.

5 Alternative spelling Kilmakerrill

G Location goods only as at 31·12·47

H These locations were, or became Halts. Few of the locations had HALT as part of the title, but as they were numerous have been shown in this way.

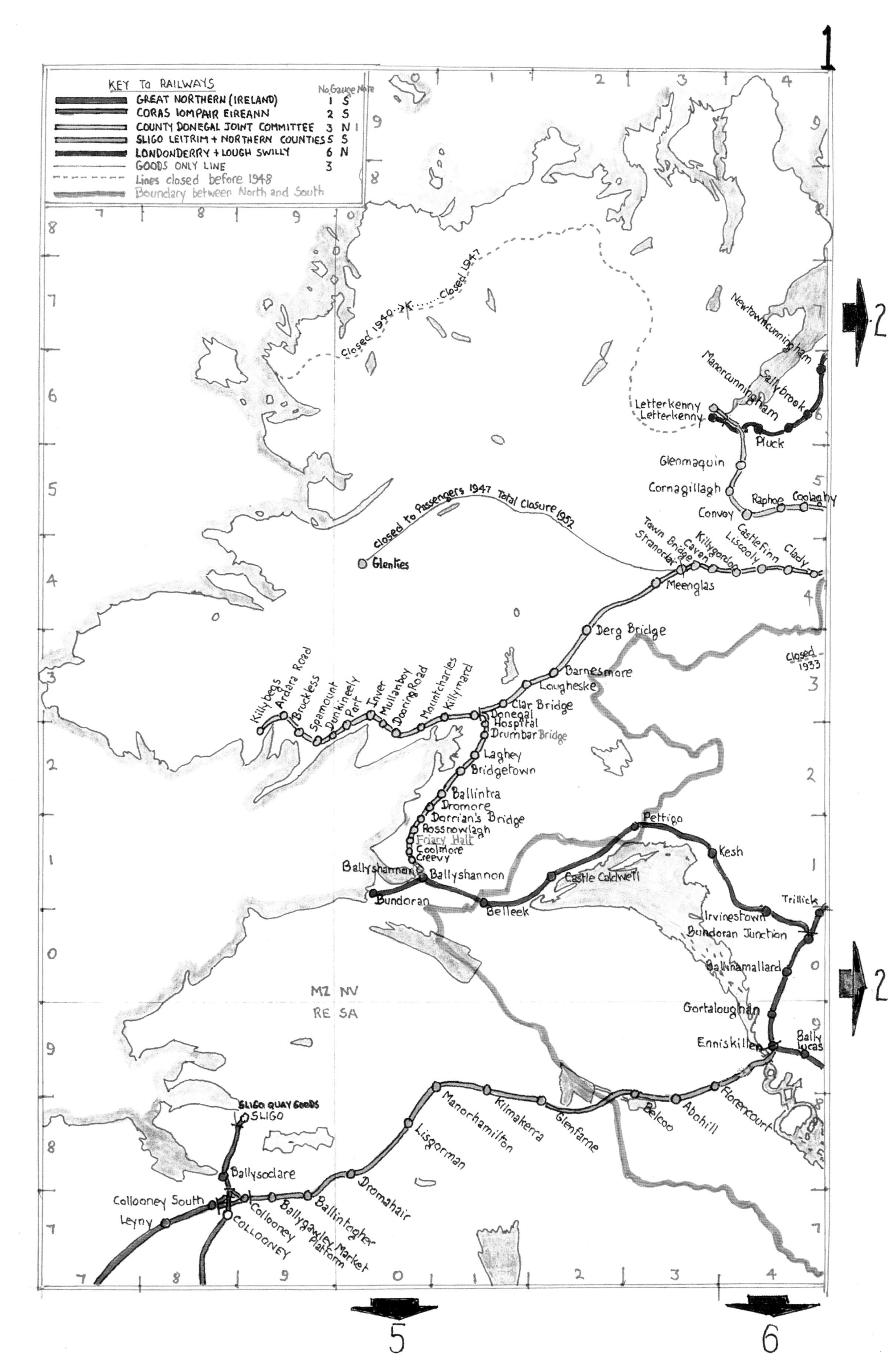

KEY TO RAILWAYS
No. Gauge Note
GREAT NORTHERN (IRELAND) 1 S
CORAS IOMPAIR EIREANN 2 S
COUNTY DONEGAL JOINT COMMITTEE 3 N 1
SLIGO LEITRIM + NORTHERN COUNTIES 5 S
LONDONDERRY + LOUGH SWILLY 6 N
GOODS ONLY LINE 3
Lines closed before 1948
Boundary between North and South
Closed 1940
Closed 1947
Newtowncunningham
Manorcunningham
Sallybrook
Letterkenny
Letterkenny
Pluck
Glenmaquin
Cornagillagh
Convoy
Raphoe
Coolaghy
Closed to Passengers 1947 Total Closure 1952
Glenties
Town Bridge
Stranorlar
Cavan
Killygordon
Liscooly
Castlefinn
Clady
Meenglas
Derg Bridge
Barnesmore
Lougheske
Clar Bridge
Closed 1933
Killybegs
Ardara Road
Bruckless
Spamount
Dunkineely
Port
Inver
Mullanboy
Doorin Road
Mountcharles
Killymard
Donegal
Hospital
Drumbar Bridge
Laghey
Bridgetown
Ballintra
Dromore
Dorrian's Bridge
Rossnowlagh
Friary Halt
Coolmore
Creevy
Ballyshannon
Ballyshannon
Bundoran
Belleek
Castle Caldwell
Pettigo
Kesh
Trillick
Irvinestown
Bundoran Junction
Ballinamallard
Gortaloughan
Enniskillen
Bally lucas
MZ NV
RE SA
SLIGO QUAY GOODS
SLIGO
Ballysodare
Collooney South
Leyny
Collooney
COLLOONEY
Ballygawley Market Platform
Ballintogher
Dromahair
Lisgorman
Manorhamilton
Kilmakerra
Glenfarne
Belcoo
Abohill
Florencecourt
2
2
5
6

LONDONDERRY + STRABANE

RAILWAYS

Railway	Note	No	Gauge[2]
GREAT NORTHERN (IRELAND)		1	S
COUNTY DONEGAL JOINT COMMITTEE	1	3	N
LONDON MIDLAND + SCOTTISH		4	
Standard gauge lines 5'3"		A	S
Narrow gauge lines 3'0"		B	N
GIANT'S CAUSEWAY + PORTRUSH		5	N
LONDONDERRY + LOUGH SWILLY		6	N

STATIONS

Station	Note	Opened closed	Ry Ref
Agadhowey		50	ANW07
Annaghmore		65	1NW10
Annakerra Crossing	H	65	1NW10
(Armagh)		57	1SB09
Armoy		50	BNW28
(Ballindrait)	H	60	3NV55
(Ballybay)		57	1SA97
Ballycastle		50	BNW29
Ballyheather	H	54	BNV55
Ballykelly	H	54	BNV87
Ballymaggory		54	BNV55
BALLYMENA			ANW25
BALLYMONEY			ANW17
Ballymoney		50	BNW17
(Ballymoney Road)	H	49	5NW09
(Beach Halt)	H	48	6NV58
BELLARENA	3	76 82	ANV88
Beragh		65	1NV71
Bessbrook	A §	65 84	1SB27
(Bridge End)		53	6NV57
Bridge Street		51	ASB27
Brimages Crossing	H	60	1NV92
Broighter	H	50	ANV87
(Buncrana)		53	6NV58
(Burnfoot)		53	6NV57
(Bushmills)		49	5NW19
Capecastle	H	50	BNW28
Carrichue	H	54	ANV77
Carrickmore		59	1NV82
(Carrigans)		56	1NV56
(Carrowen)		53	6NV57
(Castleblaney)		57	1SB07
Castledawson		50	ANW14
CASTLEROCK			ANV89
(Clones)		57	1SA77
(Coalisland)		56	1NW01
COLERAINE			ANW08
(Cookstown)	4	56	1NW02
Cookstown	4	50	ANW02
Cookstown Junction		76	BNW34
(Coolane Crossing)	H	57	1SA59
CRAIGAVON EAST	B §		1NW21
CRAIGAVON WEST	C §		1NW20
Cromore	H D §	69 88	1NW08
Cullion		54	BNV65
CULLYBACKEY			ANW25
Culmore	5	73	ANV67
Curraghbridge Halt	H	50	ANW07
Derrycoose Crossing	H	60	1NW01
Dervock		50	BNW18
Desertone		54	BNV66
DHU VARREN		69	ANW08
Donaghmore		59	1NV91
Donemana		54	BNV65
Downhill		76	ANV98
Draperstown	G	50	ANW94
(Dromore Road)		57	1NV51
(Drumhork Crossing)		55	1SB29
Dublin Bridge, Newry		64	1SB27
Dungannon		65	1NV91
Dungannon Junction Halt		64	1NV91
Dungiven	G	50	ANW86
Dunloy		76	ANW27
(Dunluce Castle)	H	49	5NW19
Edenderry Crossing	H	60	1NV72
Edward Street, Newry		65	1SB27
Eglinton		73	ANV77
(Fahan)		53	6NV57
(Fintona		57	1NV61
(Fintona Junction)		57	1NV61
Foyle Road, Londonderry		65	1NV66
(Gallagh Road)		53	6NV67
Garvagh		50	ANW06
Garvagh Crossing	H	60	1NV62
(Giant's Causeway)		49	5NW19
Glarryford		73	ANW26
(Glaslough)		57	1SA99
Goodyear		70 83	1NW20
Goraghwood		65	1SB28
Gracehill Halt	H	50	BNW28
(Graving Dock, Londonderry)		53	6NV66
(Inch Road)		53	6NV57
Keady	G	51	1SB08
Kellswater		71	ANW24
Killagan		73	ANW26
(Killylea)		57	1SB09
Kilrea		54	ANW16
(Knockarney Crossing)	H	55	1SB28
Knockloughrim		50	ANW04
(Lamberton's Halt)	H	53	6NV57
(Lawrencetown)		55	1SB99
(Lifford Halt)		60	3NV55
Limavady		50	ANV87
Limavady Junction		76	ANV87
(Lisbellaw)		57	1SA59
(Lisfannon Links)	H	53	6NV58
(Lisnagole Crossing)	H	57	1SA58
(Lisnanock Crossing)	H	57	1SA58
(Lisnaskea)		57	1SA58
LONDONDERRY			NV66
LONDONDERRY	E §		A NV66
Foyle Road	6	65	NV66
(Graving Dock)		53	6NV66
Victoria Road		54	BNV66
Waterside	E §		A NV66
LURGAN	B §		1NW21
Macfin		54	ANW07
Maghera		50	ANW05
Magherafelt		50	ANW04
MAGILLIGAN	3	76 80	ANV98
(Maguiresbridge)		57	1SA58
Markethill	G	55	1SB19
(Martin's Bridge Halt)	H	55	1SB29
(Monaghan)		57	1SA88
(Monaghan Road)		57	1SA87
Moneycarrie	H	50	ANW07
Moneymore		50	ANW03
Mullafurtherland	H	60	1NV91
(Newbliss)		57	1SA77
New Buildings	H	54	BNV66
NEWRY			SB29
NEWRY	A §	84	1SB29
Bessbrook	A §	84	1SB29
Bridge Street		51	A SB29
Dublin Street		64	1SB29
Edward Street		65	1SB29
(Newtownbutler)		51	1SA67
Newtonstewart		65	1NV63
Omagh		65	1NV62
(Pennyburn)		53	6NV67
Pomeroy		65	1NV92
Portadown		70	1NW20
PORTADOWN	§	70	1NW20
Portballintrae	H	49	5NW19
Porthall		65	1NV55
(Portrush)		49	5NW09
PORTRUSH			ANW09
Portstewart	D §	63	ANW09
POYNTZPASS		65 82	1SB29
Randalstown		56	ANW29
(Retreat)	H	57	1SB19
Reynolds	H	60	1NV91
(Richhill)		57	1NW10
Rollingford Crossing	H	60	1NV82
St Johnston		65	1NV56
(Sallaghy Crossing)	H	57	1SA58
SCARVA		65 84	1SB29
Shanmullagh Crossing	H	52 65	1NV51
Shaw's Crossing	H	64	1NW01
Sion Mills		65	1NV54
Sixmilecross		65	1NV71
(Smithborough)		57	1SA78
Staffordstown		50	ANW23
(Stewartstown)		56	1NW02
(Strabane)		60	3NV54
Strabane		65	1NV54
Stranocum	H	50	BNW18
Tamlaght	H	50	ANW05
Tanderagee		65	1SB28
Tattykeeran Crossing	H	60	1NV71
(Tooban Junction)		53	6NV57
Toome Bridge		50	ANW14
Trew + Moy		65	1NW01
(Trillick)		57	1NV50
(Tynan + Caledon)		57	1SA99
UNIVERSITY		68	ANW08
Upperlands		50	ANW05
Vernersbridge		65	1NW01
Victoria Bridge		65	1NV54
Victoria Road, Londonderry		54	BNV66
Waterside LONDONDERRY			ANV66
(Whiterocks)	H	49	NW09

NOTES

1 Joint owners at 31.12.47 were GNI and LMS
2 S = Standard 5'3"; N = Narrow 3'0"
3 Closed but re-opened for excursions only
4 Joint station with separate closure dates
5 Regular services finished '71.
§ Change of name later version.
§ Change of name earlier version, similar identifying letter gives other name. CRAIGAVON EAST + WEST are modern alternative names.
H Locations were Halts or became Halts.
G Goods location as at 31-12-47. Closing date shown is date of complete closure.
6 Station reopened as terminus for 3'0" gauge line. Planned to go as far as Carrigans in due course. FOYLE VALLEY RAILWAY.

JUNCTIONS

Junction	Ry Ref
Shantona	1SA87

TUNNELS

Tunnel	length	Ry Ref
Dungannon	814	1NW01
Castlerock Tunnels	308+668	ANV98

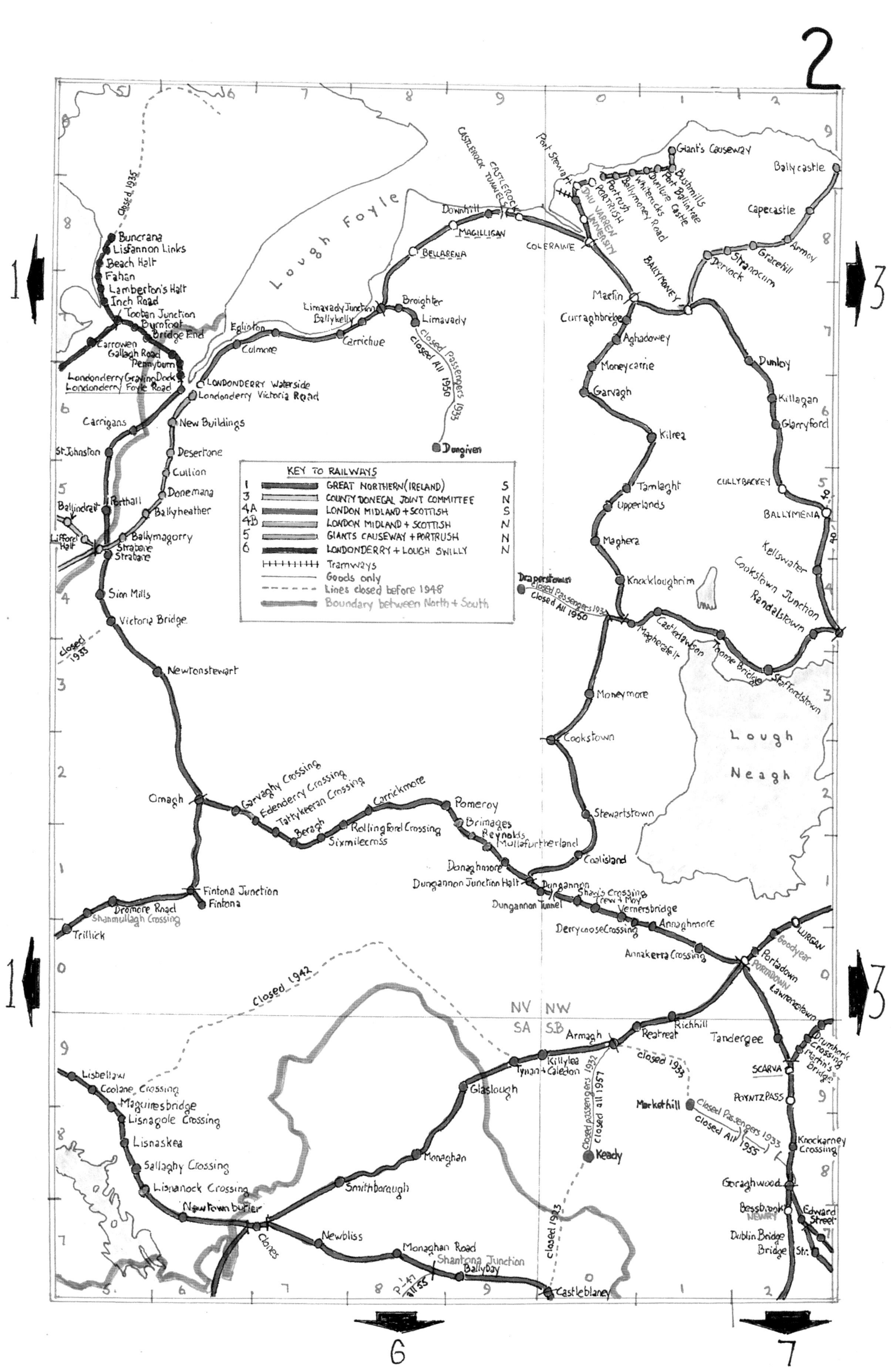
KEY TO RAILWAYS
1 GREAT NORTHERN (IRELAND) S
3 COUNTY DONEGAL JOINT COMMITTEE N
4A LONDON MIDLAND + SCOTTISH S
4B LONDON MIDLAND + SCOTTISH N
5 GIANTS CAUSEWAY + PORTRUSH N
6 LONDONDERRY + LOUGH SWILLY N
Tramways
Goods only
Lines closed before 1948
Boundary between North + South
Lough Foyle
Lough Neagh
Buncrana
Lisfannon Links
Beach Halt
Fahan
Lamberton's Halt
Inch Road
Tooban Junction
Burnfoot
Bridge End
Carrowen
Gallagh Road
Pennyburn
Londonderry Graving Dock
Londonderry Foyle Road
LONDONDERRY Waterside
Londonderry Victoria Road
Closed 1935
Eglinton
Culmore
Carrichue
Limavady Junction
Ballykelly
Broighter
Limavady
Closed Passengers 1933
Closed All 1950
Dungiven
Bellarena
Magilligan
Downhill
Castlerock Tunnels
Castlerock
Coleraine
Port Stewart
Portrush
Dhu Varren
University
Ballymoney Road
Whitebricks
Dunluce Castle
Port Ballintrae
Bushmills
Giant's Causeway
Ballycastle
Capecastle
Armoy
Gracehill
Stranocum
Dervock
Ballymoney
Macfin
Curraghbridge
Aghadowey
Moneycarrie
Garvagh
Kilrea
Tamlaght
Upperlands
Maghera
Knockloughrim
Draperstown
Closed Passengers 1930
Closed All 1950
Magherafelt
Castledawson
Toome Bridge
Staffordstown
Randalstown
Cookstown Junction
Kellswater
Ballymena
Cullybackey
Glarryford
Killagan
Dunloy
Carrigans
St. Johnston
Ballindrait
Lifford Halt
Porthall
Strabane
New Buildings
Desertone
Cullion
Donemana
Ballyheather
Ballymagorry
Sion Mills
Victoria Bridge
closed 1933
Newtonstewart
Omagh
Garvaghy Crossing
Edenderry Crossing
Tattykeeran Crossing
Beragh
Sixmilecross
Rolling Ford Crossing
Carrickmore
Pomeroy
Brimages
Reynolds
Mullafurtherland
Donaghmore
Dungannon Junction Halt
Dungannon
Dungannon Tunnel
Moneymore
Cookstown
Stewartstown
Coalisland
Shaw's Crossing
Trew + Moy
Vernersbridge
Derrycoose Crossing
Annaghmore
Annakerra Crossing
Fintona Junction
Fintona
Dromore Road
Shanmullagh Crossing
Trillick
Closed 1942
Lurgan
Goodyear
Portadown
Lawrencetown
Richhill
Retreat
Armagh
Tandergee
Killylea
Tynan + Caledon
Glaslough
closed 1933
Closed passengers 1932
Closed all 1957
Keady
Markethill
Closed Passengers 1933
Closed All 1955
Drumhork Crossing
Martin's Bridge
Scarva
Poyntzpass
Knockarney Crossing
Goraghwood
Bessbrook
Newry
Edward Street
Dublin Bridge
Bridge St.
Lisbellaw
Coolane Crossing
Maguiresbridge
Lisnagole Crossing
Lisnaskea
Sallaghy Crossing
Lisnanock Crossing
Newtownbutler
Clones
Monaghan
Smithborough
Newbliss
Monaghan Road
Shantona Junction
Ballybay
closed 1923
Castleblaney
P. 1947
All 55
NV NW
SA SB
1
3
6
7

BELFAST

RAILWAYS

No	Company	(1) Gauge
1	GREAT NORTHERN (IRELAND)	S
3	BELFAST + COUNTY DOWN	S
4A	LONDON MIDLAND + SCOTTISH (LMS) Standard gauge lines	S
4B	LONDON MIDLAND + SCOTTISH (LMS) Narrow gauge lines	N
X	BELFAST HABOUR COMMISSIONERS	S
O	New lines (post 1948)	S

STATIONS

Stations	Opened Closed	Ry	Ref
ADELAIDE		1	NW52
Aldergrove	60	1	NW33
ANTRIM		1	NW33
Ardglass	50	3	SB97
Ashfield	H 56	1	NW30
BALLINDERRY	60 74	1	NW32
Ballyboley	G 50	B	NW34
BALLYCARRY		A	NW64
Ballycastle	50	B	NW39
Ballyclare	G 50	A	NW44
Ballyclare Junction	54	A	NW43
Ballygowan	50	3	NW61
(Ballygowan)	H 56	1	NW41
Ballykinlar	H 50	3	SB69
Ballymacarrett	H 77	3	NW52
BALLYMENA		A	NW35
Ballynahinch	50	3	NW50
Ballynahinch Junction	50	3	NW60
Ballynoe	50	3	SB69
Ballyrobert	54	A	NW43
(Ballyroney)	55	1	SB48
(Ballyward)	55	1	SB49
BALMORAL		1	NW52
Banbridge	56	1	SB39
BANGOR		3	NW63
BANGOR WEST	H	3	NW63
Barn Halt	H 77	A	NW64
BELFAST	2		NW52
ADELAIDE		1	NW52
Ballymacarret	77	3	NW52
Bloomfield	50	3	NW52
BOTANIC	76	0	NW52
BRIDGE END	77	0	NW52
CENTRAL	76	0	NW52
CITY HOSPITAL	86	0	NW52
DONEGAL QUAY proposed		0	NW52
Fraser Street	50	3	NW52
Great Victoria Street	76	1	NW52
GREAT VICTORIA ST proposed to re-open		0	NW52
Neill's Hill	50	3	NW52
Queens Quay	76	3	NW52
SYDENHAM		3	NW52
Victoria Park	88	3	NW52
YORKGATE	92	0	NW52
York Road	92	A	NW52
Bleach Green Halt	H 77	A	NW53
Bloom Field	50	3	NW52
BOTANIC	76	0	NW52
BRIDGE END	77	0	NW52
Bright Halt	H 50	3	SB79
Brookhill	H 60	1	NW31
Brookmount	H 60	1	NW41
(Broomhedge)	H 53	1	NW41
CARNALEA		3	NW63
CARRICKFERGUS		A	NW64
(Castlewellan)	55	13	SB58
CITY HOSPITAL	86	0	NW52
CLIPPERSTOWN	H	A	NW54
Comber	50	3	NW62
Coney Island	H 50	3	SB79
Cookstown Junction	76	1	NW34
(Corbet)	55	1	SB39
CRAIGAVAD	57 60	3	NW63
CRAWFORDSBURN Hospital	60	3	NW63
Creevyargon Halt	50	3	NW50
Crossgar	50	3	NW60
CRUMLIN	60 74	1	NW32
CULTRA	51 78	3	NW63
Damhead	H 73	1	NW31
DERRIAGHY	H 53 56	1	NW42
Doagh	54	A	NW44
Doaghadee	50	3	NW73
DONEGAL QUAY proposed		0	NW52
DOWNSHIRE Park	H	A	NW64
Downpatrick	50	3	SB69
Downpatrick Loop Platform	50	3	SB69
Downpatrick Racecourse	H 50	3	SB69
(Dromore)	56	1	NW40
(Drumadonald)	H 55	1	SB49
Dunadry	54	A	NW33
Dundonald	50	3	NW62
Dundrum	50	3	SB69
DUNMURRY		1	NW42
Eden Hall	H 71	A	NW64
FINAGHY	H	1	NW52
Fraser Street	50	3	NW52
GLENAVY	60 74	1	NW32
GLYNN		A	NW65
(Gortnagallon Factory)	50	1	NW32
Great Victoria Street	76	1	NW52
GREAT VICTORIA STREET proposed to re-open		0	NW52
GREENISLAND		A	NW53
Groomsport Road	50	3	NW73
HELEN'S BAY		3	NW63
HILDEN	H	1	NW41
(Hillsborough)	56	1	NW41
HOLYWOOD		3	NW63
JORDANSTOWN		A	NW53
(Katesbridge)	55	1	SB49
Kellswater	71	A	NW24
Killough	50	3	SB68
Kilroot	H 77	A	NW64
Kinnegar Halt	H 57	3	NW53
Knock	50	3	NW62
KNOCKMORE	H 60 74	1	NW41
LAMBEG		1	NW42
LARNE HARBOUR		A	NW65
Larne	G 50	B	NW55
LARNE TOWN		A	NW55
Legatiriff Halt	60	1	NW32
(Leitrim)	55	1	SB59
(Lenaderg)	55	1	NW30
LISBURN		1	NW41
(Magherabeg)	H 56	1	NW41
MAGHERAMORNE		A	NW65
MARINO		3	NW63
Maze	74	1	NW41
Meeting House	H 60	1	NW32
Millar's Bridge	H 60	1	NW33
Millisle Road	H 50	3	NW73
MOIRA		1	NW31
Monkstown	3 H	A	NW53
Mossley	3	A	NW53
(Mount Halt)	H 30	A	NW53
Muckamore	H 63	A	NW33
Narrow Water	64	1	SB37
Neill's Hill	50	3	NW52
Newcastle	55	3	SB58
Newtonards	50	3	NW62
Omeath	51	A	SB36
(Poland's Bridge)	H 55	1	SB39
Queens Quay	76	3	NW52
Saintfield	62	3	NW61
Savage's Bridge	H 55	1	SB59
SEAHILL	66	3	NW63
Shepherd's Bridge	50	3	NW61
SYDENHAM		3	NW52
Templepatrick	3 54	A	NW43
TROOPERS LANE		A	NW53
Tullymurry	50	3	SB69
Victoria Park	88	3	NW52
Warrenpoint	65	1	SB37
WHITEABBEY		A	NW53
WHITEHEAD		A	NW46
WHITEHEAD RPSI		A	NW46
Whitehouse	56	A	NW53
YORKGATE	92	0	NW52
York Road	92	A	NW52

BRIDGES

Bridges	Ry	Ref
DARGAN BRIDGE	0	NW52
LAGAN BRIDGE	1	NW52

JUNCTIONS

Junctions	Ry	Ref
Dufferin Dock	AX	ALL IN NW52
Donegal Quay	1X	
East Bridge Street	1	
CENTRAL	10	
WEST LANE	0	
CITY	0	
LAGAN	0	

NOTES:

1. S = Standard 5'3"
   N = Narrow 3'0"
2. BELFAST stations are often also indexed under own name
3. These stations opened for a time in early '80s but now closed. Line is scheduled to be upgraded from goods only to all traffic.

H Station so marked was a 'Halt' for a time, even though 'Halt' might have never been part of title

G Goods locations (with goods closure dates) on lines which were reduced to goods only from all traffic lines before 1.1.1948.

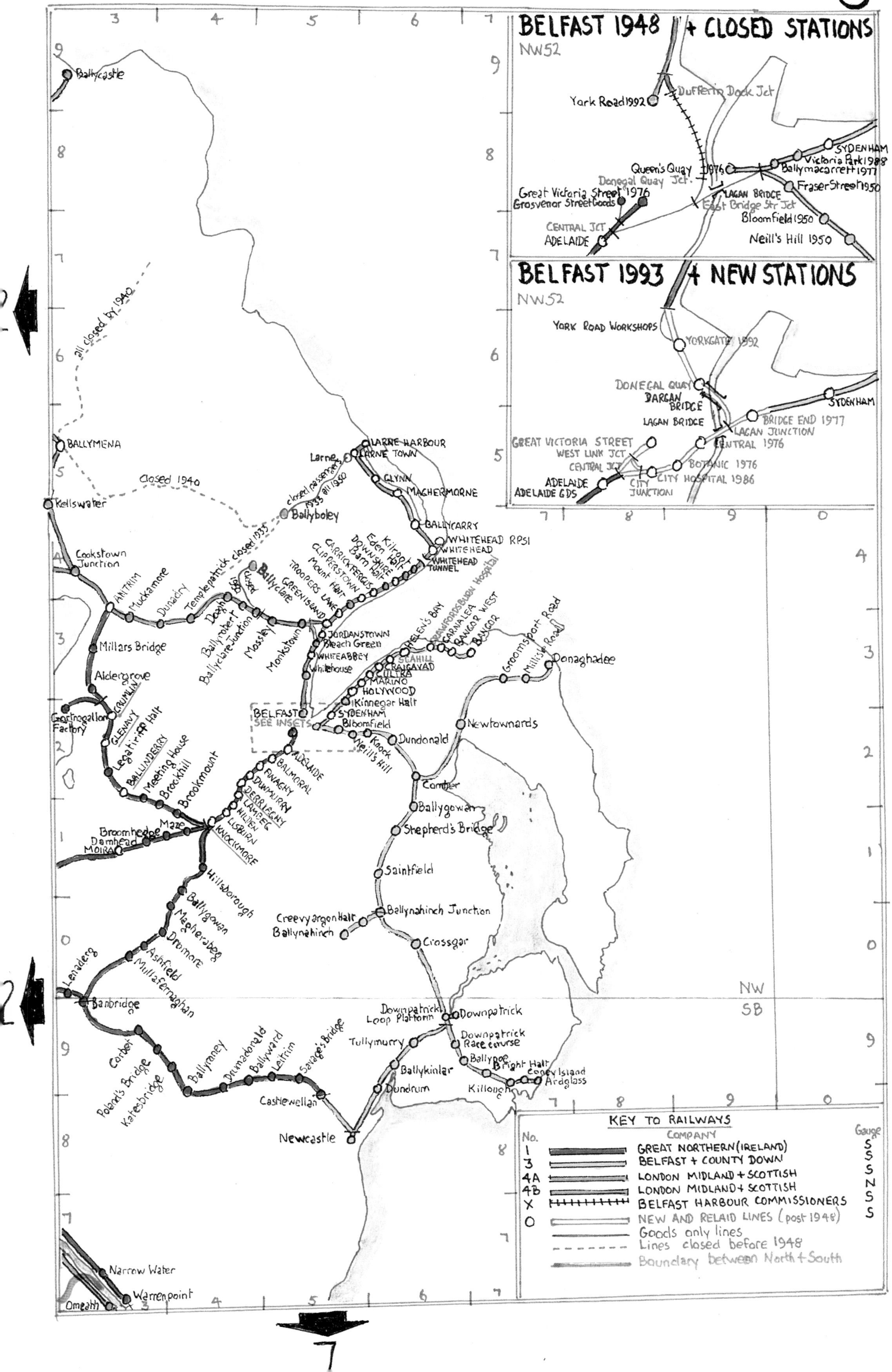

BELFAST 1948 + CLOSED STATIONS

NW52

Dufferin Dock Jct
York Road 1992
Queen's Quay 1976
Donegal Quay Jct.
Great Victoria Street 1976
Grosvenor Street Goods
LAGAN BRIDGE
East Bridge Str Jct
SYDENHAM
Victoria Park 1988
Ballymacarrett 1977
Fraser Street 1950
Bloomfield 1950
Neill's Hill 1950
CENTRAL JCT
ADELAIDE

BELFAST 1993 + NEW STATIONS

NW52

YORK ROAD WORKSHOPS
YORKGATE 1992
DONEGAL QUAY
DARGAN BRIDGE
LAGAN BRIDGE
SYDENHAM
BRIDGE END 1977
LAGAN JUNCTION
GREAT VICTORIA STREET
CENTRAL 1976
WEST LINK JCT
CENTRAL JCT
BOTANIC 1976
ADELAIDE
ADELAIDE GDS
CITY JUNCTION
CITY HOSPITAL 1986

Ballycastle
all closed by 1940
BALLYMENA
Kellswater
closed 1940
Ballyboley
closed passenger 1933 all 1950
LARNE HARBOUR
LARNE TOWN
Larne
GLYNN
MAGHERMORNE
BALLYCARRY
WHITEHEAD RPSI
WHITEHEAD
WHITEHEAD TUNNEL
Kilroot
Eden Halt
DOWNSHIRE
Barn Halt
CARRICKFERGUS
CLIPPERSTOWN
Mount Halt
TROOPERS LANE
GREENISLAND
Cookstown Junction
ANTRIM
Muckamore
Dunadry
Templepatrick closed 1935
Doagh
closed
Ballyclare
Ballyrobert
Ballyclare Junction
Mossley
Monkstown
JORDANSTOWN
Bleach Green
WHITEABBEY
Whitehouse
Millars Bridge
Aldergrove
CRUMLIN
Gortnagallon Factory
GLENAVY
Legatiriff Halt
BALLINDERRY
Meeting House
Brookhill
Brookmount
BELFAST
SEE INSETS
HELEN'S BAY
CRAWFORDSBURN Hospital
CARNALEA
BANGOR WEST
BANGOR
SEAHILL
CULTRA
CRAIGAVAD
MARINO
HOLYWOOD
Kinnegar Halt
SYDENHAM
Bloomfield
Knock
Neill's Hill
Dundonald
Groomsport Road
Millisle Road
Donaghadee
Newtownards
Comber
Ballygowan
Shepherd's Bridge
Saintfield
Ballynahinch Junction
Creevyargon Halt
Ballynahinch
Crossgar
ADELAIDE
BALMORAL
FINAGHY
DUNMURRY
DERRIAGHY
LAMBEG
HILDEN
LISBURN
KNOCKMORE
Maze
Broomhedge
Damhead
MOIRA
Hillsborough
Ballygowan
Magheraberg
Dromore
Ashfield
Mullafernaghan
Lenaderg
Banbridge
Corbet
Poland's Bridge
Katesbridge
Ballyroney
Drumadonald
Ballyward
Leitrim
Savage's Bridge
Castlewellan
Newcastle
Dundrum
Ballykinlar
Tullymurry
Downpatrick Loop Platform
Downpatrick
Downpatrick Race course
Ballynoe
Bright Halt
Coney Island
Ardglass
Killough
Narrow Water
Warrenpoint
Omeath
NW
SB

KEY TO RAILWAYS

No.	COMPANY	Gauge
1	GREAT NORTHERN (IRELAND)	S
3	BELFAST + COUNTY DOWN	S
4A	LONDON MIDLAND + SCOTTISH	S
4B	LONDON MIDLAND + SCOTTISH	N
X	BELFAST HARBOUR COMMISSIONERS	S
O	NEW AND RELAID LINES (post 1948)	S
	Goods only lines	
	Lines closed before 1948	
	Boundary between North + South	

2
2
7

WESTPORT + CLAREMORRIS

RAILWAYS

	Note	No	Gauge
CORAS IOMPAIR EIREANN	1	2	S

STATIONS

	Note	Opened closed	Ry.	Ref.
Ardrahan		76	2	RK66
Balla		63	2	RE43
BALLINA			2	RE46
Ballindine		63	2	RE51
Ballinrobe		60	2	RE41
Ballyglunin		76	2	RK79
Ballyvary		63	2	RE43
Bekan		63	2	RE62
CASTLEBAR			2	RE33
Castlegrove		63	2	RE60
Charlestown		63	2	RE75
CLAREMORRIS			2	RE52
FOXFORD		63 88	2	RE45
GALWAY CEANNT	2		2	RK57
Gort		76	2	RK65
Hollymount		60	2	RE41
Islandeady		63	2	RE33
Kiltimagh		63	2	RE54
MANULLA JUNCTION	3	63 88	2	RE43
Milltown		63	2	RE61
Oranmore		63	2	RK67
Swinford		63	2	RE65
Tuam		63	2	RE60
WESTPORT			2	RE23
WESTPORT QUAY	6		2	RE23

NOTES

1 Standard gauge in Ireland is 5' 3"

2 Title addition 1966

3 Title addition when re-opened in 1988.

6 Goods location still in use.

Although Beeching didn't apply in Ireland it is interesting to note how many places had station closed in 1963, the year of the report.

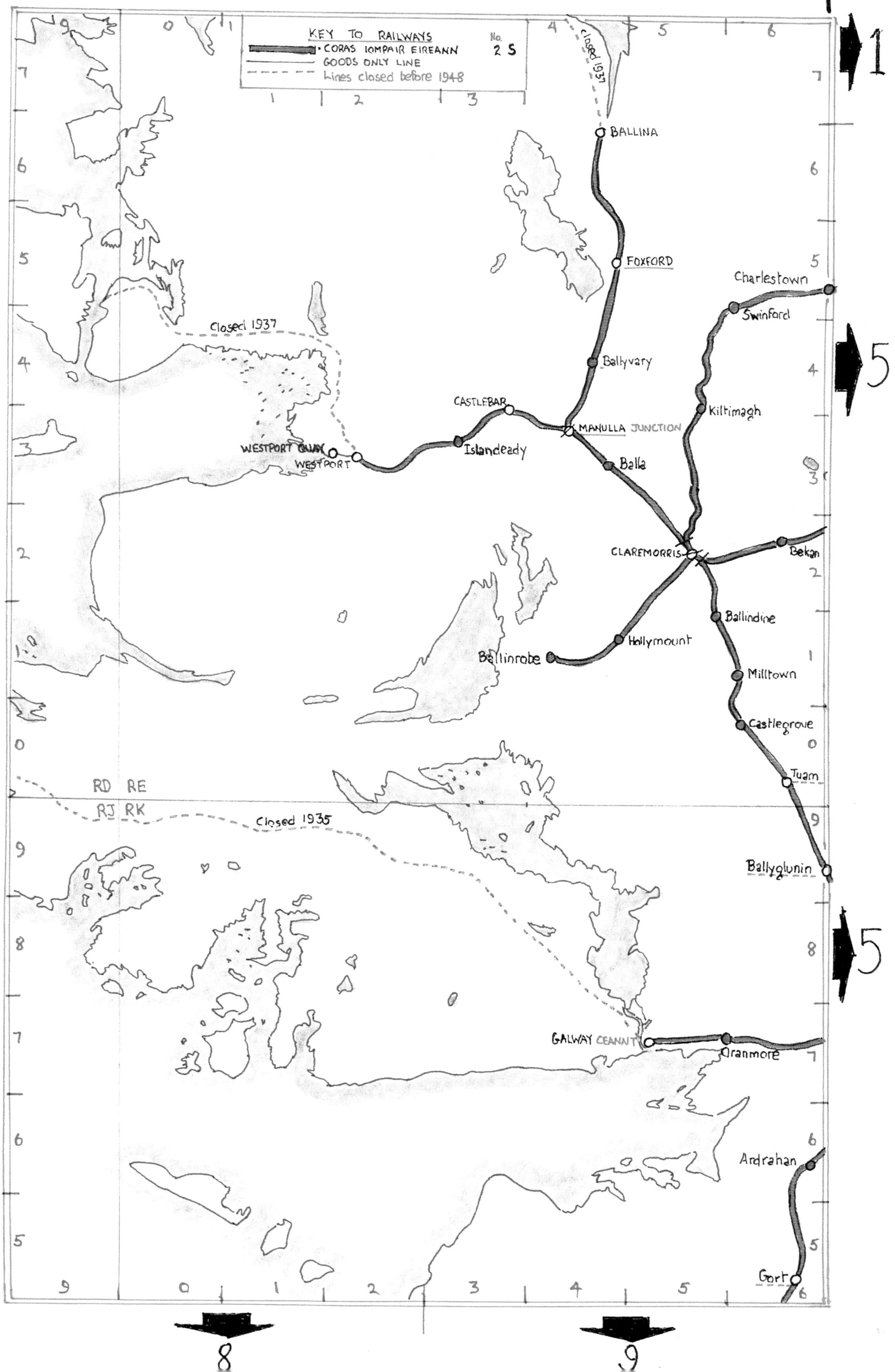

KEY TO RAILWAYS

No. 2 S

CORAS IOMPAIR EIREANN
GOODS ONLY LINE
Lines closed before 1948

closed 1937
BALLINA
FOXFORD
Charlestown
Swinford
Ballyvary
Kiltimagh
Closed 1937
CASTLEBAR
MANULLA JUNCTION
WESTPORT QUAY
WESTPORT
Islandeady
Balla
CLAREMORRIS
Bekan
Ballindine
Ballinrobe
Hollymount
Milltown
Castlegrove
Tuam
RD RE
RJ RK
Closed 1935
Ballyglunin
GALWAY CEANNT
Oranmore
Ardrahan
Gort

1
5
5
8
9

ATHLONE + ATHENRY

RAILWAYS

Railways	No	Gauge[1]
CORAS IOMPAIR EIREANN	A	S
CORAS IOMPAIR EIREANN	B	N

STATIONS

Stations	Opened Closed	Ry. Ref
Adoon	59	BSA35
Annadale	59	BSA26
Arigna	59	BSA16
ATHENRY		ARK77
ATHLONE	2 85	ASF29
Athlone	2 85	ASF29
ATTYMON Junction		ARK87
Ballaghaderreen	63	ARE84
Ballinamore	59	BSA36
BALLINASLOE		ASF08
Ballinlough	67	ARE82
Ballyduff	59	BSA36
Ballyglunin	76	ARK79
BALLYHAUNIS		ARE72
Ballymoe	63	ARE92
BALLYMOTE		ARE86
Ballymurry	63	ASA11
Banagher	3 G 62	ASF26
Birr	63	ASF25
BOYLE		ASA05
CARRICK-ON-SHANNON		ASA15
Carrowduff	63	ASF18
Carrowmore	63	ARE77
CASTLEREA		ARE93
Charlestown	63	ARE75
Cornabrone	59	BSA26
Craughwell + Loughrea	76	ARK76
Creagh	59	BSA26
Curry	63	ARE75
Dereen	59	BSA34
Donamon	63	ASA01
DROMOD		ASA24
Dromod	59	BSA24
Drumshanbo	59	BSA16
Drumsna	63	ASA24
Dunsandle	75	ARK87
Edmondstown	63	ARE84
Fenagh	59	BSA35
Gardice	59	BSA36
Island Road	63	ARE85
Kilfree Junction	63	ARE95
Kiltoom	63	ASA20
Kiltubrid	59	BSA26
Knockcroghery	63	ASA10
Lawderdale	59	BSA36
LONGFORD		ASA32
Loughrea	75	ARK86
Moate	87	ASF38
Mohill	59	BSA34
Newtownforbes	63	ASA33
ROSCOMMON		ASA01
Tubbercurry	63	ARE76
WOODLAWN		ARK98

NOTES

1 S = Standard 5'3", N = Narrow 3'0"

2 Change of site. Date of change is strange as the line via Moate did not lose its passenger service until 1987.

3 Line closed to passengers in 1947, but the station had occasional passenger trains until complete closure in 1962.

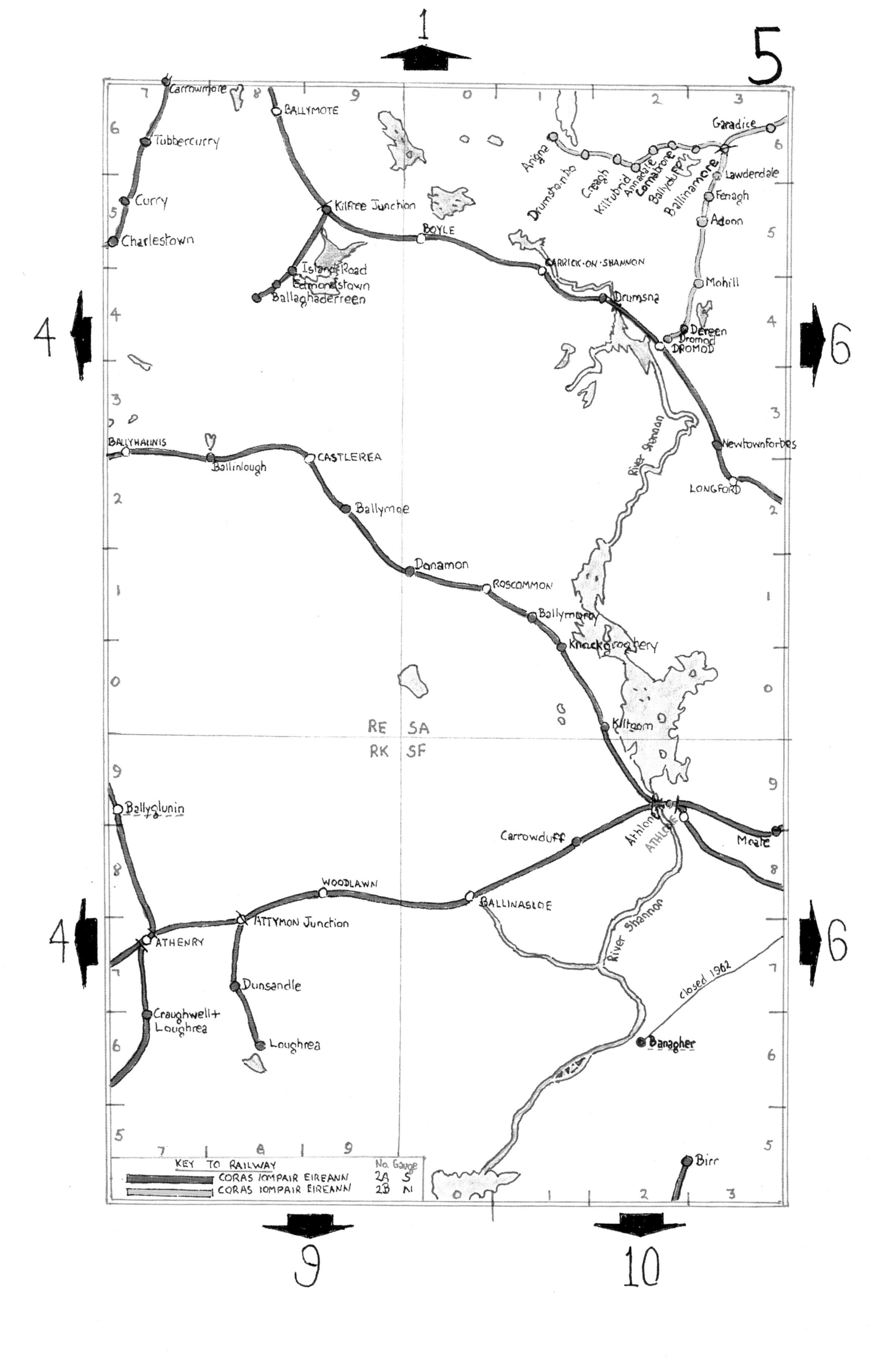
1
5
4
6
4
6
9
10
Carrowmore
Tubbercurry
Curry
Charlestown
BALLYMOTE
Kilfree Junction
BOYLE
Island Road
Edmondstown
Ballaghaderreen
Arigna
Drumshanbo
Creagh
Kiltubrid
Annadale
Cornabrone
Ballyduff
Ballinamore
Garadice
Lawderdale
Fenagh
Adoon
Mohill
Dereen
Dromod
DROMOD
CARRICK-ON-SHANNON
Drumsna
Newtownforbes
LONGFORD
River Shannon
BALLYHAUNIS
Ballinlough
CASTLEREA
Ballymoe
Donamon
ROSCOMMON
Ballymurry
Knockcroghery
Kiltoom
RE SA
RK SF
Ballyglunin
Carrowduff
Athlone
ATHLONE
Moate
WOODLAWN
BALLINASLOE
ATTYMON Junction
ATHENRY
Dunsandle
Craughwell + Loughrea
Loughrea
River Shannon
closed 1962
Banagher
Birr
KEY TO RAILWAY
No. Gauge
CORAS IOMPAIR EIREANN 2A S
CORAS IOMPAIR EIREANN 2B N

NAVAN, CLARA + MARYBOROUGH

RAILWAYS

	No.	Gauge[1]
GREAT NORTHERN (IRELAND)	1	S
CORAS IOMPAIR EIREANN	2A	S
CORAS IOMPAIR EIREANN	2B	N

STATIONS

Station	Opened/Closed	Ry	Ref
AN UAIMH	A§		1 SB01
(Ardbraccan)	H 58		1 SB02
(Ballybeg)	58		1 SA92
Ballyconnell	59		B SA46
Ballycumber	63		A SF48
(Ballyhaise)	57		1 SA66
Ballyheady	59		B SA46
(Beauparc)	58		1 SB12
(Belturbet)	57		1 SA56
Belturbet	59		B SA56
(Blackstaff)	H 57		1 SB16
Carrickmacross	G 60		1 SB05
(Castlemartin)	H 58		1 SB02
Castletown	63		A SF59
(Cavan)	57		1 SA65
Cavan	G 59		A SA65
(Ceannus Mor)	B§ 58		1 SA92
CLARA			A SF48
Crossdoney	G 59		A SA55
(Culloville)	57		1 SB06
CURRAGH	77		A SF96
Curragh Racecourse	77		A SF96
DROICEAD NUA	C§		A SG06
Dunlavin	3 57		A SG05
EDGEWORTHSTOWN	D§		A SA42
ENFIELD	63 88		A SF99
(Factory Crossing)	58		1 SB12
Fern's Lock	63		A SG09
Geashill	63		A SF67
Hazelhatch + Celbridge	4 94		A SG18
Hill of Down	63		A SF89
(Inniskeen)	57		1 SB15
(Kells)	B§ 58		1 SA92
(Kellybridge)	H 57		1 SB15
Kilcock	63		A SG09
Kildangan	63		A SF85
KILDARE			A SF96
Killucan	63		A SA70
Killyran	59		B SA46
Kilmessan	G 6 61		A SB00
KINGSCOURT	G		A SB04
(Loreto College)	H 57		1 SA66
MARYBOROUGH	E§		A SF64
MAYNOOTH	63 81		A SG18
MEATHIAS TRUIM	D§		A SA42
Monasterevan	67		A SF86
Moyvalley	63		A SF99
MULLINGAR			A SA60
Multyfarnham	63		A SA61
Naas	3 57		A SG16
(Navan)	A§ 58		1 SB01
NEWBRIDGE	C§		A SG06
(Newgate Crossing)	H 58		1 SB02
(Oldcastle)	58		1 SA73
(Phoenixtown)	H 58		1 SB02
PORTARLINGTON			A SF76
PORTLAOISE	7 E§		A SF64
(Redhills)	57		1 SA66
Sallins	5 63 94		A SG17
Straffan	63		A SG17
Streamstown	63		A SF59
Street + Rathowen	63		A SA52
Templeport for Bawnboy + Swanlibar	59		B SA46
Tomkin Road	59		B SA56
TULLAMORE			A SF57
(Virginia Road)	58		1 SA83

JUNCTIONS

Junction	Ry	Ref
CHERRYVILLE	A	SF96
Connibery	A	SF64
Inny	A	SA52
Nesbitt	A	SF99

NOTES

H	Halt – may or may not be part of title.
G	Goods location. Date is for closure to goods traffic. IN CAPITALS still open.
§	Change of name – later version
§	Change of name – earlier version.
	Similar identifying letter gives alternative. In this map area both names continue in use.
1	S = Standard 5'3"; N = Narrow 3'0"
2	Goods traffic may have lasted into early 50's
3	Station closed for regular traffic (passenger) in 1947
4	Proposed to re-open, was closed in 1947
5	Proposed for re-opening
6	Not taken out of use until 1963 but all regular goods services as date shown.
7	Alternative style PORT LAOISE.

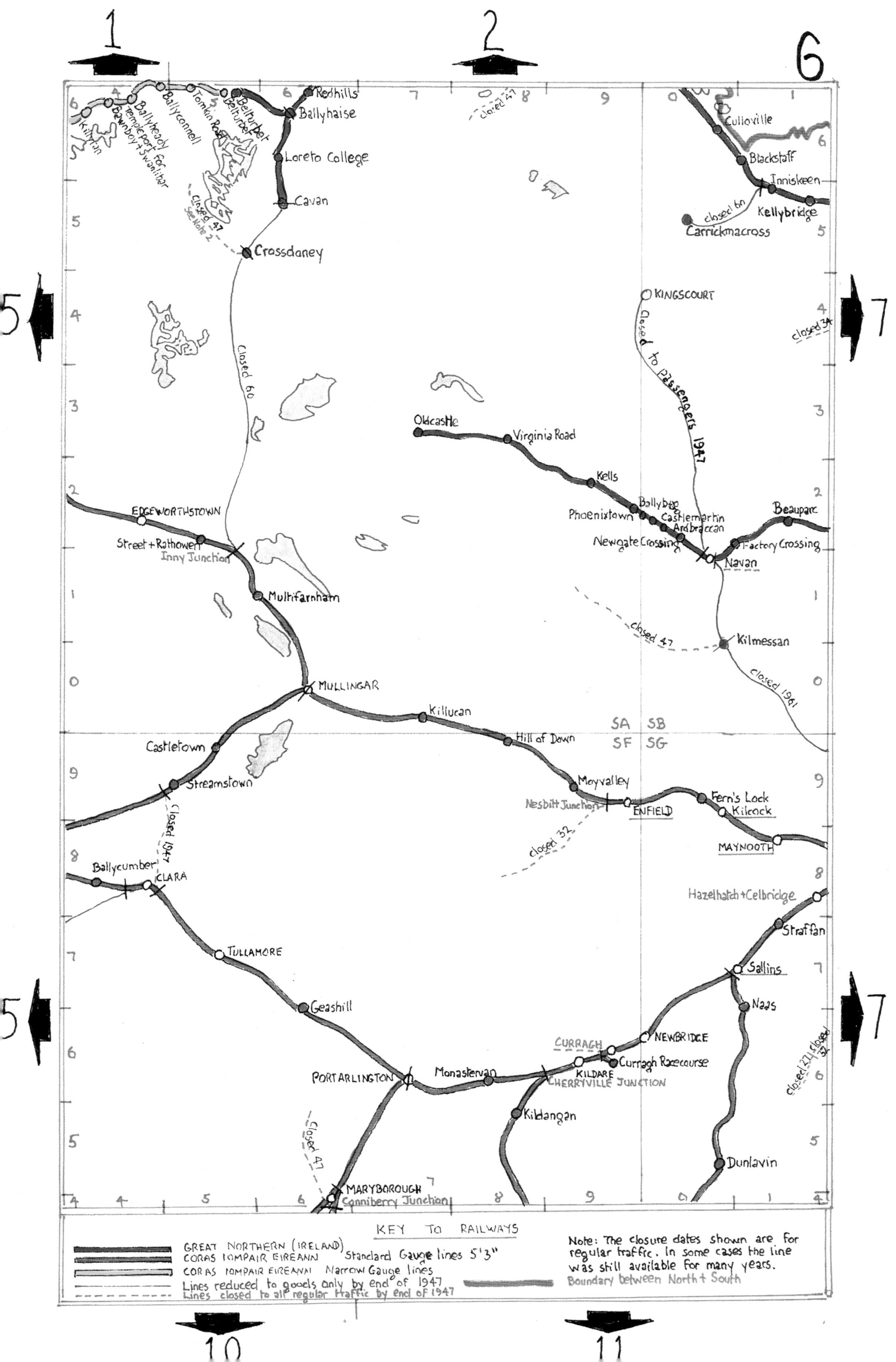

1
2
6
5
7
5
7
10
11
Killeshandra
Ballyheady
Templeport for Bawnboy + Swanlinbar
Ballyconnell
Tomkin Road
Belturbet
Redhills
Ballyhaise
Loreto College
Cavan
closed 47 See Note 2
Crossdoney
Closed 60
closed 47
Culloville
Blackstaff
Inniskeen
closed 60
Kellybridge
Carrickmacross
KINGSCOURT
Closed to passengers 1947
closed 34
Oldcastle
Virginia Road
Kells
Ballybeg
Phoenixtown
Castlemartin
Ardbraccan
Newgate Crossing
Navan
Beauparc
Factory Crossing
EDGEWORTHSTOWN
Street + Rathowen
Inny Junction
Multifarnham
closed 47
Kilmessan
closed 1961
MULLINGAR
Killucan
Hill of Down
SA SB
SF SG
Castletown
Streamstown
Moyvalley
Nesbitt Junction
ENFIELD
Fern's Lock
Kilcock
MAYNOOTH
closed 32
Closed 1947
Ballycumber
CLARA
Hazelhatch + Celbridge
Straffan
TULLAMORE
Sallins
Naas
Geashill
NEWBRIDGE
CURRAGH
Curragh Racecourse
KILDARE
closed 27 closed 32
PORTARLINGTON
Monasterevan
CHERRYVILLE JUNCTION
Kildangan
Closed 47
Dunlavin
MARYBOROUGH
Conniberry Junction
KEY TO RAILWAYS
GREAT NORTHERN (IRELAND)
CORAS IOMPAIR EIREANN
Standard Gauge lines 5'3"
CORAS IOMPAIR EIREANN Narrow Gauge lines
Lines reduced to goods only by end of 1947
Lines closed to all regular traffic by end of 1947
Note: The closure dates shown are for regular traffic. In some cases the line was still available for many years.
Boundary between North + South

DUBLIN + DUNDALK

No.	RAILWAYS [1]
1	GREAT NORTHERN (IRELAND)
2	CORAS IOMPAIR EIREANN
4	LONDON MIDLAND + SCOTTISH

STATIONS

Station	Opened closed	Ry	Ref
Amiens Street	2 59	1	3784
AMIENS STREET Junction	A§ 2 66	2	3784
Annaloughan	H 51	4	SB35
ASHTOWN	79 82	2	SG38
BALBRIGAN		1	SB41
Balglass	59	1	SG58
BALLYFERMONT		2	SG38
BARROW STREET		2	3881
BAYSIDE	73	1	SG48
Bellurgan	51	4	SB35
Bellurgan Point	H 51	4	SB35
BLACKROCK	H	2	SG47
BLANCHARDSTOWN	B § 34 90	2	SG38
BOOTERSTOWN	60	2	SG48
BRAY DALY	3 66	2	SG46
Broadstone	4G 61	2	3584
BROOMBRIDGE	90	2	3488
Bush	51	4	SB48
CABRA		2	3486
Carlingford	H 51	4	SB46
Carrickmines	59	2	SG47
Castlebellingham	76	1	SB24
CASTLEKNOCK	B§ 90	2	SG38
CHERRY ORCHARD	94	2	SG28
Clondalkin	47 94	2	SG28
CLONSILLA Junction	63 81	2	SG28
Clontarf	C§ 56	1	3986
CONNOLLY	A§ 66	2	3784
COOLMINE	90	2	SG28
Crossalaney	H 51	4	SB45
DALKEY		2	SG47
DONABATE		1	SB40
DROGHEDA MACBRIDE	66	1	SB32
(Dromin Junction)	55	1	SB24
DRUMCONDRA		2	3786
DUBLIN			
Amiens Street	2 59	1	3784
AMIENS STREET Junction	A§ 2 66	2	3784
BARROW STREET		2	3881
Broadstone	4 G 61	2	3584
BROOMBRIDGE	90	2	3488
CABRA		2	3486
Clontarf	C§ 56	1	3986
CONNOLLY	A§ 66	2	3784
DRUMCONDRA		2	3786
FAIRVIEW	C§	1	3986
Harcourt Street	59	2	3680
HEUSTON	D§ 66	2	3483
HEUSTON SUBURBAN		2	3483
KINGSBRIDGE	D§ 66	2	3483
LANSDOWNE ROAD		2	3882
Milltown	59	2	3779
NORTH WALL		124	3883
PEARSE	E§ 66	2	3882
PHOENIX PARK		2	3484
Ranelagh	59	2	3779
SANDYMOUNT	60 84	2	3980
TARA STREET		2	3781
WESTLAND ROW	E§ 66	2	3882
(Duleek)	58	1	SB22
DUNDALK Junction CLARKE	66	1	SB25
Dundalk Quay Street	51	4	SB25
Dundrum	59	2	SG37
DUNLAOGHAIRE MALLIN	66	2	SG47
Dunleer	84	1	SB23
Dunstable's Crossing	H 51	4	SB46
FAIRVIEW	C§	1	3986
Foxrock	59	2	SG47
GLENGEARY		2	SG47
GORMANSTON		1	SB31
Greenore	51	4	SB46
GREYSTONES	H	2	SG46
Gyles Quay	H 51	4	SB35
Harcourt Street	59	2	3680
HARMONSTOWN	57	1	SG48
HEUSTON	D§ 66	2	3483
HEUSTON SUBURBAN		2	3483
HOWTH		1	SG48
HOWTH JUNCTION		1	SG48
Inchicore	5 55	2	SG38
KILBARRACK	69	1	SG48
KILCOOLE		2	SG55
KILLESTER		1	SG48
KILLINEY		2	SG47
KINGSBRIDGE		2	3483
LANSDOWNE ROAD		2	3881
LAYTOWN + Bettystown		1	SB32
LEIXLIP LOUISA BRIDGE	63 91	2	SG28
LEIXLIP CONFEY	90	2	SG28
Lougher	H 60	1	SB21
Lucan South	63	2	SG28
MALAHIDE		1	SG49
Milltown	59	2	3778
MOSNEY Holiday Camp	48 58	1	SB32
Newcastle	64	2	SG55
NORTH WALL	G	124	3883
Omeath	51	4	SB36
PEARSE	E§ 66	2	3882
PHOENIX PARK		2	3484
PORTMARNOCK		1	SG49
RAHENY		1	SG48
Ranelagh	59	2	3779
RUSH + LUSK		1	SB40
St Fintans	59	1	SG48
SALTHILL + MONKSTOWN	60 84	2	SG47
SANDYCOVE + GLASTHULE		2	SG47
SANDYMOUNT	60 84	2	3980
SEAPOINT + Monkstown		2	SG47
SHANKILL	6 77	2	SG47
Shankill	59	2	SG47
SKERRIES		1	SB41
Stillorgan	59	2	SG37
Summit	59	1	SG48
SUTTON		1	SG48
SYDNEY PARADE	60 72	2	SG38
TARA STREET		2	3781
WESTLAND ROW	E§	2	3882
White's Crossing	H 51	4	SB36
Woodbrook	H 60	4	SG47

COMPANY WORKS

At Inchicore south of station

TUNNELS

No.	Name	Ry	length yds	Ref
1	Cross Guns	2	292	3686
2	Phoenix Park	2	757	3484
3	BRABAZON	2	300	SG46
4	BRANDY HOLE	2	143	SG46
5	CABLE ROCK	2	210	SG46
6	LONG	2	1084	SG46

JUNCTIONS

No.	Name	Ry	Ref
1	Island bridge	2	3483
2	Liffey	2	3487
3	Drumcondra	2	3587
4	GLASNEVIN	2	3687
5	Newcomen Bridge	2	3785
6	North Strand Road	2	3885
7	East Wall	12	3885
8	Church Road	2	3884

NOTES

1 All railways open, on this map as at 31·12·1947 were standard gauge 5'3"
2 When GN(I) nationalised stayed open as part of CIE station + Junction suffix dropped.
3 The 1966 addition not normally used.
4 Regular goods traffic finished in 1994.
5 After closure continued as a halt for railway workers at adjoining works.
6 Replacement for station on Harcourt Str. line closed 1959.
H Halt, although 'Halt' not always part of title.
G Goods location
§ } change of name – letter shows to or from other name

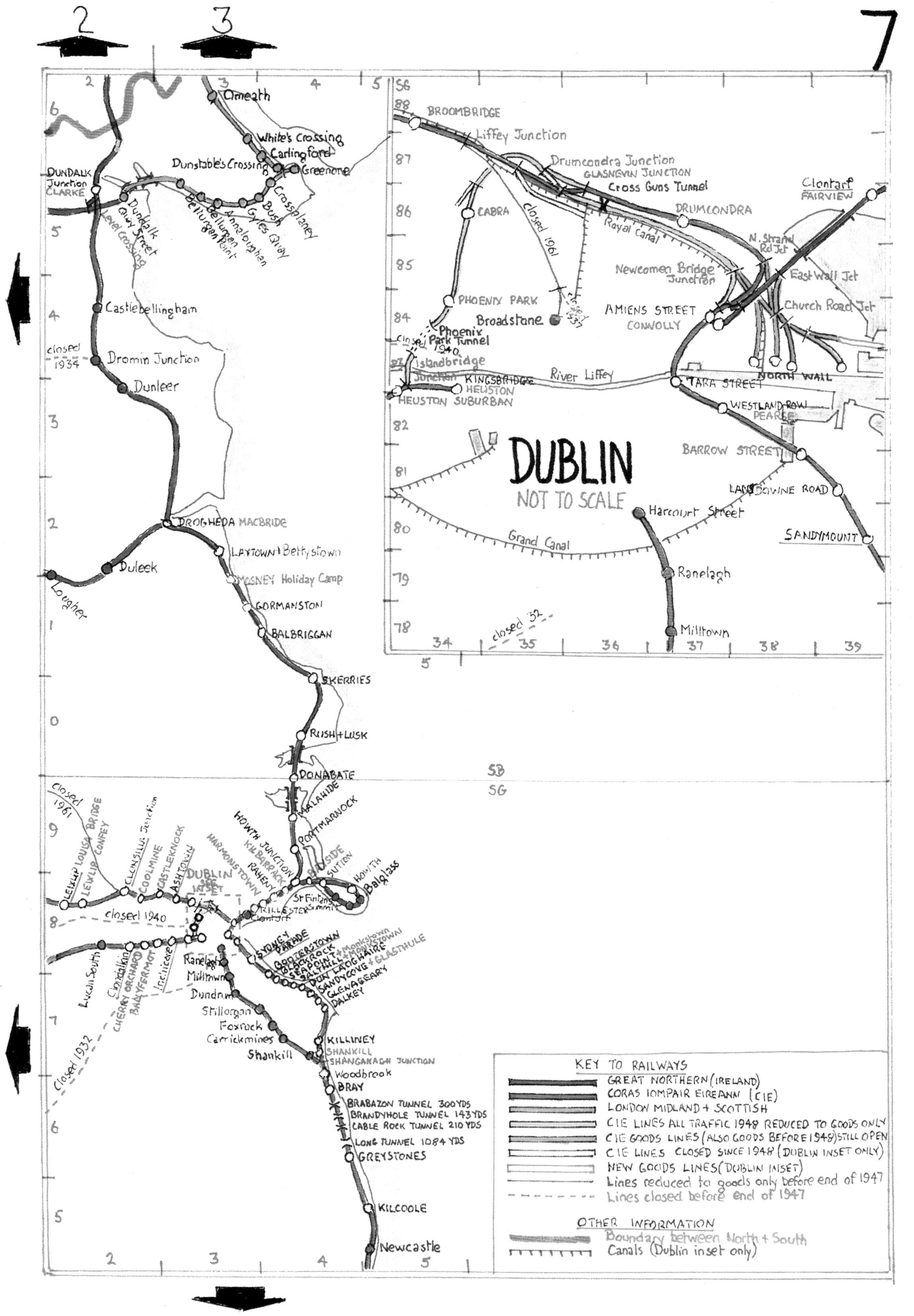
7
2
3
Omeath
White's Crossing
Carlingford
Greenore
Dunstable's Crossing
Crossplaney
Bush
Gyles Quay
Annaloughan
Bellurgan
Bellurgan Point
DUNDALK Junction
CLARKE
Dundalk Quay Street
Level Crossing
Castlebellingham
closed 1934
Dromin Junction
Dunleer
DROGHEDA MACBRIDE
LAYTOWN + Bettystown
MOSNEY Holiday Camp
GORMANSTON
BALBRIGGAN
SKERRIES
RUSH + LUSK
DONABATE
MALAHIDE
PORTMARNOCK
Duleek
Lougher
5B
5G
closed 1961
LEIXLIP LOUISA BRIDGE
LEIXLIP CONFEY
CLONSILLA Junction
COOLMINE
CASTLEKNOCK
ASHTOWN
DUBLIN INSET
closed 1940
HOWTH JUNCTION
KILBARRACK
RAHENY
HARMONSTOWN
KILLESTER
Clontarf
BAYSIDE
SUTTON
St Fintans Summit
HOWTH
Balglass
SYDNEY PARADE
BOOTERSTOWN
BLACKROCK
SEAPOINT
SALTHILL + MONKSTOWN
DUN LAOGHAIRE
SANDYCOVE + GLASTHULE
GLENAGEARY
DALKEY
Lucan South
Clondalkin
CHERRY ORCHARD
BALLYFERMOT
Inchicore
Ranelagh
Milltown
Dundrum
Stillorgan
Foxrock
Carrickmines
Shankill
closed 1932
KILLINEY
SHANKILL
SHANGANAGH JUNCTION
Woodbrook
BRAY
BRABAZON TUNNEL 300 YDS
BRANDYHOLE TUNNEL 143 YDS
CABLE ROCK TUNNEL 210 YDS
LONG TUNNEL 1084 YDS
GREYSTONES
KILCOOLE
Newcastle
BROOMBRIDGE
Liffey Junction
Drumcondra Junction
GLASNEVIN JUNCTION
Cross Guns Tunnel
CABRA
closed 1961
DRUMCONDRA
Royal Canal
Clontarf
FAIRVIEW
N. Strand Rd Jct
East Wall Jct
Newcomen Bridge Junction
Church Road Jct
PHOENIX PARK
Broadstone
closed 1937
AMIENS STREET
CONNOLLY
Phoenix Park Tunnel
closed 1940
Islandbridge Junction
KINGSBRIDGE
HEUSTON
HEUSTON SUBURBAN
River Liffey
TARA STREET
NORTH WALL
WESTLAND ROW
PEARSE
BARROW STREET
DUBLIN
NOT TO SCALE
LANSDOWNE ROAD
Harcourt Street
SANDYMOUNT
Grand Canal
Ranelagh
Milltown
closed 32
KEY TO RAILWAYS
GREAT NORTHERN (IRELAND)
CORAS IOMPAIR EIREANN (CIE)
LONDON MIDLAND + SCOTTISH
CIE LINES ALL TRAFFIC 1948 REDUCED TO GOODS ONLY
CIE GOODS LINES (ALSO GOODS BEFORE 1948) STILL OPEN
CIE LINES CLOSED SINCE 1948 (DUBLIN INSET ONLY)
NEW GOODS LINES (DUBLIN INSET)
Lines reduced to goods only before end of 1947
Lines closed before end of 1947
OTHER INFORMATION
Boundary between North + South
Canals (Dublin inset only)

11

KILRUSH + TRALEE

RAILWAYS	No	Gauge [1]
CORAS IOMPAIR EIREANN	A	S
CORAS IOMPAIR EIREANN	B	N
TRALEE + DINGLE	X	N

STATIONS		Opened Closed	Ry	Ref
Abbeydorney		63	A	RP07
Annagh	H	52 63	B	RK22
Ardfert		63	A	RP06
Ballybrack		63	A	RP14
Blackweir		61	B	RK10
Blennerville			X	RP06
Cahirciveen		60	A	R062
Cappa Pier	2 G	61	B	RK20
Caragh Lake		60	A	R094
Castleisland	G	77	A	RP15
Castlemaine		60	A	RP05
Craggaknock		61	B	RK21
Dingle	G	53	B	R065
Dooks		60	A	R094
Doonbeg		61	B	RK21
FARRANFORE			A	RP15
Fenit	3 G	75	A	R096
Glenbeigh		60	A	R084
Gortatlea		63	A	RP15
Hanrahan's Bridge	H	58 61	B	RK23
Headford Junction		63	A	RP23
Kells		60	A	R073
Kilkee		61	B	RK10
KILLARNEY			A	RP13
Killorglin		60	A	R094
Kilmorna		63	A	RP28
Kilmurry		61	B	RK22
Kilrush		61	B	RK20
Listowel		63	A	RP28
Lixnaw		63	A	RP17
Loo Bridge		60	A	RP23
Milltown		60	A	RP05
Miltown Malbay		61	B	RK22
Molahiffe		60	A	RP15
Morley's Bridge		60	A	RP22
Mountain Stage		60	A	R083
Moyasta Junction		61	B	RK10
Quilty		61	B	RK22
Rineen	H	52 61	B	RK23
Shragh	H	52 61	B	RK11
Tralee Ballyard			X	RP06
TRALEE			A	RP06
Valentia Harbour		60	A	R062

TUNNELS	Ry	Ref
Druagh Hill	A	R073

NOTES

1 S = Standard gauge 5'3"
N = Narrow gauge 3'0"

2 Regular traffic finished 1935. But some goods and passenger excursions to date shown

3 Passenger services and regular goods until 1935. But passenger excursions lasted until the date shown. As at 31·12·1993 the full line was proposed for preservation, however this project now appears lost.

G Goods location date is for line closure to goods

H Halts opened in the '50s.

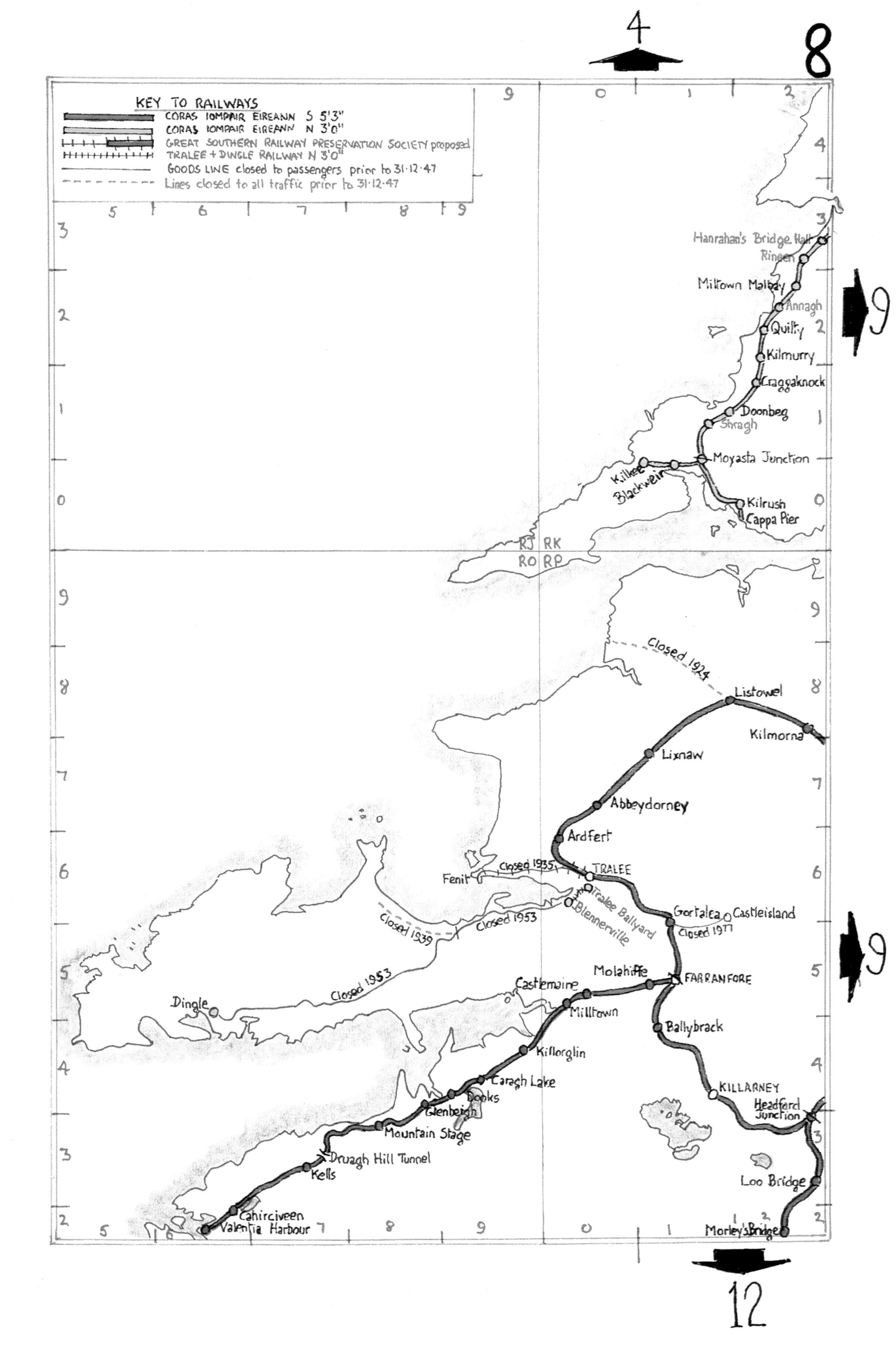
4
KEY TO RAILWAYS
CORAS IOMPAIR EIREANN S 5'3"
CORAS IOMPAIR EIREANN N 3'0"
GREAT SOUTHERN RAILWAY PRESERVATION SOCIETY proposed
TRALEE + DINGLE RAILWAY N 3'0"
GOODS LINE closed to passengers prior to 31·12·47
Lines closed to all traffic prior to 31·12·47
Hanrahan's Bridge Halt
Rineen
Miltown Malbay
Annagh
Quilty
Kilmurry
Craggaknock
Doonbeg
Shragh
Moyasta Junction
Kilkee
Blackweir
Kilrush
Cappa Pier
RJ RK
RO RP
Closed 1924
Listowel
Kilmorna
Lixnaw
Abbeydorney
Ardfert
Closed 1935
TRALEE
Fenit
Tralee Ballyard
Blennerville
Gortalea
Castleisland
Closed 1977
Closed 1939
Closed 1953
Closed 1953
Molahiffe
FARRANFORE
Castlemaine
Dingle
Milltown
Ballybrack
Killorglin
Caragh Lake
KILLARNEY
Headford Junction
Dooks
Glenbeigh
Mountain Stage
Druagh Hill Tunnel
Kells
Loo Bridge
Cahirciveen
Valentia Harbour
Morley's Bridge
9
9
12

LIMERICK, LIMERICK JUNCTION + MALLOW

RAILWAYS	No.	Gauge [1]
CORAS IOMPAIR EIREANN	A	S
CORAS IOMPAIR EIREANN	B	N

STATIONS

Station	Opened Closed	Ry Ref
Abbeyfeale	63	ARP37
Adare	63	ARP69
Annacotty	63	ARK80
Ardagh	63	ARP48
Ardsollus + Quin	63	ARK62
Askeaton	63	ARP59
Ballingrane	63	ARP59
Ballycar	63	ARK61
Ballyhooly	67	ARP94
BANTEER		ARP54
Barnagh	63	ARP47
BIRDHILL		ARK91
Boher	63	ARK90
Buttevant	77	ARP75
CASTLECONNEL	63 89	ARK81
Castletownroche	67	ARP84
CHARLEVILLE	A§	ARP77
Clare Castle	63	ARK52
Clondulane	67	ASL04
Clouna	H 54 61	BRK43
Corofin	61	BRK43
Cratloe	63	ARK60
Crusheen	63	ARK53
Devon Road	63	ARP37
Dromkeen	76	ARP99
Emly	63	ARP98
Ennis	61	BRK52
ENNIS	2 76 80	ARK52
Ennistymon	61	BRK33
Fermoy	67	ASL04
Foynes	3 63	ARK40
Hanrahan's Bridge	H 58 61	BRK23
Kilgobbin	63	ARP69
Killaloe	G 52	ARK92
Killonan	63	ARK80
Kilmallock	77	ARP87
Knocklong	4 79	ARP97
Lahinch	61	BRK33
Lifford	H 52 61	BRK53
LIMERICK COLBERT	66	ARK70
LIMERICK JUNCTION		ASL08
Lisnagry	63	ARK80
Lombardstown	63	ARP64
Long Pavement	63	ARK70
MALLOW		ARP74
MILLSTREET		ARP44
Mitchelstown	G 53	ASL06
Monreal	52 61	BRK33
Mourne Abbey	63	ARP74
NENAGH		ASF02
Newcastle West	63	ARP48
Newmarket	G 63	ARP55
Oola	63	ASL09
Pallas	63	ARP99
Patrick's Well	63	ARP79
Rathcoole	63	ARP54
Rathduff	76	ARP73
Rathkeale	62	ARP59
RATH LUIRC	A§	ARP77
RATHMORE		ARP34
Ruan	52 61	BRK53
Shallee	63	ARK92
Sixmilebridge	63	ARK61
TIPPERARY		ASL08
Tubber	63	ARK64
Willbrook	61	BRK43
Workhouse	53 61	BRK33

TUNNELS

Tunnel	Ry	Ref
Barnagh	A	RP48

JUNCTIONS

Junction		Ref
Check	Limerick	RK70
Ennis	Limerick	RK70
Foynes	Limerick	RK70
Cement Fatory	Limerick	RK70
KILLARNEY		RP74
KEANE'S POINTS		SL08
MILLTOWN CROSSING		SL08
KYLE CROSSING		SL08

NOTES

1 S = Standard 5'3" N = Narrow 3'0"
2 Now re-opened for regular services
3 Still open for goods
4 regular services ended in 1977
§ Change of name older version
§ Change of name modern version
H Halt
G Goods location date shows closed for entire line.

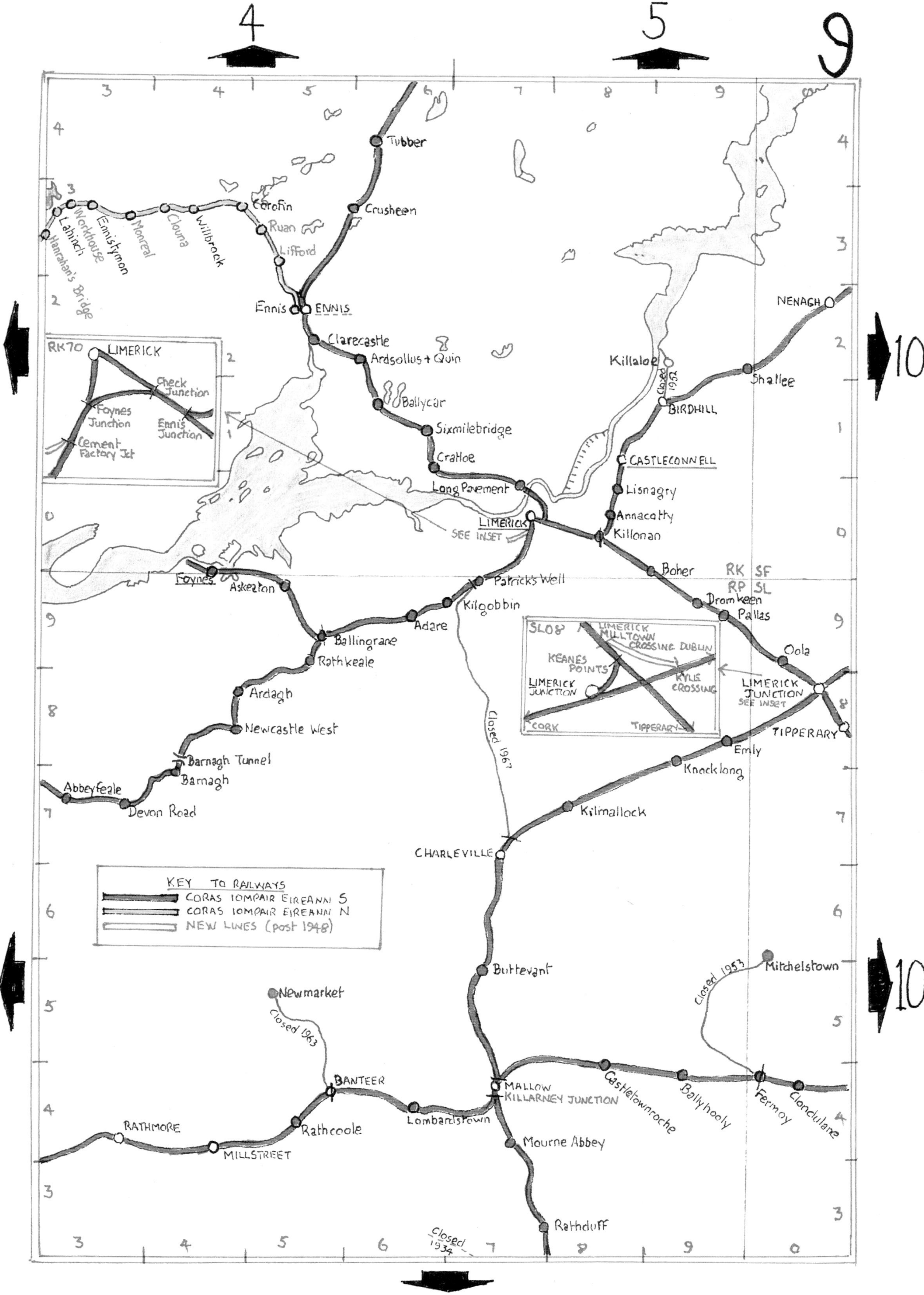

4
5
8
10
12
Tubber
Crusheen
Corofin
Ruan
Lifford
Lahinch
Hanrahan's Bridge
Workhouse
Ennistymon
Monreal
Clouna
Willbrock
Ennis
ENNIS
Clarecastle
Ardsollus + Quin
Ballycar
Sixmilebridge
Cratloe
Long Pavement
LIMERICK
SEE INSET
RK70
LIMERICK
Check Junction
Foynes Junction
Ennis Junction
Cement Factory Jct
NENAGH
Shallee
Killaloe
Closed 1952
BIRDHILL
CASTLECONNELL
Lisnagry
Annacotty
Killonan
Boher
RK SF
RP SL
Dromkeen
Pallas
Oola
Foynes
Askeaton
Patrick's Well
Kilgobbin
Adare
Ballingrane
Rathkeale
Ardagh
Newcastle West
Barnagh Tunnel
Barnagh
Abbeyfeale
Devon Road
SL08
LIMERICK MILLTOWN CROSSING
DUBLIN
KEANES POINTS
KYLES CROSSING
LIMERICK JUNCTION
CORK
TIPPERARY
LIMERICK JUNCTION
SEE INSET
TIPPERARY
Emly
Knocklong
Kilmallock
Closed 1967
CHARLEVILLE
KEY TO RAILWAYS
CORAS IOMPAIR EIREANN S
CORAS IOMPAIR EIREANN N
NEW LINES (post 1948)
Buttevant
Mitchelstown
Closed 1953
Newmarket
Closed 1963
BANTEER
MALLOW
KILLARNEY JUNCTION
Castletownroche
Ballyhooly
Fermoy
Clondulane
RATHMORE
MILLSTREET
Rathcoole
Lombardstown
Mourne Abbey
Rathduff
Closed 1934

KILKENNY + WATERFORD

RAILWAYS

CORAS IOMPAIR EIREANN	S	1

STATIONS

Station	Opened Closed	Ref
Abbeyleix	63	SF63
Attanagh	63	SF62
BALLYBROPHY		SF43
Ballyduff	67	SL14
Ballyhale	63	SL78
Ballyraggett	63	SF62
Bansha	63	SL18
Bennettsbridge	63	SF70
Bronsa	63	SF24
CAHIR		SL27
Cappagh	67	SL44
Cappoquin	67	SL35
CARRICK-ON-SUIR		SL67
Carroll's Cross	67	SL65
Cashel	2 G 54	SL29
Castlecomer	G 62	SF72
CLONMEL		SL47
CLOUGHJORDAN		SF13
Dundrum	76	SL19
Dungarvan	67	SL44
Durrow + Stradbally	67	SL54
Farranalleen	63	SL49
Fethard	63	SL48
Fiddown	63	SL67
Glenmore	63	SL87
Goold's Cross	76	SF20
Gowran	63	SF80
Grange	63	SL76
Horse + Jockey	63	SF30
KILKENNY MCDONAGH	3 66	SF70
Killeagh	63	SL22
Kilmacow	63	SL77
Kilmacthomas	67	SL65
Kilmeadan	67	SL76
Kilsheelan	63	SL57
Laffan's Bridge	63	SL49
Lisduff	63	SF42
Lismore	57	SL24
Mageney	63	SL12
MARYBOROUGH	A §	SF64
Midletown	6 63	SL12
Mogeely	6 63	SL12
Mountrath + Castletown	76	SF54
Mullinavat	63	SL77
PORT LAOISE	4 B §	SF64
Powerstown Park Racecourse	H 63	SL47
ROSCREA		SF33
Tallow Road	67	SL24
TEMPLEMORE		SF32
THOMASTOWN		SL79
THURLES		SF31
TIPPERARY		SL86
Tramore	61	SL75
WATERFORD North PLUNKETT	5 66	SL86
Waterford, The Manor	61	SL86
Wolfhill	G 63	SF13
Youghal	6 63	SL32

BRIDGES

Bridge	Ref
Suir Bridge	SL86

TUNNELS

Tunnel		Ref
Durrow	418	SL54
Snow Hill	217	SL86

JUNCTIONS

Junction		Ref
Conniberry		SF64
LAVISTOWN West	KILKENNY	SF70
North	KILKENNY	SF70
South	KILKENNY	SF70
Suir Bridge	WATERFORD	SL86
West	WATERFORD	SL86
New Wharf	WATERFORD	SL86
Abbey	WATERFORD	SL86

NOTES

1 All lines standard gauge 5'3"
2 Used for passenger excursions until closure
3 Addition 1966
4 Sometimes one word
5 Change North to PLUNKETT 1966
6 Closed to regular passenger year shown
§ Change of name old version } Both used
§ Change of name new version } Both used
G Goods
H Halt

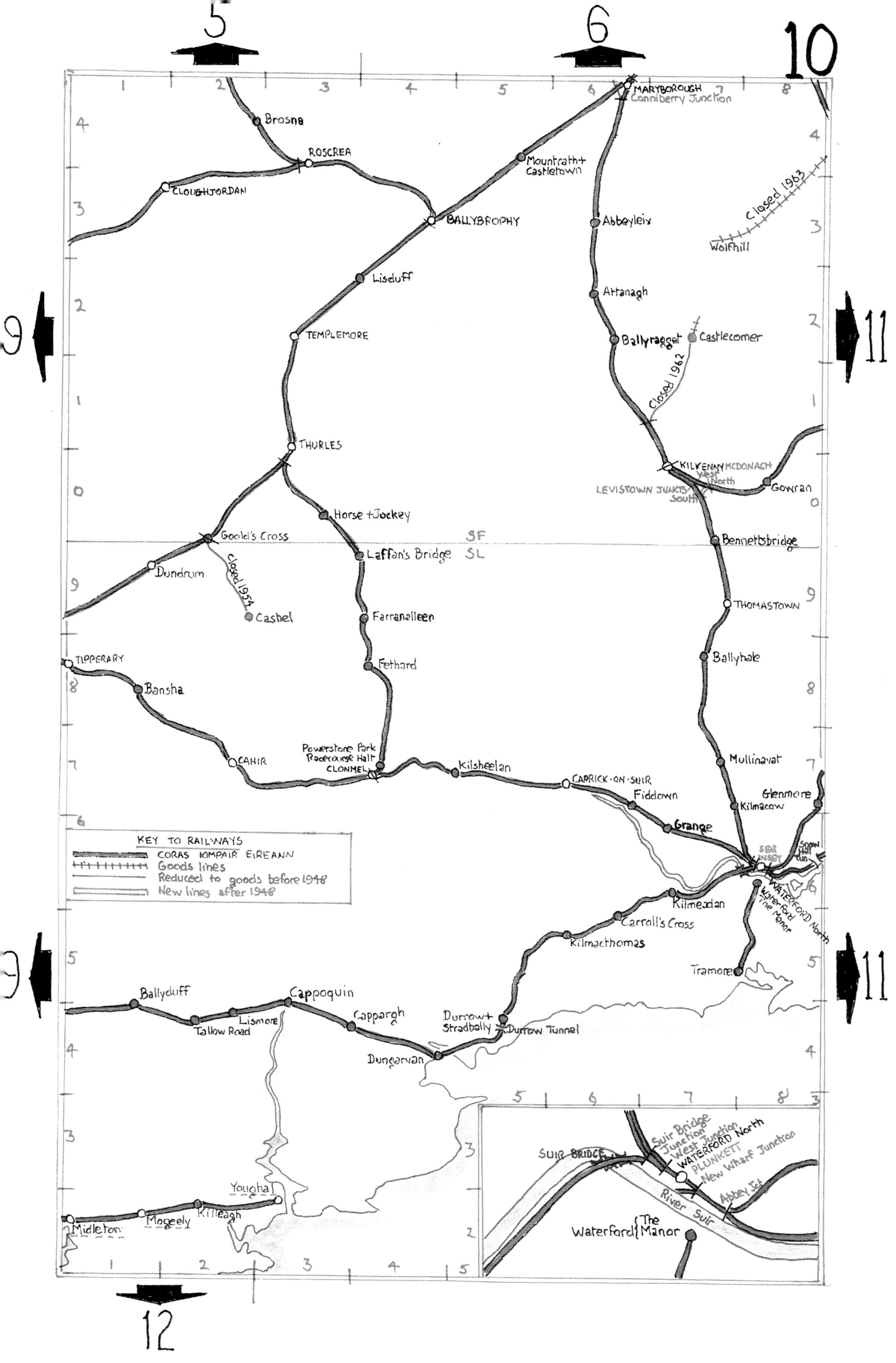

5
6
10
9
11
12
Brosna
ROSCREA
CLOUGHJORDAN
MARYBOROUGH
Conniberry Junction
Mountrath + Castletown
BALLYBROPHY
Abbeyleix
Closed 1963
Wolfhill
Lisduff
Attanagh
TEMPLEMORE
Ballyragget
Castlecomer
Closed 1962
THURLES
KILKENNY
MCDONAGH
West
North
LEVISTOWN JUNCTS. South
Gowran
Horse + Jockey
Goold's Cross
SF
SL
Laffan's Bridge
Bennettsbridge
Dundrum
closed 1954
Cashel
Farranalleen
THOMASTOWN
TIPPERARY
Fethard
Ballyhale
Bansha
Mullinavat
Powerstone Park Racecourse Halt
CLONMEL
CAHIR
Kilsheelan
CARRICK-ON-SUIR
Fiddown
Glenmore
Kilmacow
Grange
KEY TO RAILWAYS
CORAS IOMPAIR EIREANN
Goods lines
Reduced to goods before 1948
New lines after 1948
SEE INSET
WATERFORD North
Waterford The Manor
Kilmeadan
Carroll's Cross
Kilmacthomas
Tramore
Ballyduff
Cappoquin
Lismore
Tallow Road
Cappagh
Durrow + Stradbally
Durrow Tunnel
Dungarvan
Youghal
Killeagh
Mogeely
Midleton
SUIR BRIDGE
Suir Bridge Junction
West Junction
WATERFORD North
PLUNKETT
New Wharf Junction
Abbey Jct
River Suir
Waterford The Manor

WICKLOW, WEXFORD + ROSSLARE

RAILWAY	Note
CORAS IOMPAIR EIREANN	1

STATIONS	Note	Opened / Closed	Ref
ARKLOW			SG42
ATHY			SF94
AVOCA	2	64	SG42
BAGENALSTOWN	A§		SF91
BALLYCULLANE			SM06
Ballygeary	3B§	77	SM36
BRIDGETOWN			SM26
Camolin		64	SG20
CAMPILE			SL96
CARLOW			SF92
Chapel		63	SM18
Duncormick	4	76	SM16
Edermine Ferry		64	SM28
ENNISCORTHY			SM19
Ferns		77	SG20
Glenealy		64	SG44
GOREY			SG31
Inch		64	SG41
Killinick	4	76	SM26
Killurin		64	SM27
Kilmokea	H	66 67	SL96
Kilrane	5	71	SM36
Macmine Junction		64	SM18
Mageney		63	SF93
Milford		63	SF92
MUINE BHEAG	A§		SF91
New Ross		63	SL97
Palace East		63	SM08
RATHDRUM			SG43
Rathgarogue		63	SL98
Rathnew		64	SG44
ROSSLARE HARBOUR		89	SM36
Rosslare Harbour Mainland	3B§	77 89	SM36
Rosslare Harbour Pier			SM36
ROSSLARE STRAND			SM36
WELLINGTON BRIDGE			SM06
WEXFORD North O'HANRAHAN	6	66	SM27
Wexford South		77	SM27
WICKLOW			SG45
Wicklow Murrough		69 76	SG45
Woodenbridge		64	SG42

BRIDGE	Length yards	Ref
BARROW BRIDGE	2131	SL96

TUNNELS	Length yards	Ref
ENNISCORTHY	405	SM19
KILLURIN	89	SM27
FERRYCRAIG	296	SM27
RATHDRUM No. 1	190	SG43
RATHDRUM No. 2	25	SG43
RATHDRUM No. 3	99	SG43

JUNCTIONS	Ref
FELTHOUSE	SM26

NOTES

1 All open track on map at 31·12·1947 was 5'3"

NOTES continued

2 Has remained open for excursion traffic.

3 May not have been passenger station under this name but car unloading location when name changed. It may have been adjoining site. But new station of 89 is situated at a midway point between the two it replaced covering both functions

4 Closure date prior to 1984.

5 Original name Rosslare Harbour!

6 Suffix change 1966.

§ Change of name newer version

§ Change of name older version

Identifying letter shows other name.

H Halt. Open for use of workmen only.

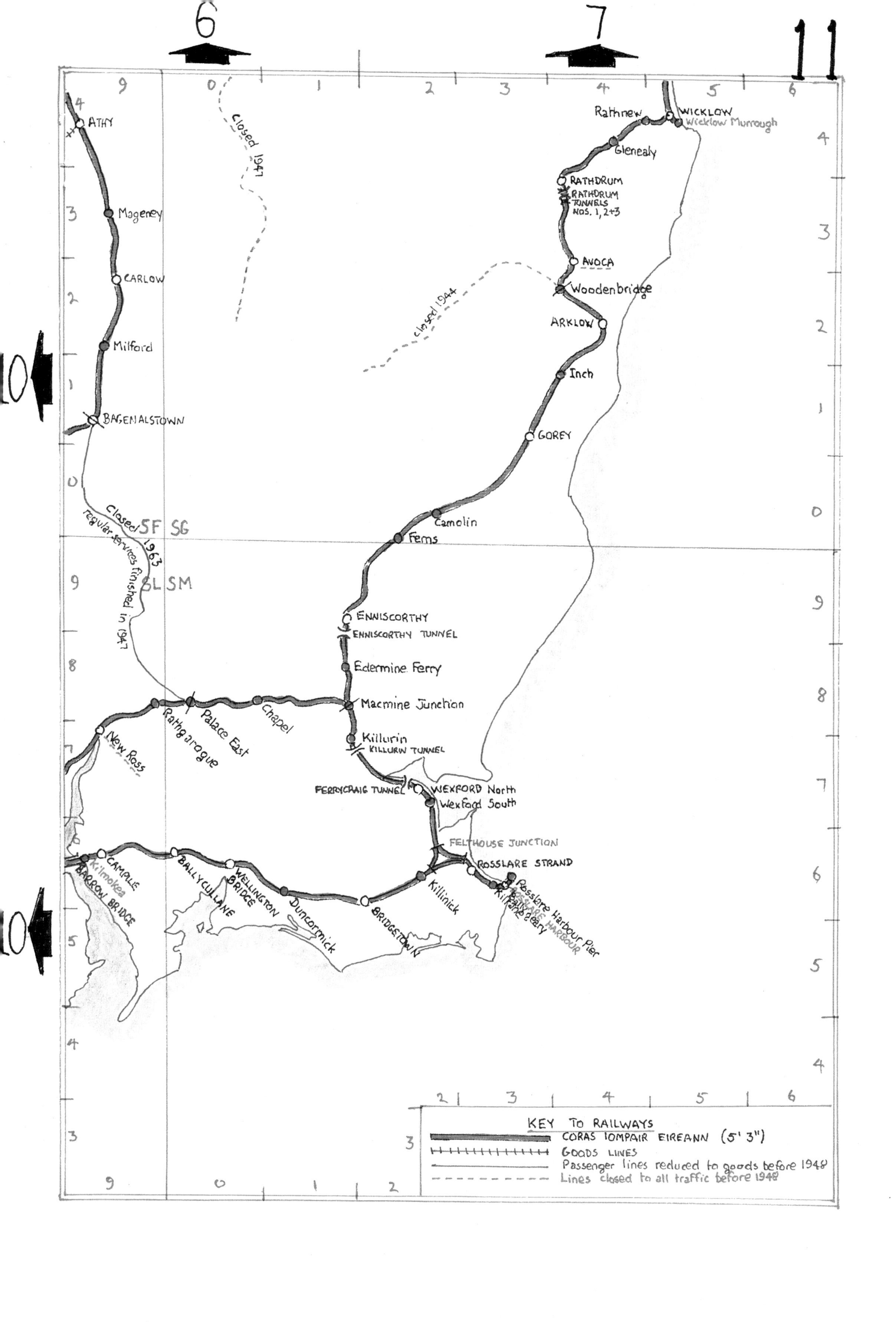
6
7
10
10
ATHY
Mageney
CARLOW
Milford
BAGENALSTOWN
Closed 1947
closed 1944
Closed 1963
regular services finished in 1947
5F SG
SL SM
WICKLOW
Rathnew
Wicklow Murrough
Glenealy
RATHDRUM
RATHDRUM TUNNELS NOS. 1, 2+3
AVOCA
Woodenbridge
ARKLOW
Inch
GOREY
Camolin
Ferns
ENNISCORTHY
ENNISCORTHY TUNNEL
Edermine Ferry
Macmine Junction
Killurin
KILLURIN TUNNEL
Chapel
Palace East
Rathgarogue
New Ross
FERRYCARRIG TUNNEL
WEXFORD North
Wexford South
FELTHOUSE JUNCTION
ROSSLARE STRAND
Rosslare Harbour Pier
ROSSLARE HARBOUR
Ballygeary
Killinick
BRIDGETOWN
Duncormick
WELLINGTON BRIDGE
BALLYCULLANE
CAMPILE
Kilmokea
BARROW BRIDGE
KEY TO RAILWAYS
CORAS IOMPAIR EIREANN (5' 3")
GOODS LINES
Passenger lines reduced to goods before 1948
Lines closed to all traffic before 1948

CORK + BALTIMORE

RAILWAYS

	Note	
CORAS IOMPAIR EIREANN	1	

STATIONS	Opened Closed	Ref
Albert Quay	61	RP92
Aughaville	61	RU29
Ballinascarthy	61	RU69
Ballinhassig	61	RP81
Ballineen + Enniskean	60	RP50
Baltimore	61	RU27
Bandon	61	RP70
Bantry	61	RU29
Blarney (North)	2 63	RP82
Capwell	3G 53	RP92
CARRIGALOE		RP91
Carrigtwohill	76	SL02
Clonakilty	61	RU68
Clonakilty Junction	61	RP60
COBH		SL01
COBH JUNCTION		RP92
CORK	4	RP92
Albert Quay	61	RP92
Capwell	3G 53	RP92
Glanmire Road	§ 66	RP92
THOMAS KENT	§ 66	PR92
Courtmacsherry	G 61	RU79
Creagh	61	RU38
Crossbarry	61	RP71
Desert	61	RP50
Drimoleague	61	RU39
Dunkettle	63	RP92
Durrus Road	61	RU29
FOTA		RP92
Glanmire Road	§ 66	RP92
Kenmare	60	RP21
Kilgarvan	60	RP22
Killeagh	63	SL22
Knockbue Halt	63	RU49
LITTLE ISLAND		RP92
Madore	61	RU39
Midleton	5 63	SL02
Mogeely	5 63	SL12
Morley's Bridge	60	RP22
RUSHBROOKE		RP91
Skibbereen	61	RU38
THOMAS KENT CORK		RP92
Upton + Innishannon	61	RP71
Waterfall	61	RP81

NOTES

1 Although several narrow gauge lines radiated from Cork all had closed to all traffic before 31·12·1947

2 Blarney became North when both its stations came under the same management in the 20's. North may have been dropped when the narrow gauge South was closed in 1934

3 Was closed in 1925 when passengers were diverted to Albert Quay. The goods services were diverted at the same time but continued to be used for some goods until 1946 and may have continued to 1953.

NOTES continued

4 The Cork inset enlargement shows all terminals including those closed before World War II. The Capwell goods connection is mentioned in Note 3. The other goods lines in the city centre closed by 1976.

5 Continued in use for excursions until circa 1993

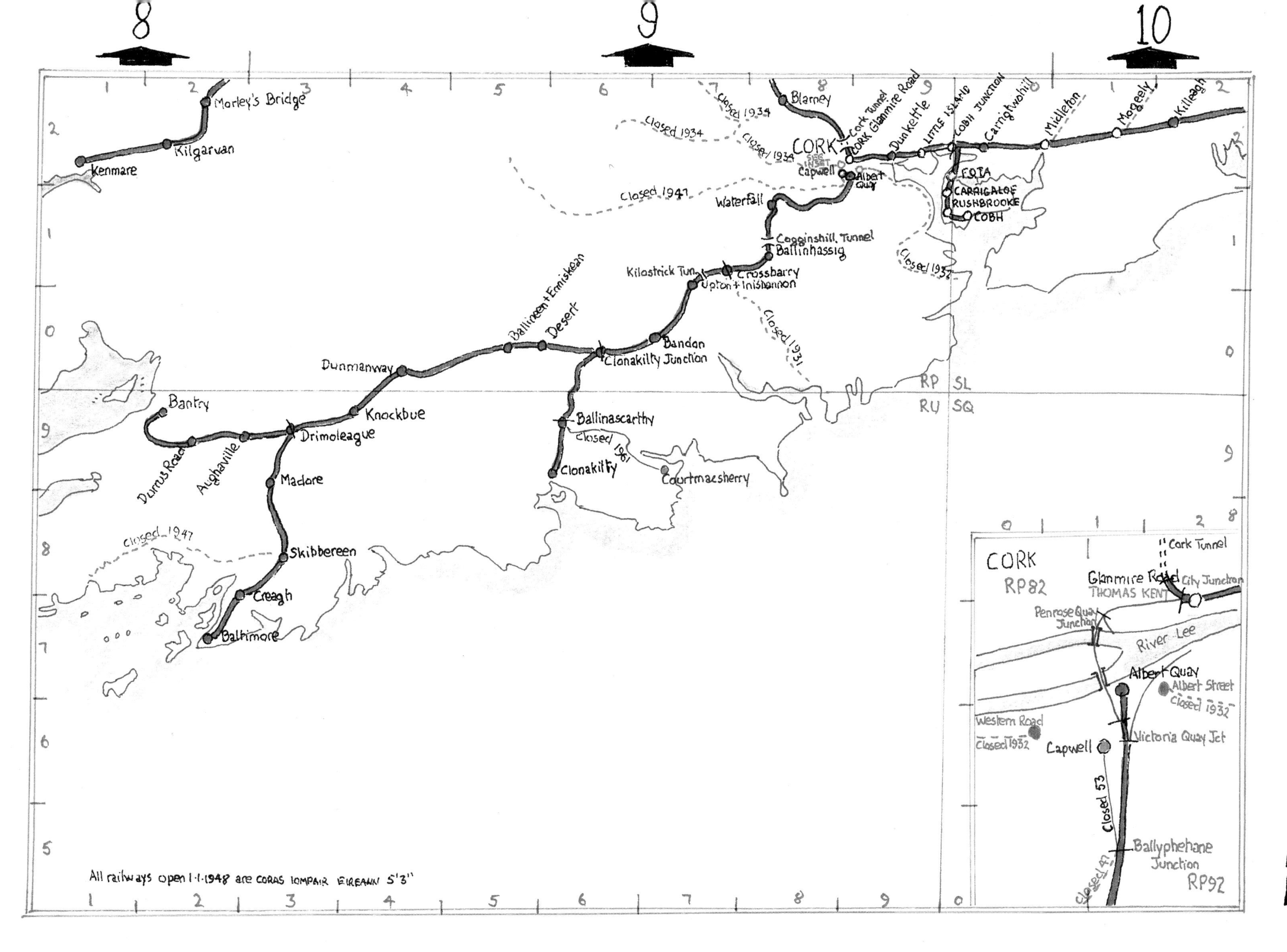
8
9
10
Morley's Bridge
Kilgarvan
Kenmare
Blarney
Closed 1934
Closed 1934
Closed 1934
CORK
SEE INSET
Cork Tunnel
CORK Glanmire Road
Dunkettle
LITTLE ISLAND
COBH JUNCTION
Carrigtwohill
Midleton
Mogeely
Killeagh
Capwell
Albert Quay
FOTA
CARRIGALOE
RUSHBROOKE
COBH
Closed 1947
Waterfall
Cogginshill Tunnel
Ballinhassig
Closed 1932
Kilostrick Tun.
Crossbarry
Upton + Inishannon
Closed 1931
Ballineen + Enniskean
Desert
Bandon
Clonakilty Junction
Dunmanway
RP SL
RU SQ
Bantry
Knockbue
Drimoleague
Ballinascarthy
Closed 1961
Clonakilty
Courtmacsherry
Durrus Road
Aughaville
Madore
Closed 1947
Skibbereen
Creagh
Baltimore
All railways open 1·1·1948 are CORAS IOMPAIR EIREANN 5'3"
CORK
RP82
Cork Tunnel
Glanmire Road
THOMAS KENT
City Junction
Penrose Quay Junction
River Lee
Albert Quay
Albert Street
Closed 1932
Western Road
Closed 1932
Capwell
Victoria Quay Jct
Closed 53
Ballyphehane Junction
Closed 47
RP92

THURSO, WICK + DORNOCH

RAILWAY

LONDON MIDLAND + SCOTTISH

STATIONS

Station	Notes	Closed	Ref
ALTNABREAC	*		NC94
ARDGAY	§77		NH59
Bilbster		60	ND25
BONAR BRIDGE	* §77		NH59
Borrobol Platform	2 *	65	NC82
Bower	·1	60	ND15
BRORA	*		NC80
Cambusavie Platform		60	NH79
CULRAIN	*		NH59
Delny		60	NH77
Dornoch		60	NH78
DUNROBIN CASTLE	1 *	65 85	NC80
Edderton		60	NH68
Embo		60	NH79
FEARN	*		NH77
FORSINARD	*		NC84
GEORGEMAS JUNCTION	3 *		ND16
GOLSPIE	*		NH89
Halkirk		60	ND16
HELMSDALE	*		ND01
Hoy	*	65	ND16
INVERSHIN	*		NH59
Kildary		60	NH77
KILDONAN	*		NC82
KINBRACE	*		NC83
LAIRG	*		NC50
Loth		60	NC91
Mound, The		60	NH79
Nigg		60	NH77
ROGART Halt	4 *	60 61	NC70
Salzcraggie Platform	*	65	NC91
SCOTSCALDER	*		ND50
Skelbo		60	NH79
TAIN	*		NH78
The Mound		60	NH79
THURSO	5 *		ND16
Watten		60	ND26
WICK	5 *		ND35

No.	ENGINE SHEDS	Notes	Closed	Ref
1	Wick	6	62	ND35
2	Thurso	6	62	ND16
3	Helmsdale	6	62	ND01
4	Golspie		50	NH89
5	Dornoch		60	NH78
6	Tain		60	NH78

No.	SUMMITS	Height Feet	Ref
1	COUNTY MARCH	708	NC94
2	LAIRG	488	NC60

NOTES:

§ Change of name - modern version.
§ Change of name - older version.
1 Private station re-opened for use in the shooting season
2 Platform dropped from name 62
3 JUNCTION added to title in the early 50s.
4 HALT part of title 61-9.
5 Underlining shows still used for some goods traffic at 31.12.93.
6 Used for short time as diesel depot.

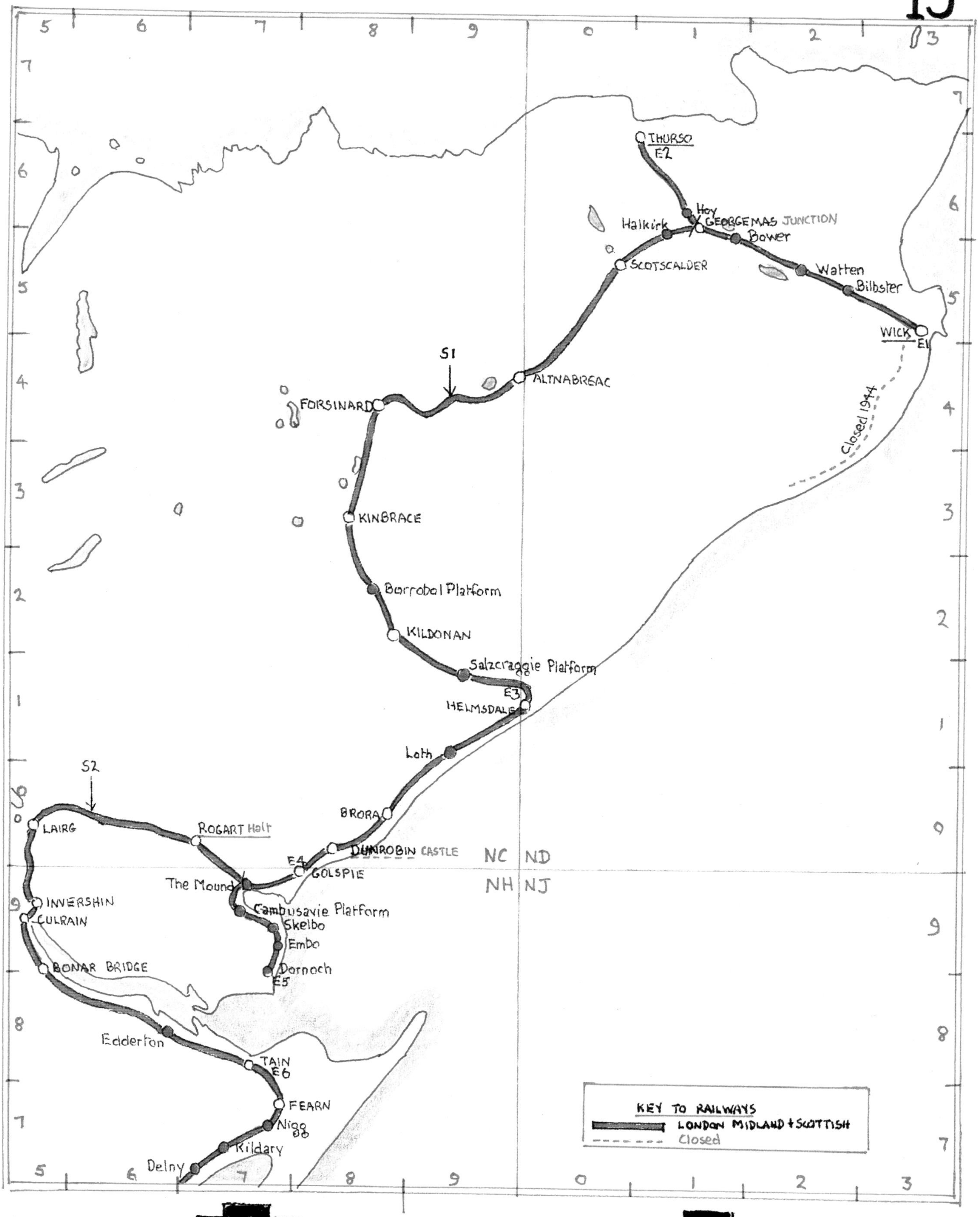

THURSO
E2
Hoy
GEORGEMAS JUNCTION
Halkirk
Bower
SCOTSCALDER
Watten
Bilbster
WICK
E1
S1
ALTNABREAC
FORSINARD
Closed 1944
KINBRACE
Borrobol Platform
KILDONAN
Salzcraggie Platform
E3
HELMSDALE
Loth
S2
BRORA
LAIRG
ROGART Halt
DUNROBIN CASTLE
NC ND
E4
GOLSPIE
The Mound
NH NJ
INVERSHIN
CULRAIN
Cambusavie Platform
Skelbo
Embo
Dornoch
E5
BONAR BRIDGE
Edderton
TAIN
E6
FEARN
Nigg
Kildary
Delny

KEY TO RAILWAYS
LONDON MIDLAND + SCOTTISH
Closed

14
15

INVERNESS, KYLE OF LOCHALSH + MALLAIG

RAILWAYS

No	Company
1	LONDON + NORTH EASTERN
2	LONDON MIDLAND + SCOTTISH

STATIONS

Station	Opened Closed	Ry Ref [8]
ACHANALT	*	2H26
ACHNASHEEN	*	2H15
ACHNASHELLAC	*	2H04
Achterneed	* 65	2H45
Allanfearn	* 65	2H74
Allangrange	51	2H55
ALNESS	60 73	2H66
ATTADALE	6 *	2G93
AVIEMORE		2H81
(AVIEMORE SPEYSIDE)	10 78	2H91
Avoch	51	2H65
Beauly	60	2H55
Bunchrew	60	2H64
CARR BRIDGE	* § 83	2H82
CARRBRIDGE	§ 83	2H82
Clunes	60	2H54
Conon	60	2H53
Craig Houses	3 51 73	2H04
Culloden Moor	* 65	2H74
Dalcross	* 65	2H75
Daviot	* 65	2H74
DINGWALL	*	2H55
DUIRINISH	*	2G72
DUNCRAIG Platform	1 * 49 62	2G83
Evanton	60	2H66
Fort George	G 58	2H75
Fortrose	51	2H75
Foulis	60	2H56
GARVE	*	2H36
Glencarron Platform	1 * 62 64	2H05
Gollanfield Junction	* 65	2H75
Imber Houses	2 3 53 72	2G53
INVERGORDON	*	2H66
INVERNESS		2H64
Kincraig	* 65	2H80
KINGUSSIE		2H70
KYLE OF LOCHALSH	*	2G72
Lentran	7 60	2H54
LOCHLUICHART	*	2H36
Luib Houses	3 51 72	2H15
MALLAIG		1M69
MORAR		1M69
Moy	* 65	2H73
MUIR OF ORD	60 76	2H55
Munlochy	51	2H65
NAIRN		2H85
NEWTONMORE		2N79
PLOCKTON	*	2G83
Redcastle	51	2H55
STRATHCARRON	*	2G94
Strathpeffer	G 51	2H45
STROME FERRY	* §	2G83
STROMEFERRY	§	2G83
Tomatin	* 65	2H72

GOODS

The principal goods locations, all still in use are at INVERNESS, MUIR OF ORD and INVERGORDON indicated by the purple underline at those stations.

COMPANY WORKS

Name	Closed	Ry Ref
Lochgorm	59	2H64

ENGINE SHEDS

No	Name	Closed	Ry Ref
E1	INVERNESS		2H64
2	Dingwall	61	2H55
3	Fortrose	50	2H75
4	Fort George	4 48	2H75
5	Aviemore	66	2H91
6	Kyle of Lochalsh	61	2G72
7	Mallaig	?	1M69

BRIDGES + VIADUCTS

No	Name	Ry
V1	Achanalt Viaduct	2H26
2	Ness Viaduct	2H64
3	Nairn Viaduct	2H74
4	Findorn Viaduct	2H82
5	Spey Viaduct	2N69

TUNNELS

No	Name	Length	Ry Ref
T	Rock Fall Tunnel		2G93

SUMMITS

No	Name	Height	Ry Ref
S1	LUIB	646	2H15
2	CORRIEMOILLIE	429	2H36
3	RAVEN'S ROCK	458	2H46
4	SCHLOD	1315	2H82

JUNCTIONS

No	Name		Ry Ref
J1	Harbour Branch		2 H64
2	Rose Street		2 H64
3	Welsh's Bridge		2 H64
4	Station		2 H64
5	Millburn	9	2 H64
6	Fodderly		2 H56

NOTES:

§ Old Version } Change of name
§ New Version }
Date of change to STROMEFERRY is not known

1 Platform dropped from title '62
2 Earlier version (to '65) Imeer Houses.
3 Opened to enable railway wives to shop.
4 Practical closure '44 but remained officially open until nationalised.
5 Continued in use for diesels until '66.
6 Shown as halt in Beeching
7 Re-opened for two days in 1982.
8 Refs are in NG, NH, NM or NN and initial N is omitted
9 Closed Junction of Nairn line is at Welsh's Bridge
10 New STRATHSPEY station see on map 15.

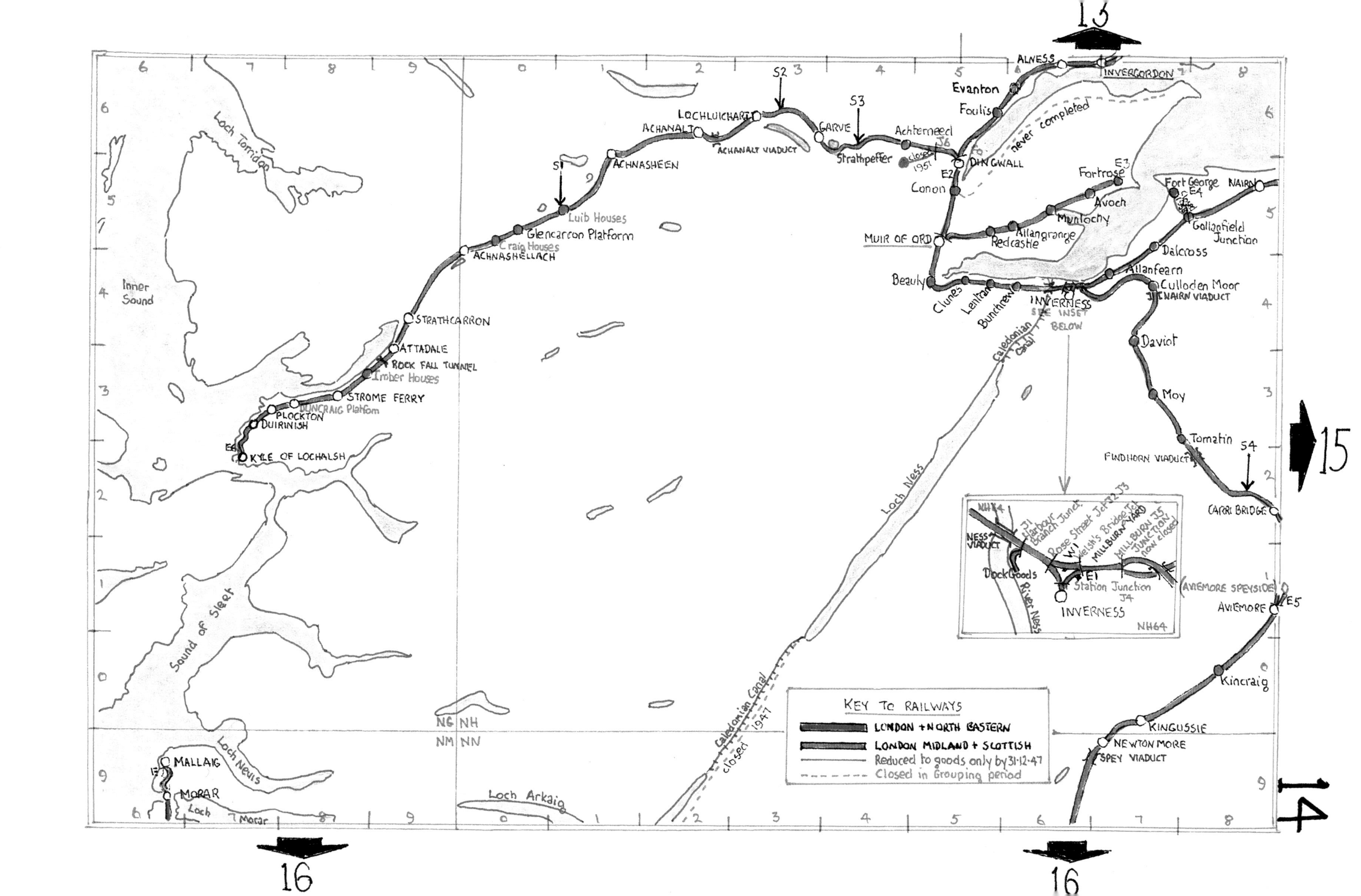
14
13
15
16
16
KEY TO RAILWAYS
LONDON + NORTH EASTERN
LONDON MIDLAND + SCOTTISH
Reduced to goods only by 31-12-47
Closed in Grouping period
ALNESS
INVERGORDON
Evanton
Foulis
never completed
DINGWALL
Achterneed
J6
closed 1951
Strathpeffer
GARVE
S3
S2
LOCHLUICHART
ACHANALT VIADUCT
ACHANALT
ACHNASHEEN
S1
Luib Houses
Glencarron Platform
Craig Houses
ACHNASHELLACH
STRATHCARRON
ATTADALE
ROCK FALL TUNNEL
Imber Houses
STROME FERRY
DUNCRAIG Platform
PLOCKTON
DUIRINISH
KYLE OF LOCHALSH
E6
Loch Torridon
Inner Sound
Sound of Sleat
Loch Nevis
MALLAIG
MORAR
Loch Morar
Loch Arkaig
NG NH
NM NN
E2
Conon
MUIR OF ORD
Redcastle
Allangrange
Munlochy
Avoch
Fortrose
E3
Fort George
E4
NAIRN
Gollanfield Junction
Dalcross
Allanfearn
Culloden Moor
NAIRN VIADUCT
Beauly
Clunes
Lentran
Bunchrew
INVERNESS
SEE INSET BELOW
Caledonian Canal
Loch Ness
Caledonian Canal
closed 1947
Daviot
Moy
Tomatin
FINDHORN VIADUCT
S4
CARR BRIDGE
NH64
NESS VIADUCT
J1
Harbour Branch Junct.
Rose Street Jct J2 J3
Welsh's Bridge Jct.
W1
MILLBURN YARD
MILLBURN J5 JUNCTION now closed
Dock Goods
River Ness
E1
Station Junction
J4
INVERNESS
(AVIEMORE SPEYSIDE)
AVIEMORE
E5
Kincraig
KINGUSSIE
NEWTON MORE
SPEY VIADUCT

ABERDEEN

RAILWAYS

No	Company
1	LONDON + NORTH EASTERN
2	LONDON MIDLAND + SCOTTISH
3	STRATHSPEY

STATIONS

Name		Opened Closed	Ry Ref [1]
ABERDEEN			J90
CRAIGINCHES			2J90
GUILD STREET			2J90
Joint	2	52	12J90
Kittybrewster	*	68	1J90
WATERLOO			1J90
Aberlour	*	65	1J24
Aboyne	*	66	1059
Advie	*	65	1J13
Alford		50	1J51
Alves	5 *	65	2J16
Arnage	*	65	1J93
Auchindachy	*	68	1J44
Auchnagatt	*	65	1J94
Auchterless		51	1J74
Auldearn		60	2H95
Aultmore		66	2J45
AVIEMORE			2H81
(AVIEMORE SPEYSIDE)		78	3H81
Ballater	*	66	1039
Ballifurth Farm Halt	*	59 65	2J02
Ballindalloch	*	65	1J13
Banchory	*	66	1069
Banff	*	64	1J66
Banff Bridge		51	1J66
Banff Golf Club House Halt	*	64	1J66
Birchfield Halt		56	1J25
Blacksboat	*	65	1J14
Boat of Garten	*	65 78	123H91
Bridgefoot Halt	*	64	1J66
Brodie	*	65	2H95
Broomhill	*	65	2H92
Brucklay	*	65	1J95
Buckie	*	68	1J46
Buckpool		60	1J46
Bucksburn		56	1J81
Cairnbulg	*	65	1K06
Cairnie Junction	*	68	1J45
Calcots	*	63	1J26
Cambus o' May	*	66	1049
CARR BRIDGE	§	83	2H82
CARRBRIDGE	$	83	2H82
Carron	*	65	1J24
Cornhill	*	68	1J56
Cove Bay		65	2J90
Craigellachie	*	68	1J24
CRAIGINCHES			2J90
Crathes	*	66	1079
Cromdale	*	65	1J03
Cullen	*	68	1J56
Culter	*	65	1J80
Cults	*	66	1J80
Dailuaine Halt	*	65	1J24
Dalvey Farm Halt	*	59 65	1J13
Dandaleith		62	1J24
Dava	*	65	2J04
Dee Street Halt	*	61 65	1069
Dess	*	66	1J50
Dinnet	*	66	1049
Drum		51	1J70
Drummuir	*	68	1J34
Dufftown	*	68	1J34
Dunphail	*	65	2J04
DYCE	*	68 84	1J81
ELGIN			2J26
Ellon	*	65	1J93
Esslemont		52	1J92
Findochty	*	63	1J46
Fochabers		66	2J36
FORRES			2J06
Fraserburgh	*	65	1J96
Fyvie		51	1J74
Garmouth	*	68	1J36
Gartly	*	68	1J53
Gibley's Cottages Halt	*	59 65	1J24
Glassaugh		53	1J56
Glassel	*	66	1069
Glenbarry	*	68	1J55
Golf Club House Halt (Banff)	*	64	1J66
Grange	*	64	1J45
Grantown-on-Spey East	*	50 65	1J02
Grantown-on-Spey West	*	50 65	2J02
GUILD STREET			J90
HUNTLY			1J54
Imperial Cottages Halt	*	59 65	1J24
INSCH	*		1J62
Inveramsay		51	1J72
Inverugie	*	65	1K14
INVERURIE	*		1J72
KEITH Junction	3	80	12J45
Keith Town	*	68	1J45
Kemnay		50	1J71
Kennethmont	*	68	1J53
Kinaldie	*	64	1J81
King Edward		51	1J75
Kinloss	*	65	2J06
Kintore	*	64	1J71
Kirkton Bridge Halt	*	65	1J96
Kittybrewster	*	68	1J90
Knock	*	68	1J55
Knockando	*	65	1J24
Ladysbridge	*	64	1J66
Lhanbryde	*	64	2J26
Logierieve	*	65	1J92
Longmorn	*	68	1J25
Longside	*	65	1K04
Lonmay	*	65	1J96
Lossiemouth	*	64	1J27
Lumphanan	*	66	1J50
Macduff		51	1J66
Maud	*	65	1J94
Mintlaw	*	65	1J94
Monymusk		50	1J61
Mormond Halt	*	65	1J95
Mosstowie		55	2J16
Muchalls		50	2089
Mulben	*	64	2J35
Nethy Bridge	*	65	1H92
Newmachar	*	65	1J81
Newseat Halt	*	65	1K04
Newtonhill		56	2099
Old Meldrum		64	1J72
Orbliston Junction	*	64	2J35
Ordens Halt	*	64	1J66
Orton	*	64	2J35
Oyne	*	68	1J62
Park	*	66	1079
Parkhill		50	1J81
Peterhead	*	65	1K14
Philorth Bridge Platform	4 *	65	1K06
Philorth Halt	*	65	1J96
Pitcaple	*	68	1J72
Pitmedden	*	64	1J81
Portessie	*	68	1J46
Portgordon	*	63	1J36
Portknockie	*	68	1J46
PORTLETHEN		56 85	2099
Portsoy	*	63	1J56
Rathen	*	65	1J96
Rothes	*	68	1J25
Rothiemay	*	68	1J54
Rothienorman		51	1J73
St Combs	*	65	1K06
Spey Bay	*	68	1J36
Strichen	*	65	1J95
Taucher's Platform	4 *	64	2J35
Tillyfourie		50	1J61
Tillynaught	*	68	1J56
Tochieneal		51	1J56
Torphins	*	64	1J60
Towiemore Halt	*	68	1J34
Turriff		51	1J75
Udny	*	65	1J92
Urquhart	*	68	1J26
Wardhouse		61	1J53
Wartle		51	1J73
Whitehouse		56	1J61

COMPANY WORKS

No	Name	Closed	Ry Ref
1	Inverurie	69	1J72

ENGINE SHEDS

No	Name	Closed [6]	Ry Ref
E1	FERRYHILL		2J90
2	Kittybrewster	61	1J90
3	Inverurie		1J72
4	Keith	61	1J45
5	Forres	62	2J06
6	Elgin		1J26
7	Keith	48	2J45
8	Boat of Garten	65	1H91
9	Ballater		1039
10	Peterhead		1K14
11	Fraserburgh		1J96
12	Alford	50	1J51
13	Banff		1J76

SUMMITS

No	Location	Ht	Ry Ref
S1	Dava	1052	2J03
2	Newmachar		1J81
3	Dufftown		1J34

BRIDGES + VIADUCTS

No	Location	Ry Ref
V1	FINDHORN VIADUCT	2J06
2	ROTHIEMAY	1J54
3	SPEY	2J35

TUNNELS

No	Name/Location	Length	Ry Ref
T1	HUTCHEON STREET	280	1J90
2	SCHOOLHILL	250	1J90

JUNCTIONS

No	Name/Location	Ry Ref
J1	FERRYHILL	12 J90

NOTES:

1. References are all in NH, NJ, NK NO or NP. The initial N omitted
2. Joint was dropped from title in 1952
4. Shown as Halt in Beeching.
5. Goods only line ran to Hopeman but closed to that point in 57 remained open to BURGHEAD to 1993, but not now in use
6. Some shed closures with no closure date shown may have closed in the grouping period

§ Old Name } Change of name
$ New Name }

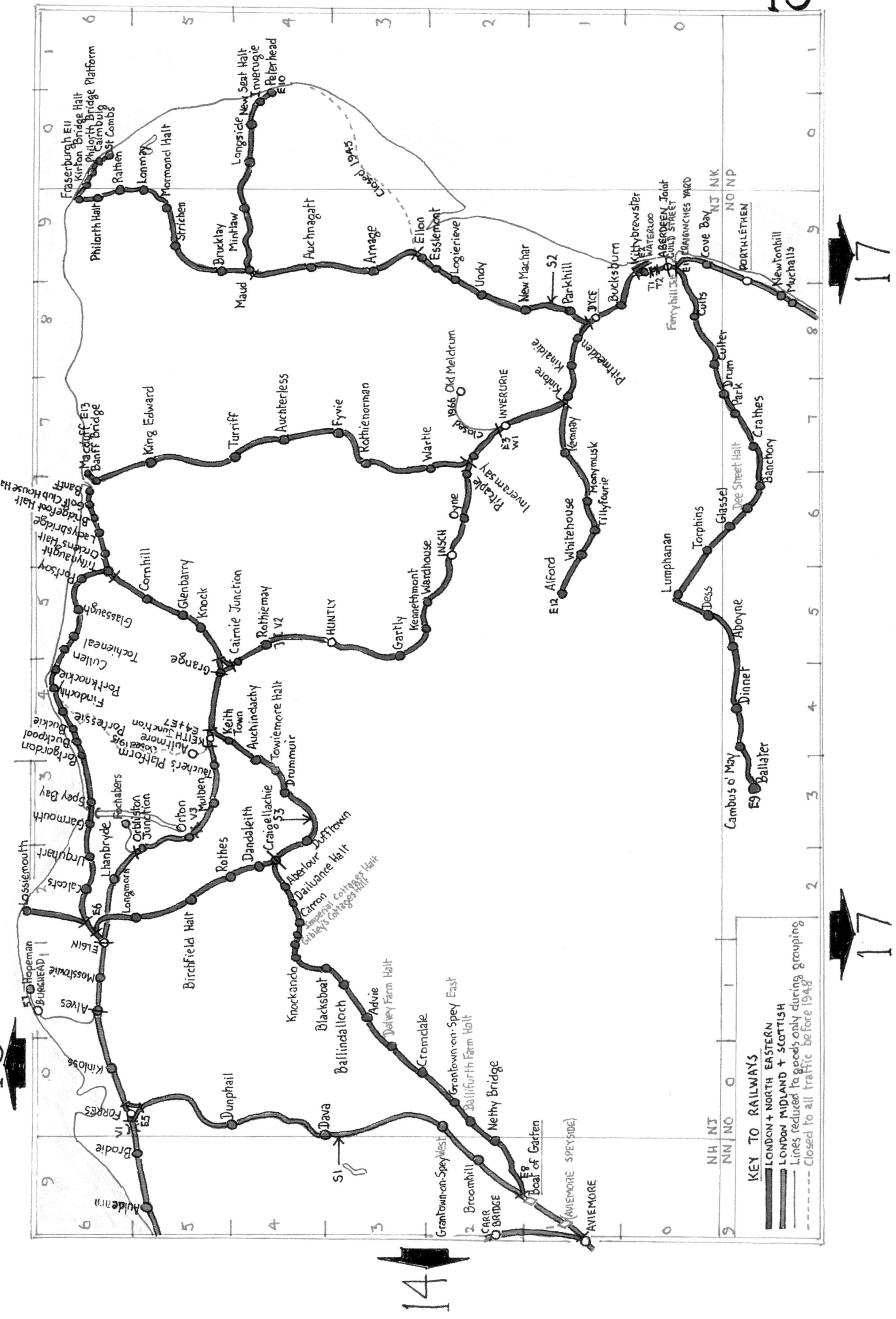

KEY TO RAILWAYS
- LONDON + NORTH EASTERN
- LONDON MIDLAND + SCOTTISH
- Lines reduced to goods only during grouping
- Closed to all traffic before 1948

Hopeman
Lossiemouth
E1 BURGHEAD
Alves
Mosstowie
ELGIN
E6
Calcots
Urquhart
Garmouth
Spey Bay
Portgordon
Buckpool
Buckie
Portessie
Findochty
Portknockie
Cullen
Tochieneal
Glassaugh
Portsoy
Tillynaught
Ordens Halt
Ladysbridge
Bridgefoot Halt
Golf Club House Halt
Banff
Macduff E13
Banff Bridge
Auldearn
Brodie
V1
FORRES
E5
Kinloss
Lhanbryde
Fochabers
Longmorn
Orbliston Junction
Orton
V3
Mulben
Taucher's Platform
Aultmore
Closed 1915
KEITH Junction
E4 + E7
Keith Town
Grange
Cairnie Junction
Cornhill
Glenbarry
Knock
Birchfield Halt
Rothes
Dandaleith
Craigellachie
S3
Auchindachy
Towiemore Halt
Drummuir
Dufftown
Knockando
Aberlour
Dailuaine Halt
Carron
Imperial Cottages Halt
Gilbey's Cottages Halt
Blacksboat
Ballindalloch
Advie
Dalvey Farm Halt
Cromdale
Grantown-on-Spey East
Ballifurth Farm Halt
Nethy Bridge
E8
Boat of Garten
(AVIEMORE SPEYSIDE)
AVIEMORE
CARR BRIDGE
Broomhill
Grantown-on-Spey West
Dava
S1
Dunphail
Rothiemay
V2
HUNTLY
Gartly
Kennethmont
Wardhouse
INSCH
Oyne
Pitcaple
Inveramsay
Closed 1966
Old Meldrum
E3
W1
INVERURIE
Kintore
Kinaldie
Pitmedden
DYCE
E12 Alford
Whitehouse
Tillyfourie
Monymusk
Kemnay
King Edward
Turriff
Auchterless
Fyvie
Rothienorman
Wartle
Fraserburgh E11
Kirkton Bridge Halt
Philorth Bridge Platform
Cairnbulg
St Combs
Philorth Halt
Rathen
Lonmay
Mormond Halt
Strichen
Brucklay
Maud
Mintlaw
Longside
New Seat Halt
Inverugie
Peterhead
E10
Auchnagatt
Arnage
Closed 1945
Ellon
Esslemont
Logierieve
Udny
New Machar
S2
Parkhill
Bucksburn
Kittybrewster
E2
WATERLOO
T1
T2
ABERDEEN Joint
GUILD STREET
Ferryhill Jct
E1
CRAIGINCHES YARD
Cove Bay
PORTHLETHEN
Newtonhill
Muchalls
Lumphanan
Torphins
Glassel
Dee Street Halt
Banchory
Crathes
Park
Drum
Culter
Cults
Dess
Aboyne
Dinnet
Cambus o' May
E9
Ballater

NH NJ
NN NO
NJ NK
NO NP

Grid numbers along the edges: 9, 0, 1, 2, 3, 4, 5, 6, 7, 8, 9, 0, 1 (left to right); 6, 5, 4, 3, 2, 1, 0 (top to bottom)

13
14
17
17

FORT WILLIAM, OBAN + CRIANLARICH

RAILWAYS

No	Company
1	LONDON + NORTH EASTERN
2	LONDON MIDLAND + SCOTTISH

STATIONS

Name	Opened Closed	Ry Ref
Aberfeldy	*65	2N85
Ach-na-Cloich	*65	2M93
Appin	*66+	2M94
ARDLUI		1N31
ARISAIG		1M68
Ballachulish Ferry	*66+	2N05
Ballachulish (Glencoe) For Kinlochleven	*66+	2N05
Balquidder	*65	2N52
BANAVIE	*	1N07
Barcaldine Halt	*66+	2M94
BEASDALE	*	1M78
Benderloch	*66+	2M83
Black Island Platform 1	59	2N86
BLAIR ATHOLL		2N86
BRIDGE OF ORCHY		1N24
Comrie	*64	2N72
CONNEL FERRY		2M93
CORPACH		1N07
CORROUR		1N36
Creagan	*66+	2M94
CRIANLARICH		1N32
Crianlarich Lower	*65 53	2N32
Crieff	*64	2N82
Dalchonzie Halt	51	2N72
DALMALLY		2N12
Dalnaspidal	*65	2N67
DALWHINNIE	*	2N68
Duror	*66+	2M95
6 FALLS OF CRUACHAN	*2 65 88	2N02
Fort William	75	1N07
FORT WILLIAM	75	1N07
GLENFINNAN for Loch Shiel		1M88
Gorton	3	1N34
Grandtully	*65	2N85
Highlandman	*64	2N52
Innerpeffray	51	2N82
Kentallen	*66+	2N05
Killin	5 *65	2N53
Killin Junction	*65	2N52
Kingshouse Platform	4 *65	2N52
LOCHAILORT		1M78
LOCH AWE	* 88	2N12
Lochearnhead	51	2N52
LOCH EIL OUTWARD BOUND	85	1N07
LOCHEILSIDE	*	1M97
Luib	*65	2N42
Muthill	*64	2N81
North Connel	*66+	2M93
OBAN		2M83
Pittenzie Halt	*58 64	2N81
RANNOCH		1N46
ROY BRIDGE		1N28
Strageath Halt	*58 64	1N81
Strathyre	*65	2N51
Struan	*65	2N76
TAYNUILT		2M93
TULLOCH		1N38
TYNDRUM LOWER	53	2N32
TYNDRUM UPPER	56	1N33

ENGINE SHEDS

No	Name/Location	Closed	Ry Ref
1	Oban	62	2M83
2	FORT WILLIAM		1N07
3	Aberfeldy	61	2N85
4	Blair Athol	62	2N86
5	Loch Tay	65	2N53
6	Ballachulish	62	2N05
7	Crieff	65	2N82

SUMMITS

No	Location	ft	Ry Ref
1	COUNTY MARCH	1024	1N33
2	GORTON		1N35
3	CORROUR	1350	1N36
4	DRUIMUACHDAR	1484	2N67
5	Glenoglehead	941	2N52
6	TYNDRUM	840	2N22
7	GLENCRUITTEN	361	2M82

TUNNELS

No	Name	yds	Ry Ref
1	BORRODALE	350	1M68
2	BLEASDALE No1	154	1M78
3	BLEASDALE No2	192	1M78
4	LOCHAILORT	176	1M78
5	LEACHABHUIDH No.2	66	1M88
6	LEACHABHUIDH No.1	88	1M88
7	FERSIT	140	1N37
8	CRUACH ROCK SNOWSHED	220	1N45

BRIDGES + VIADUCTS

No	Name/Location	Ry Ref
V1	LARICH MOR VIADUCT	1M68
2	BORRODALE VIADUCT	1M68
3	GLENFINNAN VIADUCT	1M98
4	SPEAN VIADUCT	1N28
5	GARBH GHADIR VIADUCT	1N45
6	HORSESHOE VIADUCT	1N33
7	SUCCOTH VIADUCT	2N22
8	TULLOCH VIADUCT	1N38
9	Connel Ferry Bridge	2M83
10	Creagan Bridge	2M94

NOTES

1. Opening date not known. Thought to be for railway workers wives.
2. Open seasonally.
3. Private station now closed.
4. Listed as Halt in Beeching.
5. line to Tay Bridge remained in use as far as shed but not for goods.
6. Initial N omitted in references, as

NOTES continued

all are in either NM or NN.

+ this symbol in opened and closed column indicates all stations so marked closed for three months in 1953.

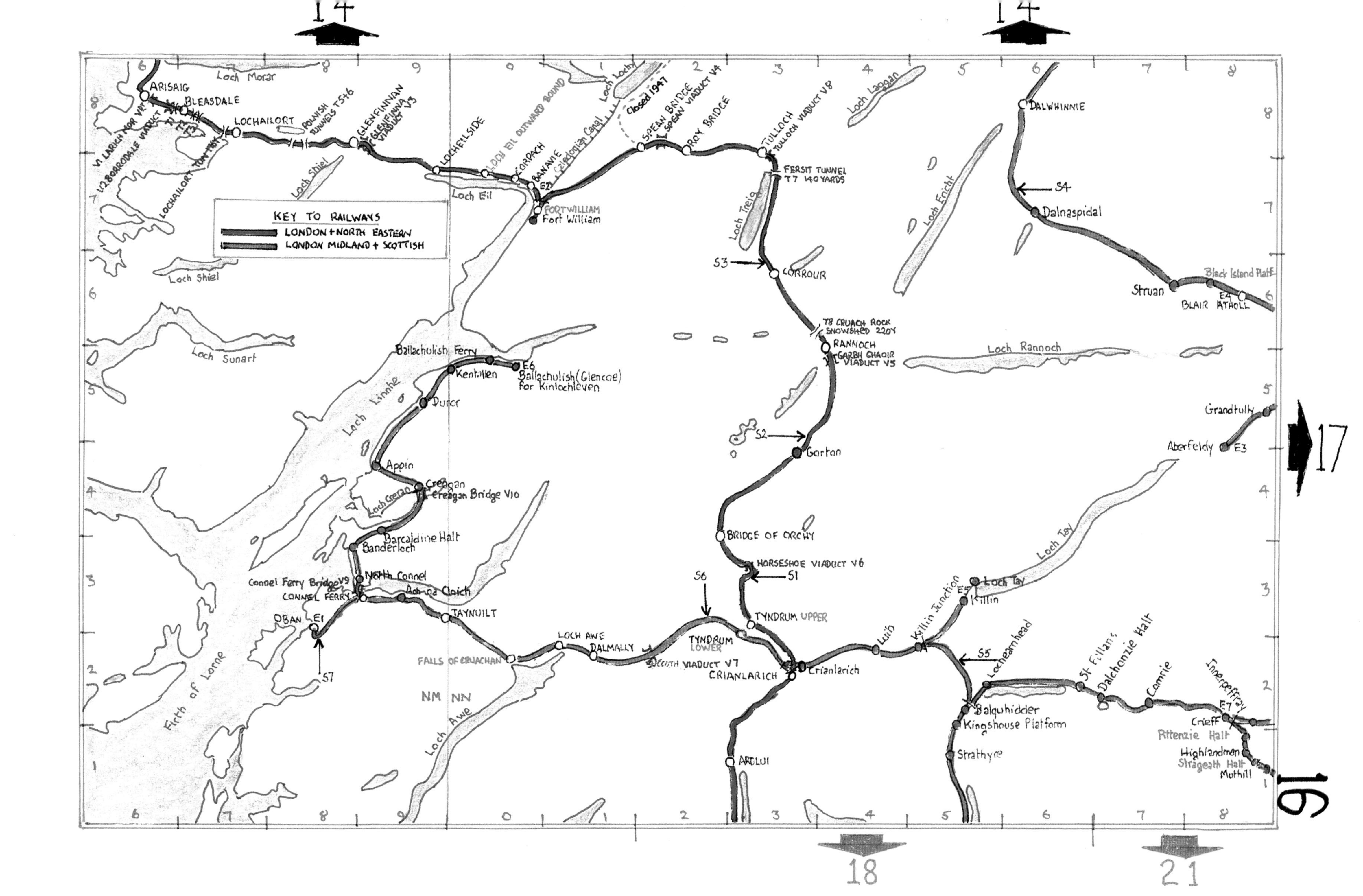

KEY TO RAILWAYS
LONDON + NORTH EASTERN
LONDON MIDLAND + SCOTTISH
14
17
18
21
ARISAIG
BLEASDALE
LOCHAILORT
POLNISH TUNNELS T5+6
GLENFINNAN
GLENFINNAN VIADUCT V3
LOCHEILSIDE
LOCH EIL OUTWARD BOUND
CORPACH
BANAVIE
E2
FORT WILLIAM
Fort William
Caledonian Canal
Closed 1947
SPEAN BRIDGE
SPEAN VIADUCT V4
ROY BRIDGE
TULLOCH
TULLOCH VIADUCT V8
FERSIT TUNNEL
T7 140 YARDS
CORROUR
S3
T8 CRUACH ROCK SNOWSHED 220Y
RANNOCH
GARBH CHAOIR VIADUCT V5
S2
Gorton
BRIDGE OF ORCHY
HORSESHOE VIADUCT V6
S1
TYNDRUM UPPER
TYNDRUM LOWER
S6
CRIANLARICH
Crianlarich
ARDLUI
DALMALLY
LOCH AWE
FALLS OF CRUACHAN
TAYNUILT
Ach-na-Cloich
Connel Ferry Bridge V9
CONNEL FERRY
North Connel
OBAN
E1
S7
Banderloch
Barcaldine Halt
Creagan
Creagan Bridge V10
Loch Creran
Appin
Duror
Kentallen
Ballachulish Ferry
Ballachulish (Glencoe)
for Kinlochleven
E6
DALWHINNIE
S4
Dalnaspidal
Struan
BLAIR ATHOLL
E4
Black Island Halt
Grandtully
Aberfeldy
E3
Luib
Killin Junction
E5
Killin
Loch Tay
S5
Lochearnhead
Balquhidder
Kingshouse Platform
Strathyre
St Fillans
Dalchonzie Halt
Comrie
Innerpeffray
E7
Crieff
Pittenzie Halt
Highlandman
Strageath Halt
Muthill
Loch Morar
Loch Shiel
Loch Eil
Loch Lochy
Loch Treig
Loch Laggan
Loch Ericht
Loch Rannoch
Loch Sunart
Loch Linnhe
Loch Awe
Firth of Lorne
NM
NN

MONTROSE DUNDEE + PERTH

RAILWAYS

1 LONDON + NORTH EASTERN (LNE)
2 LONDON MIDLAND + SCOTTISH (LMS)
3 DUNDEE + ARBROATH JOINT (LNE+LMS)
4 DUNDEE HARBOUR LINE

STATIONS

Name	Opened/Closed	Ry	Ref
Abercairney	51	2	92
Abernethy	55	1	11
Almond Bank	51	2	02
Alyth	51	2	24
Alyth Junction	* 67	2	24
ARBROATH		3	64
Ardler	56	2	24
Auchterarder	56	2	91
Auchterhouse	55	2	33
Auchtermuchty	50	1	21
Auldbar Road	56	2	55
Baldovan + Downfield 3	55	2	33
Baldragon	55	2	33
Balgowan	51	2	92
Ballinluig	* 65	2	95
BALMOSSIE	62	3	43
Balnaguard	* 65	2	95
Bankfoot	64	2	03
Barnhill Angus	52 55	2	43
BARRY LINKS		3	53
Birnie Road	51	1	67
Blackford	56	2	90
Blairgowrie	55	2	14
Brechin	51 ?	2	56
Bridge of Dun	* 67 ?	2	66
Bridge of Earn	* 64	1	11
BROUGHTY FERRY	56	2	43
Burrelton	56	2	13
Careston	56	2	56
Cargill	56	2	13
Carmyllie	65	3	54
CARNOUSTIE		3	53
Clocksbriggs	55	2	45
Collessie	55	1	21
Colliston	55	2	64
Coupar Angus	* 67	2	24
Craigo	56	2	66
CUPAR		1	31
Dairsie	54	1	41
Dalguise	* 65	2	94
Dronley	55	2	33
Drumlithie	56	2	78
Dubton	52	2	66
Dundee East	59	3	43
DUNDEE Tay Bridge	2 ?	1	43
Dundee West	* 65	2	43
DUNKELD + Birnam	80		
+BIRNAM	4 91	2	04
Dunning	56	2	91
Eassie	56	2	34
Easthaven	* 67	3	53
East Newport	A § 50?	1	42
Edzell	64	2	57
Elliot Junction	* 67	3	64
Errol	85	2	22
Farnell Road	56	2	65
Fordoun	56	2	77
Forfar	* 67	2	45
Forgandenny	56	2	01
Forteviot	56	2	01
Friockheim	55	2	55
Gagie	55	2	43
Glamis	56	2	34
Glasterlaw	51	2	55
Glencarse	56	2	12
GLENEAGLES		2	91
Glenfarg	* 64	1	11
GOLF STREET Halt	60 83	3	53
Gourdon	51	1	77
Grandtully	* 65	2	85
Guard Bridge	* 65	1	41
Guay	59	2	94
Guthrie	55	2	55
Inchture	56	2	22
Inverbervie	51	1	87
INVERGOWRIE		2	33
Johnshaven	51	1	76
Jordanstone	51	2	24
Justinhaugh	52	2	45
Killiecrankie	* 65	2	96
Kilmany	51	2	32
Kinfauns	50	2	12
Kingennie	55	2	43
Kingsmuir	55	2	45
Kirkbuddo	55	2	44
Kirriemuir	52	2	35
LADYBANK		1	31
Laurencekirk	* 67	2	67
Lauriston	51	1	76
LEUCHARS Junction		1	42
Leysmill	55	2	54
Liff	55	2	33
Lindores	51	1	21
Lochee	55	2	33
Longforgan	56	2	32
Luncarty	51	2	03
Luthrie	51	1	32
Madderty	51	2	92
Magdalen Green	56	2	33
Marykirk	56	2	66
Meigle	51	2	24
Methven	65	2	02
Methven Junction Halt	51	2	02
MONIFIETH		3	53
Monikie	55	2	54
MONTROSE		1	65
Muirton Halt	59	2	02
Murthly	* 65	2	03
Newburgh	55	1	21
Newport-on-Tay East	A § 50 69	1	42
Newport-on-Tay West	B § 50 69	1	42
Newtyle	55	2	24
North Waterbridge	51	1	76
PERTH General		2	12
Perth Prince's Street	* 66	2	12
Pitcronkie Platform	51	2	24
PITLOCHRY		2	95
Rosemount Halt	55	2	14
Ruthven Road	51	2	02
St Andrews	69	2	41
St Cyrus	51	1	76
St Fort	* 65		42
SPRINGFIELD	*	1	31
Stanley	56	2	03
STONEHAVEN		2	88
Strathmiglo	50	1	21
Tannadice	52	1	46
Tayport	66	1	42
Tibbermuir	51	2	02
Tulliebardine	* 64	2	91
West Ferry	* 67	3	43
West Newport	B § 50	1	42
Wormit	69	1	32

ENGINE SHEDS

No	Name/Location	Ry	Ref
E1	PERTH	2	12
2	Dundee Tay Bridge	1	43
3	Dundee West	2	43
4	Forfar	2	45
5	Arbroath	2	64
6	Brechin	2	56
7	Montrose	1	65
8	St Andrews	1	41
9	Ladybank	1	31

PRESERVED LINE

CALEDONIAN RAILWAY (BRECHIN) runs from Brechin to Bridge of Dun on seasonable basis

TUNNELS

No	Name/Location	Length yards	Ry	Ref
T1	KILLIECRANKIE	244	2	96
2	INVER	350	2	04
3	KINGSWOOD	350	2	04
4	MONCRIEFF	1210	2	12
5	DOCK STREET	616	2	43

BRIDGES + VIADUCTS

No	Name	Ry	Ref
V1	TAY BRIDGE	2	32
2	GLENURY	2	88
3	BERVIE WATER	2	78
4	NORTH ESK VIADUCT	2	66
5	SOUTH ESK VIADUCT	1	75
6	ROSSIE VIADUCT	1	75
7	KILLIECRANKIE VIADUCT	2	96
8	RIVER TAY VIADUCT	2	94
9	INVER VIADUCT	2	94

JUNCTIONS

No	Name	Ry	Ref
J1	Aberfeldy Branch	2	95
2	Almond Valley	2	02
3	HILTON	12	12
4	St Vigeans	123	64
5	Kinnaber	12	66
6	Tay Bridge South	1	32
7	Newburgh	1	42
8	St Fort North	1	42
9	St Fort South	1	42
10	Ninewells	1	33
11	BUCKINGHAM WEST	12	33
12	Camperdown East	12	43
13	Forfar Line	23	43

NOTES

1 All in NN or NP and on this map the letter prefix is not needed to give each place a unique reference.

2 Tay Bridge suffix probably dropped 65 when the other DUNDEE stations closed.

3 + Downfield not shown on the map

4 + Birnam was dropped from title in 1980. Restored in 1991

§ Old Name } Change of
§ New Name } Name

Letter shows other name.

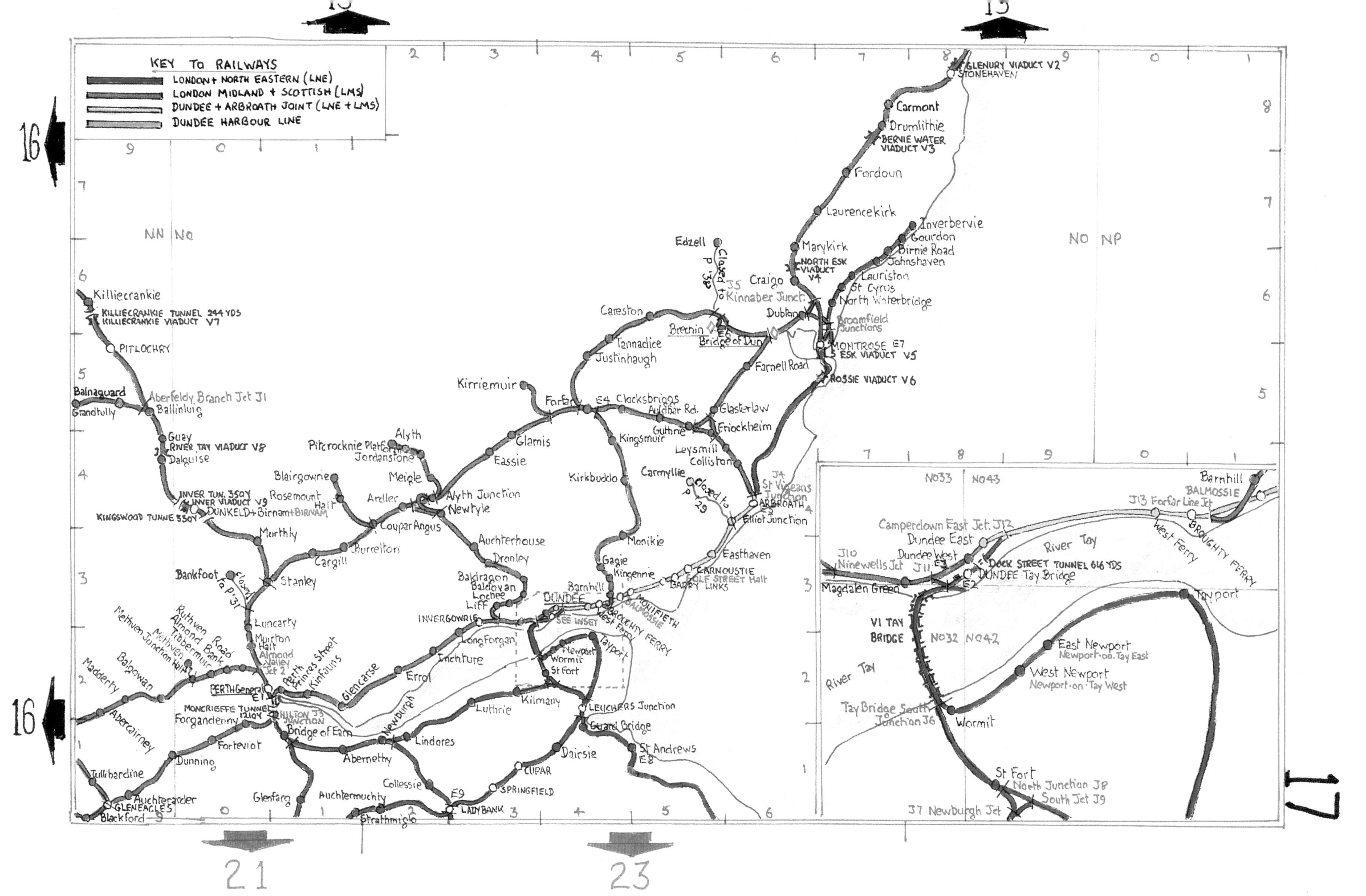

KEY TO RAILWAYS
LONDON + NORTH EASTERN (LNE)
LONDON MIDLAND + SCOTTISH (LMS)
DUNDEE + ARBROATH JOINT (LNE + LMS)
DUNDEE HARBOUR LINE
NN NO
NO NP
GLENURY VIADUCT V2
STONEHAVEN
Carmont
Drumlithie
BERVIE WATER VIADUCT V3
Fordoun
Laurencekirk
Marykirk
NORTH ESK VIADUCT V4
Craigo
Inverbervie
Gourdon
Birnie Road
Johnshaven
Lauriston
St Cyrus
North Waterbridge
Broomfield Junctions
Dubton
Kinnaber Junct.
J5
Edzell
Closed to P '38
Careston
Brechin
E6
Bridge of Dun
Tannadice
Justinhaugh
MONTROSE E7
ESK VIADUCT V5
Farnell Road
ROSSIE VIADUCT V6
Kirriemuir
Forfar
E4
Clocksbriggs
Auldbar Rd.
Guthrie
Glasterlaw
Friockheim
Kingsmuir
Leysmill
Colliston
Carmyllie
Closed to P '29
J4
St Vigeans Junction
ARBROATH
E3
Elliot Junction
Kirkbuddo
Monikie
Easthaven
CARNOUSTIE
GOLF STREET Halt
BARRY LINKS
MONIFIETH
BALMOSSIE
BROUGHTY FERRY
West Ferry
Gagie
Kingennie
Barnhill
DUNDEE
SEE INSET
Killiecrankie
KILLIECRANKIE TUNNEL 244 YDS
KILLIECRANKIE VIADUCT V7
PITLOCHRY
Balnaguard
Grandtully
Aberfeldy Branch Jct J1
Ballinluig
Guay
RIVER TAY VIADUCT V8
Dalguise
INVER TUN. 350Y
INVER VIADUCT V9
DUNKELD + Birnam
KINGSWOOD TUNNEL 350Y
Murthly
Blairgowrie
Rosemount Halt
Pitcrocknie Platform
Jordanstone
Alyth
Meigle
Ardler
Alyth Junction
Newtyle
Coupar Angus
Glamis
Eassie
Auchterhouse
Dronley
Burrelton
Cargill
Stanley
Bankfoot
Closed to P '31
Luncarty
Muirton Halt
Almond Valley Jct 2
Baldragon
Baldovan
Lochee
Liff
INVERGOWRIE
Longforgan
Inchture
Errol
Glencarse
Perth Princes Street
Kinfauns
PERTH General
E1
MONCRIEFFE TUNNEL 1210Y
HILTON J3 JUNCTION
Forgandenny
Bridge of Earn
Forteviot
Dunning
Newburgh
Lindores
Abernethy
Ruthven Road
Almond Bank
Tibbermuir
Methven
Methven Junction Halt
Balgowan
Madderty
Abercairney
Tullibardine
Auchterarder
GLENEAGLES
Blackford
Glenfarg
Auchtermuchty
Strathmiglo
Collessie
E9
LADYBANK
SPRINGFIELD
CUPAR
Dairsie
Luthrie
Kilmany
LEUCHARS Junction
Guard Bridge
St Andrews
E8
Tayport
Newport
Wormit
St Fort
Barnhill
BALMOSSIE
J13 Forfar Line Jt
West Ferry
BROUGHTY FERRY
Camperdown East Jct. J12
Dundee East
Dundee West
J11
E2
J10
Ninewells Jct
DOCK STREET TUNNEL 616 YDS
DUNDEE Tay Bridge
Magdalen Green
River Tay
V1 TAY BRIDGE
NO33
NO43
NO32
NO42
East Newport
Newport-on-Tay East
West Newport
Newport-on-Tay West
Tay Bridge South Junction J6
Wormit
St Fort
North Junction J8
South Jct J9
J7 Newburgh Jct
15
16
21
23

18 GREENOCK, GLASGOW + KILMARNOCK

RAILWAYS

No	Company
1	LONDON + NORTH EASTERN (LNE)
2	LONDON MIDLAND + SCOTTISH (LMS)
3	LNE + LMS JOINT

STATIONS

Station	Opened closed	Ry	Ref
Aberfoyle	51	1	[50]
ALEXANDRA PARADE	§		19
ALEXANDRIA + Bonhill	62	3	37
ANDERSTON Cross	§		19
ANNIESLAND		1	56
ARDROSSAN			24
HARBOUR	87	2	24
Montgomerie Pier	* 68	2	24
SOUTH BEACH		2	24
TOWN	* 53 87	2	24
Winton Pier	68	2	24
ARGYLE STREET	§		20
ARROCHAR + TARBET		1	[20]
ASHFIELD	§		19
BALLIESTON	* 64 93	2	66
Balfron	51	1	58
BALLOCH Central	88	3	38
Balloch Pier	* 86	3	38
Balmore	51	1	57
BARASSIE	*	2	33
9			
BARNHILL	§		19
BARRHEAD	*	2	45
Barrmill	† 62	2	35
BEARSDEN		1	57
Bellahouston	A § 54	2	56
Beith Town	† 53 62	2	35
Beith North	51	2	35
BELLGROVE	§		19
BISHOPBRIGGS	*	1	67
BISHOPTON		2	46
Blanefield	51	1	57
BLANTYRE		2	65
Bogside Race Course	* 52 67	2	34
BOGSTON		2	37
Bothwell	B 55	1	65
Bothwell	B 50	2	65
BOWLING	*	1	47
Bowling	51	2	47
BRANCHTON	67	2	27
Bridge of Weir	* 83	2	36
BRIDGE STREET	§		20
Bridgeton Cross	§		19
BRIDGETON CROSS	§		19
Buchanan Street	* 66	2	56
BUCHANAN STREET	§		20
Buchlyvie	51	1	59
Burnbank	52	1	65
BURNSIDE		2	65
BUSBY	*	2	55
Calderpark Halt for Zoo	51 62	2	66
Caldwell	62	2	45
Callander	* 65	2	[60]
CAMBUSLANG	§		19
Campsie Glen	51	1	67
CARDONALD		2	56
CARDROSS		1	37
CARMYLE	* 64 93	2	66
CARNTYNE		1	66
CARTSDYKE		2	27
CATHCART		2	56
CESSNOCK	§		20
CHARING CROSS	§		19
CLARKSTON + Stamperland	52 73	2	55
CLYDEBANK Central	§		19
Clydebank East	§		19
Clydebank Riverside	§		19
Copland Road	§		20
CORKERHILL	* 83 90	2	
COWCADDENS	§		20
Cowlairs	§		19
CRAIGENDORAN		1	28
Craigendoran West Highland	64	1	28
CROFTFOOT		2	65
CROOKSTON	* 82 90	3	46
CROSSHILL	§		19
Crosshouse	* 66	2	33
CROSSMYLOOF	§		19
Crow Road	§		19
Cumberland Street	§		20
Cunninghamhead	51	2	34
DALMARNOCK	§		19
DALMUIR Park	52 73	1	47
Dalmuir Riverside	* 52 64	2	47
DALREOCH		3	37
DALRY		2	24
Darvel	* 64	2	53
Dreghorn	* 64	2	33
DRUMCHAPEL		1	57
DRUMRY	53	1	57
Drybridge	* 69	2	33
DUKE STREET		1	66
DUMBARTON CENTRAL	52	3	37
DUMBARTON EAST		2	47
DUMBRECK	A § 90	2	56
Dumgoyne	51	1	58
DUNLOP	* 66 67	2	44
EASTERHOUSE		1	66
EAST KILBRIDE	*	2	65
Eglinton Street	§		20
Elderslie	* 66	2	46
EXHIBITION	§		20
FAIRLIE Town/High	C 52 53 73	2	25
Fairlie Pier	72	3	25
Fallside	53	2	66
FINNIESTON			20
Fort Matilda	93	2	27
Gailes	* 67	2	33
Galston	* 64	2	43
GARELOCHHEAD		1	29
Garnkirk	60	2	66
GARROWHILL Halt		1	66
GARSCADDEN			19
Gartcosh	† 62	2	66
Gartmore	50	1	59
Gatehead	* 69	3	33
Georgetown	59	2	46
GIFFNOCK	*	2	55
GLASGOW			
Buchanan Street	* 66	2	56
CENTRAL	§		19
QUEEN STREET		1	56
St Enoch	§		19
Glasgow Cross	§		20
Glasgow Green	§		19
Glen Douglas Halt	* 61 64	1	29
GLENGARNOCK		2	35
Gourock	93	2	27
Govan Cross	§		20
GREENOCK			27
CENTRAL		2	27
Lynedoch	59	2	27
Princes Pier	* 65	2	27
Upper	67	2	27
WEST		2	27
HAIRMYRES		2	65
HAWKHEAD	* 66 91	2	46
HELENSBURGH CENTRAL		1	28
HELENSBURGH UPPER		1	28
HIGH STREET	§		19
HILLFOOT		1	55
HILLHEAD	§		20
HILLINGTON EAST	§		19
HILLINGTON WEST	§		19
Houston + Crosslee	* 83	2	46
Howwood	53	2	35
Hurlford	55	2	43
Hyndland	§		19
HYNDLAND	§		19
IBM Halt	78	2	27
Ibrox	67	2	56
IBROX	§		20
INVERKIP		2	27
IRVINE		2	33
JOHNSTONE High		2	46
Johnstone North	55	2	46
JORDANHILL	§		19
Kelvin Bridge	§		19
KELVIN BRIDGE	§		20
Kelvin Hall	§		19
KELVINHALL	§		20
KENNISHEAD		2	56
Kilbirnie	* 66	2	35
Kilbarchan	* 66	2	36
Kilbowie	* 64	2	46
Killearn	51	1	48
Kilmacolm	* 83	2	36
KILMARNOCK		2	43
KILMAURS	* 66 84	2	44
KILPATRICK		1	47
KILWINNING		2	24
KINGS PARK		2	55
KINNING PARK			20
KIRKHILL		2	65
Kirkintilloch	* 64	1	67
LAMBSHILL	93	1	56
LANGBANK		2	37
LANGSIDE + Newlands	§		19
LARGS		2	25
Lennoxtown	51	1	67
LENZIE		1	67
LOCHSIDE	D § 55 66 85	2	35
LOCHWINNOCH	D § 85	2	35
Lochwinnoch	* 66	2	35
Lugton	* 66	2	45
Maryhill Central	* 52 64	2	56
MARYHILL	51 60 64 93	1	56
MAXWELL PARK			19
MERKLAND STREET			20
MILLIKEN PARK	* 66 89	2	36
MILNGAVIE		1	57
Milton of Campsie	51	1	67
Montgreenan	55	2	34
MOSSPARK WEST	* 74 83 90	2	56
MOUNT FLORIDA	§		19
Mount Vernon North	52 55	1	66
MOUNT VERNON	93	2	66
MUIREND		2	55
NEILSTON High	74	2	45
Neilston Low	* 53 64	2	45
Newmilns	* 64	2	53
NEWTON		2	65
NITSHILL	*	2	56
Old Kilpatrick	* 64	2	47
PAISLEY			46
Abercorn	67	2	46
CANAL	* 83 90	2	46
GILMOUR STREET		2	46
ST JAMES		2	46
West	* 66	2	46
Parkhead North	52 58	1	66
Parkhead Stadium	* 52 64	2	66
PARTICK	§		19
Partick Central	§		19
Partick Cross	§		20
Partick Hill	§		19
Partick West	* 64	2	56
PATTERTON for Darnley Rifle Range		2	55
POLLOKSHAWS EAST	§		19
POLLOKSHAWS WEST	52	2	56
POLLOKSHIELDS EAST	§		19
POLLOKSHIELDS WEST	§		19
PORT GLASGOW		2	37
Possil North	§		19
POSSILPARK + PARKHOUSE	§		19
PRIESTHILL + DARNLEY		2	56
Princes Pier	* 65	2	27
QUEEN STREET		1	56
Renfrew			46
Fulbar Street	67	2	46
South	67	2	46
Wharf	67	2	46
RENTON		3	37
Rhu	* 56 60 64	1	28
Robroyston	56	2	66
RUTHERGLEN	64 79	2	66
St Enoch			19
ST ENOCH			20
ST GEORGE'S CROSS			20
St Rollox			19
SALTCOATS Central	52 65	2	24
Sandyford Platform	67	2	46
Scotstoun East	§		19
SCOTSTOUNHILL	§		19
Scotstoun West	§		19
Shandon	* 64	1	28
SHAWLANDS	§		19
SHETTLESTONE		1	66
Shields Road	§		19
SHIELDS ROAD	§		20
SINGER		1	47
SOUTH BEACH		2	24
SPRINGBURN	§		19
Springside	* 64	2	33
Stepps	† 62	2	66
STEPPS	89	2	66
STEVENSTON		2	24
STEWARTON	* 66 67	2	44
STOBCROSS	§		19
Strathaven Central	* 65	2	64
Strathblane	51	1	57
Strathbungo	§		19
Summerston	51	1	57
SUMMERSTON	93	1	56
THORNLIEBANK	*	2	55
THORNTONHALL		2	55
Tollcross	§		19
Torrance	51	2	67
TROON		2	33
Twechar	51	1	67
UDDINGSTON Central	§		19
Uddingston East	§		19
Uddingston West	§		19
Uplawmoor	* 62	2	45
WEMYSS BAY		2	16
WESTERTON		1	56
WEST GREENOCK		2	27
WEST KILBRIDE		2	24
WEST STREET	§		20
WHINHILL	90	2	27
Whistlefield Halt	* 60 64	1	29
WHITECRAIGS		2	55
Whiteinch Riverside	§		19
Whiteinch Victoria Park	§		19
Winton Pier	68	2	24
WILLIAMWOOD		2	55
WOODHALL Halt		2	37
YOKER High	53 65	1	56
Yoker Ferry	§		19

GOODS

No	Location	Closed	Ry	Ref
G1	Chryston	65	1	67
2	Port Glasgow Upper	59	2	37
3	Riccarton + Craigie	65	2	43

ENGINE SHEDS (8)

No	Name/Location	Closed	Ry	Ref
E2	Beith	62	2	35
4	Lennoxtown	?	1	67
5	Aberfoyle	?	1	[50]
6	Arrochar	?	1	[20]
7	Hurlford	66	2	43
8	Ardrossan	65	2	24
10	Princes Pier Greenock	60	2	27

TUNNELS

No	Name	Length	Ry	Ref
T1	Fairlie	990	2	25
2	Inverkip	200	2	17
3	Newbury Street	2110	2	27

NOTES

1 Ref: Mainly in NS. Those in NN are distinguished-box round the Ref.

2 All passenger stations in the area the map covers are included. Those which are unnamed on the map are in brown and the map on which they are named is show in brown in the ref column. The Glasgow Subway is NOT shown on this map or on MAP 19. It appears only on map 20.

3 Features other than passenger stations are NOT featured in this gazetteer if they are in an area that is covered by an enlargement.

4 Name changes: Old § New § Letter gives reference to other name where the identical letter will be used.

5 B Two stations at Bothwell. One LNE, the other LMS

6 C Name Changes

to 52	FAIRLIE
52-53	FAIRLIE Town
53-57	FAIRLIE High
From 57	FAIRLIE

7 Goods shown in separate list on most subsequent maps

8 The numbered Engine Sheds not in this gazetteer had been closed before 1948.

9 Additional station:
Barleith * 64 2 43

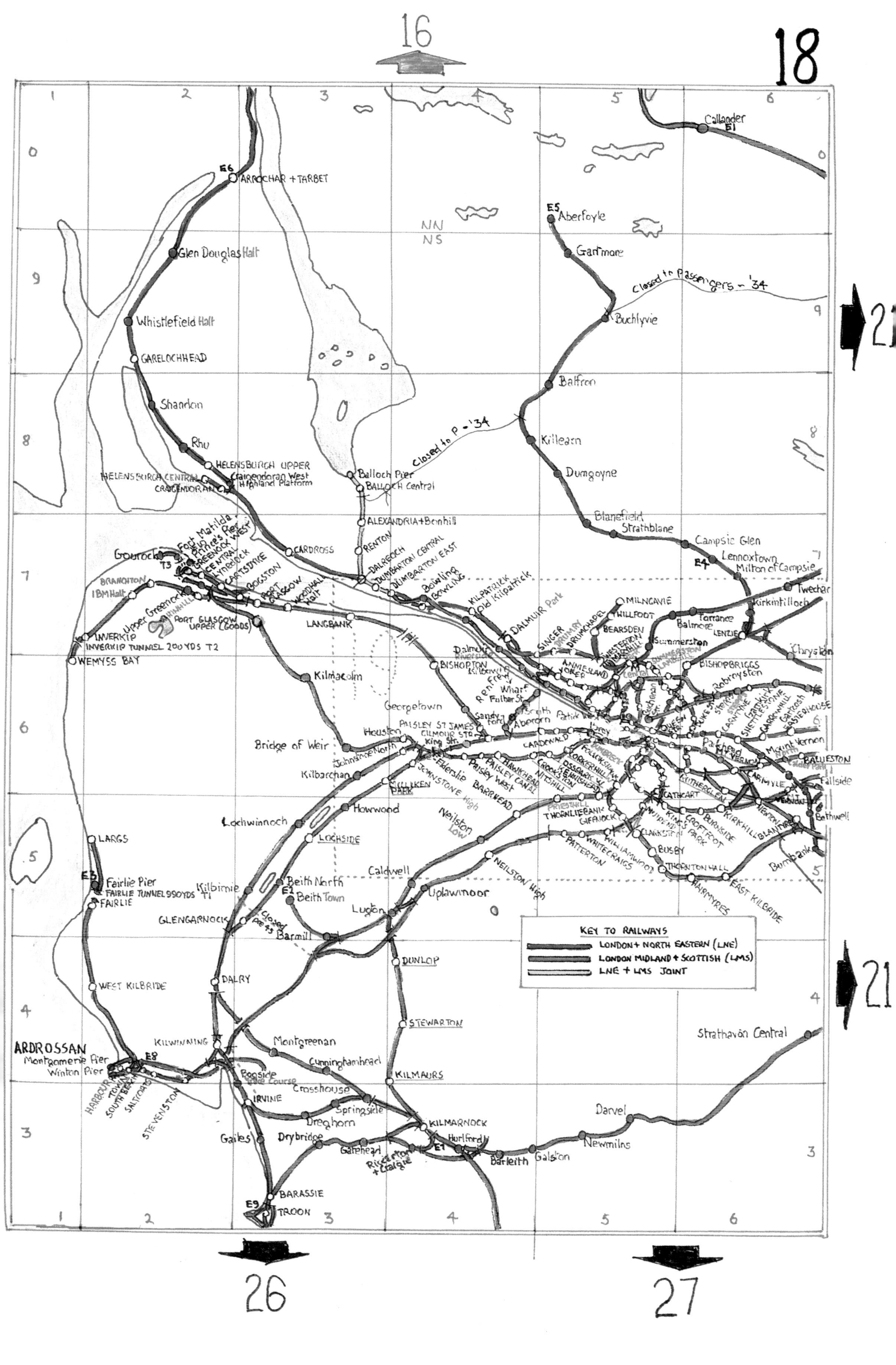
18
16
21
21
26
27
Callander
E1
E6
ARROCHAR + TARBET
NN
NS
E5
Aberfoyle
Gartmore
Glen Douglas Halt
Closed to Passengers - '34
Buchlyvie
Whistlefield Halt
GARELOCHHEAD
Balfron
Shandon
Closed to P - '34
Killearn
Rhu
HELENSBURGH UPPER
HELENSBURGH CENTRAL
Craigendoran West
Highland Platform
CRAIGENDORAN
Balloch Pier
BALLOCH Central
Dumgoyne
ALEXANDRIA + Bonhill
RENTON
Blanefield
Strathblane
Campsie Glen
Lennoxtown
E4
Milton of Campsie
Gourock
T3
Fort Matilda
Prince's Pier
GREENOCK WEST
CENTRAL
CARTSDYKE
BOGSTON
PORT GLASGOW
WOODHALL Halt
CARDROSS
DALREOCH
DUMBARTON CENTRAL
DUMBARTON EAST
Bowling
BOWLING
KILPATRICK
Old Kilpatrick
Twechar
BRANCHTON
IBM Halt
Upper Greenock
PORT GLASGOW UPPER (GOODS)
LANGBANK
DALMUIR Park
MILNGAVIE
HILLFOOT
BEARSDEN
Kirkintilloch
Torrance
Balmore
LENZIE
INVERKIP
INVERKIP TUNNEL 200YDS T2
WEMYSS BAY
Kilmacolm
BISHOPTON
SINGER
DRUMCHAPEL
WESTERTON
Summerston
ANNIESLAND
YOKER
BISHOPBRIGGS
Robroyston
Chryston
Georgetown
Renfrew Wharf
Fulbar St.
Sandyford
Aberdeen
Houston
PAISLEY ST JAMES
GILMOUR STR.
King St.
Bridge of Weir
Johnstone North
CARDONALD
Elderslie
JOHNSTONE High
Paisley West
PAISLEY CANAL
HAWKHEAD
CROOKSTON
NITSHILL
BARRHEAD
Kilbarchan
MILLIKEN PARK
Howwood
Parkhead
Mount Vernon
BAILLIESTON
Fallside
CARMYLE
Bothwell
BLANTYRE
CATHCART
RUTHERGLEN
KIRKHILL
Lochwinnoch
LOCHSIDE
Neilston Low
THORNLIEBANK
GIFFNOCK
CLARKSTON
BUSBY
WHITECRAIGS
PATTERTON
THORNTON HALL
Burnbank
LARGS
E3
Fairlie Pier
FAIRLIE TUNNEL 990YDS T1
FAIRLIE
Kilbirnie
E2
Beith North
Beith Town
Caldwell
Uplawmoor
NEILSTON High
HAIRMYRES
EAST KILBRIDE
Lugton
GLENGARNOCK
Closed pre 43
Barmill
KEY TO RAILWAYS
LONDON + NORTH EASTERN (LNE)
LONDON MIDLAND + SCOTTISH (LMS)
LNE + LMS JOINT
DUNLOP
DALRY
WEST KILBRIDE
STEWARTON
Strathavon Central
ARDROSSAN
Montgomerie Pier
Winton Pier
E8
KILWINNING
Montgreenan
Cunninghamhead
HARBOUR
TOWN
SOUTH BEACH
SALTCOATS
STEVENSTON
Bogside
Race Course
Crosshouse
IRVINE
Springside
KILMAURS
Dreghorn
KILMARNOCK
Darvel
Gailes
Drybridge
Gatehead
Riccarton + Craigie
E1
Hurlford
Barleith
Galston
Newmilns
BARASSIE
E9
TROON

GLASGOW + PAISLEY

No.	RAILWAYS
1	LONDON + NORTH EASTERN (LNE)
2	LONDON MIDLAND + SCOTTISH (LMS)
3	LNE + LMS JOINT
4	GLASGOW SUBWAY (2)
0	BRITISH RAILWAYS (BR)

STATIONS

Station	Opened/Closed	Ry Ref
ALEXANDRA PARADE		166
ANDERSTON Cross	77	256
ANNIESLAND		156
ARGYLE STREET	§	20
ASHFIELD	93	156
BALLIESTON	* 6493	266
Balmore	51	157
BARNHILL Glasgow	5365	166
BARRHEAD	*	255
BEARSDEN		157
Bellahouston	A § 5490	256
BELLGROVE		166
BISHOPBRIGGS	*	167
BISHOPTON		247
BLANTYRE		265
Bothwell	50	165
Bothwell	50	265
BOWLING	*	147
Bowling	51	247
Bridge of Weir	* 83	236
BRIDGE STREET	§	20
Bridgeton Cross Central	546579	166
BRIDGETON Cross	6479	266
Buchanan Street	* 66	256
BUCHANAN STREET	§	20
Burnbank	52	165
BURNSIDE		266
BUSBY	*	255
Calderpark Halt for The Zoo	5162	266
Caldwell	62	245
CAMBUSLANG		266
CARDONALD		256
CARMYLE	* 6493	266
CARNTYNE		166
CATHCART		256
CESSNOCK	§	20
CHARING CROSS		156
CLARKSTON + Stamperland	* 5273	255
CLYDEBANK Central	65	157
Clydebank East	59	156
Clydebank Riverside	* 5364	246
Copland Road	§	20
CORKERHILL	* 8390	256
COWCADDENS	§	20
Cowlairs	* 64	156
CROFTFOOT		266
CROOKSTON	8390	266
CROSSHILL		256
CROSSMYLOOF	*	256
Crow Road	60	256
Cumberland Street	§	20
DALMARNOCK	* 6479	266
DALMUIR Park	5273	147
Dalmuir Riverside	* 5264	247
DALREOCH		1337
DAWSHOLM		056
DRUMCHAPEL		157
DRUMRY	53	157
DUKE STREET		166
DUMBARTON CENTRAL	52	347
DUMBARTON EAST		247
DUMBRECK	A § 90	256
EASTERHOUSE		166
EAST KILBRIDE	*	265
Eglinton Street	§	20
Elderslie	* 66	246
EXHIBITION CENTRE	B § 86	256
Fallside	53	266
Finnieston	B § § 7986	156
Garnkirk	60	266
GARROWHILL Halt		166
GARSCADDEN	?	156
Gartcosh	+ 62	266
Georgetown	59	246
GIFFNOCK	*	255
GLASGOW		56
Buchanan Street	* 66	256
CENTRAL		256
QUEEN STREET		156
St Enoch	* 66	256
Glasgow Cross	§	20
Glasgow Green	53	256
GOVAN Cross	§	20
HAIRMYRES		265
HAWKHEAD	6691	256
HIGH STREET	7781	156
HILLFOOT		157
HILLHEAD	§	20
HILLINGTON EAST		256
HILLINGTON WEST	52	256
Houston + Crosslee	* 7383	246
Howwood	53	246
Hyndland	C 60	156
HYNDLAND	C 60	156
Ibrox	67	256
Ibrox Football Platform	D 65	2
IBROX	§	20
JOHNSTONE High	5152	246
Johnstone	55	246
JORDANHILL		156
Kelvin Bridge	52	256
KELVINBRIDGE	§	20
Kelvin Hall	* E § 5964	256
KELVIN HALL	§	20
KENNISHEAD	*	256
Kilbarchan	* 66	246
Kilbowie	* 64	247
KILPATRICK		147
KING'S PARK		256
KINNING PARK	§	20
KIRKHILL		266
Kirkintilloch	64	167
LAMBHILL	93	156
LANGSIDE + Newlands		256
LENZIE		167
Maryhill Central	5264	257
MARYHILL Park (60-64)	51 60 6493	257
MAXWELL PARK		256
MERKLAND STREET	§	20
MILLIKEN PARK	* 6689	246
MILNGAVIE		157
MOSSPARK West	* 8390	256
MOUNT FLORIDA		256
Mount Vernon North	5255	166
MOUNT VERNON	93	266
MUIREND		255
NEILSTON High	74	245
Neilston Low	* 5366	245
NEWTON	*	266
NITSHILL	*	256
Old Kilpatrick	* 64	247
PAISLEY		46
Abercorn	67	246
CANAL	* 8390	246
GILMOUR STREET		246
ST JAMES		246
West	* 66	246
Parkhead North	5258	166
Parkhead Stadium	* 5264	266
PARTICK	79	1456
Partick Central	E § 59	256
Partick Cross	§	20
Partick Hill	F 5379	156
Partick West	* 64	256
PATTERTON For Darnley Rifle Range		255
POLLOKSHAWS WEST	* 52	256
POLLOKSHAWS EAST		256
POLLOKSHIELDS EAST	§	20
POLLOKSHIELDS WEST		256
Possil North	* 5464	256
POSSILPARK + PARKHOUSE	6493	156
PRIESTHILL + DARNLEY	90	227
QUEENS PARK		256
Renfrew		
Fulbar Street	67	256
South	67	246
Wharf	67	256
Robroyston	* 56	266
RUTHERGLEN	6479	266
St Enoch	* 66	256
ST ENOCH	§	20
ST GEORGE'S CROSS	§	20
St Rollox	+ 62	256
Sandyford Platform	67	246
Scotstoun East	* 5764	256
SCOTSTOUNHILL		156
Scotstoun West	* 64	256
SHAWLANDS		256
SHETTLESTON		166
Shields Road	* 66	256
SHIELDS ROAD	§	20
SINGER		146
South Renfrew	67	246
SPRINGBURN		156
Stepps	+ 62	266
STEPPS	89	266
Stobcross	B § 7959	256
Strathbungo	62	256
Summerston	51	157
SUMMERSTON	93	156
THORNLIEBANK	*	256
THORNTONHALL	*	255
Tollcross	* 64	266
Torrance	51	167
UDDINGSTON Central	58	266
Uddingston East	5355	166
Uddingston West	55	166
WESTERTON		157
WEST STREET	§	20
WHITECRAIGS		255
Whiteinch Riverside	* 5364	256
Whiteinch Victoria Park	51	156
WILLIAMWOOD		255
YOKER High	5365	156
Yoker Ferry	* 5364	256

GOODS

Name	Closed	Ry Ref
Barrhead South	63	255
Basin Kirkintilloch	66	167
Burnbank	52	165
Canal, Paisley	?	246
Cambuslang	66	266
Chryston	65	167
Dawsholm	64	256
Dumbarton Central	66	147
Dumbarton East	?	247
Dumbuck	59	147
Gallowhill, Paisley	65	246
Glenfield	66	246
Gleniffer	59	245
Govan	66	256
King Street, Paisley	65	246
Limwood	67	246
Netherton	59	255
Potter Field, Renfrew	64	246
Potterhill, Paisley	65	246
Rutherglen	66	266
Saucel, Paisley	65	246
Shieldhall	66	256
Springburn Park	65	266
Thornliebank	62	255

ENGINE SHEDS

No	Name	Closed	Ry Ref
1	Dawsholm	64	256
2	Yoker	64	256
3	Yoker	61	156
5	Eastfield	*	156
6	Cowlairs	*	156

* Continued as shed after steam but now closed.

TUNNELS

No.	Name/Location		Ry Ref
1	DALREOCH	550	137
2	BISHOPTON No.1	330	247
3	BISHOPTON No.2	350	247

NOTES

(1) Refs: All in NS

(2) Glasgow Subway not shown on this map or on map 18 but PARTICK is shown as ordinary station and is also on GLASGOW SUBWAY.

(3) Name Change § old name, § Modern name. Letter indicates other name. In one case B there are two changes of name as follows

Start Date	Name	End Date
1896	Stobcross (closed)	1959
1979	Finnieston	1986
1986	EXHIBITION CENTRE	

C Replacement Station was nearby but on a different line

D Exact location unclear and not on the map.

(4) All junctions not named after adjoining stations shown on the map are named and have therefore been excluded from this gazetteer.

(5) All items except passenger stations within the area covered by the enlargement of map 20 are normally excluded from map and gazetteer.

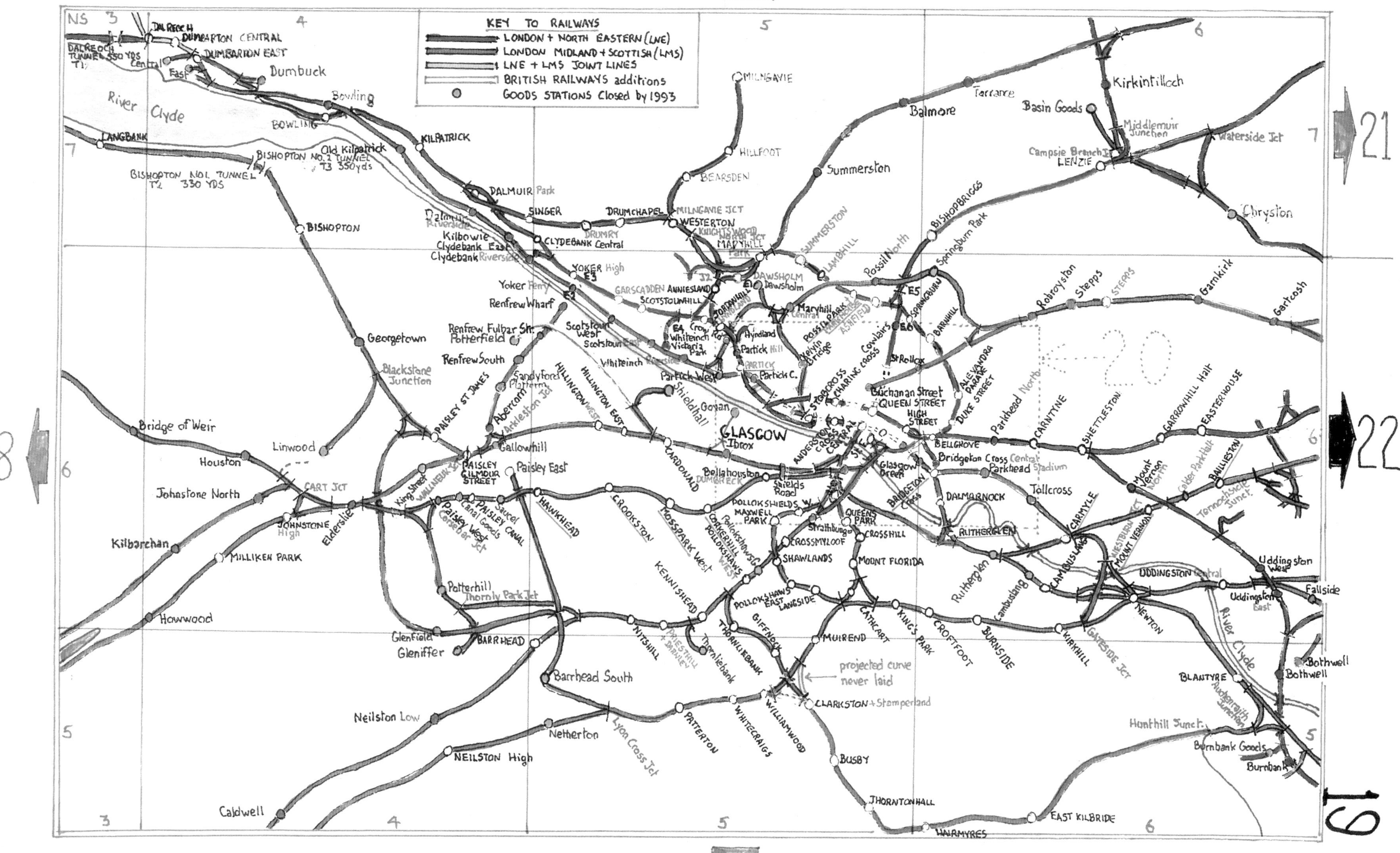
KEY TO RAILWAYS
LONDON + NORTH EASTERN (LNE)
LONDON MIDLAND + SCOTTISH (LMS)
LNE + LMS JOINT LINES
BRITISH RAILWAYS additions
GOODS STATIONS Closed by 1993
GLASGOW
River Clyde
Dalreoch
Dumbarton Central
Dumbarton East
Dumbuck
Bowling
Langbank
Kilpatrick
Bishopton
Dalmuir Park
Singer
Drumchapel
Westerton
Milngavie
Hillfoot
Bearsden
Summerston
Balmore
Terrance
Basin Goods
Kirkintilloch
Lenzie
Waterside Jct
Chryston
Bishopbriggs
Springburn Park
Robroyston
Stepps
Garnkirk
Gartcosh
Georgetown
Blackstone Junction
Yoker
Renfrew Wharf
Renfrew South
Anniesland
Scotstounhill
Maryhill
Hyndland
Partick West
Whiteinch
Shieldhall
Govan
Ibrox
Charing Cross
Buchanan Street
Queen Street
High Street
Bellgrove
Duke Street
Alexandra Parade
Parkhead North
Carntyne
Shettleston
Garrowhill Halt
Easterhouse
Baillieston
Mount Vernon
Bridgeton Cross
Dalmarnock
Tollcross
Rutherglen
Carmyle
Cambuslang
Uddingston
Fallside
Newton
Blantyre
Bothwell
Hunthill Junct.
Burnbank Goods
Burnbank
Bridge of Weir
Houston
Linwood
Johnstone North
Johnstone High
Kilbarchan
Milliken Park
Howwood
Elderslie
Paisley St James
Paisley Gilmour Street
Paisley East
Gallowhill
Hillington West
Hillington East
Cardonald
Hawkhead
Crookston
Mosspark West
Bellahouston
Shields Road
Pollokshields West
Maxwell Park
Crossmyloof
Shawlands
Queens Park
Crosshill
Mount Florida
Cathcart
King's Park
Croftfoot
Burnside
Kirkhill
Potterhill
Glenfield
Gleniffer
Barrhead
Barrhead South
Nitshill
Kennishead
Thornliebank
Giffnock
Muirend
Clarkston + Stamperland
projected curve never laid
Williamwood
Whitecraigs
Patterton
Netherton
Lyon Cross Jct
Neilston Low
Neilston High
Caldwell
Busby
Thorntonhall
Hairmyres
East Kilbride

GLASGOW

RAILWAY

No.	Company	Abbreviation
1	LONDON + NORTH EASTERN	(LNE)
2	LONDON MIDLAND + SCOTTISH	(LMS)
3	LNE + LMS JOINT	
4	GLASGOW SUBWAY	
0	BRITISH RAIL	(BR)

STATIONS

Station	Opened Closed	Ry	Ref
ALEXANDRA PARADE		1	6165
ANDERSTON Cross	77	2	5765
ARGYLE STREET	79	2	5965
BARNHILL Glasgow	53 65	1	6067
Bellahouston	A§ 54 90	2	5664
BRIDGE STREET	77 80	4	5865
Bridgeton Cross Central	79	1	6664
BRIDGETON Cross	64 79	2	6664
Buchanan Street	* 66	2	5966
BUCHANAN STREET	77 80	4	5865
CARNTYNE		1	6265
CENTRAL HIGH LEVEL		2	5865
CENTRAL LOW LEVEL	64 79	2	5865
CESSNOCK	77 80	4	5665
CHARING CROSS		1	5766
Copland Road	B§ 77	4	5565
COWCADDENS	77 80	4	5866
Cowlairs	* 64	1	5967
Crow Road	60	2	5567
Cumberland Street	* 66	2	5864
DALMARNOCK	* 64 79	2	6064
DUKE STREET		1	6065
DUMBRECK	A§ 90	2	5664
Eglinton Street	* 65	2	5864
EXHIBITION CENTRE	C§ 86	2	5665
Finnieston	C§ 79 86	1	5665
Glasgow Cross	* 64	2	5965
Glasgow Green	53	2	5964
GOVAN Cross	77 80	4	5566
HIGH STREET	77 81	1	5965
HILLHEAD	77 80	4	5767
Hyndland	60	1	5567
HYNDLAND	60	1	5567
Ibrox	67	2	5564
Ibrox Football Platform	65	2	
(IBROX)	B§ 80	4	5565
Kelvin Bridge	52	2	5666
KELVINBRIDGE	77 80	4	5766
Kelvin Hall	D§ 59 64	2	5566
(KELVINHALL)	E§ 80	4	5666
KINNING PARK	77 80	4	5664
MAXWELL PARK		2	5663
Merkland Street	F§ 77	4	5566
Parkhead North	52 58	1	6165
Parkhead Stadium	* 52 64	2	6164
PARTICK	F§ 79 80	1 4	5566
Partick Central	D§ 59	2	5566
Partick Cross	E§ 77	4	5666
Partick Hill	53 79	1	5566
Partick West	G* 64	2	19
POLLOKSHIELDS EAST		2	5763
POLLOKSHIELDS WEST		2	5763
QUEEN STREET HIGH LEVEL		1	5965
QUEEN STREET LOW LEVEL		1	5966
St Enoch	* 66	2	5865
ST ENOCH	77 80	4	5865
ST GEORGE'S CROSS	77 80	4	5866
St Rollox	+ 62	2	6066
SHIELDS ROAD	77 80	4	5764
Shields Road	* 66	2	5764
SPRINGBURN		1	6067
Stobcross	C§ 79 59	2	5665
Strathbungo	62	2	5763
Tallcross	* 64	2	6264
WEST STREET	77 80	4	5864

GOODS

Name/Location	Closed	Ry	Ref
Bellahouston	64	2	5664
BRIDGETON		2	6064
Camlachie	?	1	6165
College	68	2	5965
Craighall	?	1	5867
Eglinton Street	57	2	5864
General Terminus	?	2	5765
Govan	66	2	5565
Gushetfaulds	?	2	5864
Haghill	65	1	6165
High Street	?	1	5965
Kennyhill	64	2	6165
Kinning Park	?	2	5664
LONDON ROAD	⌇	2	6164
Partick	65	2	5566
Pinkston North	?	1	5966
Pinkston South	?	1	5966
Port Dundas	64	1 2	5966
Port Eglinton	57	2	5764
Princes Dock	?	3	5765
Queens Dock	?	2	5665
St Rollox East	64	2	5966
St Rollox West	68	2	5966
Sighthill	⌇	1	6066
South Side	64	2	5864
Stobcross Joint	68	3	5665
West Side	64	2	5864

WORKS

Name	Ry	Ref
ST ROLLOX GLASGOW WORKS	2	5966

ENGINE SHEDS

No	Name/Location	Closed	Ry	Ref
1	BOLORNOCK		2	6167
2	St Enoch	35X	2	5965
3	POLMADIE		2	5963
4	Parkhead	65	1	6165
5	Stobcross	66	1	5665
6	CORKERHILL		2	5564
7	Hyndland	85	1	5567

TUNNELS

No	Name/Location	Length yds	Ry	Ref
1	STOBCROSS STREET	640	2	5765
2	ANDERSTON	2170	2	5865
3	CANNING STREET	460	2	6064
4	DALMARNOCK ROAD	790	2	6064
5	FINNIESTON	530	1	5766
6	CHARING CROSS	1114	1	5866
7	HIGH STREET	680	1	5965
8	BELLGROVE	213	1	6065
9	DUKE STREET	220	1	6065
10	BLOCHAIRN	110	1	6066
11	BARNHILL	130	1	6066
12	EGLINTON STREET	200	2	5863
13	QUEEN STREET HIGH LEVEL	990	1	5966
14	KELVINHAUGH	945	2	5666

all above still in use

JUNCTIONS

No	Name	Ry	Ref
1	Kelvinside	2	5667
2	Pinkston	1	5967
3	Robroyston West	2	6267
4	Balornock	2	6167
5	FINNIESTON WEST	10	5566
6	FINNIESTON EAST	1	5666
7	Blackhill	2	6166
8	Moorepark	2	5565
9	Cathcart Road	2	5863
10	Clyde	2	5965
11	Saltmarket	2	5965
12	Barrack Street	1	5965
13	HIGH STREET	12	6065
14	St John's	12	6065
15	SWORD STREET	1	6065
16	SHIELDS	2	5664
17	Bridge Street	2	5864
18	Cumberland Street	2	5864
19	Terminus	2	5764
20	MUIRHOUSE NORTH	2	5763
21	MUIRHOUSE CENTRAL	2	5763
22	MUIRHOUSE SOUTH	2	5763
23	Strathclyde	2	6063
24	CLYDE	2	6063

NOTES:

(1) REF: All in NS

(2) NAME CHANGE: § OLD NAME
§ NEW NAME
Adjoining letter gives reference to the other name.

(3) ⌇ Closed by BR but in private use.

(4) All subway stations were closed 1977 but re-opened after renovation in 1980. Some re-opened under a changed name.

(5) Some other stations also closed and later re-opened on same site but with a change of name. The sequence etc with the marked station is as follows:

A Bellahouston closed 54, re-opened in 90 as DUMBRECK

B Copland Road closed for renovation in 77 re-opened 90 as (IBROX)

C Stobcross closed 1959 reopened on same site 1979 as Finnieston but then name changed 1986 to EXHIBITION CEN.

D Partick Central closed 1959 but was renamed Kelvin Hall which closed 64

E Partick Cross closed 77 for renovation re-opened (KELVINHALL) 80

F Merkland Street closed 1977 for renovation but re-opened PARTICK in 80. But in the meantime 79 it had opend as a normal station replacing Partick Hill

G This station not on map. See 19 but included to give comprehensive cover to all stations under PARTICK

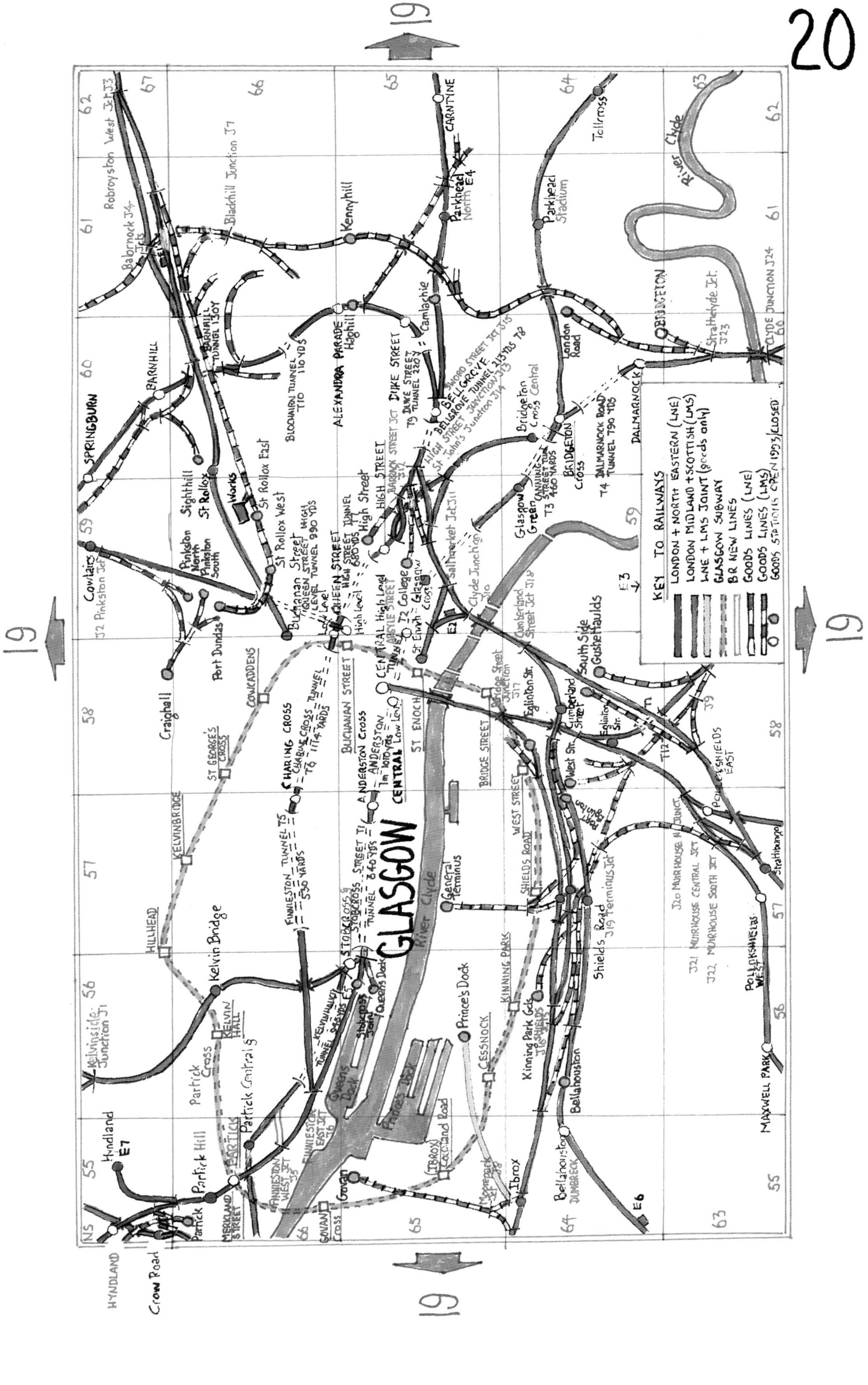

GLASGOW

River Clyde

HYNDLAND
Crow Road
Hyndland E7
Partick
Partick Hill
Partick Cross
MERKLAND STREET
PARTICK
Partick Central 8
KELVIN HALL
Kelvinside Junction J1
Kelvin Bridge
HILLHEAD
KELVINBRIDGE
ST GEORGE'S CROSS
COWCADDENS
Craighall
Port Dundas
Cowlairs
J2 Pinkston Jct
Pinkston North
Pinkston South
Sighthill
St Rollox
Works
St Rollox East
St Rollox West
SPRINGBURN
BARNHILL
BARNHILL TUNNEL 130Y
Babrnock J4 Jcts
Robroyston West Jct J3
Blackhill Junction J7
BLOCHAIRN TUNNEL T10 110 YDS
ALEXANDRA PARADE
Haghill
Kennyhill
Camlachie
DUKE STREET
T9 DUKE STREET TUNNEL 220Y
Parkhead North E4
CARNTYNE
FINNIESTON WEST JCT J5
FINNIESTON EAST JCT J6
FINNIESTON TUNNEL T5 530 YARDS
CHARING CROSS
CHARING CROSS TUNNEL T6 1114 YARDS
Buchanan Street
QUEEN STREET HIGH LEVEL TUNNEL 990 YDS
Low Level
QUEEN STREET
High Level
HIGH STREET TUNNEL 680 YDS T7
High Street
HIGH STREET
BARRACK STREET JCT J12
BELLGROVE
BELLGROVE TUNNEL 213 YDS T8
SWORD STREET JCT J15
HIGH STREET JUNCTION J13
St John's Junction J14
KELVINHAUGH TUNNEL 645 YDS
E5
STOBCROSS
STOBCROSS STREET T1 TUNNEL 340 YDS
Stobcross Joint
Queens Dock
Queens Dock
ANDERSTON Cross
ANDERSTON Tm 1010 yds
CENTRAL Low Level
BUCHANAN STREET
CENTRAL High Level
ARGYLE STREET TUNNEL
ST ENOCH
St Enoch
T2 College
Glasgow Cross
Saltmarket Jct J11
Clyde Junction J10
E2
GOVAN Cross
Govan
Prince's Dock
(IBROX) Copland Road
Prince's Dock
General Terminus
CESSNOCK
Moorepark Jct J8
Ibrox
KINNING PARK
Kinning Park Gds
J16 SHIELDS J15
SHIELDS ROAD
WEST STREET
BRIDGE STREET
Bridge Street Junction J17
Eglinton Str.
Cumberland Street Jct J18
Glasgow Green
CANNING STREET TUNNEL T3 460 YARDS
Bridgeton Cross Central
BRIDGETON Cross
London Road
Parkhead Stadium
Tollcross
Bellahouston
DUMBRECK
Bellahouston
E6
Shields Road
J19 Terminus Jct
Port Eglinton
West Str.
Cumberland Street
Eglinton Str.
South Side
Gushetfaulds
E3
59
T4 DALMARNOCK ROAD TUNNEL 790 YDS
DALMARNOCK
BRIDGETON
Strathclyde Jct. J23
CLYDE JUNCTION J24
River Clyde
J20 MUIRHOUSE N. JUNCT.
J21 MUIRHOUSE CENTRAL JCT
J22 MUIRHOUSE SOUTH JCT
T12
J9
POLLOKSHIELDS EAST
POLLOKSHIELDS WEST
MAXWELL PARK
Strathbungo

NS 55 56 57 58 59 60 61 62
67 66 65 64 63
19

KEY TO RAILWAYS
- LONDON + NORTH EASTERN (LNE)
- LONDON MIDLAND + SCOTTISH (LMS)
- LNE + LMS JOINT (goods only)
- GLASGOW SUBWAY
- BR NEW LINES
- GOODS LINES (LNE)
- GOODS LINES (LMS)
- GOODS STATIONS OPEN 1993 / CLOSED

21 STIRLING DUNFERMLINE + MOTHERWELL

RAILWAYS

No	Company
1	LONDON + NORTH EASTERN (LNE)
2	LONDON MIDLAND + SCOTTISH (LMS)
3	LNE + LMS JOINT
4	BO'NESS + KINNEIL ◊

STATIONS

Name	Opened/Closed	Ry	Ref
ABERDOUR		1	T18
ADDIEWELL	*	2	S96
AIRBLES	89	2	S75
AIRDRIE South	52	1	S76
Airth	54	2	S88
Alloa	* 68	1	S89
Alva	54	1	S89
Armadale	56	1	S96
Auchengray	* 66	2	S95
Auchenheath	51	2	S84
Auchlochen Halt	A 65	2	S83
Balado	* 64	1	O00
Balerno	49	2	T16
Bannockburn	50	2	S89
BARGEDDIE	93	1	S76
Barnton	51	2	T17
BATHGATE Upper	56 86	1	S96
Bellshill	51	1	S76
BELSHILL		2	S76
Biggar	50	2	T03
(BIRKHILL)	◊	14	S97
Blackford	56	2	N80
Blackwood	* 65	2	S74
BLAIRHILL + Gartsherrie	§		22
Bogside (Fife)	54 58	1	S99
Bo'ness	◊ 56 ?	14	T08
Bonnybridge High 53/65	* 67	1	S87
Braidwood	62	2	S84
BREICH	*	2	S96
BRIDGE OF ALLAN	* 65 85	2	S79
Brocketsbrae	51	2	S84
Broughton	50	1	T03
Caldercruix	56	1	S86
Cambus	* 68	1	S89
Camelon	** 67 94	1	S88
CARFIN Halt	* 83	2	S75
CARLUKE		2	S84
Carnwath	* 66	2	S94
CARSTAIRS		2	S94
Castlecary	* 67	1	S77
Causewayhead	* 55	1	S89
Clarkston Lanark	* 53 56	1	S76
Cleghorn	* 65	2	S84
CLELAND	*	2	S85
Coalburn	* 65	2	S83
COATBRIDGE CENTRAL	53	2	S76
Coatbridge Central	51	1	S76
COATBRIDGE SUNNYSIDE		1	S76
COATDYKE		1	S76
Cobbinshaw	* 66	2	T05
Coulter	50	2	T03
COWDENBEATH		1	T19
Crook of Devon	* 64	1	O00
Crossgates	49	1	T18
CROY	*	1	S77
CUMBERNAULD	*	2	S77
CURRIE HILL	B 51 87	2	T16
DALMENY		1	T17
Dalserf	51	2	S75
Dollar	* 64	1	S99
Douglas West	* 64	2	S83
Doune	* 65	2	N70
DRUMGELLOCH	89	1	S76
Drumpark	C 64	2	S76
Drumshoreland	51	1	T07
Dullatur	* 67	1	S77
DUNBLANE		2	N70
DUNFERMLINE Lower	69	1	T88
Dunfermline Upper	68	1	T08
East Grange	58	1	T08
EDINBURGH AIRPORT	*	1	T17
FALKIRK			
Camelon	* 67	1	S88
GRAHAMSTON		1	S88
HIGH		1	S87
Fallside	53	2	S76
FAULDHOUSE North	* 52 86	2	S96
Flemington	* 65	2	S75
Gateside	50	1	O10
Glenboig	56	2	S76
Grangemouth	68	2	S98
GREENFAULDS	89	2	S77
Greenhill	* 66	2	S87
Greenloaning	56	2	N80
Hamilton	51	1	S75
HAMILTON CENTRAL			S75
HAMILTON WEST		2	S75
Happendon	* 64	2	S83
Harburn	* 66	2	T06
HARTWOOD	*	2	S85
Haywood	51	2	S95
HOLYTOWN	*	2	S76
INVERKEITHING		1	T18
Kilsyth	51	3	S77
Kinbuck	56	2	N70
(KINNIEL)	◊ 79	14	S98
Kinross Junction	70	1	O10
KIRKNEWTON	C § 82	2	T16
Lamington	* 65	2	S93
LANARK		2	S84
Lanark Racecourse	64	2	S84
Langloan	§		22
LARBERT		2	S88
Larkhall Central	* 1 64 65	2	S75
Larkhall East	51	2	S76
Law Junction	* 65	2	S85
Lesmahagow	* 65	2	S84
LINLITHGOW		1	T07
LIVINGSTON NORTH	48 86	1	T06
LIVINGSTON SOUTH	84	2	T06
LOCHGELLY		1	T19
Manuel High Level	* 67	1	S97
Mawcarse Junction	* 62 64	1	O10
Menstrie + Glenochil	54 54	1	S89
Midcalder	D § * 82	2	T16
Milnathort	* 64	1	O10
Mossend	+ 62	2	S76
MOTHERWELL		2	S75
Netherburn	51	2	S84
Newpark	59	2	T06
NORTH QUEENSFERRY		1	T18
Oakley	68	1	T08
Philipstoun	51	1	T07
Plains	51	1	S76
Plean for Cowrie	56	2	S88
POLMONT		1	S97
Ponfeigh	* 64	2	S83
Ratho	51	1	T17
ROSYTH Halt	83	1	T18
Rumbling Bridge	* 64	1	T09
Sandilands	* 64	2	T83
SHIELDMUIR	90	2	S75
SHOTTS	*	2	S86
SOUTH GYLE	85	1	T17
STIRLING		2	S89
Stobo	50	2	T13
Stonehouse	* 65	2	S74
Symington	* 65	2	S93
Thankerton	* 65	2	S93
Throsk	* 66	2	S89
Tillicoultry	* 64	1	S99
Tillietudlem	51	2	S84
UPHALL	56 86	1	T07
WEST CALDER	*	2	T06
Westcraigs	56	1	S96
WESTER HAILES	87	2	T16
WHIFFLET	92	2	S76
Whifflet High Level	§		22
Whifflet Low Level	§		22
Wilsontown	51	2	S95
WISHAW Central	65	2	S75
Wishaw South	58	2	S75

TUNNELS

No	Name/Location	Length in yards	Ry	Ref
T1	KIPPENCROSS	616	2	N70
2	FALKIRK	876	1	S87
3	ABRONHILL	176	2	S77
4	NORTH QUEENSFERRY	460	1	T18
5	INVERKEITHING	418	1	T18

BRIDGES + VIADUCTS

No	Name/Location	Ry	Ref
V1	FORTH BRIDGE	1	T18
2	Alloa Bridge	2	S89

JUNCTIONS

No	Name/Location	Ry	Ref
J1	Kincardine	1	S99
2	Lilliehills	1	T18
3	Bonnywater	2 3	S88
4	CARMUIRS WEST	1 2	S88
5	CARMUIRS NORTH	1 2	S88
6	CARMUIRS EAST	1	S88
7	Bainsford	1 2	S98
8	Fouldubs	2	S98
9	Winchburgh	1	T07
10	Blackstone	1	S97
11	Slamannan	1	S87
12	Broxburn Branch	1	T07
13	MIDCALDER	2	T06
14	Silvermuir Junctions	2	S94
15	Alton Heights	2	S83
16	Poneil	2	S83
17	STRAWFRANK	2	S94
18	Douglas Junctions	2	S84

GOODS

No	Name of Depot	Closed	Ry	Ref
1	Addiewell	55	1	S96
2	Castlehill	?	1	S85
3	Charlestown	64	1	T08
4	Crofthead	64	1	S96
5	East Calder	59	1	T06
6	Falkirk Lime Road	63	1	S87
7	Gartshore	64	1	S77
8	GRANGEMOUTH DOCKS	O	2	S98
9	Holygate	65	1	T07
10	Lochmill	65	1	S97
11	Morningside	65	1	S85
12	Morningside	51	2	S85
13	Port Edgar	66	1	T17
14	Redding	64	1	S97
15	Steel End	41	1	T09

ENGINE SHEDS

No	Name/Location	Closure if known	Ry	Ref
1	Bathgate	66	1	S96
2	Carstairs	66	2	S94
3	Loch Leven		1	O10
4	Kinniel	63?	1	S97
5	Kilsyth		1	S77
6	Stirling	66	2	S89
7	Grangemouth	65	2	S97
8	Stirling North	51	1	S89
9	Dunfermline	67	1	T18
10	Polmont	64	1	S97
11	Alloa Shore Road	51	1	S89

Closure dates are to steam. Some depots continued to serve as depots for diesels.

NOTES

To distinguish preserved railways and proposed opening of stations
◊ shows preserved station (as map)
* indicates proposed to re-open. If open occurred after atlas terminal date indicated by green opening date
§ Old Name } Change of name
§ New Name }
Identical letters indicate detail
blue date shows timing
A Not advertised to public and not therefore in Beeching
B On re-opening became one word- i.e. CURRIEHILL
ALL Passenger Stations in area are included in the gazetteer. Those not named are shown in brown and brown number indicates map on which they will be found.
Other features within the area enlarged are not normally shown on this map or included in the gazetteer. See Map 22
On this map and on map 22 a fair number of good stations are shown and are accordingly listed separately.
D Re-opened '93 as KIRKWOOD

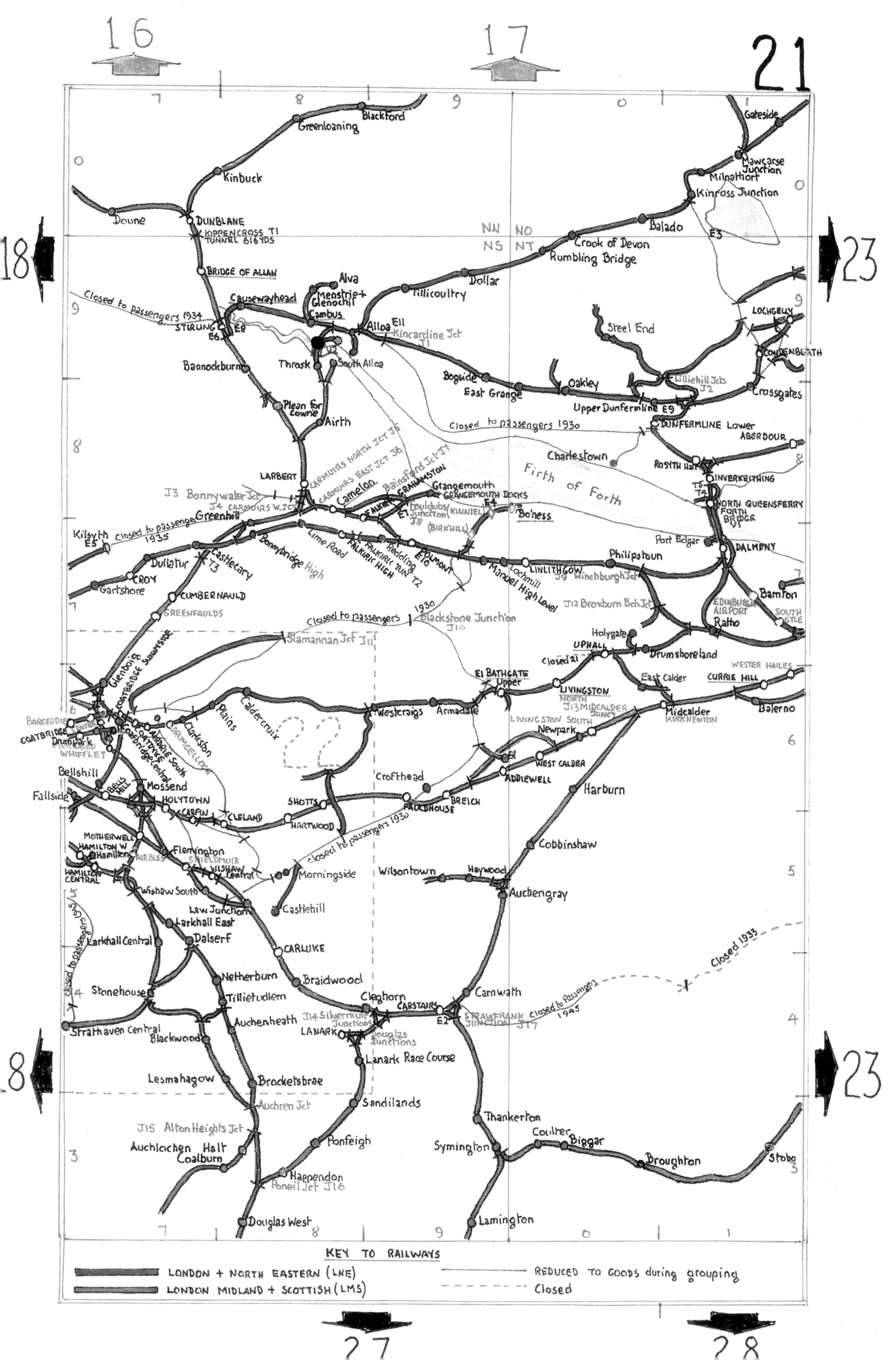
16
17
18
23
27
28
Blackford
Greenloaning
Kinbuck
Doune
DUNBLANE
KIPPENCROSS T1 TUNNEL 616YDS
BRIDGE OF ALLAN
Causewayhead
STIRLING
Closed to passengers 1934
Bannockburn
Plean for Cowie
Alva
Menstrie + Glenochil
Cambus
Alloa
Kincardine Jct
Thrask
South Alloa
Airth
Tillicoultry
Dollar
Crook of Devon
Rumbling Bridge
Balado
Kinross Junction
Milnathort
Mawcarse Junction
Gateside
Steel End
Lochgelly
Cowdenbeath
Lilliehill Jcts
Crossgates
Bogside
East Grange
Oakley
Upper Dunfermline
DUNFERMLINE Lower
Closed to passengers 1930
Charlestown
ABERDOUR
ROSYTH Halt
INVERKEITHING
NORTH QUEENSFERRY
FORTH BRIDGE
Firth of Forth
Port Edgar
DALMENY
LARBERT
J3 Bonnywater Jct
J4 CARMUIRS W. JCT
Camelon
GRAHAMSTON
Grangemouth
GRANGEMOUTH DOCKS
Bo'ness
Kilsyth
closed to passengers 1935
Greenhill
Dullatur
CROY
Gartshore
Castlecary
Bonnybridge High
Lime Road
FALKIRK HIGH
Redding
POLMONT
Manuel High Level
Linlithgow
Philipstoun
Winchburgh Jct
J12 Broxburn Bch Jct
Bamton
EDINBURGH AIRPORT
Ratho
SOUTH GYLE
CUMBERNAULD
GREENFAULDS
Closed to passengers 1930
Blackstone Junction
Slamannan Jct
Holygate
UPHALL
Drumshoreland
Closed 21
BATHGATE Upper
LIVINGSTON NORTH
East Calder
CURRIE HILL
WESTER HAILES
Balerno
Midcalder
KIRKNEWTON
Glenboig
COATBRIDGE SUNNYSIDE
Plains
Caldercruix
Westcraigs
Armadale
LIVINGSTON SOUTH
Newpark
WEST CALDER
ADDIEWELL
BAREDDIE
COATBRIDGE
Drumpark
KIRKWOOD
WHIFFLET
Clarkston
DRUMGELLOCH
Airdrie South
Coatbridge Central
Bellshill
Fallside
Mossend
HOLYTOWN
CARFIN
CLELAND
SHOTTS
HARTWOOD
Crofthead
FAULDHOUSE
BREICH
Harburn
Cobbinshaw
MOTHERWELL
HAMILTON W
Hamilton
HAMILTON CENTRAL
Flemington
SHIELDMUIR
WISHAW Central
closed to passengers 1930
Morningside
Wilsontown
Haywood
Auchengray
Wishaw South
Law Junction
Larkhall East
Larkhall Central
Dalserf
Casthill
CARLUKE
Braidwood
Netherburn
Tillietudlem
Stonehouse
Strathaven Central
Blackwood
Auchenheath
Cleghorn
CARSTAIRS
Carnwath
STRAWFRANK JUNCTION
closed to passengers 1945
Closed 1933
LANARK
Lanark Race Course
Douglas Junctions
Lesmahagow
Brocketsbrae
Auchren Jct
Sandilands
J15 Alton Heights Jct
Auchlochan Halt
Coalburn
Ponfeigh
Happendon
Poneil Jct J16
Douglas West
Thankerton
Symington
Coulter
Biggar
Broughton
Stobo
Lamington
KEY TO RAILWAYS
LONDON + NORTH EASTERN (LNE)
LONDON MIDLAND + SCOTTISH (LMS)
REDUCED TO GOODS during grouping
Closed

AIRDRIE + MOTHERWELL

RAILWAYS

No.	Company
1.	LONDON + NORTH EASTERN (LNE)
2	LONDON MIDLAND + SCOTTISH (LMS)
3	LNE + LMS JOINT

STATIONS

Name		Opened Closed	Ry Ref.
AIRBLES		89	275
AIRDRIE South		52	176
Auchenheath		51	284
BARGEDDIE		93	176
Bellshill		51	175
BELLSHILL			275
Blackwood	*	65	274
BLAIRHILL + Gartsherrie			176
Bothwell		55	175
Bothwell		50	275
Braidwood		62	284
Brocketsbrae		51	284
Burnbank		52	175
Caldercruix		56	186
CARFIN Halt		83	275
CARLUKE			284
Clarkston		5356	176
CLELAND			285
COATBRIDGE			76
Central		51	176
CENTRAL		53	276
SUNNYSIDE			176
COATDYKE			176
Dalserf		51	275
DRUMGELLOCH		89	176
Drumpark	B *	64	276
Fallside		53	275
Flemington	*	65	275
Gartcosh	†	62	276
Glenboig		56	276
HAMILTON			75
Hamilton		51	175
CENTRAL			275
WEST			275
HARTWOOD	*		285
HOLYTOWN	*		275
LANARK			284
Lanark Racecourse		64	294
Langloan	*	64	276
Larkhall Central	*	6465	275
Larkhall East		51	275
Law Junction	*	65	285
Lesmahagow	*	65	284
Mossend	†	62	276
MOTHERWELL			275
Netherburn		51	284
Plains		51	186
SHIELDMUIR		90	275
SHOTTS	*		285
Stonehouse	*	65	274
Strathaven Central	*	65	274
Tillietudlem		51	284
Uddingston East		5355	175
Westcraigs		51	296
WHIFFLET		92	76
Whifflet High Level Upper	*	5364	276
Whifflet Low Level Lower	†	5362	276
WISHAW Central		65	275
Wishaw South		58	275

GOODS

No	Name/Location	Opened Closed	Ry Ref
1	Airdrie	64	276
2	Airdrie North	64	176
3	Auchenheath	53	284
4	Blackwood	64	274
5	Castlehill	?	185
6	Ferniegair	64	275
7	Greengairs	?	177
8	Morningside	65	185
9	Morningside	51	285
10	MOSSEND	O	276
11	Motherwell	66	275
12	Newarthill	64	275
13	RAVENSCRAIG	O	275
14	Sheepford	?	176
15	Shotts	63	185
16	Strathaven North	64	274

ENGINE SHEDS

No	Name/Location			
1	MOTHERWELL			275
2	Hamilton	A	62	275
3	Morningside		?	185
4	Kipps Coatbridge		63	176

TUNNELS

No	Name/Location	Length yards	Ry Ref
1	BARNCLUITH	375	275

BRIDGES + VIADUCTS

No	Name/Location	Ry Ref
1	CAMPS VIADUCT	275

JUNCTIONS

No	Name/Location	Ry Ref
1	GARNQUEEN NORTH	276
2	Garnqueen South	1276
3	SUNNYSIDE	176
4	Gartsherrie North	276
5	GARTSHERRIE SOUTH	276
6	Rosehall	276
7	Dykehead Branch	176
8	Brownieside	176
9	Hartwoodhill	186
10	Merryton	275
11	Stonehouse	275
12	Belside	285
13	Langbyres	285
14	Langridge	285
15	Castlehill Branch	185
16	Blackhall	185
17	Iron Works	285
18	Danduff Branch	274
19	Southfield	284
20	Craigenhill	284
21	Douglas East	284
22	Douglas	284
23	Drumbowie	285

NOTES

This map which has many goods only lines has these distinguished in addition to down graded lines.

A The closing date shown is for closure to steam. Shed continued in use for diesels.

REF. All in NS

B Reopened '93 as KIRKWOOD

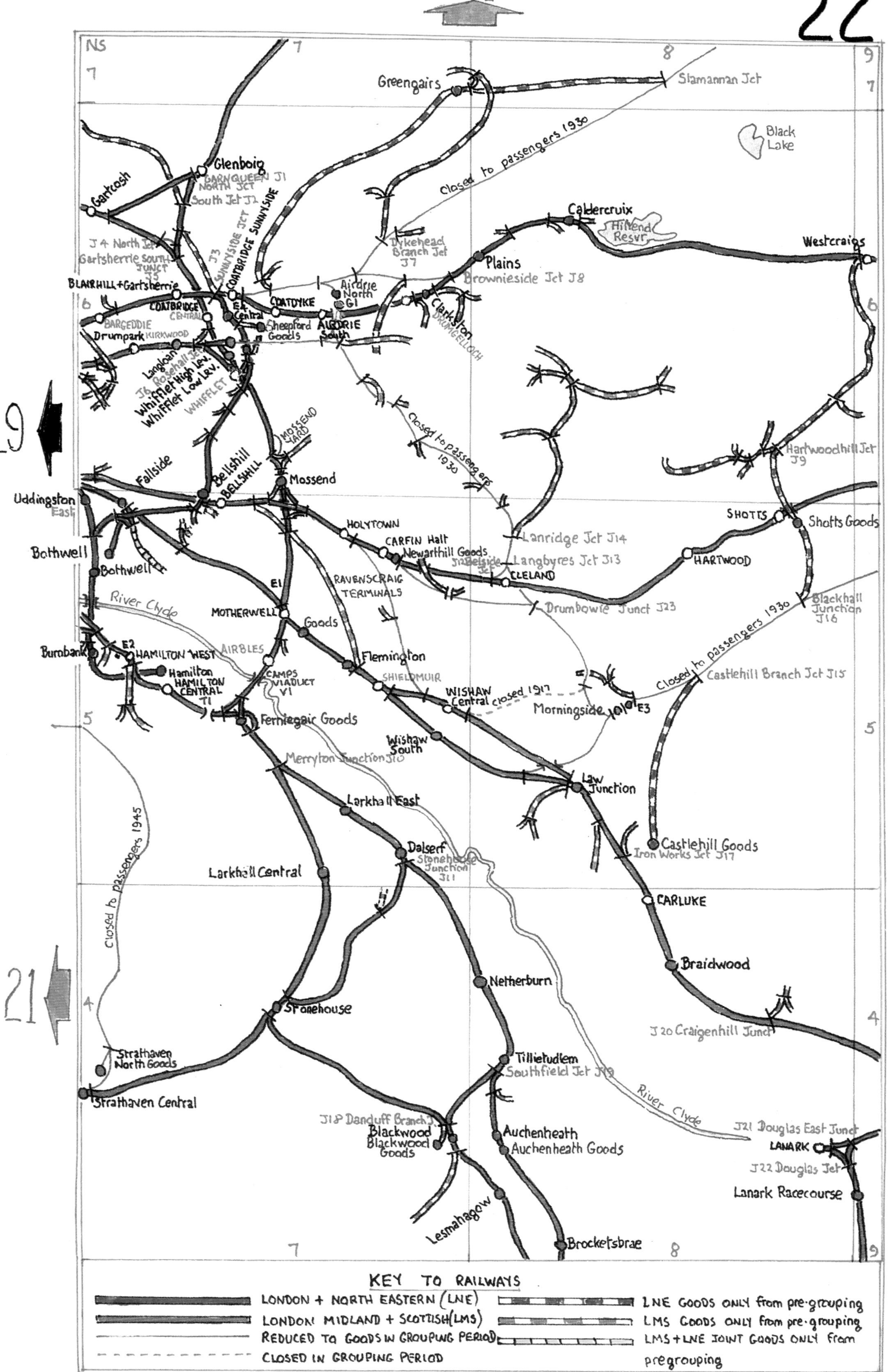
21
19
21
NS
7
8
9
Greengairs
Slamannan Jct
Black Lake
Glenboig
Garnqueen J1 North Jct
South Jct J2
Gartcosh
Closed to passengers 1930
Caldercruix
Hillend Resvr
Westcraigs
J4 North Jct
Gartsherrie South Junct J5
Sunnyside Jct J3
Coatbridge Sunnyside
Dykehead Branch Jct J7
Plains
Brownieside Jct J8
Blairhill+Gartsherrie
Coatbridge Central
E1 Central
Coatdyke
Airdrie North G1
Airdrie South
Clarkston
Drumgelloch
Bargeddie
Drumpark
Kirkwood
Sheepford Goods
Langloan
Rosehall Jct
J6
Whifflet High Lev.
Whifflet Low Lev.
Whifflet
Closed to passengers 1930
Mossend Yard
Hartwoodhill Jct J9
Fallside
Bellshill
Mossend
Uddingston East
Bothwell
Bothwell
Holytown
Carfin Halt
Newarthill Goods
Lanridge Jct J14
J12 Belside Jct
Langbyres Jct J13
Cleland
Shotts
Shotts Goods
Hartwood
Ravenscraig Terminals
E1
Motherwell
River Clyde
Drumbowie Junct J23
Blackhall Junction J16
Goods
Burnbank
E2
Hamilton West
Airbles
Flemington
Closed to passengers 1930
Castlehill Branch Jct J15
Hamilton
Hamilton Central T1
Camps Viaduct V1
Shieldmuir
Wishaw Central
closed 1917
Morningside
E3
Fernieqair Goods
Wishaw South
5
Merryton Junction J10
Law Junction
Larkhall East
Castlehill Goods
Iron Works Jct J17
Dalserf
Stonehouse Junction J11
Larkhall Central
Closed to passengers 1945
Carluke
Braidwood
Netherburn
4
Stonehouse
J20 Craigenhill Junct
Strathaven North Goods
Tillietudlem
Southfield Jct J19
Strathaven Central
River Clyde
J18 Danduff Branch J
Blackwood
Blackwood Goods
Auchenheath
Auchenheath Goods
J21 Douglas East Junct
Lanark
J22 Douglas Jct
Lanark Racecourse
Lesmahagow
Brocketsbrae
KEY TO RAILWAYS
LONDON + NORTH EASTERN (LNE)
LONDON MIDLAND + SCOTTISH (LMS)
REDUCED TO GOODS IN GROUPING PERIOD
CLOSED IN GROUPING PERIOD
LNE GOODS ONLY from pre-grouping
LMS GOODS ONLY from pre-grouping
LMS + LNE JOINT GOODS ONLY from pregrouping

21

21

EDINBURGH + GALASHIELS

RAILWAYS

No	Company
1	LONDON + NORTH EASTERN
2	LONDON MIDLAND + SCOTTISH
3	LOCHTY PRIVATE

STATIONS

Station	Opened Closed	Ry Ref
Abbeyhill	§	24
ABERDOUR		1 T28
Anstruther	* 65	1 050
Auchendinny	51	1 T26
Auchtermuchty	50	1 021
Balgreen Halt		24
Barnton	51	2 T17
Blackford Hill	† 62	1 T27
Bonnyrigg	† 62	1 T36
Bowland	53	1 T43
Broomieknowe	51	1 T36
Buckhaven	55	1 T39
BURNTISLAND		1 T28
Cameron Bridge	69	1 030
CARDENDEN		1 T29
Cardrona	62	1 T33
Clovenfords	62	1 T43
Corstorphine	68	1 T27
Craigleith	62	2 T27
Craiglockhart	† 62	1 T27
Crail	* 65	1 060
Dalry Road	§	24
Davidson's Mains	51	2 T27
Direlton	54	1 T58
DREM		1 T57
Duddingston + Craigmillar	† 62	1 T27
DUNBAR		1 T67
Dysart	69	1 T39
Earleston	48	1 T53
Easter Road Park Halt	§	24
East Fortune	* 64	1 T57
East Linton	* 64	1 T57
East Pilton	§	24
Eddleston	62	1 T24
EDINBURGH		T27
Abbeyhill	§	24
Dalry Road	§	24
HAYMARKET		1 T27
Merchiston	* 65	2 T27
Murrayfield	62	2 T27
Prince's Street		24
Waverley	A 66	1 T27
Elie	* 65	1 T40
Eskbank + Dalkeith	* 54 69	1 T36
Falkland Road	58	1 020
Fountainhall Junction	* 59 69	1 T44
Fushiebridge	K 59	1 T36
GLENROTHES with THORNTON	92	1 T29
Gordon	48	1 T64
Gorebridge	* 69	1 T36
Gorgie East	† 52 62	1 T27
Granton Road	62	2 T27
Greenlaw	48	1 T64
Haddington	49	1 T54
HAYMARKET		1 T27
Heriot	* 69	1 T45
House o' Hill	51	2 T27
Innerleithen	62	1 T33
Inveresk	* 64	1 T37
Joppa	* 64	1 T37
Junction Road	§	24
Kilconquhar	* 65	1 040
KINGHORN		1 T28
Kingskettle	* 67	1 030
KINGSKNOWE	* 67 71	2 T27
KIRKCALDY		1 T29
LADYBANK		1 031
Largo	* 65	1 040
Lasswade	51	1 T36
Leadburn	55	1 T25
LEITH		T27
Central	52	1 T27
Junction Road		24
North	B § 52 62	1 T27
Leven	69	1 030
Lindean	51	1 T43
LONGNIDDRY		1 T47
Lundin Links	* 65	1 040
Lyne	50	2 T23
MARKINCH		1 020
Maxton	† 64	1 T62
Melrose	* 69	1 T53
Merchiston	* 65	2 T27
Methill	55	1 030
Millerhill	55	1 T37
Morningside Road	† 62	1 T27
Murrayfield	62	2 T27
Musselburgh	* 64	1 T37
MUSSELBURGH	88	1 T37
Newhailes	50	1 T37
Newhaven	62	2 T27
Newington	† 62	1 T27
Newtongrange	* 69	1 T36
NORTH BERWICK		1 T58
North Leith	B § 52	1 T27
Peebles	50	2 T23
Peebles East	C 50 58 62	1 T24
Penicuik	51	1 T26
Piershill	* 64	1 T27
Pinkhill	68	1 T27
Pittenweem	* 63	2 050
Polton	51	1 T36
Pomathorn Halt	62	1 T25
Portobello	64	1 T37
PRESTONPANS		1 T37
Princes Street	§	24
Rosewell + Hawthorden	† 62	1 T26
Rosslyn Castle	51	1 T26
Rosslynlee	62	1 T26
Rosslynlee Hospital Halt	58	1 T26
Roxburgh	† 64	1 T62
Rutherford	E † 64	1 T63
St Boswells	*	1 T53
St Monace	* 65	1 050
Selkirk	51	1 T42
Sinclairtown	69	1 T29
SLATEFORD	*	2 T27
Stow	* 69	1 T44
Strathmiglow	50	1 020
Thornilee	50	1 T43
Thornton Junction	69	1 T39
Tynehead	* 69	2 T35
Walkerburn	62	1 T33
WALLYFORD	proposed	1 T37
WAVERLEY	D § 66	1 T27
Wemyss Castle	55	1 T39
West Wemyss	64	1 T39

GOODS

No	Name/Location	Closed	Ry Ref
G 1	Auchtertool	60	1 T29
2	Beltonford	64	1 T67
3	Falahill	60	1 T45
4	Gifford	59	1 T56
5	Glencorse	59	1 T26
6	Granton East	60	1 T27
7	Granton High	68	2 T27
8	Kennoway	64	1 030
9	Largoward	64	1 040
10	Lauder	58	1 T54
11	LEITH SOUTH		12 T27
12	Leslie	67	1 020
13	Lochty	F O 64 3	1 050
14	Mamerry	60	1 T47
15	MILLERHILL		O T37
16	Montrave	64	1 030
17	St Leonards	68	1 T27
18	THORNTON YARD		O T29

SUMMITS

No	Location	Height	Ry Ref
S 1	Falahill	900	1 T45

TUNNELS

No	Name/Location	Length	Ry Ref
T 1	Kinghorn	265	1 T28

ENGINE SHEDS H

No	Name	Ry	Ref
E 1	Thornton	1	T39
2	Dunbar	1	T67
3	Galashiels	1	T43
4	Hardengreen	1	T36
5	Longniddry	1	T47
6	Peebles	1	T24
7	Penicuik	1	T26
8	Methill	1	030

JUNCTIONS

No	Name	Ry	Ref
J 1	Redford	O	T29
2	Clunybridge	O	T29
3	Inverkiel	1	T28
4	Thornton North	1	T39
5	Thornton West	1	T29
6	Thornton East	1	T39
7	THORNTON SOUTH	1	T39
8	Pilton West	2	T27
9	MONKTONHALL	10	T37
10	Tranent	1	T47
11	Aberlady	1	T47
12	Ormiston	1	T46
13	Smeaton	1	T36
14	Hardengreen	1	T36
15	Kilnknowe	1	T43
16	Gala Foot	1	T53
17	Ravenswood	1	T53
18	Kelso	1	T53

NOTES:

O In railway column indicates British Rail (new line)

A EDINBURGH WAVERLEY lost its famous suffix in 1966

B North Leith became Leith North in 1952

C Peebles (ex LNE) had East added to title 1950 - 1958. This appears odd as the ex LMS station was closed to passengers in 1950, but both stations were open for goods until about '58

D See A above.

E Beeching shows as 'Halt'.

F Re-opened a Lochty Private Railway as far as new station Knightwood, but not shown on recent maps. So may be closed

G The line leaving the main line to the south, rejoined it at Ravelrig just to the west of CURRIE HILL on map 21. On this line just one station is shown at Balerno (see map 21). There were other passenger stations at Colinton and Juniper Green (on this map area) and a Currie (map 21). The official closure date was 1949 but last passenger train ran in 1943. The stations are therefore not shown.

H Thornton shed closed in '67. Methill which was a sub-shed to Thornton was closed earlier. The other sheds were sub-sheds to St Margaret's and it is difficult to distinguish closure as several locations could continue as signing on points after closure, so no closure dates for sheds are shown for this area.

K Additional station

Galashiels *69 1 T43

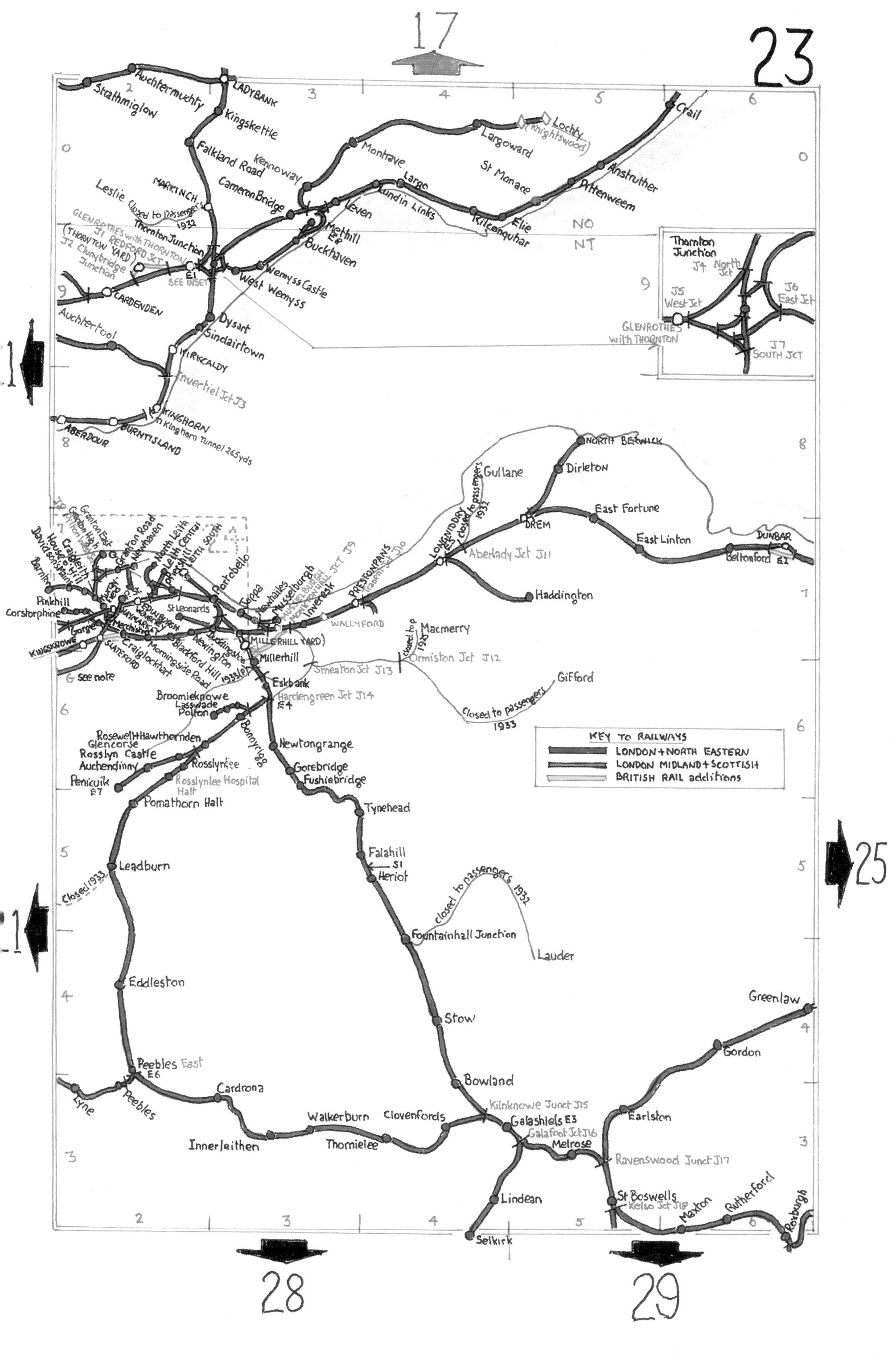
17
Auchtermuchty
Strathmiglow
LADYBANK
Kingskettle
Falkland Road
Kennoway
Montrave
Largoward
Lochty
(Knightswood)
Crail
Anstruther
Pittenweem
St Monance
Elie
Kilconquhar
Largo
Lundin Links
Leven
Methil
Buckhaven
Cameron Bridge
MARKINCH
Leslie Closed to passengers 1932
Thornton Junction
GLENROTHES with THORNTON
J1 REDFORD JCT
(THORNTON YARD)
J2 Clunybridge Junction
SEE INSET
CARDENDEN
Wemyss Castle
West Wemyss
Dysart
Sinclairtown
Auchtertool
KIRKCALDY
Invertiel Jct J3
KINGHORN
Kinghorn Tunnel 265yds
ABERDOUR
BURNTISLAND
NO
NT
Thornton Junction
J4 North Jct
J5 West Jct
J6 East Jct
J7 SOUTH JCT
GLENROTHES with THORNTON
NORTH BERWICK
Dirleton
Gullane
Closed to passengers 1932
LONGNIDDRY
DREM
East Fortune
East Linton
DUNBAR
Beltonford
Aberlady Jct J11
Haddington
PRESTONPANS
Musselburgh
Inveresk
WALLYFORD
Macmerry
Ormiston Jct J12
Smeaton Jct J13
Gifford
Closed to passengers 1933
Portobello
Joppa
Newhailes
Granton Road
Newhaven
North Leith
Leith Central
Piershill
Corstorphine
Pinkhill
Barnton
Davidson's Mains
House o' Hill
Craigleith
EDINBURGH WAVERLEY
St Leonards
Duddingston
Newington
Blackford Hill
Morningside Road
Craiglockhart
Merchiston
SLATEFORD
KINGSKNOWE
see note
MILLERHILL YARD
Millerhill
Eskbank
Hardengreen Jct J14
Broomieknowe
Lasswade
Polton
Bonnyrigg
Newtongrange
Gorebridge
Fushiebridge
Rosewell+Hawthornden
Glencorse
Rosslyn Castle
Auchendinny
Rosslynlee
Rosslynlee Hospital Halt
Penicuik
Pomathorn Halt
Tynehead
Falahill
Heriot
Leadburn
Closed 1933
Fountainhall Junction
Closed to passengers 1932
Lauder
KEY TO RAILWAYS
LONDON + NORTH EASTERN
LONDON MIDLAND + SCOTTISH
BRITISH RAIL additions
Eddleston
Stow
Peebles East
Lyne
Peebles
Cardrona
Innerleithen
Walkerburn
Thornielee
Clovenfords
Bowland
Kilnknowe Junct J15
Galashiels E3
Galafoot Jct J16
Melrose
Ravenswood Junct J17
Lindean
Selkirk
St Boswells
Kelso Jct J18
Maxton
Rutherford
Roxburgh
Earlston
Gordon
Greenlaw
25
28
29

EDINBURGH

RAILWAYS

No	Company
1	LONDON + NORTH EASTERN
2	LONDON MIDLAND + SCOTTISH
0	BRITISH RAIL additions

STATIONS

Station		Opened Closed	Ry Ref
Abbeyhill	*	63	1 2774
Balgreen Halt		68	1 2173
Blackford Hill	†	62	1 2671
Corstorphine		68	1 2073
Craigleith		62	2 2274
Craiglockhart	†	62	1 2371
Dalry Road		62	2 2473
Davidson's Mains		51	2 2075
Duddingston + Craigmillar	†	62	1 2872
Easter Road Park Halt		50 67	1 2775
East Pilton		62	2 2376
EDINBURGH			
Abbeyhill	*	63	1 27746
Dalry Road		62	2 2473
HAYMARKET			1 2473
Merchiston	*	65	2 2372
Murrayfield		62	2 2373
Prince's Street	*	65	2 2473
Waverley	A §	66	1 2574
Gorgie East		52 62	1 2372
Granton Road		62	2 2476
HAYMARKET			1 2473
House o' Hill		51	2 2275
Joppa	*	64	1 3173
Junction Road	B	57	1 2676
LEITH			
Central		52	1 2776
Junction Road	B	57	1 2676
North	C §	52 62	1 2777
Merchiston	*	65	2 2372
Morningside Road	†	62	1 2471
Murrayfield		62	2 2373
Newhaven		62	2 2577
Newington	†	62	1 2772
North Leith	C §	52	1 2777
Piershill	*	64	1 2874
Pinkhill		68	1 2173
Portobello		64	1 3073
Prince's Street	*	65	2 2473
SLATEFORD	*		2 2271
WAVERLEY	A §	66	1 2574

GOODS

No	Name/Location	Closed	Ry Ref
1	Bonnington	68	1 2676
2	Bonnington Rose Bank	65	1 2577
3	Craigleith	60	2 2275
4	Gorgie West	59	2 2272
5	Granton East	60	1 2477
6	Granton High	68	2 2377
7	Heriothill	67	1 2375
8	LEITH SOUTH		1 22876
9	LEITH SOUTH + DOCKS		1 22877
10	Leith Walk	?	1 2675
11	Lothian Road	64	2 2473
13	North Leith	?	2 2677
14	Portobello	85	1 3173
15	Rose Lane	68	1 2774
16	St Leonards	68	1 2673
17	Scotland Street	67	1 2575

ENGINE SHEDS

No	Name/Location	Closed	Ry Ref
E 1	St Margaret's	67	1 2874
2	Leith Central	?	1 2776
3	Dalry Road	65	2 2473
4	South Leith (Seafield)	62	2 2877

TUNNELS

No	Name	Length	Ry Ref
T 1	Haymarket	1040	1 2473
2	Mound	130	1 2574
3	Calton North	476	1 2674
	Calton South	397	1 2674
4	Heriothill		1 2575
5	St Leonards		1 2773
6	Craiglockhart	60	1 2373

JUNCTIONS

No	Name	Ry	Ref
J 1	Haymarket East	10	2473
2	Haymarket Central	1	2373
3	Haymarket West	1	2273
4	Breakwater	2	2377
5	Lochend	1	2874
6	Lochend South	1	2874
7	Easter Road	1	2775
8	Trinity	1	2577
9	Pilton East	2	2376
10	Pilton West	2	2276
11	Crewe	2	2376
12	Warriston	1	2575
13	Seafield	2	2876
14	South Leith	1	2976
15	Barnton	2	2274
16	Bailey Field	1	3074
17	Leith Docks Branch	1	3074
18	Saughton	1	2072
19	Barnton Branch	2	2373

NOTES:

REF All in NT

- § Old } Change of name
- § New }
- A Waverley dropped from title 66
- B Same station
- C North Leith became Leith North 52

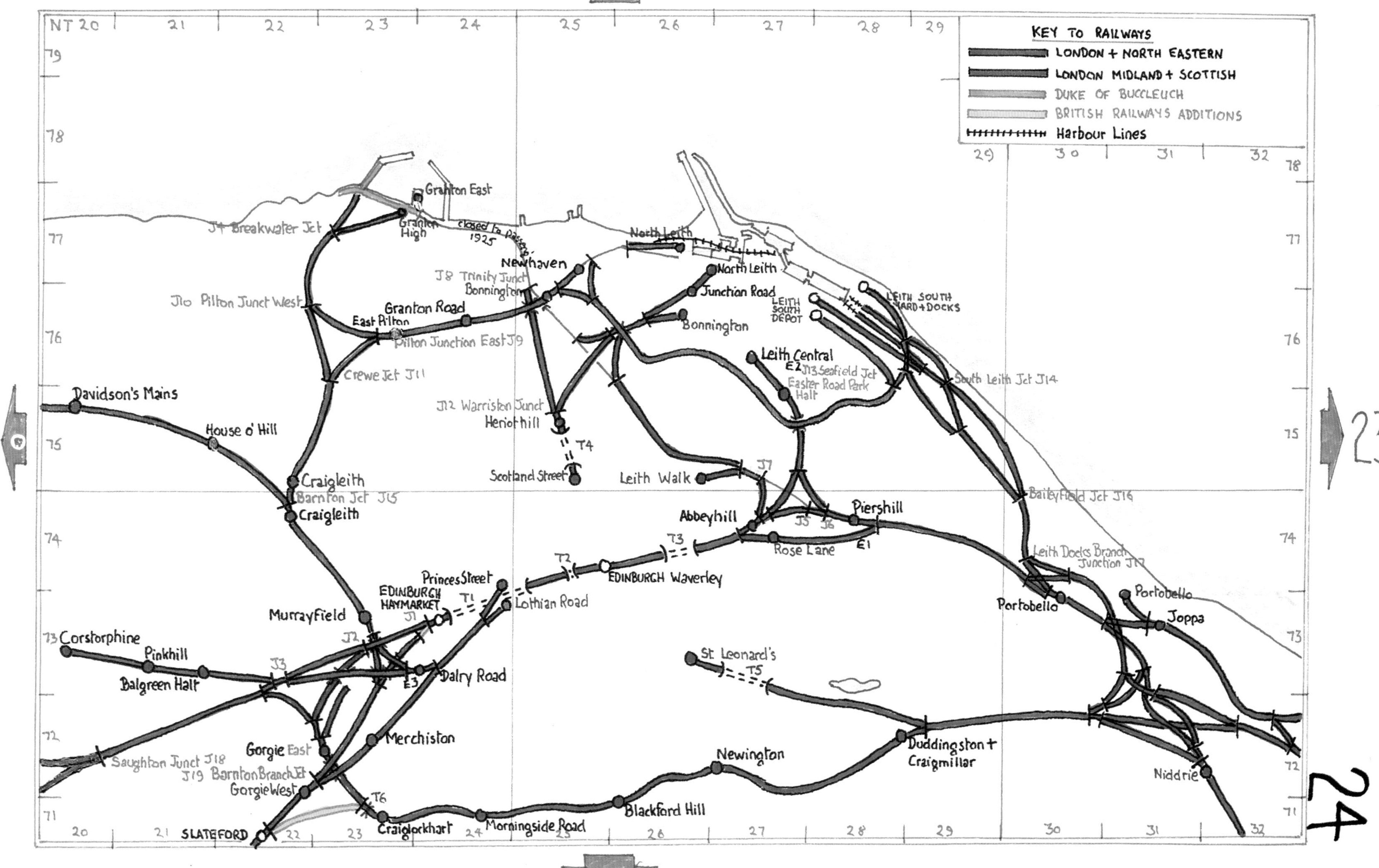

KEY TO RAILWAYS
LONDON + NORTH EASTERN
LONDON MIDLAND + SCOTTISH
DUKE OF BUCCLEUCH
BRITISH RAILWAYS ADDITIONS
Harbour Lines
Granton East
Granton High
closed to passengers 1925
J4 Breakwater Jct
North Leith
Newhaven
J8 Trinity Junct
Bonnington
North Leith
Junction Road
Bonnington
LEITH SOUTH DEPOT
LEITH SOUTH YARD + DOCKS
J10 Pilton Junct West
Granton Road
East Pilton
Pilton Junction East J9
Crewe Jct J11
Leith Central
E2
J13 Seafield Jct
Easter Road Park Halt
South Leith Jct J14
Davidson's Mains
House o' Hill
J12 Warriston Junct
Heriothill
T4
Scotland Street
Leith Walk
J7
Craigleith
Barnton Jct J15
Craigleith
Baileyfield Jct J16
Abbeyhill
Piershill
J5
J6
Rose Lane
E1
T3
T2
EDINBURGH Waverley
Leith Docks Branch Junction J17
Princes Street
Lothian Road
EDINBURGH HAYMARKET
T1
J1
Murrayfield
Portobello
Portobello
Joppa
Corstorphine
Pinkhill
Balgreen Halt
J2
J3
E3
Dalry Road
St Leonard's
T5
Merchiston
Gorgie East
Saughton Junct J18
J19 Barnton Branch Jct
Gorgie West
Newington
Duddingston + Craigmillar
Niddrie
T6
SLATEFORD
Craiglockhart
Morningside Road
Blackford Hill
23
23
23
23

BERWICK-UPON-TWEED + KELSO

RAILWAYS

No.	Company
1	LONDON + NORTH EASTERN
2	NORTH SUNDERLAND

STATIONS

Station	Opened / Closed	Ry. Ref.
Ayton	62	1NT96
Beal	68	1NU04
Belford	68	1NU13
BERWICK-UPON-TWEED	55	1NU05
Burnmouth	62	1NT96
Carham	55	1NT73
Chirnside	51	1NT85
Cockburnspath	51	1NT77
Coldstream	+ 64	1NT83
Duns	51	1NT75
Edrom	51	1NT85
Eyemouth	48 62	1NT96
Goswick	58	1NU04
Grantshouse	* 64	1NT87
Greenlaw	48	1NT64
Innerwick	51	1NT77
Kelso	+ 64	1NT73
Lucker	53	1NU13
Marchmont	48	1NT74
Norham	+ 64	1NT84
North Sunderland	51	2NU23
Reston	* 64	1NT86
Scremerston	51	1NU04
Seahouses	51	2NU23
Sprouston	55	1NT73
Sunilaws	55	1NT83
Tweedmouth	+ 64	1NU05
TWEEDMOUTH DOCKS		1NU05
Twizell	55	1NT84
Velvet Hall	55	1NT94

ENGINE SHEDS

No.	Name/Location	Closed	Ry Ref
1	Tweedsmouth	66	1NU05
2	Duns	?	1NT75

BRIDGES + VIADUCTS

No	Name/Location	Ry. Ref.
1	PEASE DEAN VIADUCT	1NT76
2	ROYAL BORDER BRIDGE	1NU05

NOTES:

NORTH SUNDERLAND was a private line and was worked by LNE, was not nationalised!! It was however always regarded as part of the national network and on this map is shown as such.

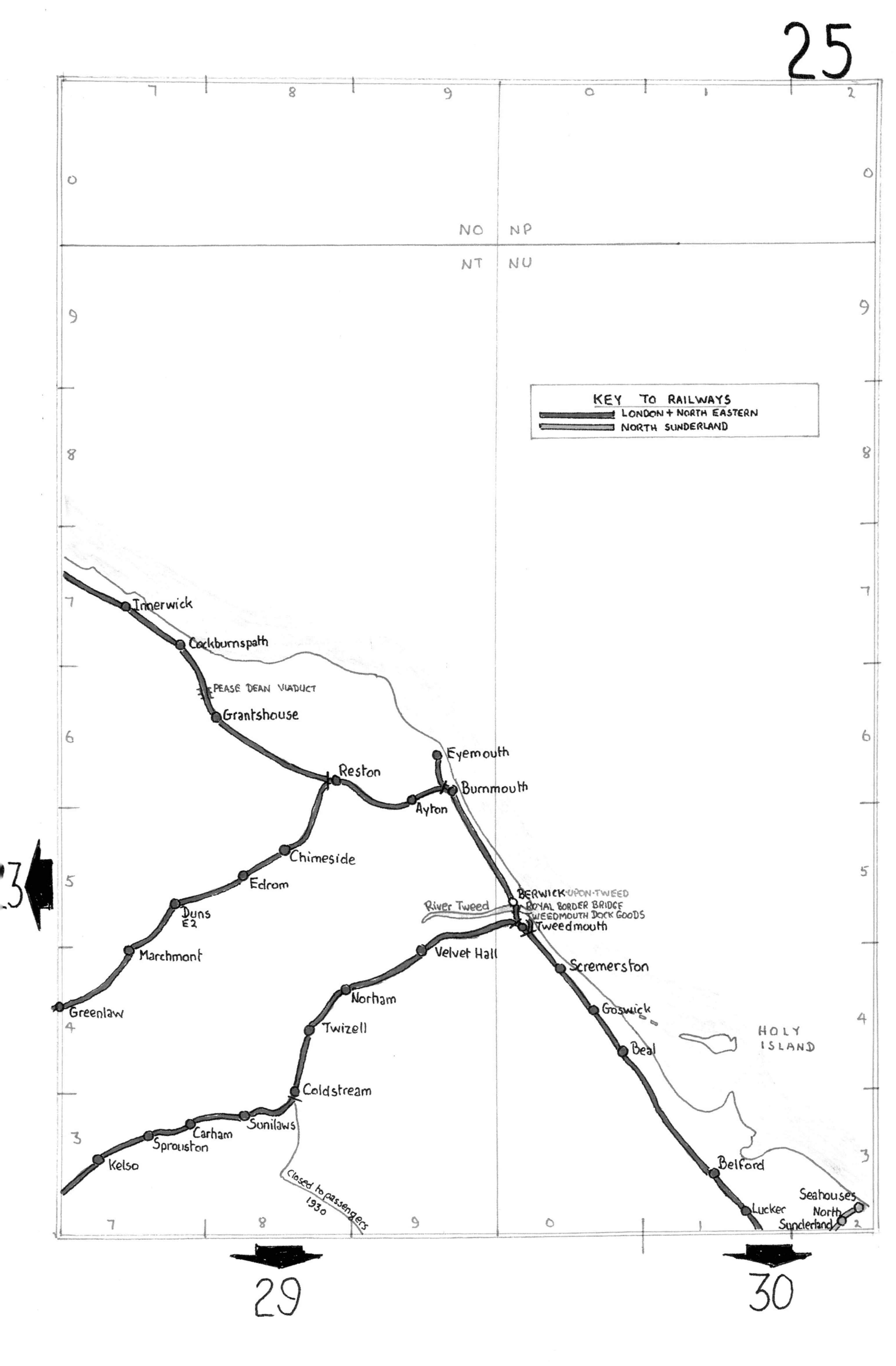
KEY TO RAILWAYS
LONDON + NORTH EASTERN
NORTH SUNDERLAND
NO
NP
NT
NU
Innerwick
Cockburnspath
PEASE DEAN VIADUCT
Grantshouse
Reston
Eyemouth
Burnmouth
Ayton
Chirnside
Edrom
Duns
E2
Marchmont
Greenlaw
BERWICK-UPON-TWEED
River Tweed
ROYAL BORDER BRIDGE
TWEEDMOUTH DOCK GOODS
Tweedmouth
Velvet Hall
Scremerston
Norham
Goswick
Twizell
Beal
HOLY ISLAND
Coldstream
Sunilaws
Carham
Sprouston
Kelso
Closed to passengers 1930
Belford
Lucker
Seahouses
North Sunderland
23
29
30

AYR GIRVAN + STRANRAER

RAILWAYS

No	Company
2	LONDON MIDLAND + SCOTTISH

STATIONS

Station		Opened Closed	Ref
Annbank		51	NS32
Auchincruive		51	NS32
AYR			NS32
BARRHILL	*		NX28
Cairntable Halt		50	NS41
Cassillis		54	NS31
Castle Kennedy	*	65	NX15
Colfin		50	NX05
Creetown	*	65	NX46
Dailly	*	65	NS20
Dalmellington	*	64	NS40
Dalrymple		54	NS31
Dipple		55	NS20
Drongan		51	NS41
Dunragit	*	65	NX15
FALKLAND YARD			NS32
Garlieston		64	NX44
GIRVAN	*		NX19
Girvan Harbour		? B	NX19
Glenluce	*	65	NX25
Glenwhilly	*	65	NX17
Greenan Castle		59	NS31
Heads of Ayr Holiday Camp		68	NS31
Holehouse Junction		50	NS31
Hollybush	*	64	NS31
Kilkerran	*	65	NS20
Killochan		51	NS20
Kirkcowan	*	65	NX36
Kirkinner		50	NX45
Mauchline	*	65	NS42
MAYBOLE	*		NS21
Millisle For Garlieston		50	NX44
New Luce	*	65	NX16
NEWTON-ON-AYR			NS32
Newton Stewart	*	65	NX46
Palnure		51	NX46
Patna	*	64	NS41
Pinmore	*	65	NX29
Pinwherry	*	65	NX18
Portpatrick		50	NW95
PRESTWICK			NS32
Rankinston		50	NS41
Scorbie		50	NX44
STRANRAER Harbour	*		NX06
Stranraer Town	*	53 66	NX05
Trabboch		51	NS42
Waterside	*	64	NS40
Whauphill		50	NX44
Whithorn		50	NX44
Wigtown		50	NX45

ENGINE SHEDS

No.	Name/Location	Closure to steam	Ref
1	Ayr	66 A	NS32
2	Newton Stewart	59	NX46
3	Stranraer	66	NX06

SUMMITS

No	Name/Location	Height feet	Ref
1	Chirmorie		NX27
2	Pinmore	394	NX29

VIADUCTS

Name/Location	Ref
Cree Viaduct	NX46

TUNNELS

No	Name/Location	Length yards	Ref
1	MOSSGIEL	680	NS42
2	PINMORE	440	NX29

JUNCTIONS

No	Name/Location	Ref
1	Monkton	NS32
2	Mossblown	NS32
3	Annbank	NS32
4	Falkland	NS32
5	Hawkhill	NS32
6	Alloway	NS32
7	Belston	NS41
8	Maidens Branch	NX19
9	Harbour Branch	NX19
10	Withorn Branch	NX46
11	Harbour Branch	NX05
12	Challoch	NX15

NOTES:

A Closure date is for steam. Remains open

B Closure date is unclear

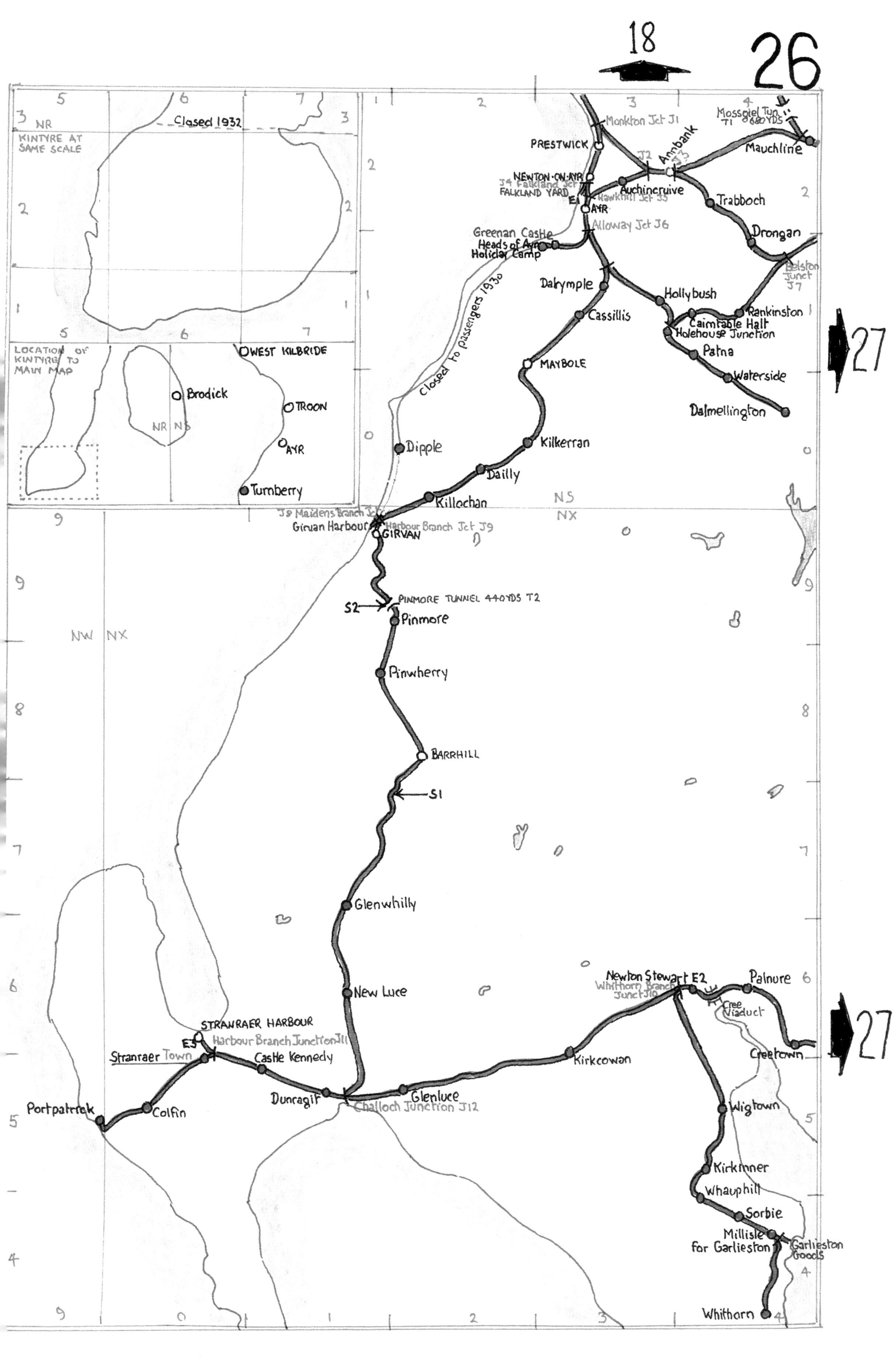
18
KINTYRE AT SAME SCALE
Closed 1932
LOCATION OF KINTYRE TO MAIN MAP
WEST KILBRIDE
Brodick
TROON
AYR
Turnberry
Monkton Jct J1
Mossgiel Tun T1 680 YDS
PRESTWICK
Annbank J3
J2
Mauchline
NEWTON-ON-AYR
J4 Falkland Jct
FALKLAND YARD
Auchincruive
Hawkhill Jct J5
E1
AYR
Trabboch
Alloway Jct J6
Greenan Castle
Heads of Ayr Holiday Camp
Drongan
Belston Junct J7
Dalrymple
Hollybush
Cassillis
Rankinston
Cairntable Halt
Holehouse Junction
Patna
Waterside
Dalmellington
MAYBOLE
Closed to passengers 1930
Dipple
Kilkerran
Dailly
Killochan
J8 Maidens Branch Jct
Girvan Harbour
Harbour Branch Jct J9
GIRVAN
NS
NX
PINMORE TUNNEL 440YDS T2
S2
Pinmore
Pinwherry
NW NX
BARRHILL
S1
Glenwhilly
New Luce
Newton Stewart E2
Whithorn Branch Junct J10
Palnure
Cree Viaduct
Creetown
STRANRAER HARBOUR
E3
Harbour Branch Junction J11
Stranraer Town
Castle Kennedy
Kirkcowan
Portpatrick
Colfin
Dunragit
Glenluce
Challoch Junction J12
Wigtown
Kirkinner
Whauphill
Sorbie
Millisle for Garlieston
Garlieston Goods
Whithorn
27
27

CUMNOCK + DUMFRIES

RAILWAYS

No.	Company
2	LONDON MIDLAND + SCOTTISH

STATIONS

Station	Opened Closed	Ref.
Abington	* 65	NS92
Amisfield	52	NX98
AUCHINLECK	* 65 84	NS52
Auldgirth	52	NX98
Bridge of Dee	49	NX75
Carronbridge	53	NS80
Castle Douglas	* 65	NX76
Catrine	64	NS52
Closeburn	61	NX99
Commondyke	50	NS52
Crawford	* 65	NS92
Cronberry	51	NS62
Crossmichael	* 65	NX76
Cumnock	51	NS51
Cumnock	* A § 55 65	NS52
Dalbeattie	* 65	NX86
DUMFRIES		NX97
Dumfries House	49	NS51
Elvanfoot	* 65	NS91
Gatehouse of Fleet	* 49 50 65	NX56
Glenbuck	52	NS72
Holywood	49	NX98
Inches	* 64	NS72
Killywan	59	NX86
KIRKCONNEL	*	NS71
Kirkcudbright	* 65	NX65
Kirkgunzeon	50	NX86
Locharbriggs	52	NX97
Lochskerrow	* 63	NX66
Lugar	50	NS52
Moniaive	49	NX79
Muirkirk	* 64	NS62
NEW CUMNOCK	* 65 91	NS61
New Galloway	* 65	NX66
Ochiltree	51	NS51
Old Cumnock	A § 55	NS52
Parton	* 65	NX66
Sanquhar	* 65 94	NS71
Skares	51	NS51
Southwick	* 65	NX86
Tarff	* 65	NX65
Thornhill	* 65	NX89

ENGINE SHEDS

No	Name/Location	Closed to steam	Ref
1	Kirkcudbright	55	NX65
2	Dumfries	66	NX86

BRIDGES + VIADUCTS

No	Name/Location	Ref
1	Water of Fleet Viaduct	NX56
2	Rea Viaduct	NX66

TUNNELS

No	Name/Location	Length Yards	Ref
1	DRUMLANRIG	1410	NS80

SUMMITS

No	Name/Location	Height feet	Ref
1	Dromore (Gatehouse of Fleet)		NX56
2	Polquhap	616	NS51

JUNCTIONS

No	Name/Location	Ref
1	Brackenhill	NS52
2	Logan	NS52
3	Pathead	NS51
4	Bank	NS51
5	Cairn Valley	NX97

NOTES:

§ Change of Name Old
§ Change of Name New
A Old Cumnock 'lost Old of title in 1955 following closure of Cumnock (1951)

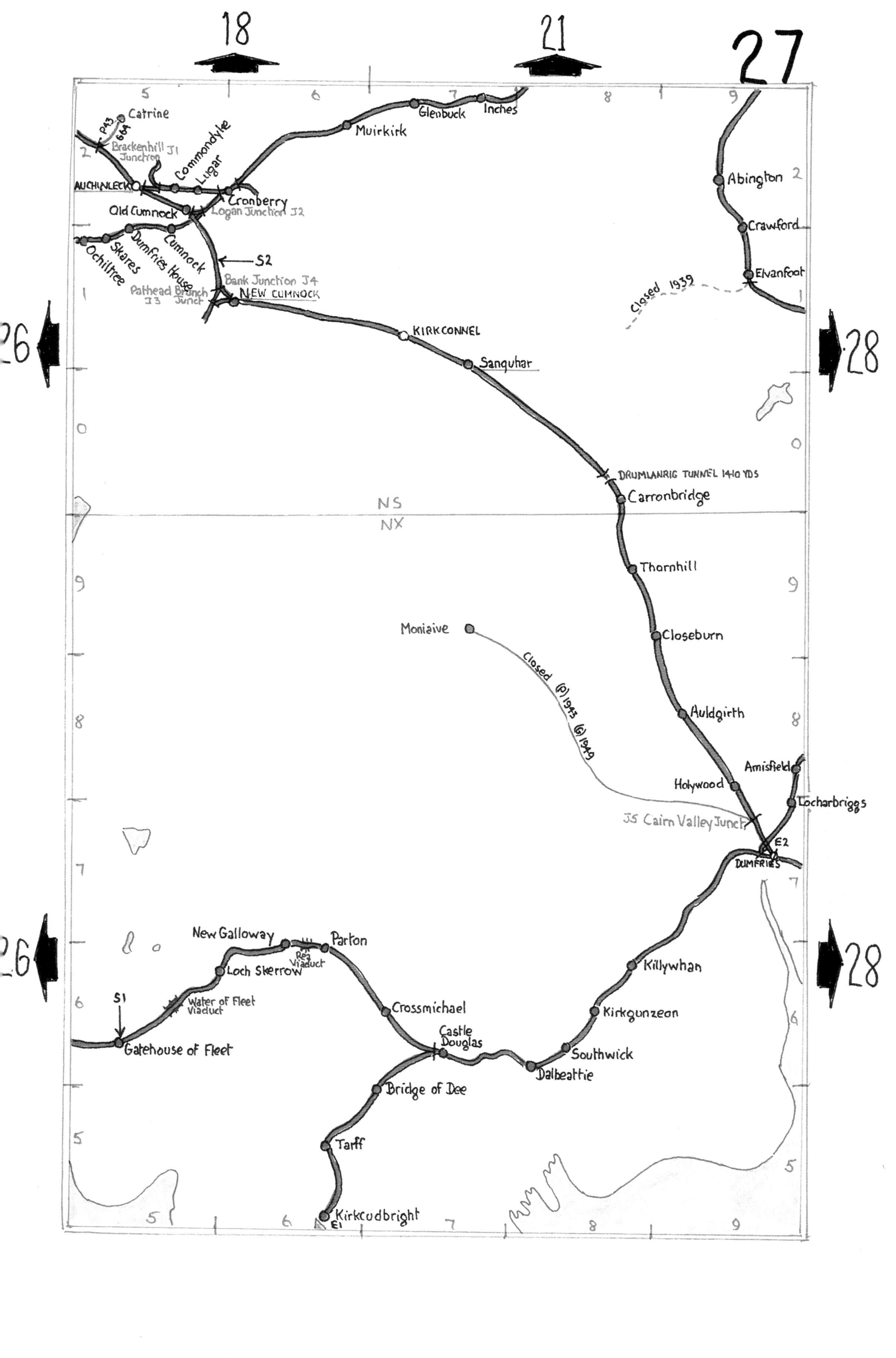
18
21
27
26
28
Catrine
Brackenhill Junction J1
AUCHINLECK
Commondyke
Lugar
Cronberry
Old Cumnock
Logan Junction J2
Muirkirk
Glenbuck
Inches
Ochiltree
Skares
Dumfries House
Cumnock
S2
Bank Junction J4
Pathead Branch Junct J3
NEW CUMNOCK
KIRKCONNEL
Sanquhar
Abington
Crawford
Elvanfoot
Closed 1939
DRUMLANRIG TUNNEL 1410 YDS
Carronbridge
NS
NX
Thornhill
Moniaive
Closeburn
Closed (P) 1943 (G) 1949
Auldgirth
Amisfield
Holywood
Locharbriggs
J5 Cairn Valley Junct
E2
DUMFRIES
New Galloway
Parton
Loch Skerrow
Water of Fleet Viaduct
S1
Gatehouse of Fleet
Crossmichael
Castle Douglas
Killywhan
Kirkgunzeon
Southwick
Dalbeattie
Bridge of Dee
Tarff
Kirkcudbright
E1

CARLISLE + MOFFAT

RAILWAYS

No	Company
1	LONDON + NORTH EASTERN (LNE)
2	LONDON MIDLAND + SCOTTISH (LMS)
3	DENTHOLME JOINT COMMITTEE (LNE + LMS)

STATIONS

Station		Opened Closed	Ry	Ref
Abbey Town	*	64	1	NY15
ANNAN			2	NY16
Beattock		72	2	NT00
Blackdyke Halt	*	64	1	NY15
Burgh-by-Sands	*	64	1	NY35
Canonbie	*	64	1	NY47
CARLISLE Citadel			2	NY45
Cummersdale		51	2	NY35
Cummertrees		55	2	NY16
Cumwhinton		56	2	NY45
DALSTON			2	NY35
Dinwoodie		60	2	NY19
Drumburgh		55	1	NY25
Eastriggs	*	65	2	NY26
Ecclefechan		60	2	NY17
Floriston		50	2	NY36
Gilnockie	*	64	1	NY47
Gretna		51	2	NY36
GRETNA GREEN	*	65 93	2	NY36
Kershope Foot	*	69	1	NY48
Kirkandrews	*	64	1	NY35
Kirkbride	*	64	1	NY25
Kirkpatrick		60	2	NY26
Kirtlebridge		60	2	NY27
Langholm	*	64	1	NY38
Lochmaben		52	2	NY08
LOCKERBIE			2	NY18
Longtown	*	69	1	NY36
Moffat		54	2	NT00
Nethercleugh		60	2	NY18
Newcastleton	*	69	1	NY48
Parkhouse Halt	*	69	1	NY35
Penton	*	69	1	NY47
Racks	*	65	2	NY07
Riddings Junction	*	64	1	NY47
Rockcliffe Halt		50 65	2	NY36
Ruthwell	*	65	2	NY06
Scotby		59	1	NY45
Scotch Dyke		49	1	NY37
Selkirk	*	51 3	1	23
Shieldhill		52	2	NY08
Silloth	*	64	1	NY15
Wamphrey		60	2	NY19
WETHERAL	*	67 81	1	NY45

GOODS

No	Name/Location		Closed	Ry	Ref
G1	Canal		63	1	4057
2	Crown Street (LNW)		66	2	4255
3	Crown Street (M+C) - Bog	A	70	2	4255
4	Dentholme		85	3	4156
5	LONDON ROAD			1	4355
6	Petteril		63	2	4355
7	Viaduct		65	2	4256
8	(Cattle) St Nicholas	B	70	2	4354
9	KINGMOOR	C		0	NY35

SUMMITS

No	Name	Height Feet	Ry	Ref
S1	Beattock	1015	2	NT01

ENGINE SHEDS

No	Name/Location		Closed	Ry	Ref
E1	Kingmoor (steam)		68	2	NY35
2	KINGMOOR		91	2	NY35
3	Beattock		67	2	NT00
4	Silloth	D	?	1	NY15
5	Langholm	D	?	1	NY38
6	Durran Hill		59	2	4454
7	Upperby		66	2	4354
8	Canal		63	1	3958

VIADUCTS

No	Name	Ry	Ref
V2	Esk Viaduct	2	NY36

JUNCTIONS

No	Name	Ry	Ref
J1	Canal Shed	1	3958
2	Canal	12	3958
3	Canal Goods	1	3958
4	Willowholme	2	4058
5	Port Carlisle Branch	2	4058
6	Caldew	2	4158
7	Caldew South	2	4157
8	Dentholme North	23	4157
9	Dentholme South	23	4156
10	Rome Street	12	4155
11	Forks	2	4155
12	Bog	2	4255
13	Currock	2	4055
14	London Road West	1	4355
15	London Road	12	4355
16	Petteril	12	4455
17	Durran Hill Goods	1	4455
18	Upperby Shed	2	4354
19	Upperby	2	4354
20	Upperby Bridge	2	4453

NOTES:

* This station is located in the area covered by the Carlisle Enlargement. It is shown on map 23.

A Bog official name from 1923 but still known also as Crown Street.

B Known as Carlisle Cattle but also often referred to as its old name: St Nicholas.

C New station opened by BR.

D Appears to have closed prior to BR days.

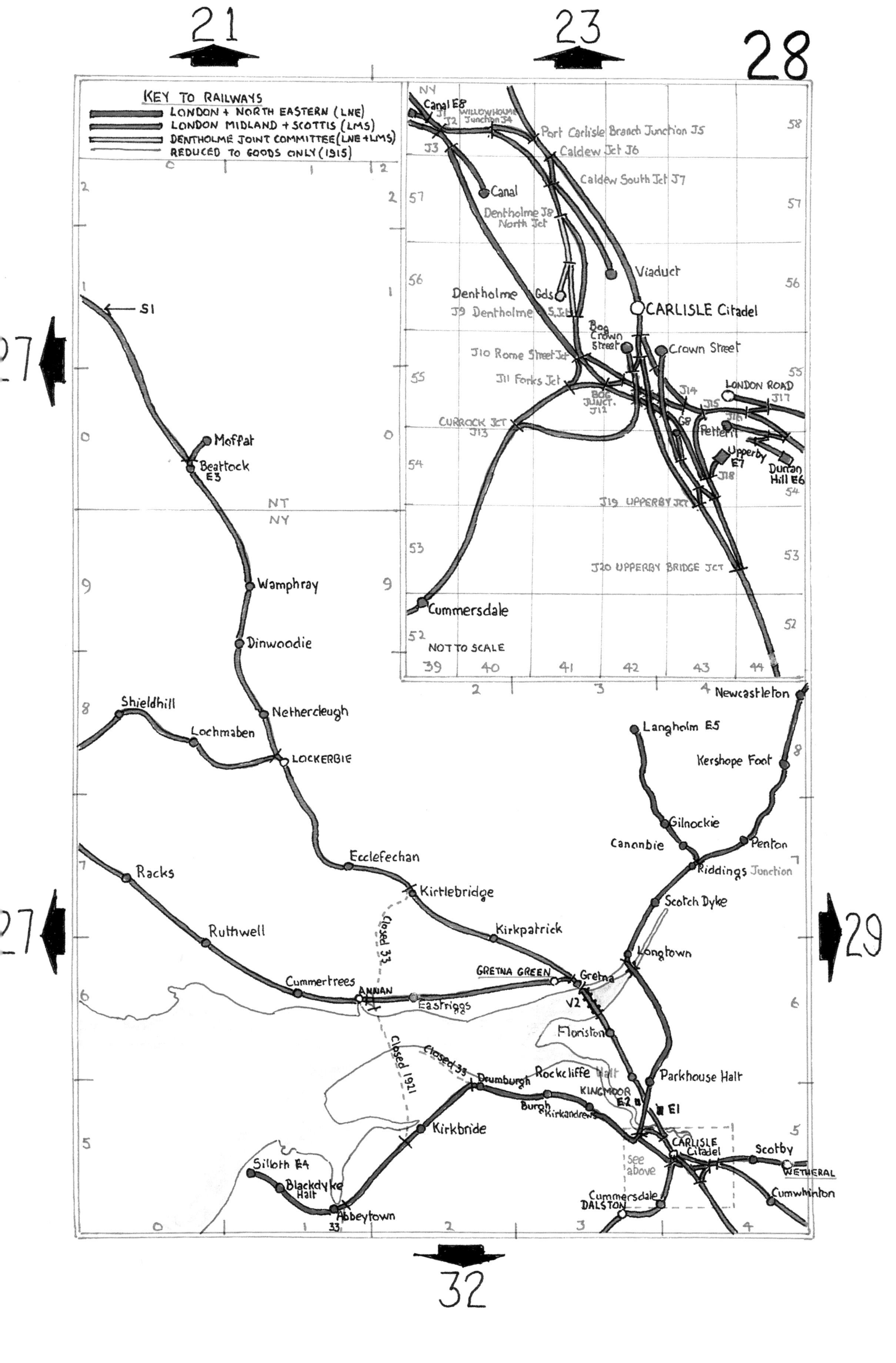

21
23
27
27
29
32
KEY TO RAILWAYS
LONDON + NORTH EASTERN (LNE)
LONDON MIDLAND + SCOTTIS (LMS)
DENTHOLME JOINT COMMITTEE (LNE + LMS)
REDUCED TO GOODS ONLY (1915)
S1
Moffat
Beattock
E3
NT
NY
Wamphray
Dinwoodie
Nethercleugh
Shieldhill
Lochmaben
LOCKERBIE
Ecclefechan
Kirtlebridge
Racks
Ruthwell
Kirkpatrick
Closed 33
Cummertrees
ANNAN
Eastriggs
GRETNA GREEN
Gretna
V2
Floriston
Closed 1921
Closed 33
Drumburgh
Rockcliffe Halt
Parkhouse Halt
KINGMOOR
E2
E1
Burgh
Kirkandrews
Kirkbride
Silloth E4
Blackdyke Halt
Abbeytown
33
See above
CARLISLE Citadel
Scotby
WETHERAL
Cumwhinton
Cummersdale
DALSTON
Newcastleton
Langholm E5
Kershope Foot
Gilnockie
Canonbie
Penton
Riddings Junction
Scotch Dyke
Longtown
Canal E8
J1
J2
WILLOWHOLME Junction J4
J3
Port Carlisle Branch Junction J5
Caldew Jct J6
Caldew South Jct J7
Canal
Dentholme J8 North Jct
Viaduct
Dentholme
Gds
J9 Dentholme S.Jct
CARLISLE Citadel
Bog Crown Street
Crown Street
J10 Rome Street Jct
J11 Forks Jct
BOG JUNCT. J12
J14
LONDON ROAD
J17
J15
J16
G8
Petteril
CURROCK JCT J13
Upperby E7
J18
Durran Hill E6
J19 UPPERBY JCT
J20 UPPERBY BRIDGE JCT
Cummersdale
NOT TO SCALE
39
40
41
42
43
44

JEDBURGH + HEXHAM

RAILWAYS

1 LONDON + NORTH EASTERN

STATIONS

Name	Opened / closed	Ref
Allendale	50	NY85
BARDON MILL	*	NY76
Barrasford	56	NY97
Belses	* 69	NT52
BRAMPTON Junction	71	NY55
Charlesfield Halt	61	NT52
Chollerton	56	NY97
Coanwood	† 76	NY65
CORBRIDGE	*	NY96
Deadwater	56	NY69
Falstone	56	NY78
Featherstone Park	† 76	NY66
Fourstones	* 67	NY86
Gilsland	* 67	NY66
Greenhead	* 67	NY66
HALTWHISTLE		NY66
Hassendean	* 69	NT51
Hawick	* 69	NT51
Hawick	69	NT51
HAYDON BRIDGE		NY86
Heads Nook	* 67	NY55
HEXHAM		NY96
How Mill	59	NY55
Humshaugh	56	NY96
Jedburgh	48	NT62
Jedfoot	48	NT62
Kielder Forest	48 56	NY69
Kirkbank	48	NT72
Knowesgate	52	NY98
Lambley	† 76	NY65
Lewiefield Halt	56	NY69
Long Row	59	NY56
Maxton	64	NT62
Naworth	52	NY56
Nisbet	48	NT62
Plashetts	56	NY68
Reedsmouth	56	NY88
Riccarton Junction	* 69	NY59
Roxburgh Junction	C † 64	NT72
Rutherford Halt	A † 64	NT63
St Boswells	* 69	NT53
Saughtree	48 56	NY59
Shankend	* 69	NT50
Slaggyford	B † 76	NY65
Steele Road	* 69	NY59
Stobs	* 69	NT50
Tarset	56	NY88
Thorneyburn	56	NY78
Wall	55	NY96
Wark	56	NY87
Woodburn	52	NY98

ENGINE SHEDS

No	Name/Location	Closure if known	Ref
E1	Hawick	66	NT51
2	St Boswells		NT53
3	Riccarton		NY59
4	Jedburgh		NT62
5	Hexham	59	NY96

TUNNELS

No	Name	Length	Ref
T1	Whitrope		NT50
2	Whitchester	202	NT70

SUMMITS

No	Name	Height in feet	Ref
S1	Gilsland		NY66
2	Whitrope		NT50

JUNCTIONS

No	Name	Ref
J1	Alston Branch	NY66
2	Allendale Branch	NY96
3	Reedsmouth Line	NY96

NOTES:

A Halt addition is as shown in Beeching.

B Proposed to re-open as extension of the SOUTH TYNEDALE RAILWAY 2'0" gauge

C Junction addition is as shown in Beeching.

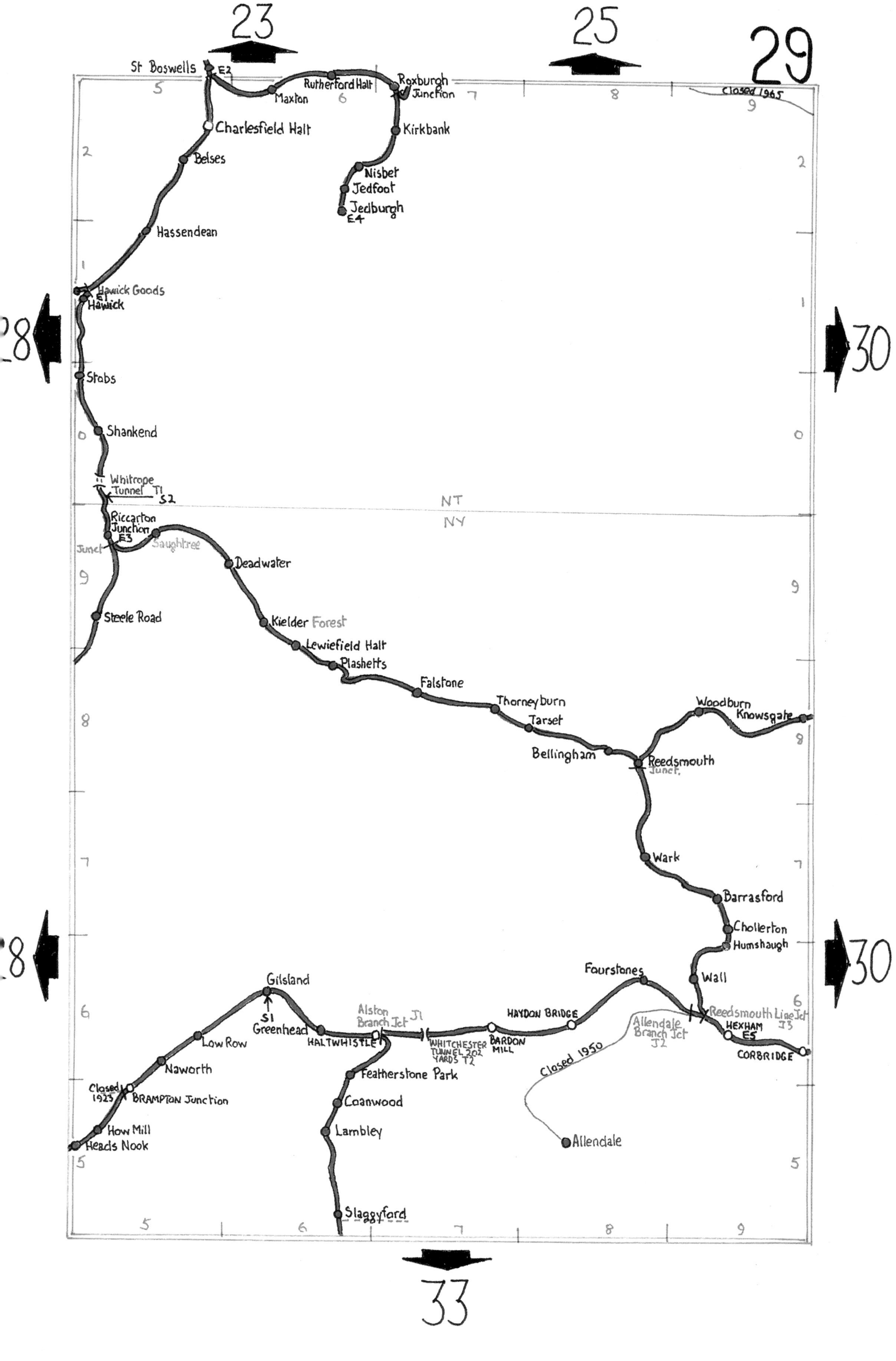

23
25
29
St Boswells
E2
Maxton
Rutherford Halt
Roxburgh Junction
Closed 1965
Charlesfield Halt
Belses
Kirkbank
Nisbet
Jedfoot
Jedburgh
E4
Hassendean
Hawick Goods
E1
Hawick
28
30
Stobs
Shankend
Whitrope Tunnel T1
S2
NT
NY
Riccarton Junction
E3
Junct
Saughtree
Deadwater
Steele Road
Kielder Forest
Lewiefield Halt
Plashetts
Falstone
Thorneyburn
Tarset
Bellingham
Woodburn
Knowsgate
Reedsmouth
Junct.
Wark
Barrasford
Chollerton
Humshaugh
Wall
Fourstones
Reedsmouth Line Jct J3
Allendale Branch Jct J2
HEXHAM
E5
CORBRIDGE
Gilsland
S1
Greenhead
HALTWHISTLE
Alston Branch Jct J1
WHITCHESTER TUNNEL 202 YARDS T2
BARDON MILL
HAYDON BRIDGE
Closed 1950
Allendale
Low Row
Naworth
Closed 1923
BRAMPTON Junction
How Mill
Heads Nook
Featherstone Park
Coanwood
Lambley
Slaggyford
33

MORPETH NEWCASTLE + SUNDERLAND

RAILWAYS

No	Railway
1	LONDON + NORTH EASTERN
2	NORTH SUNDERLAND
3	SOUTH SHIELDS MARSDEN + WHITBURN COLLIERY
X	TYNE + WEAR METRO

STATIONS

Station	Opened / Closed	Ry	Ref
ACKLINGTON		1	U20
ALNMOUTH		1	U21
Alnwick	68	1	U11
Amble	64	1	U20
Angerton	52	1	Z08
Annfield Plain	55	1	Z15
Annitsford	58	1	Z27
Ashington	* 64	1	Z28
Backworth	77	1	Z37
(BANKFOOT)	81	X	Z26
Beamish	A 53	1	Z25
Bebside	* 64	1	Z28
(BEDE)	84	X	Z36
Bedlington	* 64	1	Z28
Bensham	54	1	Z26
BENTON	78 80	X	Z26
Birtley	55	1	Z25
Blackhill	55	1	Z15
BLAYDON	*	1	Z16
Blyth	* 64	1	Z38
Boldon Colliery	B § 91	1	Z36
Brinkburn	52	1	Z99
BROCKLEY WHINS	B § 91	1	Z36
Byker	§		31
(BYKER)	§		31
(CALLERTON PARKWAY)	91	X	Z17
Carville	§		31
CHATHILL		1 2	U12
CHESTER-LE-STREET	*	1	Z25
Chevington	58	1	Z29
(CHICHESTER)	84	X	Z36
Choppington	50	1	Z28
Christon Bank	58	1	U22
Consett	55	1	Z15
CORBRIDGE		1	Z06
Cox Green	* 64	1	Z35
CRAMLINGTON		1	Z27
CULLERCOATS	79 80	X	Z37
DUNSTON	84	1	Z26
EAST BOLDON		1	Z36
Ebchester	53	1	Z15
Elswick	* 67	1	Z26
Ewesley	52	1	Z09
(FAWDON)	81	X	Z26
FELLING	79 81	X	Z26
Fencehouses	* 64	1	Z35
Fontburn Halt	52	1	Z09
Forest Hall	58	1	Z27
(FOUR LANE ENDS)	86	X	Z26
Gateshead East	65 81	1	Z26
(GATESHEAD)	81	X	Z26
GATESHEAD METRO CENTRE	87	1	Z26
(GATESHEAD STADIUM)	81	X	Z26
(HADRIAN ROAD)	82	X	Z36
Hartley	* 64	1	Z26
(HAYMARKET)	80	X	Z26
Heaton	80	1	Z26
HEBBURN	81 84	X	Z36
Heddon-on-the-Wall	58	1	Z16
Hepscott	50	1	Z28
HEWORTH	C 79 81	1 X	Z26
Holywell	65	1	Z37
HOWDON-on-Tyne	80 80 82	X	Z36
Hylton	* 64	1	Z35
(ILFORD ROAD)	80	X	Z26
JARROW	81 84	X	Z36
Jesmond	78	1	Z36
(JESMOND)	80	X	Z36
Killingworth	58	1	Z27
(KINGSTON PARK)	85	X	Z26
Knitsley	D 54	1	Z14
Lamesley	54	1	Z25
Leadgate	55	1	Z15
Lemington	58	1	Z16
Lintz Green	53	1	Z15
Little Mill	58	1	U21
LONG BENTON	78 80	X	Z26
Longhirst	51	1	Z28
Longhoughton	62	1	U21
Longwitton	52	1	Z09
Low Fell	52	1	Z26
Lucker	53	1	U13
MANORS East	E 69	1	Z26
(MANORS)	82	X	Z26
Marsden Cottage	53	3	Z36
Meldon	52	1	Z18
Middleton North	51	1	Z08
Millfield	55	1	Z35
MONKSEATON	79 80	X	Z37
Monkwearmouth	67	1	Z35
MORPETH		1	Z28
(MONUMENT)	§		31
Newbiggin-by-the-Sea	* 64	1	Z38
Newburn	58	1	Z16
NEWCASTLE		1 X	Z26
Central	F §	1	Z26
(HAYMARKET)	§		31
Heaton	80	1	Z26
MANORS East	E 69	1	Z26
(MANORS)	§		31
(MONUMENT)	§		31
(ST JAMES)	§		31
(NEWCASTLE AIRPORT)	G 91	X	Z17
Newham	50	1	U12
Newsham	* 64	1	Z37
North Blyth	?	1	Z38
North Seaton	* 64	1	Z28
NORTH SHIELDS	80 82		Z36
North Sunderland	51	2	U13
North Wylam	* 68	1	Z16
Pallion	* 64	1	Z35
(PALMERSVILLE)	86	X	Z27
PEGSWOOD	*	1	Z28
PELAW Junction	H 79 79 85	X	Z26
Pelton	53	1	Z25
Penshaw	* 64	1	Z35
PERCY MAIN	80 82	X	Z36
Plessey	58	1	Z27
Point Pleasant	§		31
PRUDHOE		1	Z06
(REGENT CENTRE)	81	X	Z26
RIDING MILL	*	1	Z06
Rothbury	52	1	U00
Rowlands Gill	54	1	Z15
Ryhope	53	1	Z45
Ryhope East	59 60	1	Z45
Ryton	54	1	Z16
St Anthony's	§		31
(ST JAMES)	§		31
St Peter's	§		31
Scotsgap	52	1	Z08
Scotswood	* 67	1	Z26
SEABURN		1	Z35
SEAHAM		1	Z44
Seahouses	51	2	U23
Seaton Delaval	* 64	1	Z37
Seghill	* 64	1	Z37
(SHIREMOOR)	80	X	Z37
Shotley Bridge	53	1	Z15
(SMITH'S PARK)	J 82	X	Z36
SOUTH GOSFORTH	78 80	X	Z26
SOUTH SHIELDS	81 84	X	Z36
South Shields Westoe Lane	53	3	Z36
Stannington	58	1	Z28
STOCKSFIELD		1	Z06
SUNDERLAND Central	69	1	Z35
Swalwell	53	1	Z16
TYNE DOCK	81 84	X	Z36
TYNEMOUTH	79 80	X	Z36
TYNE YARD		(1)	Z25
Usworth	* 63	1	Z35
Walker	§		31
WALKERGATE	80 82	X	Z26
WALLSEND	80 82	X	Z36
(WANSBECK ROAD)	81	X	Z26
Warkworth	58	1	U20
Washington	* 63	1	Z35
Westoe Lane	53	3	Z36
WEST JESMOND	78 80	X	Z26
WEST MONKSEATON	79 80	X	Z37
Whitburn Colliery	53	3	Z46
WHITLEY BAY	79 81	X	Z37
WIDDRINGTON		1	Z29
Willington Quay			31
WYLAM	* 66 67	1	Z16

ENGINE SHEDS

No	Name	Closed	Ry	Ref
E1	Alnmouth	66	1	U21
2	Blyth, South	67,68	1	Z38
3	Consett Junction	65	1	Z15
4	North Blyth	67,68	1	Z38
5	Rothbury	52	1	U00

BRIDGES + VIADUCTS

No	Name/Location	Ry	Ref
V1	Wansbeck Viaduct	1	Z28

JUNCTIONS

No	Name	Ry	Ref
J1	Marchey's House	1	Z28
2	West Sleekburn East	1	Z28
3	West Sleekburn South	1	Z28
4	Hownesgill	1	Z04
5	Reedsmouth Branch	1	Z28

NOTES:

Although on the map two minor railways are shown, these are both shown in this gazetteer as main line railways and were in fact in use as such. The North Sunderland was worked by the LNE and later by BR as part of the national system and is therefore shown in that way. It remained private until closure in 1951. The other railway, the South Shields Marsden + Whitburn Colliery had a rather different fate. It was national-ised but into the coal board!!

Although all stations within the map area are included in this gazetteer those not named on the map are shown in brown, and the map on which they appear is shown in brown in the reference column. Other features are only included if they are in the unenlarged area.

REF All in NU or NZ, therefore the initial N is omitted.

§ Old Name } Name change
§ New Name

A Museum here includes working tramway and colliery railway

B Name change

C The two opening dates are for ordinary railway (79) and Tyne + Wear Metro (81). The two systems are parallel but independent.

D Closure date is official but it was only used by excursions from 1939

E Was also a North station but this was replaced by Metro.

F Central dropped became just NEWCASTLE

G Not included under NEWCASTLE which is restricted to the central stations.

J Became Meadow Well but not until '94.

K two closing dates, first is for steam, other for diesels.

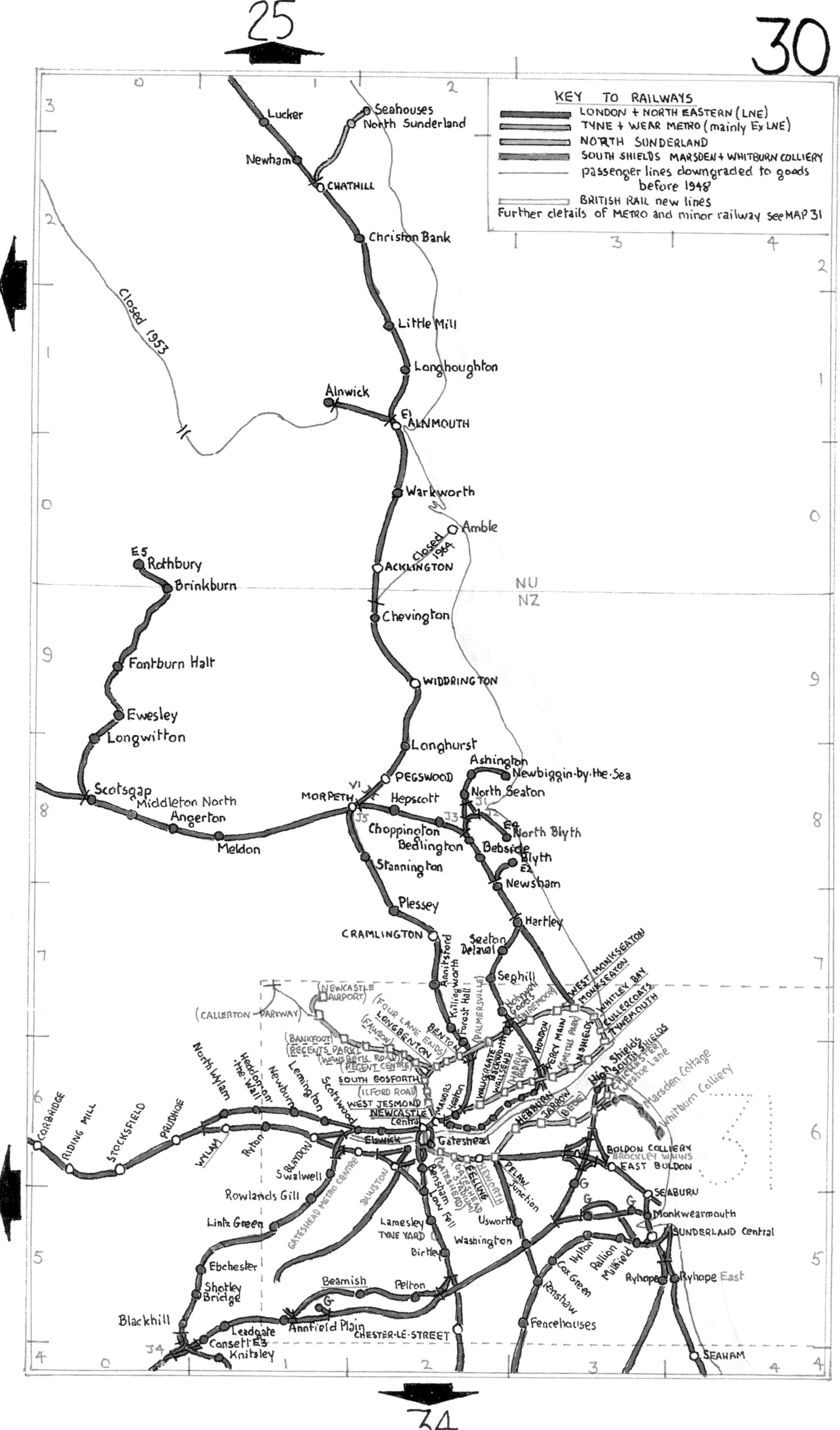

25
30
29
29
34
KEY TO RAILWAYS
LONDON + NORTH EASTERN (LNE)
TYNE + WEAR METRO (mainly Ex LNE)
NORTH SUNDERLAND
SOUTH SHIELDS MARSDEN + WHITBURN COLLIERY
passenger lines downgraded to goods before 1948
BRITISH RAIL new lines
Further details of METRO and minor railway see MAP 31
Lucker
Seahouses
North Sunderland
Newham
CHATHILL
Christon Bank
Closed 1953
Little Mill
Longhoughton
Alnwick
ALNMOUTH
Warkworth
Amble
Closed 1964
ACKLINGTON
Rothbury
Brinkburn
Chevington
NU
NZ
Fontburn Halt
WIDDRINGTON
Ewesley
Longwitton
Longhurst
Ashington
Newbiggin-by-the-Sea
PEGSWOOD
North Seaton
Scotsgap
Middleton North
MORPETH
Hepscott
Angerton
Meldon
Choppington
Bedlington
Bebside
North Blyth
Blyth
Stannington
Newsham
Plessey
Hartley
CRAMLINGTON
Seaton Delaval
Seghill
WEST MONKSEATON
MONKSEATON
WHITLEY BAY
CULLERCOATS
TYNEMOUTH
(NEWCASTLE AIRPORT)
(CALLERTON PARKWAY)
(BANKFOOT)
(REGENTS PARK)
(WANSBECK ROAD)
(REGENT CENTRE)
SOUTH GOSFORTH
(ILFORD ROAD)
WEST JESMOND
NEWCASTLE Central
LONGBENTON
(FOUR LANE ENDS)
BENTON
Forest Hall
Killingworth
Annitsford
(PALMERSVILLE)
Holywell
MANORS
Heaton
WALKERGATE
WALLSEND
HOWDON
PERCY MAIN
N SHIELDS
High Shields
SOUTH SHIELDS
Westoe Lane
Marsden Cottage
Whitburn Colliery
HEBBURN
JARROW
(BEDE)
CORBRIDGE
RIDING MILL
STOCKSFIELD
PRUDHOE
WYLAM
North Wylam
Heddon-on-the-Wall
Newburn
Lemington
Scotswood
Ryton
BLAYDON
Swalwell
Elswick
Gateshead
Rowlands Gill
GATESHEAD METRO CENTRE
DUNSTON
Lintz Green
Bensham
Low Fell
FELLING
HEWORTH
PELAW
Pelaw Junction
BOLDON COLLIERY
BROCKLEY WHINS
EAST BOLDON
SEABURN
Monkwearmouth
SUNDERLAND Central
Lamesley
TYNE YARD
Usworth
Washington
Birtley
Hylton
Pallion
Millfield
Cox Green
Ryhope
Ryhope East
Ebchester
Shotley Bridge
Beamish
Pelton
Penshaw
Fencehouses
Blackhill
Leadgate
Annfield Plain
CHESTER-LE-STREET
Consett
Knitsley
SEAHAM

NEWCASTLE SOUTH SHIELDS + SUNDERLAND

RAILWAYS

No	Company
1	LONDON + NORTH EASTERN
2	SOUTH SHIELDS, MARSDEN + WHITBURN COLLIERY G
3	TANFIELD
4	BOWES
X	TYNE + WEAR METRO

STATIONS

Name	Note	Opened closed	Ry Ref
(ANDREWS HOUSE)			325
Annfield Plain		55	115
Annitsford		58	127
Backworth		77	137
(BANKFOOT)		81	X26
Beamish	B	53	125
(BEDE)		84	X36
Bensham		54	126
BENTON		7880	X26
Birtley		55	125
(BLACKHAMS HILL)			425
BLAYDON	*		116
Boldon Colliery	A§	91	136
BROCKLEY WHINS	A§	91	136
Byker		54	126
(BYKER)		82	X26
(CALLERTON PARKWAY)		91	X17
Carville	*	73	136
(CAUSEY ARCH)			325
CHESTER·LE·STREET	*		125
(CHICHESTER)		84	X36
Cox Green	*	64	135
CULLERCOATS		7980	X37
DUNSTON		84	126
EAST BOLDON			136
(EAST TANFIELD)			315
Elswick	*	67	126
(FAWDON)		81	X26
FELLING		7981	X26
Fencehouses	*	64	135
Forest Hall		58	127
(FOUR LANE ENDS)		86	X26
Gateshead East		81	126
(GATESHEAD)		81	X26
GATESHEAD METRO CENTRE		87	126
(GATESHEAD STADIUM)		81	X26
(HADRIAN ROAD)		82	X36
(HAYMARKET)		80	X26
Heaton		80	126
HEBBURN		81 84	X36
HEWORTH	C	79 81	X26
High Shields		81	136
HOWDON-on-Tyne		80 8082	X36
Hylton		64	135
(ILFORD ROAD)		80	X26
JARROW		8184	X36
Jesmond		78	126
(JESMOND)		80	X26
Killingworth		58	127
(KINGSTON PARK)		85	X26
Lamesley		54	125
Lemington		58	116
Lintz Green		53	115
LONGBENTON		7880	X26
Low Fell		52	126
MANORS East	D	69	126
(MANORS)		82	X26
(MARLEY HILL)			325
Marsden Cottage		53	236
Millfield		55	135
MONKSEATON		7980	X37
Monkwearmouth		67	135
(MONUMENT)		81	X26
Newburn		58	116
NEWCASTLE			1X26
Central	E§		126
(HAYMARKET)		80	X26
Heaton		80	126
MANORS East	D		126
NEWCASTLE			26
(MANORS)		82	X26
(MONUMENT)		81	X26
(ST JAMES)		82	X26
(NEWCASTLE AIRPORT)		91	X17
NORTH SHIELDS		8082	X36
Pallion	*	64	135
(PALMERSVILLE)		86	X27
PELAW Junction	H	79 7985	X26
Penshaw	*	64	135
PERCY MAIN		8082	X36
Point Pleasant	*	73	136
(REGENT CENTRE)		81	X26
Rowlands Gill		54	115
Ryhope		53	145
Ryhope East		5960	145
Ryton		54	116
St Anthony's		60	126
(ST JAMES)		82	X26
St Peter's	*	73	126
Scotswood	*	67	126
SEABURN			135
(SHIREMOOR)		80	X37
(SMITH'S PARK)	F	82	X26
SOUTH GOSFORTH		7880	X26
SOUTH SHIELDS		8184	X36
South Shields Westoe Lane		53	236
(SPRINGWELL)			425
SUNDERLAND Central		69	135
(SUNNISIDE)			325
Swalwell		53	116
TYNE DOCK		8184	X36
TYNEMOUTH		7980	X36
Usworth	*	63	135
Walker	*	73	126
WALKERGATE		8082	X26
WALLSEND		8082	X36
(WANSBECK ROAD)		81	X26
Washington	*	63	135
Westoe Lane		53	236
WEST JESMOND		7880	X26
WEST MONKSEATON		7980	X37
Whitburn Colliery		53	246
WHITLEY BAY		7980	X37
Willington Quay	*	73	136

GOODS

No.	Name	Closure if date known	Ref
1	New Bridge Street	67	26
2	GATESHEAD		26
3	Quayside		26
4	Forth	83	26
5	Redheugh	65	26
6	Holywell	65	37
7	Blaydon		16
8	Derwenthaugh		26
9	Tynemouth	71	36
10	Albert Dock		36
11	South Shields	70	36
12	Tyne Dock	60	36
13	Boldon	67	36
14	North Dock (Monkw'm'th)	65	45
15	Hylton Lane	65	35
16	Southwick	65	35
17	South Dock Sunderland	65	45
18	West Stanley		15
19	TYNE YARD		25

WORKS

No	Name		Ref
W1	Gateshead	J	26

ENGINE SHEDS

No	Name/Location	Closed	Ref
E1	Gateshead	90	26
2	Bowes Bridge	62	25
3	HEATON	K	26
4	Blaydon	63	16
5	Borough Gardens	59	26
6	Percy Main	65	36
7	Sunderland	67	45
8	Tyne Dock	67	36
9	Annfield Plain	L 40	15
10	Pelton Level	48	25
11	GOSFORTH	X	26

BRIDGES + VIADUCTS

No	Name/Location	Ry Ref
1	KING EDWARD BRIDGE	1 26
2	QUEEN ELIZABETH II BRIDGE	X26
3	HIGH LEVEL BRIDGE	1 26
4	Scotswood Bridge	1 16

TUNNELS

No	Name	Length yards	Ry Ref
T1	BENSHAM	125	126
2	RED BARNS	98	126
3	NORTH SHIELDS		X36

JUNCTIONS

No	Name	Rys	Ref
J1	CASTLE	1	26
2	WEST	1	26
3	KING EDWARD BRIDGE NORTH	1	26
4	KING EDWARD BRIDGE EAST	1	26
5	KING EDWARD BRIDGE SOUTH	1	26
6	Dunston East	1	26
7	Greensfield	1	26
8	GREENSFIELD	1	26
9	HIGH LEVEL BRIDGE	1	26
10	HIGH STREET	1	26
11	PARK LANE	1	26
12	Redheugh Bankfoot	1	26
13	NORWOOD	1	26
14	GREEN LANE	1	36
15	Castletown	1	35
16	Diamond Hall	1	35
17	Wickham	1	26
18	Southwick	1	35
19	Ryhope Grange	1	45

NOTES:

§ New Name } Identical letters refer
§ Old Name } to other name or give other details

A Name change

B Museum + working colliery line + electric tramway

C Two opening dates: ordinary 79 and Metro 81 on parallel but independent lines

D There was also a North station (different platforms of basically the same station). This was replaced by Metro station.

E Central dropped by BR, station became simply NEWCASTLE.

F Became MEADOW WELL but not until 1994

G Railway Nationalised but became part of NCB not BR!!

H Junction dropped when converted to Metro station

J Closed in 1920's but re-opened during war years to deal with some major repairs

K Open at Map Terminal date i.e. 31-12-1993 but since closed.

30

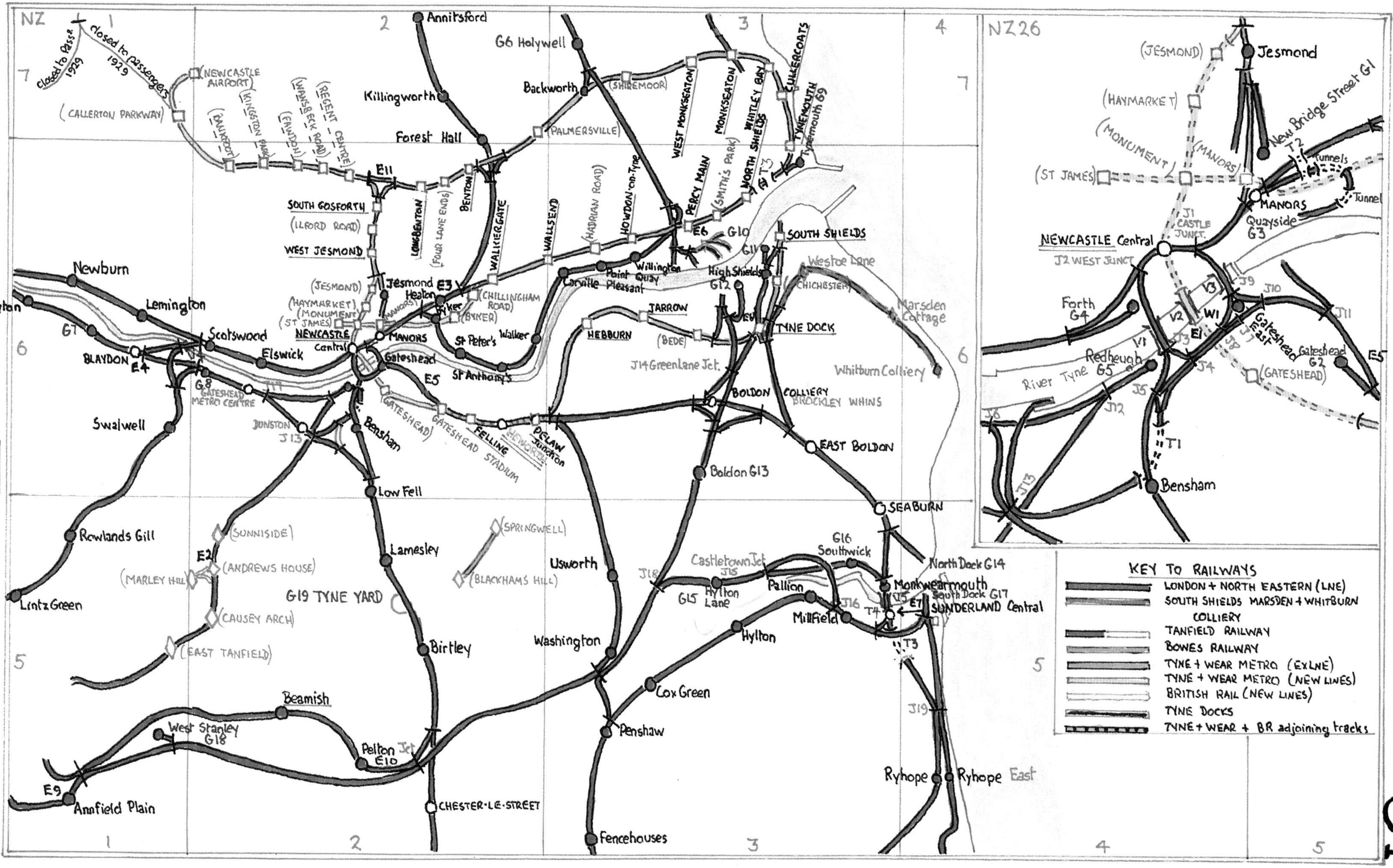

NZ 26

(JESMOND)
Jesmond
(HAYMARKET)
New Bridge Street G1
(MONUMENT)
(MANORS)
T2
Tunnels
(ST JAMES)
MANORS
Tunnel
J1 CASTLE JUNCT.
Quayside G3
NEWCASTLE Central
J2 WEST JUNCT
J9
J10
J11
V3
Forth G4
W1
V2
E1
Gateshead East
Gateshead G2
E5
V1
J3
J7
J8
Redheugh G5
J4
(GATESHEAD)
River Tyne
J5
J6
J12
T1
J13
Bensham

NZ
1
2
3
4
7
closed to Pass[a] 1929
closed to passengers 1929
(NEWCASTLE AIRPORT)
(CALLERTON PARKWAY)
(BANKFOOT)
(KINGSTON PARK)
(FAWDON)
(WANSBECK ROAD)
(REGENT CENTRE)
Annitsford
G6 Holywell
Killingworth
Backworth
(SHIREMOOR)
WEST MONKSEATON
MONKSEATON
WHITLEY BAY
CULLERCOATS
TYNEMOUTH
Tynemouth G9
(PALMERSVILLE)
Forest Hall
E11
BENTON
(FOUR LANE ENDS)
LONGBENTON
WALKERGATE
WALLSEND
(HADRIAN ROAD)
HOWDON-on-Tyne
PERCY MAIN
(SMITH'S PARK)
NORTH SHIELDS
T3
SOUTH GOSFORTH
(ILFORD ROAD)
WEST JESMOND
E6
G10
G11
SOUTH SHIELDS
Westoe Lane
(JESMOND)
Jesmond E3
Heaton
(CHILLINGHAM ROAD)
Willington
Point Quay
Carville
Pleasant
High Shields
G12
(CHICHESTER)
Newburn
Rytan
Lemington
(HAYMARKET)
(MONUMENT)
(ST JAMES)
MANORS
Byker
(BYKER)
Walker
TARROW
Marsden Cottage
G7
Scotswood
NEWCASTLE Central
St Peter's
HEBBURN
(BEDE)
TYNE DOCK
6
BLAYDON E4
Elswick
Gateshead
St Anthony's
J14 Greenlane Jct.
Whitburn Colliery
G8
GATESHEAD METRO CENTRE
E5
BOLDON
COLLIERY
BROCKLEY WHINS
Swalwell
DUNSTON
J13
Bensham
(GATESHEAD)
FELLING
GATESHEAD STADIUM
HEWORTH
PELAW Junction
EAST BOLDON
Boldon G13
Low Fell
SEABURN
Rowlands Gill
(SUNNISIDE)
(SPRINGWELL)
E2
(ANDREWS HOUSE)
Lamesley
G16 Southwick
(MARLEY HILL)
(BLACKHAMS HILL)
Usworth
Castletown Jct J15
North Dock G14
J18
Monkwearmouth
Lintz Green
G19 TYNE YARD
G15
Hylton Lane
Pallion
South Dock G17
(CAUSEY ARCH)
Millfield
J16
T4
E7
SUNDERLAND Central
J17
Birtley
Washington
Hylton
T3
(EAST TANFIELD)
5
Cox Green
J19
Beamish
West Stanley G18
Penshaw
Pelton Jct E10
Ryhope
Ryhope East
E9
Annfield Plain
CHESTER-LE-STREET
Fencehouses

KEY TO RAILWAYS
LONDON + NORTH EASTERN (LNE)
SOUTH SHIELDS MARSDEN + WHITBURN COLLIERY
TANFIELD RAILWAY
BOWES RAILWAY
TYNE + WEAR METRO (EXLNE)
TYNE + WEAR METRO (NEW LINES)
BRITISH RAIL (NEW LINES)
TYNE DOCKS
TYNE + WEAR + BR adjoining tracks

30
30

THE LAKE COUNTIES

RAILWAYS

No	Company
1	LONDON + NORTH EASTERN (LNE)
2	LONDON MIDLAND + SCOTTISH (LMS)
3	RAVENGLASS + ESKDALE (gauge 1'3")
4	LAKESIDE + HAVERTHWAITE (ex LMS line)

STATIONS

Station	Opened / Closed	Ry	Ref
ARMATHWAITE	* 70 86	2	NY54
ARNSIDE		2	SD47
ASKAM	*	2	SD17
ASPATRIA		2	NY14
BARROW Central IN FURNESS	59	2	SD26
Bassenthwaite Lake	* 66	2	NY12
BECKFOOT		3	SD19
Blencow	* 52 56 72	2	NY42
Bolton-le-Sands	* 69	2	SD46
BOOTLE	*	2	SD08
Braithwaite	* 66	2	NY22
Bransty, WHITEHAVEN	68	2	NX91
BRAYSTONES	*	2	NY00
Brayton	50	2	NY14
Brigham	* 66	2	NY03
Broughton-in-Furness	58	2	SD28
Bullgill	60	2	NY03
BURNESIDE		2	SD59
Calthwaite	52	2	NY43
Camerton	A 66	2	NY03
CARK + CARTMEL		2	SD37
CARNFORTH	B	2	SD46
Cockermouth	* 66	2	NY13
Coniston	58	2	SD29
CORKICKLE	*	2	NX91
Cotehill	52	2	NY44
Curthwaite	50	2	NY34
DALEGARTH	§ C 79	3	NY10
DALTON		2	SD27
Dearham Bridge	50	2	NY03
DRIGG	*	2	SD09
Egremont	G * 69	2	NY01
Embleton	58	2	NY13
(ESKDALE DALEGARTH)	§ C 79	3	NY10
ESKDALE GREEN	§ D 79	3	SD19
Eskmeals	59	2	SD09
(FISHERGROUND)	91	3	SD19
FLIMBY		2	NY03
FOXFIELD	*	2	SD28
Furness Abbey	50	2	SD27
GRANGE-OVER-SANDS		2	SD47
Greenodd	E 55	2	SD38
GREEN ROAD	*	2	SD18
HARRINGTON		2	NX92
Haverthwaite	E 55 73	24	SD38
Hest Bank	* 69	2	SD46
Heversham	E 53	2	SD48
IRTON ROAD		3	SD19
KENTS BANK		2	SD37
Keswick	* 72	2	NY22
KIRKBY-IN-FURNESS	*	2	SD28
(LAKESIDE)	F § 73	24	SD38
Leegate	50	2	NY24
Lindal	51	2	SD27
MARYPORT		2	NY03
MILLOM	*	2	SD18
Moresby Junction Halt	G 52	2	NX91
Monk Moors Halt	58	2	SD09
(MUNCASTER MILL)	67	3	SD19
NETHERTOWN	*	2	NX90
Newby Bridge	E 49 73		SD38
PARTON		2	NX92
PENRITH		2	NY52
Penruddock	* 72	2	NY42
Plumpton	48	2	NY53
RAVENGLASS for Eskdale	* 74	2	SD09
RAVENGLASS		3	SD09
ROOSE		2	SD26
ST BEES	*	2	NX91
Sandside	E 53	2	SD47
St Thomas Cross Platform	G 52	2	NY01
SEASCALE	*	2	NY00
SELLAFIELD	*	2	NY00
SILECROFT	*	2	SD18
SILVERDALE		2	SD47
Southwaite	52	2	NY44
STAVELEY		2	SD49
(THE GREEN)	§ D 79	3	SD19
Threlkeld	* 72	2	NY32
Torver	58	2	SD29
Troutbeck	* 72	2	NY42
ULVERSTON		2	SD27
WHITEHAVEN Bransty	68	2	NX91
CORKICKLE	*	2	NX91
WIGTON		2	NY24
WINDERMERE	H	2	SD49
Windermere Lakeside	* F § 65 73	24	SD38
Woodend	G 55	2	NY01
Woodland	58	2	SD28
WORKINGTON		2	NX92
Workington Bridge	51	2	NY02

GOODS

No	Location	Closed	Ref
1	Ramsden Dock	?	SD26
2	Barrow	71	SD16
3	Hodbarrow	?	SD17
4	Seaton	64	NY03
5	Mealsgate	52	NY24
6	Preston Street	69	NX91

ENGINE SHEDS

No	Location	Closed	Ref
1	Carnforth	68	SD46
2	Coniston	58	SD29
3	Barrow	77	SD26
4	Penrith	62	NY52
5	Moor Row	54	NX91
6	Workington	68	NX92

TUNNELS

No	Name / Location	Length Yards	Ref
1	FURNESS ABBEY	76	SD26
2	LINDAL	439	SD27
3	Haverthwaite West	200	SD78
4	WHITEHAVEN	1333	NX91
5	DALTON	225	

BRIDGES + VIADUCTS

No	Name	Ref
1	KENT VIADUCT	SD47
2	LEVEN VIADUCT	SD37
3	DUDDON FOXFIELD VIADUCT	SD27

JUNCTIONS

No	Name	Ref
1	Buccleuch	SD26
2	St Lukes	SD26
3	Salthouse	SD26
3A	Thwaite Flat	SD27
4	Oak Lea	SD27
5	Goldmire North	SD27
6	Goldmire South	SD27
7	Millwood	SD27
12	Eamont Bridge	NY42
14	Redhills	NY52

NOTES:

A Regular services finished in '52

B The main line platforms unused prior to '70

C Name change ESKDALE to front.

D Name change

E Last train pre nationalisation.

F Name change when station re-opened by Lakeside + Haverthwaite.

G All these stations were closed to regular traffic before nationalisation but some passenger trains ran and Egremont had also the distinction of being in the Beeching report.

§ Old name } Change of name. Letter
§ New name } shows other name.

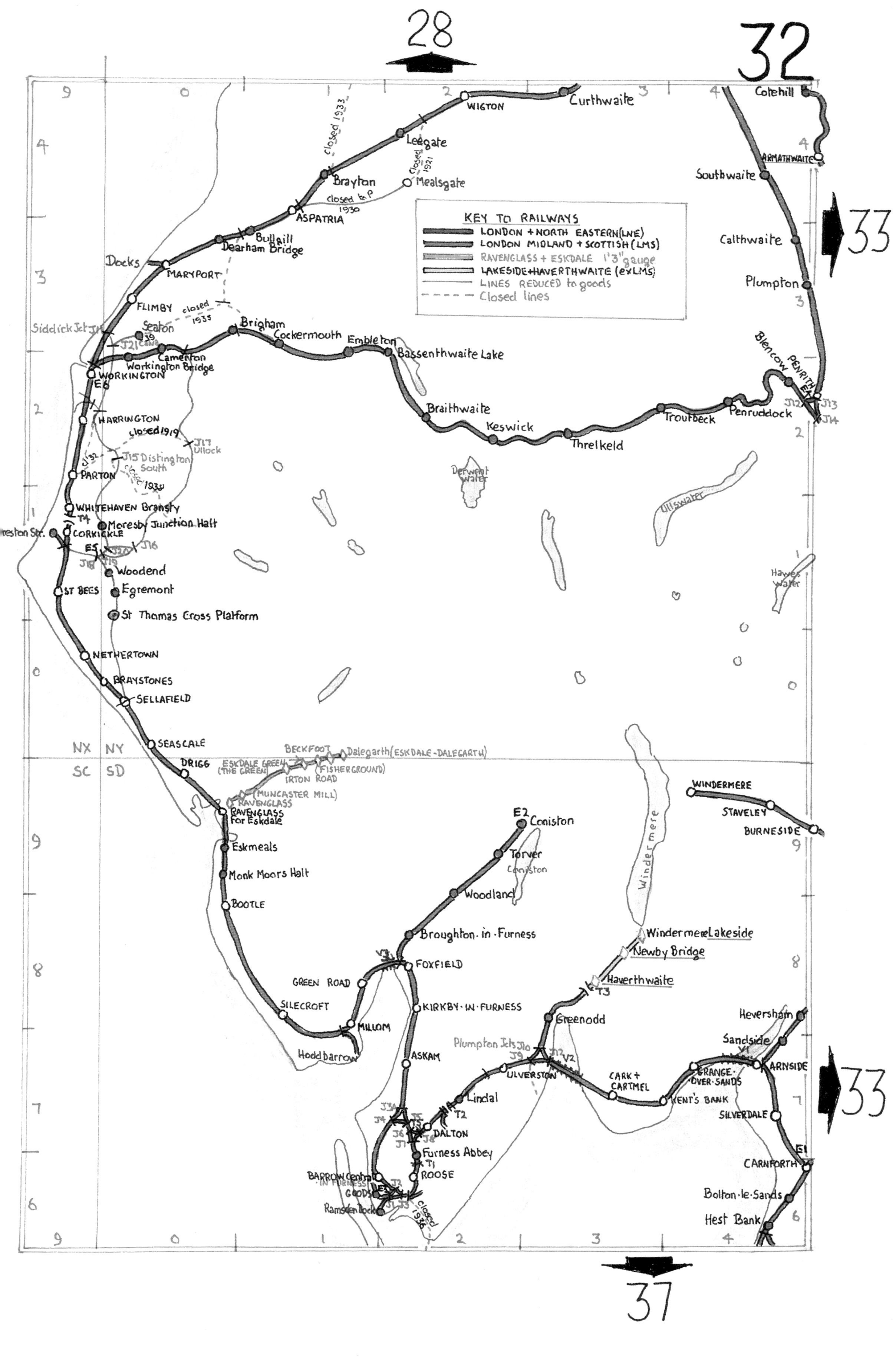
28
33
33
37
KEY TO RAILWAYS
LONDON + NORTH EASTERN (LNE)
LONDON MIDLAND + SCOTTISH (LMS)
RAVENGLASS + ESKDALE 1'3" gauge
LAKESIDE + HAVERTHWAITE (ex LMS)
LINES REDUCED to goods
Closed lines
Curthwaite
WIGTON
Leegate
Brayton
Mealsgate
closed 1933
closed 1921
closed to P 1930
ASPATRIA
Bullgill
Dearham Bridge
Docks
MARYPORT
FLIMBY
closed 1935
Siddick Jct
Seaton
Brigham
Cockermouth
Embleton
Bassenthwaite Lake
Camerton
Workington Bridge
WORKINGTON
HARRINGTON
closed 1919
Distington South
Ullock
PARTON
WHITEHAVEN Bransty
Moresby Junction Halt
CORKICKLE
Woodend
Egremont
ST BEES
St Thomas Cross Platform
NETHERTOWN
BRAYSTONES
SELLAFIELD
SEASCALE
DRIGG
Braithwaite
Keswick
Threlkeld
Troutbeck
Penruddock
Blencow
PENRITH
Cotehill
ARMATHWAITE
Southwaite
Calthwaite
Plumpton
Derwent water
Ullswater
Hawes Water
BECKFOOT
Dalegarth (ESKDALE-DALEGARTH)
ESKDALE GREEN (THE GREEN)
IRTON ROAD
(FISHERGROUND)
(MUNCASTER MILL)
RAVENGLASS
RAVENGLASS for Eskdale
Eskmeals
Monk Moors Halt
BOOTLE
Coniston
Torver
Woodland
Broughton-in-Furness
FOXFIELD
GREEN ROAD
SILECROFT
MILLOM
Hodbarrow
KIRKBY-IN-FURNESS
ASKAM
DALTON
Furness Abbey
ROOSE
BARROW Central (IN FURNESS)
GOODS
Ramsden Dock
closed 1936
Windermere
WINDERMERE
STAVELEY
BURNESIDE
Windermere Lakeside
Newby Bridge
Haverthwaite
Greenodd
Plumpton Jcts
ULVERSTON
Lindal
CARK + CARTMEL
KENT'S BANK
GRANGE-OVER-SANDS
Heversham
Sandside
ARNSIDE
SILVERDALE
CARNFORTH
Bolton-le-Sands
Hest Bank
NX NY
SC SD

PENRITH KENDAL + KIRKBY STEPHEN

RAILWAYS

No	Company
1	LONDON + NORTH EASTERN
2	LONDON MIDLAND + SCOTTISH

STATIONS

Station		Opened Closed	Ry	Ref
Alston	†	76	1	NY74
APPLEBY West	*	5268	2	NY62
Appleby East		52 62	1	NY72
Arkholme for Kirkby Lonsdale		60	2	SD57
ARMATHWAITE		70 86	2	NY54
Askrigg		54	1	SD99
Barbon		54	2	SD68
Barras		62	1	NY81
BENTHAM	*		2	SD66
Borwick		60	2	SD57
Bowes		62	1	NY91
BURNESIDE			2	SD59
Burton + Holme		50	2	SD57
CARNFORTH			2	SD57
CLAPHAM	*		2	SD76
Cliburn		56	1	NY52
Clifton Moor		62	1	NY52
Crosby Garrett		52	2	NY70
Culgaith	*	70	2	NY62
DENT	A *	70 86	2	SD78
Eastgate		53	1	NY93
Gaisgill		52	1	NY60
GARSDALE	A *	70	2	SD79
Grayrigg		54	2	SD59
Hawes		59	12	SD88
Heversham		53	2	SD58
Hornby		57	2	SD56
HORTON·IN·RIBBLESDALE	A *	70 86	2	SD87
Ingleton		57	2	SD77
KENDAL			2	SD59
Kirkby Lonsdale		54	2	SD67
Kirkby Stephen East		50 62	1	NY70
KIRKBY STEPHEN West	A * 53 68	70 86	2	NY70
Kirkby Thore		63	1	NY62
LANGWATHBY	A *	70 86	2	NY53
LAZONBY + Kirkoswald	A *	70 86 86	2	NY53
Little Salkeld	*	70	2	NY53
Long Marton	*	70	2	NY62
Low Gill		60	2	SD69
Melling		52	2	SD67
Mickleton	*	64	1	NY92
Middleton·in·Teesdale	*	64	1	NY92
Milnthorpe	*	68	2	SD58
Musgrave		52	1	NY71
New Biggin	*	70	2	NY62
Ormside		52	2	NY71
OXENHOLME (LAKE DISTRICT)			2	SD58
PENRITH			2	NY52
Ravenstonedale		52	1	NY70
RIBBLEHEAD	A *	70 86	2	SD77
Romaldkirk	*	64	1	NY92
St John's Chapel		53	1	NY83
Sedbergh		54	2	SD69
Shap	*	68	2	NY51
Shap Summit		58	2	NY50
Smardale		52	1	NY70
Stainmore		49	1	NY91
STANHOPE		53 88	1	NY93
Tebay	*	68	2	NY60
Temple Sowerby		53	1	NY62
Warcop		62	1	NY71
Wearhead		53	1	NY83
WENNINGTON	*		2	SD66
Westgate·in·Weardale		53	1	NY93

ENGINE SHEDS

No	Name/Location		Closed	Ry	Ref
1	Oxenholme		62	2	SD58
2	Penrith		62	2	NY52
3	Kirkby Stephen	B	61	1	NY70
4	Tebay		68	2	NY60
5	Ingleton		54	2	SD77
6	Wearhead		53	1	NY83
7	Alston		59	1	NY74
8	Middleton·in Teesdale		57	1	NY92
9	Carnforth		68	2	SD57

SUMMITS

No	Location	Ht in feet	Ry.	Ref.
1	Shap	916	2	NY50
2	Aisgill	1166	2	SD79
3	Stainmore	1370	1	NY91

TUNNELS

No	Name/Location	Length in yds	Ry	Ref
1	ARMATHWAITE	330	2	NY54
2	BARON WOOD No.2	251	2	NY54
3	BARON WOOD No.1	207	2	NY54
4	LAZONBY	99	2	NY53
5	WASTE BANK	164	2	NY63
6	CULGAITH	661	2	NY62
7	HELM	571	2	NY7
8	CROSBY GARRETT	181	2	NY70
9	BIRKETT	424	2	NY70
10	SHOTLOCK HILL	106	2	SD89
11	MOORCOCK	98	2	SD89
12	RISE HILL	1213	2	SD78
13	BLEA MOOR	2629	2	SD78
14	Moss Dale Head	245	2	SD89
15	MELLING	1230	2	SD67

BRIDGES + VIADUCTS

No	Name/Location	Ry	Ref
V1	DRY BECK VIADUCT	2	NY54
2	ARMATHWAITE VIADUCT	2	NY54
3	LITTLE SALKELD VIADUCT	2	NY53
4	NEW BIGGIN VIADUCT	2	NY62
5	LONG MARTON VIADUCT	2	NY62
6	ORMSIDE VIADUCT	2	NY61
7	CROSBY GARRETT VIADUCT	2	NY70
8	SMARDALE VIADUCT	2	NY70
9	AISGILL VIADUCT	2	SD79
10	LUNDS VIADUCT	2	SD79
11	MOORCOCK VIADUCT	2	SD79
12	ARTEN GILL VIADUCT	2	SD78
13	DENT HEAD VIADUCT	2	SD78
14	BLEA MOOR/RIBBLEHEAD VIADUCT	2	SD77

JUNCTIONS

No.	Name	Ry	Ref
1	Redhills	12	NY42
2	Eamont Bridge	12	NY52
3	Eden Valley	12	NY63
4	Appleby North	12	NY62
5	Hawes Branch	2	SD79
6	Hincaster	2	SD58

NOTES

This map which includes the major part of the Settle - Carlisle line includes a rather full selection of its engineering features and includes all its tunnels. A number of stations which re-opened and are annotated A were opened for excursion traffic during the period they were closed.

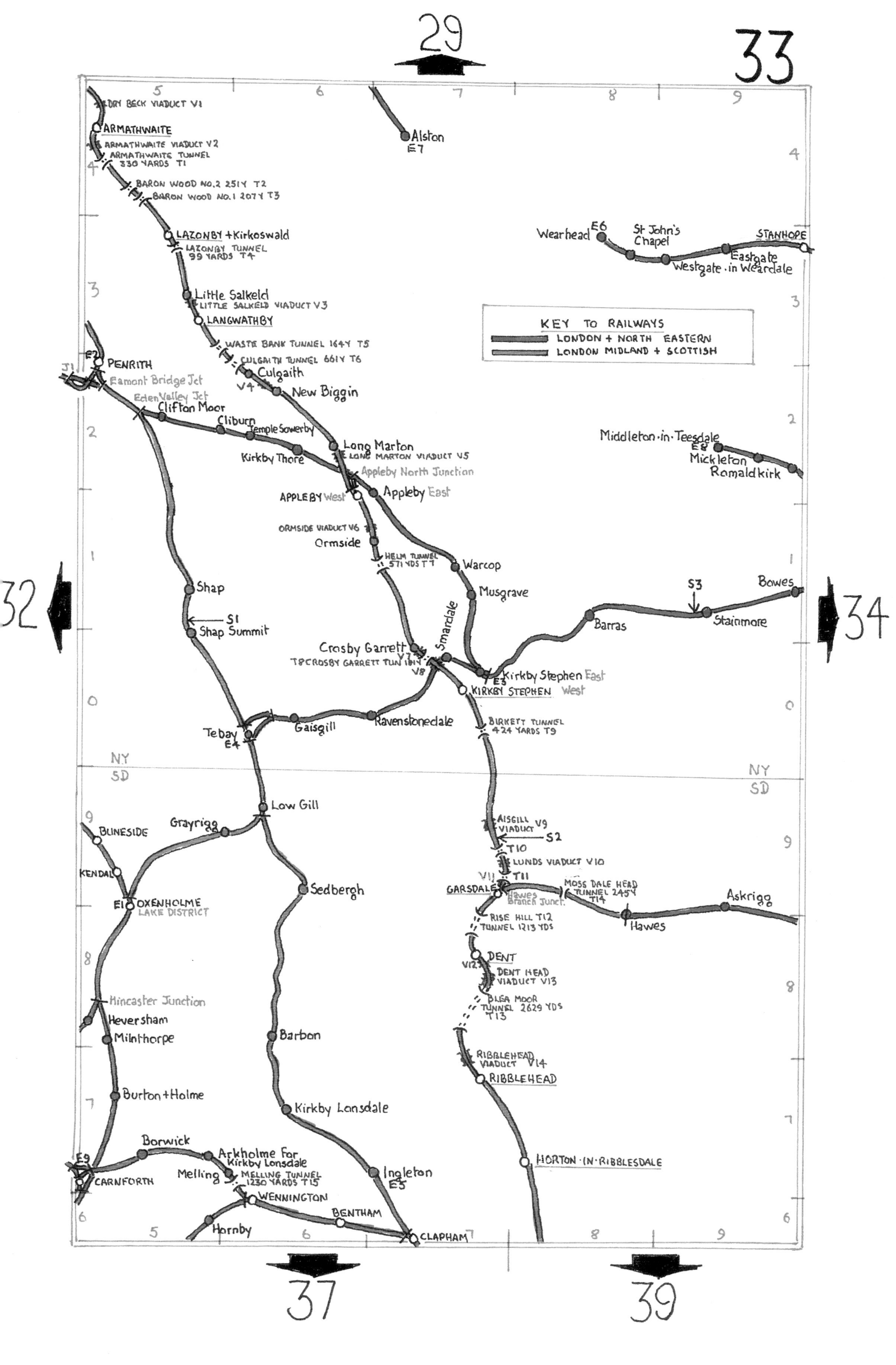
29
32
34
37
39
KEY TO RAILWAYS
LONDON + NORTH EASTERN
LONDON MIDLAND + SCOTTISH
DRY BECK VIADUCT V1
ARMATHWAITE
ARMATHWAITE VIADUCT V2
ARMATHWAITE TUNNEL 330 YARDS T1
BARON WOOD NO.2 251Y T2
BARON WOOD NO.1 207Y T3
LAZONBY + Kirkoswald
LAZONBY TUNNEL 99 YARDS T4
Little Salkeld
LITTLE SALKELD VIADUCT V3
LANGWATHBY
WASTE BANK TUNNEL 164Y T5
CULGAITH TUNNEL 661Y T6
Culgaith
V4
New Biggin
PENRITH
E2
J1
Eamont Bridge Jct
Eden Valley Jct
Clifton Moor
Cliburn
Temple Sowerby
Kirkby Thore
Long Marton
LONG MARTON VIADUCT V5
Appleby North Junction
APPLEBY West
Appleby East
ORMSIDE VIADUCT V6
Ormside
HELM TUNNEL 571 YDS T7
Warcop
Musgrave
Alston
E7
Wearhead
E6
St John's Chapel
Westgate in Weardale
Eastgate
STANHOPE
Middleton in Teesdale
E8
Mickleton
Romaldkirk
Shap
S1
Shap Summit
Smardale
Crosby Garrett
V7
T8 CROSBY GARRETT TUN 181Y
V8
Kirkby Stephen East
E3
KIRKBY STEPHEN West
Barras
S3
Stainmore
Bowes
Tebay
E4
Gaisgill
Ravenstonedale
BIRKETT TUNNEL 424 YARDS T9
NY
SD
Low Gill
Grayrigg
BURNESIDE
KENDAL
E1
OXENHOLME LAKE DISTRICT
Sedbergh
AISGILL VIADUCT V9
S2
T10
LUNDS VIADUCT V10
V11
T11
GARSDALE
Hawes Branch Junct.
MOSS DALE HEAD TUNNEL 245Y T14
Hawes
Askrigg
RISE HILL T12 TUNNEL 1213 YDS
DENT
V12
DENT HEAD VIADUCT V13
BLEA MOOR TUNNEL 2629 YDS T13
Hincaster Junction
Heversham
Milnthorpe
Barbon
RIBBLEHEAD VIADUCT V14
RIBBLEHEAD
Burton + Holme
Kirkby Lonsdale
E9
CARNFORTH
Borwick
Arkholme For Kirkby Lonsdale
Melling
MELLING TUNNEL 1230 YARDS T15
Ingleton
E5
WENNINGTON
Hornby
BENTHAM
CLAPHAM
HORTON IN RIBBLESDALE

DURHAM MIDDLESBROUGH + NORTHALLERTON

RAILWAYS

LONDON + NORTH EASTERN

STATIONS

Station	Opened / Closed	Ref
Ainderby	54	E39
ALLEN'S WEST Halt	70	Z41
Aycliffe	53	Z22
Aysgarth	62	E08
Baldersby	59	E37
Bank Top	A § ?	Z21
Barnard Castle	* 64	Z01
Bearpark	B 54	Z24
Bedale	C 54	E28
Beechburn	* 65	Z13
Billingham-on-Tees	D 66	Z42
BILLINGHAM	D 66	Z42
BISHOP AUCKLAND	*	Z22
Blackhall Colliery	* 64	Z43
Blackhall Rocks	60	Z43
Bowes	62	Z01
Bradbury	50	Z32
Brancepeth	* 64	Z23
Brandon Colliery	* 64	Z23
Brompton	* 65	E39
Broomielaw	* 64	Z01
Castle Eden	52	Z43
Catterick Bridge	* 69	Z20
Cockfield Fell	58	Z12
Constable Burton	54	E19
Cotherstone	* 64	Z01
Cowton	58	Z30
Coxhoe Bridge	52	Z33
Crakehall	54	E28
Croft Spa	* 69	Z20
Crook	* 65	Z13
Danby Wiske	58	E39
DARLINGTON Bank Top	A § ?	Z21
Darlington NORTH ROAD	* E § ?	Z21
DINSDALE		Z31
DURHAM		Z24
EAGLESCLIFFE		Z41
Easington	* 64	Z44
Etherley	* F § 65	Z13
Evenwood	57	Z12
Ferryhill	* 67	Z33
Finghall Lane	C 54	E19
Frosterley	53	Z03
Gainford	* 64	Z11
Greatham	91	Z42
Harperley	53	Z13
Hart	53	Z43
Hartlepool	64	Z53
HARTLEPOOL	G § 67	Z53
Haswell	52	Z34
Haverton Hill	61	Z42
HEIGHINGTON	*	Z22
Hesleden	52	Z43
Hetton	53	Z34
Horden	* 64	Z44
Hulands	H 49	Z01
Hunwick	* 64	Z13
Jervaulx	54	E28
Knitsley	B 54	Z14
Lanchester	B 54	Z14
Lartington	62	Z01
Leamside	53	Z34
Leeming Bar	54	E28
Leyburn	C 54	E19
Melmerby	* 67	E37
MIDDLESBROUGH		Z42
Moulton	* 66	Z20
Murton Junction	53	Z34
NEWTON AYCLIFFE	78	Z22
NORTHALLERTON		E39
NORTH ROAD	E § ?	Z21
Norton-on-Tees	60	Z42
Otterington	58	E38
Pickhill	59 62	E38
Picton	60	Z40
Piercebridge	* 64	Z21
Pilmoor	58	E47
Pittington	53	Z34
Plawsworth	52	Z24
Potto	54	Z40
Redmire	C 54	E09
Redmarshall	52	Z42
Richmond	* 69	Z10
Ripon	* 67	E37
Scorton	* 69	Z20
Scruton	54	E39
SEAHAM		Z44
Seaton	52	Z34
SEATON CAREW		Z52
Sedgefield	52	Z32
Sessay	58	E47
Sexhow	54	Z40
SHILDON	*	Z22
Shotton Bridge	52	Z34
Sinderby	62	E38
South Hetton	52	Z34
Spennithorne	54	E19
Spennymoore	B 53	Z23
STANHOPE	J 53 88	Z03
Stillington	52	Z32
STOCKTON-on-Tees	64	Z41
TEESSIDE AIRPORT	71	Z31
THIRSK		E48
THORNABY		Z41
Thornley	52	Z43
Topcliffe	59	E37
Tow Law	56	Z13
Trenholme Bar	54	Z40
Trimdon	52	Z33
Ushaw Moor	58	Z24
Waterhouses	60	Z14
Welbury	54	Z40
Wellfield	52	Z43
Wensley	54	E09
West Auckland	62	Z12
West Cornforth	52	Z33
West HARTLEPOOL	G § 67	Z53
Willington	* 64	Z13
Wingate	52	Z43
Winston	* 64	Z11
Witton Gilbert	B 54	Z24
Witton-le-Wear	53	Z13
WITTON PARK For ENSCOMB	J F § 91	Z13
Wolsingham	53	Z03
Yarm	60	Z41

GOODS

No	Name/Location	Closed	Ref
G1	Barton	50	Z21
2	Coxhoe	66	Z33
3	Croft	64	Z21
4	Durham Elvet	64	Z24
5	Durham Gilesgate	66	Z24
6	Eryholme	?	Z30
7	Fighting Cocks	64	Z31
8	Forcett	64	Z11
9	Hartlepool	63	Z53
10	Masham	63	E28
11	Middlesbrough	73	Z42
12	Northallerton Town	?	E39
13	North Shore Stockton	68	Z41
14	Parkhead	65	Z04
15	South (Bank) Stockton	72	Z41
16	TEES YARD		Z41
17	Waskerley	65	Z04
18	Water-houses	64	Z14
19	Butterknowle	63	Z21

ENGINE SHEDS

No	Name/Location	Opened / Closed	Ref
E1	Durham	58	Z24
2	Darlington Bank Top	66	Z21
3	Haverton Hill	59	Z42
4	Leyburn	54	E19
5	Middlesbrough	58	Z42
6	Newport	58	Z41
7	Northallerton	63	E39
8	Stockton	59	Z41
9	THORNABY	58	Z41
10	West Auckland	54	Z12

WORKS

No	Name/Location	Closed	Ref
W1	Darlington	66	Z21

TUNNELS

No	Name	Length	Ref
T1	Shildon	1220	Z22

JUNCTIONS

No	Name	Ref
J1	Bishophouse	E47
2	Sunbeck	E47
3	Sessay Wood	E47
4	Longlands Northallerton	E39
5	Cordio	E39
6	Boroughbridge Gates	E39
7	High Northallerton	E39
8	Low Northallerton	E39
9	Castle Hills	E39
10	Northallerton South	E39
11	Northallerton West	E39
12	Middleton	Z01
13	Merrybent	Z21
14	Charity Darlington	Z21
15	Hopetown	Z21
16	Stooperdale	Z21
17	Albert Hill	Z21
18	Parkgate	Z21
19	South Darlington	Z41
20	Bowesfield	Z41
21	Cemetery Road North	Z53
22	Cemetery Road South	Z53
23	Cemetery Road East	Z53
24	Carlton North	Z42
25	Carlton East	Z42
26	Carlton South	Z42
27	Carlton West	Z42
28	Wear Valley	Z13
29	Burnhill	Z04
30	Belmont	Z34
31	Broomside Branch	Z34
32	Sim Pasture	Z22

NOTES:

Ref All in NZ or SE. The initial N or S is omitted.

§ Old Name } Change of name
§ New Name

Other name indicated by use of identical letter.

A Bank Top dropped from title. The date this happened is unclear.

B These stations lost a regular passenger service before the nationalisation of railways. But date shown closed is official date.

C Re-opened for a handful of passenger services after closure. Line is now disused.

D Change of site

E Darlington dropped from title. Date unclear.

F Name change on re-opening

G West dropped from title.

H Non-advertised station used by workpeople.

J Re-opened on a seasonal Sunday service basis

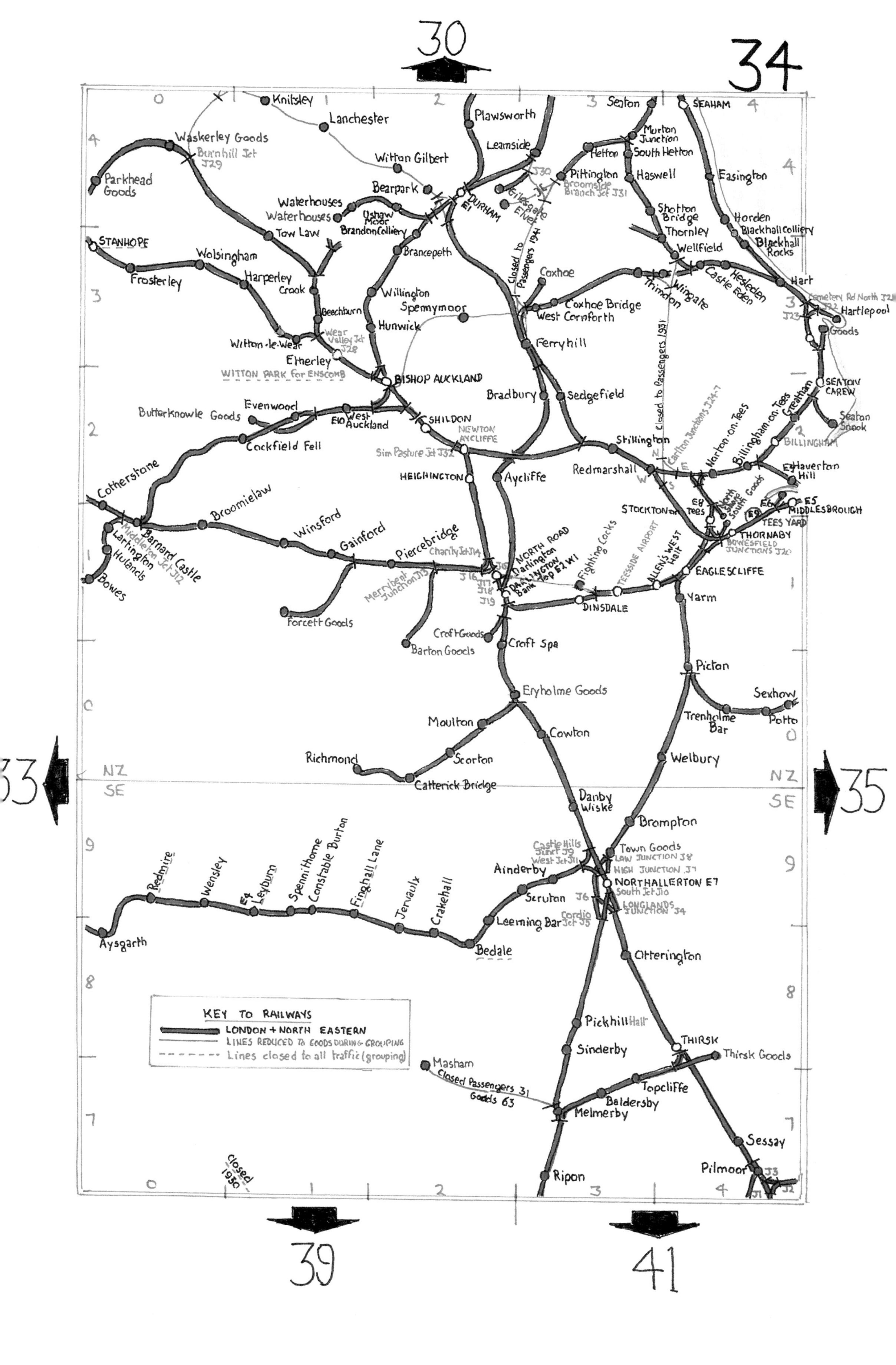
30
34
33
35
39
41
KEY TO RAILWAYS
LONDON + NORTH EASTERN
LINES REDUCED TO GOODS DURING GROUPING
Lines closed to all traffic (grouping)
Knitsley
Lanchester
Witton Gilbert
Bearpark
Waskerley Goods
Burnhill Jct J29
Parkhead Goods
STANHOPE
Frosterley
Wolsingham
Harperley
Tow Law
Crook
Beechburn
Waterhouses
Ushaw Moor
Brandon Colliery
Brancepeth
Willington
Hunwick
Spennymoor
Witton-le-Wear
Wear Valley Jct J28
Etherley
WITTON PARK for ENSCOMB
BISHOP AUCKLAND
SHILDON
NEWTON AYCLIFFE
Sim Pasture Jct J32
HEIGHINGTON
Aycliffe
West Auckland
Evenwood
Butterknowle Goods
Cockfield Fell
Cotherstone
Barnard Castle
Middleton Jct J12
Lartington
Hulands
Bowes
Broomielaw
Winsford
Gainford
Piercebridge
Charity Jct J14
Merrybent Junction J15
Forcett Goods
Barton Goods
Croft Goods
Croft Spa
NORTH ROAD Darlington
DARLINGTON Bank Top E2 W1
Fighting Cocks
TEESSIDE AIRPORT
ALLEN'S WEST Halt
DINSDALE
EAGLESCLIFFE
Yarm
Picton
Trenholme Bar
Sexhow
Potto
Welbury
Eryholme Goods
Moulton
Cowton
Richmond
Scorton
Catterick Bridge
Danby Wiske
Brompton
Castle Hills Junct J9
West Jct J11
Town Goods
LOW JUNCTION J8
HIGH JUNCTION J7
NORTHALLERTON E7
South Jct J10
LONGLANDS JUNCTION J4
Ainderby
Scruton
Leeming Bar
Cordio Jct J5
Bedale
Crakehall
Jervaulx
Finghall Lane
Constable Burton
Spennithorne
Leyburn
Wensley
Redmire
Aysgarth
Otterington
Pickhill Halt
Sinderby
THIRSK
Thirsk Goods
Topcliffe
Baldersby
Melmerby
Masham
Closed Passengers 31 Goods 63
Ripon
Sessay
Pilmoor
closed 1950
Plawsworth
Leamside
DURHAM
Gilesgate Elvet
Closed to Passengers 1941
Pittington
Broomside Branch Jct J31
Hetton
South Hetton
Murton Junction
Seaton
SEAHAM
Easington
Haswell
Shotton Bridge
Thornley
Wellfield
Horden
Blackhall Colliery
Blackhall Rocks
Hesleden
Castle Eden
Wingate
Trimdon
Hart
Cemetery Rd North
Hartlepool
Goods
SEATON CAREW
Seaton Snook
Coxhoe
Coxhoe Bridge
West Cornforth
Ferryhill
Bradbury
Sedgefield
Closed to Passengers 1931
Stillington
Redmarshall
Carlton Junctions J24-7
Norton-on-Tees
Billingham-on-Tees
Greatham
BILLINGHAM
Haverton Hill
MIDDLESBROUGH
TEES YARD
THORNABY
BOWESFIELD JUNCTIONS J20
STOCKTON
North Shore
South Goods
NZ
SE

WHITBY + MALTON SCARBOROUGH + FILEY

RAILWAYS

No	Company
1	LONDON + NORTH EASTERN (LNE)
X	NORTH YORKSHIRE MOORS (ex LNE)

STATIONS

Name		Opened / Closed	Ry	Ref
Amotherley	A	58	1	SE77
Ampleforth		50	1	SE57
Barton-le-Street	A	58	1	SE77
BATTERSBY	*		1	NZ50
BEMPTON			1	TA17
Boosbeck		60	1	NZ61
BRITISH STEEL REDCAR	P	78	1	NZ52
Brotton		60	1	NZ62
Cargo Fleet		90	1	NZ52
CASTLETON MOOR	*	?	1	NZ60
Cayton		52	1	TA08
Cloughton	*	65	1	TA09
COMMONDALE	*		1	NZ60
Coxwold	B	58	1	SE57
DANBY	*		1	NZ70
Ebberston		50	1	SE88
EGTON	*		1	NZ80
Farworth	C §	?	X	SE88
FILEY			1	TA17
Filey Holiday Camp		77	1	TA17
Forge Valley		50	1	SE98
Fyling Hall	*	65	1	NZ90
Ganton	D	49	1	SE97
Gilling	E	63	1	SE67
GLAISDALE	*		1	NZ70
Goathland	*	65 73	X	NZ80
Grangetown		91	1	NZ52
GREAT AYTON	*		1	NZ51
Greatham		91	1	NZ52
Gristhorpe		59	1	TA08
GROSMONT	F *	65 73	1X	NZ80
Guisborough	*	64	1	NZ61
GYPSY LANE		76	1	NZ51
Hartlepool	G		1	NZ53
HARTLEPOOL	H §	67	1	NZ53
Hawsker	*	65	1	NZ90
Hayburn Wyke	*	65	1	TA09
Helmsley		53	1	SE68
Hinderwell		58	1	NZ81
Hovingham Spa	A	58	1	SE67
HUNMANBY			1	TA17
Husthwaite Gate		53	1	SE57
Hutton Gate	*	64	1	NZ61
Ingleby		54	1	NZ50
Kettleness		58	1	NZ81
KILDALE	*		1	NZ60
Kirby Moorside	J §	48 53	1	SE68
LEALHOLM	*		1	NZ70
Levisham	*	65 73	X	SE89
Loftus		60	1	NZ71
LONGBECK		85	1	NZ62
MALTON			1	SE77
Marishes Road	*	65	1	SE87
MARSKE			1	NZ62
MARTON	K §	82	1	NZ51
MIDDLESBROUGH			1	NZ52
Nawton		53	1	SE68
Newtondale Halt		48 80	1	SE89
North Skelton		51	1	NZ61
Nunnington		53	1	SE67
NUNTHORPE	*		1	NZ51
Ormesby	* K §	82		NZ51
Pickering	*	65 73	X	SE88
Pinchingthorpe		51	1	NZ51
Ravenscar	*	65	1	NZ90
REDCAR				
BRITISH STEEL		78	1	NZ52
CENTRAL			1	NZ62
EAST			1	NZ62
Robin Hood's Bay	*	65	1	NZ90
RUSWARP	*		1	NZ80
SALTBURN			1	NZ62
Sandsend		58	1	NZ81
Sawdon		50	1	SE98
Scalby		64	1	TA09
SCARBOROUGH Central		69	1	TA08
Scarborough Londesborough Road		66	1	TA08
SEAMER			1	TA08
SEATON CAREW			1	NZ52
Sinnington		53	1	SE78
Skinningrove		58		NZ72
SLEIGHTS	*		1	NZ80
Slingsby	A	58	1	SE77
Snainton		50	1	SE98
SOUTH BANK	M		1	NZ52
Speeton	*	70	1	TA17
Stainton Dale	*	65	1	TA09
Staithes		58	1	NZ71
Stokesley		54	1	NZ50
Thornton Dale		50	1	SE88
West HARTLEPOOL	H	67	1	NZ53
WHITBY Town	*	51	1	NZ81
Whitby West Cliff		61	1	NZ81
Wykeham		50	1	SE98

GOODS

No	Name / Location	Closed	Ry	Ref
G1	BRITISH STEEL - TEESSIDE	N	1	NZ52
2	Eston	66	1	NZ51
3	Hartlepool	63	1	NZ53
4	Scarborough	81	1	TA08
5	Seaton Snook (Seaton-on-Tees)	57	1	NZ52
6	Skinningrove BRITISH STEEL	N	1	NZ72
7	TEES DOCK	N	1	NZ52

ENGINE SHEDS

No	Name / Location	Closed	Ry	Ref
E1	Guisborough	54	1	NZ61
2	Malton	63	1	SE77
3	Pickering	59	1	SE88
4	Saltburn	58	1	NZ62
5	Scarborough	63	1	TA08
6	Whitby	59	1	NZ81

TUNNELS

No	Name / Location	Length (yds)	Ry	Ref
T1	Grinkle	992	1	NZ71
2	Kettleness		1	NZ81
3	Sandsend Ness	1651	1	NZ81
4	Ravenscar		1	NZ90
5	GROSMONT	146	X	NZ80

JUNCTIONS

No	Name	Ref
1	Cemetery Road North	NZ53
2	Cemetery Road South	NZ53
3	Cemetery Road West	NZ53
4	Newburn	NZ53
5	Priestcrofts	NZ61
6	Lumpey Mines	NZ61
7	Prospect Hill	NZ81
8	Boghall	NZ81
9	Rillington	SE87
10	Royal Oak North	TA17
11	Royal Oak South	TA17

NOTES:

- § Old name } Identical letters give
- § New name } alternative name
- § Name changed when re-opened by NORTH YORKSHIRE MOORS RAILWAY to (FARWATH)
- A Closed to regular passenger traffic in 1931
- B Closed to regular passenger traffic in 1953.
- C Change of name see § above.
- D Used only for excursion after nationalised.
- E Excursion traffic only after 1933.
- F Re-opening was both for ordinary traffic and by NORTH YORKSHIRE MOORS RAILWAY
- G Not used for regular services after nationalisation.
- H Change of name (West dropped)
- J Change of name to Kirbymoorside (ie just one word) 1948
- K Change of Name.
- L Excursion station to deal with heavy summer holiday traffic.
- M Rebuilt in 1984.
- N Still open.
- P Unadvertised 'halt' Warrenby until '78

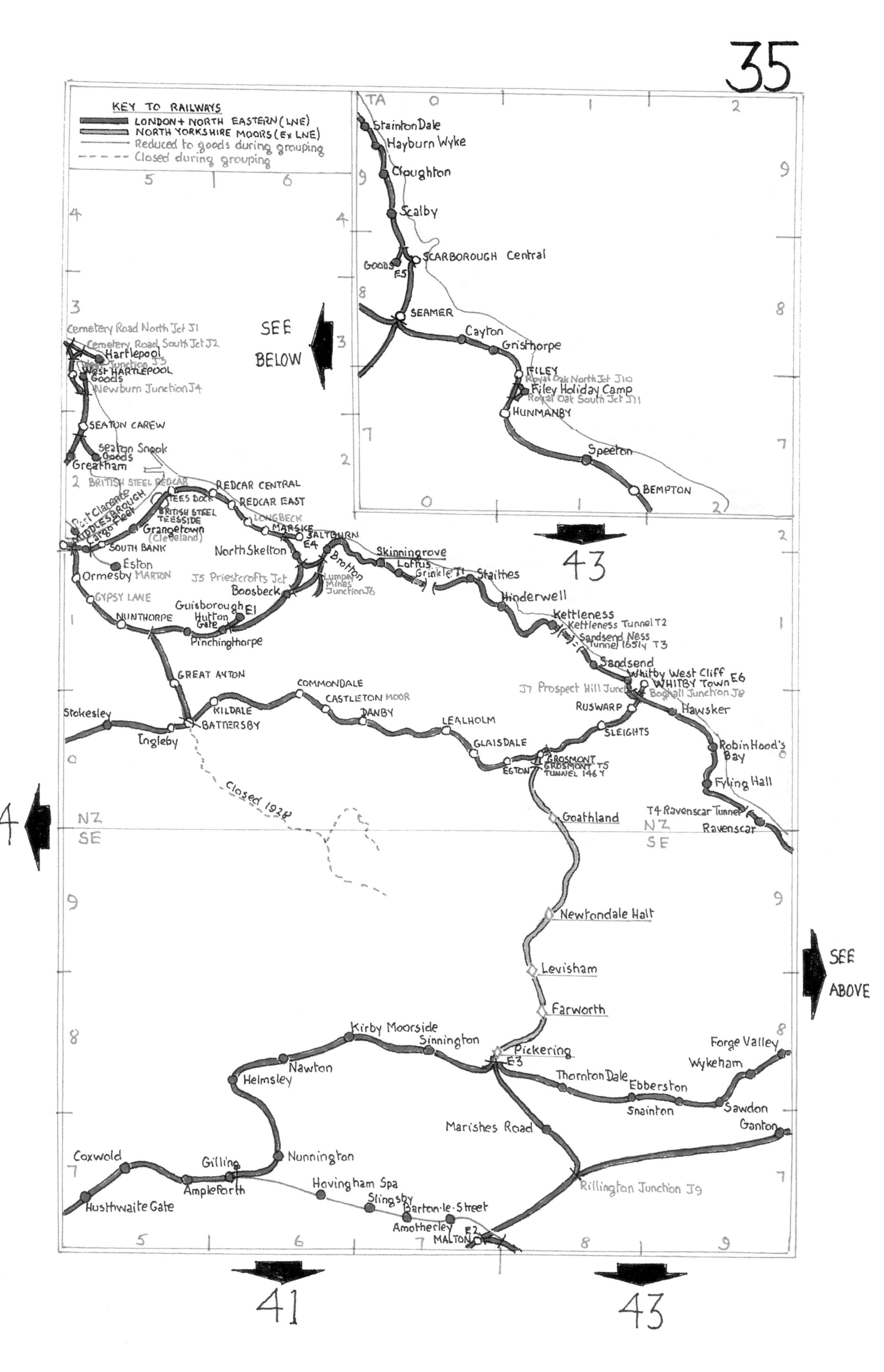

KEY TO RAILWAYS
LONDON + NORTH EASTERN (LNE)
NORTH YORKSHIRE MOORS (Ex LNE)
Reduced to goods during grouping
Closed during grouping
SEE BELOW
SEE ABOVE
Stainton Dale
Hayburn Wyke
Cloughton
Scalby
SCARBOROUGH Central
Goods
E5
SEAMER
Cayton
Gristhorpe
FILEY
Royal Oak North Jct J10
Filey Holiday Camp
Royal Oak South Jct J11
HUNMANBY
Speeton
BEMPTON
Cemetery Road North Jct J1
Cemetery Road South Jct J2
Hartlepool
West HARTLEPOOL Goods
Newburn Junction J4
SEATON CAREW
Seaton Snook Goods
Greatham
BRITISH STEEL REDCAR
TEES DOCK
BRITISH STEEL TEESSIDE
Port Clarence
MIDDLESBROUGH
Cargo Fleet
Grangetown (Cleveland)
SOUTH BANK
Eston
Ormesby MARTON
GYPSY LANE
NUNTHORPE
REDCAR CENTRAL
REDCAR EAST
LONGBECK
MARSKE
SALTBURN
E4
North Skelton
J5 Priestcrofts Jct
Boosbeck
Guisborough E1
Hutton Gate
Pinchinghorpe
Brotton
Lumpsey Mines Junction J6
Skinningrove
Loftus
Grinkle T1
Staithes
Hinderwell
Kettleness
Kettleness Tunnel T2
Sandsend Ness Tunnel 1651y T3
Sandsend
Whitby West Cliff
WHITBY Town E6
J7 Prospect Hill Junct
Boghall Junction J8
Hawsker
Robin Hood's Bay
Fyling Hall
T4 Ravenscar Tunnel
Ravenscar
RUSWARP
SLEIGHTS
GREAT AYTON
COMMONDALE
CASTLETON MOOR
KILDALE
DANBY
LEALHOLM
GLAISDALE
Stokesley
Ingleby
BATTERSBY
GROSMONT
GROSMONT TUNNEL 146 Y T5
EGTON
Closed 1928
Goathland
Newtondale Halt
Levisham
Farworth
Pickering
E3
Kirby Moorside
Sinnington
Nawton
Helmsley
Thornton Dale
Ebberston
Snainton
Forge Valley
Wykeham
Sawdon
Ganton
Marishes Road
Nunnington
Coxwold
Gilling
Ampleforth
Husthwaite Gate
Hovingham Spa
Slingsby
Barton-le-Street
Amotherley
MALTON
E2
Rillington Junction J9
TA
NZ
SE
34
43
41
43

ISLE OF MAN

RAILWAYS

No	Company	Gauge	Traction
1	ISLE OF MAN (preserved)	3'0"	Steam
2	ISLE OF MAN (closed)	3'0"	Steam
3	MANX ELECTRIC (ME)	3'0"	Electric
4	SNAEFELL MOUNTAIN (ME)	3'6"	Electric
5	DOUGLAS CORPORATION HORSE TRAMS	3'0"	Horses
6	GROUNDLE GLEN	2'0"	Various

STATIONS

Station		Opened Closed	Ry	Ref
BALDRINE			3	48
(BALDROMMA, HALFWAY)	?		3	48
BALLABEG		48 80	1	27
BALLABEG			3	48
BALLAGLASS		75 77	3	48
BALLAJORA		75 77	3	49
BALLARAGH		75 77	3	48
BALLASALLA	A	65 77	1	27
Ballaugh		65 67 68	2	39
BELLEVUE		75 77	3	49
BUNGALOW	B		4	38
CASTLETOWN	A	65 77	1	26
COLBY	A	65 77	1	27
CORNAA		75 77	3	49
Crosby		65 67 68	2	37
DERBY CASTLE, Douglas			3	37
DERBY CASTLE, Douglas	B		5	37
DHOON GLEN		75 77	3	48
DHOON QUARRY		75 77	3	48
DOUGLAS		65 77	1	37
DOUGLAS PIER	B		5	37
DREEMSKERRY		75 77	3	49
FAIRY COTTAGE			3	48
GARWICK GLEN			3	48
GLEN MONA		75 77	3	48
GROUNDLE GLEN			3	47
(HALFWAY (BALDROMMA))	?		3	48
HOWSTRAKE			3	47
Kirkmichael		65 67 68	2	39
LAXEY			34	48
LEWAIGUE		75 77	3	49
Lezayre		61 67 68	2	49
MINORCA		75 77	3	48
ONCHAN HEAD			3	37
Peel		65 67 68	2	28
Peel Road		61	2	28
PORT ERIN	A	65 77	1	16
PORT ST MARY	A	65 77	1	26
PORT SODERICK	A	65 77	1	37
Ramsey		65 67 68	2	49
RAMSEY		75 77	3	49
(RONALDSWAY HALT)	C	67	1	26
St Germain's		61	2	28
St John's		65 67 68	2	28
SANTON	A	58 77	1	37
SNAEFELL	B		4	38
SOUTH CAPE			3	48
Sulby Bridge		65 67 68	2	39
Sulby Glen		65 67 68	2	39
Union Mills	D	68	2	37

ENGINE SHEDS + DEPOTS

No	Name/Location	Ry	Ref
E 1	DOUGLAS	1	37
2	Peel	2	28
3	PORT ERIN	1	16
4	Ramsey	2	49
5	DERBY CASTLE	5	37
6	DERBY CASTLE	3	37
7	LAXEY	4	48

SUMMITS

No	Location	Height Feet	Ry	Ref
S 1	SNAEFELL	1990	4	38
2	SANTON	230	1	37

BRIDGES + VIADUCTS

No	Name/Location	Ry	Ref
V 1	Glen Wyllin Viaduct	2	39
2	Glen Mooar Viaduct	2	39

NOTES:

The railways of the Isle of Man do not fit into the pattern shown elsewhere in the British Isles. There are differences in gauge nationalisation date, and even the 'tramway' system had its unique features.

The only proper railway was the IOM railway built to a 3'0" gauge and steam operated. But it is impossible to say when this became a preserved railway and this has led to the method to show stations still in use in black with a green underline.

Turning to the electric lines, these might well be described as tramways except tickets issued were of railway type. They have therefore been classified as METRO.

It was also felt appropriate to include the Douglas Horse Tram which has been in continuous seasonal use for over 100 years.

Notes on the map show nationalisation of the steam and electric lines.

A Station so marked closed in 1965 and re-opened in 1977 for summer season only and for shopper service out of season. In the interim period there were many openings and closings.

B Seasonal Service only has always been operated – usually May to September.

C From opening service was irregular and often unadvertised

D Last train 61.

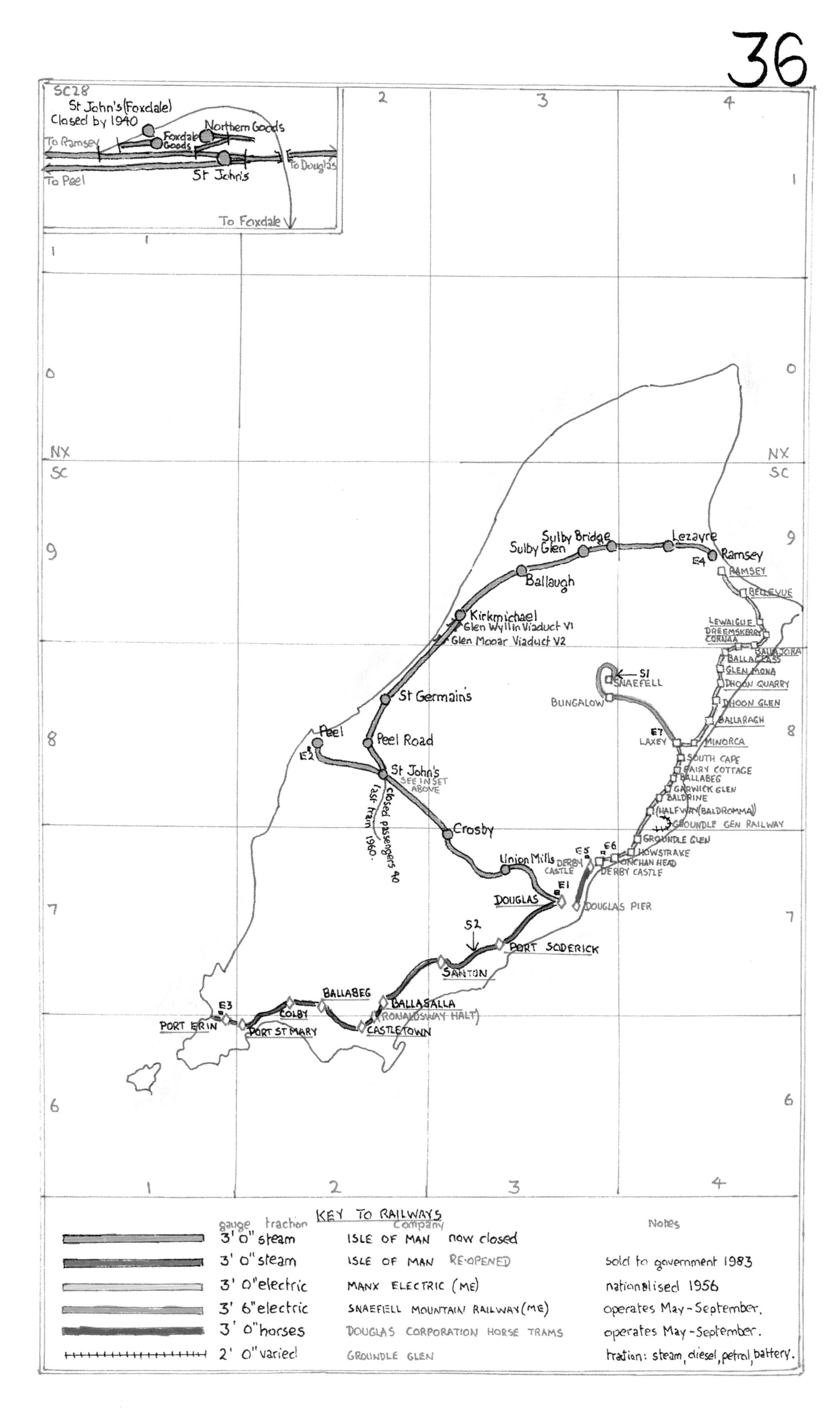
SC28
St John's (Foxdale)
Closed by 1940
Northern Goods
Foxdale Goods
To Ramsey
To Peel
St John's
To Douglas
To Foxdale
NX
SC
Sulby Bridge
Sulby Glen
Lezayre
Ramsey
E4
Ballaugh
Kirkmichael
Glen Wyllin Viaduct V1
Glen Mooar Viaduct V2
St Germain's
Peel
E2
Peel Road
St John's
SEE INSET ABOVE
closed passengers 40
last train 1960.
Crosby
Union Mills
DOUGLAS
E1
RAMSEY
BELLEVUE
LEWAIGUE
DREEMSKERRY
CORNAA
BALLAJORA
BALLAGLASS
GLEN MONA
DHOON QUARRY
DHOON GLEN
BALLARAGH
S1
SNAEFELL
BUNGALOW
E7
LAXEY
MINORCA
SOUTH CAPE
FAIRY COTTAGE
BALLABEG
GARWICK GLEN
BALDRINE
(HALFWAY (BALDROMMA))
GROUNDLE GEN RAILWAY
GROUNDLE GLEN
HOWSTRAKE
ONCHAN HEAD
DERBY CASTLE
E5
E6
DERBY CASTLE
DOUGLAS PIER
S2
PORT SODERICK
SANTON
BALLASALLA
(RONALDSWAY HALT)
CASTLETOWN
BALLABEG
COLBY
PORT ST MARY
E3
PORT ERIN
KEY TO RAILWAYS
gauge traction company Notes
3' 0" steam ISLE OF MAN now closed
3' 0" steam ISLE OF MAN RE-OPENED sold to government 1983
3' 0" electric MANX ELECTRIC (ME) nationalised 1956
3' 6" electric SNAEFELL MOUNTAIN RAILWAY (ME) operates May-September.
3' 0" horses DOUGLAS CORPORATION HORSE TRAMS operates May-September.
2' 0" varied GROUNDLE GLEN traction: steam, diesel, petrol, battery.

LANCASTER, PRESTON + WIGAN

RAILWAYS

No	Company
1	LONDON + NORTH EASTERN (LNE)
2	LONDON MIDLAND + SCOTTISH (LMS)
3	CHESHIRE LINES COMMITTEE (LNE+LMS)
4	EAST LANCASHIRE (ex LMS)

STATIONS

Station	Note	Opened / Closed	Ry	Ref
ACCRINGTON			2	72
ADDLINGTON			2	61
AINSDALE	*		2	31
Ainsdale Beach		52	3	31
Ainsworth Road		53	2	70
Altcar + Hillhouse		52	3	30
ANSDELL + FAIRHAVEN			2	32
APPLEY BRIDGE			2	50
Aspull, Dicconson Lane +	A	54	2	60
Atherton Bag Lane		54	2	60
ATHERTON Central		54	2	60
AUGHTON PARK			2	40
Balshaw Lane + Euxton	*	69	2	51
BAMBER BRIDGE			2	52
Bam Furlong		50	2	60
Banks	*	64	2	32
BARE LANE			2	46
Baxenden		51	2	72
Bay Horse		60	2	45
BENTHAM			2	66
BESCAR LANE			2	31
Bickershaw + Abram				38
BIRKDALE	*		2	31
Birkdale Palace		52	3	31
BLACKBURN			2	62
Black Lane Radcliffe		70	2	70
BLACKPOOL				33
Central		64	2	33
NORTH	*		2	33
PLEASURE BEACH		87	2	33
SOUTH			2	33
BLACKROD	*		2	61
Boar's Head		49	2	50
Bolton Great Moor Street		54	2	70
BOLTON Trinity Street		54	2	70
Bolton-le-Sands	*	69	2	46
Bradley Fold		70	2	70
Brandlesholme Road Halt		52	2	71
Brinscall		60	2	62
BROMLEY CROSS			2	71
BRYN	*		2	50
Burn Naze Halt		70	2	34
BURSCOUGH BRIDGE			2	41
BURSCOUGH JUNCTION			2	41
Bury Bolton Street	* B	71 80 80	4	70
CARNFORTH			2	47
Caton		61	2	56
Chapel Street SOUTHPORT	C §	?	2	31
Chatburn		62	2	74
Chequerbent		52	2	60
CHERRY TREE			2	62
CHORLEY			2	51
CHURCH + OSWALDTWISTLE			2	72
Churchtown	*	64	2	31
CLAPHAM			2	76
CLIFTON Junction		74	2	70
CLITHEROE	D	71 90	2	74
Coppull	*	69	2	51
Crossens	*	64	2	31
CROSTON			2	41
Daisyfield		58	2	62
DAISY HILL			2	60
Darcy Lever		51	2	70
DARWEN			2	62
Dicconson Lane + Aspull Halt	A	54	2	60
Ellenbrook		61	2	70
ENTWISTLE	*		2	71
Ewood Bridge + Edenfield	*	72	2	71
Farington		60	2	52
FARNWORTH + Halshaw Moor		74	2	70
Feniscowles		60	2	62
Fleetwood	*	66	2	34
Fleetwood	E §	66 70	2	34
FORMBY	*		2	20
FRESHFIELD	*		2	20
Garstang + Catterall	*	69	2	54
GATHURST for Shevington		75	2	50
GIGGLESWICK	*		2	76
Great Harwood		57	2	73
Great Moor Street Bolton		54	2	70
Greenmount		52	2	71
HAG FOLD		87	2	60
HALL-I'-TH'-WOOD		86	2	71
HALL ROAD	*		2	30
Halton (Lancs)	*	66	2	56
HAPTON			2	73
Haslingden		60	2	72
Heapey		60	2	61
Helmshore	*	66	2	72
Hesketh Bank	*	64	2	42
Hesketh Park	*	64	2	31
Hest Bank	*	69	2	46
Heys Crossing Halt		51	2	40
HEYSHAM Harbour FORT	F §	75 87	2	45
HIGHTOWN	*		2	30
HILLSIDE	*		2	31
Hilton House Halt		54	2	60
HINDLEY North		50 78	2	60
Hindley + Platt Bridge	G §	52	1	60
Hindley South	G §	52 64	1	60
Hindley Green		61	2	60
Hoghton		60	2	62
Holcombe Brook		52	2	71
Hoole	*	64	2	42
Hornby		57	2	56
Horwich	*	65	2	61
HOSCAR			2	41
Howe Bridge		59	2	60
HUNCOAT			2	73
Hundred End		62	2	42
INCE			2	50
Irlams-o'-th'-Height		56	2	70
(IRWELL VALE)		87	4	71
KEARSLEY			2	70
KIRKHAM + WESHAM			2	43
LANCASTER Castle			2	46
Lancaster Green Ayre	*	66	2	46
Langho		56	2	73
LAYTON	*		2	33
LEYLAND			2	52
Little Hulton		54	2	70
Longton Bridge	*	64	2	42
Lord Street Southport		52	3	31
LOSTOCK HALL		69	2	52
Lostock Junction	*	66	2	60
LOSTOCK PARKWAY		88	2	60
Lower Darwen		58	2	62
Lower Ince	§			38
Lydiate		52	3	30
LYTHAM			2	32
MAGHULL			2	30
MEOLS COP			2	31
Midge Hall		61	2	52
MILL HILL	*		2	62
MOORSIDE + Wardley		74	2	70
Morecambe Euston Road	*	63	2	46
MORECAMBE Promenade		68	2	46
MOSES GATE			2	70
MOSS SIDE		61 63	2	33
NEW LANE			2	41
New Longton + Hutton	*	64	2	52
Oaks, The		50	2	71
ORMSKIRK	H		2	40
ORRELL	*		2	50
Padiham		57	2	73
PARBOLD for Newburgh		75	2	41
PEMBERTON	*		2	50
Pendlebury		60	2	70
Penwortham Cop Lane	*	64	2	52
Platt Bridge	§			38
PLEASINGTON	*		2	52
Plodder Lane		54	2	70
Poulton Curve Halt		52	2	33
POULTON-LE-FYLDE			2	33
Preston Junction	J §	52	2	52
PRESTON			2	52
RADCLIFFE				70
Black Lane		70	2	70
Bridge		59	2	70
Central	* K §	71	2	70
RADCLIFFE	K §	71	2	70
RAINFORD Junction	*		2	40
Rainford Village		51	2	40
Ramsbottom	*	72 87	4	71
RAMSGREAVE + WILPSHIRE	S §	94 94	2	63
Red Rock		49	2	51
Rimington		58	2	74
Ringley Road		53	2	70
RISHTON			2	72
RUFFORD			2	41
Rumworth + Daubhill		52	2	60
ST. ANNES-ON-THE-SEA			2	32
St Lukes		68	2	31
SALWICK			2	43
Scale Hall	*	57 66	2	46
Sefton + Maghull		52	3	30
Simonstone		57	2	73
Skelmersdale		56	2	40
SOUTHPORT				31
BIRKDALE			2	31
Birkdale Palace		52	3	31
Chapel Street	C §	?	2	31
Hesketh Park		64	2	31
Lord Street		52	3	31
MEOLS COP			2	31
St Lukes		68	2	31
SOUTHPORT	C §	?	2	31
Spring Vale		58	2	71
SQUIRES GATE			2	33
Standish		49	2	51
Stubbins	*	72 87	4	71
Summerseat	*	72 87	4	71
Sunny Wood		52	2	71
SWINTON			2	70
The Oaks		50	2	71
Thornton (for) Cleveleys	L	53 70	2	34
Todd Lane Junction	* J §	52 68	2	52
Tottington		52	2	71
TOWN GREEN + Aughton		75	2	40
Turton + Edgworth		61	2	71
Tyldesley	*	69	2	60
UPHOLLAND	*		2	50
WALKDEN High Level		55	2	70
Walkden Low Level		54	2	70
WENNINGTON			2	66
WESTHOUGHTON			2	60
Westhead Halt		51	2	40
West Leigh		54	2	60
Whalley		62 94	2	73
White Bear		60	2	51
White Moss Crossing Halt		51	2	40
WIGAN				50
Central	*	64	1	50
NORTH WESTERN			2	50
WALLGATE			2	50
Wilpshire		62 94	2	63
Withnell		60	2	71
Woodhill Road Halt		52	2	62
Woodvale		52	3	31
Woolfold		52	2	71
Worsley	*	69	2	70
Wrea Green		61	2	33
Wyre Dock	F §	66	2	34

GOODS

No	Name	Note	Closed	Ry	Ref
G1	Astley Bridge		61	2	71
2	Glasson Dock		64	2	45
3	Grane Road		64	2	72
4	Hoddlesden		50	2	72
5	Hollins		68	2	62
6	Knott End		50	2	34
7	Longridge		67	2	53
8	Lytham Dock		63	2	32
9	Poulton		68	2	33
10	Preston Butler Street		71	2	52
11	Preston Deepdale		68	2	52
12	PRESTON DOCKS	M		X	52
13	Maudlands (Preston)		?	2	52
14	Preston West Lancs		65	2	52
15	Southport Blowick		64	2	31
16	Southport Kensington Rd		73	2	31
17	Southport Lord Street		52	3	31
18	Whelley		?	2	50
19	Wyre Dock		64	2	34

WORKS

No	Name	Closed	Ry	Ref
W1	Horwich	R	2	61

ENGINE SHEDS

No	Name / Location	Note	Closed	Ry	Ref
E1	Accrington	N	61	2	72
2	Agecroft		66	2	70
3	Blackpool North		64	2	33
4	Blackpool Central		64	2	33
5	Bolton		68	2	70
6	Bury	N	65	2	71
7	Carnforth	P	68	2	47
8	Fleetwood		66	2	34
9	Lancaster		66	2	46
10	Lostock Hall		68	2	52
11	Lower Darwen		66	2	62
12	Plodder Lane		54	2	70
13	Preston		61	2	52
14	Southport		52	3	31
15	Southport	P	66	2	31
16	SPRINGS BRANCH	N		2	50
17	Wigan		64	2	50
18	Wigan Central		50	1	50

TUNNELS

No	Name / Location	Length	Ry	Ref
T1	Sough	2011	2	71
2	Deepdale No 1	162	2	52
3	Deepdale No 2	272	2	52
4	Deepdale No 3	384	2	52
5	Fishergate	140	X	52
6	Wilpshire	327	2	63
7	Blackburn	435	2	62

JUNCTIONS

No	Name / Locations	Ry	Ref
J1	Southport Roe Lane	2	31
2	Southport Meols Cop	2	31
3	Southport Ash Street	2	31
4	Southport Butt Lane	2	31
5	Southport New Line	2	31
6	Preston Strand Road	X	52
7	Preston Middleforth	2	52
8	Preston Whitehouse North	2	52
9	Preston Whitehouse South	2	52
10	Farington West	2	52
11	Moss Lane	2	52
12	Preston Ribble	2	52
13	Hillhouse	23	30
14	Euxton	2	52
15	Blackburn King Street	2	62
16	Newchurch Branch	24	71
17	Preston P+W Junction	2	52
18	Bushey Lane	2	40
19	Randle	2	40

NOTES:

REF All in SO therefore letters omitted

ALL stations in the area are included but those not named on the map shown in brown with map number (38) where full details are shown. Some other stations in the enlarged are are in abbreviated form.

§ Old Name } Change of name
§ New Name

Corresponding letters show alternative name

A Shown as Aspull on map

B Closed when trains diverted to a new station near to closed Knowsley Street. But station continues in use as preserved East Lancashire station.

C Changed after Lord Street closed.

D Regular services ended '62. Reopen for irregular services. Now (99) fully re-opened.

E Name change when 'Old' Fleetwood was closed.

F HARBOUR until 75 (rebuilt 70 nearby site). re-opened 87 as SEA TERMINAL. then became PORT from 92.

G Change of name.

H Operated as two back to back terminal stations.

J Change of name.

K Change of name Central dropped.

L Change of name: Thornton for Cleveleys became Thornton Cleveleys.

M Docks long abandoned. But the area has been developed as industrial estate. Railway (x) belonged to PRESTON CORPORATION and was approached by a short section of line owned LMS + PRESTON CORPORATION. Line was still in use at atlas terminal date.

N Closure dates are for steam. Of the sheds so marked Accrington continued as a diesel depot and Bury as electric depot, many others had short life as diesel depot after closure for steam. SPRINGS BRANCH still in use as at atlas terminal date

P Preserved Steam Depots currently in use.

R Sold 1987

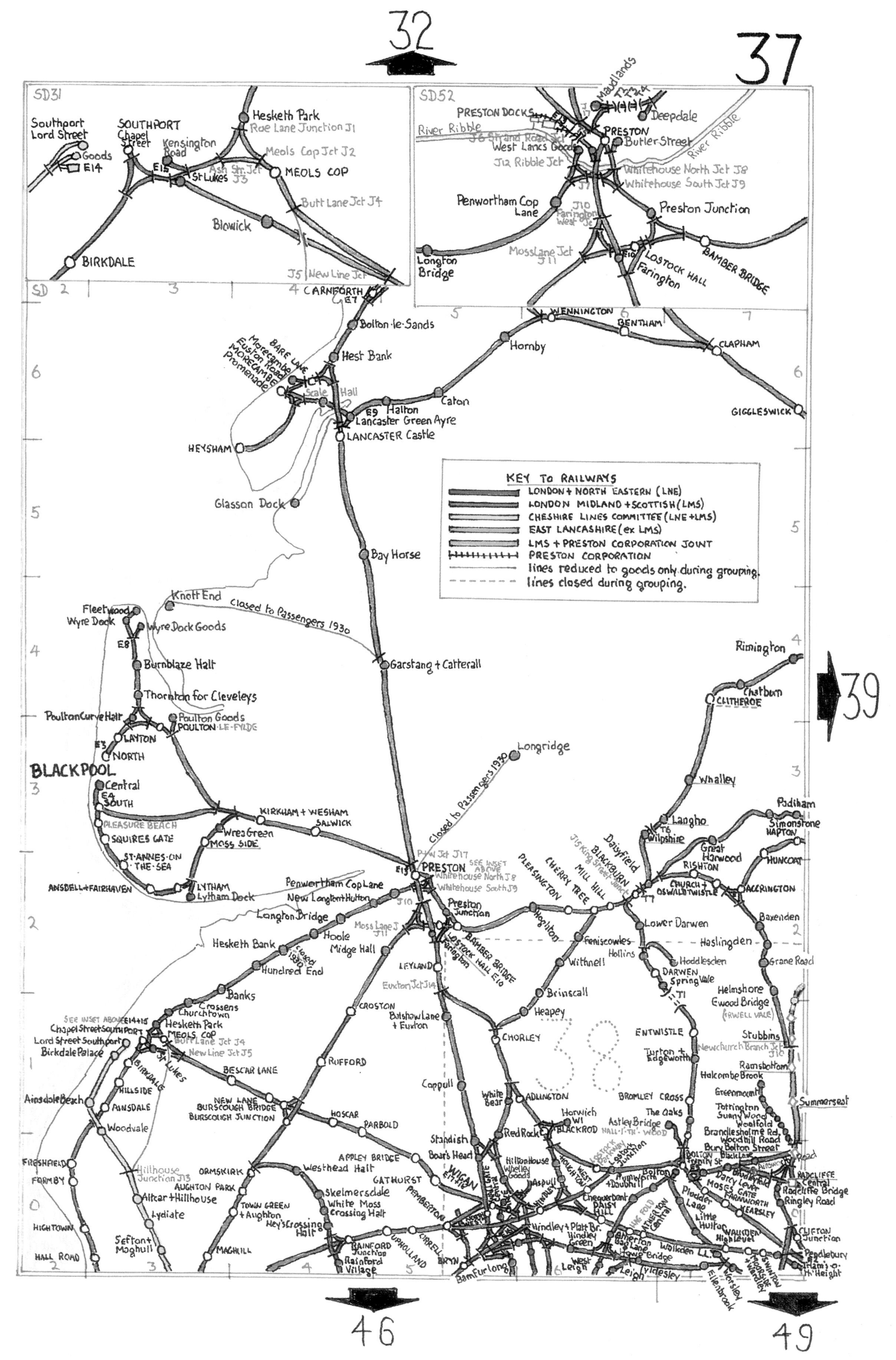
32
SD31
Southport Lord Street
Goods
E14
SOUTHPORT Chapel Street
Kensington Road
E15
St Lukes
Hesketh Park
Roe Lane Junction J1
Meols Cop Jct J2
Ash Str. Jct J3
MEOLS COP
Butt Lane Jct J4
Blowick
BIRKDALE
J5 New Line Jct
SD52
PRESTON DOCKS
Maudlands
Deepdale
River Ribble
J6 Strand Road Jct
PRESTON
Butler Street
West Lancs Goods
J12 Ribble Jct
Whitehouse North Jct J8
Whitehouse South Jct J9
J7
Penwortham Cop Lane
J10 Farington West Jct
Preston Junction
Moss Lane Jct J11
Longton Bridge
LOSTOCK HALL
Farington
BAMBER BRIDGE
CARNFORTH
E7
Bolton-le-Sands
Hest Bank
WENNINGTON
BENTHAM
CLAPHAM
Hornby
BARE LANE
Morecambe Euston Road
MORECAMBE Promenade
Scale Hall
Caton
GIGGLESWICK
E9
Halton
Lancaster Green Ayre
LANCASTER Castle
HEYSHAM
KEY TO RAILWAYS
LONDON + NORTH EASTERN (LNE)
LONDON MIDLAND + SCOTTISH (LMS)
CHESHIRE LINES COMMITTEE (LNE+LMS)
EAST LANCASHIRE (ex LMS)
LMS + PRESTON CORPORATION JOINT
PRESTON CORPORATION
lines reduced to goods only during grouping.
lines closed during grouping.
Glasson Dock
Bay Horse
Knott End
Closed to Passengers 1930
Fleetwood
Wyre Dock
Wyre Dock Goods
E8
Burn Naze Halt
Thornton for Cleveleys
Garstang + Catterall
Rimington
Chatburn
CLITHEROE
39
Poulton Curve Halt
Poulton Goods
POULTON-LE-FYLDE
LAYTON
E3
NORTH
BLACKPOOL
Central
E4
SOUTH
Longridge
Closed to Passengers 1930
Whalley
KIRKHAM + WESHAM
SALWICK
PLEASURE BEACH
Wrea Green
MOSS SIDE
SQUIRES GATE
ST. ANNES-ON-THE-SEA
Langho
Padiham
Simonstone
Wilpshire
Great Harwood
RISHTON
HUNCOAT
ACCRINGTON
CHURCH + OSWALDTWISTLE
Daisyfield
BLACKBURN
J15 King Street Junct
MILL HILL
CHERRY TREE
PLEASINGTON
Hoghton
PRESTON
E13
SEE INSET ABOVE
Whitehouse North J8
Whitehouse South J9
ANSDELL + FAIRHAVEN
LYTHAM
Lytham Dock
Penwortham Cop Lane
New Longton + Hutton
Longton Bridge
J10
Preston Junction
Moss Lane J J11
LOSTOCK HALL E10
BAMBER BRIDGE
Farington
Lower Darwen
Baxenden
Feniscowles
Haslingden
Hollins
Hoddlesden
Hesketh Bank
Hoole
Midge Hall
Closed 1930
Hundred End
LEYLAND
Withnell
DARWEN
Spring Vale
T1
Grane Road
Banks
Crossens
Churchtown
Euxton Jct J14
CROSTON
Brinscall
Heapey
Helmshore
Ewood Bridge
(IRWELL VALE)
SEE INSET ABOVE E14+15
Chapel Street Southport
Lord Street Southport
Birkdale Palace
Hesketh Park
MEOLS COP
Butt Lane Jct J4
New Line Jct J5
St Lukes
Bulshaw Lane + Euxton
CHORLEY
38
ENTWISTLE
Stubbins
Newchurch Branch Jct J16
Turton + Edgeworth
Ramsbottom
BIRKDALE
BESCAR LANE
RUFFORD
HILLSIDE
Ainsdale Beach
AINSDALE
NEW LANE
BURSCOUGH BRIDGE
BURSCOUGH JUNCTION
Coppull
White Bear
ADLINGTON
BROMLEY CROSS
Holcombe Brook
Summerseat
The Oaks
Woodvale
HOSCAR
PARBOLD
Horwich
Astley Bridge
Standish
Boar's Head
Red Rock
BLACKROD
Hilton House
APPLEY BRIDGE
Westhead Halt
FRESHFIELD
FORMBY
Hillhouse Junction J13
ORMSKIRK
AUGHTON PARK
GATHURST
WIGAN
Aspull
Chequerbent
DAISY HILL
Altcar + Hillhouse
Lydiate
Skelmersdale
White Moss Crossing Halt
TOWN GREEN + Aughton
Hey's Crossing Halt
PEMBERTON
BOLTON
Bolton
Moses Gate
Farnworth
Kearsley
Radcliffe Central
Radcliffe Bridge
Ringley Road
Bury Bolton Street
Tottington
Woolfold
HIGHTOWN
Sefton + Maghull
MAGHULL
RAINFORD Junction
Rainford Village
UPHOLLAND
ORRELL
BRYN
Bamfurlong
Hindley + Platt Br.
Hindley Green
Atherton Central
Bag Lane
Howe Bridge
Leigh
West Leigh
Tyldesley
Walkden Low Level
Walkden High Level
Little Hulton
Plodder Lane
Ellenbrook
Worsley
Clifton Junction
Pendlebury
HALL ROAD
46
49

BOLTON, BURY + WIGAN

RAILWAYS

No	Company
1	LONDON + NORTH EASTERN (LNE)
2	LONDON MIDLAND + SCOTTISH (LMS)
3	EAST LANCASHIRE (ex LMS)
4	GREATER MANCHESTER LIGHT RAPID TRANSPORT (ex LMS)

STATIONS

Name	Opened Closed	Ry	Ref
ADDLINGTON	H	2	51
Ainsworth Road	53	2	70
Aspull, Dicconson Lane +	54	2	60
ATHERTON Central	54	2	60
Atherton Bag Lane	54	2	60
Balshaw Lane + Euxton	* 69	2	51
Bamfurlong	50	2	50
BESSES-O'-TH'-BARN	G	4	80
Bickershaw + Abram	* 50	2	60
Black Lane, Radcliffe	70	2	70
BLACKROD	*	2	61
Boar's Head	49	2	50
Bolton, Great Moor Street	54	2	70
BOLTON Trinity Street	54	2	70
Bradley Fold	70	2	70
Brandlesholme Road Halt	52	2	71
Brinscall	60	2	62
BROMLEY CROSS		2	71
BRYN		2	50
(BURY)	G 80	4	81
Bury Bolton Street	* 71 80 87	3	71
Bury Knowsley Street	70	2	81
BURY SOUTH	A	4	71
Chequerbent	52	2	60
CHORLEY		2	51
CLIFTON Junction		2	70
Coppull	* 69	2	51
DAISY HILL		2	60
Darcy Lever	51	2	70
DARWEN		2	62
Dicconson Lane + Aspull Halt	54	2	60
Ellenbrook	61	2	70
ENTWISTLE	*	2	71
Ewood Bridge + Edenfield	* 72	2	72
FARNWOOD + Halshaw Moor	B 74	2	70
Great Moor Street, Bolton	54	2	70
Greenmount	52	2	71
HAG FOLD	87	2	60
HALL-I'-TH'-WOOD	86	2	71
Haslingden	60	2	72
Heapey	60	2	62
Helmshore	* 66	2	72
Hilton House Halt	54	2	60
Hindley + Platt Bridge South	D * 52 64	2	60
Hindley Green	61	2	60
HINDLEY North	C 50 78	2	60
Holcombe Brook	52	2	71
Horwich	* 65	2	61
Howe Bridge	59	2	60
INCE		2	50
Irlams-o'-th'-Height	56	2	70
(IRWELL VALE)	87	3	71
KEARSLEY		2	70
Leigh	* 69	2	60
Little Hulton	54	2	70
Lostock Junction	* J 66	2	60
LOSTOCK PARKWAY	J 88	2	60
Lower Ince	* 64	1	50
MOORSIDE + Wardley	74	2	70
MOSES GATE		2	70
Oaks, The	50	2	71
PEMBERTON	*	2	50
Pendlebury	60	2	70
Platt Bridge	61	2	50
Plodder Lane	54	2	70
PRESTWICH	G	4	80
RADCLIFFE			70
Black Lane	70	2	70
Bridge	59	2	70
Central	* E § 71	2	70
RADCLIFFE	G E § 71	4	70
Ramsbottom	* 72 87	3	71
Rawtenstall	* 72 87	3	82
Red Rock	49	2	51
Ringley Road	53	2	70
Rumworth + Daubhill	52	2	70
Spring Vale	58	2	62
Standish	49	2	51
Stubbins	* 71 87	2	71
Summerseat	* 72 87	2	71
Sunny Wood Halt	52	2	70
SWINTON		2	70
The Oaks	50	2	71
Tottington	52	2	71
Trinity Street BOLTON	54	2	70
Turton + Edgworth	61	2	71
Tyldesley	* 69	2	60
WALKDEN High Level	55	2	70
Walkden Low Level	54	2	70
WESTHOUGHTON		2	60
West Leigh	54	2	60
White Bear	60	2	51
WHITEFIELD	G	2	80
WIGAN			50
Central	* 64	1	50
NORTH WESTERN		2	50
WALLGATE		2	50
Withnell	60	2	62
Worsley	* 69	2	70

GOODS

No	Name/Location	Closed	Ry	Ref
G1	Atherton Bag Lane	63	2	60
2	Bolton Astley Bridge	61	2	71
3	Bolton Craddock Lane	64	2	70
4	Bolton Crook Street	65	2	70
5	Chorley Friday Street	75	2	51
6	Coppull	65	2	51
7	Grane Road	64	2	72
8	Hindley + Amberswood	55	2	60
9	Hindley + Platt Bridge	D 54	1	60
10	Hoddlesden	50	2	72
11	Leigh	67	2	60
12	Little Hulton Mineral	?	2	70
13	Rumworth	65	2	60
14	Springs Branch	?	2	60
15	Stonehill	?	2	70
16	Westhoughton	64	2	60
17	Whelley	?	2	50
18	Wigan Central	65	1	60
19	Wigan North Western	?	2	50

ENGINE SHEDS

No	Name/Location	Closed	Ry	Ref
E1	Agecroft	66	2	70
2	Bolton	68	2	70
3	Bury	F 65	2	70
4	Plodder Lane	54	2	70
5	SPRINGS BRANCH	C	2	50
6	Wigan	64	2	50
7	Wigan Central	50	1	50

TUNNELS

No	Name/Location	Length	Ry	Ref
T1	Saugh	2011	2	72
2	Nutball	c100	3	71
3	Brooksbottom	c420	3	71
4	Whitfield	161	4	70
5	Bradshawgate	88	2	70
6	Pendlebury	201	2	70
7	Chorley	124	2	51
8	Farnworth	295	2	70
9	Bury	80	3	71

BRIDGES + VIADUCTS

No	Name/Location	Ry	Ref
V1	Brooksbottom Viaduct	3	71
2	Bradshaw Brook Viaduct	2	71
3	Huyton Viaduct	2	51
4	Yarrow Viaduct	2	51

JUNCTIONS

No	Name	Ry	Ref
J1	Haigh	2	50
2	Whelley	2	50
3	Roundhouse Branch	2	50
4	Kirkless	2	50
5	de Trafford	2	60
6	Amberswood East	12	60
7	Amberswood West	12	60
8	Strangeways East	12	60
9	Bickershaw West	2	60
10	Bickershaw Central	2	60
11	Bickershaw East	2	60
12	Bickershaw South	2	60
13	Springs Branch	2	50
14	St Helens Line	2	50
15	Ince Moss	2	50
16	Park Lane	2	50
17	Crow Nest	2	50
18	Red Moss	2	61
19	Dobbs Brow	2	60
20	Astley Bridge	23	50
21	Newchurch Branch	23	71
22	Brindle Heath	2	70
23	Chowbent West	2	60
24	Chowbent East	2	60
25	Goose Green	2	50

NOTES:

REF All the map is within SD so the letters are omitted from the reference.
§ Name change - old name
§ Name change - new name
Identical letter indicates alternative
A Proposed New Station
B + Halshaw Moor portion of name is not shown on the map. It was dropped from the title in 74.
C North added in 50, dropped in 78
D + Platt Bridge substituted by South in 52 and continued with this title until the station was closed.
E Name change (Central dropped from title).
F Closure dates are for steam. But the Bury shed was replaced by a depot for electric units and this remains in use. SPRINGS BRANCH is also still in use.
G These stations all closed in August '91, before re-opening in April '92 as part of GREATER MANCHESTER LIGHT RAPID TRANSPORT.
J Re-opened with change of name. Lostock Junction closed 66, LOSTOCK PARKWAY re-opened 88 with change of name, but identical site.

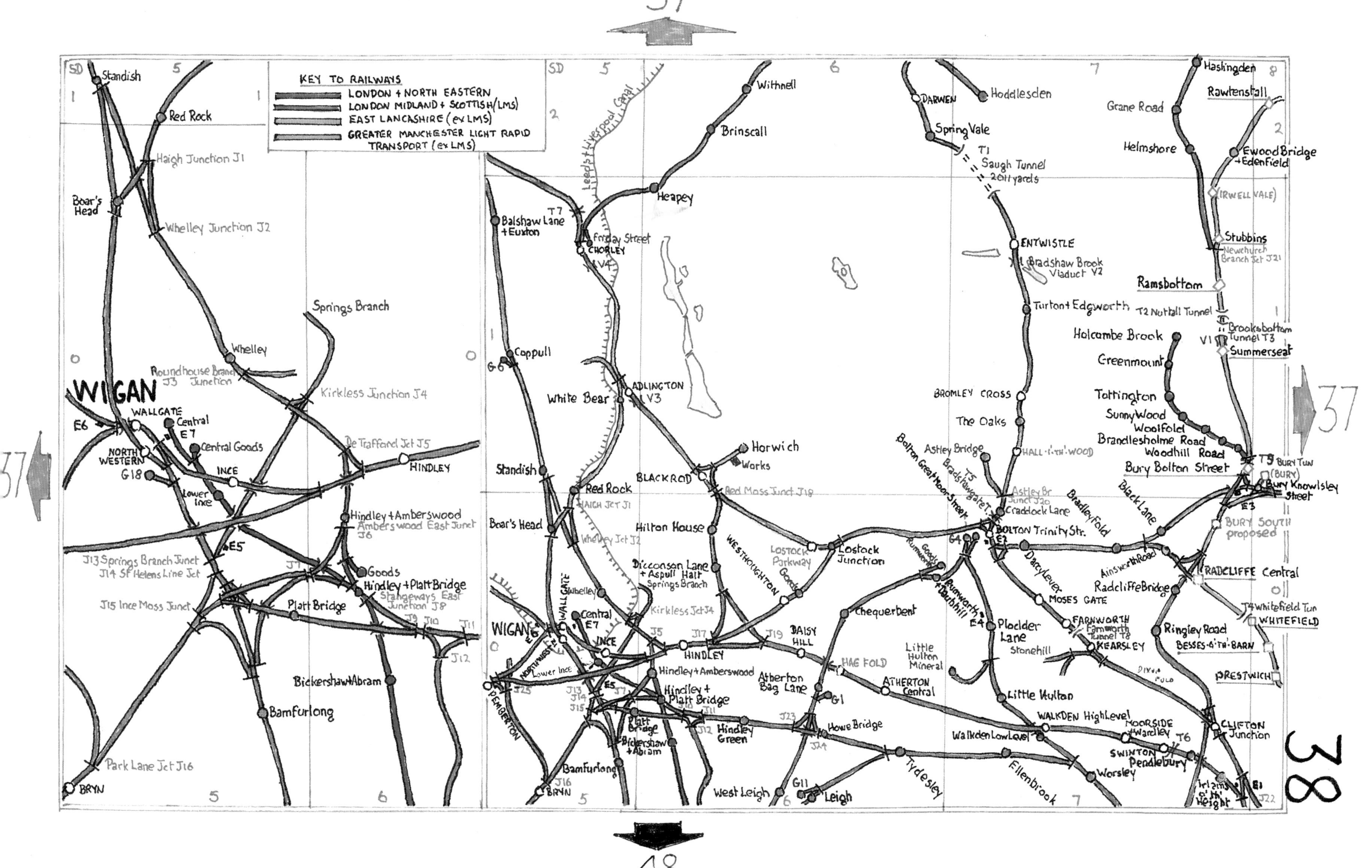

KEY TO RAILWAYS
LONDON + NORTH EASTERN
LONDON MIDLAND + SCOTTISH (LMS)
EAST LANCASHIRE (ex LMS)
GREATER MANCHESTER LIGHT RAPID TRANSPORT (ex LMS)
37
48
WIGAN
Standish
Red Rock
Haigh Junction J1
Boar's Head
Whelley Junction J2
Whelley
Roundhouse Branch Junction J3
Kirkless Junction J4
Springs Branch
WALLGATE
Central E7
Central Goods
NORTH WESTERN
G18
E6
INCE
Lower Ince
De Trafford Jct J5
HINDLEY
Hindley + Amberswood
Amberswood East Junct J6
E5
Goods
Hindley + Platt Bridge
Strangeways East Junction J8
J13 Springs Branch Junct
J14 St Helens Line Jct
J15 Ince Moss Junct
Platt Bridge
Bickershaw + Abram
Bamfurlong
Park Lane Jct J16
BRYN
Leeds + Liverpool Canal
Withnell
Brinscall
Heapey
Balshaw Lane + Euxton
T7
Friday Street
CHORLEY
V4
Coppull
G6
ADLINGTON
V3
White Bear
Horwich
Works
BLACKROD
Red Moss Junct J18
Hilton House
Haigh Jct J1
Whelley Jct J2
Dicconson Lane + Aspull Halt
Springs Branch
Kirkless Jct J4
WESTHOUGHTON
LOSTOCK Parkway
Lostock Junction
Chequerbent
DAISY HILL
HAG FOLD
J17
J19
Atherton Bag Lane
G1
ATHERTON Central
Little Hulton Mineral
Howe Bridge
J23
J24
Hindley Green
Tydesley
West Leigh
G11
Leigh
Ellenbrook
PEMBERTON
J25
J16
DARWEN
Hoddlesden
Spring Vale
T1 Saugh Tunnel 2011 yards
ENTWISTLE
Bradshaw Brook Viaduct V2
Turton + Edgworth
BROMLEY CROSS
The Oaks
HALL-i-th'-WOOD
Astley Bridge
Astley Br Junct J20
Craddock Lane
Bolton Great Moor Street
T5 Bradshawgate T.
BOLTON Trinity Str.
E1
G4
Bradley Fold
Black Lane
Darcy Lever
MOSES GATE
FARNWORTH
Farnworth Tunnel T8
KEARSLEY
Stonehill
Plodder Lane
E4
Rumworth + Daubhill
Little Hulton
WALKDEN High Level
Walkden Low Level
MOORSIDE + Wardley
T6
SWINTON
Pendlebury
Worsley
CLIFTON Junction
Irlams o' th' Height
E1
J22
Haslingden
Rawtenstall
Grane Road
Helmshore
Ewood Bridge + Edenfield
(IRWELL VALE)
Stubbins
Newchurch Branch Jct J21
Ramsbottom
T2 Nuttall Tunnel
Brooksbottom Tunnel T3
V1
Summerseat
Holcombe Brook
Greenmount
Tottington
Sunnywood
Woolfold
Brandlesholme Road
Woodhill Road
Bury Bolton Street
T9
BURY TUN
(BURY)
Bury Knowsley Street
E3
BURY SOUTH proposed
Ainsworth Road
Radcliffe Bridge
RADCLIFFE Central
T4 Whitefield Tun
WHITEFIELD
Ringley Road
BESSES-o'-TH'-BARN
PRESTWICH
DIXON FOLD

SKIPTON, LEEDS + OLDHAM

RAILWAYS

No	Company
1	LONDON+NORTH EASTERN (LNE)
2	LONDON MIDLAND+SCOTTISH (LMS)
	LNE + LMS JOINT LINES
A	HALIFAX+OVENDEN JOINT
B	HALIFAX HIGH LEVEL
C	Leeds Joint Lines
D	OTLEY+ILKLEY JOINT
E	OLDHAM ASHTON+GUIDE BRIDGE
	Preserved Lines (all ex LMS
F	KEIGHLEY+WORTH VALLEY
G	EMBSAY STEAM
H	EAST LANCASHIRE
5	GREATER MANCHESTER LIGHT RAPID TRANSPORT (exLMS)

STATIONS

Station	Note	Opened Closed	Ry	Ref
Addingham	*	65	2	05
Apperley Bridge+Rawdon		61 65	2	13
Armley+Wortley	A §	50	1	23
Armley Canal Road	*	50 65	2	23
Armley Moor	* A §	50 66	1	23
Arthington	*	65	1	24
BAILDON		53 73	2	14
Bacup	*	66	2	82
Barnoldswick	*	65	2	84
BARRACKS Burnley			2	83
Batley		64	1	22
BATLEY			2	22
Batley Carr		50	1	22
Batley, Upper	§			40
Battyeford		53	2	22
Beeston		55	1	23
Bell Busk		59	2	95
BEN RHYDDING	*		D	14
BERRY BROW	*	66 92	2	11
BESSES-O'-TH'-BARN	* C		5	80
BINGLEY			2	14
Birkenshaw+Tong		53	1	23
Birstall Town		51	2	22
Birstwith		51	1	25
Bolton Abbey	D *	65 97	2	05
BOWKER VALE	* C		5	80
Bowling Junction		51	2	13
BRADFORD				
Bowling Junction		51	2	13
Dudley Hill				13
Exchange	B §	83	12	13
FORSTER SQUARE			2	13
Great Horton		55	1	13
Horton Park		52	1	13
INTERCHANGE	B §	83	2	13
Laisterdyke		66	1	13
Manningham	*	65	2	13
St Dunstans		52	1	13
Bradley		50	2	12
BRAMLEY		66 83	1	23
BRIERFIELD			2	83
Brighouse (for Rastrick)		70	2	12
Broadfield		70	2	81
BROCKHOLES	*		2	11
BURLEY-IN-WHARFEDALE	*		D	14
BURLEY PARK		88	1	23
BURNLEY				
BARRACKS			2	83
CENTRAL			2	83
MANCHESTER ROAD		61 86	2	83
Bury Knowsley Street		70	2	81
BURY	E	80	C 5	81
Calverley+Rodley	*	65	2	23
CASTLETON			2	81
Clayton		55	1	13
Clayton West	*	83	2	21
Cleckheaton Central	*	61 65	2	12
Cleckheaton Spen	F	53	2	12
Clegg Street		59	E	90
Clough Fold	*	66	2	82
COLNE			2	84
CONONLEY	*	65 88	2	94
Cooper Bridge		50	2	12
COTTINGLEY	G	88	2	23
CROSSFLATTS		82	2	04
CRUMPSALL	* C		5	80
Cullingworth		55	1	03
Dacre		51	1	16
Damems		49 68	F	04
Darley		51	1	16
DEAN LANE (Newton Heath)			2	80
DEIGHTON		82	2	11
Delph		55	2	90
DENBY DALE+Cumberworth	*	61	2	20
DERKER	H	85		
Denholme			1	03
Dewsbury Central	§			40
DEWSBURY Wellington Road		69	2	22
Diggle	*	63	2	00
Dobcross		55	2	90
Drighlington+Adwalton		61 62	1	22
Dudley Hill		52	1	13
Dunford Bridge		70	1	10
Earby		70	2	94
Earlsheaton		53	2	22
Eastwood		51	2	92
Elland		62	2	12
Elslack		52	2	95
Embsay	*	65 81	G	05
FAILSWORTH			2	90
Farnley+Wortley		52	2	23
FORSTER SQUARE			2	13
Foulridge		59	2	84
FRIZINGHALL	*	65 87	2	13
GARGRAVE	*		2	95
GIGGLESWICK	*		2	86
Gildersome West		51 55	1	22
Gisburn		62	2	84
Glodwick Road Oldham		55	2	90
Golcar	*	68	2	01
Gomersal		53	2	22
Grasscroft		55	2	90
Great Horton		55	1	13
GREENFIELD	*		2	90
Greenside Pudsey	*	64	1	23
Greetland		62	2	02
Grotton+Springhead		55	2	90
GUISELEY	*		2	14
HALIFAX				
HALIFAX	J	61	2	02
North Bridge		55	A	02
Old	J §	51	2	02
Ovenden		55	A	02
Town	J §	51 61	2	02
Hampsthwaite		50	1	26
HAPTON			2	83
HARROGATE			1	25
Haworth		62 68	F	03
Hazlehead Bridge		50	1	10
HEADINGLEY			1	23
Healey House		49	2	11
HEATON PARK	* C		5	80
HEBDEN BRIDGE			2	92
Heckmondwike Central	*	61 65	2	22
Heckmondwike Spen				40
HELLIFIELD	*		2	85
Heywood		70	2	81
Hipperholme	K	53	2	12
Holbeck High Level		51 58	1	23
Holbeck Low Level		51 58	1	23
HOLLINWOOD			2	90
Holme		30	2	82
Holmfield		55	AB	02
Holmfirth		59	2	10
(HOLYWELL HALT)		?	G	05
HONLEY			2	11
Horbury+Ossett		62 70	2	20
HORSFORTH			1	24
Horton Park		52	1	13
Howden Clough		52	1	22
HUDDERSFIELD			2	11
ILKLEY	*		2D	14
Ingrow East		51 55	1	04
Ingrow West 51-61		62 68	F	04
KEIGHLEY			2F	04
Kildwick+Crosshills	*	65	2	04
Kirkstall	*	65	2	23
Laisterdyke		66	1	13
LEEDS				23
Armley+Wortley	A §	50	1	23
Armley Canal Road	*	50 65	2	23
Armley Moor	* A §	50 66	1	23
Beeston		55	1	23
BURLEY PARK		88	1	23
Central		67	12	23
City	L §	66	12	23
Farnley+Wortley		52	2	23
HEADINGLEY			1	23
Holbeck High Level		51 58	1	23
Holbeck Low Level		51 58	12	23
Kirkstall	*		2	23
LEEDS	L §	66	C	23
Lees		55	2	90
Lightcliffe	*	65	2	12
LITTLEBOROUGH			2	91
Liversedge Central	*	61 65	2	12
Liversedge Spen	§			40
LOCKWOOD	*		2	11
LONG PRESTON	*		2	85
Longwood+Milnsbridge	*	61 68	2	11
Low Moor	*	65	2	13
Luddendenfoot		62	2	02
MANCHESTER ROAD Burnley			2	83
Manningham	*	65	2	13
MARSDEN	*		2	01
Measurements Halt		55	2	90
Meltham		49	2	11
MENSTON	*		2	14
Middleton	*	64	2	80
Middleton Junction	*	66	2	80
MILES PLATTING	*		2	80
MILLS HILL		85	2	80
MILNROW			2	91
MIRFIELD			2	22
Moorgate		55	2	90
MORLEY Low		51 63	2	22
Morley Top		51 61	1	22
MOSSLEY	*		2	90
MOSTON			2	80
MUMPS, Oldham			1	90
MYTHOLMROYD			2	02
NELSON			2	83
Netherton		49	2	11
New Hall Bridge Halt		48	2	83
NEW HEY			2	91
Newlay+Horsforth	*	65 61	2	23
NEW PUDSEY		67	1	23
Newsholme		57	2	85
Newton Heath	*	66	2	80
Nidd Bridge		62	1	26
Northorpe Higher		53	2	22
Northorpe North Road	§			40
Oakworth		62 68	F	04
OLDHAM				
Central		66	2	90
Clegg Street		59	E	90
Glodwick Road		55	2	90
MUMPS			2	90
WERNETH			2	90
Ossett	*	64	1	22
Otley	*	65	2	14
Ovenden		55	A	02
Oxenhope		62 68	2	03
Padiham		57	2	73
PANNAL			1	25
Park Bridge		59	E	90
Pateley Bridge		51	1	16
PENISTONE			12	20
Pool-in-Wharfedale	*	65	1	24
Portsmouth		58	2	82
PRESTWICH	* C		5	80
PUDSEY				
Greenside	*	64	1	23
Lowtown	*	64	1	23
NEW		67	1	23
Queensbury		55	1	13
RAVENSTHORPE+Thornhill		60	2	22
Ravensthorpe Lower	§			40
Rawtenstall	*	72 87	14	82
Reedley Hallows Halt		56	2	83
Rimington		58	2	84
Ripley Valley		51	1	26
ROCHDALE			2	91
ROSE GROVE			2	83
Royton	*	66	2	90
Royton Junction	H	78 87	2	90
Saddleworth	*	68	2	90
St Dunstans		52	1	13
SALTAIRE	*	65 84	2	13
SETTLE	*		2	86
SHAW+Crompton	M §	74 89	2	91
SHAW+CROMPTON	M §	89	2	91
SHEPLEY+Shelley	*	61	2	11
SHIPLEY	N		2	13
SILKSTONE COMMON	Q	59 84 84	1	20
Skelmanthorpe	*	83	2	21
SKIPTON			2	95
SLAITHWAITE	*	68 82	2	01
SMITHY BRIDGE		60 85	2	91
SOWERBY BRIDGE			2	02
Stacksteads	*	66	2	82
Staincliffe+Batley Carr		52	2	22
Stanningley for Farsley		61 68	1	23
Stansfield Hall	P	49	2	92
STEETON+SILSDEN	*	65 90	2	04
STOCKSMOOR	*		2	11
Thongs Bridge		59	2	11
Thornhill	§			40
Thornton		55	1	03
Thornton-in-Craven	*	70	2	94
Tingley		54	1	22
TODMORDEN			2	92
Towneley		52	2	83
Upper Batley	§			40
WALSDEN		61 90	2	92
Waterfoot	* R	66	2	82
WEETON			1	24
WERNETH, Oldham			2	90
WHITEFIELD	* C		5	80
Wilsden		55	1	03
Woodhead		64	1	10
WOODLANDS ROAD	* C		5	80
Wormald Green		62	1	26
Wyke+Norwood Green		53	2	12

GOODS

No	Name/Location	Closed	Ry	Ref
G1	Birstall	62	2	22
2	Bradford Adolphus Str	72	1	13
3	Brindle Heath	65	2	80
4	Dewsbury (exMid)	50	2	22
5	Friezland	65	2	90
6	Grassington+Threshfield	69	2	06
7	Halifax St Pauls	60	B	02
8	HEALEY MILLS	O	2	22
9	Heap Bridge	67	2	81
10	Keighley GN	61	1	04
11	Kirkburton	65	2	11
12	Linthwaite	58	2	01
13	Oldham Clegg Str	68	12	90
14	Micklehurst	62	2	90
15	Newtown Huddersfield	68	2	11
16	Rishworth	53	2	02
17	Shipley GN	68	1	13
18	Strainland+Holywell G	59	2	02
19	Staley+Millbrook	64	2	90
20	Yeadon	S 64	2	24

ENGINE SHEDS

No	Name/Location	Closed	Ry	Ref
E1	Agecroft	66	2	80
2	Bacup	54	2	82
3	Bowling Junction	T 61	1	13
	(Hammerton Street)			13
4	Hellifield	63	2	85
5	Huddersfield	67	2	11
6	Ilkley	59	D	14
7	Ingrow	55	1	04
8	Keighley	62	2	04
	LEEDS			
9	NEVILLE HILL	O	1	33
10	Copley Hill	64	1	23
11	Farnley Junction	66	2	23
12	Holbeck	67	2	23
13	Lees	64	2	90
14	Low Moor	67	2	13
15	Manningham	67	2	13
16	Mirfield	67	2	22
17	Newton Heath	68	2	80
18	Pateley Bridge	51	1	16
18A	Rose Grove	68	2	83
19	Skipton	67	2	95
20	Sowerby Bridge	64	2	02

TUNNELS

No	Name/Location	Length	Ry	Ref
T1	Gisburn	156	2	85
2	Thrutch No.1	592	2	82
3	Thrutch No.2	290	2	82
4	Bacup	114	2	82
5	Towneley	389	2	83
6	Holme	265	2	82
7	Hall Royd Tun.	274	2	92
8	Castle Hill	194	2	92
9	Horsfall	274	2	92
10	Summit	2795	2	01
11	Ingrow	150	F	04
12	Mytholmes	75	F	04
13	Lees Moor	1553	1	04
14	Weasel Hall	109	2	92
15	Sowerby Bridge	657	2	02
16	Ripponden	593	2	02
17	Haw Bank	218	2	05
18	Doe Park	140	1	03
19	Hamer's Hill	153	1	03
20	Wellhead	622	1	0
21	Queensbury	2501	1	0
22	Wheatley	800	B	0
23	Beacon Hill	1105	2	1
24	Meltham		2	1
25	Bramhope	3761	1	2
26	Woodhead	5302	1	1
27	Lydgate	1332	2	9
28	Scout	202	2	9
29	Werneth	471	2	9
30	Central (Oldham)	499	2	9
31	Butterhouse	329	2	0
32	Clayton	1057	1	1
33	Morley	3369	2	2
34	Gildersome	2331	2	2
35	Thackley	1496	2	1
36	Winterbutlee	306	2	9
37	Bingley	151	2	1
38	Esholt	548	2	1
39	Bowling	1648	2	1
40	Wyke	1365	2	1
41	Stanedge	5344	2	0

JUNCTIONS

No	Name/Location	Ry	Re
J1	Nidd	1	2
2	Bilton Road	1	2
3	Dragon	1	2
4	Milnerwood	2D	1
5	Worth Valley	2E	0
6	Cutlers	1	1
7	Gannow	2	8
8	Whiteplatts	2	9
9	Hall Royd	2	9
10	Dryclough	2	0
11	Delph Branch	2	9

NOTES

REF Map in SD or SE but due t space shortage and number only providing a unique re letters not used.

§ Old name } Change of name
§ New name

A Name change.

B Name change, present station on adjoining site.

C Closed Aug 1991 and reopene April 1992 on conversion t GMLRT

D Due to extend to this station (re-opened 1998).

E Re-opened on new site and new line then converted t GMLRT

F Excursion traffic continued after closure

G Near to closed Churwell (closed pre-nationalisation)

H Opened 1/4 mile from Royton Junction (DERKER) and both stations opened at the perio 85-87 but although in the index of BR timetable both stations did not appear at the same time in the table

J Name changes: Old to 51, Town 51-61, thereafter just HALIFAX.

K Excursion traffic continued after closure.

L Name change

M Name change: Crompton dropped from title and the restored.

N At nationalisation there we no platforms on Bingley Leed side of triangle. But later all sides of triangle had platforms

Q Common added when station re-opend.

R For Newchurch had been dropped from title pre '48

S had occasional passenger service during annual holiday week.

T continued in use for some time as a diesel depot known as Hammerton Street

40 in map reference column as indication that location not named on map but full details are shown on the enlargement at page 40.

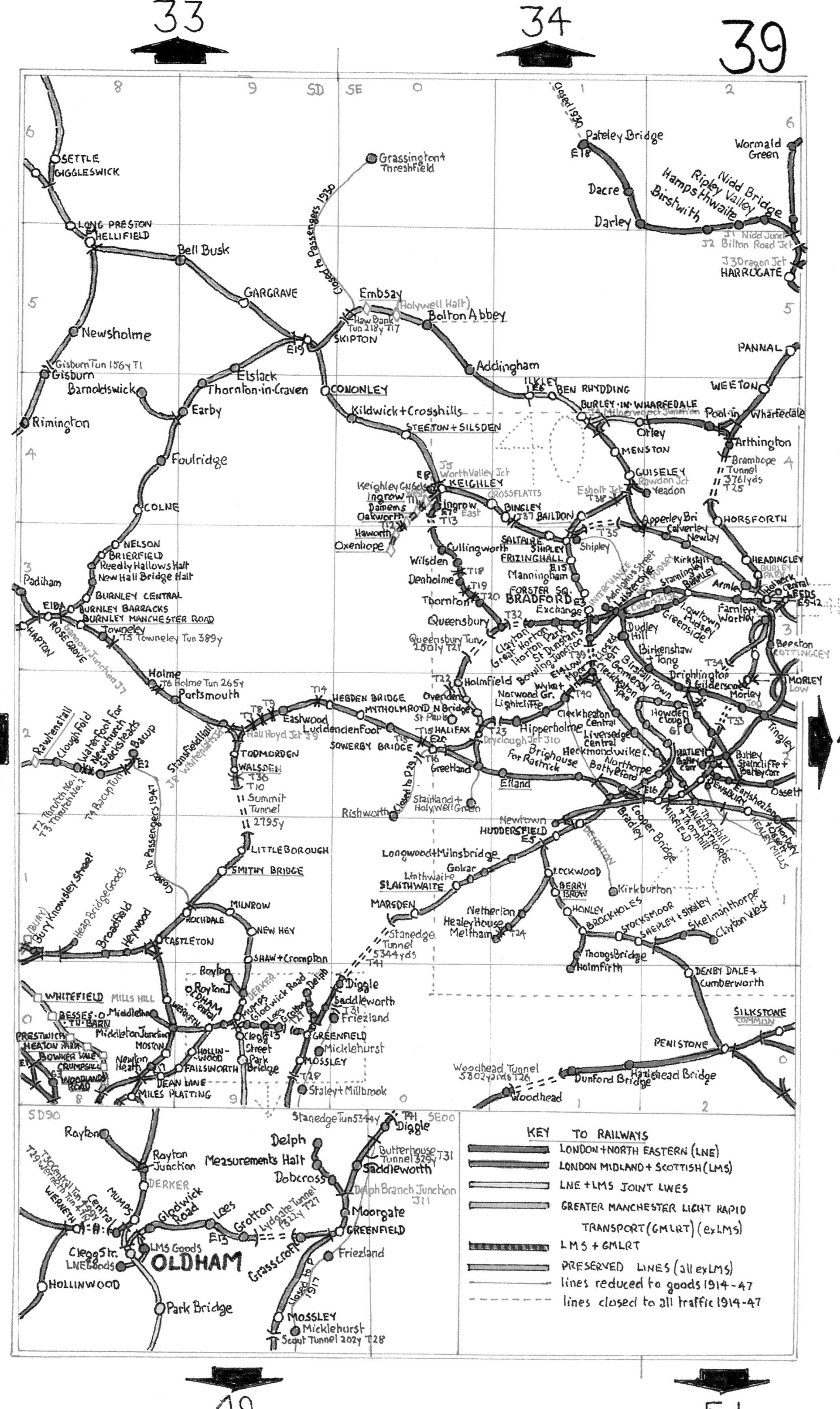
33
34
37
41
49
51
SETTLE
GIGGLESWICK
LONG PRESTON
HELLIFIELD
Bell Busk
GARGRAVE
Newsholme
Gisburn Tun 156y T1
Gisburn
Barnoldswick
Rimington
Elslack
Thornton-in-Craven
Earby
Foulridge
COLNE
NELSON
BRIERFIELD
Reedly Hallows Halt
New Hall Bridge Halt
BURNLEY CENTRAL
BURNLEY BARRACKS
BURNLEY MANCHESTER ROAD
Towneley
T5 Towneley Tun 389y
Padiham
HAPTON
ROSE GROVE
Gannow Junction J7
Holme
T6 Holme Tun 265y
Portsmouth
Grassington+ Threshfield
Closed to Passengers 1930
Embsay
Holywell Halt
Haw Bank Tun 218y T17
SKIPTON
E19
Bolton Abbey
Addingham
CONONLEY
Kildwick + Crosshills
STEETON + SILSDEN
J5 Worth Valley Jct
KEIGHLEY
Keighley GN Goods
Ingrow
Damems
Oakworth
Haworth
Oxenhope
Ingrow East
T13
CROSSFLATTS
BINGLEY
T37
BAILDON
SALTAIRE
SHIPLEY
FRIZINGHALL
E15
Shipley
Cullingworth
Wilsden
T18
Denholme
T19
Thornton
T20
Queensbury
T32
Queensbury Tun 2501y T21
Manningham
FORSTER SQ.
BRADFORD
Exchange
E3
ILKLEY
BEN RHYDDING
BURLEY-IN-WHARFEDALE
Milnerwood Junction
Otley
MENSTON
GUISELEY
Rawdon Jct
Yeadon
Esholt Jct
T38
Apperley Bri
Calverley
Newlay
T35
Kirkstall
Stanningley
Bramley
Armley
Holbeck
LEEDS Central
E9-12
Farnley + Wortley
Beeston
COTTINGLEY
MORLEY
Low
Morley
Tingley
Ossett
Pateley Bridge
Closed 1930
E18
Dacre
Darley
Birstwith
Hampsthwaite
Ripley Valley
Nidd Bridge
Wormald Green
J1 Nidd Junct
J2 Bilton Road Jct
J3 Dragon Jct
HARROGATE
PANNAL
WEETON
Pool-in-Wharfedale
Arthington
Bramhope Tunnel 3761yds T25
HORSFORTH
HEADINGLEY
BURLEY PARK
Dudley Hill
Birkenshaw + Tong
Drighlington + Adwalton
Gildersome
Laisterdyke
Pudsey
Greenside
Clayton
Great Horton
Horton Park
St Dunstans
Bowling Junction
T39
Holmfield
Ovenden
T22
North Bridge
St Pauls
HALIFAX
T15
E20
Dryclough Jct J10
T23
Norwood Gr.
Lightcliffe
Wyke
Low Moor
Hipperholme
Cleckheaton Central
Liversedge Central
Heckmondwike
Brighouse
for Rastrick
Northorpe
Battyeford
E16
Howden Clough
Batley Carr
BATLEY
Staincliffe + Batley Carr
DEWSBURY
Earlsheaton
Horbury
HEALEY MILLS
Mirfield
Ravensthorpe + Thornhill
Thornhill
Cooper Bridge
Bradley
Elland
Greetland
T16
Stainland + Holywell Green
Rishworth
Closed to P 1929
SOWERBY BRIDGE
Luddendenfoot
MYTHOLMROYD
HEBDEN BRIDGE
T14
Eastwood
T9
T8
Hall Royd Jct J9
Stansfield Hall
TODMORDEN
WALSDEN
T36
T10
Summit Tunnel 2795y
LITTLEBOROUGH
SMITHY BRIDGE
ROCHDALE
MILNROW
NEW HEY
SHAW + Crompton
CASTLETON
Heywood
Broadfield
Heap Bridge Goods
Bury Knowsley Street
BURY
Rawtenstall
Cloughfold
Waterfoot for Newchurch
Stacksteads
Bacup
E2
T2 Thrutch No.1
T3 Thrutch No.2
T4 Bacup Tun
Closed to Passengers 1947
Newtown
HUDDERSFIELD
E5
Longwood + Milnsbridge
Golcar
Linthwaite
SLAITHWAITE
MARSDEN
Standedge Tunnel 5344yds
T41
LOCKWOOD
BERRY BROW
HONLEY
BROCKHOLES
STOCKSMOOR
SHEPLEY + SHELLEY
Skelmanthorpe
Clayton West
Kirkburton
Netherton
Healey House
Meltham
T24
Thongs Bridge
Holmfirth
DENBY DALE + Cumberworth
SILKSTONE COMMON
PENISTONE
Woodhead Tunnel 5302yards T26
Dunford Bridge
Hazlehead Bridge
Woodhead
Royton
Royton Jct
DERKER
OLDHAM Central
MUMPS
Gladwick Road
Lees
Grotton
Delph
Diggle
Saddleworth
T31
Friezland
GREENFIELD
Micklehurst
MOSSLEY
T28
Staley + Millbrook
Clegg Street
Park Bridge
WHITEFIELD
MILLS HILL
BESSES-O-TH-BARN
PRESTWICH
HEATON PARK
BOWKER VALE
CRUMPSALL
WOODLANDS ROAD
Middleton
Middleton Junction
MOSTON
WERNETH
HOLLINWOOD
FAILSWORTH
Newton Heath
DEAN LANE
MILES PLATTING
SD90
SE00
Stanedge Tun 5344y T41
Butterhouse Tunnel 329y T31
Measurements Halt
Dobcross
Delph Branch Junction J11
Moorgate
Lydgate Tunnel 1332y T27
Grasscroft
Closed to P 1917
Scout Tunnel 202y T28
T30 Central Tun 429y
T29 Werneth Tun 471y
Clegg Str.
LNE Goods
LMS Goods
E13
OLDHAM
Park Bridge
KEY TO RAILWAYS
LONDON + NORTH EASTERN (LNE)
LONDON MIDLAND + SCOTTISH (LMS)
LNE + LMS JOINT LINES
GREATER MANCHESTER LIGHT RAPID TRANSPORT (GMLRT) (ex LMS)
LMS + GMLRT
PRESERVED LINES (all ex LMS)
lines reduced to goods 1914-47
lines closed to all traffic 1914-47

BRADFORD + HUDDERSFIELD

RAILWAYS

No. Company

1 LONDON + NORTH EASTERN (LNE)
2 LONDON MIDLAND + SCOTTISH (LMS)
3 LNE + LMS JOINT LINES
  A HALIFAX + OVENDEN JOINT
  B HALIFAX HIGH LEVEL
  C Leeds Joint Lines
  D OTLEY + ILKLEY JOINT
4 Preserved lines:
  F KEIGHLEY + WORTH VALLEY (ex LMS)

STATIONS

Station	Opened / Closed	Ry Ref
Apperley Bridge + Rawdon	* 61 65	2 13
Armley + Wortley	A § 50	1 23
Armley Canal Road	* 50 65	2 23
Armley Moor	* A § 50 66	1 23
Arthington	* 65	1 24
BAILDON	B 53 13	2 13
Batley	64	1 22
BATLEY		2 22
Batley Carr	50	1 22
Batley, Upper	52	1 22
Battyeford	53	2 11
Beeston	55	1 23
BERRY BROW	* 66 69	2 11
BINGLEY		2 13
Birkenshaw + Tong	53	1 22
Birstall Town	51	2 22
Bowling Junction	51	2 13
BRADFORD		
Bowling Junction	51	2 13
Dudley Hill	52	1 13
Exchange	C § 83	12 13
FORSTER SQUARE	L	2 13
Great Horton	55	1 13
Horton Park	52	1 13
INTERCHANGE	C § 83	12 13
Laisterdyke	66	1 13
Manningham	* 65	2 13
St Dunstan's	52	1 13
Bradley	50	2 11
BRAMLEY	66 83	1 23
BROCKHOLES	*	2 11
BURLEY-IN-WHARFEDALE	*	D 14
BURLEY PARK	88	1 13
Calverley + Rodley	65	2 23
Clayton	55	1 13
Clayton West	* 83	2 21
Cleckheaton Central	* 61 65	2 12
Cleckheaton Spen	D 53	12
Cooper Bridge	50	2 12
COTTINGLEY	88	2 22
Crigglestone West	* 61 65	2 21
CROSSFLATTS	82	2 13
Cullingworth	55	1 03
DEIGHTON	82	2 11
DENBY DALE + Cumberworth	61	2 20
Denholme	55	1 03
Dewsbury Central	* 64	1 22
DEWSBURY Wellington Road	69	2 22
Drighlington + Adwalton	62	1 22
Dudley Hill	52	1 13
Earlsheaton	53	2 22
Elland	62	2 12
Farnley + Wortley	52	2 23
FORSTER SQUARE		2 13
FRIZINGHALL	* 65 87	2 13
Gildersome West	51 55	1 22
Golcar	* 68	2 11
Gomersal	53	2 22
Great Horton	55	1 13
Greenside, Pudsey	* 64	1 23
Greetland	62	2 02
GUISELEY	*	2 14
Haigh	* 65	2 21
HALIFAX		02
HALIFAX	J 61	2 02
North Bridge	55	A 02
Old	J § 51	2 02
Ovenden	55	A 02
Town	J § 51 61	2 02
HEADINGLEY		1 23
Healey House	49	2 11
Heckmondwike Central	61 65	2 22
Heckmondwike Spen	53	2 22
Hipperholme	E 53	2 12
Holbeck High Level	51 58	2 23
Holbeck Low Level	51 58	C 23
Holmfield	55	A 02
Holmfirth	59	2 10
HONLEY	*	2 11
Horbury + Ossett	62 70	2 21
HORSFORTH		1 23
Horton Park	52	1 13
Howden Clough	52	1 22
HUDDERSFIELD		2 11
Ingrow East	51 55	1 03
KEIGHLEY		2 04
Kirkstall	* 65	2 23
Laisterdyke	66	1 13
LEEDS		23
Armley + Wortley	A § 50	1 23
Armley Canal Road	50 65	2 23
Armley Moor	* A § 50 66	1 23
Beeston	55	1 23
BURLEY PARK	88	1 23
Central	61	C 23
City	B § 66	C 23
Farnley + Wortley	52	2 23
HEADINGLEY		1 23
Holbeck High Level	51 58	2 23
Holbeck Low Level	51 58	C 23
Kirkstall	* 65	23
LEEDS	B § 66	23
Lightcliffe	* 65	2 12
Liversedge Central	* 61 65	2 22
Liversedge Spen	53	2 22
LOCKWOOD	*	2 11
Longwood + Milnsbridge	* 61 68	2 11
Low Moor	* 65	2 12
Manningham	* 65	2 13
Meltham	49	2 11
MENSTON	*	2 14
MIRFIELD		2 21
MORLEY Low	51 63	2 22
Morley Top	51 61	1 22
Netherton	49	2 11
Newlay + Horsforth	* 61 65	2 23
NEW PUDSEY	P 67	23
Northorpe Higher	53	2 22
Northorpe North Road	* 65	2 22
Ossett	* 64	1 21
Otley	* 65	D 14
Ovenden	55	A 02
Pool-in-Wharfedale	* 65	1 24
PUDSEY		23
Greenside	* 64	1 23
Lowtown	* 64	1 23
NEW	67	1 23
Queensbury	55	1 13
RAVENSTHORPE + Thornhill	60	2 21
Ravensthorpe Lower	51 52	2 22
St Dunstan's	52	1 13
SALTAIRE	* 65 84	2 13
SHEPLEY + Shelley	* 61	2 10
SHIPLEY	E	2 13
Skelmanthorpe	* 83	2 21
SLAITHWAITE	* 68 82	2 01
SOWERBY BRIDGE		2 02
Staincliffe + Batley Carr	52	2 22
Stanningley for Farsley	P 61 68	1 23
STOCKSMOOR	*	2 10
Thongs Bridge	59	2 10
Thornhill	62	2 21
Thornton	55	1 03
Tingley	54	1 22
Upper Batley	52	2 22
Wilsden	55	1 03
Wyke + Norwood Green	53	2 12

GOODS

No	Name/Location	Closed	Ry Ref
G1	Birstall	62	2 22
2	Bradford Adolphus Street	72	1 13
3	Bradford Bowling	64	1 13
4	Bradford City Road	72	1 13
5	Dewsbury GN	?	1 22
6	Dewsbury Midland	50	2 22
7	Dewsbury Market Place	61	2 22
8	Halifax St Pauls	60	B 02
9	Halifax Shaw Syke	?	2 02
10	Halifax South Parade	?	1 02
11	HEALEY MILLS	O	2 21
12	Heckmondwike	64	2 22
13	Huddersfield Hillhouse	70	2 11
14	Huddersfield Newtown	68	2 11
15	Keighley	61	1 04
16	Kirkburton	65	2 11
17	Kirkstall Forge	59	2 23
18	Leeds Cardigan Road	72	1 23
19	Linthwaite	58	2 01
20	Longwood	66	2 11
21	Shipley GN	68	1 13
22	Stainland + Holywell Green	59	2 01
23	Wheatley	60	B 02
24	Yeadon	G 64	2 24

ENGINE SHEDS

No	Name/Location	Closed	Ry Ref
E3	Bowling Junction (Hammerton Street)	H 61	1 13
5	Huddersfield	67	2 11
7	Ingrow	55	1 03
8	Keighley	62	2 04
	LEEDS		
9	NEVILLE HILL	K	1 33
10	Copley Hill	64	1 23
11	Farnley Junction	66	2 23
12	Holbeck	67	2 23
14	Low Moor	67	2 12
15	Manningham	67	2 13
16	Mirfield	67	2 21
20	Sowerby Bridge	64	2 02

TUNNELS R

No	Name/Location	length	Ry Ref
T1	Otley		1 24
2	Bingley	151	2 13
3	Shipley	55	2 13
4	Baildon No.1	156	2 13
5	Baildon No.2	274	2 13
6	Esholt	548	2 14
7	Springs	77	2 13
8	Apperley Lane	75	2 13
9	Thackley	1496	2 13
10	Headingley	70	1 23
11	Clayton	1057	1 13
12	Manchester Road	312	1 13
13	Lees Moor	1533	1 03
14	Banker Sidings		1 13
15	Wakefield Road	132	1 13
16	Ripponden	593	2 02
17	Doe Park	140	1 03
18	Hillfoot or Stanningley	455	1 23
19	Hamers Hill	53	1 03
20	Wellhead	622	1 03
21	Queensbury	2501	1 02
22	Wheatley	800	B 02
23	Greenside	616	1 23
24	Bowling	1648	2 12
25	Bramhope	3761	1 24
26	Bank House	214	2 02
27	Salterhebble	91	2 02
28	Beacon Hill	1105	2 12
29	Hipperholme	388	2 12
30	Wyke	1365	2 12
31	Low Moor		2 12
32	Elland	420	2 12
33	Huddersfield	695	2 11
34	Gledholt	243	2 11
35	Lockwood	205	2 11
36	Robin Hood	228	2 11
37	Thurstonland	1631	2 11
38	Shelley Woodhouse	511	2 20
39	Cumberworth	906	2 20
40	Woolley	1745	2 21
41	Gomersal	819	2 22
42	Gildersome	2331	2 22
43	Morley	3369	2 22
44	Ardsley	297	1 22
45	Greenbottom	134	2 14
46	Lightcliffe	70	2 12

BRIDGES + VIADUCTS

No	Name / Location	Ry	Ref
V1	Hewenden Viaduct	1	03
2	Thornton Viaduct	1	03
3	Charlestown Viaduct	2	13
4	Bolton Hall Viaduct	2	12
5	Apperley Viaduct	2	13
6	Tong Park Viaduct	2	13
7	Esholt Viaduct	2	13
8	Stanningley Viaduct	1	23

JUNCTIONS

No	Name / Location	Ry	Ref
1	Milnerwood	2D	14
2	Worth Valley	2F	04
3	Esholt	2	14
4	Rawdon	2	14
5	Guiseley	2	13
6	Apperley	2	23
7	Hammerton Street	1	13
8	Laisterdyke West	1	13
9	Quarry Gap	1	13
10	Cutlers	1	13
11	Tyersal	1	13
12	Wortley West	1	23
13	Wortley South	1	23
14	Wortley East	1	23
15	Broad Lane	1	13
16	Halifax High Level (Line)	AB	02
17	Milneroyd	2	02
18	Dryclough	2	02
19	Bradley Wood	2	12
20	Heaton Lodge	2	11
21	Springwood	2	11
22	Holmfirth Branch	2	11
23	Dewsbury	2	21
24	Middlestown	2	21
25	Runtlings	1	21

NOTES:

REF All map in SE so numbers alone used in the Reference

§ Old name } Name Change
§ Later name

A Name change

B Station was opened for the summer months of 1957

C Name change. New station was on an adjoining site

D Excursion traffic continued after closure

E Some excursion traffic after '53.

F In 1947 platforms on Bradford lines only. Subsequently platforms on all sides of the triangle.

G Used for passenger trains on local annual holiday week into the 50's

H Closure date shown is for steam continued in use as a diesel depot for some time

J Name changes:
Old to 51
from 51 Town to 61
from 61 No addition ie HALIFAX

K Still in use

P Stanningley was replaced by NEW PUDSEY opened by Beeching !!

B Name change. From 66 station became just LEEDS.

R Some additional Tunnels not in the gazetteer are included on the map.

39

KEY TO RAILWAYS

- LONDON + NORTH EASTERN (LNE)
- LONDON MIDLAND + SCOTTISH (LMS)
- LNE + LMS JOINT LINES
- KEIGHLEY + WORTH VALLEY (ex LMS)

SE 0 1 2

BURLEY-IN-WHARFEDALE
Milnerwood Jct J1
Otley
Otley Tunnel T1
Pool-in-Wharfedale
Arthington
Bramhope Tunnel 3761 yards T25
MENSTON
GUISELEY
Greenbottom Tunnel T45 134 yards
Rawdon Jct J4
Esholt Jct J3
Esholt Tunnel 548y J6
Yeadon
Springs Tun 77y T7
Baildon No.2 Tun 274y T5
V6
V7
BAILDON
Baildon No.1 156y T4
Worth Valley Junction J2
E8
KEIGHLEY
Goods
E7
Ingrow East
CROSSFLATTS
BINGLEY
Bingley Tunnel 151y T2
Charlestown Viaduct V3
Guiseley Junction J5
Thackley Tunnel 1496y T9
Closed to Pass. 32
Apperley Lane Tun 75y T8
Apperley Bridge + Rawdon
Apperley Junction J6
HORSFORTH
Lees Moor Tunnel 1553 yards T13
SALTAIRE
T3 Shipley Tun 55y
SHIPLEY
FRIZINGHALL
Calverley + Rodley
Newlay + Horsforth
Cullingworth
Hewenden Viaduct V1
Wilsden
Apperley Viaduct V5
Kirkstall Forge Goods
HEADINGLEY
Headingley Tunnel 70yds T10
Cardigan Road Goods
E9-12
Kirkstall
BURLEY PARK
LEEDS
Manningham
E15
BRADFORD
INTERCHANGE
Exchange
Adolphus Street
Hammerton Street T17
Wakefield Rd Tun 132y T15
Laisterdyke West Jct J8
Laisterdyke
Hillfoot or Stanningley Tunnel 435 yards T18
NEW PUDSEY
Stanningley Viaduct V8
Stanningley
BRAMLEY
Armley Canal Road
Holbeck
HL
LL
Central
LEEDS City
T17 Doe Park Tunnel 140y
Denholme
Hamers Hill Tunnel 53y T19
T20 Wellhead Tunnel 662y
Thornton
Thornton Viaduct V2
FORSTER SQUARE
City Road Goods
E3
Quarry Gap Jct J9
Cutlers Jct J10
Tyersal Jct J11
Lowtown Pudsey
Greenside
Greenside Tun 616y T23
Armley + Wortley
Wortley Jcts J12 J13 South
J14
Farnley + Wortley
Queensbury
Clayton Tunnel 1057 yards T11
Clayton
Great Horton
Horton Park
T12 Manchester Road Tun 312yds
Bankfoot Sidings Tun T16
St Dunstans
Bowling Goods
Broad Lane Jct J15
Dudley Hill
Beeston
COTTINGLEY
Queensbury Tunnel 2501y T21
Bowling Tunnel 1648y T24
Closed 1917
Bowling Junction
Tunnel
Birkenshaw + Tong
Gildersome Tunnel 2331y T42
Gildersome West
MORLEY Low
Morley Top
Ardsley Tunnel 297y T44
Holmfield
Halifax High Level Junction J16
Wheatley Tun 800y T22
to P 1917
Wheatley Goods
Ovenden
Lee Bank Tunnel 267yds
Beacon Hill Tunnel 1105y T28
Old Lane Tun 402y
North Bridge
St Pauls
South Parade
Shaw Syke
HALIFAX Old Town
E14
Low Moor
Low Moor Tunnel T31
Wyke Tunnel 1365y T30
Hipperholme
Lightcliffe
Wyke + Norwood Green
V4 Bolton Hall Viaduct
Lightcliffe Tun 70y T40
Hipperholme Tunnel 388y T29
Closed to P 31
Drighlington + Adwalton
Birstall Town
Howden Clough
Gomersal Tunnel 819y T41
Gomersal
Birstall
Upper Batley
Morley Tunnel 3369y T43
Tingley
Cleckheaton Spen
Cleckheaton Central
Liversedge Central
Liversedge Spen
Heckmondwike Spen
Heckmondwike Central
BATLEY
Batley
Goods
Batley Carr
Staincliffe + Batley Carr
Dewsbury Central
Market Place
DEWSBURY
Goods
Dewsbury GN Goods
Earlsheaton
Runtlings Lane J25
Ossett
E20
SOWERBY BRIDGE
Milner Royd Jct J17
Ripponden Tunnel 593y T16
Dryclough Junction J18
Salterhebble Tuns 91y T27
Bank House Tun 214 T26
Greetland
Elland Tun 420y T32
Elland
Closed to P 1929
Stainland + Holywell Green
Brighouse for Rastrick
Bradley Wood Jcts J19
Cooper Bridge
Northorpe Higher
Northorpe North Rd
J20
Bradley
Battyeford
MIRFIELD
Ravensthorpe
RAVENSTHORPE + Thornhill
Thornhill
Dewsbury Jct J23
Middlestown Jct J24
HEALEY MILLS
Horbury + Ossett
DEIGHTON
Newtown Goods
Hillhouse Goods
E5
HUDDERSFIELD
Huddersfield Tunnels 695y T33
Springwood Junction J21
Closed to Passengers 1930
Kirkburton
Gledholt Tun 243y T34
Longwood + Milnsbridge
Longwood Goods
Golcar
Linthwaite
SLAITHWAITE
Lockwood Tunnel 205y T35
LOCKWOOD
Tunnel
Tunnel
Netherton
BERRY BROW
Robin Hood Tun 228y T36
HONLEY
Healey House Tunnel
Meltham
BROCKHOLES
Holmfirth Branch Junction J22
Thurstonland Tun 1631y T37
Thong's Bridge
Holmfirth
STOCKSMOOR
SHEPLEY + Shelley
Skelmanthorpe
Shelley Woodhouse Tunnel 511y T38
Clayton West
Cumberworth Tunnel 906 yards T39
DENBY DALE + Cumberworth
Crigglestone West
Woolley Tunnel 1745y T40
Haigh

41
59
42

HARROGATE, YORK + DONCASTER

RAILWAYS

No Company
1 LONDON + NORTH EASTERN (LNE)
2 LONDON MIDLAND + SCOTTISH (LMS)
3 LNE + LMS Joint Lines
A AXHOLME
B METHLEY
C SOUTH YORKSHIRE
D SWINTON + KNOTTINGLEY
E others
4 EASINGWOLD (worked by LNE)
5 DERWENT VALLEY (Light)
6 BRITISH RAIL (new lines)

STATIONS

Opened Closed Ry Ref

Ackworth 59 D 41
ADWICK-le-Street, Carcroft + * 67 93 1 50
AGBRIGG SANDAL + 57 87 87 1 31
Airmyn + Rawcliffe * 61 64 1 62
Alne 58 1 56
Altofts + Whitwood * 70 90 2 32
Alverthorpe 54 1 32
Ardsley * 64 1 32
Arksey 52 1 50
Armley Canal Road * 50 65 2 E
Askern X 48 2 51
BAGHILL PONTEFRACT D 42
Balne 58 1 51
Bardsey * 64 1 34
Barlow * 64 1 62
Barnby Dun 67 1 60
Barnsley Court House 60 2 30
BARNSLEY Exchange 60 2 30
Beningbrough 58 1 55
BENTLEY 92 1 50
Birdwell + Hoyland Common 51 53 1 30
BOLTON-ON-DEARNE D 40
Bolton Percy * 65 1 54
Boroughbridge 50 1 36
Bowers Halt 51 1 42
Bubwith X 54 1 73
Burton Salmon 59 1 42
Carcroft + ADWICK-le-Street * 67 93 1 50
CASTLEFORD Central 69 1 42
Castleford Cutsyke * 52 68 2 42
CATTAL * 1 45
CHURCH FENTON 1 53
Cliff Common A 57 1 63
Collingham Bridge * 64 1 34
Copgrove 50 1 36
Copmanthorpe 59 1 54
Crigglestone West * 81 65 1 21
CROSS GATES 1 33
CROWLE Central 69 1 71
Cudworth * 68 2 30
Cutsyke Castleford * 52 68 2 42
Darfield * 63 2 40
DARTON 2 31
Denby Halt 49 2 40
DODWORTH 59 89 1 30
DONCASTER 1 50
Dovecliffe 53 1 30
Drax Hales * 61 64 1 62
Dunnington 79 5 65
Earswick * 65 1 65
Easingwold 48 4 56
EAST GARFORTH 87 1 43
Eastrington, North 55 1 73
EASTRINGTON, South * 61 1 72
ELSECAR + Hoyland 71 2 30
Escrick 53 1 64
Fangfoss 59 1 75
FEATHERSTONE B* 67 92 2 42
Ferrybridge for Knottingley 65 D 42
Finningley B 61 1 60
FITZWILLIAM * 67 82 1 60
Foggathorpe 57 1 73
Frickley 53 D 40
GARFORTH 1 43
Gascoigne Wood Junction 59 1 53
Goldsborough 58 1 35
GOLDTHORPE 88 D 40
Goldthorpe + Thurnscoe Halt 51 2 40
GOOLE Town 61 1 72
Great Houghton Halt 51 2 40
Grimethorpe Halt 51 2 30
Haigh * 65 2 21
Hambleton 59 1 53
HAMMERTON * 1 45
Hampole 52 1 41
Hare Park + Crofton 52 1 31
Harlington Halt 51 2 40
HARROGATE 1 35
HATFIELD + STAINFORTH C § 92 1 61
Heck 58 1 51
Hemingbrough * 61 1 63
Hemsworth * 67 1 41
HENSALL * 2 52
Hessay 58 1 55
High Field 54 1 73
Holbeck High Level 51 58 E E
Holbeck Low Level 51 58 E E
Holme Moor B 54 1 73
Horbury, Millfield Road 61 2 31
HORNBEAM PARK 92 1 35
HOWDEN North 61 1 72
Howden South 55 1 72
Hoyland, ELSECAR + 71 2 30
Hoyland Common, Birdwell + 51 53 1 30
Hunslet 60 2 33
Joan Croft Halt 52 1 51
Kippax 51 1 42
KIRK SANDALL 92 1 60
KNARESBOROUGH * 1 35
KNOTTINGLEY * 2 42
Layerthorpe, York 79 5 65
Ledston 51 1 42
LEEDS E
  Armley 65 2 E
  Central 67 E E
  City D § 66 E E
  Holbeck 51 58 E E
  Holbeck 51 58 E
  LEEDS D § 66 E E
  Marsh Lane 58 1 33
Lofthouse + OUTWOOD E 60 88 B 32
Marsh Lane 58 1 33
Marston Moor 58 1 55
Medge Hall 60 1 71
Menthorpe Gate 53 1 63
Methley North 50 57 2 32
Methley South 51 60 B 32
MICKLEFIELD 1 43
Millfield Road Horbury 61 2 31
Monk Fryston 59 1 42
MONKHILL PONTEFRACT 2 42
MOORTHORPE + South Kirkby 61 D 41
Moss 53 1 51
Nabum 53 1 54
Newton Kyme * 64 1 44
Nidd Bridge 62 1 36
NORMANTON 2 32
North Eastrington 55 1 73
North, HOWDEN 61 1 72
Norton F 48 2 51
Nostell 51 1 31
Osmondthorpe Halt 60 1 33
OUTWOOD, Lofthouse E 60 88 B 32
PANNAL 1 35
Pendas Way * 64 1 33
Pocklington * 65 1 74
PONTEFRACT 42
  BAGHILL D 42
  MONKHILL 2 42
  TANSHELF * 67 92 2 42
POPPLETON * 1 55
Raskelf 58 1 46
RAWCLIFFE * 2 62
Rawcliffe, Airmyn + 61 64 1 62
Riccall 58 1 63
Rowntree Halt 88 1 63
Royston + Notton * 68 2 31
Ryhill Halt 51 2 31
SALTMARSHE * 1 72
SANDAL + AGBRIGG 57 87 1 31
Sandal + Walton G § 51 2 31
Scholes * 64 1 33
SELBY 1 63
Sharlston 63 2 31
SHERBURN-IN-ELMET * 65 84 1 53
SNAITH * 2 62
South EASTRINGTON * 61 1 72
SOUTH ELMSALL * 1 41
South Howden 55 1 72
South Kirkby, MOORTHORPE + 61 D 41
SOUTH MILFORD 1 43
Spofforth * 64 1 35
STAINFORTH + HATFIELD C § 92 1 61
Stairfoot for Ardsley 57 1 30
Stamford Bridge * 65 1 75
Stanley * 64 B 32
STARBECK * 1 35
STREETHOUSE 92 2 32
Summer Lane 59 1 30
Tadcaster * 64 1 44
TANSHELF PONTEFRACT * 67 92 2 42
Temple Hirst 61 1 52
THORNE NORTH 1 61
Thorner * 64 1 34
THORNE SOUTH 1 61
Thorp Arch * 64 1 44
THURNSCOE 88 D 40
Tollerton * 65 1 56
ULLESKELF * 1 54
WAKEFIELD KIRKGATE 2 32
WAKEFIELD WESTGATE 1 32
Walton G § 51 61 2 31
Warthill 59 1 65
Wath-on-Dearne Central 50 68 1 40
Wath-on-Dearne North § 42
Wetherby * 64 1 34
Wetherby Race Course 59 1 44
WHITLEY BRIDGE * 2 52
Whitwood, Altofts + * 70 90 2 32
Wombwell Central 50 59 1 30
WOMBWELL WEST § 42
WOODLESFORD * 2 32
Womersley F 48 2 51
Wormald Green 62 1 36
Worsborough Bridge H 65 1 30
WRESSLE * 1 73
YORK 1 55
York Layerthorpe 79 5 65

GOODS

No Name/Location Closed Ry Ref
G1 Birdwell + Pilley Wharf 54 2 30
2 Bramwith 61 1 60
3 Cawood 60 1 53
4 Cliff Common 61 5 63
5 Cudworth 65 1 31
DONCASTER 50
6 BELMONT YARD O 1 50
7 York Road 65 1 50
8 Elsecar East 63 1 30
9 Epworth 65 A 70
10 Fryston 60 1 42
11 GOOLE DOCKS O 2 72
12 Harlington 56 2 40
13 Hatfield Moor 63 A 70
LEEDS E
14 Copley Hill 58 2 E
15 Hunslet Lane 72 2 E
16 Whitehall Road ? 2 E
17 Wellington Street 74 E E
18 Maud's Bridge 62 1 71
19 Robin Hood 64 1 32
20 Reedness 65 A 71
21 Rothwell 65 1 32
22 Stourton 63 1 32
23 Thorpe Gates 64 1 53
24 Warmsworth 64 1 50
25 YORK O 1 55
26 York Foss Islands 88 1 65
26A Wath L 33 1 40

WORKS

No Name/Location Ry Ref
W1 DONCASTER 1 50
2 YORK 1 55

BRIDGES + VIADUCTS

No Name/Location Ry Ref
V1 Crimple Viaduct 1 35
2 Goole Swing Bridge 1 72
3 Farnley Viaduct 2 E

TUNNELS

No Name Length Ry Ref
T1 Prospect 825 1 35
2 Woolley 1745 2 21
3 Bamsdale 1226 1 51
4 Brierley 685 1 41
5 Richmond Hill 118 1 33

ENGINE SHEDS

No Name/Location Closed Ry Ref
E1 Ardsley ? 1 32
2 Barnsley ? 1 30
3 Cudworth ? 1 31
4 DONCASTER O 1 50
5 Goole 67 2 72
6 Knottingley 70 2 42
LEEDS
7 Copley Hill 64 1 E
8 Holbeck 67 2 E
9 NEVILLE HILL O 1 33
10 Stourton 67 2 33
11 Normanton 68 2 32
12 Royston (Carlton) 67 2 31
13 Selby 59 1 63
14 Starbeck 59 1 35
15 Wakefield 67 2 32
16 Wath ? 1 40
17 York 67 1 55

JUNCTIONS

No. Name Ry Ref
J1 Burton Lane 1 55
2 Skelton 1 55
3 Nidd 1 34
4 Bilton Road 1 34
5 Dragon 1 34
6 Crimple 1 34
7 Pilmoor 1 34
8 Botham 1 55
9 Holgate Bridge 1 55
10 Challoner's Whin 1 54
11 Colton 10 54
12 Brayton North 1 63
13 Brayton East 1 63
14 Barlby 1 63
15 Milford 1 43
16 Wrenthorpe North 2 32
17 Wrenthorpe South 1 32
18 Wrenthorpe West 1 32
19 Royston 2 31
20 Oakhill 2 72
21 Marshland 1A 72
22 Aire 1 62
23 Wrangbrook 1 41
24 Wrangbrook West 1 41
25 Joan Croft 1 51
26 Shaftholme 1 51
27 Applehurst 1 51
28 Goose Hill 2 32
29 Potteric Carr 1C 50
30 Low Ellers C 50
31 Askern 12 51
32 Holbeck 12 E
33 Whitehall 2 E
34 Exchange Sidings 12 E
35 Geldard 1 E
36 Three Signal Bridge 12E E
37 Wortley 12 E
38 Holbeck South 1 E
39 Wortley West 1 E
40 Wortley South 1 E
41 Canal (or West) 2E E
42 Farnley Line 2E E
43 Engine Shed 2 E

NOTES:

REF All in SE therefore numeric only. Items on LEEDS inset marked E in reference column. Two stations in the area are not named on the map but are on map 42 shown in this gazetteer by 42 in reference col.
§ Old name } change
§ New name } of name
other name identified by having corresponding letter.
A Although closed in 57, regular services finished in 54.
B Irregular services called at the station after it closed.
C Change of name.
D City dropped by 66
E Re-opened as OUTWOOD
F last passenger train to call was in 47.
G Name change.
H Just used for works outings. Line otherwise was always goods only may actually have been in use for a longer period
X After closure was used for a passenger service on an ad hoc basis.
L Line from Thurnscoe to Wath may have closed entirely in 1933 but there may have been some goods between HB Wath to the LNE line as shown on map.

34
35

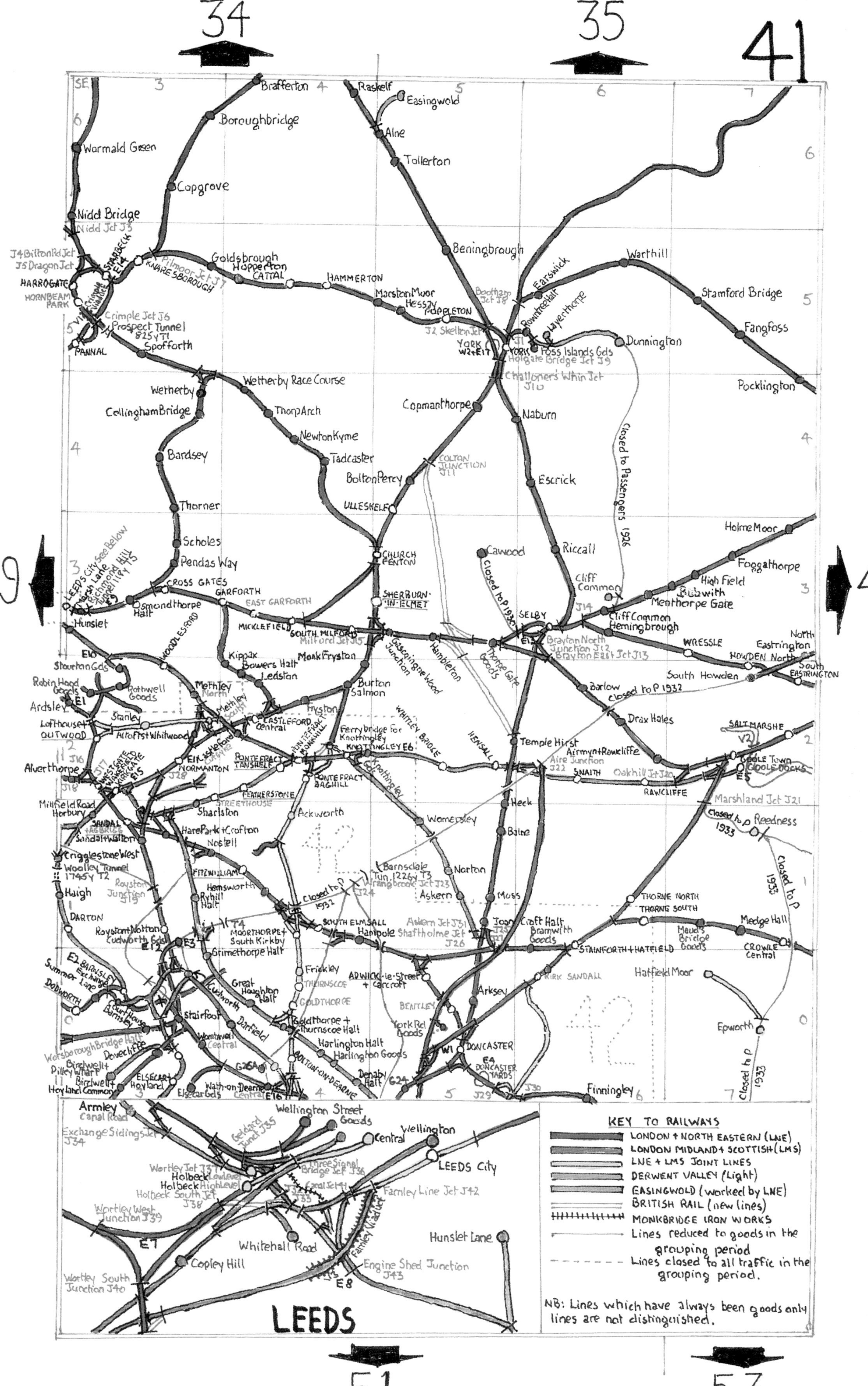

39
43
51
53

METHLEY, BARNSLEY + DONCASTER

RAILWAYS
No Company
1 LONDON + NORTH EASTERN (LNE)
2 LONDON MIDLAND + SCOTTISH (LMS)
3 LNE + LMS JOINT LINES:
B METHLEY
C SOUTH YORKSHIRE
D SWINTON + KNOTTINGLEY
E Others
O BRITISH RAIL (New Lines)

STATIONS

Ackworth
ADWICK-le-Street, Carcroft +
AGBRIGG, SANDAL +
Altofts + Whitwood
Alverthorpe
Arksey
BAGHILL, PONTEFRACT
Barnby Dun
Barnsley Court House
BARNSLEY Exchange
BENTLEY
Birdwell + Hoyland Common
BOLTON-ON-DEARNE
Carcroft + ADWICK-le-Street
Castleford Cutsyke
Cudworth
Cutsyke, Castleford
Darfield
DARTON
Denaby Halt
DODWORTH
DONCASTER
Dovecliffe
ELSECAR + Hoyland
FEATHERSTONE
Ferrybridge For Knottingley
FITZWILLIAM
Frickley
GOLDTHORPE
Goldthorpe + Thurnscoe
Great Houghton Halt
Grimethorpe Halt
Hampole
Hare Park + Crofton
Harlington Halt
HATFIELD + STAINFORTH
Hemsworth
Horbury, Millfield Road
Hoyland, ELSECAR +
Hoyland Common, Birdwell
Joan Croft Halt
KIRK SANDALL
KNOTTINGLEY
Lofthouse + OUTWOOD

Methley North
Methley South
Millfield Road Horbury
MONKHILL, PONTEFRACT
MOORTHORPE + South Kirkby
NORMANTON
Nostell
OUTWOOD, Lofthouse +
PONTEFRACT
BAGHILL
MONKHILL
TANSHELF
Opened Closed Ry Ref Royston + Notton
59 D 41 Ryhill Halt
A * 67 93 1 50 SANDAL + AGBRIGG
57 87 87 1 31 Sandal + Walton
* 70 90 2 A Sharlston
54 1 32 SOUTH ELMSALL
52 1 50 South Kirkby, MOORTHORPE +
D 42 STAINFORTH + HATFIELD
67 1 60 Stairfoot For Ardsley
60 2 30 Stanley
2 30 STREETHOUSE
92 1 50 Summer Lane
51 53 1 30 TANSHELF, PONTEFRACT
D 40 THORNE SOUTH
A * 67 93 1 50 THURNSCOE
* 52 68 2 A WAKEFIELD KIRKGATE
* 68 2 30 WAKEFIELD WESTGATE
* 52 68 2 A Walton
* 63 2 40 Wath-on-Dearne Central
2 30 Wath-on-Dearne North
49 2 40 Whitwood, Altofts +
59 89 1 30 Wombwell Central
1 50 WOMBWELL West
53 1 30 Worsborough Bridge
71 2 30
B * 67 92 2 42 GOODS
65 D 42 No Name/Location
* 67 82 1 41 G1 Ackworth Moor Top
53 D 40 2 Birdwell + Pilley Wharf
88 D 40 3 Bramwith
51 2 40 4 Crigglestone
51 2 40 5 Cudworth
51 2 30 6 Doncaster Cherry Tree Lane
52 1 51 7 DONCASTER YARDS (BELMONT)
52 1 31 8 Doncaster Marsh Gate
51 2 40 9 Doncaster York Road
C § 92 1 61 10 Harlington
* 67 1 41 11 Knottingley
61 2 31 12 Oakenshaw
71 2 30 13 Old Mill Lane
51 53 1 30 14 Oakwell
52 1 51 15 Pickburn + Brodsworth
91 1 60 16 Thorpe-in-Balne
* 2 42 17 Wakefield
D 60 88 1B 32 18 Wath Coal Yard

50 57 2 A 19 Worsborough
51 60 B A
61 2 31 COMPANY WORKS
* 2 42 No Location
61 D 41 W1 DONCASTER
2 32
51 1 31 ENGINE SHEDS
D 60 88 1B 32 No Name/Location
42 E2 Barnsley
D 42 3 Cudworth
* 2 42 4 DONCASTER
* 67 92 2 42 6 Knottingley
* 68 2 31 11 Normanton
51 2 31 12 Royston
87 87 1 31 15 Wakefield
E § 51 2 31 16 Wath
63 2 31
* 1 41 COLLIERY LOCATIONS
61 D 41 1 Don Pedro
C § 92 1 61 2 Featherstone
57 1 30 3 New Monckton Main
* 64 B 32 4 Hemsworth
92 2 42 5 Whitwood
59 1 30 6 Grimethorpe
67 92 2 42 7 Houghton
1 61 8 Brodsworth Main
88 D 40 9 Bullcroft
2 32 10 Bentley New
1 32 11 Rossington Main
E § 51 61 2 31
50 68 1 40 TUNNELS
* 50 68 2 40 No Name/Location
70 90 2 A T1 Barnsdale
50 59 1 30 2 Brierley
50 69 2 30 3 Chevet
F 65 68 1 30 4 Ardsley

JUNCTIONS
Closed Ry Ref No Name
62 1 41 J1 Whitwood
54 2 30 2 Altofts
61 1 60 3 Methley Line
64 2 31 4 Potteric Carr
54 2 31 5 Low Ellers
67 1 50 6 Black Carr
O 0 50 7 Bessacarr
71 1 50 8 Loversall Carr
65 1 50 9 St Catherine's Junctions
56 2 40 10 Black Carr East Junctions
70 2 52 11 Black Carr West
64 2 31 12 Wrenthorpe West
59 1 30 13 Wrenthorpe North
59 1 30 14 Wrenthorpe South
63 1 50 15 Balne Lane
58 1 51 16 Ings Lane
67 E 32 17 Goose Hill
G 86 1 40 18 St John's Colliery

60 1 30 19 Cutsyke
20 Horbury
21 Oakenshaw
Ry Ref 22 Royston
1 50 23 Snydale Branch
24 Shafton
H 25 Brierley
Closed Ry Ref 26 South Kirkby
? 1 27 Moorthorpe
? 1 28 Moorthorpe North
O 1 29 Brackenhill
70 2 30 Wrangbrook
68 2 31 Wrangbrook West
67 2 32 Moorhouse
67 2 33 Joan Croft
? 1 34 Applehurst
35 Silkstone Branch
Ry Ref 36 Monk Spring
2 42 37 Aldam
2 42 38 Chapeltown Line
12 31 39 Elsecar
1 41 40 Dearne North
1 A 41 Dearne South
12 40 42 Sprotborough Junctions
12 40 43 Avoiding Lines
1 50 44 Hexthorpe
1 50 45 Bridge
1 50 46 Bentley
1 B 47 Skelton
48 Shaftholme
49 Askern
Length Ry Ref
12 26 1 41
6 85 1 41
7 02 2 31
2 25 2 30
Ry Ref
1 A
12 A
1B A
1C B
C B
1 B
12 B
12 B
2CE B
2E B
2 B

12 42
2 31
12 31
2 31
2 31
2 31
12 31
1D 41
D 41
D 41
1D 41
1 41
1 41
1 41
1 51
1 50
2 30
2 30
1 30
2 30
1 40
DE 40
D 40
1 50
1 50
1 50
1 50
1 50
1 50
1 50
12 50
1 32
1 32
1 32
1 32
12 32
2 32
2 32

NOTES:

REF All the map is within SE so for the main map a numerical reference only is required. The two inset maps marked A and B have these letters shown in reference column if appropriate. It should be noted that if a location appears both on inset and main map only the inset reference is used.

§ Earlier name } Change of name
§ Later name }

A Carcroft + Adwick-le-Street closed in 1967 but was re-opened as ADWICK in 1993.

B Official closure was 1975 but from date shown ie 68 regular services ceased.

C Change of Name: STAINFORTH + HATFIELD became HATFIELD + STAINFORTH.

D Lofthouse + Outwood re-opened OUTWOOD.

E Change of name Sandal + Walton became Walton in 1951 and retained this name until closure.

F Used for works outings only. Exact location is unclear.

G Exact closure date is unclear it fell gradually into dis-use on the closure of collieries, abandoned feeder lines and the advent of merry-go-round trains.

H Repeat of numbers from map 41. But restricted to the sheds in this map's area.

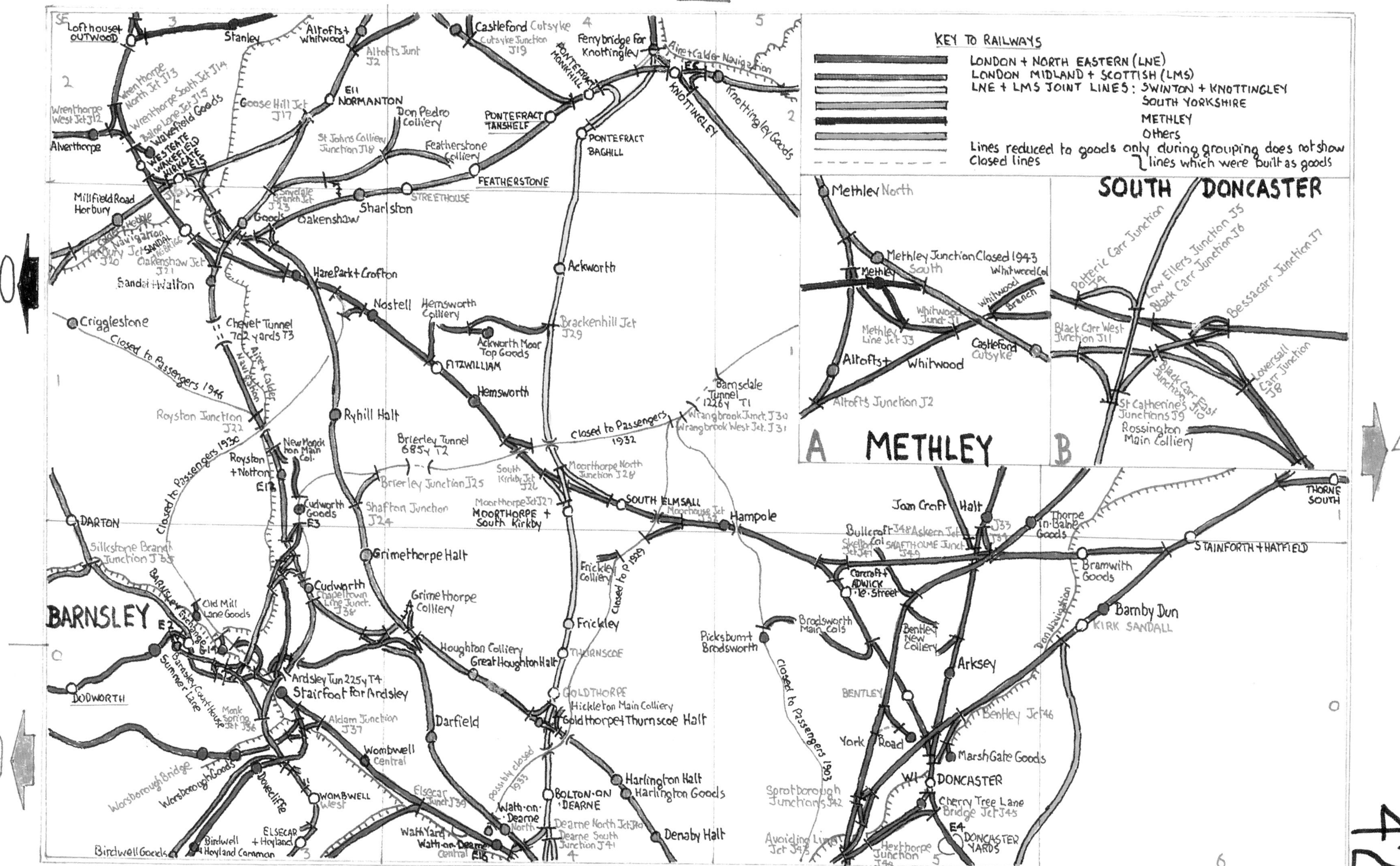

41
KEY TO RAILWAYS
LONDON + NORTH EASTERN (LNE)
LONDON MIDLAND + SCOTTISH (LMS)
LNE + LMS JOINT LINES: SWINTON + KNOTTINGLEY
SOUTH YORKSHIRE
METHLEY
Others
Lines reduced to goods only during grouping does not show lines which were built as goods
Closed lines
A METHLEY
Methley North
Methley Junction Closed 1943
Methley South
Whitwood Col
Whitwood Branch
Whitwood Junct J1
Methley Line Jct J3
Castleford Cutsyke
Altofts + Whitwood
Altofts Junction J2
B SOUTH DONCASTER
Potteric Carr Junction J4
Low Ellers Junction J5
Black Carr Junction J6
Bessacarr Junction J7
Black Carr West Junction J11
Loversall Carr Junction J8
Black Carr East Junction J10
St Catherine's Junctions J9
Rossington Main Colliery
Lofthouse + OUTWOOD
Stanley
Altofts + Whitwood
Altofts Junt J2
Castleford Cutsyke
Cutsyke Junction J19
Ferrybridge for Knottingley
Aire + Calder Navigation
KNOTTINGLEY
Knottingley Goods
PONTEFRACT MONKHILL
PONTEFRACT TANSHELF
PONTEFRACT BAGHILL
Wrenthorpe North Jct J13
Wrenthorpe South Jct J14
Wrenthorpe West Jct J12
Balne Lane Jct J15
Wakefield Goods
Alverthorpe
WESTGATE WAKEFIELD KIRKGATE
Goose Hill Jct J17
NORMANTON
Don Pedro Colliery
St Johns Colliery Junction J18
Featherstone Colliery
FEATHERSTONE
Millfield Road
Horbury
Sharlston
STREETHOUSE
Oakenshaw
Oakenshaw Jct J21
Sandal + Walton
Hare Park + Crofton
Nostell
Hemsworth Colliery
Ackworth
Brackenhill Jct J29
Ackworth Moor Top Goods
FITZWILLIAM
Hemsworth
Crigglestone
Closed to Passengers 1946
Chevet Tunnel 702 yards T3
Aire + Calder Navigation
Royston Junction J22
Ryhill Halt
Barnsdale Tunnel 1226 y T1
Wrangbrook Junct. J30
Wrangbrook West Jct. J31
Closed to Passengers 1932
Brierley Tunnel 685 y T2
New Monckton Main Col.
Royston + Notton
Closed to Passengers 1930
Brierley Junction J25
Moorthorpe North Junction J28
South Kirkby Jct J26
Cudworth Goods
Shafton Junction J24
Moorthorpe Jct J27
MOORTHORPE + South Kirkby
SOUTH ELMSALL
Moorhouse Jct
Hampole
Joan Croft Halt
Thorpe in Balne Goods
THORNE SOUTH
DARTON
Silkstone Branch Junction J35
Grimethorpe Halt
Bullcroft Jct J48
Askern Jct J33
Skellow Col
SHAFTHOLME Junct. J49
STAINFORTH + HATFIELD
Bramwith Goods
Frickley Colliery
Closed to P 1929
Carcroft + ADWICK le Street
BARNSLEY
Old Mill Lane Goods
Barnsley Exchange
Cudworth
Chapeltown Line Junct. J38
Grimethorpe Colliery
Frickley
Picksburnt Brodsworth
Brodsworth Main Cols
Bentley New Colliery
Barnby Dun
KIRK SANDALL
Don Navigation
Houghton Colliery
Great Houghton Halt
THURNSCOE
Arksey
Barnsley Court House
Summer Lane
DODWORTH
Ardsley Tun 225 y T4
Stairfoot for Ardsley
GOLDTHORPE
Hickleton Main Colliery
Goldthorpe + Thurnscoe Halt
BENTLEY
Monk Spring Jct J36
Aldam Junction J37
Darfield
Closed to Passengers 1903
Bentley Jct J46
York Road
Marsh Gate Goods
Wombwell Central
Worsborough Bridge
Worsborough Goods
Dovecliffe
WOMBWELL West
Elsecar Junct J39
possibly closed 1933
Harlington Halt
Harlington Goods
Sprotborough Junctions J42
DONCASTER
Cherry Tree Lane Bridge Jct J45
BOLTON-ON-DEARNE
Wath-on-Dearne North
Dearne North Jct J40
Dearne South Junction J41
ELSECAR + Hoyland
Wath Yard
Wath-on-Dearne Central
Denaby Halt
Avoiding Line Jct J43
Hexthorpe Junction J44
DONCASTER YARDS
Birdwell Goods
Birdwell + Hoyland Common
40
39

HULL, IMMINGHAM + GRIMSBY

RAILWAYS

No	Company
1	LONDON + NORTH EASTERN (LNE)
A	AXHOLME (LNE + LMS JOINT)
X	GRIMSBY + IMMINGHAM ELECTRIC (LNE) See Note B

STATIONS

Station	Note	Opened	Closed	Ry	Ref
ALTHORPE				1	SE81
Appleby			67	1	SE91
ARRAM		*		1	TA04
Bainton			54	1	SE95
BARNETBY				1	TA00
BARROW HAVEN		*		1	TA02
BARTON-ON-HUMBER		*		1	TA02
BEVERLEY				1	TA03
Boothferry Park Halt	*1 A	51	93	1	TA02
Botanic Gardens Hull	*1	*	64	1	TA02
BRIDLINGTON				1	TA16
BRIGG				1	TA00
Brocklesby			93	1	TA11
BROOMFLEET		*		1	SE82
BROUGH				1	SE92
Burdale			50	1	SE86
Burton Agnes		*	70	1	TA16
Carnaby		*	70	1	TA16
Cherry Burton			59	1	SE94
CLEETHORPES				1	TA30
Cleveland Bridge	*2		61	X	TA21
Cleveland Street			56	X	2
Corporation Bridge	*2		56	X	TA21
COTTINGHAM	*1			1	TA03
DRIFFIELD				1	TA05
East Halton Halt	T	48	63	1	TA12
Ellerby		*	64	1	TA13
Elsham			93	1	TA01
Enthorpe			54	1	SE94
Everingham			54	1	SE84
FERRIBY				1	SE92
Flamborough			55	1	TA16
Garton			50	1	SE95
GILBERDYKE	C §			1	SE82
GOXHILL		*		1	TA02
GREAT COATES	*2			1	TA21
Great Coates Level Crossing				X	2
GRIMSBY					2
Cleveland Bridge	*2		56	X	TA21
Cleveland Street			61	X	2
Corporation Bridge	*2		56	X	TA21
DOCKS	*2			1	TA21
Hainton Street Halt	*2		61	1	TA20
Jackson Street			56	X	2
NEW CLEE	*2			1	TA21
Stortford Street	*2		56	X	TA21
TOWN	*2			1	TA20
Weelsby Road Halt	D		52	1	TA20
Yarborough Street	*2		56	X	TA21
Hainton Street Halt	*2		61	1	TA20
HARBROUGH	*2			1	TA11
HEALING	*2			1	TA21
Hedon		*	64	1	TA12
HESSLE				1	TA02
Holton-le-Clay			55	1	TA20
Holton Village Halt			61	1	TA20
Hornsea Town		*	50 64	1	TA24
Hornsea Bridge		*	64	1	TA24
Howsham			65	1	TA00
HULL					
Boothferry Park	*1	51	93	1	TA02
Botanic Gardens	*1		64	1	TA02
HULL	*1 E §		?	1	TA02
Newington	*1 F		?	1	TA02
Paragon	*1 E §		?	1	TA02
Southcoates	*1	*	64	1	TA12
Stepney	*1	*	64	1	TA03
Wilmington	*1	*	64	1	TA02
HUTTON CRANSWICK				1	TA05
IMMINGHAM					2
Dock	T *2	64	69	1	TA11
Dock	*2		61	X	TA11
Town	*2		61	X	TA11
Jackson Street			56	X	2
Keyingham		*	64	1	TA22
Killingholme Halt	T	56	63	1	TA11
Kiln Lane Stallingborough			61	X	2
Kipling Cotes		*	65	1	SE94
KIRTON LINDSEY				1	SE90
Little Weighton			55	1	SE93
Lockington			60	1	TA04
Londesborough		*	65	1	SE84
Lowthorpe		*	70	1	TA06
Marfleet	*1	*	64	1	TA12
Market Weighton		*	65	1	SE84
Marsh Road Crossing			61	X	2
Melton (Crossing) Halt	K	65	89	1	SE92
Middleton-on-the-Wolds			54	1	SE95
Moortown for Caistor			65	1	TA00
NAFFERTON				1	TA05
NEW CLEE				1	TA21
NEW HOLLAND	H		81		TA02
New Holland Pier	J	*	81	1	TA02
New Holland Town	J	*	81	1	TA02
Newington	*1 F		?	1	TA02
North Cave			55	1	SE93
North Grimston			50	1	SE86
North Kelsey			65	1	TA00
No.5 Passing Place			61	X	2
Nunburnholme			51	1	SE84
Ottringham		*	64	1	TA22
Paragon	*1 E §		?	1	TA02
Patrington		*	64	1	TA32
Rye Hill + Burstwick		*	64	1	TA22
Sandholme			55	1	SE83
Scawby + Hibaldstow			68	1	SE90
SCUNTHORPE + Frodingham			63	1	SE81
Settrington			50	1	SE86
Sigglesthorne		*	64	1	TA14
Skirlaugh			57	1	TA13
Sledmere + Fimber			50	1	SE96
Southburn			54	1	SE95
South Cave			55	1	SE93
Southcoates	*1	*	64	1	TA12
Springhead Halt			55	1	TA02
STADDLETHORPE	C §		74	1	SE82
STALLINGBOROUGH	*2			1	TA11
Stepney	*1	*	64	1	TA03
Stortford Street	*2		56	X	TA21
Sutton-on-Hull	*1	*	64	1	TA13
Swine		*	64	1	TA13
THORNTON ABBEY		*		1	TA11
ULCEBY		*		1	TA11
Walling Fen			55	1	SE83
Waltham			61	1	TA20
Wassand			53	1	TA14
Weelsby Road Halt	D		52	1	TA20
Wetwang			50	1	SE95
Wharram			50	1	SE86
Whitedale		*	64	1	TA14
Willerby + Kirk Ella			55	1	TA03
Wilmington		*	64	1	TA02
Withernsea		*	64	1	TA32
Yarborough Street	*2		56	X	TA21

GOODS

Note L

No	Name/Location	Note	Closed if known	Ry	Ref
G 1	Fockerby		65	A	SE81
	GRIMSBY				2
2	Coal Depot	*2		1	TA21
3	Dock	*2		1	TA21
4	Pier	*2		1	TA21
5	Town			1	2
6	Gunness + Burringham		63	1	SE81
	HULL				1
7	Alexandra Dock	*1		1	TA12
8	Burleigh Street			1	1
9	Cannon Street	*1	68	1	TA02
10	Cattle Dock			1	1
11	Dairycoates		57	1	1
12	Drypool		69	1	1
13	Drypool Victoria Dock		69	1	1
14	HULL COAL TERMINAL	*1	O	1	TA12
15	King George Dock	*1		1	TA12
16	Kingston Street			1	1
17	Neptune Street	*1	68	1	TA02
18	Stoneferry	*1	65	1	TA13
	IMMINGHAM				2
19	Coal	*2		1	TA11
20	Dock	*2		1	TA11
21	YARD	*2	O	1	TA11
22	Keadby		71	1	SE81
23	Kilnwick Gates		60	1	TA04
24	Whitton		51	1	SE82
25	Winestead		56	1	TA22

ENGINE SHEDS

No	Name/Location	Note	Closed if known	Ry	Ref
E 1	Barnetby			1	TA00
2	Bridlington		58	1	TA16
3	Frodingham		?	1	TA81
4	Grimsby	*2	?	1	TA20
	HULL				1
5	Alexandra Dock		63	1	1
6	Botanic Gardens		59	1	1
7	Dairycoates		67	1	1
8	Springhead		58	1	1
9	IMMINGHAM		0	1	TA11
10	New Holland		?	1	TA02
11	Pyewipe	*2	61	X	TA21

TUNNELS

No	Name/Location	Length	Ry	Ref
T 1	Burdale	1734	1	SE86
2	Weedly	132	1	SE93
3	Sugar Loaf	132	1	SE93
4	Drewton	2114	1	SE93
5	Kirton	1334	1	SE90

JUNCTIONS

No	Name	Ry	Ref
J 1	West Parade	1	1
2	Victoria Dock Branch	1	1
3	Hessle	1	1
4	Cottingham Bridge	1	1
5	Hessle Road	1	1
6	Dairycoates	1	1
7	Walton Street	1	1
8	Pasture Street	1	2
9	Garden Street	1	2
10	Frodingham	1	SE91
11	Wrawby South	1	TA00
12	Wrawby North	1	TA00
13	Hedon Road	1	1

NOTES:

REF There are two insets. When an item is on both the main map and an inset the main map reference is used, and the gazetteer entry also has number of inset shown. If on inset only, the number of inset is in ref column.

§ Old name } change of name
§ New name }

identifying letter shows the other name

A Open only for excursion traffic. Halt is close to sports ground. Exact closure date is unclear.

B This was a rail operated tramway along streets at either end with central section in open country. The compulsory stops (in Bradshaw) are shown on main map. Request stops on inset only. Additional request stop at Boulevard Recreation Ground not shown as exact location unclear.

C Change of name.

D Closure date as shown but last train to call at halt was in 1940.

E Date Paragon dropped from title is unclear.

F Private station when opened, later use was mainly excursion traffic to avoid reversals. Closure date is unclear.

G May have closed earlier.

H Replaced earlier station which was of no use when ferry service was discontinued on opening of the HUMBER BRIDGE.

J Closed when Humber Bridge opened see Note H.

K Change of name was dropping of "Crossing" in 65.

L Some closure dates unclear, whilst in other cases although maybe closed several sidings remained in use.

M Where closure date is shown ? date of closure unclear and may in fact have closed prenationalisation.

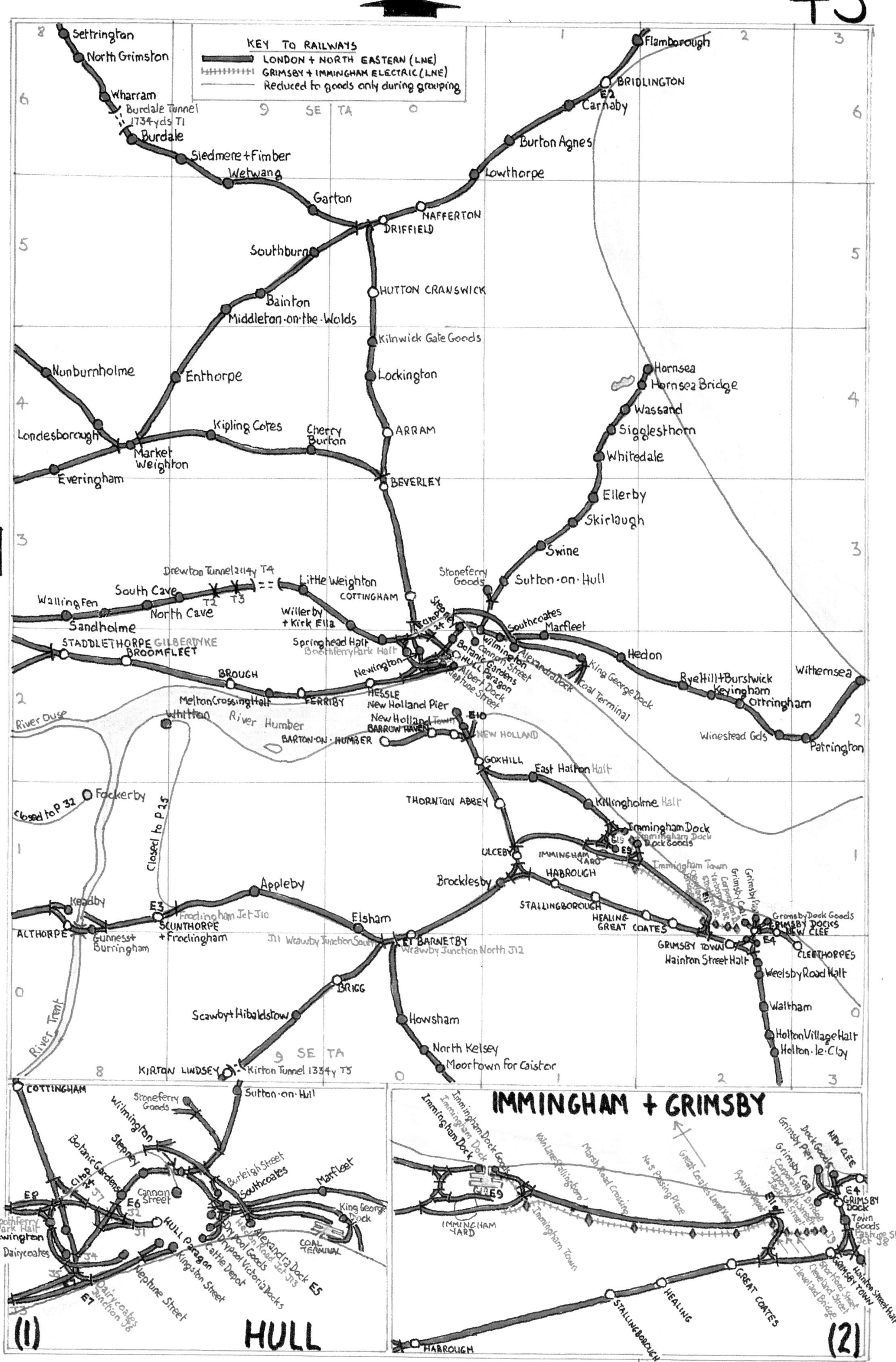
35
41
53
54
KEY TO RAILWAYS
LONDON + NORTH EASTERN (LNE)
GRIMSBY + IMMINGHAM ELECTRIC (LNE)
Reduced to goods only during grouping
Settrington
North Grimston
Wharram
Burdale Tunnel 1734yds T1
Burdale
Sledmere + Fimber
Wetwang
Garton
Flamborough
BRIDLINGTON
Carnaby
Burton Agnes
Lowthorpe
NAFFERTON
DRIFFIELD
Southburn
Bainton
Middleton-on-the-Wolds
HUTTON CRANSWICK
Kilnwick Gate Goods
Lockington
ARRAM
BEVERLEY
Nunburnholme
Enthorpe
Londesborough
Market Weighton
Everingham
Kipling Cotes
Cherry Burton
Hornsea
Hornsea Bridge
Wassand
Sigglesthorne
Whitedale
Ellerby
Skirlaugh
Swine
Sutton-on-Hull
Stoneferry Goods
Drewton Tunnel 2114y T4
South Cave
North Cave
Walling Fen
Sandholme
Little Weighton
COTTINGHAM
Willerby + Kirk Ella
Springhead Halt
Boothferry Park Halt
STADDLETHORPE
GILBERDYKE
BROOMFIELD
BROUGH
FERRIBY
HESSLE
Newington
Southcoates
Marfleet
Hedon
Ryehill + Burstwick
Keyingham
Ottringham
Withernsea
Patrington
Winestead Gds
King George Dock
Coal Terminal
River Ouse
River Humber
Melton Crossing Halt
Whitton
New Holland Pier
New Holland Town
BARROW HAVEN
BARTON-ON-HUMBER
NEW HOLLAND
GOXHILL
East Halton Halt
THORNTON ABBEY
Killingholme Halt
Immingham Dock
Immingham Dock Goods
ULCEBY
IMMINGHAM YARD
Brocklesby
HABROUGH
STALLINGBOROUGH
HEALING
GREAT COATES
Fockerby
Closed to P 32
Closed to P 25
Keadby
ALTHORPE
Gunness + Burringham
SCUNTHORPE + Frodingham
Frodingham Jct J10
Appleby
Elsham
BARNETBY
J11 Wrawby Junction South
Wrawby Junction North J12
BRIGG
Scawby + Hibaldstow
Howsham
North Kelsey
Moortown for Caistor
KIRTON LINDSEY
Kirton Tunnel 1334y T5
River Trent
GRIMSBY TOWN
Hainton Street Halt
Grimsby Dock Goods
GRIMSBY DOCKS
NEW CLEE
CLEETHORPES
Weelsby Road Halt
Waltham
Holton Village Halt
Holton-le-Clay
IMMINGHAM + GRIMSBY
HULL
(1)
(2)
Wilmington
Stepney
Botanic Gardens
Cannon Street
HULL Paragon
Burleigh Street
Kingston Street
Neptune Street
Alexandra Dock
Dairycoates
Dairycoates Junction J6
Cattle Depot
Drypool Goods
Drypool Victoria Docks
COAL TERMINAL
Immingham Town
Kiln Lane, Stallingboro'
Marsh Road Crossing
Great Coates Level Xing
Pyewipe Road
Grimsby Pier
Grimsby Coal
Corporation Bridge
Dock Goods
Town Goods
Pasture St Jct J8
Cleveland Bridge
Stortford Street

ANGLESEY + SNOWDONIA

RAILWAYS

No	Company
1	FFESTINIOG
2	LONDON MIDLAND + SCOTTISH
3	GREAT WESTERN
4	WELSH HIGHLAND
5	SNOWDON MOUNTAIN
X	LLANBERIS LAKE
O	BRITISH RAIL additions

STATIONS

Gauge	Station	Opened / Closed	Ry Ref
	Aber	60	2 67
	ABERERCH Halt	A 56 68	3 43
	Afon Wen	64	3 43
	Amlwch	* 64	2 49
	BANGOR		2 57
	BARMOUTH		3 61
	Bethesda	63	2 66
	Black Rock Halt	B 77	3 53
	Blaenau Festiniog Central	51 60	3 64
	Blaenau Festiniog North	* C § 51 82	2 64
	BLAENAU FFESTINIOG	§ C 82	1 2 64
	BODORGAN	*	2 37
	(BOSTON LODGE)	56	1 53
	Brynkir	* 64	2 44
	Caernarvon	* 70	2 46
	(CAMPBELL'S PLATFORM)	65	1 64
	(CEI LLYDAN)	71	X 56
	Chwilog	* 64	2 43
	Clogwyn	78	5 65
	CRICCIETH		3 43
	(DDUALLT)	68	1 64
	Dinas	51	2 45
	DYFFRYN-on-Sea ARDUDWY	48	3 52
	Felin Hen	51	2 56
	Festiniog	60	3 64
	Gaerwen	* 66	2 47
	(GILFACH DDU)	71	X 56
	Groeslon	* 64	2 45
	HALFWAY	D	5 65
	HARLECH		3 53
	HEBRON		5 55
	Holland Arms	52	2 47
	HOLYHEAD		2 28
	LLANABER Halt	68	3 61
	LLANBEDR	E § 78	3 52
	Llanbedr + PENSARN	78	3 52
	Llanberis	F 62	2 56
	LLANBERIS		5 56
	LLANDANWG Halt	68	3 52
	LLANDECWYN Halt	A 68	3 63
	Llanerchymedd	* 64	2 48
	LLANFAIRFECHAN	*	2 67
	LLANFAIRPWLL	G * 66 73	2 57
	Llangefni	* 64	2 47
	Llangwyllog	* 64	2 48
	Llangybi	* 64	2 43
	Llanwnda	* 64	2 45
	Maentwrog Road	H 60	3 64
	Manod	60	3 64
	Menai Bridge	* 66	2 57
	MINFFORDD		3 53
	(MINFFORDD)	56	1 54
	Nantlle	F 63	2 45
	Padarn Halt	F 62	2 56
	Pant Glas	57	2 44
	Penmaenpool	* 65	3 61
1'11½"	(PENLLYN)	71	X 56
S	(PENRHYN)	57	1 64
S	PENRHYNDEUDRAETH		3 63
2'0"	PENSARN, Llanbedr	78	3 52
RACK 2'7½"	PENYCHAIN		3 43
1'11½"	Penygroes	* 64	2 45
S	(PEN-Y-MOUNT)	80	4 54
	(PLAS HALT)	63	1 64
	Port Dinorwic	60	2 56
	Portmadoc	J § 75	3 54
	(Portmadoc)	K § 55 73	1 53
	PORTHMADOG	J § 75	3 54
	(PORTHMADOG)	K § 73	1 53
	(PORTHMADOG)	80	4 54
	PWLLHELI		3 33
	Rhosgoch	* 64	2 48
	RHOSNEIGR	*	2 37
	SNOWDON SUMMIT		5 65
	TALSARNAU		3 63
	Talwrn Bach Halt	E § 78	3 52
	TALYBONT Halt	68	3 52
	(TAN-Y-BWLCH)	58	1 64
	(TAN-Y-GRISIAU)	78	1 64
	Teigl Halt	60	3 64
	Trawsfynydd	60	3 63
	Trawsfynydd Lake Halt	60	3 63
	Treborth	59	2 56
	Tregarth	51	2 66
	TY CROES	*	2 37
	TYGWYN Halt	A 68	3 63
	VALLEY	* 66 82	2 27
	WATERFALL		5 55
	Ynys	* 64	2 44

GOODS

No	Name/Location	Closed	Ry Ref
G1	Holyhead Cattle Dock		2 28
2	HOLYHEAD SEALINK CONTAINER TERMINAL		2 28
3	Red Wharf Bay + Benllech	50	2 58

ENGINE SHEDS ETC

No.	Name/Location	Closed	Ry Ref
E1	HOLYHEAD	O	2 28
2	Bangor	65	2 57
3	Portmadoc	63	3 54
4	Pwllheli	66	3 33
5	Trawsfynydd	61	3 63
6	BOSTON LODGE	L O	1 53
7	MINFFORDD	M O	1 54
8	LLANBERIS	O	5 56
9	GILFACH DDU	O	X 56

TUNNELS

No	Name/Location	Length	Ry Ref
T1	Bodorgan No. 1	413	2 46
2	Bodorgan No 2	115	2 46
3	Britannia Bridge	498	2 57
4	Belmont	613	2 57
5	Bangor	912	2 57
6	Llandegai	506	2 57
7	Vaynol	497	2 56
8	Carnarvon	164	2 46
9	Cwm-y-Glo	106	2 56
10	Moelwyn	730	1 64
11	Festiniog	38 58	2 64

BRIDGES + VIADUCTS

No	Name/Location	Ry	Ref
V1	Britannia Bridge	2	57
2	Stanley Embankment	2	28
3	Barmouth Bridge	3	61
4	Bryn-Yr-Odyn Viaduct	3	64
5	Pensarn River Bridge	3	52

NOTES:

Ref All in SH therefore numerals only are used

§ Old Name } Change of name identical
§ New Name } letters identify other name

SPELLING The variation used is normally that used by the companies as at 1/1/48. When a place received a new name this is often shown. But it should be noted when the name changed and when railway showed the change can be very different

- A Closed 1994
- B Last train 1976
- C Rebuilt on closely adjoining site and the FFESTINOG also used same site when it re-opened. All FFESTINIOG stations are in fact re-openings, but closure was in pre nationalisation period. Also name change.
- D Disused.
- E Name change.
- F Regular passenger services finished 1932
- G Also opened 1970-72 LLANFAIR PG on map
- H Re-opened 89 for specials.
- J Name Change } Note different dates
- K Name Change } of change !!
- L Also Works
- M PW Depot and carriage sheds.

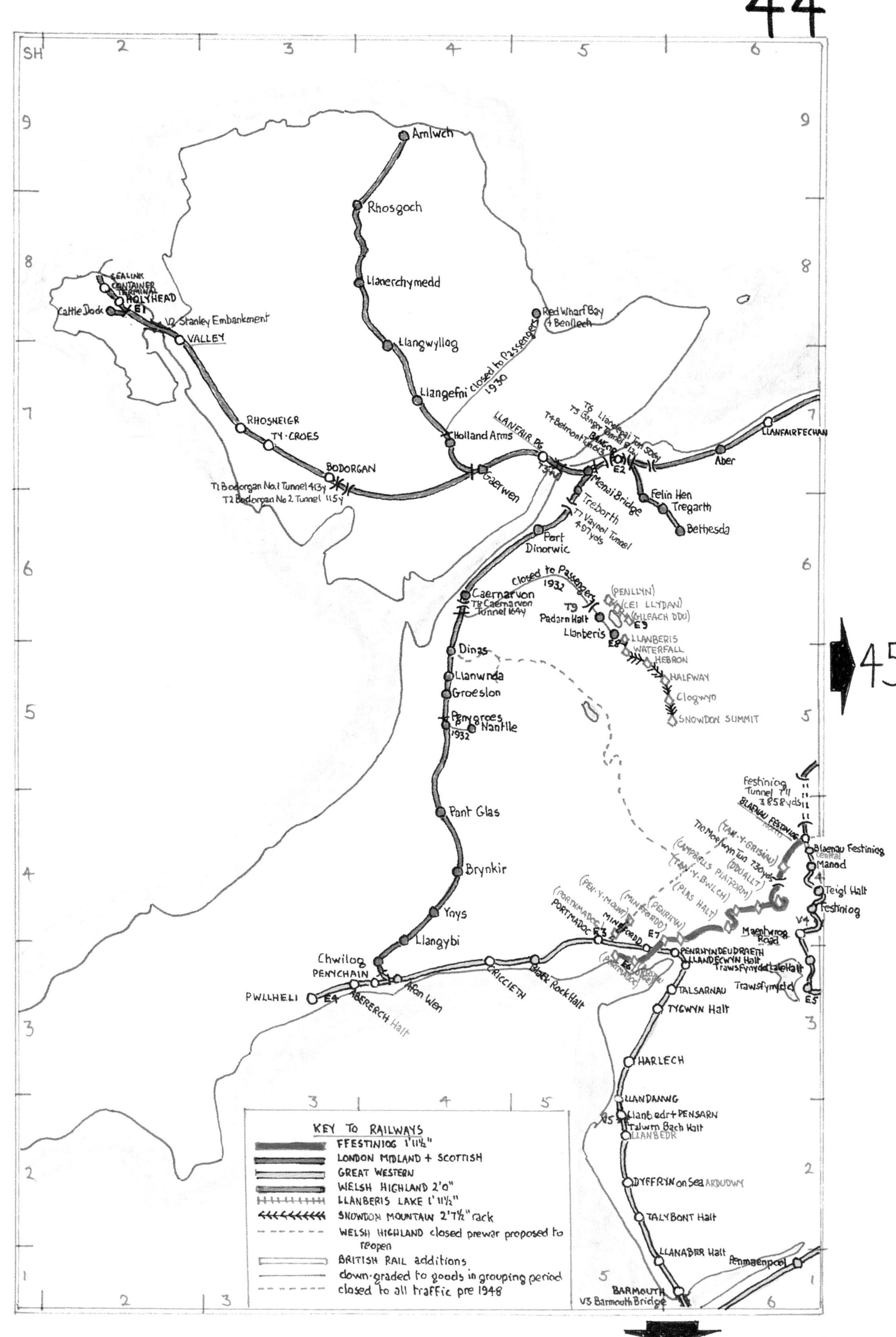
SH
Amlwch
Rhosgoch
Llanerchymedd
Llangwyllog
Llangefni
Holland Arms
Gaerwen
Red Wharf Bay + Benllech
closed to Passengers 1930
SEALINK CONTAINER TERMINAL
HOLYHEAD
Cattle Dock
E1
V2 Stanley Embankment
VALLEY
RHOSNEIGR
TY-CROES
BODORGAN
T1 Bodorgan No.1 Tunnel 413y
T2 Bodorgan No.2 Tunnel 115y
LLANFAIR PG
T3
T4 Belmont Tunnel
T5 Bangor Tunnel
T6 Llandegai Tunnel
BANGOR
E2
Menai Bridge
Treborth
T7 Vaynol Tunnel 497yds
Felin Hen
Tregarth
Bethesda
Aber
LLANFAIRFECHAN
Port Dinorwic
Caernarvon
T8 Caernarvon Tunnel 164y
closed to Passengers 1932
T9
Padarn Halt
Llanberis
E8
E9
(PENLLYN)
(CEI LLYDAN)
(GILFACH DDU)
LLANBERIS
WATERFALL
HEBRON
HALFWAY
Clogwyn
SNOWDON SUMMIT
Dinas
Llanwnda
Groeslon
Penygroes
Nantlle
1932
Pant Glas
Brynkir
Ynys
Llangybi
Chwilog
PENYCHAIN
Afon Wen
PWLLHELI
E4
ABERERCH Halt
CRICCIETH
Black Rock Halt
Ffestiniog Tunnel 3858yds
BLAENAU FFESTINIOG
Blaenau Ffestiniog Central
Manod
Teigl Halt
Ffestiniog
V4
Maentwrog Road
Trawsfynydd Lake Halt
Trawsfynydd
E5
T10 Moelwyn Tun. 730yds
(TAN-Y-GRISIAU)
(DDUALLT)
(CAMPBELLS PLATFORM)
(TAN-Y-BWLCH)
(PLAS HALT)
(PENRHYN)
(MINFFORDD)
(PEN-Y-MOUNT)
(PORTMADOC)
PORTMADOC
MINFFORDD
E3
E6
E7
PENRHYNDEUDRAETH
LLANDECWYN Halt
TALSARNAU
TYGWYN Halt
HARLECH
LLANDANWG
Llanbedr + PENSARN
V5
Talwrn Bach Halt
LLANBEDR
DYFFRYN on Sea
ARDUDWY
TALYBONT Halt
LLANABER Halt
Penmaenpool
BARMOUTH
V3 Barmouth Bridge
KEY TO RAILWAYS
FFESTINIOG 1'11½"
LONDON MIDLAND + SCOTTISH
GREAT WESTERN
WELSH HIGHLAND 2'0"
LLANBERIS LAKE 1'11½"
SNOWDON MOUNTAIN 2'7½" rack
WELSH HIGHLAND closed prewar proposed to reopen
BRITISH RAIL additions
down-graded to goods in grouping period
closed to all traffic pre 1948
45

56

NORTH WALES

RAILWAYS

No.	Company
2	LONDON MIDLAND + SCOTTISH (LMS)
3	GREAT WESTERN (GW)
4	BALA LAKE (ex GW) now 1'11½" gauge
5	LLANGOLLEN (ex GW)

STATIONS

Name	Opened Closed	Ry Ref
ABERGELE + PENSARN	*	2 H97
Arenig	60	3 H83
Bala	* 65	3 H93
Bala Junction	* 65	3 H93
Bala Lake Halt	A 39	3 H93
(BALA (LLYN TEGID))	A 76	4 H93
BETTWS·Y·COED	* B § 53	2 H75
BETWS·Y·COED	B § 53	2 H75
Bodfari	62	2 J07
Bontnewydd	* 65	3 H73
Bonwm Halt	* 64	3 J14
Bryncelynog Halt	60	3 H73
Bryngwyn	* 65	3 J11
(BRYN HYNOD HALT)	75	4 H93
Caerwys	62	2 J17
Capel Celyn Halt	60	3 H83
Carrog	5 C * 64	3 J14
COLWYN BAY		2 H87
CONWAY	* D § 66	2 H77
CONWY	D § 87	2 H77
Corwen	5 C * 64	3 J04
Cwm Prysor Halt	53 60	3 H73
Cynwyd	* 64	3 J04
(DEESIDE)	?	5 J14
DEGANWY	*	2 H78
Denbigh	62	2 J06
Derwen	53	2 J05
DOLGARROG	* 64 65	2 H76
Dolgelley	E § 60	3 H71
Dolgellau	* E § 60 65	3 H71
Dolserau Halt	51	3 H71
DOLWYDDELAN	F § 80	2 H75
DOLWYDDELEN	* F § 80	2 H75
Drws·y·Nant	* 65	3 H82
Eyarth	53	2 J15
Flag Station Halt	G § 50	3 H93
(FLAG STATION (GLANLLYN))	H § 80	4 H93
Frongoch	60	3 H93
Garneddwen Halt	* 65	3 H82
GLAN CONWAY	*	2 H77
Glan Llyn Halt	J * G § 50 64	3 H93
(Glan Llyn Halt)	J H § 72 80	4 H93
Glyndyfrdwy	* 64 ?	5 J14
Gwyddelwern	53	2 J04
Holywell Junction	* 66	2 J17
Holywell Town	54	2 J17
Llafar Halt	60	3 H73
Llandderfel	* 64	3 H93
Llandrillo	* 64	3 J03
LLANDUDNO		2 H78
LLANDUDNO JUNCTION		2 H77
Llandulas	52	2 H97
Llanfechain	* 65	3 J11
Llanfyllin	* 65	3 J11
Llangedwyn	51	1 J12
Llangower Halt	* K § 65	3 H93
Llangynog	51	3 J02
(LLANGYWAIR)	§ K 72	5 H93
Llanrhaiadr	53	2 J06
Llanrhaiadr Mochnant	51	3 J12
LLANRWST + Trefriw NORTH	* 74 89	2 H76
LLANRWST	89	H76
Llanuwychillyn	* 65 72	4 H83
Llys Halt	* 65	3 H82
Mostyn	* 66	2 J18
Nannerch	62	2 J16
Nantclwyd	53	2 J15
Old Colwyn	52	2 H87
Pedair Ffordd	51	3 J12
PENMAENMAWR	*	2 H77
Pentrefelin	51	3 J12
(PENTREPIOD HALT)		4 H83
Penybontfawr	51	3 J02
PONT·Y·PANT	*	2 H75
PRESTATYN	*	2 J08
Rhewl	62	2 J16
Rhuddlan	55	2 J07
RHYL		2 J08
ROMAN BRIDGE	*	2 H75
Ruthin	62	2 J15
St Asaph	55	2 J07
St Winefrides Halt	54	2 J17
Star Crossing Halt	62	2 J16
Talacre	* 66	2 J18
TAL·Y·CAFN + Eglwysbach	* 74	2 H77
Trawsfynydd	60	3 H63
Trawsfynydd Lake Halt	60	3 H63
Trefnant	55	2 J07
Tyddyn Bridge Halt	60	3 H83
Wnion Halt	* 65	3 H82

GOODS

No	Name/Location	Closed	Ry Ref
G 1	Deganwy	64	2 H77
2	Dyserth	64	2 J08

ENGINE SHEDS

No	Name/Location	Closed	Ry Ref
E 1	Trawsfynydd	61	3 H73
2	LLANDUDNO JUNCTION	O	2 H77
3	Bala	65	3 H93
4	Rhyl	63	2 J08
5	Denbigh	55	2 J06
6	Llanuwychillyn	O	4 H83

TUNNELS

No	Name/Location	Length	Ry Ref
T 1	Penclip	452	2 H77
2	Penmaenbach	718	2 H77
3	Conway	74	2 H77
4	Conway Tubular Bridge	149	2 H77
5	Penmaenrhos	485	2 H87
6	Llanrwst	85	2 H76
7	Beaverpool	110	2 H75
8	Pont·y·Pant Lower	144	2 H75
9	Pont·y·Pant Upper	66	2 H75
10	Llandderfel	159	3 H93

JUNCTIONS

No	Name	Ry	Ref
J 1	Foryd	2	J08
2	Pier Branch	2	J07
3	For Mold	2	J06
4	Corwen LMS + GW	23	J04

BRIDGES + VIADUCTS

No	Name / Location	Ry	Ref
V 1	Conway Tubular Bridge	2	H77
2	Blaen·y·Cwm Viaduct	3	H73

NOTES

Ref All in SH or SJ therefore initial S is omitted.

§ Name change old name } letter gives ref
§ Name change new name } to other name

A This Halt although closed in 39 is shown as it was both, site of Bala first station + is terminal station for new BALA LAKE RAILWAY now BALA (LLYN TEGID)

B Name change

C Proposed re-opening on the extended LLANGOLLEN.

D Name change.

E Name change.

F Name change

G Name change

H Name change

J Re-opened after change of name and then followed by a further name change.

K Name changed when re-opened by the BALA LAKE railway

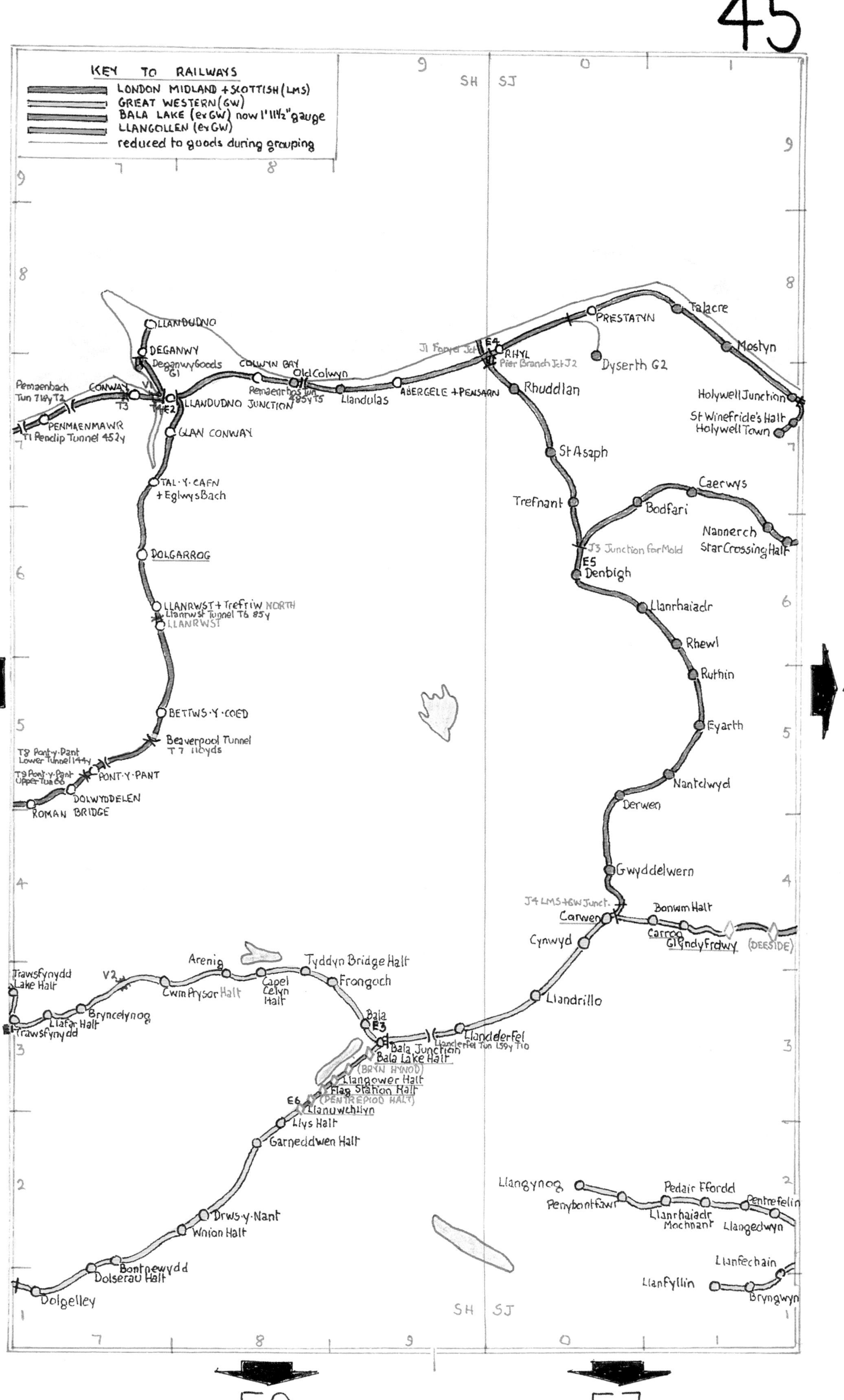
KEY TO RAILWAYS
LONDON MIDLAND + SCOTTISH (LMS)
GREAT WESTERN (GW)
BALA LAKE (ex GW) now 1'11½" gauge
LLANGOLLEN (ex GW)
reduced to goods during grouping
SH
SJ
LLANDUDNO
DEGANWY
Deganwy Goods G1
CONWAY
Penmaenbach Tun 718y T2
PENMAENMAWR
T1 Pendip Tunnel 452y
LLANDUDNO JUNCTION
COLWYN BAY
Old Colwyn
Penmaenrhos Tun 485y T5
Llandulas
ABERGELE + PENSARN
J1 Foryd Jct
RHYL
Pier Branch Jct J2
PRESTATYN
Dyserth G2
Talacre
Mostyn
Holywell Junction
St Winefride's Halt
Holywell Town
Rhuddlan
St Asaph
Trefnant
Caerwys
Bodfari
Nannerch
Star Crossing Halt
J3 Junction for Mold
Denbigh
Llanrhaiadr
Rhewl
Ruthin
Eyarth
Nantclwyd
Derwen
Gwyddelwern
J4 LMS + GW Junct.
Corwen
Bonwm Halt
Carrog
Glyndyfrdwy
(DEESIDE)
Cynwyd
Llandrillo
Llandderfel
Llandderfel Tun 159y T10
GLAN CONWAY
TAL-Y-CAFN + Eglwysbach
DOLGARROG
LLANRWST + Trefriw NORTH
Llanrwst Tunnel T6 85y
LLANRWST
BETTWS-Y-COED
Beaverpool Tunnel T7 110yds
T8 Pont-y-Pant Lower Tunnel 144y
T9 Pont-y-Pant Upper Tun 66
PONT-Y-PANT
DOLWYDDELEN
ROMAN BRIDGE
Trawsfynydd Lake Halt
Trawsfynydd
Llafar Halt
Bryncelynog
Cwm Prysor Halt
Arenig
Capel Celyn Halt
Tyddyn Bridge Halt
Frongoch
Bala
Bala Junction
Bala Lake Halt
(BRYN HYNOD)
Llangower Halt
Flag Station Halt
(PENTREPIOD HALT)
Llanuwchllyn
Llys Halt
Garneddwen Halt
Drws-y-Nant
Wnion Halt
Bontnewydd
Dolserau Halt
Dolgelley
Llangynog
Penybontfawr
Pedair Ffordd
Llanrhaiadr Mochnant
Pentrefelin
Llangedwyn
Llanfechain
Llanfyllin
Bryngwyn

44
46
56
57

LIVERPOOL WREXHAM + OSWESTRY

RAILWAYS see note 6

No	Company
1	LONDON + NORTH EASTERN (LNE)
2	LONDON MIDLAND + SCOTTISH (LMS)
A	WIRRAL (LMS)
23	BIRKENHEAD JOINT (LMS + GW)
23	WREXHAM + MINERA (LMS + GW)
3	GREAT WESTERN (GW)
4	CHESHIRE LINES COMMITTEE (LNE+LMS)
12	OTHER LNE + LMS Joint Lines
5	MERSEY
6	LIVERPOOL OVERHEAD
7	LLANGOLLEN (ex GW)

STATIONS

Name	Opened / Closed	Ry Ref
Acrefair	* 65	3 24
ACTON BRIDGE		2 67
Adderley	† 63	3 64
AIGBURTH, Mersey Road +	72 78	4 38
AINTREE Sefton Arms	? 68	2 39
Aintree Central	1 51 63	4 39
Alexandra Dock	56	6 47
Alexandra Dock	2 49	2 39
ALLERTON for Garston + Woolton	74	2 48
Appleton	51	2 58
Arddleen Halt	* 64 65	3 21
Arpley	58	2 68
Ashton-in-Makerfield	75	1 59
Audlem	† 63	3 64
BACHE	3 84	23 46
Bagillt	* 66	2 27
Balderton	53	3 36
Balliol Road Bootle	48	2 47
Bangor-on-Dee	† 62	2 34
BANK HALL	*	2 47
Barrow for Tarvin	53	4 47
Baschurch	60	3 42
BEBINGTON + New Ferry	74	23 38
Beeston Castle + Tarporley	*	2 56
Berwyn Halt	* 54 64	7 24
Bettisfield	* 65	3 43
BIDSTON		1A 29
BIRCHWOOD	80	4 69
BIRKENHEAD		47
CENTRAL		5 38
CONWAY PARK	*	5 47
HAMILTON SQUARE		5 38
NORTH		A 29
PARK		5A 39
Woodside	* 67	23 38
Blacon	* 68	1 36
Blodwell Junction	51	3 22
BLUNDELLSANDS + CROSBY	*	2 39
BOOTLE		47
Balliol Road	48	2 47
MARSH LANE + STRAND RD.	A § * 67	2 47
NEW STRAND	A § 67	2 47
ORIEL ROAD	*	2 47
Breck Road	48	2 39
BROAD GREEN	*	2 49
Brocklebank Dock	56	6 47
BROMBOROUGH		23 38
BROMBOROUGH RAKE	85	23 38
Broughton + Bretton	62	2 36
Broxton	57	2 45
Brunswick Dock	56	6 47
Brymbo	50	3 35
BUCKLEY Junction	* 74	1 36
Burton Point for Burton + Puddington	55	1 37
CAERGWRLE Castle + Wells	* 74	1 35
Caldy	54	23 28
Calveley	60	2 55
Canada Dock	56	6 47
Canning	56	6 47
CAPENHURST		23 37
Carreghofa Halt	* 65	3 22
Cefn	60	3 24
CEFN-Y-BEDD	*	1 35
CHESTER		48
BACHE	3 84	23 46
GENERAL	4 69	23 46
Liverpool Road	51	1 36
Northgate	* 69	4 46
Upton-by-Chester	3 84	23 46
CHIRK		3 23
Clarence Dock	56	6 47
Clock Face	51	2 59
Clay Halt	† 62	3 34
Clubmoor	60	4 47
Coed Talon	50	2 26
Collins Green	51	2 59
Connah's Quay + SHOTTON	B § 53	1 27
Connah's Quay	* 66	2 27
Coole Pilate Halt	† 63	3 64
Coxbank Halt	† 63	3 64
Crank Halt	51	2 49
CRESSINGTON	* 72 78	4 38
CREWE		2 75
Crudgington	† 63	3 61
CUDDINGTON		4 67
Culcheth	* 64	1 69
Daresbury	52	23 58
DELAMERE		4 57
Dingle	56	6 47
DITTON Junction	73 94	2 48
Dunham Hill	52	23 47
EARLESTOWN Junction	* 50	2 59
ECCLESTON PARK	*	2 49
EDGE HILL	*	2 39
Edge Lane	48	2 47
Ellerdine Halt	† 63	3 62
Ellesmere	* 65	3 33
ELLESMERE PORT	*	23 47
Elson Halt	† 62	3 33
FARNWORTH	C § 59	4 58
Farnworth + Bold	51	2 58
FAZAKERLEY	*	2 39
Fenn's Bank	* 65	3 53
Ffrith	50	23 25
Fiddler's Ferry + Penketh	50	2 58
FLINT	*	2 27
Ford	51	2 39
Four Crosses	* 65	3 21
Frankton	* 65	3 33
FRODSHAM	*	23 57
GARSTON	* 72 78	4 48
GARSWOOD	*	2 59
Gateacre for Woolton	* 72	4 48
Gladstone Dock	56	6 47
Glanyrafon	51	3 22
GLAZEBROOK		4 69
Glazebury + Bury Lane	58	2 69
GOBOWEN		3 33
Golborne North	49 52	1 69
Golborne South	49 61	2 69
GREENBANK, Hartford +	73	4 67
GREEN LANE		5 38
Gresford for Llay Halt	55 62	3 35
Grindley Brook Halt	57	2 54
GWERSYLLT + Wheatsheaf	59	1 35
Hadlow Road	56	23 37
Hadnall	60	2 52
Halebank	58	2 48
Halewood	51	4 48
HALEWOOD	88	4 48
Halton	52	23 58
HARTFORD		2 67
Hartford + GREENBANK	73	4 67
Haughton Halt	60	3 32
HAWARDEN	*	1 36
HAWARDEN BRIDGE		1 37
Haydock	52	1 59
Haydock Park Racecourse	65	1 59
HELSBY	*	23 47
Helsby + Alvanley	63 64	4 47
Herculaneum Dock	56	6 47
Heswall	56	23 28
HESWALL Hills	* 56	1 28
Hightown Halt	† 62	3 35
Hodnet	† 63	3 62
Holywell Junction	* 66	2 17
HOOTON		23 37
Hope + Penyffordd	62	2 36
Hope Exchange	D § 53	1 36
Hope Exchange	E § 53	2 36
Hope High Level	D § 53 58	1 36
Hope Low Level	E § 53 58	2 36
HOPE Village	* 74	1 35
HOUGH GREEN		4 48
HOYLAKE		A 28
HUNTS CROSS		4 48
Huskisson Dock	56	6 47
HUYTON	*	2 48
Huyton Quarry	58	2 48
INCE + ELTON		23 47
James Street	56	6 47
JAMES STREET		5 39
Johnstown + Hafod	60	3 34
Kenyon Junction	61	2 69
Kinnerton	62	2 36
Kirby Park	56	23 28
KIRKBY	* 5	2 39
KIRKDALE		2 47
Knotty Ash + Stanley	60	4 49
Latchford	62	2 68
Lea Green	55	2 59
LEASOWE		A 29
Leaton	60	3 41
Ledsham	59	23 37
Linacre Road	51	2 39
Liscard + Poulton	60	A 39
LITTLE SUTTON	*	23 37
LIVERPOOL	6	47
(CENTRAL DEEP LEVEL)	77	0 47
CENTRAL LOW LEVEL	* 14	4 39
Central Low Level	75	5 47
Exchange	77	2 39
JAMES STREET		5 39
LIME STREET		2 39
(LIME STREET DEEP LEV)	77	0 47
MOORFIELDS LOW LEVEL	77	0 47
(MOORFIELDS DEEP LEVEL)	78	0 47
Riverside	49 50 71	X 47
Llanfechain	* 65	3 22
Llanfynydd	50	23 25
Llangollen	* 65	7 24
Llansaintffraid	* 65	3 22
Llansilin Road	51	3 22
Llanyblodwell	51	3 22
Llanymynech	* 65	3 22
Llanymynech Junction	7 60	3 22
Llong	62	3 26
Llynclys	* 65	3 22
LOSTOCK GRALAM		3 67
Lowton	49	2 69
Lowton St Mary's	* 64	1 69
Lymm	62	2 68
Malpas	57	2 54
MANOR ROAD		A 29
Marchwiel	† 62	3 34
Market Drayton	† 63	3 63
MARSH LANE see BOOTLE	67	2 47
MEOLS		A 29
Mersey Road + AIGBURTH	* 72 78	4 38
Mickle Trafford	51	23 47
Mickle Trafford East	50 51	4 47
Mold	62	2 26
Mollington	60	23 37
Moore	8 52	2 58
MORETON		A 29
Moss Bank	51	2 59
MOSSLEY HILL for Aigburth	74	2 38
MOULDSWORTH		4 57
NANTWICH	*	2 65
Nelson Dock	56	6 47
NESTON + Parkgate North	* 52 68	1 37
Neston South	52 56	23 27
NEW BRIGHTON		A 39
NEW STRAND	A §	2 47
NEWTON-LE-WILLOWS	*	2 59
NORTHWICH		4 67
Norton	9 52	23 58
Old Mill Lane Halt	51	2 49
OLD ROAN		2 39
Oldwoods Halt	60	3 42
ORIEL ROAD see BOOTLE		2 47
ORRELL PARK Halt	68	2 39
Oswestry	66	3 33
Otterspool	51	4 38
OVERPOOL	88	23 38
Overton-on-Dee	† 62	3 34
Padeswood + Buckley	58	2 26
PADGATE		4 69
Pant	* 65	3 22
Parkgate	56	23 27
Park Hall Halt	66	3 33
Peasley Cross	51	2 59
Pennington	54	2 69
PEN-Y-FFORDD + Leeswood	* 74	1 36
Peplow	† 63	3 62
Pickhill Halt	† 62	3 34
Pier Head	56	6 47
Porthywaen	51	3 22
PORT SUNLIGHT		23 38
PREES	*	2 53
PRESCOT	*	2 49
Preston Brook	2 52	2 58
PRESTON ROAD	* F § 84	2 47
Queensferry	* 66	2 36
RAINHILL	*	2 49
Rednal + West Felton	66	3 32
Rhos	7 52	3 24
Rhosymedre	59	3 24
Rhydymwyn	62	2 26
RICE LANE	F § 84	2 47
Risley	15 52	4 69
Risley	60	4 69
Riverside	6 49 50 71	X 47
ROBY	*	2 49
ROCK FERRY		23 38
Rookery	51	2 49
Rossett	* 64	3 35
Rowton Halt	† 63	3 62
RUNCORN		2 58
RUNCORN EAST	9 83	23 58
St Helens Central	49 52	1 59
ST HELENS JUNCTION		2 59
ST HELENS Shaw Street CENTRAL	* 49 87	2 59
ST MICHAEL'S	* 72 78	4 38
Saltney	60	3 36
Saltney Ferry	62	2 36
SANDHILLS		2 47
Sandycroft	61	2 36
Sankey Bridges	49	2 58
SANKEY FOR PENKETH		4 58
Saughall	54	1 36
Seacombe + Egremont	53 60	A 39
SEAFORTH + LITHERLAND	*	2 39
Seaforth Sands	56	26 39
Sealand	* 68	1 37
Sefton Park	52	2 38
Sesswick Halt	† 62	3 34
SHOTTON High Level	* 10 B § 53 72	1 36
SHOTTON Low Level	* 10 52 66 72	2 37
Shrawardine	7 60	3 31
Spellow	48	2 39
SPITAL		23 38
Stanley	48	2 47
STANLOW + THORNTON	*	23 47
Stanwardine Halt	60	3 42
Storeton for Barnston	51	2 28
Sun Bank Halt	50	3 24
Sutton Oak	51	2 59
Tanhouse Lane	* 64	12 48
Tattenhall	57	2 46
Tattenhall Road	* 66	2 56
Tern Hill	† 63	3 63
THATTO HEATH	*	2 49
Thelwall	56	2 68
Thurstaston	54	23 28
Tinkers Green Halt	* 65	3 33
Toxteth Dock	56	6 47
Trench Halt	† 62	3 33
Trevor	* 65	3 24
Trehowel Halt	51	3 23
Tue Brook	48	2 47
Union Farm Bank Halt	51	2 59
UPTON	*	1 28
Upton-by-Chester	84	23 46
Vulcan Halt	* 65	2 59
WALLASEY (GROVE ROAD)		A 29
WALLASEY VILLAGE		A 29
Walton + Anfield	48	2 39
WALTON Junction	?	2 47
WALTON Preston Road	F § 84	2 47
WALTON RICE LANE	F § 84	2 47
Wapping Dock	56	6 47
Warbreck	60	4 47
WARRINGTON		48
Arpley	58	2 68
BANK QUAY High Level	63	2 58
Bank Quay Low Level	63	2 58
CENTRAL		4 68
WATERLOO	*	2 39
Waverton	59	2 46
Wavertree	58	2 38
Welshampton	* 65	3 43
WEM	*	2 52
WEST ALLERTON		2 38
West Derby	60	4 39
WEST KIRBY		A 28
West Kirby	56	23 28
West Leigh + Bedford	16 * 64	2 69
WHISTON	90	2 49
WHITCHURCH		2 54
Whitehurst	60	3 24
Whittington High Level	60	3 33
Whittington Low Level	60	3 33
WIDNES		48
Appleton	51	2 58
Central	* 64	12 48
Farnworth North	C § 59 68	4 58
South	59 62	2 58
Tanhouse Lane	64	12 48
WIDNES North	C § 59 68	4 58
Willaston	54	2 65
WINSFORD		2 66
Wollerton Halt	† 63	3 62
Worleston	52	2 65
WRENBURY	*	2 64
WREXHAM CENTRAL		13 35
WREXHAM Exchange	11 81	1 35
WREXHAM GENERAL		3 35
Wynville Halt	60	3 34
YORTON	*	2 52

WORKS

No	Location	Co	Ref
W1	CREWE	2	65

GOODS

No	Name/Location	Closed	Co Ref
G1	Buckley	50	1 26
2	Criggion	49	3 21
3	Manley	61	4 57
4	Oswestry	71	3 23
5	Overt Wharton	68	2 66
6	Porthywaen	64	3 22
7	Rhydmeredydd	12 ?	3 22
8	Winnington + Anderton	69	4 67
9	Winsford + Over	68	4 66
10	Woodside	61	2 48

ENGINE SHEDS see Note 13

No	Name/Location	Closed	Ry Ref
E6	Chester GW	60	3 46
7	Chester LNW	67	2 46
8	Chester Northgate	60	4 46
9	Crewe Gresty Lane	63	3 65
10	Crewe North	65	2 65
11	Crewe South	66	2 75
12	CREWE ELECTRIC	O	0 65
13	CREWE DIESEL	O	0 65
21	Mold Junction	66	2 26
22	Northwich	68	4 67
23	Oswestry	65	3 38
24	Sutton Oak	67	2 59
25	Warrington Arpley	63	2 68
26	Warrington Central	66	4 68
27	Warrington Dallam	67	2 68
28	Whitchurch	57	2 54
29	Widnes	64	2 58
30	Widnes Tanhouse Ln	12 ?	1 58
31	Wrexham Croes Newydd	67	3 35
32	Wrexham Rhosddu	?	1 35

TUNNELS

No	Name	Length	Ry Ref
T1	Sutton	1936	23 58
2	Christleton	160	2 46

VIADUCTS + BRIDGES

No	Name	Ry	Ref
V1	Runcorn Bridge	2	58

NOTES:

REF All in SJ so letters omitted
§ Old Name } change of name
§ New Name }
Corresponding letters refer to the alternative name.
1 Still open for excursions and full re-opening is planned.
2 Last passenger train was pre-nationalisation.
3 Upton-by-Chester replaced by BACHE (nearby site).
4 became just CHESTER in 69.
5 This is two back to back terminal stations!!
6 New lines and stations see MAP 47. Two non listed railways: MERSEY DOCKS + HARBOUR X, BRITISH RAIL O only NEW stations on NEW lines
7 Closed pre-war for regular passenger traffic.
8 Regular services ended 1943
9 Norton closed but re-opened as RUNCORN EAST
10 Distinction between High + Low Level made 52-3. Low was closed 66, re-opened 72 when distinction dropped.
11 Exchange and GENERAL have for many years been effectively one. From 81 Exchange dropped from title of LNE platforms
12 May have closed entirely before nationalisation
13 Sheds 1-5 and 14-20 see map 47
14 Rebuilt on adjoining site 76-77.
* Proposed to open
Stations located but not named on the map have the appropriate page in Brown in the reference column.
Also a brown number against town or city gives page reference where that town or city is enlarged.
15 Originally Newchurch Halt.
16 Additional station: Weston Rhyn 60 3 23

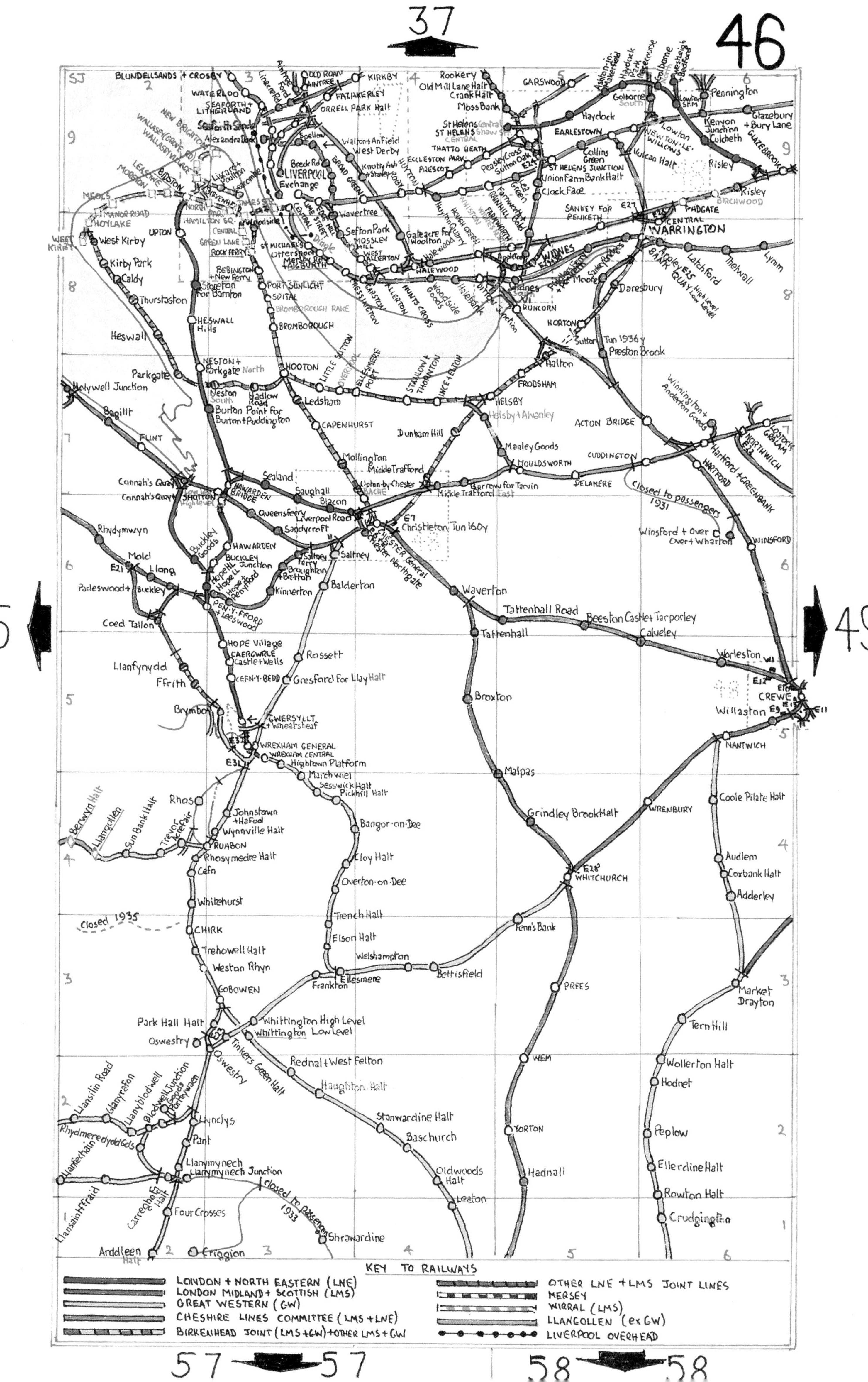

46
37
45
49
57
57
58
58
SJ
KEY TO RAILWAYS
LONDON + NORTH EASTERN (LNE)
LONDON MIDLAND + SCOTTISH (LMS)
GREAT WESTERN (GW)
CHESHIRE LINES COMMITTEE (LMS + LNE)
BIRKENHEAD JOINT (LMS + GW) + OTHER LMS + GW
OTHER LNE + LMS JOINT LINES
MERSEY
WIRRAL (LMS)
LLANGOLLEN (ex GW)
LIVERPOOL OVERHEAD
BLUNDELLSANDS + CROSBY
WATERLOO
SEAFORTH + LITHERLAND
KIRKBY
FAZAKERLEY
ORRELL PARK Halt
Rookery
Old Mill Lane Halt
Crank Halt
Moss Bank
GARSWOOD
Haydock
Golborne
Pennington
Glazebury + Bury Lane
Kenyon Junction
Culcheth
GLAZEBROOK
Risley
EARLESTOWN
Vulcan Halt
Collins Green
ST HELENS JUNCTION
Union Farm Bank Halt
Clock Face
THATTO HEATH
ECCLESTON PARK
PRESCOT
West Derby
LIVERPOOL
Exchange
Wavertree
Sefton Park
MOSSLEY HILL
WEST ALLERTON
Gateacre for Woolton
HALEWOOD
SANKEY FOR PENKETH
PADGATE
CENTRAL
WARRINGTON
Latchford
Thelwall
Lymm
Daresbury
WIDNES
RUNCORN
NORTON
Preston Brook
Halton
FRODSHAM
HELSBY
Helsby + Alvanley
ACTON BRIDGE
Dunham Hill
Manley Goods
MOULDSWORTH
CUDDINGTON
DELAMERE
HARTFORD
Hartford + Greenbank
NORTHWICH
Closed to passengers 1931
Winsford + Over
Over + Wharton
WINSFORD
BIDSTON
HOYLAKE
West Kirby
Kirby Park
Caldy
Thurstaston
Heswall
UPTON
Storeton for Barnston
HESWALL Hills
Parkgate
NESTON + Parkgate North
Neston South
Hadlow Road
Burton Point for Burton + Puddington
PORT SUNLIGHT
SPITAL
BROMBOROUGH RAKE
BROMBOROUGH
HOOTON
Ledsham
CAPENHURST
Mollington
Holywell Junction
Bagillt
FLINT
Connah's Quay
SHOTTON
HAWARDEN BRIDGE
Sealand
Saughall
Blacon
Queensferry
Sandycroft
Liverpool Road
Upton-by-Chester
Mickle Trafford
Barrow for Tarvin
Christleton Tun 160y
CHESTER General
Chester Northgate
Rhydymwyn
Mold
Llong
Padeswood + Buckley
Coed Talon
HAWARDEN
Buckley Junction
Hope + Penyffordd
Kinnerton
Saltney
Balderton
Waverton
Tattenhall Road
Tattenhall
Beeston Castle + Tarporley
Calveley
Worleston
CREWE
Willaston
NANTWICH
HOPE Village
CAERGWRLE Castle + Wells
CEFN-Y-BEDD
Rossett
Gresford for Llay Halt
Llanfynydd
Ffrith
Brymbo
GWERSYLLT + Wheatsheaf
WREXHAM GENERAL
WREXHAM CENTRAL
Hightown Platform
Marchwiel
Sesswick Halt
Pickhill Halt
Bangor-on-Dee
Broxton
Malpas
Grindley Brook Halt
WRENBURY
Coole Pilate Halt
Audlem
Coxbank Halt
Adderley
WHITCHURCH
Rhos
Johnstown + Hafod
Wynnville Halt
RUABON
Rhosymedre Halt
Cefn
Berwyn Halt
Llangollen
Sun Bank Halt
Trevor
Acrefair
Whitehurst
Closed 1935
CHIRK
Trehowell Halt
Weston Rhyn
GOBOWEN
Cloy Halt
Overton-on-Dee
Trench Halt
Elson Halt
Welshampton
Frankton
Ellesmere
Bettisfield
Fenn's Bank
PREES
Market Drayton
Tern Hill
Park Hall Halt
Oswestry
Whittington High Level
Whittington Low Level
Rednal + West Felton
Haughton Halt
Tinkers Green Halt
WEM
Wollerton Halt
Hodnet
Llansilin Road
Glanyrafon
Llanyblodwell
Blodwell Junction
Porthywaen
Llynclys
Pant
Llanymynech
Llanymynech Junction
Stanwardine Halt
Baschurch
YORTON
Peplow
Llanfechain
Oldwoods Halt
Hadnall
Ellerdine Halt
Carreghofa Halt
Four Crosses
Closed to passengers 1933
Leaton
Rowton Halt
Crudgington
Llansantffraid
Shrawardine
Arddleen Halt
Criggion

LIVERPOOL + BIRKENHEAD

RAILWAYS

No.	Company
1	LONDON + NORTH EASTERN (LNE)
2	LONDON MIDLAND + SCOTTISH (LMS)
23	BIRKENHEAD JOINT (LMS + GW)
3	GREAT WESTERN (GW)
4	CHESHIRE LINES COMMITTEE (LNE+LMS)
5	MERSEY
A	WIRRAL (LMS)
6	LIVERPOOL OVERHEAD
X	MERSEY DOCKS + HARBOUR BOARD
0	BRITISH RAIL (new lines)

STATIONS

Station	Opened Closed	Ry	Ref
AIGBURTH, Mersey Road +	72 78	4	38
AINTREE Sefton Arms	? 68	2	39
Aintree Central	1 51 63	4	39
Alexandra Dock	56	6	B
Alexandra Dock	2 49	2	39
ALLERTON for Garston + Woolton	74	2	48
Balliol Road Bootle	48	2	39
BANK HALL	*	2	39
BEBINGTON + New Ferry	74	23	38
BIDSTON		1A	29
BIRKENHEAD			A
CENTRAL		5	38
CONWAY PARK	*	5	38
HAMILTON SQUARE		5	38
NORTH		A	29
PARK		5A	38
Woodside	* 67	23	38
BLUNDELLSANDS + CROSBY	*	2	39
BOOTLE			B
Balliol Road		2	39
Marsh Lane + Strand Rd	A § * 67	2	39
NEW STRAND	A § 67	2	39
ORIEL ROAD	*	2	39
Breck Road	48	2	39
BROAD GREEN		2	49
Brocklebank Dock	56	6	B
Brunswick Dock	56	6	B
Canada Dock	56	6	B
Canning	56	6	B
Clarence Dock	56	6	B
Clubmoor	60	4	39
CRESSINGTON	* 72 78	4	38
Dingle	56	6	B
EDGE HILL	*	2	39
Edge Lane	48	2	39
FAZAKERLEY	*	2	39
Ford	51	2	39
GARSTON	* 72 78	4	48
Gateacre for Woolton	* 72	4	48
Gladstone Dock	56	6	B
GREEN LANE		5	38
Herculaneum Dock	56	6	B
HUNTS CROSS		4	48
Huskisson Dock	56	6	B
James Street	56	6	B
JAMES STREET		5	39
KIRKBY	* 3	2	49
KIRKDALE		2	39
Knotty Ash + Stanley	60	4	49
Linacre Road	51	2	39
Liscard + Poulton	60	A	39
LIME STREET		2	39
LIVERPOOL			B
(CENTRAL DEEP LEVEL)		0	B
CENTRAL Low Level	* 4	4	39
Central Low Level	75	5	B
Exchange		2	39
JAMES STREET		5	39
LIME STREET		2	39
(LIME STREET DEEP LEVEL)	77	0	B
MOORFIELDS LOW LEVEL	77	0	B
(MOORFIELDS DEEP LEVEL)	78	0	B
Riverside	49 50 71	X	B
Marsh Lane + Strand Road	A § * 67	2	39 G
Mersey Road + AIGBURTH	* 72 78	4	38
MOORFIELDS LOW LEVEL	77	0	B
(MOORFIELDS DEEP LEVEL	78	0	B
MOSSLEY HILL for Aigburth	74	2	38
Nelson Dock	56	6	B
NEW BRIGHTON		A	39
NEW STRAND	A §	2	39
OLD ROAN		2	39
ORRELL PARK Halt	68	2	39
ORIEL ROAD		2	39
Otterspool	51	4	38
Pier Head	56	6	B
Preston Road	* B § 84	2	39
RICE LANE	B § 84	2	39
Riverside	49 50 71	X	B
ROBY	*	2	49
ROCK FERRY		23	38
ST MICHAEL'S	72 78	4	38
SANDHILLS		2	39
Seacombe + Egremont	53 60	A	39
SEAFORTH + LITHERLAND	*	2	39
Seaforth Sands	56	26	39
Sefton Park	52	2	38
Spellow	48	2	39
Stanley	48	2	39
Storeton for Barnton	51	2	28
Toxteth Dock	56	6	B
Tue Brook	48	2	39
WALLASEY GROVE ROAD		A	29
WALLASEY VILLAGE		A	29
WALTON			B
+ Anfield	48	2	39
Junction	5 ?	2	39
Preston Road	B § 84	2	39
RICE LANE	B § 84	2	39
Wapping Dock	56	6	B
Warbreck	60	4	39
WATERLOO	*	2	39
Wavertree	58	2	38
WEST ALLERTON		2	48
West Derby	60	4	39

GOODS

No	Name/Location	Closed if known Note 6	Ry	Ref
	BIRKENHEAD MAP			A
1	Bidston	68	1	
2	Birkenhead North		2	
3	Cathcart Street	61	23	
4	Dock Road	55	1	
5	Duke Street	59	1	
6	Egerton Dock	61	2	
7	Great Float West		4	
8	Monks Ferry		23	
9	Morpeth Dock	72	3	
10	Seacombe	63	A	
11	Shore Road	61	4	
12	Tranmere Pool		23	B
	LIVERPOOL MAP			
13	Alexandra Dock	67	2	
14	Bankfield	65	2	
15	Bootle Canada Dock		2	
16	Brunswick		4	
17	Brunswick Dock		2	
18	Crown Street	72	2	
19	Edge Hill		2	
20	Great Howard Street	63	2	
21	Huskisson		4	
22	Langton Dock	70	2	
23	North Docks	66	2	
24	North Mersey	68	2	
25	Park Lane	65	2	
26	Rathbone Road	72	2	
27	Sandon Dock	69	2	
28	South Docks		2	
29	Stanley Cattle		2	
30	Waterloo Dock	63	2	
31	Wavertree + Edge Hill	73	4	
	OTHERS			C
32	Garston Dock		2	38
33	SPEKE YARD	0	2	48

ENGINE SHEDS

No.	Name/Location	Closed	Ry	Ref
E1	Bidston	63	1	A
2	Birkenhead LMS	7 67	2	A
3	Birkenhead GW	8 67	3	A
4	Birkenhead Shore Rd	61	4	A
5	Birkenhead NORTH	9 0	5	A
14	Aintree	67	2	B
15	Bank Hall	66	2	B
16	Brunswick	61	4	B
17	Central	66	4	B
18	Edge Hill	68	2	B
19	Speke Junction	68	2	48
20	Walton-on-the-Hill	63	4	B
33	ALLERTON	0	0	48

TUNNELS

No.	Name/Location	Length	Ry	Ref
T1	Dingle	1082	4	B
2	Dingle	10 506	6	B
3	St Michael's	103	4	B
4	Fulwood	200	4	B
5	Mount Pleasant	134	2	B
6	Crown Street	170	2	B
7	Bootle	481	2	B
8	Kirkdale No.1	497	2	B
9	Kirkdale No.2	210	2	B
10	Alexandra Dock	288	2	B
11	Spellow No.2	348	2	B
12	Wapping		2	B
13	Corporation Road	64	A	A
14	Cavendish Street	71	A	A
15	Central	29 32	40	B

JUNCTIONS

No	Name Location	Ry	Ref
J1	New Brighton No.1	A	A
2	New Brighton No.2	A	A
3	Slopes Branch	2	A
4	Seacombe	A	A
5	Bidston North	A	A
6	Bidston South	12	A
7	Bidston East	A	A
8	Bidston West	A	A
9	Mersey + Birkenhead	235	A
10	Brook Street	23	A
11	Dee	1	A
12	Canning Street	23	A
13	Egerton Street	4	B
14	Olive Mount	2	B
15	Derby Square	50	B
16	Paradise	0	B
17	Picton Road	2	B
18	Sefton	2	B

NOTES:

REF Only on Map C otherwise just shown as A or B

§ Old name } Change of name
§ New name }

Identical letter gives identity to alternative name

* Proposed to open

1 Still opened for excursions. Full re-opening planned

2 Last passenger train was before nationalisation.

3 This is two back-to-back termini.

4 Rebuilt on adjoining site 76-77.

5 Junction dropped from title in BR period.

6 Many of goods location still in use some privately.

7 continued after closure to steam as diesel depot

8 Effective closure date was 51 after which time ex LMS depot used.

9 Depot for EMUs

10 Length is to station which was in continuation of enlarged tunnel and this continued beyond the station (used for 'turning' purposes.

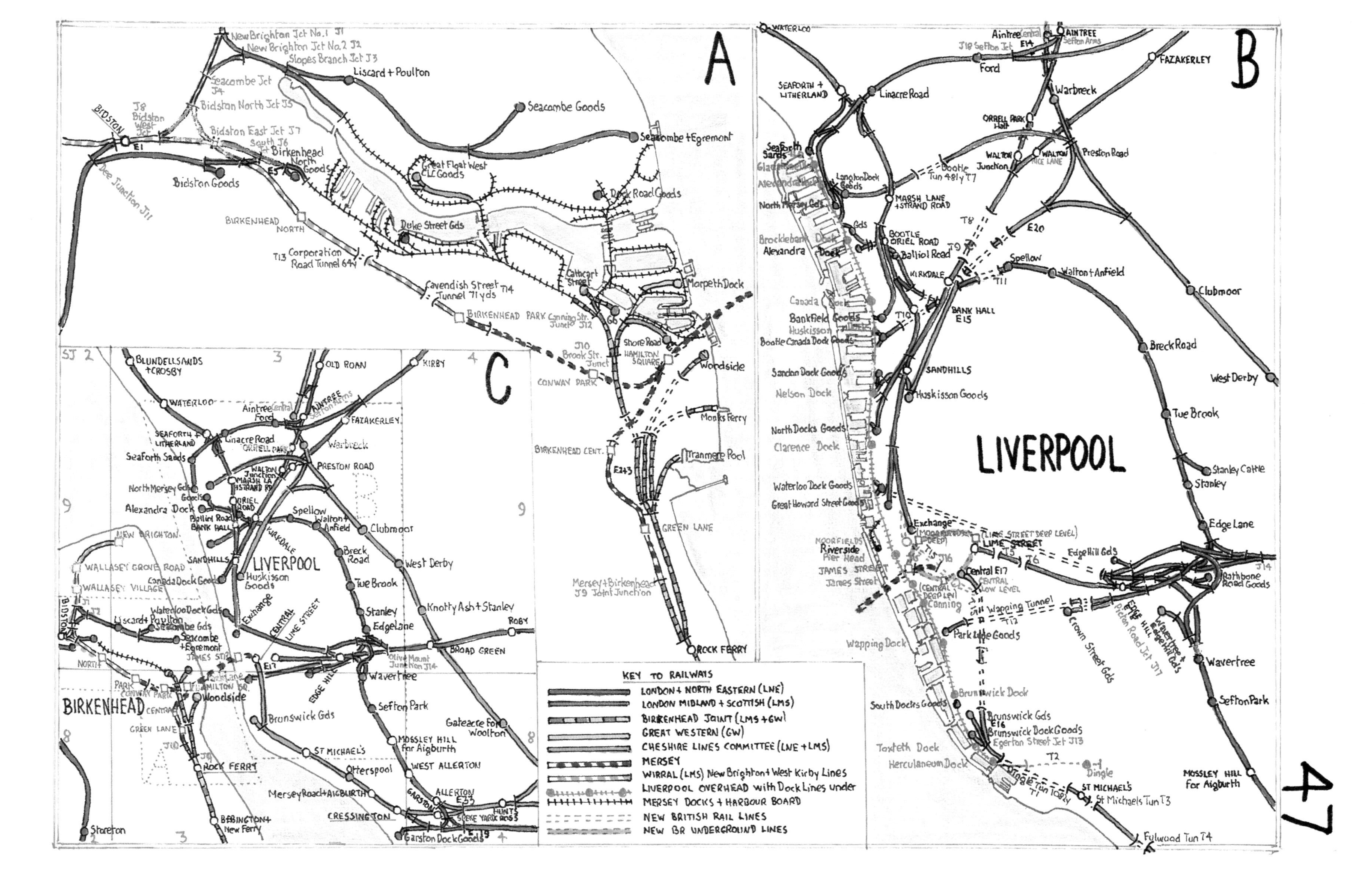
A
B
C
LIVERPOOL
BIRKENHEAD
KEY TO RAILWAYS
LONDON + NORTH EASTERN (LNE)
LONDON MIDLAND + SCOTTISH (LMS)
BIRKENHEAD JOINT (LMS + GW)
GREAT WESTERN (GW)
CHESHIRE LINES COMMITTEE (LNE + LMS)
MERSEY
WIRRAL (LMS) New Brighton + West Kirby Lines
LIVERPOOL OVERHEAD with Dock Lines under
MERSEY DOCKS + HARBOUR BOARD
NEW BRITISH RAIL LINES
NEW BR UNDERGROUND LINES
New Brighton Jct No.1 J1
New Brighton Jct No.2 J2
Slopes Branch Jct J3
Liscard + Poulton
Seacombe Jct J4
Bidston North Jct J5
Seacombe Goods
Bidston East Jct J7
South J6
Seacombe + Egremont
BIDSTON
J8 Bidston West Jct
E1
Birkenhead North Goods
Great Float West CLC Goods
Dock Road Goods
Bidston Goods
Dee Junction J11
BIRKENHEAD NORTH
Duke Street Gds
T13 Corporation Road Tunnel 64y
Cathcart Street
Morpeth Dock
Cavendish Street Tunnel 71 yds T14
BIRKENHEAD PARK
Canning Str. Junct J12
Shore Road
J10 Brook Str. Junct
HAMILTON SQUARE
Woodside
CONWAY PARK
Monks Ferry
BIRKENHEAD CENT.
Tranmere Pool
E243
GREEN LANE
Mersey + Birkenhead J9 Joint Junction
ROCK FERRY
WATERLOO
Aintree Central
AINTREE Sefton Arms
J18 Sefton Jct
E14
FAZAKERLEY
Ford
SEAFORTH + LITHERLAND
Linacre Road
Warbreck
ORRELL PARK Halt
Seaforth Sands
WALTON Junction
WALTON RICE LANE
Preston Road
Langton Dock Goods
Bootle Tun 481y T7
MARSH LANE + STRAND ROAD
North Mersey Gds
Gds
T8
E20
BOOTLE ORIEL ROAD
Brocklebank Dock
Alexandra Dock
Balliol Road
T9
Spellow
Walton + Anfield
KIRKDALE
T11
Clubmoor
Canada Dock
T10
BANK HALL E15
Bankfield Goods
Huskisson
Bootle Canada Dock Goods
Breck Road
Sandon Dock Goods
SANDHILLS
West Derby
Nelson Dock
Huskisson Goods
Tue Brook
North Docks Goods
Clarence Dock
Stanley Cattle
Waterloo Dock Goods
Stanley
Great Howard Street Goods
Edge Lane
Exchange
(LIME STREET DEEP LEVEL)
LIME STREET
Edge Hill Gds
MOORFIELDS
Riverside Pier Head
T5
T6
JAMES STREET
James Street
Central E17
CENTRAL LOW LEVEL
Rathbone Road Goods
J14
(CENTRAL DEEP LEVEL)
Canning
Wapping Tunnel
T12
Crown Street Gds
EDGE HILL E18
Picton Road Jct J17
Wavertree + Edge Hill Gds
Park Lane Goods
Wapping Dock
Wavertree
Brunswick Dock
South Docks Goods
Brunswick Gds
E16
Brunswick Dock Goods
Egerton Street Jct J13
Sefton Park
Toxteth Dock
T2
Herculaneum Dock
Dingle
Dingle Tun 1040y T1
MOSSLEY HILL for Aigburth
ST MICHAEL'S
St Michaels Tun T3
Fulwood Tun T4
SJ 2
3
4
9
8
BLUNDELLSANDS + CROSBY
OLD ROAN
KIRBY
WATERLOO
Aintree Central
Ford
AINTREE Sefton Arms
FAZAKERLEY
SEAFORTH + LITHERLAND
Linacre Road
ORRELL PARK
Warbreck
Seaforth Sands
PRESTON ROAD
WALTON Junction
MARSH LA + STRAND RD
North Mersey Gds
Goods
ORIEL ROAD
Alexandra Dock
Balliol Road
BANK HALL
KIRKDALE
Spellow
Walton + Anfield
Clubmoor
NEW BRIGHTON
WALLASEY GROVE ROAD
SANDHILLS
LIVERPOOL
Huskisson Goods
Breck Road
West Derby
Canada Dock Goods
WALLASEY VILLAGE
Tue Brook
BIDSTON
Waterloo Dock Gds
Exchange
CENTRAL
LIME STREET
Stanley
Knotty Ash + Stanley
Liscard + Poulton
Seacombe Gds
Edge Lane
ROBY
Seacombe + Egremont
JAMES ST
BROAD GREEN
NORTH
E17
Olive Mount Junction J14
PARK
CONWAY PARK
HAMILTON SQ
Wavertree
Woodside
EDGE HILL
CENTRAL
Brunswick Gds
Sefton Park
GREEN LANE
Gateacre for Woolton
ST MICHAEL'S
MOSSLEY HILL for Aigburth
ROCK FERRY
Otterspool
WEST ALLERTON
MerseyRoad + AIGBURTH
ALLERTON E33
GARSTON
HUNTS CROSS
CRESSINGTON
SPEKE YARDS
Storeton
BEBINGTON + New Ferry
Garston Dock Goods

48 ST HELENS, WIDNES, WARRINGTON, CHESTER + CREWE

RAILWAYS

No.	Company
1	LONDON + NORTH EASTERN (LNE)
12	SHEFFIELD + MIDLAND (LNE + LMS)
2	LONDON MIDLAND + SCOTTISH (LMS)
23	BIRKENHEAD JOINT (LMS + GW)
3	GREAT WESTERN (GW)
4	CHESHIRE LINES COMMITTEE (LNE + LMS)
0	BRITISH RAIL new lines

STATIONS

Note	Station	Opened/Closed	Ry	Ref
	Appleton	51	2	B
	Arpley	58	2	C
	Ashton-in-Makerfield	75	1	A
1	BACHE	84	23	D
*	Blacon	68	1	D
	CHESTER General	69	23	D
	Chester Liverpool Street	51	1	D
*	Chester Northgate	69	4	D
	Clock Face	51	2	A
	Collins Green	51	2	A
	Crank Halt	51	2	A
	CREWE		2	E
*	Culcheth	64	1	A
	DITTON Junction	73 94	2	B
*	EARLESTOWN Junction	50	2	A
*	ECCLESTON PARK		2	A
A §	Farnsworth	59	4	B
	Golborne North	49 52	1	A
	Golborne South	49 61	2	A
	Haydock	52	1	A
	Haydock Park	65	1	A
	HOUGH GREEN		4	B
	Kenyon Junction	61	2	A
	Lea Green	55	2	A
	Lowton	49	2	A
*	Lowton St Mary's	64	1	A
2	Mickle Trafford	51	23	D
2	Mickle Trafford East	50 51	4	D
	Moss Bank	51	2	A
*	NEWTON-LE-WILLOWS		2	A
	Peasley Cross	51	2	A
	Pennington	54	2	A
*	RAINHILL		2	A
	St Helens Central	49 52	1	A
B §	ST HELENS Shaw Street	49 87	2	A
B §	ST HELENS CENTRAL	87	2	A
	ST HELENS		2	A
	Saltney	60	3	D
	Sankey Bridges	49	2	C
	Sutton Oak	51	2	A
*	Tanhouse Lane	64	12	B
*	THATTO HEATH		2	A
	Union Farm Bank Halt	51	2	A
1	Upton-by-Chester	84	23	D
*	Vulcan Halt	65	2	A
	WARRINGTON BANK QUAY High Level	63	2	C
	Warrington Bank Quay Low Level	63	2	C
	WARRINGTON CENTRAL		4	C
*	Widnes Central	64	12	B
A §	WIDNES North	59 68	4	B
	Widnes South	59 62	2	B
	Willaston	54	2	E

GOODS

No	Location	Closure if known	Ry	Ref
G1	Chester GW		3	
2	Chester Northgate	65	4	
3	CREWE BASFORD YARD	3	2	
4	CREWE GRESTY LANE	3	2	
5	St Helens		2	
6	Warrington	65	2	
7	WARRINGTON YARD	3	0	
8	Widnes	64	12	

ENGINE SHEDS

No	Name/Location	Closed Steam	Ry	Ref
E6	Chester GW	60	3	D
7o	Chester LMS	see note 4	2	D
7N	Chester LMS	67	2	D
8	Chester Northgate	60	4	D
9	Crewe Gresty Lane	63	3	E
10	Crewe North	65	2	E
11	Crewe South	66	2	E
12	CREWE ELECTRIC	3	0	E
13	CREWE DIESEL	3	0	E
24	Sutton Oak	67	2	A
25	Warrington Arpley	63	2	C
26	Warrington Central	66	4	C
27	Warrington Dallam	67	2	C
29	Widnes	5 64	2	B

WORKS

No	Location		Ry	Ref
W1	CREWE	6	2	E

TUNNELS

No	Name	Length	Ry	Ref
T1	Windmill Lane	104	2	D
2	Northgate Street	218	2	D
3	Christleton	160	2	D

BRIDGES + VIADUCTS

No	Name	Ry	Ref
V1	Runcorn Bridge	2	D
2	Roodee Viaduct	2	D

JUNCTIONS

No	Location	Ry	Ref
J1	Carr Mill	2	A
2	Gerards Bridge	2	A
3	Ashton Green North	2	A
4	Ashton Green South	2	A
5	Winnick	2	A
6	Parkside East	2	A
7	Parkside West	2	A
8	Dallam Branch	2	C
9	Sankey	2	C
10	Brook Lane	23	D
11	Tunnel	223	D
12	Holyhead	23	D
13	Gresty Lane	2	E

NOTES

REF Map designation only

§ Old name } Change of name
§ New name }

Corresponding letters indicate other name

1 Upton-by-Chester was replaced by BACHE
2 The BR cross-over was the re-instatement of an old pregrouping one never used and taken up following inter-company dispute
3 Open at end of period.
4 o Old N New. Old taken over by GW in the pre-nationalisation era.
5 Map 46 shows 30 shed at Tanhouse Lane, but this appears to have closed pre-nationalisation.
6 Still open but privatised.

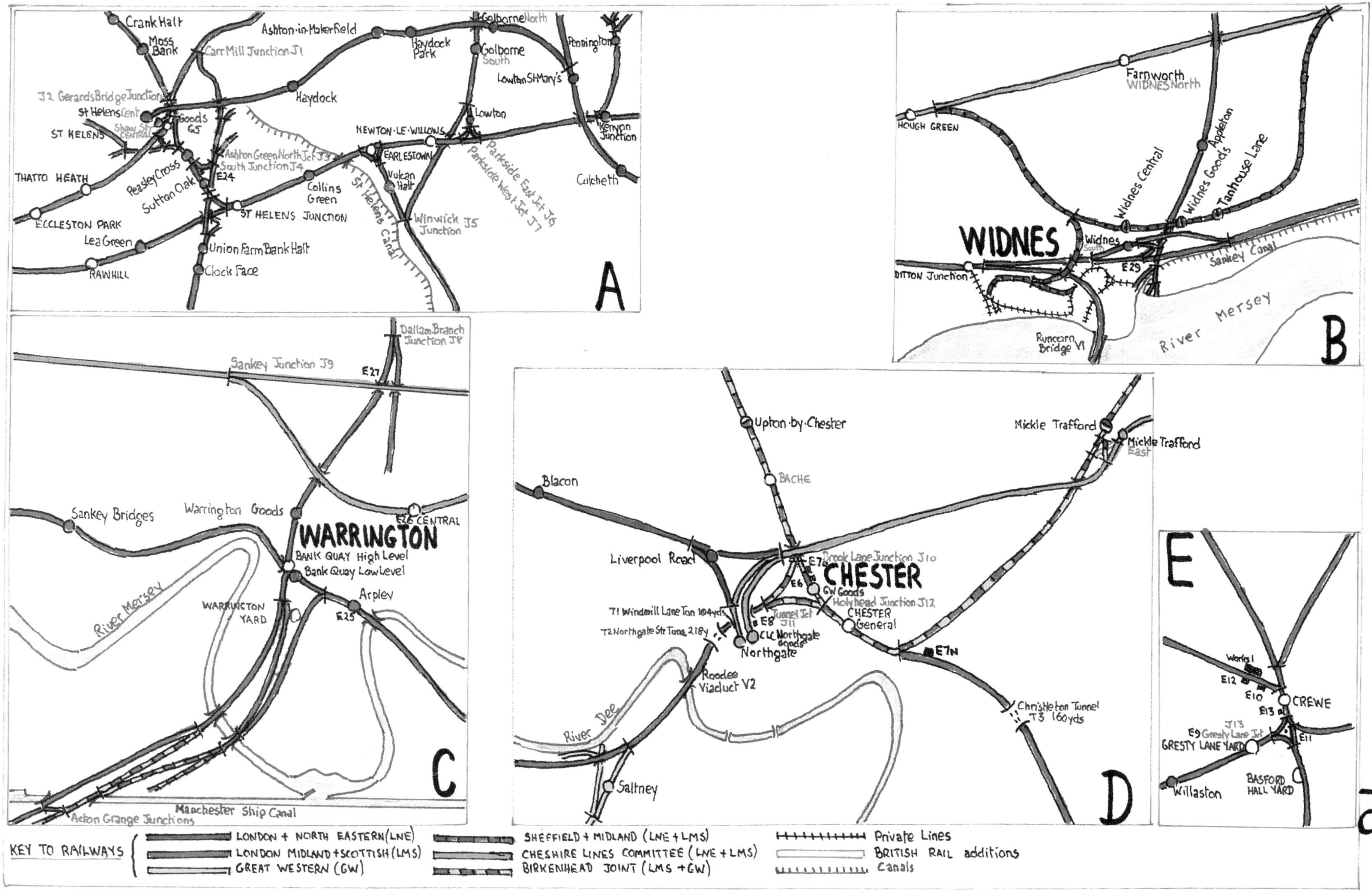

A

Crank Halt
Moss Bank
Ashton-in-Makerfield
Carr Mill Junction J1
J2 Gerards Bridge Junction
St Helens Cent
Shaw St Central
ST HELENS
Goods G5
Haydock
Haydock Park
Golborne North
Golborne South
Lowton St Mary's
Pennington
Lowton
Kenyon Junction
Culcheth
NEWTON-LE-WILLOWS
EARLESTOWN
Parkside East Jct J6
Parkside West Jct J7
Vulcan Halt
Winwick Junction J5
St Helens Canal
Collins Green
Ashton Green North Jct J3
South Junction J4
E24
THATTO HEATH
Peasley Cross
Sutton Oak
ECCLESTON PARK
ST HELENS JUNCTION
Lea Green
Union Farm Bank Halt
Clock Face
RAWHILL

B

HOUGH GREEN
Farnworth
WIDNES North
Widnes Central
Appleton
Widnes Goods
Tanhouse Lane
WIDNES
Widnes South
E29
Sankey Canal
DITTON Junction
Runcorn Bridge V1
River Mersey

C

Dallam Branch Junction J8
Sankey Junction J9
E27
Sankey Bridges
Warrington Goods
WARRINGTON
E26 CENTRAL
BANK QUAY High Level
Bank Quay Low Level
River Mersey
WARRINGTON YARD
Arpley
E25
Acton Grange Junctions
Manchester Ship Canal

D

Upton-by-Chester
Mickle Trafford
Mickle Trafford East
BACHE
Blacon
Liverpool Road
E7
Brook Lane Junction J10
CHESTER
E6
GW Goods
Holyhead Junction J12
T1 Windmill Lane Tun 104yds
Tunnel Jct J11
E8
CHESTER General
T2 Northgate St Tunl 218y
CLC Northgate Goods
Northgate
E7N
Roodee Viaduct V2
River Dee
Christleton Tunnel T3 160yds
Saltney

E

Works 1
E12
E10
CREWE
E13
J13
E9 Gresty Lane Jct
GRESTY LANE YARD
E11
BASFORD HALL YARD
Willaston

KEY TO RAILWAYS
LONDON + NORTH EASTERN (LNE)
LONDON MIDLAND + SCOTTISH (LMS)
GREAT WESTERN (GW)
SHEFFIELD + MIDLAND (LNE + LMS)
CHESHIRE LINES COMMITTEE (LNE + LMS)
BIRKENHEAD JOINT (LMS + GW)
Private Lines
BRITISH RAIL additions
Canals

MANCHESTER + STAFFORD

RAILWAYS

No	Company
1	LONDON + NORTH EASTERN (LNE)
2	LONDON, MIDLAND + SCOTTISH (LMS)
3	CHESHIRE LINES COMMITTEE (LNE+LMS)
4	other Joint lines (LNE+LMS)
M	now GREATER MANCHESTER METROLINK
M	NEW METROLINK
O	NEW BRITISH RAIL (new lines)

STATIONS

Station	Opened Closed	Ry Ref
ADLINGTON		2 J98
ALDERLEY EDGE		2 J87
ALSAGER		2 J75
Alsop-en-le-Dale	63	2 K15
Alton Towers	* 54 65	2 K04
ALTRINCHAM + Bowden	74 M	3 J78
ALTRINCHAM, NAVIGATION ROAD	M	3 J78
ARDWICK	*	1 J89
Ashbourne	1 63	2 K14
ASHBURYS for Belle Vue	*	1 50
ASHLEY		3 J78
ASHTON Charlestown UNDER-LYNE	* 68	2 J99
Ashton Oldham Road	59	4 J99
Ashton Park Parade	56	1 50
Astley	56	2 J79
Audenshaw	50	2 J99
Baguley	* 64	3 J78
BARLASTON + Tittensor	72	2 J83
BELLE VUE		4 50
Birch Vale	* 70	4 K08
Blackwell Mill	2 66	2 K07
BLYTHE BRIDGE		2 J94
Bollington	* 70	4 J97
Bosley	64	2 J96
BRAMHALL		2 J88
BREDBURY		4 J99
BRINNINGTON	77	4 J99
BROADBOTTOM, Mottram +	* 54	1 K09
Broadheath	62	2 J78
BROOKLANDS	M	4 J79
Bucknall + Northwood	62	2 J94
BURNAGE		2 50
Burslem	* 64	2 J85
BUXTON		2 K07
Buxton	* 67	2 K07
Cadishead	* 64	3 J79
Chapel-en-le-Frith Central	* 67	2 K08
CHAPEL-EN-LE-FRITH South	* 68	2 K07
CHASSEN ROAD		3 J79
Chatterley	48	2 J85
Cheadle North	* 50 64	3 J89
Cheadle Heath	* 67	2 J88
CHEADLE HULME		2 J88
Cheadle (Staffs)	† 63	2 K04
Cheddleton	* 65	2 J95
Cheedale Halt	3 87	2 K07
CHELFORD		2 J87
CHINLEY		2 K08
Chorlton-cum-Hardy	* 67	3 J89
Clayton Bridge	* 68	2 J89
Cliffe Park Halt	2 64	2 J96
Clifton (Mayfield	2 58	2 K14
Cobridge	* 64	2 J84
Coldmeece	4 58	2 J83
Colwich	58	2 K02
CONGLETON		2 J86
Consall	* 65	2 J94
Cresswell	66	2 J94
Cross Lane	59	2 J89
Crowden	57	1 K09
Crown Street Halt	49	2 J84
DANE ROAD	M	4 J79
DAVENPORT	*	2 J88
Denstone	* 65	2 K04
DENTON	*	2 J99
Didsbury	* 67	2 J89
DINTING		1 K09
DISLEY	*	2 J98
DOVE HOLES	*	2 K07
Dowlow Halt	54	2 K16
Droylsden	* 68	2 J99
Dukinfield + Ashton	50	2 J99
Dukinfield Central	59	1 50
Dunham Massey	62	2 J78
EAST DIDSBURY + Parr's Wood	74	2 J89
ECCLES	*	2 J79
EDALE	*	2 K18
Endon	62	2 J95
ETRURIA		2 J84
FAIRFIELD for Droylsden	* 74	1 J99
Fallowfield	58	1 J89
Fenton	62	2 J94
Fenton Manor	56	2 J84
FLIXTON		3 J79
FLOWERY FIELD	85	1 J99
Ford Green	5 60 62	2 J85
FURNESS VALE	*	2 K08
GATLEY for Cheadle	74	2 J88
GLOSSOP Central	* 74	1 K09
Gnosall	* 64	2 J82
Godley Junction East	* 7 74 86 90	1 J99
GODLEY	86	1 J99
GOOSTREY		2 J77
GORTON + Openshaw	* 6	1 J89
Great Bridgeford	52	2 J92
Great Longstone	8 † 67	2 K17
GUIDE BRIDGE		1 J99
HADFIELD		1 K09
HALE		3 J88
HANDFORTH		2 J88
Hanley	* 64	2 J84
Hartington	63	2 K16
HATTERSLEY	78	1 J99
Haughton	49	2 J82
Hayfield	* 70	4 K08
HAZEL GROVE	*	2 J98
HEALD GREEN		2 J88
Heatley + Warburton	62	2 J78
HEATON CHAPEL + Heaton Moor	74	2 J89
Heaton Mersey	61	2 50
Heaton Norris	59	2 J89
Hibel Road Macclesfield	60	2 J97
Higher Buxton	51	2 K07
Higher Poynton	* 70	4 J98
High Lane	* 70	4 J98
Hindlow	1 63	2 K16
HOLMES CHAPEL		2 J76
HOPE	*	2 K18
HUMPHREY PARK	84	3 J79
Hurdlow	9 52	2 K16
HYDE CENTRAL	* 51	4 J99
HYDE Junction NORTH	* 51	1 J99
Hyde Road	58	1 J89
IRLAM For/+ Cadishead	54 74	4 J79
Keele	56	2 J74
KIDSGROVE Central	65?	J85
Kidsgrove Halt	50	2 J85
Kidsgrove Liverpool Road	* 64	2 J85
Kingsley + Froghall	* 65	2 K04
Knott Mill + DEANSGATE	71	4 J89
KNUTSFORD		4 J77
Leek	* 65	2 J95
Leek Brook Halt	10 59	2 J95
Leigh	* 66	2 K03
LEVENSHULME North	52 60	2 50
Levenshulme South	52 58	1 50
Liverpool Road Halt	* 64	2 J84
LONGPORT		2 J94
LONGSIGHT	13 58 80	2 50
LONGTON		2 J94
MACCLESFIELD Central		2 J97
Macclesfield Hibel Road	60	2 J97
Madeley	52	2 J74
MANCHESTER		J89
Central	69	3 J89
DEANSGATE, Knott Hill +	12	4 J89
Exchange	69	2 J89
(G MEX (DEANSGATE))	12 92	M 50
(HIGH STREET)	92	M 50
London Road	11A § 60(1)	2 J89
(MARKET STREET)	92	M 50
Mayfield	60	2 50
(MOSLEY STREET)	92	M 50
OXFORD ROAD		4 J89
PICCADILLY	11A § 60	4 J89
(PICCADILLY GARDENS)	92	M 50
(ST PETER'S SQUARE)	92	M 50
VICTORIA		2 J89
MANCHESTER AIRPORT	93	0 J88
MANCHESTER UNITED FC GROUND		3 J89
Marchington	58	2 K13
MARPLE		4 J99
MAULDETH ROAD For Withington	74	2 J89
Meir	* 66	2 J94
Middlewich		2 J76
Middlewood Higher	51 60	4 J98
MIDDLEWOOD Lower	* 51 61	2 J98
MILES PLATTING		2 J89
Milford + Brocton	50	2 J92
Miller's Dale for Tidswell	*	2 K17
Milton	62	2 J95
MOBBERLEY		3 J78
Monsal Dale	60	2 K17
Monton Green	* 69	2 J79
Mottram + BROADBOTTOM	54	1 J99
MOTTRAM STAFF HALT	14	1 K09
Mow Cop + Scholar Green	* 64	2 J85
NAVIGATION ROAD	M	3 J78
Newcastle-under-Lyme	* 64	2 J84
Newchapel + Goldenhill	* 64	2 J85
NEW MILLS CENTRAL	52	4 J98
NEW MILLS NEWTOWN	*	2 J98
NEWTON FOR HYDE	*	1 J99
Norbury + Ellaston	58	2 K14
Normacot	* 64	2 J94
Northenden	* 64	3 J88
North Rode	62	2 J96
NORTON BRIDGE	*	2 J82
Norton-in-Hales	56	2 J73
Oakamoor	* 65	2 K04
Old TRAFFORD (BAR)	B § 92 M	4 J89
(OLD TRAFFORD)	C § 92 M	4 J89
Ordsall Lane	57	2 50
PARK	*	2 J89
Parsley Hay	67	2 K16
Partington	* 64	4 J79
PATRICROFT	*	2 J79
Peak Forest for Peak Dale	* 65 67	2 K07
Pendleton	* 66	2 J89
PENDLETON Broad Street	66	2 J89
Pipe Gate for Woore	56	2 J74
Pitts Hill	* 64	2 J85
PLUMLEY		3 J77
POYNTON		2 J98
PRESTBURY		2 J97
Radway Green + Barthomley	* 66	2 J75
REDDISH NORTH	51	4 J89
REDDISH SOUTH	* 52	2 J89
Rocester	* 65	2 K03
ROMILEY		4 J99
ROSE HILL (MARPLE)	*	4 J98
Rudyard Lake	15 64	2 J95
Rushton	15 64	2 J96
RYDER BROW	85	4 50
SALE	M	4 J79
SALFORD CENTRAL	88	2 J89
SALFORD CRESCENT	87	2 J89
SANDBACH		2 J76
Seedley	56	2 J89
Silverdale	* 64	2 J84
STAFFORD		2 J92
Stafford Common Air Ministry Sidings	16 52	1 J92
STALYBRIDGE		4 J99
Standon Bridge	52	2 J83
STOCKPORT		2 J89
Stockport Tiviot Dale	* 67	3 J99
Stockton Brook	56	2 J95
STOKE-ON-TRENT		2 J84
STONE		2 J93
STRETFORD	M	4 J79
STRINES	*	4 J98
STYAL		2 J88
Sudbury	66	2 K13
Tean	53	2 J94
Thorpe Cloud	63	2 K15
TIMPERLEY	M	4 J79
Tissington	63	2 K15
Tiviot Dale, Stockport	* 67	3 J99
(TRAFFORD BAR)	B § 92 M	4 J89
TRAFFORD PARK + Stretford	74	3 J79
Trentham	* 64	2 J84
Trentham Gardens	16 57	2 J84
Tunstall	* 64	2 J85
URMSTON		3 J79
UTTOXETER		2 K03
Wall Grange + Longsdon	56	2 J95
Warwick Road (OLD TRAFFORD)	C § 92 M	4 J89
WEDGWOOD Halt	65	2 J83
West Timperley	* 64	3 J79
WHALEY BRIDGE	*	2 K08
Whitmore	52	2 J74
WILMSLOW		2 J88
Withington + West Didsbury		2 J89
Woodhead	64	1 K19
WOODLEY	*	4 J99
WOODSMOOR	90	2 J98

GOODS

No	Name/Location	Closed	Ry Ref
G1	Badnall Wharf	59	2 J83
2	Caldon Low	68	2 K05
3	Congleton Brunswick Street	68	2 J86
4	Fenny Bentley	63	2 K15
5	Friden	67	2 K16
6	Kingsley + Froghall	64	2 K04
7	Ladmanlow	54	2 K07
8	Manchester Docks	72	2 J89
9	Stafford Doxey Road	64	1 J92
10	Weston Coyney	63	2 J94

ENGINE SHEDS

No	Name/Location	Closed Steam	Ry Ref
E1	Alsager	62	2 J79
2	Ashbourne	32	2 K14
3	BUXTON	17 68	2 K07
5	Macclesfield	61	2 J97
6	Stafford	65	2 J92
7	Stockport	68	2 J89
8	Stoke	67	2 J85
9	Uttoxeter	64	2 K03

TUNNELS

No	Name/Location	Length	Ry Ref
T1	Shugborough	777	2 J92
2	Keele	321	2 J74
3	Silverdale	684	2 J84
4	Newcastle		2 J84
5	Hartshill		2 J84
6	Harecastle	260	2 J85
7	Harecastle No.2 (Middle)	180	2 J85
8	Harecastle No.3 (South)	1763	2 J85
9	Ashwood Dale	100	2 K07
10	Rusher Cutting	121	2 K17
11	Chee Tor No.2	94	2 K17
12	Chee Tor No.1	401	2 K17
13	Litton	515	2 K17
14	Cressbrook	471	2 K17
15	Ashbourne		2 K14
16	Great Rocks	161	2 K07
17	Dove Holes	2984	2 K07
18	Barmoor Clough	111	2 K07
19	Eaves	431	2 K07
20	Hayfield	197	4 K08
21	New Mills	120	2 K08
22	Cowburn	3702	2 K08
23	Hibel Road	343	2 J97
24	Prestbury	273	2 J97
25	Headstone	533	2 K17
26	Woodhead	5302	1 K19
27	Disley	3866	2 J98
28	Hindlow	514	2 K06
29	Marple North	99	4 J99
30	Marple South	224	2 J98

JUNCTIONS

No	Name/Location	Ry	Ref
J1	Trent Valley	2	J92
2	Swynnerton	2	J83
3	Broomshall	12	K03
4	Miller's Dale	2	K17

NOTES

REF All in SJ or SK, initial S omitted

§ Old name } Change of name, identical
§ New name } letter gives alternative.

M In open and closed column. These stations (all 4's) closed 91 and reopened in 92 as METRO

1 Regular services ended earlier
2 Staff and Railway families halt.
3 On goods only line and opened for excursions
4 Opened 41 to service Ordnance Factory.
5 Re-opened for 'wakes' traffic, one week for each of three years
6 Addition to title '+ Openshaw' shown in Beeching to distinguish station?
7 Was replaced by GORTON, closure unclear.
8 Regular services ceased in 62.
9 Regular services ended in 49.
10 Served workpeople and hospital.
11 London Road became PICCADILLY and merged with existing station. Then in 92 became METRO also.
12 There is also an adjoining Metro.
13 Re-opened as staff halt also it was used whilst PICCADILLY reorganised.
14 Staff Halt
15 Regular Services ended 60
16 N/A workmens service only.
17 Closure date is for steam. But is an existing modern shed still open.

Stations located on the map but not named have 50 in reference column as an indication of map on which station is named

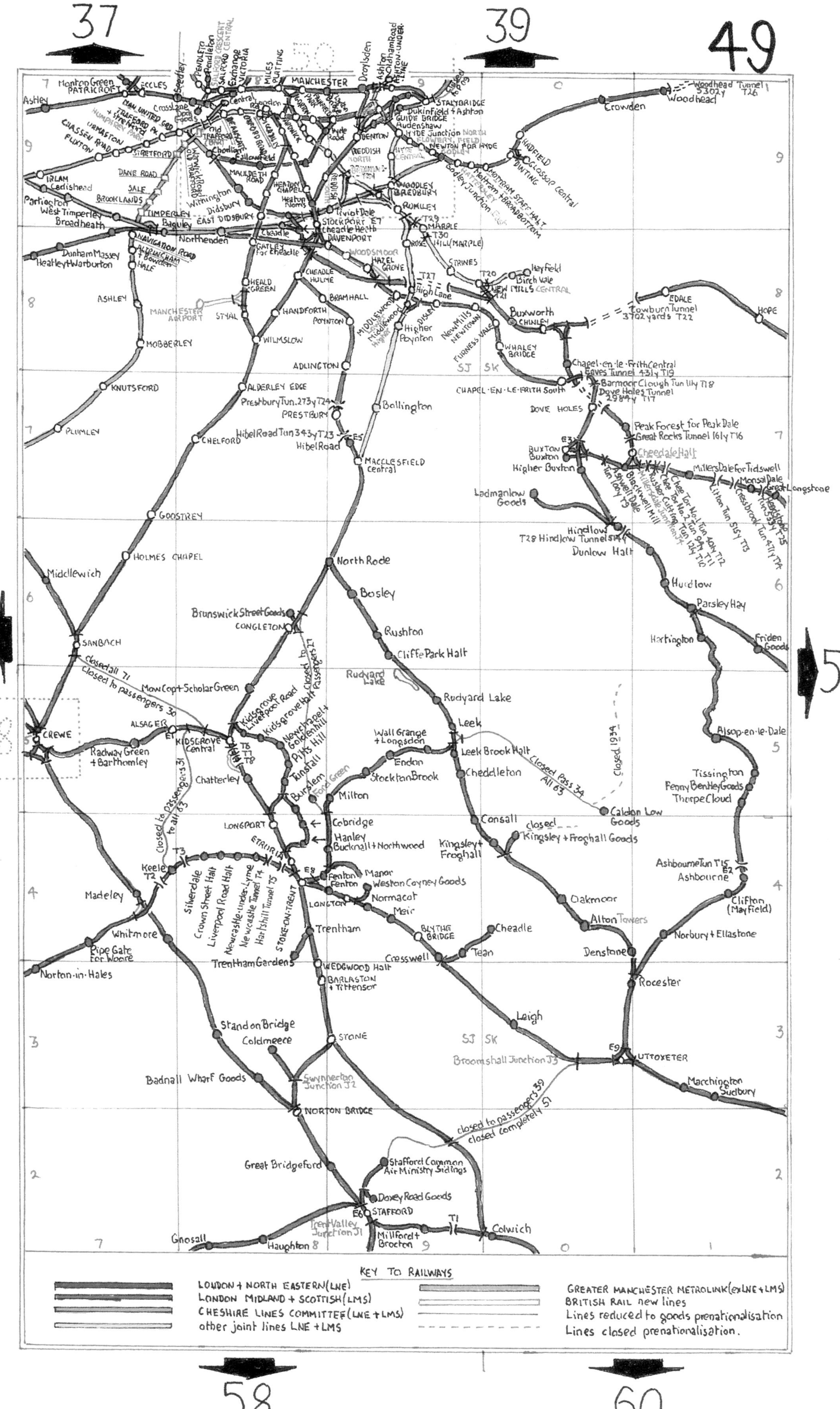
37
39
49
46
51
58
60
MANCHESTER
Droylsden
Ashton Oldham Road
ASHTON-UNDER-LYNE
Monton Green
PATRICROFT
ECCLES
Seedley
Pendleton
SALFORD CRESCENT
SALFORD CENTRAL
Exchange
VICTORIA
MILES PLATTING
Ashley
Cross Lane
MAN. UNITED GRD
+ STRETFORD PK
HUMPHREY PARK
URMSTON
CHASSEN ROAD
FLIXTON
Central
Old Trafford
STRETFORD
DANE ROAD
SALE
BROOKLANDS
IRLAM
Cadishead
Partington
West Timperley
Broadheath
TIMPERLEY
Baguley
Northenden
NAVIGATION ROAD
ALTRINCHAM + Bowdon
HALE
Dunham Massey
Heatley + Warburton
ASHLEY
MOBBERLEY
KNUTSFORD
PLUMLEY
Chorlton
Withington
Didsbury
EAST DIDSBURY
MAULDETH ROAD
HEATON CHAPEL
Heaton Norris
Tiviot Dale
STOCKPORT
Cheadle Heath
DAVENPORT
Cheadle
GATLEY For Cheadle
HEALD GREEN
MANCHESTER AIRPORT
STYAL
HANDFORTH
WILMSLOW
CHEADLE HULME
BRAMHALL
POYNTON
ADLINGTON
ALDERLEY EDGE
Prestbury Tun. 273y T24
PRESTBURY
Hibel Road Tun 343y T23
Hibel Road
MACCLESFIELD Central
CHELFORD
GOOSTREY
HOLMES CHAPEL
Middlewich
SANBACH
STALYBRIDGE
Dukinfield + Ashton
GUIDE BRIDGE
Audenshaw
HYDE Junction
NEWTON FOR HYDE
DENTON
REDDISH
WOODLEY
BREDBURY
ROMILEY
MARPLE
ROSE HILL (MARPLE)
STRINES
WOODSMOOR
HAZEL GROVE
High Lane
MIDDLEWOOD
Higher Poynton
DISLEY
New Mills NEWTOWN
FURNESS VALE
WHALEY BRIDGE
NEW MILLS CENTRAL
Hayfield
Birch Vale
Buxworth
CHINLEY
Crowden
Woodhead
Woodhead Tunnel 5302y T26
HADFIELD
Dinting
GLOSSOP Central
EDALE
HOPE
Cowburn Tunnel 3702 yards T22
Bollington
SJ SK
Chapel-en-le-Frith Central
Eaves Tunnel 431y T19
CHAPEL-EN-LE-FRITH South
Barmoor Clough Tun 114y T18
Dove Holes Tunnel 2984y T17
DOVE HOLES
Peak Forest for Peak Dale
Great Rocks Tunnel 161y T16
BUXTON
Buxton
Higher Buxton
Cheedale Halt
Millers Dale for Tideswell
Monsal Dale
Great Longstone
Ladmanlow Goods
Hindlow
T28 Hindlow Tunnel
Dunlow Halt
Hurdlow
Parsley Hay
Hartington
Friden Goods
Alsop-en-le-Dale
Tissington
Fenny Bentley Goods
Thorpe Cloud
Ashbourne Tun T15
Ashbourne
Clifton (Mayfield)
Norbury + Ellastone
North Rode
Bosley
Rushton
Cliffe Park Halt
Rudyard Lake
Rudyard Lake
Leek
Leek Brook Halt
Cheddleton
Consall
Brunswick Street Goods
CONGLETON
Mow Cop + Scholar Green
Kidsgrove Liverpool Road
Kidsgrove Halt
Newchapel + Goldenhill
Pitts Hill
Tunstall
Burslem
Ford Green
Milton
Cobridge
Hanley
Bucknall + Northwood
Wall Grange + Longsdon
Endon
Stockton Brook
Closed Pass 34 All 63
Closed 1934
Caldon Low Goods
Kingsley + Froghall Goods
Kingsley + Froghall
Oakmoor
Alton Towers
Denstone
Rocester
UTTOXETER
Marchington
Sudbury
Broomshall Junction J3
Leigh
Cresswell
Tean
Cheadle
BLYTHE BRIDGE
Meir
Normacot
Weston Coyney Goods
Fenton Manor
Fenton
LONGTON
CREWE
Radway Green + Barthomley
ALSAGER
KIDSGROVE Central
Chatterley
LONGPORT
ETRURIA
closed all 71
closed to passengers 30
closed to passengers 31 to all 63
Keele
Madeley
Silverdale
Crown Street Halt
Liverpool Road Halt
Newcastle-under-Lyme
Newcastle Tunnel T4
Hartshill Tunnel T5
STOKE-ON-TRENT
Trentham
Trentham Gardens
WEDGWOOD Halt
BARLASTON + Tittensor
Whitmore
Pipe Gate For Woore
Norton-in-Hales
Standon Bridge
Coldmeece
STONE
Swynnerton Junction J2
Badnall Wharf Goods
NORTON BRIDGE
closed to passengers 39
closed completely 51
Great Bridgeford
Stafford Common Air Ministry Sidings
Doxey Road Goods
STAFFORD
Trent Valley Junction J1
Gnosall
Haughton
Milford + Brocton
Colwich
KEY TO RAILWAYS
LONDON + NORTH EASTERN (LNE)
LONDON MIDLAND + SCOTTISH (LMS)
CHESHIRE LINES COMMITTEE (LNE + LMS)
other joint lines LNE + LMS
GREATER MANCHESTER METROLINK (ex LNE + LMS)
BRITISH RAIL new lines
Lines reduced to goods prenationalisation
Lines closed prenationalisation.

MANCHESTER

RAILWAYS
No Company
1 LONDON + NORTH EASTERN (LNE)
2 LONDON MIDLAND + SCOTTISH (LMS)
3 CHESHIRE LINES COMMITTEE (LNE + LMS)
M GREATER MANCHESTER METRO LINK (GMML) (ex 2 or ex 4)
4 other Joint Lines LNE + LMS
M GMM New Lines.
○ BRITISH RAIL New lines

STATIONS
Opened Closed Ry Ref
ARDWICK 1 89
ASHBURYS FOR BELE VUE 1 89
ASHTON Charlestown A § 68 2 99
Ashton Oldham Road 59 4 99
Ashton Park Parade 56 1 99
ASHTON · UNDER · LYNE A § 68 2 99
Audenshaw 50 2 99
BELLE VUE 4 89
BREDBURY 4 99
BRINNINGTON 77 4 99
BURNAGE 2 89
Chorlton · cum · Hardy ✳ 67 3 89
Clayton Bridge ✳ 68 2 89
Cross Lane 59 2 89
DENTON ✳ 2 99
Didsbury ✳ 67 2 89
Droylsden ✳ 68 2 99
Dukinfield + Ashton 50 2 99
Dukinfield Central 59 1 99
EAST DIDSBURY + Parr's Wood 74 2 89
FAIRFIELD for Droylsden ✳ 74 1 99
Fallowfield 58 1 89
FLOWERY FIELD 85 1 99
GODLEY 1 86 1 99
Godley Junction East 1 74 86 87 1 99
GORTON + Openshaw 2 1 89
GUIDE BRIDGE 1 99
HEATON CHAPEL + Heaton Moor 74 2 89
Heaton Mersey 2 89
Heaton Norris 59 2 89
HYDE CENTRAL ✳ 51 4 99

HYDE Junction NORTH
Hyde Road
Knott Mill + DEANSGATE
LEVENSHULME North
Levenshulme South
LONGSIGHT
MANCHESTER
Central
DEANSGATE, Knott Hill + Exchange
(G MEX (DEANSGATE))
(HIGH STREET)
London Road
(MARKET STREET)
Mayfield
(MOSELEY STREET)
OXFORD ROAD
PICCADILLY
(PICCADILLY GARDENS)
(ST PETER'S SQUARE)
VICTORIA
MANCHESTER UNITED FC GROUND
MAULDETH ROAD for Withington
MILES PLATTING
NEWTON FOR HYDE
Old TRAFFORD (BAR)
(OLD TRAFFORD)
Ordsall Lane
PARK
Pendleton
PENDLETON Broad Street
REDDISH NORTH
REDDISH SOUTH
ROMILEY
RYDER BROW
SALFORD CENTRAL
SALFORD CRESCENT
STALY BRIDGE
STOCKPORT
Stockport Tiviot Dale
(TRAFFORD BAR)
TRAFFORD PARK + Stretford
Warwick Road (OLD TRAFFORD)

✳51 1 99 Wilbraham Road
58 1 89 Withington + West Didsbury
3 71 4 89 WOODLEY
52 60 2 89
52 58 1 89
4 80 2 89

GOODS
No Station / Location
89 6 1 Ancoats
69 3 89 2 Ardwick South
5 4 89 3 Ashton Oldham Road
69 2 89 4 Ashton Road
5 92 M 89 5 Bayley Street Staleybridge
92 M 89 6 Beswick
6 B § 12 89 7 Brindle Heath
92 M 89 8 Central
60 2 89 9 Cornbrook
92 M 89 10 Deansgate
4 89 11 Docks
6 B § (12)4 89 12 Dulcie Street
92 M 89 13 Liverpool Road
92 M 89 14 Liverpool Street
2 89 15 London Road
3 89 16 Longsight
74 2 89 17 Oldham Road
2 80 18 Openshaw
1 99 19 Portwood
C § 92 M 89 20 Salford
§ 92 M 89 21 Staly + Millbrook
57 2 89 22 Stalybridge (ex LY pass)
✳ 2 89 23 Wellington Road Stockport
✳ 66 2 89 24 Windsor Bridge
66 2 89
51 4 89

COMPANY WORKS
✳52 2 89 No Name
4 99 W 1 Gorton
85 4 89
88 2 89

TUNNELS
87 2 89 No Name
4 99 T 1 Stalybridge
2 89 2 Scout
67 3 89 3 Katherine Street
C § 92 M 89 4 Stalybridge New
74 3 89 5 Hooley Hill
D § 92 M 89 6 Bredbury High Level

58 1 89 7 Old Trafford
61 2 89 8 Brinnington
✳ 4 99 9 Collyhurst
10 Queens Road

ENGINE SHEDS
Closed Ry Ref No Name
72 2 89
66 2 89 E 1 Gorton
66 2 99 2 Heaton Mersey
66 2 89 3 LONGSIGHT
67 2 99 4 Trafford Park
67 2 89
65 2 80

VIADUCTS + BRIDGES
64 3 89 No Name
67 3 89 V 1 Collyhurst Viaduct
64 1 89 2 Stockport Viaduct
72 2 89
67 1 89

JUNCTIONS
75 2 89 No Name / Location
66 2 89 J 1 Ashton Moss
65 2 89 2 Crowthorn
65 2 89 3 Dewsnap
68 2 89 4 Apethorn
65 1 89 5 George's Road
72 3 89 6 Oldfield Road
67 2 89 7 Cornbrook
64 2 99 8 Cheetham Hill
65 2 99 9 Queens Road
67 3 89 10 Thorpe's Bridge
56 2 89 11 Windsor Bridge North
12 Windsor Bridge South
13 Brewery
Closed Ry Ref 14 Philips Park No.1
62 1 89 15 Philips Park No.2
16 Baguley Fold
17 Ashton Moss North
Length Ry Ref 18 Micklehurst Line
668 2 99
202 2 99

NOTES:
94 2 99 REF No letters used (in SD or SJ).
592 2 99 § Old Name } change of name
2 99 § New Name
160 4 99 Identical letter shows alternative

142 M4 89
4 99
4 26 2 89
2 62 2 80

Closed Steam Ry Ref
? 1 89
68 3 89
7 65 2 89
68 3 89

Ry Ref
2 80
2 89

Ry Ref
2 99
24 99
1 99
34 99
3 89
2 89
34 89
2M 80
2M 80
2 80
2 89
2 89
2 80
2 89
2 89
2 89
12 99
2 99

1 Godley Junction until 74
East added 86
when new station opened. The two stations were very close together, it has been presumed the old station closed in the following year.
2 It appears + Openshaw dropped in early BR days, although shown in Beeching. But this may have been necessary to distinguish it from the West Highland station.
3 On Map 49 DEANSGATE is shown as METRO - also. However there are two separate adjoining stations as shown here.
4 Opened as staff halt, but was also used by PICCADILLY traffic whilst alterations to the latter were taking place.
5 Adjoining stations see note 3 above.
6 London Road changed its name and merged with its earlier namesake PICCADILLY. As mentioned above under note 4 LONGSIGHT was in temporary regular use for some trains during a substantial re-ordering.
7 Still open as a diesel depot.

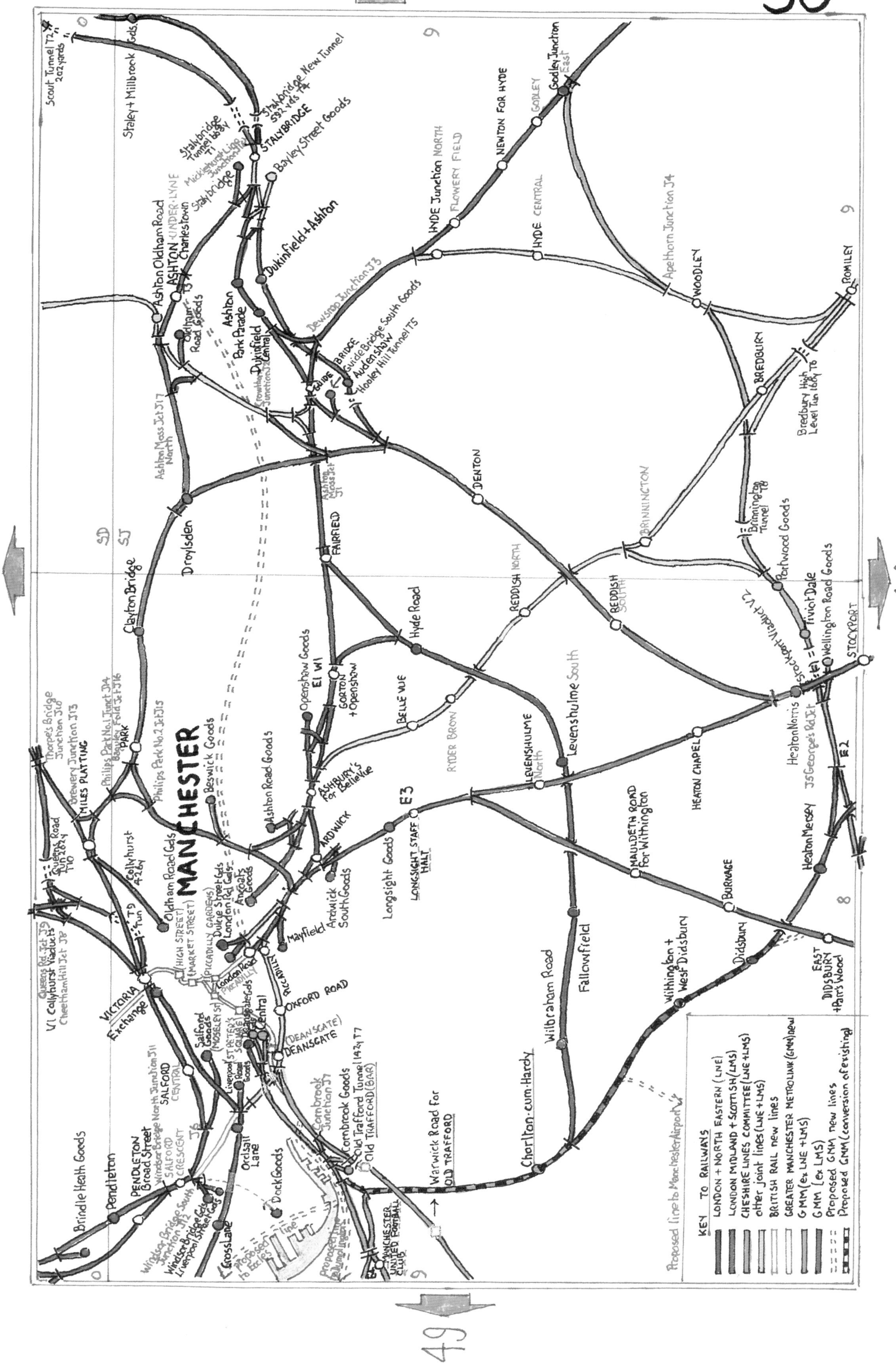

39

49

49

49

MANCHESTER

SD
SJ

Queens Rd. Jct J9
V1 Collyhurst Viaducts
Cheetham Hill Jct J8
Queens Road Tun 262y T10
Thorpe's Bridge Junction J10
Brewery Junction J13
MILES PLATTING
Philips Park No.1 Junct J14
Baguley Fold Jct J16
PARK
Philips Park No.2 Jct J15
Clayton Bridge
Droylsden
Ashton Moss Jct J17 North
Ashton Oldham Road
ASHTON UNDER-LYNE
Charlestown
T3
Oldham Road Goods
Stalybridge Tunnel 169y T1
Micklehurst Line Junction J1
Stalybridge
Staley + Millbrook Gds.
Scout Tunnel T2 202 yards
Stalybridge New Tunnel 532 yds T4
STALYBRIDGE
Bayley Street Goods
Ashton Park Parade
Dukinfield Central
Crowthorn Junction J2
Dukinfield + Ashton
Dewsnap Junction J3
GUIDE BRIDGE
Guide Bridge South Goods
Audenshaw
Hooley Hill Tunnel T5
Ashton Moss Jct J1
FAIRFIELD
HYDE Junction NORTH
FLOWERY FIELD
NEWTON FOR HYDE
GODLEY
Godley Junction East
HYDE CENTRAL
DENTON
Apethorn Junction J4
WOODLEY
ROMILEY
BREDBURY
Bredbury High Level Tun 166y T6
Brinnington Tunnel T8
BRINNINGTON
Portwood Goods
Tiviot Dale
Wellington Road Goods
Stockport Viaduct V2
STOCKPORT
Heaton Norris
J5 George's Rd Jct
E2
Heaton Mersey
EAST DIDSBURY + Parr's Wood
HEATON CHAPEL
REDDISH NORTH
REDDISH SOUTH
RYDER BROW
BELLE VUE
Hyde Road
GORTON + Openshaw
E1 W1
Openshaw Goods
ASHBURY'S for Belle Vue
ARDWICK
Ardwick South Goods
Longsight Goods
LONGSIGHT STAFF HALT
E3
LEVENSHULME North
Levenshulme South
MAULDETH ROAD for Withington
BURNAGE
Didsbury
Withington + West Didsbury
Fallowfield
Wilbraham Road
Chorlton-cum-Hardy
Warwick Road for OLD TRAFFORD
Proposed line to Manchester Airport
MANCHESTER UNITED FOOTBALL CLUB
Old TRAFFORD (BAR)
Old Trafford Tunnel 142y T7
Cornbrook Goods
Cornbrook Junction J7
Proposed line (Pomona Docks)
Dock Goods
Proposed to Eccles
Grosslane
Ordsall Lane
Windsor Bridge South Junction J12
Windsor Bridge Gds
Liverpool Street Gds
SALFORD CRESCENT
J6
Windsor Bridge North Junction J11
PENDLETON Broad Street
Pendleton
Brindle Heath Goods
SALFORD CENTRAL
Salford Goods (MOSELEY ST)
Liverpool Road Goods
ST PETER'S SQUARE
G-Mex
Central
Deansgate Gds
DEANSGATE
(DEANSGATE)
OXFORD ROAD
PICCADILLY
London Road
(PICCADILLY)
Mayfield
Dulcie Street Gds
London Rd Gds
Ancoats Goods
Ashton Road Goods
Beswick Goods
(PICCADILLY GARDENS)
(MARKET STREET)
(HIGH STREET)
Oldham Road Gds
Collyhurst 426y
T9 Tun
VICTORIA
Exchange

0
0
9
9
9
9
8

KEY TO RAILWAYS
- LONDON + NORTH EASTERN (LNE)
- LONDON MIDLAND + SCOTTISH (LMS)
- CHESHIRE LINES COMMITTEE (LNE + LMS)
- other joint lines (LNE + LMS)
- BRITISH RAIL new lines
- GREATER MANCHESTER METROLINK (GMM) new
- GMM (ex LNE + LMS)
- GMM (ex LMS)
- Proposed GMM new lines
- Proposed GMM (conversion of existing)

SHEFFIELD, DERBY + NOTTINGHAM

RAILWAYS

No	Company
1	LONDON + NORTH EASTERN (LNE)
2	LONDON MIDLAND + SCOTTISH (LMS)
3	SOUTH YORKSHIRE JOINT (LNE + LMS)
4	other joint lines LNE + LMS
5	PEAK (ex LMS) 'preserved'
6	MIDLAND RAILWAY CENTRE (ex LMS)
0	BRITISH RAIL new lines

STATIONS

Station	Opened Closed	Ry Ref
ALFRETON + MANSFIELD PARKWAY	1 73 73	2 45
Alfreton + South Normanton	1 * 67 73	2 45
AMBERGATE	*	2 35
Annesley	53	2 55
Annesley Sidings	2 56	1 55
Annesley South Junction Halt	2 56	1 55
Arkwright Street	† 63 67 69	1 53
Arkwright Town	51	1 46
ATTENBOROUGH		2 53
ATTERCLIFFE ROAD	3 94	2 38
Awsworth	* 64	1 44
Bakewell	67	2 26
BAMFORD	*	2 28
Barnby Moor + Sutton	49	1 68
Barrow Hill + Staveley Works	51 54	2 47
BASFORD Vernon	52 63 93	2 54
Basford + Bulwell North	* 53 64	1 54
Bawtry	4 65	1 69
Beauchief	61	2 38
BEESTON		2 53
Beighton	54	1 48
BELPER	*	2 34
BINGHAM		1 64
Bingham Road	† 64	2 63
Bolsover Castle	77 81	2 47
Bolsover South	50 51	1 46
Borrowash	* 66	2 43
Boughton	55	1 66
Breadsall	53	1 33
BRIGHTSIDE	3	2 38
Brimington	A § 51 56	1 37
Broughton Lane	56	1 38
Bulwell Market	* 52 64 94	2 54
Bulwell Common	† 63	1 54
BURTON JOYCE	*	2 64
BURTON-ON-TRENT		2 22
Butterley	5 63 81	6 35
CARLTON + NETHERFIELD	* 74	2 24
Castle Donnington + Shardlow	5	2 42
CHAPELTOWN South	7 51 69	2 38
Chapeltown + Thorncliffe Central	51 53	1 38
Chellaston	6 59 60	2 32
Chesterfield Central	† 63	1 37
Chesterfield Market Place	51	1 37
CHESTERFIELD St Marys	50 51	2 37
Midland	51 64	2 37
Clay Cross	* 67	2 36
Clipstone Colliery Sidings	2 68	1 56
Clowne + Barlborough	51 54	2 47
Clowne South	51 64	1 47
Codnor Park + Ironville	* 67	2 45
Codnor Park + Selston for		45
Ironville + Jacksdale	B § 50	1 45
CONISB(O)ROUGH	50	1 59
CROMFORD	*	2 35
Darley Dale	* 67 ?	5 26
DARNALL		1 38
Daybrook	60	1 54
Deepcar for Stocksbridge	8 68	1 29
Denby	5 61	2 34
DERBY Midland	50 68	2 33
Derby Friargate	* 64	1 33
Derby Nottingham Road	* 67	2 33
Doe Hill	60	2 45
DORE + TOTLEY	* 71	2 38
Draycott + Breaston	* 66	2 43
DRONFIELD	* 67 81	2 37
DUFFIELD	*	2 34
East Leake	* 69	1 52
Eastwood + Langley Mill	† 63	1 44
Ecclesfield East	50 53	1 39
Ecclesfield West	50 68	2 39
Eckington + Renishaw	51	2 47
Eckington + Renishaw	C § 50	1 47
Edlington	9 63	2 59
Edwinstowe	10 67	1 66
Egginton Junction	62	2 22
Elmton + Creswell	* 64	2 57
Etwall	5 61	1 23
Farnsfield	5 49	2 65
Finningley	11 61	1 69
Gedling + Carlton	60	1 64
Gedling Colliery Halt	2 54	2 64
Grange Lane	53	1 39
GRINDLEFORD	*	2 27
(HAMMERSMITH)	?	6 35
Harworth Colliery Sidings	2 61	3 69
Hathern	60	2 52
HATHERSAGE	*	2 28
Hazlewood	5 49	2 34
Heath	† 63	1 46
Heeley	* 68	2 38
Hollinwell + Annesley	62	1 55
Holmes	55	2 49
Horninglow	49	2 22
Hucknall Byron	* 52 64	2 54
Hucknall Central	† 63	1 54
Hucknall Town	5 54	1 54
Idridgehay	5 49	2 24
Ilkeston Junction + Cossall	* 67	2 44
Ilkeston North	* 50 64	1 44
Ilkeston Town	5 50	2 44
Jacksdale	† B § 50 63	1 45
Kegworth	* 68	2 52
Killamarsh Central	† 50 63	1 48
Killamarsh West	50 54	2 48
Kilnhurst Central	50 68	1 49
Kilnhurst West	50 68	2 49
Kimberley East	* 55 64	1 44
Kirkby Bentinck	† 63	1 46
Kirkby-in-Ashfield Central	62	1 45
Kirkby-in-Ashfield East	* 59 65	2 55
KIVETON BRIDGE		1 48
KIVETON PARK		1 58
LANGLEY MILL + Eastwood	* 67 86	2 44
Langwith	* 64	2 56
Linby	* 64	2 54
Long Eaton	* 67	2 43
LONG EATON	E § 68	2 43
LOUGHBOROUGH Midland	70	2 52
LOWDHAM	*	2 64
Mansfield Central	50 62	1 56
Mansfield Town	* 52 64	2 56
Mansfield Woodhouse	* 64	2 56
MATLOCK	67 72	2 25
MATLOCK BATH	* 67 72	2 25
(MATLOCK RIVERSIDE)	?	5 26
Meadow Hall + Wincobank	51 53	1 39
MEADOWHALL	D § 90	2 39
MEXBOROUGH		1 49
Mickleover	5 56	1 23
Millhouses + Ecclesall	* 68	2 38
NETHERFIELD + Colwick	74	1 64
New Basford	* 64	1 54
NEWSTEAD	* 64 93	2 55
Newstead + Annesley	5 63	1 65
Newthorpe	† 63	1 44
(NORTHWOOD)	?	5 26
NOTTINGHAM		53
Arkwright Street	† 63 67 69	1 53
City	12 § 50 51	2 53
London Road High Level	67	1 53
Midland	12 § 51 69	2 53
NOTTINGHAM	12 § 50 69	2 53
Racecourse	59	1 63
Victoria	* 67	1 53
Nottingham Road Derby	* 61	2 33
Old Dalby	* 66	2 62
Ollerton	64	1 66
Oughty Bridge	59	1 39
Parkgate + Aldwarke	51	2 49
Parkgate + Rawmarsh	68	2 49
PEARTREE + Normanton	* 68 76	2 33
Pilsley	59	1 46
Pinxton South	† 54 63	1 45
Pinxton + Selston North	50 61	2 45
Pleasley East	50 63	1 46
Plumtree	49	2 63
Rye Bridge	* 67	2 45
Pye Hill + Somercotes	† 63	1 45
RADCLIFFE-on-Trent	74	1 63
Radford	* 64	2 53
RAMS LINE HALT	2 90	2 33
Ranskill	58	1 68
Renishaw Central	† C § 50 63	1 47
Repton + Willington	* 68	2 22
RETFORD		1 68
Ripley	5 61	2 35
Rolleston-on-Dove	49	2 22
Rossington	8 67	1 69
ROTHERHAM CENTRAL	60 87	1 49
Rotherham (Masborough)	69 87 89	2 49
Rotherham Road	53	1 49
Rotherham Westgate	52	2 49
Rowsley For Chatsworth	* 65 67	2 26
Ruddington	† 63	1 53
Rushcliffe Halt	† 63	1 52
Sawley Junction for LONG EATON	E § 68	2 43
Scarcliffe	51	1 56
Sheepbridge + Brimington	A § 51	1 37
Sheepbridge + Whittington Moor	* 51 75	2 37
SHEFFIELD		38
ATTERCLIFFE ROAD		2 38
Midland City	13 § 50 51	2 38
Midland	13 § 51 70	2 38
SHEFFIELD	13 § 70	2 38
Victoria	70	1 38
Shipley Gate	48	2 44
Shirebrook Colliery Sidings	2 54	2 56
Shirebrook North	10 69	1 56
Shirebrook South	5 63	1 56
Shirebrook West	* 54 64	2 56
SHIREOAKS		1 58
Shottle	5 49	2 34
SINFIN CENTRAL	6 76	2 33
SINFIN NORTH	6 76	2 33
Skegby	5 63	1 46
Spink Hill for Mount St Mary	5 58	1 47
SPONDON	*	2 33
Stanton Gate	* 67	2 43
Stapleford + Sandiacre	* 67	2 43
Staveley Town Central	† 50 64	1 47
Staveley Town	52	2 47
Staveley Works for Barrow Hill	† 63	1 47
Stretton	61	2 36
Stretton + Clay Mills	49	2 22
Sutton-in-Ashfield Central	14 63	1 55
Sutton-in-Ashfield Town General	50 51	2 45
Sutton-in-Ashfield Town	14 63	1 45
Sutton Junction	* 64	2 55
(SWANWICK)	?	6 45
Swinton Central	50 58	1 49
Swinton Town	50 58	2 49
Teversall East	5 53 55	1 46
Teversall Manor	5 53 63	2 46
Thrybergh	68	3 49
Thurcroft Colliery Sidings	58	3 58
THURGARTON	*	2 64
Tibshelf Town	† 63	1 64
Tinsley	51	1 49
Treeton	51	2 48
Trent	* 68	2 43
Trowell	* 67	2 43
TUTBURY + HATTON	66 89	2 22
Unstone	51	2 37
Upper Broughton	48	2 62
Wadsley Bridge	11 59	1 39
Waleswood	55	1 48
Warsop	76	1 56
Wentworth + Hoyland Common	51 59	2 39
West Hallam	* 64	1 44
Westhouses + Blackwell	* 67	2 54
WHATSTANDWELL	*	2 35
Whittington	15 77	2 47
Whitwell	* 64	2 57
Widmerpool	49	2 62
Wincobank + Meadow Hall	D § 51 56	2 39
Wingfield	* 67	2 35
Wirksworth	5 49	2 25
WOODHOUSE		1 48
Woodhouse Mill	53	2 48
WORKSOP		1 57
Wortley	55	1 29

GOODS

No	Name/Location	Closed	Ry Ref
G1	Clay Cross	63	2 36
2	Clipstone	63	1 56
3	Cromford	64	2 35
4	Dinnington + Laughton	65	3 58
5	Hasland	65	2 36
6	Heanor	63	1 44
7	Hellaby	66	4 59
8	Longcliffe	64	2 25
9	Maltby	65	3 59
10	Misson	64	1 69
11	Rowsley	68	2 26
12	Steeplehouse	64	2 25
13	Tickhill + Wadworth	64	3 59
14	TINSLEY	O	1 48
15	TOTON	O	2 43

ENGINE SHEDS

No	Name/Location	Closed	Ry Ref
E1	Rowsley	64	2 25
2	Millhouses	62	2 38
3	Canklow	65	2 49
4	Grimethorpe	61	2 38
5	Darnall	?	1 38
6	Mexborough	?	1 49
7	Westhouses	66	2 45
8	Hasland	64	2 36
9	Staveley	?	1 47
10	Mansfield	60	2 55
11	Kirkby	66	2 55
12	Langwith	?	1 56
13	Derby (also Loco Works)	67 (62)	2 33
14	NOTTINGHAM (steam 65)	16 O	2 53
15	Derby Friargate	55	1 33
16	Annesley	?	1 55
17	Colwick	66	1 64
18	TOTON (steam 65)	16 O	2 43
		18	

TUNNELS

No.	Name/Location	Length	Ry Ref
T1	Totley	6230	2 27
2	High Tor No. 2	378	2 25
3	High Tor No. 1	321	2 26
4	Willersley	764	2 35
5	Haddon	1058	2 26
6	Stanton	1330	2 62
7	Grimston	1305	2 62
8	Bradway	2027	2 37
9	Spink Hill	501	1 47
10	Norwood End	341	2 48
11	Clay Cross	1784	2 36
12	Rowtham	929	2 46
13	Bolsover	2624	1 46
14	Duckmanton	501	1 46
15	Wingfield	260	2 35
16	Victoria Street	393	1 53
17	Mansfield Road	1189	1 54
18	Thorneywood	408	1 54
19	St Ann's Well		1 54
20	Sherwood	442	1 54
21	Mapperley	1132	1 64
22	Sherwood Rise	665	1 54
23	Wirksworth		2 25
24	Holt Lane	126	2 35
25	Whatstandwell	149	2 35
26	Lea Wood	315	2 26
27	Toadmoor	129	2 35
28	Longland	17 101	2 34
29	Alfreton	840	2 45
30	Kirkby	199	2 55
31	Whitwell	544	2 57
32	Tankersley	1498	2 39
33	Milford	853	2 34
34	Annesley	1001	1 55

NOTES:

REF All in SK so letters omitted

§ Older name } change of name. Letter
§ Newer name } gives reference to the other name

1. Change of name when re-opened.
2. Unadvertised stopping place. Used by workmen and others.
3. Closed when Sheffield SUPERTRAM opened.
4. Regular service ended '58.
5. Regular service ended before nationalisation.
6. line closed to passengers in 1930 re-opened to serve works.
7. Rebuilt on adjoining site 1982.
8. Regular service ended 59
9. Regular service ended 51
10. Regular service ended 64
11. Used for passengers after closure – excursions, RAF persons etc
12. Nottingham name changes:
    NOTTINGHAM to 50
    50 NOTTINGHAM City 51
    51 NOTTINGHAM Midland 69
    69 NOTTINGHAM
13. Sheffield name changes
    SHEFFIELD Midland to 50
    50 SHEFFIELD City 51
    51 SHEFFIELD Midland 69
    69 SHEFFIELD
14. Regular services ended 56
15. Regular services ended 52
16. Still in use but new site see map 52
17. Tunnel opened out into cutting
18. There is a modern loco 'shed' at TINSLEY to SE of yard see map 52.

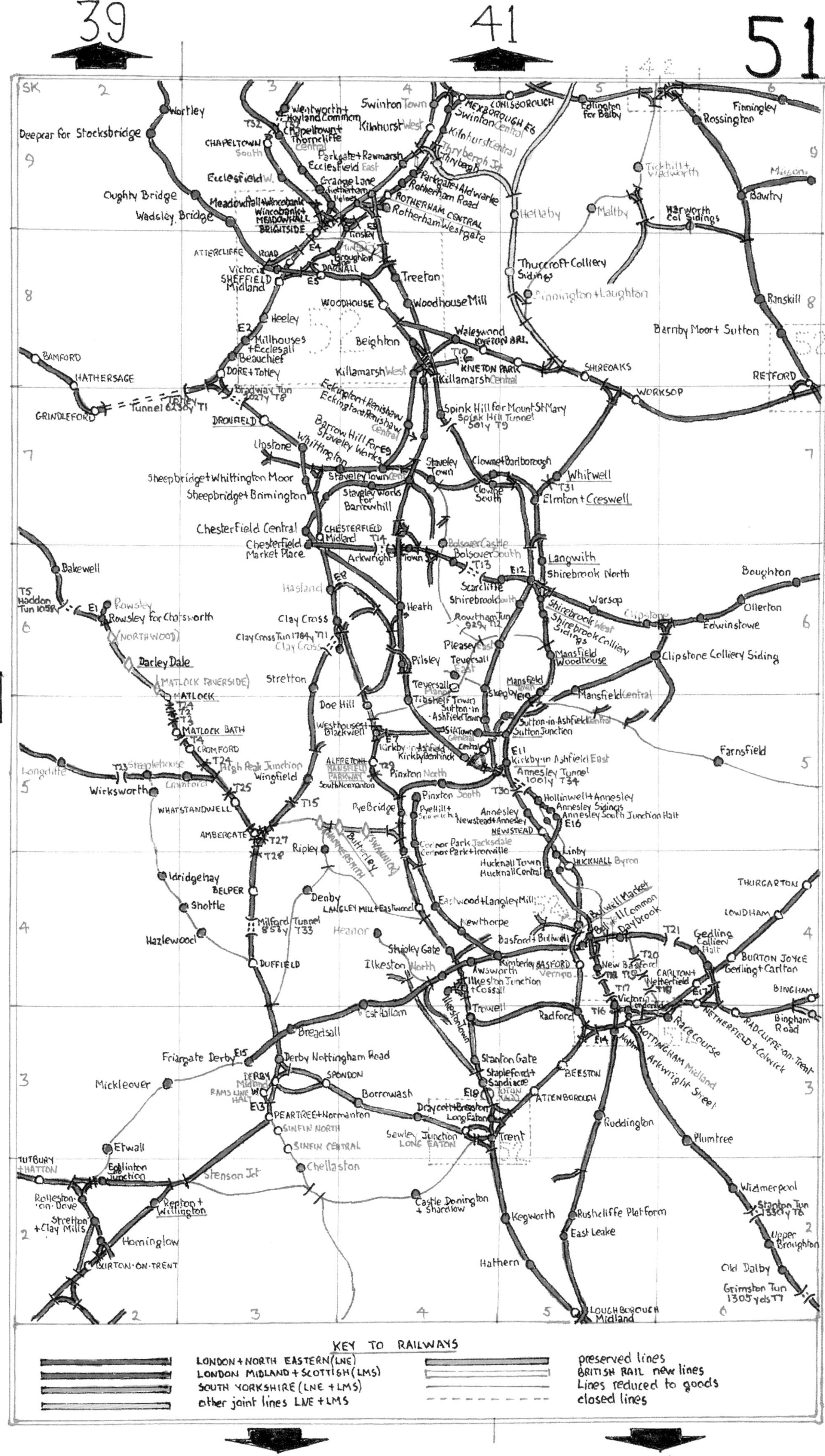
39
41
49
53
60
61
SK
Wortley
Deepcar for Stocksbridge
Oughty Bridge
Wadsley Bridge
Wentworth + Hoyland Common
Chapeltown + Thorncliffe
CHAPELTOWN South
Ecclesfield W.
Ecclesfield East
Parkgate + Rawmarsh
Grange Lane
Swinton Town
Kilnhurst West
MEXBOROUGH E6
Swinton Central
Kilnhurst Central
CONISBOROUGH
Edlington for Balby
Thrybergh Jct
Thrybergh
Parkgate + Aldwarke
Rotherham Road
ROTHERHAM CENTRAL
Rotherham Westgate
Meadowhall + Wincobank
Wincobank + MEADOWHALL
BRIGHTSIDE
Tinsley
ATTERCLIFFE ROAD
Broughton Lane
DARNALL
Victoria
SHEFFIELD Midland
Treeton
WOODHOUSE
Woodhouse Mill
Heeley
Millhouses + Ecclesall
Beauchief
DORE + TOTLEY
Beighton
Waleswood
KIVETON BRI.
KIVETON PARK
Killamarsh West
Killamarsh Central
Hellaby
Maltby
Tickhill + Wadworth
Warworth Col Sidings
Thurcroft Colliery Sidings
Dinnington + Laughton
Finningley
Rossington
Misson
Bawtry
Ranskill
Barnby Moor + Sutton
RETFORD
SHIREOAKS
WORKSOP
BAMFORD
HATHERSAGE
GRINDLEFORD
Totley Tunnel 6230y T1
DRONFIELD
Bradway Tun 2027y T8
Eckington + Renishaw
Eckington + Renishaw Central
Spink Hill for Mount St Mary
Spink Hill Tunnel 501y T9
Barrow Hill
Staveley Works
Whittington
Unstone
Sheepbridge + Whittington Moor
Sheepbridge + Brimington
Staveley Town
Staveley Central
Staveley Works for Barrow Hill
Clowne + Barlborough
Clowne South
Whitwell
Elmton + Creswell
Chesterfield Central
CHESTERFIELD Midland
Chesterfield Market Place
Arkwright Town
Bolsover Castle
Bolsover South
Scarcliffe
Shirebrook South
Langwith
Shirebrook North
Warsop
Boughton
Ollerton
Edwinstowe
Clipstone
Shirebrook West
Shirebrook Colliery Sidings
Clipstone Colliery Siding
Mansfield Woodhouse
Mansfield Town
Mansfield Central
Bakewell
Haddon Tun 1058y
Rowsley
Rowsley for Chatsworth
(NORTHWOOD)
Darley Dale
(MATLOCK RIVERSIDE)
MATLOCK
MATLOCK BATH
CROMFORD
Hasland
Clay Cross
Clay Cross Tun 1784y T11
Heath
Rowtham Tun 929y T12
Pleasley East
Teversall East
Pilsley
Teversall Manor
Tibshelf Town
Sutton-in-Ashfield Town
Stretton
Doe Hill
Westhouses + Blackwell
Kirkby-in-Ashfield Central
Kirkby Bentinck
Skegby
Sutton-in-Ashfield Central
Sutton Junction
Farnsfield
Kirkby-in-Ashfield East
Annesley Tunnel 1001y T34
ALFRETON MANSFIELD PARKWAY
South Normanton
Pinxton North
Pinxton South
Longcliffe
Steeplehouse
Wirksworth
Cromford
High Peak Junction
Wingfield
WHATSTANDWELL
AMBERGATE
Pye Bridge
Pye Hill + Somercotes
Annesley
Newstead + Annesley
NEWSTEAD
Hollinwell + Annesley
Annesley Sidings
Annesley South Junction Halt
Linby
HUCKNALL Byron
Hucknall Town
Hucknall Central
Ripley
Butterley
Hammersmith
Swanwick
Codnor Park Jacksdale
Codnor Park + Ironville
Idridgehay
Shottle
BELPER
Denby
LANGLEY MILL + Eastwood
Eastwood + Langley Mill
Hazlewood
Milford Tunnel 853y T33
Heanor
Newthorpe
Shipley Gate
Ilkeston North
Basford + Bulwell
Bulwell Market
Bulwell Common
Daybrook
Gedling Colliery Halt
THURGARTON
LOWDHAM
BURTON JOYCE
Gedling + Carlton
DUFFIELD
Kimberley
BASFORD Vernon
Awsworth
Ilkeston Junction + Cossall
New Basford
CARLTON + Netherfield
BINGHAM
Bingham Road
West Hallam
Trowell
Radford
Ilkeston Town
Victoria
NOTTINGHAM Midland
Race Course
NETHERFIELD + Colwick
RADCLIFFE-on-Trent
Breadsall
Friargate Derby
Derby Nottingham Road
SPONDON
Mickleover
DERBY Midland
RAMS LINE HALT
Borrowash
Stanton Gate
Stapleford + Sandiacre
BEESTON
Arkwright Street
PEARTREE + Normanton
SINFIN NORTH
SINFIN CENTRAL
Draycott + Breaston
Long Eaton
ATTENBOROUGH
Ruddington
Sawley Junction
LONG EATON
Trent
Chellaston
Etwall
TUTBURY + HATTON
Egginton Junction
Stenson Jct
Plumtree
Castle Donington + Shardlow
Widmerpool
Stanton Tun 1330y T6
Rolleston-on-Dove
Stretton + Clay Mills
Repton + Willington
Kegworth
Rushcliffe Platform
East Leake
Upper Broughton
Horninglow
BURTON-ON-TRENT
Hathern
Old Dalby
Grimston Tun 1305 yds T7
LOUGHBOROUGH Midland
KEY TO RAILWAYS
LONDON + NORTH EASTERN (LNE)
LONDON MIDLAND + SCOTTISH (LMS)
SOUTH YORKSHIRE (LNE + LMS)
other joint lines LNE + LMS
preserved lines
BRITISH RAIL new lines
Lines reduced to goods
closed lines

52 SHEFFIELD + ROTHERHAM, RETFORD, BASFORD + BULWELL, TRENT, LINCOLN AND NOTTINGHAM

RAILWAYS

No	Company
1	LONDON + NORTH EASTERN (LNE)
2	LONDON MIDLAND + SCOTTISH (LMS)
0	BRITISH RAIL new lines

STATIONS

Station	Opened Closed	Ry	Ref
Arkwright Street	† 63 67 69	1	F
ATTERCLIFFE ROAD	1 94	2	A
Barnaby Moor + Sutton	49	1	B
BASFORD Vernon	52 63 93	2	C
Basford + Bulwell North	* 53 64	1	C
Beighton	54	1	A
BRIGHTSIDE	1	2	A
Broughton Lane	56	1	A
Bulwell Common	† 63	1	C
Bulwell Market	* 52 64 94	2	C
DARNALL		1	A
Heeley	* 68	2	A
Holmes	55	2	A
Killamarsh Central	† 50 63	1	A
Killamarsh West	50 54	2	A
LINCOLN Central	50 91	1	E
Lincoln St Marks	* 50 85	2	E
Long Eaton	* 67	2	D
LONG EATON	A § 68	2	D
Meadow Hall + Wincobank	51 53	1	A
MEADOWHALL	B § 90	2	A
Millhouses + Ecclesall	* 68	2	A
NOTTINGHAM			F
Arkwright Street	† 63 67 69	1	F
City	2 § 50 51	2	F
London Road High Level		1	F
Midland	2 § 51 69	2	F
NOTTINGHAM	2 § 50 69	2	F
Racecourse	59	1	F
Victoria	* 67	1	F
RETFORD		1	B
LOW LEVEL	3 65	1	B
ROTHERHAM			A
CENTRAL	60 87	1	A
Masborough	69 87 89	2	A
Westgate	52	2	A
Sawley Junction for LONG EATON	A § 68	2	D
SHEFFIELD			A
ATTERCLIFFE ROAD	1 94	2	A
Midland City	6 § 50 51	2	A
Midland	6 § 51 70	2	A
SHEFFIELD	6 § 70	2	A
Victoria	70	1	A
SWALLOWNEST	4	1	A
Tinsley	51	1	A
Treeton	51	2	A
Trent	* 68	2	D
Wadsley Bridge	5 59	1	A
Wincobank + MEADOWHALL	B § 51 56	2	A
WOODHOUSE		1	A
Woodhouse Mill	53	2	A

GOODS

No	Name/Location	Closed	Ry	Ref
G1	LINCOLN HOLMES YARD	0	1	E
2	Lincoln East	65	1	E
3	Lincoln St Marks	65	2	E
4	Lincoln West Yard	65	1	E
	NOTTINGHAM			F
5	Cattle	65	1	F
6	Cattle	65	2	F
7	London Road + Exchange Sidings	72	1	F
8	Manvers Street	66	2	F
9	Nottingham (Midland)	65	2	F
10	Queens Walk	67	1	F
11	TOTON	0	2	D
	RETFORD			B
12	Babworth	66	1	B
13	Thrumpton	70	1	B
	SHEFFIELD			A
14	Bridgehouses	65	1	A
15	City	63	1	A
16	Park	63	1	A
17	Pond Street	66	2	A
18	Queens Road	63	2	A
19	Wicker	65	2	A
20	Woodhouse	71	1	A
21	TINSLEY	0	[illegible]	A
22	Sneiton		12	F

ENGINE SHEDS

No	Name/Location	Closed	Ry	Ref
E2	Millhouses	62	2	A
3	Canklow	65	2	A
4	Grimethorpe	61	2	A
5	Darnall	?	1	A
14	Nottingham	65	2	F
14A	NOTTINGHAM	7 0	2	F
18	TOTON (closed to steam 65)	7 0	2	D
19	Lincoln (Holme)	65	1	E
20	Lincoln St Marks	59	2	E
21	Lincoln Diesel Depot	91	1	E

TUNNELS

No	Name	Length	Ry	Ref
T1	Red Hill Passenger Line	154	2	D
2	Red Hill Goods Line	167	2	D
3	Victoria Street	393	1	F
4	Thorneywood	408	1	F

JUNCTIONS

No	Name/Location	Ry	Ref
J1	Grimesthorpe	12	A
2	Shepcote Lane	10	A
3	Catcliffe	10	A
4	Whiskerhill	10	B
5	Retford North	1	B
6	Retford South	1	B
7	Sheet Stores	2	D
8	North Erewash	2	D
9	South Erewash	2	D
10	Meadow Lane	2	D
11	Attenborough	2	D
12	Ratcliffe	2	D
13	Pyewipe West	1	E
14	Pyewipe	1	E
15	Boultham	1	E
16	West Holmes	1	E
17	Durham Ox	1	E
18	Sincil	1	E
19	Greetwell	1	E
20	Weekday Cross	1	F
21	Mansfield	2	F

NOTES:

REF As the page contains several small maps the grid reference is not used. Each map is given a reference letter and that letter is shown in the reference column

§ Older name } name change
§ Newer name }

B Letter gives reference to other name

1 Closed when Sheffield Super-Tram taken into use.

2 Nottingham name changes are as under:

	NOTTINGHAM	50
50	NOTTINGHAM City	51
51	NOTTINGHAM Midland	69
69	NOTTINGHAM	

3 Low Level Platforms added when alter-ations shown on map completed in 65

4 Proposed new station but evidently this was later abandoned.

5 Continued in occasional use after closure

6 Sheffield name changes as under:

	SHEFFIELD Midland	50
50	SHEFFIELD City	51
51	SHEFFIELD Midland	70
70	SHEFFIELD	

7 Although a shed at Nottingham was continuous it changed its site as shown on this map.

8 Shed at Retford is close to station and was closed in 63, gazetteered on 54

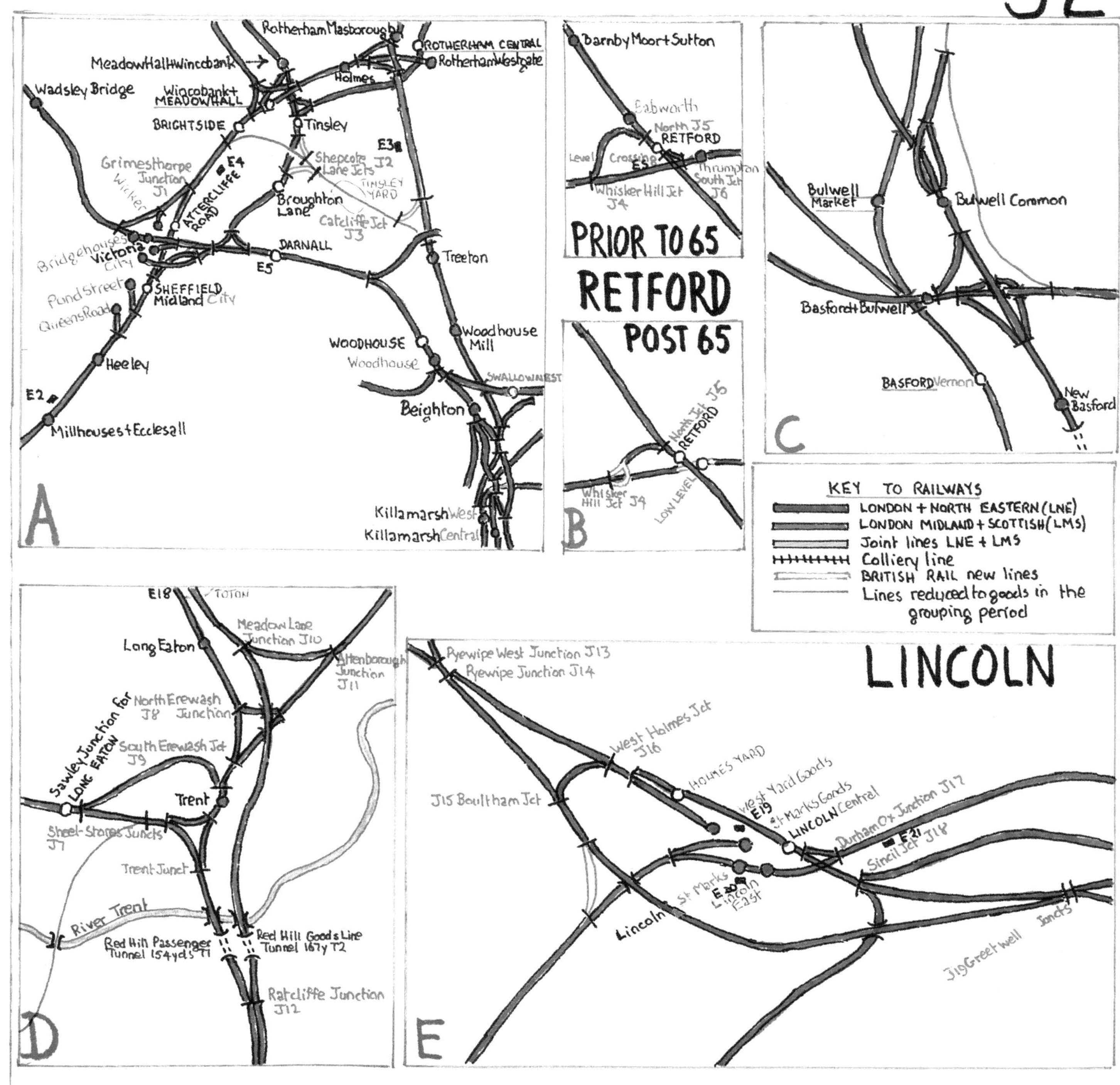
Rotherham Masborough
ROTHERHAM CENTRAL
Rotherham Westgate
Meadow Hall + Wincobank
Wadsley Bridge
Wincobank + MEADOWHALL
Holmes
BRIGHTSIDE
Tinsley
Grimesthorpe Junction J1
Wicker
E4
ATTERCLIFFE ROAD
Shepcote Lane Jcts
E3
J2
TINSLEY YARD
Broughton Lane
Catcliffe Jct J3
Bridgehouses
Victoria
City
DARNALL
E5
Treeton
Pond Street
SHEFFIELD Midland City
Queens Road
Heeley
E2
Millhouses + Ecclesall
WOODHOUSE
Woodhouse
Woodhouse Mill
SWALLOWNEST
Beighton
Killamarsh West
Killamarsh Central
A
Barnby Moor + Sutton
Eabworth
North J5
RETFORD
Level Crossing
E8
Thrumpton South Jct J6
Whisker Hill Jct J4
PRIOR TO 65
RETFORD
POST 65
North Jct J5
RETFORD
Whisker Hill Jct J4
LOW LEVEL
B
Bulwell Market
Bulwell Common
Basford + Bulwell
BASFORD Vernon
New Basford
C
KEY TO RAILWAYS
LONDON + NORTH EASTERN (LNE)
LONDON MIDLAND + SCOTTISH (LMS)
Joint lines LNE + LMS
Colliery line
BRITISH RAIL new lines
Lines reduced to goods in the grouping period
E18
TOTON
Long Eaton
Meadow Lane Junction J10
Attenborough Junction J11
Sawley Junction for LONG EATON
North Erewash Junction J8
South Erewash Jct J9
Trent
Sheet Stores Juncts J7
Trent Junct
River Trent
Red Hill Passenger Tunnel 154yds T1
Red Hill Goods Line Tunnel 167y T2
Ratcliffe Junction J12
D
LINCOLN
Pyewipe West Junction J13
Pyewipe Junction J14
West Holmes Jct J16
HOLMES YARD
West Yard Goods
E19
St Marks Goods
LINCOLN Central
Durham Ox Junction J17
E21
Sincil Jct J18
J15 Boultham Jct
St Marks
E20
Lincoln East
Lincoln
J19 Greetwell Juncts
E

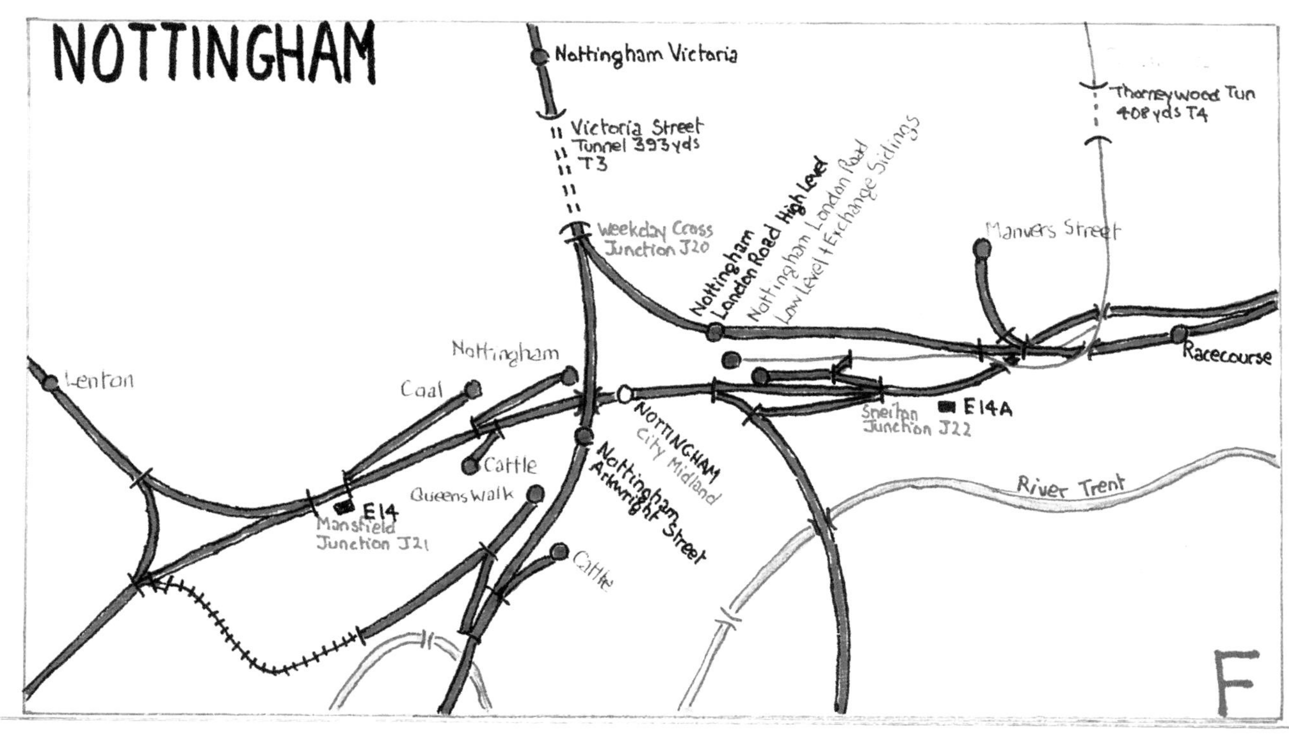
NOTTINGHAM
Nottingham Victoria
Victoria Street Tunnel 393yds T3
Thorneywood Tun 408yds T4
Weekday Cross Junction J20
Nottingham London Road High Level
Nottingham London Road Low Level + Exchange Sidings
Manvers Street
Racecourse
Lenton
Nottingham
Coal
NOTTINGHAM City Midland
Sneinton Junction J22
E14A
Cattle
Queens Walk
Nottingham Arkwright Street
Cattle
E14
Mansfield Junction J21
River Trent
F

53 LINCOLN, NEWARK + SLEAFORD

RAILWAYS

No	Company
1	LONDON + NORTH EASTERN (LNE)
2	LONDON MIDLAND + SCOTTISH (LMS)
3	MIDLAND + GREAT NORTHERN (LNE+LMS)
4	Other joint lines LNE+LMS
5	Cranwell RAF line
0	BRITISH RAIL (new lines)

STATIONS

Name	Opened Closed	Ry	Ref
ANCASTER		1	K94
ASLOCKTON		1	K74
Bardney	* 70	1	F16
Barkston	55	1	K94
Barnstone	53	4	K73
Beckingham	59	1	K78
BINGHAM		1	K74
Blankney + METHERINGHAM	61 75	1	F06
BLEASBY	*	2	K75
Blyton for Corringham	59	1	K89
BOTTESFORD		1	K83
Branston + Heighington	58	1	F06
Carlton-on-Trent	53	1	K87
Caythorpe	† 62	1	K94
Claxby + Usselby	60	1	F19
Claypole	57	1	K84
Clifton-on-Trent	57	1	K87
COLLINGHAM	*	2	K86
Corby Glen	59	1	K92
Cottam	59	1	K87
Counter Drain	59	3	F12
Cranwell	56	5	F05
Crow Park for Sutton-on-Trent	58	1	K76
Digby	61	1	F05
Doddington + Harby	55	1	K87
Donington Road	61	1	F23
Dukeries Junction High Level	50	1	K76
Dukeries Junction Low Level	50	1	K76
East Barkwith	51	1	F18
ELTON + ORSTON		1	K74
FISKERTON	*	2	K75
Five Mile House	1 * 64	1	F07
Fledborough	55	1	K77
GAINSBOROUGH CENTRAL		1	K88
GAINSBOROUGH LEA ROAD		1	K88
GRANTHAM		1	K93
Great Ponton	58	1	K92
Grimston	57	2	K72
Harby + Stathern	53	4	K73
Harmston	† 62	1	K96
Haxey + Epworth	59	1	K79
HECKINGTON		1	F14
Helpringham	55	1	F14
Holton-le-Moor	65	1	F09
Honington	† 62	1	K94
Hougham	57	1	K94
HYKEHAM	*	2	K96
Kingthorpe	51	1	F17
KIRTON LINDSEY		1	K99
Langworth for Wragby	65	1	F07
Lea	57	1	K88
Leadenham	65	1	K95
Leverton	59	1	K78
LINCOLN Central	50 91	1	K97
Lincoln St Marks	* 50 85	2	K97
Long Clawson + Hose	53	4	K72
MARKET RASEN		1	F18
METHERINGHAM, Blankney +	75 75	1	F06
Misterton	2 63	1	K79
Moortown	65	1	F09
Navenby	† 62	1	K95
NEWARK CASTLE	* 50	2	K75
NEWARK NORTHGATE	50	1	K85
Nocton + Dunston	55	1	F06
Northorpe	55	1	K99
Park Drain	55	1	K79
Potterhanworth	55	1	F06
RAUCEBY		1	F04
Redmile	53	4	K73
Reepham	65	1	F07
RETFORD	3	1	K78
ROLLESTON Junction	* 73	2	K75
RUSKINGTON	61 75	1	F05
SAXILBY		1	K87
Scalford	53	4	K72
Scopwick + Timberland	55	1	F05
Sedgebrook	56	1	K83
Skellingthorpe	55	1	K97
SLEAFORD		1	F04
Snelland	65	1	F08
Southrey	* 70	1	F16
Southwell	59	2	K75
Stixwould	* 70	2	F16
Stow Park	61	1	K88
Sturton	59	1	K78
SWINDERBY	*	2	K86
Thorpe-on-the-Hill	55	2	K96
Torksey	59	1	K87
Tuxford Central	55	1	K76
Tuxford North	55	1	K77
Waddington	† 62	1	K96
Walkeringham	59	1	K79
Wickenby	65	1	F08
Woodhall Junction	* 70	1	F16
Wragby	51	1	F17

JUNCTIONS

No	Name	Ry	Ref
J 1	Trent Bridge North	1	K88
2	Trent Bridge South	1	K88
3	Pyewipe West	1	K97
4	Pyewipe	1	K97
5	Boultham	1	K97
6	West Holmes	1	K97
7	Durham Ox	1	K97
8	Greetwell East	1	K97
9	Greetwell West	1	K97
10	Washingborough	1	F07
11	Allington	1	K83
12	Eastwell	1	K72
13	Wycombe	12	K82
14	Sykes	1	K87
15	Clarborough	1	K78

NOTES

Ref All in SK or TF. Initial letter omitted

1 Only used for excursions after 58

2 Regular service ended in 61

3 Low Level Platforms opened in 65 following alterations

4 Lincoln sheds see 52

5 Closure is for steam.

6 Continued in use for a few years as diesel depot.

GOODS

No	Location	Closed	Ry	Ref
G 1	Haxey Junction	56	4	K79
2	Waltham on the Wolds	64	1	K82

ENGINE SHEDS 4

No	Name/Location	5 Closed	Ry	Ref
E 1	Newark	59	1	K85
2	Retford	64	1	K77
3	Tuxford	?	1	K76
4	Sleaford	6 58	1	F04
5	Southwold	55	2	K75

TUNNELS

No	Name/Location	Length	Ry	Ref
T 1	Askham	57	1	K77
2	Clarborough	658	1	K78
3	Stoke	880	1	K92
4	Gonerby	506	1	K83
5	Peascliffe	967	1	K94

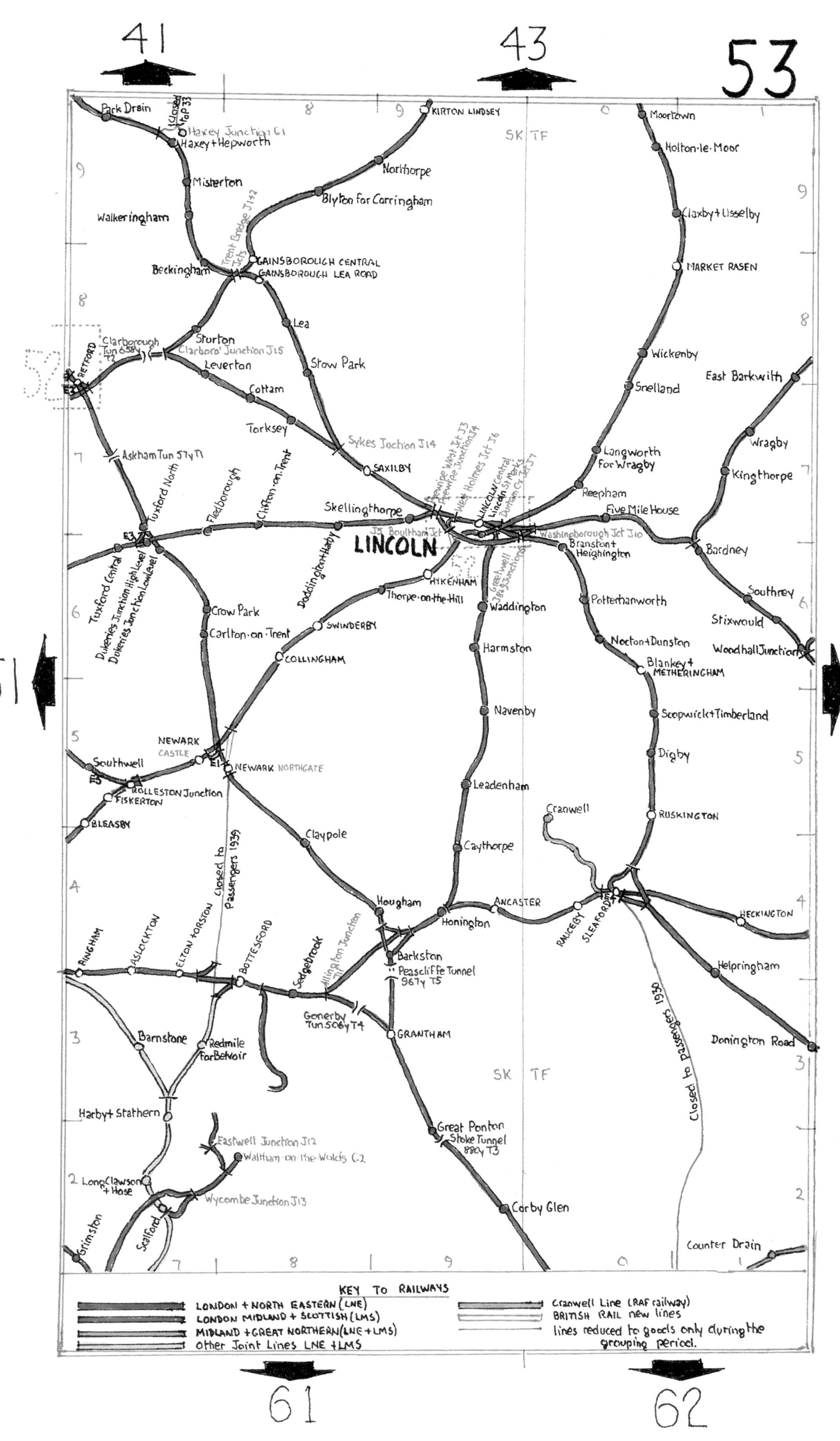
41
43
51
54
61
62
Park Drain
Haxey Junction G1
Haxey + Hepworth
Misterton
Walkeringham
Beckingham
GAINSBOROUGH CENTRAL
GAINSBOROUGH LEA ROAD
KIRTON LINDSEY
Northorpe
Blyton for Corringham
Lea
Stow Park
Sturton
Leverton
Cottam
Torksey
RETFORD
Clarborough Tun 658y T2
Clarboro' Junction J15
Askham Tun 57y T1
Tuxford North
Fledborough
Clifton-on-Trent
Sykes Junction J14
SAXILBY
Skellingthorpe
LINCOLN
Doddington + Harby
HYKENHAM
Thorpe-on-the-Hill
SWINDERBY
COLLINGHAM
Tuxford Central
Dukeries Junction High Level
Dukeries Junction Low Level
Crow Park
Carlton-on-Trent
NEWARK CASTLE
NEWARK NORTHGATE
Southwell
ROLLESTON Junction
FISKERTON
BLEASBY
Claypole
Closed to passengers 1939
Hougham
Barkston
Peascliffe Tunnel 967y T5
Honington
ANCASTER
RAUCEBY
SLEAFORD
Cranwell
HECKINGTON
Helpringham
Donington Road
Closed to passengers 1930
BINGHAM
ASLOCKTON
ELTON + ORSTON
BOTTESFORD
Sedgebrook
Allington Junction
Gonerby Tun 550y T4
GRANTHAM
Barnstone
Redmile For Belvoir
Harby + Stathern
Eastwell Junction J12
Waltham-on-the-Wolds
Long Clawson + Hose
Wycombe Junction J13
Scalford
Grimston
Great Ponton
Stoke Tunnel 880y T3
Corby Glen
Counter Drain
Moortown
Holton-le-Moor
Claxby + Usselby
MARKET RASEN
Wickenby
Snelland
Langworth for Wragby
Reepham
Five Mile House
Washingborough Jct J10
Branston + Heighington
Bardney
East Barkwith
Wragby
Kingthorpe
Southrey
Stixwould
Woodhall Junction
Potterhanworth
Nocton + Dunston
Blankney + METHERINGHAM
Scopwick + Timberland
Digby
RUSKINGTON
Waddington
Harmston
Navenby
Leadenham
Caythorpe
LINCOLN Central
Lincoln St Marks
West Holmes Jct J6
Boultham Jct
SK TF
KEY TO RAILWAYS
LONDON + NORTH EASTERN (LNE)
LONDON MIDLAND + SCOTTISH (LMS)
MIDLAND + GREAT NORTHERN (LNE + LMS)
Other Joint Lines LNE + LMS
Cranwell Line (RAF railway)
BRITISH RAIL new lines
lines reduced to goods only during the grouping period.

SKEGNESS, SPALDING + KINGS LYNN

RAILWAYS

No	Company
1	LONDON + NORTH EASTERN (LNE)
2	LONDON MIDLAND + SCOTTISH (LMS)
3	MIDLAND + GREAT NORTHERN (LNE + LMS)

STATIONS

Name	Opened / Closed	Ry Ref
Aby for Claythorpe	61	1 47
Alford Town	* 70	1 47
Algarkirk + Sutterton	61	1 23
Authorpe	61	1 48
BOSTON		1 34
Burgh-le-Marsh	* 70	1 46
Clenchwarton	59	3 51
Coningsby	* 70	1 25
Dersingham	69	1 63
Dogdyke	† 63	1 25
Donington-on-Bain	51	1 28
Donington Road	61	1 23
East Ville	61	1 45
Firsby	* 70	1 46
Fleet	59	3 32
Fotherby Halt	61	1 39
Gayton Road	59	3 61
Gedney	59	3 42
Gosberton	61	1 23
Grimoldby	60	1 48
Grimston Road	59	3 62
Hallington	51	1 38
HAVENHOUSE	*	1 56
Heacham	69	1 63
Holbeach	59	3 32
Horncastle	54	1 26
HUBBERT'S BRIDGE		1 24
Hunstanton	69	1 63
KING'S LYNN		1 62
Kirkton	61	1 33
Langrick	† 63	1 24
Legbourne Road	53	1 38
Little Steeping	58	1 46
Long Sutton	59	3 42
Louth	* 80	1 38
Ludborough	61	1 39
Mablethorpe	* 70	1 58
Middleton Towers	68	1 61
Midville	* 70	1 35
Moulton	59	3 32
Mumby Road	* 70	1 47
New Bolingbroke	* 70	1 35
North Drove	58	3 22
North Thoresby	* 70	1 39
North Wootton	69	1 62
Old Leake	56	1 35
Pinchbeck	61	1 22
Saltfleetby	60	1 49
Seacroft	53	1 56
Sedgeford	52	1 73
Sibsey	61	1 35
SKEGNESS	*	1 56
Snettisham	69	1 63
South Lynn	59	3 61
South Willingham + Hainton	51	1 28
SPALDING Town	48 70 70 71	1 22
Stickney	* 70	1 35
Surfleet	61	1 22
Sutton Bridge	59	3 42
Sutton-on-Sea	* 70	1 58
SWINESHEAD		1 24
Tattershall	† 63	1 25
Terrington	59	3 51
Theddlethorpe	60	1 48
THORPE CULVERT	*	1 46
Tumby Woodside	* 70	1 25
Tydd	59	3 41
Utterby Halt	61	1 39
WAINFLEET	*	1 45
Walpole	59	3 51
Weston	59	3 22
Whaplode	59	3 32
Willoughby	* 70	1 47
Withcall	51	1 28
Wolferton	69	1 62
Woodhall Junction	* 70	1 16
Woodhall Spa	54	1 26

GOODS

No	Name/Location	Closed	Ry Ref
G 1	Boston	?	1 34
2	Boston Wharf	?	1 34
3	Kings Lynn Harbour	68	1 62
4	Kings Lynn Hardwick Road	65	3 62
5	Spalding St Johns	66	2 22
6	Spilsby	58	1 46
7	Sutton Bridge Wharf	65	3 42
8	King's Lynn	59	1 62
9	South Lynn	?	3 61

ENGINE SHEDS

No	Name/Location	Closed [2]	Ry Ref
E 1	Boston	64	1 34
2	Louth	56	1 38
3	Mablethorpe	64	1 58
4	Spalding	60	1 22
5	Spilsby	58	1 46
6	Wainfleet	[1] ?	1 45
7	Hunstanton	58	1 63

TUNNELS

No	Name/Location	Length	Ry Ref
T 1	Withcall		1 28

JUNCTIONS

No.	Name	Ry	Ref
J 1	Cuckoo	3	22
2	Welland Bank	3	22
3	Holbeach	1	22

NOTES:

Ref All in TF so letters omitted

1 Shed destroyed but continued as a signing on point

2 Closure dates are to steam. In some cases continued for a short time as diesel depot.

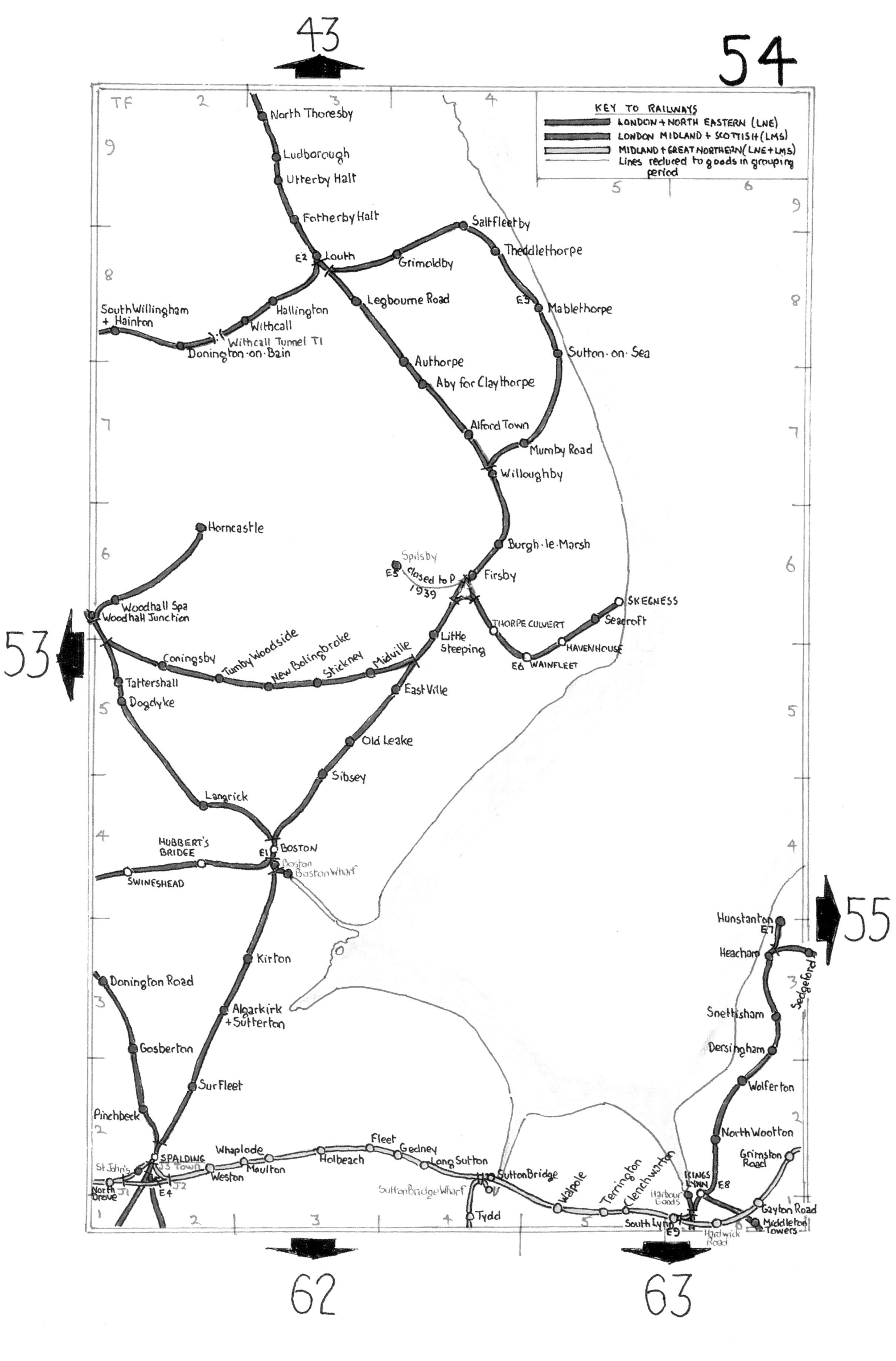

43
54
53
55
62
63
TF
KEY TO RAILWAYS
LONDON + NORTH EASTERN (LNE)
LONDON MIDLAND + SCOTTISH (LMS)
MIDLAND + GREAT NORTHERN (LNE + LMS)
Lines reduced to goods in grouping period
North Thoresby
Ludborough
Utterby Halt
Fotherby Halt
Louth
E2
Saltfleetby
Theddlethorpe
Grimoldby
Legbourne Road
E3
Mablethorpe
South Willingham + Hainton
Hallington
Withcall
Withcall Tunnel T1
Donington-on-Bain
Sutton-on-Sea
Authorpe
Aby for Claythorpe
Alford Town
Mumby Road
Willoughby
Horncastle
Burgh-le-Marsh
Spilsby
E5
closed to P 1939
Firsby
SKEGNESS
Woodhall Spa
Woodhall Junction
Seacroft
THORPE CULVERT
Little Steeping
HAVENHOUSE
E6
WAINFLEET
Coningsby
Tumby Woodside
New Bolingbroke
Stickney
Midville
Tattershall
East Ville
Dogdyke
Old Leake
Sibsey
Langrick
HUBBERT'S BRIDGE
E1
BOSTON
Boston
Boston Wharf
SWINESHEAD
Hunstanton
E7
Heacham
Kirton
Sedgeford
Donington Road
Algarkirk + Sutterton
Snettisham
Dersingham
Gosberton
Surfleet
Wolferton
Pinchbeck
North Wootton
SPALDING
Whaplode
Fleet
Gedney
Grimston Road
St John's
J3 Town
Moulton
Holbeach
Long Sutton
Sutton Bridge
Walpole
Terrington
Clenchwarton
KINGS LYNN
E8
North Drove
J1
E4
J2
Weston
Sutton Bridge Wharf
Harbour Goods
Gayton Road
Tydd
South Lynn
E9
Hardwick Road
Middleton Towers

55 A WELLS·NEXT·THE·SEA + FAKENHAM
B CROMER + NORTH WALSHAM

RAILWAYS

No	Company	
1	LONDON + NORTH EASTERN (LNE)	
3	MIDLAND + GREAT NORTHERN (MGN)	1
4	NORFOLK + SUFFOLK JOINT	1
5	NORTH NORFOLK (ex MGN)	1
6	WELLS + WALSINGHAM 10¼" (ex LNE)	
7	BURE VALLEY 1' 3" (ex LNE)	

STATIONS

Station		Opened Closed	Ry Ref
Aylsham North		48 59	3 G12
Aylsham South		48 52	17 G12
(BRAMPTON HALT)			7 G22
Burnham Market		52	1 F84
Buxton Lamas		52	17 G22
Catfield		59	3 G32
Cawston		52	1 G12
Coltishall		52	17 G22
Corpusty + Saxthorpe		59	3 G02
County School	*	64	1 F92
Cromer High		48 54	1 G24
CROMER Beach		69	3 G24
Cromer Links Halt		53	3 G23
Docking		52	1 F73
East Rudham		59	3 F82
Fakenham East	*	48 64	1 F92
Fakenham West		48 59	3 F92
Felmington		59	3 G22
Foulsham		52	1 G02
Guestwick		59	3 G02
GUNTON			1 G23
Hillington		52	3 F72
Hindolvestone		59	3 G02
Holkham		52	1 F84
Holt	*	64	35 G03
Honing For Worstead		59	3 G32
(HOVETON)			7 G31
HOVETON + WROXHAM	§	60	1 G31
(KELLING HEATH PARK)			5 G04
Massingham		59	3 F72
Melton Constable	*	64	3 G03
Mundesley·on·Sea	*	64	4 G33
NORTH WALSHAM Main		48 60	1 G22
North Walsham Town		48 59	3 G22
Overstrand		53	4 G23
Paston + Knapton	*	64	4 G33
Raynham Park		59	3 F82
Reepham	2	81	1 G02
ROUGHTON ROAD		85	1 G23
Ryburgh	*	64	1 F92
Sedgeford		52	1 F73
SHERINGHAM			3 G14
(SHERINGHAM)			5 G14
Sidestrand Halt		53	4 G23
Stalham		59	3 G32
Stanhoe		52	1 F73
Thursford		59	3 F93
Trimingham		53	4 G23
Walsingham	*	64	16 F93
(WARHAM HALT)			6 F94
Wells (on·Sea) (NEXT·THE·SEA)	*	64	16 F94
WEST RUNTON			3 G14
Weybourne	*	6	35 G14
Whitwell + Reepham		59	3 G02
Wighton Halt	*	64	16 F93
WORSTEAD			1 G22
WROXHAM	§	66	1 G31

ENGINE SHEDS

No	Name/Location	Closed	Ry Ref
E 1	Melton Constable	?	3 G03
2	Wells	55	1 F94
3	Cromer	?	3 G24
4	Cromer Beach	54	1 G24

JUNCTIONS

No	Name/Location	Ry	Ref
J 1	Antingham Road	134	G23

NOTES:

REF All in TF or TG so initial T is omitted.

§ Old version } Change of name
§ New version }

1 Joint owners: LNE and LMS

2 Regular services ended in 52.

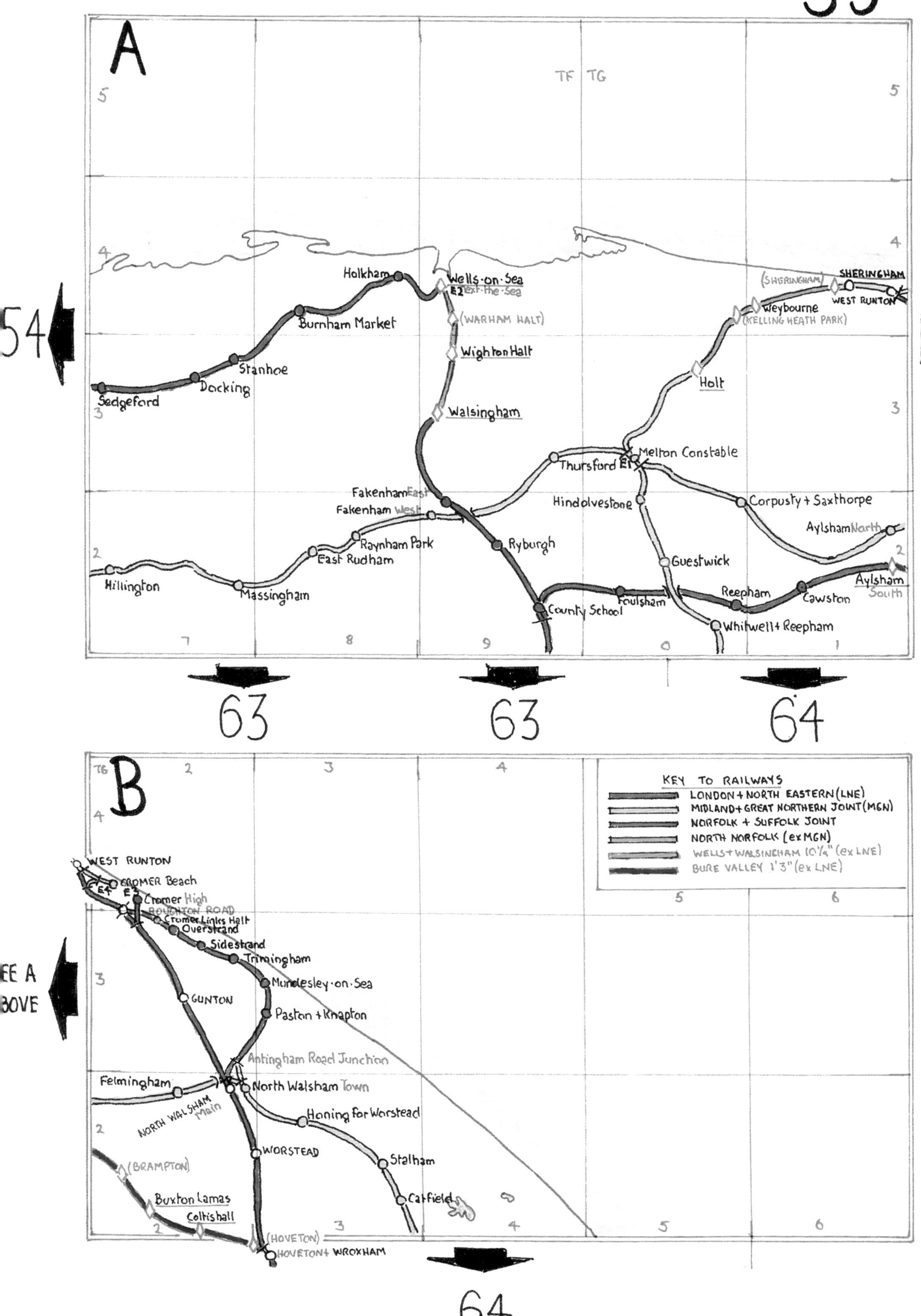
A
TF TG
Holkham
Wells-on-Sea
E2
Next-the-Sea
(WARHAM HALT)
Wighton Halt
Walsingham
Burnham Market
Stanhoe
Docking
Sedgeford
SHERINGHAM
(SHERINGHAM)
WEST RUNTON
Weybourne
(KELLING HEATH PARK)
Holt
Melton Constable
Thursford
E1
Hindolvestone
Corpusty + Saxthorpe
Aylsham North
Fakenham East
Fakenham West
Raynham Park
East Rudham
Ryburgh
Guestwick
Reepham
Cawston
Aylsham South
Hillington
Massingham
County School
Foulsham
Whitwell + Reepham
54
SEE B BELOW
63
63
64
B
TG
WEST RUNTON
CROMER Beach
E4
E3
Cromer High
ROUGHTON ROAD
Cromer Links Halt
Overstrand
Sidestrand
Trimingham
Mundesley-on-Sea
GUNTON
Paston + Knapton
Antingham Road Junction
Felmingham
North Walsham Town
NORTH WALSHAM Main
Honing for Worstead
WORSTEAD
Stalham
Catfield
(BRAMPTON)
Buxton Lamas
Coltishall
(HOVETON)
HOVETON + WROXHAM
SEE A ABOVE
KEY TO RAILWAYS
LONDON + NORTH EASTERN (LNE)
MIDLAND + GREAT NORTHERN JOINT (MGN)
NORFOLK + SUFFOLK JOINT
NORTH NORFOLK (ex MGN)
WELLS + WALSINGHAM 10¼" (ex LNE)
BURE VALLEY 1'3" (ex LNE)
64

FAIRBOURNE, ABERYSTWYTH + LLANDOVERY

RAILWAYS

No.	Company
2	LONDON MIDLAND + SCOTTISH (LMS)
23	LMS + GW JOINT
3	GREAT WESTERN (GW)
4	VALE OF RHEIDOL (GW) 1' 11½" gauge
5	TALYLLYN 2' 3" gauge
6	FAIRBOURNE 1' 3" then 1986 12¼" gauge

STATIONS

Station	Opened Closed	Ry	Ref
Aberayron	51	3	N46
ABERDOVEY		3	N69
ABERFFRWD	1	4	N67
ABERGYNOLWYN	2	5	H60
Abertafol	3 85	3	N69
ABERYSTWYTH		3	N58
ABERYSTWYTH	1	4	N58
Alltddu Halt	* 65	3	N66
Arthog	* 65	3	H61
Barmouth Ferry	A § 85	6	H61
BARMOUTH JUNCTION	B § 60	3	H61
Blaenplwyf Halt	51	3	N55
BORTH		3	N69
Bow Street	* 65	3	N68
BRYN GLAS	2	5	H60
Bryn Teify	* 65	3	N43
CAPEL BANGOR	1	4	N68
Caradog Falls Halt	* 64	3	N66
Carno	* 65	3	N99
Cemmes Road	* 65	3	H80
Ciliau Aeron Halt	51	3	N46
Commins Coch Halt	* 65	3	H80
Crossways Halt	51	3	N46
CYNGHORDY	† 49 50	2	N84
Derry Ormond	* 65	3	N55
DEVIL'S BRIDGE	1	4	N77
DOLGOCH (FALLS)	2	5	H60
DOVEY JUNCTION		3	N69
FachGoch Halt	50	5	H60
FAIRBOURNE		3	H61
FAIRBOURNE	4	6	H61
FelindyFfryn Halt	* 64	3	N67
Felin Fach	51	3	N55
GARTH	†	2	N94
Glandyfi	* 65	3	N69
GLANRAFON		4	N68
Gogarth Halt	3 85	3	N69
Hendy Halt	2	5	H60
Lampeter	* 65	3	N54
LLANBADARN	1	4	N68
Llanbrynmair	* 65	3	H90
LLANDOVERY	†	23	N73
Llandre	* 65	3	N68
Llanerch Ayron Halt	51	3	N46
LLANGAMMARCH Wells	† 80	2	N94
LLANGELYNIN Halt	68	3	H50
Llangybi	* 65	3	N65
Llanidloes	† 62	3	N98
Llanilar	* 64	3	N67
Llanrhystyd Road	* 64	3	N57
LLANWRTYD Wells	† 80	2	N94
LLANWRDA Halt	† 65 69	23	N77
Llanybyther	* 65	3	N54
LLWYNGWRIL		3	H50
MACHYNLLETH		3	H70
Maesycrugiau	* 65	3	N44
Marteg Halt	† 62	3	N97
MORFA MAWDDACH	B § 60	3	H61
(NANT GWERNOL)	2 76	5	H60
NANTYRONEN	1	4	N67
Olmarch Halt	* 65	3	N65
Pencader	* 65	3	N43
Pencarreg Halt	* 65	3	N54
PENDRE, TOWYN		5	H50
PENHELIG Halt	68	3	N69
Pont Llanio	* 65	3	N65
(PORTH PENRHYN)	A § 60	6	H61
Rhayader	† 62	3	N96
RHEIDOL FALLS	1	4	N77
RHIWFRON	1	4	N77
Silian Halt	51	3	N55
Strata Florida	* 65	3	N76
SUGAR LOAF HALT	5 49 50 65 84	2	N84
Talerddig	* 65	3	H90
Talsarn Halt	51	3	N55
TONFANAU	94	3	H50
TOWYN	C § 75	3	H50
TOWYN (TYWYN) Kings WHARF		5	H50
TOWYN (TYWYN) PENDRE		5	H50
Trawscoed	* 64	3	N67
Tregaron	* 65	3	N66
Tylwch Halt	† 62	3	N98
TYWYN	C § 75	3	H50
Ynyslas	* 65	3	N69

3 last train 84
4 closed for periods and narrowed in 86 and terminal stations rebuilt at that time
5 At present time normally open only in the summer.

GOODS

No	Location	Closed	Ry	Ref
G 1	Dinas Mawddwy	51	3	H71

ENGINE SHEDS

No	Name/Location	Closed	Ry	Ref
E 1	Aberystwyth	65	3	N58
2	Aberayron	62	3	N46
3	Llanidloes	62	3	N98
4	Machynlleth	66	3	H70

BRIDGES + VIADUCTS

No	Name/Location	Ry	Ref
V 1	Barmouth Bridge	3	H61

TUNNELS

No	Name/Location	Length	Ry	Ref
T 1	Marteg	372	3	N97
2	Rhayader	270	3	N96
3	Sugar Loaf	1000	2	N84

SUMMITS

No	Name/Location	Ht.	Ry	Ref
S 1	Talerddig		3	H90
2	Sugar Loaf	820	2	N84

NOTES:

Ref All in SH or SN therefore initial S omitted.

§ Older name } Change of name
§ newer name }

identical letters give reference to other variation

1 In grouping period ownership passed to GW was then part of BR until 1988 after short period of closure re-opened under private ownership

2 Closed for short periods and eventually it was extended to NANT GWERNOL in 76. The 'halts' shown in lower case are not normally in use. Quarry Siding is a passing loop.

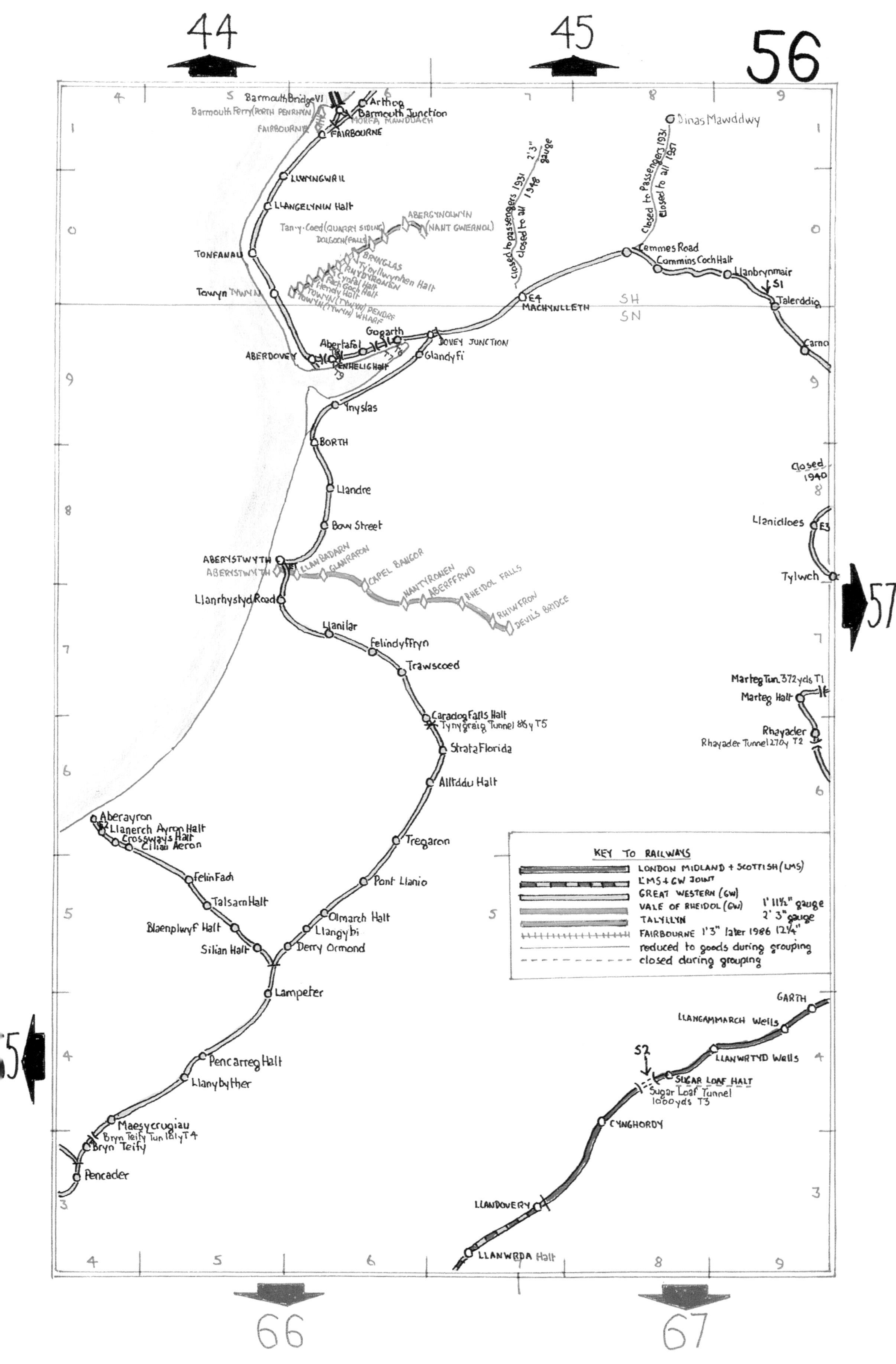
44
45
57
55
66
67
Barmouth Bridge V1
Barmouth Ferry (PORTH PENRHYN)
Arthog
Barmouth Junction
MORFA MAWDDACH
FAIRBOURNE
LLWYNGWRIL
LLANGELYNIN Halt
TONFANAU
Towyn TYWYN
Tan-y-Coed (QUARRY SIDING)
DOLGOCH (FALLS)
ABERGYNOLWYN
(NANT GWERNOL)
BRYNGLAS
Tynyllwynhen Halt
RHYDYRONEN
Cynfal Halt
Fach Goch Halt
Hendy Halt
TOWYN (TYWYN) PENDRE
TOWYN (TYWYN) WHARF
closed to passengers 1931
closed to all 1948
2'3" gauge
Dinas Mawddwy
Closed to Passengers 1931
closed to all 1951
Cemmes Road
Commins Coch Halt
Llanbrynmair
S1
Talerddig
Carno
E4
MACHYNLLETH
SH
SN
Gogarth
Abertafol
ABERDOVEY
PENHELIG Halt
DOVEY JUNCTION
Glandyfi
Ynyslas
BORTH
Llandre
Bow Street
ABERYSTWYTH
LLANBADARN
GLANRAFON
CAPEL BANGOR
NANTYRONEN
ABERFFRWD
RHEIDOL FALLS
RHIWFRON
DEVIL'S BRIDGE
Llanrhystyd Road
Llanilar
Felindyffryn
Trawscoed
Caradog Falls Halt
Tynygraig Tunnel 86y T5
Strata Florida
Alltddu Halt
Tregaron
Pont Llanio
Olmarch Halt
Llangybi
Derry Ormond
Lampeter
Aberayron
Llanerch Ayron Halt
Crossways Halt
Ciliau Aeron
Felin Fach
Talsarn Halt
Blaenplwyf Halt
Silian Halt
Pencarreg Halt
Llanybyther
Maesycrugiau
Bryn Teify Tun 181y T4
Bryn Teify
Pencader
Closed 1940
Llanidloes
E3
Tylwch
Marteg Tun 372yds T1
Marteg Halt
Rhayader
Rhayader Tunnel 270y T2
KEY TO RAILWAYS
LONDON MIDLAND + SCOTTISH (LMS)
LMS + GW JOINT
GREAT WESTERN (GW)
VALE OF RHEIDOL (GW) 1' 11½" gauge
TALYLLYN 2' 3" gauge
FAIRBOURNE 1'3" later 1986 12¼"
reduced to goods during grouping
closed during grouping
GARTH
LLANGAMMARCH Wells
LLANWRTYD Wells
S2
SUGAR LOAF HALT
Sugar Loaf Tunnel 1000yds T3
CYNGHORDY
LLANDOVERY
LLANWRDA Halt

57 SHREWSBURY, CAERSWS + BUILTH

RAILWAYS

No	Company
2	LONDON MIDLAND + SCOTTISH (LMS)
23	LMS + GW JOINT
3	GREAT WESTERN (GW)
4	WELSHPOOL + LLANFAIR (GW) 2'6" gauge 1

STATIONS

Station	Opened Closed	Ry Ref
Aberedw	† 62	3 004
Abermule	* 65	3 019
All Stretton Halt	58	23 049
Berrington + Eye	58	23 046
Boughrood + Llyswen	† 62	3 014
Breidden	60	23 J21
Bromfield	* 58	23 047
BROOME	†	2 038
BUCKNELL Halt	† 65 69	2 037
BUILTH ROAD High Level	† 50 69	2 005
Builth Road Low Level	† 50 62	3 005
Builth Wells	† 62	3 005
Buttington	60	3 J21
CAERSWS	*	3 009
(CASTLE CAEREINION)	1 63	4 J10
CHURCH STRETTON		23 049
CILMERY Halt	† B 69	2 005
Condover	58	23 J40
CRAVEN ARMS + Stokesay	74	23 048
Credenhill	† 62	2 044
(CYFRONYDD)	1 63	4 J10
DOLAU Halt	† 65 69	2 016
Doldowlod	† 62	3 N96
Dolwen Halt	† 56 62	3 N98
Dolyhir	51	3 025
Dorrington	58	23 J40
Eardisley	† 62	2 034
Erwood	† 62	3 004
Forden	* 65	3 J20
Forge Crossing Halt	51	3 036
Glan-yr-Afon Halt	† 62	3 N97
Glasbury-on-Wye	† 62	2 014
(Golfa)	1	4 J10
Hanwood	60	23 J40
Harton Road	51	3 048
Hay-on-Wye	† 55 62	2 024
(HENIARTH)		4 J10
HOPTON HEATH	†	2 037
Kingsland	55	3 046
Kington	55	3 035
Kinnersley	† 62	2 034
KNIGHTON Halt	† 65 69	2 037
KNUCKLAS Halt	† 56 69	2 027
Leebotwood	58	23 049
LEOMINSTER		23 056
Little Stretton Halt	58	23 049
LLANBISTER ROAD Halt	† 64 69	2 017
Llandinam	† 62	3 008
LLANDRINDOD Wells Halt 68-9	† 80	2 006
(LLANFAIR CAEREINION)	65	4 J10
LLANGUNLLO Halt	C † 65 69	2 027
Llanfaredd Halt	† 62	3 005
Llanstephan Halt	† 62	3 014
Marshbrook	58	23 048
Marston Halt	53	3 035
Minsterley	51	23 J30
Moat Lane Junction	† 62	3 009
Montgomery	* 65	3 029
Moorhampton	† 62	2 034
Newbridge-on-Wye	† 62	3 005
New Radnor	51	3 026
NEWTOWN		3 019
Onibury	58	23 047
Pantydwr	† 62	3 N97
Pembridge	55	3 036
PENYBONT	A † 80	2 016
Plas-y-Court Halt	60	23 J31
Plealey Road	51	23 J40
Pontdolgoch	* 65	3 009
Pontesbury	51	23 J30
Pool Quay	* 65	3 J21
Presteign	51	3 036
(RAVEN SQUARE, WELSHPOOL)	81	4 J20
St Devereux	58	3 043
St Harmons	† 62	3 N97
Scafell Halt	55	3 009
SHREWSBURY General	?	23 J41
Stanner	51	3 025
(SYLFAEN)	72	4 J10
Talgarth	† 62	3 013
Three Cocks Junction	† 62	3 013
Titley	55	3 035
Tram Inn	58	3 043
Trefeinon	† 62	2 013
Tylwch Halt	† 62	3 N98
WELSHPOOL		3 J20
(WELSHPOOL RAVEN SQUARE)	81	4 J20
Westmoor	62	2 044
Whitney-on-Wye	† 62	2 024
Wistanstow Halt	56	23 048
Yorkleton Halt	56 60	23 J31

GOODS

No	Name/Location	Closed	Ry Ref
G 1	Coton Hill Shrewsbury	2 ?	3 J41
2	Coleham Shrewsbury	66	23 J41
3	Welshpool (narrow gauge)	56	4 J20
4	Kerry	56	3 019

ENGINE SHEDS

No	Name/Location	Closed	Ry Ref
E 1	Shrewsbury Salop	67	2 J41
	Shrewsbury	67	3 J41
2	Welshpool	54	3 J20
3	Moat Lane	62	3 009
4	Craven Arms	62	2 048
5	Knighton	3 50	2 037
6	Builth Wells	57	3 005
7	Builth Road	62	2 005
8	Kington	51	3 035
9	Hereford	64	3 043
10	Leominster	62	3 055

TUNNELS

No	Name/Location	Length	Ry Ref
T 1	Penybont	440	2 016
2	Llangunllo	647	2 027
3	Red Hill	50	3 043

JUNCTIONS

No	Name/Location	Ry	Ref
J 1	Cruck Meole	23	J40
2	Marsh Farm	323	048
3	Central Wales	223	048
4	Builth Road North	23	005
5	Builth Road South	2	005
6	Golden Valley Line	23	024
7	Mid Wales		013
8	Moorfields	23	044
9	Redhill	23	043

NOTES:

REF All in SH, SJ, SN or SO therefore initial S is omitted

NAME CHANGES. Quite a few places had changes in Wales, most of them minor and all after nationalisation some are noted below:

	Name at 1.1.48	Later version
A	PENYBONT	PEN-Y-BONT
B	CILMERY	CILMERI
C	LLANGUNLLO	LLANGYNLLO

1 Welshpool + Llanfair became part of GW at the grouping. Passenger service discontinued from 1931 but some later excursions. Closed to all traffic 1956. Re-opened 1963 from Llanfair + extended in stages to RAVEN SQ WELSHPOOL. The street portion in Welshpool remained closed

2 Although yard closed as such, sidings still in use.

3 Closure date shown is date of transfer to Western region. Closure date not known.

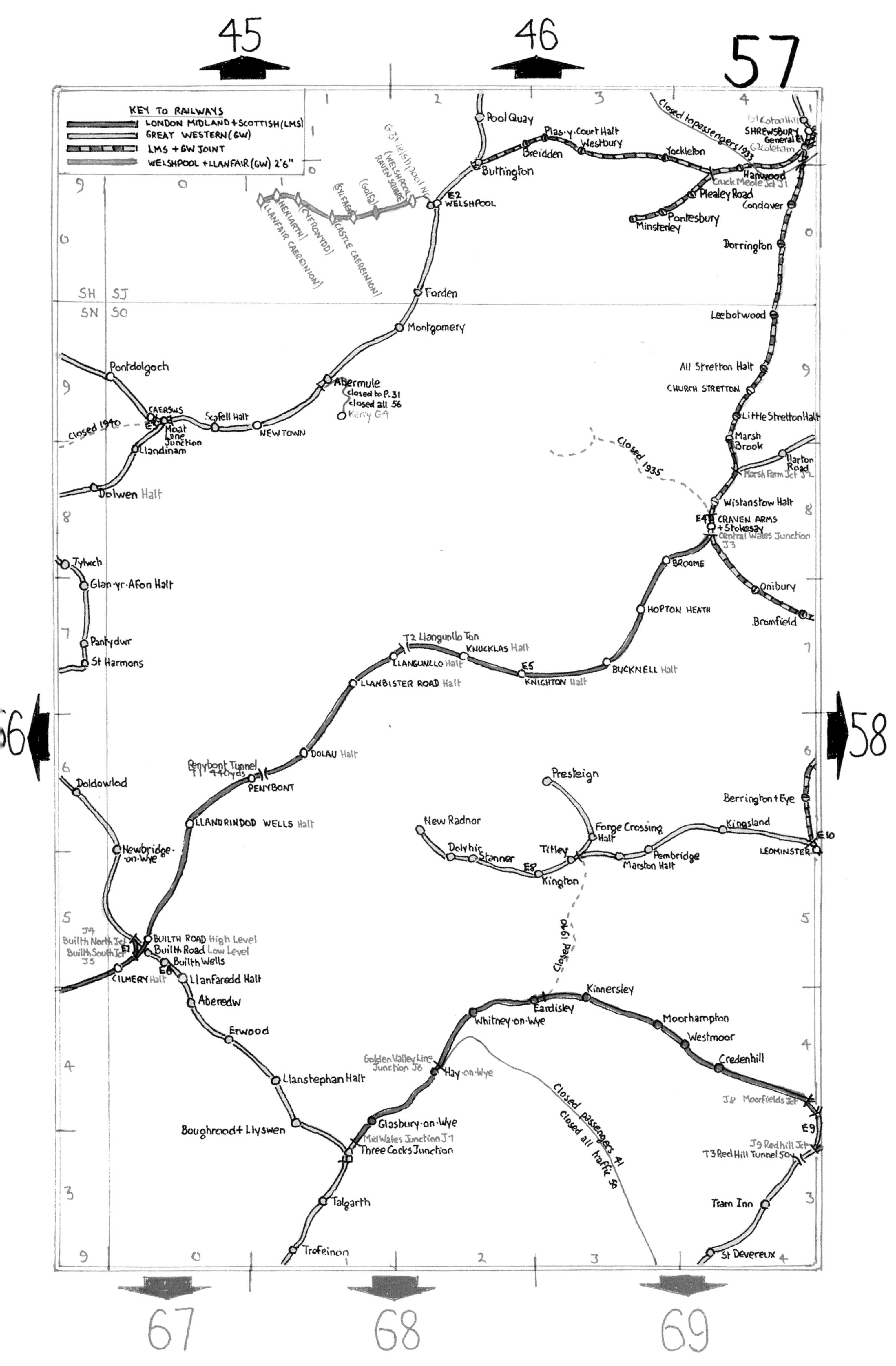

45
46
57
KEY TO RAILWAYS
LONDON MIDLAND + SCOTTISH (LMS)
GREAT WESTERN (GW)
LMS + GW JOINT
WELSHPOOL + LLANFAIR (GW) 2'6"
Pool Quay
Buttington
Breidden
Plas-y-Court Halt
Westbury
Yockleton
Closed to passengers 1933
SHREWSBURY General
Hanwood
Plealey Road
Pontesbury
Minsterley
Condover
Dorrington
E2 WELSHPOOL
(WELSHPOOL RAVEN SQUARE)
(GOLFA)
(SYLFAEN)
(CASTLE CAEREINION)
(CYFRONYDD)
(HENIARTH)
(LLANFAIR CAEREINION)
Forden
Montgomery
SH SJ
SN SO
Pontdolgoch
Abermule
closed to P. 31
closed all 56
Kerry G4
CAERSWS
Moat Lane Junction
Scafell Halt
NEWTOWN
closed 1940
Llandinam
Dolwen Halt
Leebotwood
All Stretton Halt
CHURCH STRETTON
Little Stretton Halt
Marsh Brook
Harton Road
Marsh Farm Jct J2
Closed 1935
Wistanstow Halt
E4 CRAVEN ARMS + Stokesay
Central Wales Junction J3
BROOME
Onibury
Bromfield
HOPTON HEATH
BUCKNELL Halt
E5 KNIGHTON Halt
KNUCKLAS Halt
T2 Llangunllo Tnn
LLANGUNLLO Halt
LLANBISTER ROAD Halt
Tylwch
Glan-yr-Afon Halt
Pantydwr
St Harmons
DOLAU Halt
Penybont Tunnel T1 440yds
PENYBONT
LLANDRINDOD WELLS Halt
Doldowlod
Newbridge-on-Wye
Presteign
Forge Crossing Halt
Titley
New Radnor
Dolyhir
Stanner
E8 Kington
Pembridge
Marston Halt
Kingsland
Berrington + Eye
E10 LEOMINSTER
58
Closed 1940
J4 Builth North Jct
Builth South Jct J5
BUILTH ROAD High Level
Builth Road Low Level
E6 Builth Wells
CILMERY Halt
Llanfaredd Halt
Aberedw
Erwood
Llanstephan Halt
Boughrood + Llyswen
Kinnersley
Eardisley
Whitney-on-Wye
Moorhampton
Westmoor
Credenhill
Golden Valley Line Junction J6
Hay-on-Wye
Glasbury-on-Wye
Mid Wales Junction J7
Three Cocks Junction
Closed passengers 41
Closed all traffic 56
J8 Moorfields Jct
E9
J9 Redhill Jct
T3 Red Hill Tunnel 50y
Talgarth
Tram Inn
Trefeinon
St Devereux
67
68
69

TELFORD, WOLVERHAMPTON + WORCESTER

RAILWAYS

No	Company
2	LONDON MIDLAND + SCOTTISH (LMS)
23	LMS + GW JOINT
3	GREAT WESTERN (GW)
4	SEVERN VALLEY (ex GW)

STATIONS

Station	Notes	Opened Closed	Ry	Ref
Admaston Halt		52 64	23	61
Albion		60	2	99
ALBRIGHTON			3	80
Alveley (Colliery) Halt	1 †	54 63	4	78
Arley	†	63 74	4	77
Ashperton Halt	*	64 65	3	64
Baptist End Halt	*	64	3	98
Berrington	†	63	3	50
Berrington + Eye		58	23	46
Bewdley		70 74	4	77
BILBROOK			3	80
Bilston Central		50 72	3	99
Bilston West	*	50 62	3	59
Blackwell	*	66	2	97
BLAKEDOWN, Churchill +		70	3	87
Blowers Green	†	62	3	99
Boughton Halt	*	65	3	85
Bransford Road	*	65	3	85
Brettell Lane	†	62	3	98
Bridgnorth	†	63 70	4	79
Brierley Hill	†	62	3	98
BROAD LANE		90	2	90
BROMSGROVE			2	96
Buildwas	†	63	3	60
Burlish Halt		68 70	3	87
CANNOCK	*	65 89	2	90
Churchill + BLAKEDOWN		70	3	87
Cleobury Mortimer	†	62	3	67
Coalbrookdale	2A § †	62	3	60
Coalport East		50 52	2	60
Coalport West	†	50 63	3	60
CODSALL			3	80
COLWALL			3	74
COSELEY, Deepfields +	5	?	2	99
COSFORD			3	70
Cound Halt	†	63	3	50
(COUNTRY PARK HALT)	1		4	78
CRADLEY Heath + Cradley HEATH	3	68 81	3	98
Cressage	†	63	3	50
Crudgington	†	63	3	61
Cutnall Green Halt	*	65	3	86
Daisy Bank + Bradley	†	62	3	99
Darby End Halt	*	64	3	98
Darlaston	*	65	2	99
Dawley + Stirchley		52	2	60
Deepfields + COSELEY	5	?	2	99
Defford	*	65	2	94
Dinmore		58	23	55
Donnington	*	64	2	71
Doseley Halt	†	63	3	60
DROITWICH SPA			3	86
Dudley	4 *	64	2	99
Dudley	4 *	64	3	99
DUDLEY PORT High Level		64	2	99
Dudley Port Low Level		64	2	99
Dunstall Park		68	3	90
Eardington	6 †	63 70 83	4	78
Easthope Halt		51	3	59
Easton Court		61	23	56
Eckington	*	65	2	94
Ettingshall Road + Bilston	*	64	2	99
Farley Halt	†	62	3	60
Fencote		52	3	65
Fernhill Heath	*	65	3	85
Fladbury	*	66	3	94
Foley Park Halt		68	3	87
Ford Bridge		54	23	55
Four Ashes		59	2	80
Gailey		51	2	91
Great Bridge North	*	50 64	3	59
Great Bridge South	*	50 64	3	59
GREAT MALVERN			3	74
Green Bank Halt	†	62	3	60
Hadley		64	2	61
Hadnall		60	2	51
HAGLEY			3	98
Halesowen	8	60	3	98
Hampton Loade	†	63 70	4	78
HARTLEBURY			3	87
HEDNESFORD	*	65 69	2	91
Henwick	*	65	3	85
HEREFORD			23	54
Highley	†	63 74	4	78
High Street Halt, Old Hill	*	64	3	98
Horsehay + Dawley	†	62	3	60
Hunnington	7	58	23	98
Iron Bridge + Broseley	†	63	3	60
IRONBRIDGE GORGE	2A §	88	3	60
Jackfield Halt	9 †	63	3	60
Ketley	†	62	3	60
Ketley Town Halt	†	62	3	60
KIDDERMINSTER			3	87
(KIDDERMINSTER TOWN)		84	4	87
Knightwick	*	64	3	75
LANDYWOOD		89	2	90
Lawley Bank	†	62	3	60
Leigh Court	*	64	3	75
LEOMINSTER			23	55
Lightmoor Junction Halt	†	56 62	3	60
Linley Halt	†	51 63	3	79
Longdon Halt	†	63	3	61
Longville		51	3	59
LUDLOW			23	57
LYE			3	98
Madeley		52	3	60
Madeley Market		52	3	60
Malins Lee		52	3	60
MALVERN LINK			3	74
Malvern Wells Hanley Road	10	51 52	2	74
Malvern Wells	*	65	3	74
Moreton-on-Lugg		58	23	54
Much Wenlock	†	62	3	60
Neen Sollars	†	62	3	67
New Dale Halt	†	62	3	60
New Hadley Halt	11	68 85	3	61
Newland Halt	*	65	3	74
Newnham Bridge	†	62	3	66
Newport	*	64	2	71
Northwood Halt	†	63 74	4	77
Norton Junction Halt	12 *	59 66	3	85
Oakengates Market Street		51 52	2	61
OAKENGATES West	14B §	51 56	3	61
OAKENGATES FOR TELFORD	B §	83	3	61
OLDBURY + Bromford Lane	13C §	77 83	2	99
OLD HILL			3	98
PENKRIDGE			2	91
PERSHORE			3	94
Presthope		51	3	59
Priestfield		72	3	99
Princes End + Coseley	†	62	3	99
Round Oak	†	62	3	98
Rowden Mill		52	3	65
ROWLEY REGIS + Blackheath		68	3	98
Rowton Halt	†	63	3	61
Rubery	7	64	23	97
Rushbury		51	3	59
Rushwick Halt	*	65	3	85
SANDWELL + DUDLEY	13C §	83	2	99
SHIFNAL			3	70
Shrewsbury Abbey	15	60	X	51
SHREWSBURY General			3	51
SHRUB HILL			3	85
Steens Bridge		52	3	55
Stoke Edith	*	65	3	64
Stoke Prior Halt		52	3	55
Stoke Works	*	66	3	96
Stoulton	*	66	3	95
STOURBRIDGE JUNCTION			3	98
STOURBRIDGE TOWN			3	98
Stourport-on-Severn		70	3	87
Suckley	*	64	3	75
Swan Village		72	3	99
TELFORD CENTRAL		86	3	70
Telford Coalbrookdale	2A §	79 79	3	60
Tenbury Wells	†	62	23	56
Tipton Five Ways	†	50 62	3	99
TIPTON Owen Street		50 68	2	99
Trench Crossing	*	64	2	61
Upton Magna		64	23	51
Upton-on-Severn		61	2	84
Wadborough	*	65	2	94
Walcot		64	23	51
Wednesbury Central		50 68 72	3	99
Wednesbury Town	*	60 64	2	99
WELLINGTON For Telford	D §	83 86	23	61
WELLINGTON TELFORD WEST	D §	86	23	61
Westwood Halt		51	3	69
Willenhall Bilston Street	*	65	2	99
Windmill End Halt	*	52 64	3	98
Withington		61	3	54
WOLVERHAMPTON High Level		73	2	99
Wolverhampton Low Level		72	3	99
Wooferton		61	23	56
WORCESTER FOREGATE STREET			3	85
WORCESTER SHRUB HILL			3	85
Wyre Forest	†	62	3	77
Wyre Halt	*	66	3	94
Wyrley + Cheslyn Hay	*	65	2	90

GOODS

No	Name/Location	Closed	Ry	Ref
G 1	Bushbury	65	2	90
2	Monmore Green	65	2	99
3	Walsall Street	65	3	99
4	Ditton Priors	17 65	3	68
5	Clee Hill	60	23	57
6	Stoke Works	64	2	96
7	Droitwich Road	52	2	96
8	Dunhampstead	49	2	95
9	Spetchley	61	2	95
10	Coleham	66	23	41
11	Hadley	65	2	61
12	Hollinswood	65	3	70
13	Shrewsbury	71	2	51

ENGINE SHEDS

No	Name/Location	Closed [16]	Ry	Ref
E 1	Salop/Coleham Shrewsbury	67	2	51
2	Shrewsbury	67	3	61
3	Wellington	64	3	61
4	Much Wenlock	51	3	69
5	Coalport	52	2	60
6	Clee Hill	18 60	2	57
7	Ludlow	51	23	57
8	Leominster	62	3	56
9	Worcester	65	3	85
10	Kidderminster	64	3	87
11	Bromsgrove	64	2	96
12	Wolverhampton	63	3	90
13	Stourbridge Junction	66	3	98
14	Bushbury	65	2	90
15	Tipton	56	2	99

TUNNELS

No	Name/Location	Length	Ry	Ref
T 1	Colwall	1583	3	74
2	Dinmore	1051	23	55
3	Rainbow Hill	212	3	85
4	Mount Pleasant	123	3	87
5	Bewdley	486	4	87
6	Oakengates	471	3	60
7	Dudley	948	3	99
8	Old Hill	890	3	98
9	Knowle Sand	40	4	79
10	Presthope	207	3	59
11	Swan Village	412	3	99

VIADUCTS

No	Name/Location	Ry	Ref
V 1	Kidderminster Viaduct	4	87

SUMMITS

No	Location	Ht	Ry	Ref
S 1	Blackwell	600	2	97

JUNCTIONS

No.	Name/Location	Ry	Ref
J 1	Rainbow Hill	3	85
2	Tunnel	3	85
3	Abbot's Wood	23	85
4	Shelwick	233	54
5	Barrs Court	233	54
6	Brecon Curve	23	54

NOTES:

REF All in SJ or SO therefore letters omitted.

§ Old Name, § New Name } Change of name

Corresponding letter indicates other name

1. The name change was dropping of Colliery. The location has recently re-opened as COUNTRY PARK HALT

2.

From	Name	event	to
	Coalbrookdale	closed	62
79	Telford Coalbrookdale	re-open	79
88	IRONBRIDGE GORGE	change	

Open for seasonal excursions only

3. became CRADLEY 68, CRADLEY HEATH 81
4. Different Platforms of same stations.
5. Unclear when name changed
6. Opened by Severn Valley 70 but was closed in 83.
7. Regular service ended in 1919. But used intermittently for excursions + for workmen to car Factory.
8. Regular services ended 1928
9. Rebuilt on adjoining site 1954.
10. Wells was dropped from title Hanley Road added in 1951
11. Halt dropped from title in 1968.
12. Junction dropped from title and Halt added in 1959.
13. Bromford Lane dropped before 77. Station rebuilt in 83 when name was changed to SANDWELL + DUDLEY
14. West added 51-6 the FOR TELFORD added in 1983.
15. Regular services ended 1933. Used for some troop movements. The X in the railway column indicates that operations on the line were by WD + GW Jointly.
16. Closure dates are for steam.
17. Although part of GW on nationalisation was subsequently from May 57 transferred to Admiralty.
18. Theoretically a joint shed, but as far only one engine working alternated, on nationalisation was LMS.

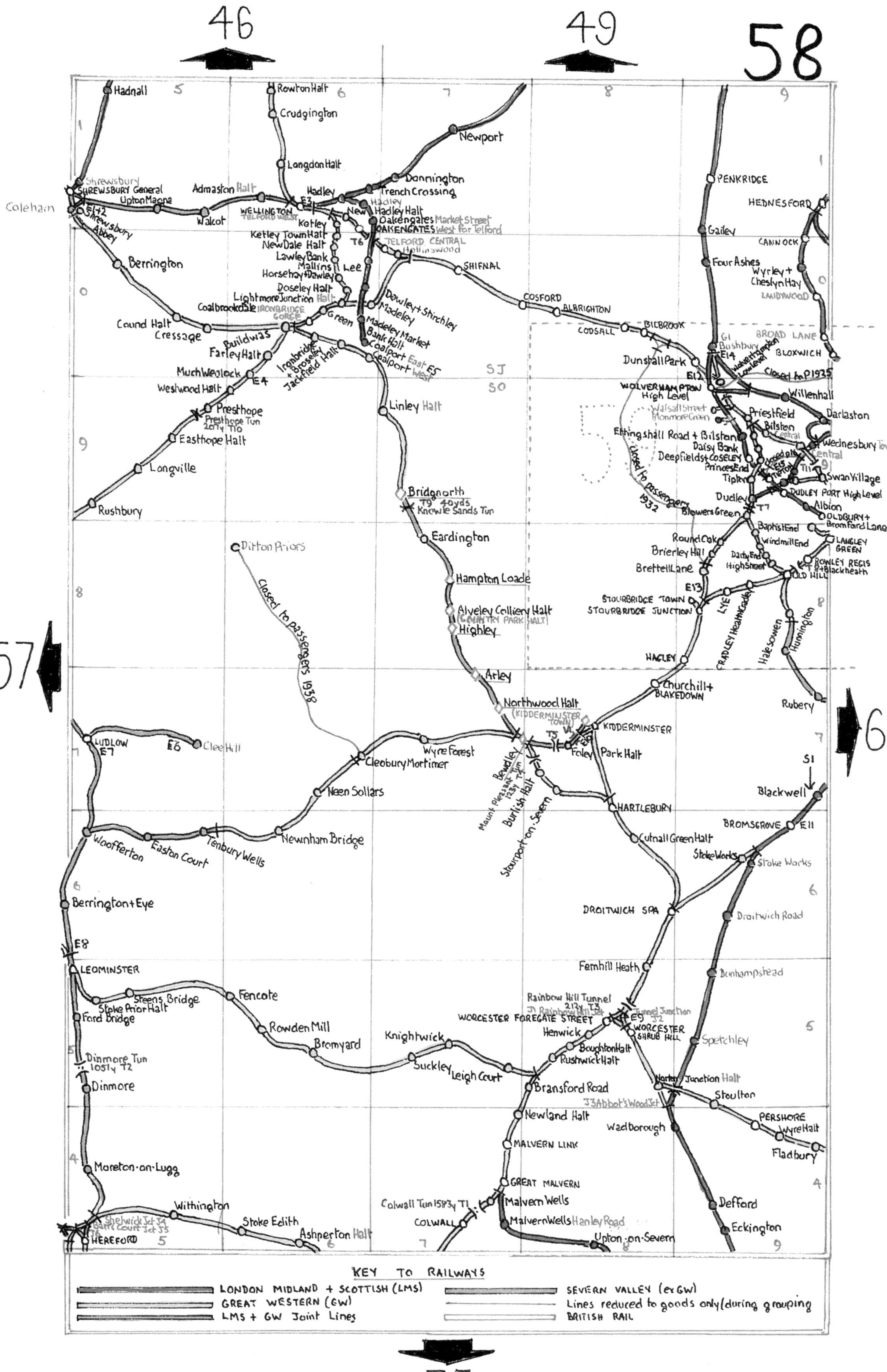

46
49
58
57
60
75
Hadnall
Rowton Halt
Crudgington
Newport
Longdon Halt
Donnington
Trench Crossing
Shrewsbury
SHREWSBURY General
Colehain
Admaston Halt
Upton Magna
Walcot
WELLINGTON
TELFORD WEST
Hadley
Hadley Halt
Ketley
Ketley Town Halt
New Dale Halt
Lawley Bank
Mallins
Horsehay + Dawley
Doseley Halt
Lightmore Junction Halt
Lee
Oakengates Market Street
OAKENGATES West for Telford
TELFORD CENTRAL
Hollinswood
SHIFNAL
Shrewsbury Abbey
Berrington
Coalbrookdale
IRONBRIDGE GORGE
Green
Dawley + Stirchley
Madeley
Madeley Market
Coalport East
Coalport West
Cound Halt
Cressage
Buildwas
Farley Halt
Much Wenlock
Westwood Halt
Presthope
Presthope Tun
Easthope Halt
Longville
Rushbury
Ironbridge + Broseley
Jackfield Halt
Linley Halt
COSFORD
ALBRIGHTON
CODSALL
BILBROOK
Dunstall Park
PENKRIDGE
Gailey
Four Ashes
HEDNESFORD
CANNOCK
Wyrley + Cheslyn Hay
LANDYWOOD
BROAD LANE
Bushbury
BLOXWICH
WOLVERHAMPTON High Level
Wolverhampton Low Level
Closed to P 1925
Willenhall
Darlaston
Walsall Street
Monmore Green
Priestfield
Bilston Central
Ettingshall Road + Bilston
Daisy Bank
Deepfields + COSELEY
Princes End
Tipton
Wednesbury Town
Wednesbury Central
Swan Village
DUDLEY PORT High Level
Albion
Dudley
OLDBURY + Bromford Lane
Blowers Green
Closed to passengers 1932
Round Oak
Brierley Hill
Brettell Lane
Baptist End
Windmill End
Darby End
High Street
LANGLEY GREEN
ROWLEY REGIS + Blackheath
OLD HILL
STOURBRIDGE TOWN
STOURBRIDGE JUNCTION
LYE
CRADLEY HEATH + Cradley
Halesowen
Hunnington
HAGLEY
Churchill + BLAKEDOWN
Rubery
SJ
SO
Bridgnorth
Knowle Sands Tun
Eardington
Hampton Loade
Alveley Colliery Halt
COUNTRY PARK HALT
Highley
Arley
Northwood Halt
KIDDERMINSTER TOWN
KIDDERMINSTER
Foley Park Halt
Ditton Priors
Closed to passengers 1938
LUDLOW
Clee Hill
Wyre Forest
Cleobury Mortimer
Bewdley
Mount Pleasant Tun
Burlish Halt
Stourport-on-Severn
HARTLEBURY
Neen Sollars
Woofferton
Easton Court
Tenbury Wells
Newnham Bridge
Cutnall Green Halt
Blackwell
BROMSGROVE
Stoke Works
DROITWICH SPA
Droitwich Road
Berrington + Eye
LEOMINSTER
Steens Bridge
Stoke Prior Halt
Ford Bridge
Fencote
Rowden Mill
Bromyard
Knightwick
Suckley
Leigh Court
Fernhill Heath
Dunhampstead
Rainbow Hill Tunnel
WORCESTER FOREGATE STREET
Henwick
Tunnel Junction
WORCESTER SHRUB HILL
Boughton Halt
Rushwick Halt
Spetchley
Bransford Road
Norton Junction Halt
Abbot's Wood Jct
Stoulton
Newland Halt
MALVERN LINK
Wadborough
PERSHORE
Wyre Halt
Fladbury
Dinmore Tun
Dinmore
Moreton-on-Lugg
GREAT MALVERN
Malvern Wells
Malvern Wells Hanley Road
Colwall Tun
COLWALL
Upton-on-Severn
Defford
Eckington
Withington
Stoke Edith
Ashperton Halt
Shelwick Jct
Barrs Court Jct
HEREFORD
KEY TO RAILWAYS
LONDON MIDLAND + SCOTTISH (LMS)
GREAT WESTERN (GW)
LMS + GW Joint Lines
SEVERN VALLEY (ex GW)
Lines reduced to goods only (during grouping
BRITISH RAIL

59 BIRMINGHAM + WOLVERHAMPTON

RAILWAYS

No	Company
2	LONDON MIDLAND + SCOTTISH (LMS)
23	LMS + GW JOINT lines
3	GREAT WESTERN (GW)

STATIONS

Station	Opened Closed	Ry Ref
ACOCKS GREEN		3 P18
ADDERLEY PARK		2 P18
Albion	60	2 099
Aldridge	*65	2 K00
ASTON		2 P08
Baptist End Halt	*64	3 098
BESCOT STADIUM		2 P09
BILBROOK		3 J80
Bilston Central	50 72	3 099
Bilston West	†50 62	3 099
BIRMINGHAM		P08
MOOR STREET		3 P08
NEW STREET		2 P08
SNOW HILL	72 87	3 P08
BIRMINGHAM INTERNATIONAL	76	2 P18
BLAKE STREET		2 K10
Blowers Green	†62	3 099
BLOXWICH		2 K00
BORDESLEY		3 P08
BOURNVILLE		2 P08
Brettell Lane	†62	3 098
Brierley Hill	†62	3 098
BROAD LANE	90	2 J90
Bromford Bridge	65	2 P19
BUTLERS LANE	57	2 P19
Castle Bromwich	68	2 P19
CHESTER ROAD		2 P19
CODSALL		3 J80
Coleshill	68	2 P19
COSELEY, Deepfieldst		2 099
CRADLEY Heath + Cradley	A§ ?	3 098
CRADLEY HEATH	A§	098
Daisy Bank + Bradley	†62	3 099
Darby End Halt	*64	3 098
Darlaston	*65	2 099
Deepfields + COSELEY	?	2 099
DUDDESTON, Vauxhall +	74	2 P09
Dudley		2 099
Dudley		3 099
DUDLEY PORT High Level	64	2 099
12 Dudley Port Low Level	64	2 099
Dunstall Park	68	3 J90
ERDINGTON		2 P19
Ettingshall Road + Bilston	64	2 099
FIVE WAYS	50 78	2 P08
FOUR OAKS		2 P19
GRAVELLY HILL		2 P19
GREAT BARR	B§74	2 P09
Great Bridge North	*50	2 099
Great Bridge South	*50	3 099
HAGLEY		3 098
Halesowen	3 60	3 098
HALL GREEN		3 P18
HAMSTEAD	B§74	2 P09
Handsworth + Smethwick	2 68 72	3 P08
Hawthorns Halt, The		3 P09
High Street Halt (Old Hill)		3 098
Hockley	72	3 P08
Hummington	1 58	23 098
KINGS NORTON		2 P07
LANGLEY GREEN, Oldbury +	68	3 P08
LEA HALL		2 P18
LYE		3 098
MARSTON GREEN		2 P18
Monument Lane	58	2 P08
MOOR STREET		3 P08
NEW STREET		2 P08
OLDBURY + Bromfield Lane	4C §77 83	2 099
Oldbury + LANGLEY GREEN	68	3 P08
OLTON		3 P18
Pelsall	*65	2 K00
Penns	*65	2 P19
PERRY BARR		2 P09
Pleck	58	2 P09
Priestfield	72	3 099
Prince's End + Coseley	†62	3 099
Round Oak	†62	3 098
ROWLEY REGIS + Blackheath	68	3 098
Saltley	68	2 P08
SANDWELL + DUDLEY	4C §83	2 099
SELLY OAK	78	2 P08
SMALL HEATH + Sparkbrook	68	3 P18
SMETHWICK ROLFE STREET	63	2 P09
SMETHWICK Junction WEST	56	3 P08
SNOW HILL	72 87	3 P08
Soho	49	2 P08
Soho + Winson Green	D§65	3 P08
SOLIHULL		3 P18
Spon Lane	*64	2 P08
SPRING ROAD		3 P18
STETCHFORD for Yardley		2 P18
STOURBRIDGE JUNCTION		3 098
STOURBRIDGE TOWN		3 098
Streetly	*65	2 P09
SUTTON COLDFIELD		2 P19
Sutton Park	*65	2 P19
Swan Village	72	3 099
TAME BRIDGE	90	2 P09
The Hawthorns Halt	68	3 P09
Tipton Five Ways	50 62	3 099
TIPTON Owen Street	53 68	2 099
TYSELEY		3 P18
UNIVERSITY	78	2 P08
Vauxhall + DUDDESTON	74	2 P08
WALSALL		2 P09
WATER ORTON		2 P19
Wednesbury Central	50 68 72	3 099
Wednesbury Town	*60 64	2 099
West Bromwich	72	3 P09
Willenall Bilston Street	65	2 099
Windmill End Halt	*52 64	3 098
Winson Green	D§65 72	3 P08
Winson Green	57	2 P08
WITTON		2 P09
WOLVERHAMPTON High Level		2 099
Wolverhampton Low Level	72	3 099
WYLDE GREEN		2 P19
YARDLEY WOOD		3 P18

GOODS

No	Name/Location	Closed	Ry Ref
G1	Bushbury	65	2 J90
2	Wednesfield Heath	65	2 J90
3	Sutton Coldfield	67	2 P19
4	Penns	65	2 P19
5	Darlaston	65	2 099
6	Water Orton	66	2 P19
7	Harborne	63	2 P08
8	Lawley Street 6		2 P08
9	Windsor Street + Aston	80	2 P08
10	Withymore	65	3 098
11	Central	67	2 P08
12	Old Hill	64	3 098
13	Monmore Green	65	3 099
14	Walsall Street	65	3 099
15	Wednesbury	68	3 099
16	Oldbury	64	3 098
17	Albion	64	2 099
18	Oldbury	?	2 P09
19	Soho	68	2 P08
20	Curzon Street	6 68	2 P08
21	Stourbridge Town	65	3 098
22	BESCOT YARD	5 C	0 P09
23	Swan Village	66	3 099
24	Walsall (ex LNW)	?	2 P09
25	Walsall (ex Midland)	?	2 P09
26	Oxley	?	3 J90

ENGINE SHEDS 8

No	Name Location	Closed	Ry Ref
E1	Wolverhampton	63	3 J90
2	TYSELEY	9 66	3 P18
3	Stourbridge Junction	66	3 098
4	SALTLEY	9 61	2 P18
5	Bournville	60	2 P08
6	Aston	65	2 P08
7	Monument Lane	62	2 P08
8	Tipton	56	2 099
9	Bushbury	65	2 J90

COMPANY WORKS

No	Name/Location	Closed	Ry Ref
10	Walsall	10 58	2 P09
11	OXLEY	9	0 J90
12	SOHO	9	0 P08
C1	Stafford Rd. Wolverhampton	64	3 J90

TUNNELS

No	Name/Location	length yards	Ry Ref
T1	Old Hill	896	3
2	Dudley	948	3
3	Galton	64	3
4	New Street North	751	2
5	Wolverhampton	377	3
6	Snow Hill	596	3
7	Bath Row	7 209	2
8	Granville Street	83	2
9	Canal	224	2
10	Holliday Street	93	2
11	Suffolk Street	176	2
12	Bath Row Goods	11 109	2
13	Granville Street Goods	11 234	2
14	New Street South	254	2
15	Hamstead	125	2
16	Swan Village	412	3
17	Park Street Walsall	143	2
18	Moseley	156	2
19	Church Road	107	2

NOTES:

REF In SJ, SK, SO or SP therefore initial S is omitted.

§ Old Name, § New Name } Change of name; corresponding letter gives ref to the other name

1 Regular services ended 1919 but in use for excursion and weekday workmen's trains.

2 Smethwick dropped from station name in 72

3 Regular services to 1928 then used by excursion and workmen's trains.

4 Bromfield Lane dropped from name in 77 change to SANDWELL + DUDLEY was in 83.

5 Open by BR. Still in use

6 Still in use for railway purposes.

7 Tunnels 7 to 11 named from the south

8 Closure date is for steam.

NOTES (continued):

9 Still in use

10 Converted for use as DMU depot, but discontinued due to inconvenient site

11 Bath Row is south of Granville Street.

12 There are two new schemes projected for this area. The first is upgrading the line from SNOW HILL to SMETHWICK WEST for passengers, currently used only for freight, the other is MIDLAND METRO from SNOW HILL to WOLVERHAMPTON MARKET STREET following the old GW route as far as Priestfield with stations at previous sites plus many intermediate stops also.

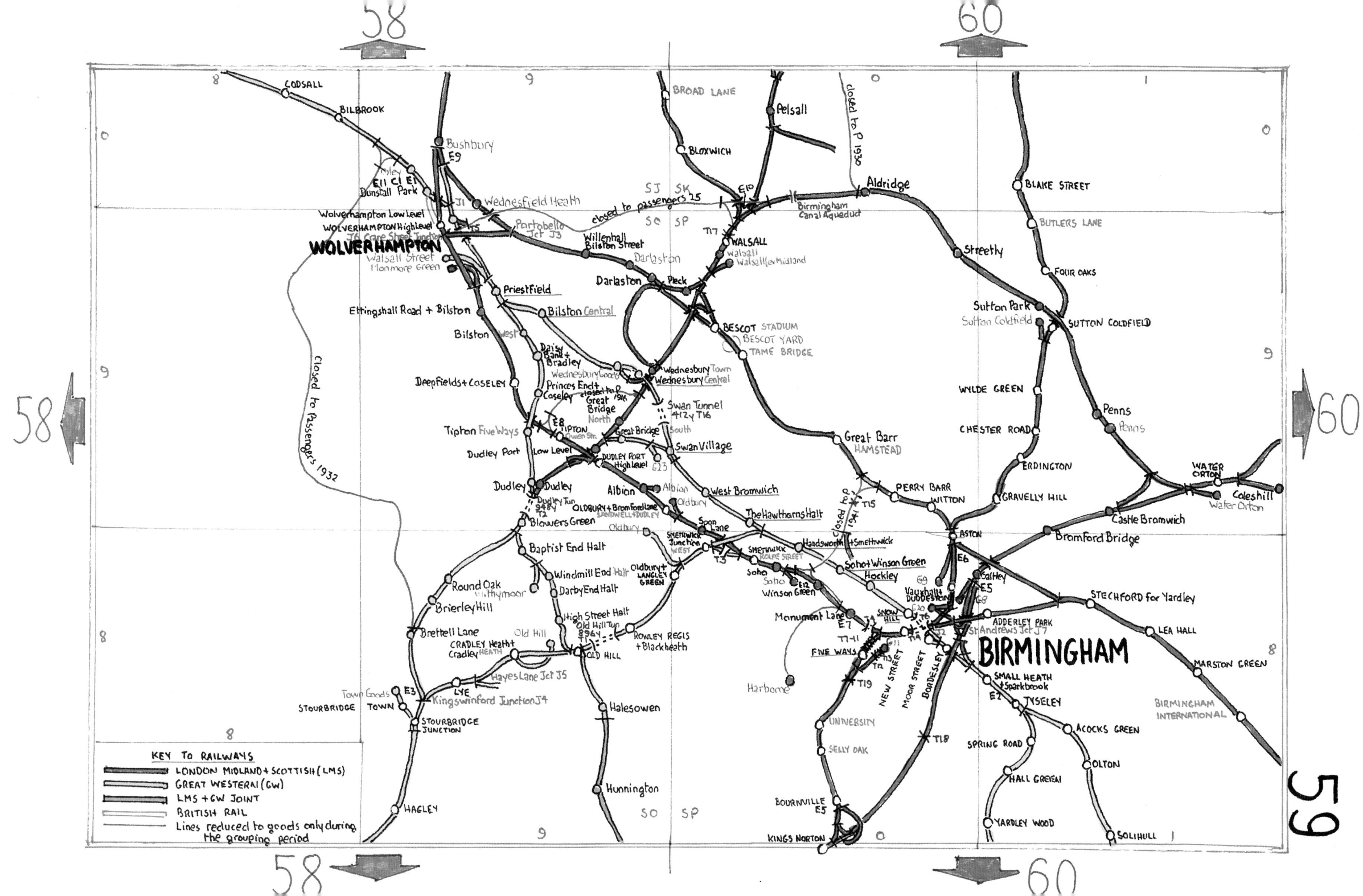
59
KEY TO RAILWAYS
LONDON MIDLAND + SCOTTISH (LMS)
GREAT WESTERN (GW)
LMS + GW JOINT
BRITISH RAIL
Lines reduced to goods only during the grouping period
WOLVERHAMPTON
BIRMINGHAM
CODSALL
BILBROOK
Bushbury
Dunstall Park
Wolverhampton Low Level
WOLVERHAMPTON High Level
Wednesfield Heath
Portobello Jct J3
Willenhall Bilston Street
Darlaston
Priestfield
Bilston Central
Ettingshall Road + Bilston
Bilston
Deepfields + Coseley
Tipton Five Ways
Dudley Port
Dudley
Blowers Green
Baptist End Halt
Windmill End Halt
Darby End Halt
Round Oak
Brierley Hill
Brettell Lane
Old Hill
Halesowen
Hunnington
Rowley Regis + Blackheath
Oldbury + Langley Green
LYE
Kingswinford Junction J4
Hayes Lane Jct J5
STOURBRIDGE JUNCTION
STOURBRIDGE TOWN
HAGLEY
BROAD LANE
BLOXWICH
Pelsall
WALSALL
Aldridge
Birmingham Canal Aqueduct
closed to P 1930
closed to passengers 25
closed to Passengers 1932
Pleck
BESCOT STADIUM
BESCOT YARD
TAME BRIDGE
Wednesbury Town
Wednesbury Central
Swan Tunnel
Great Bridge
Swan Village
West Bromwich
Albion
The Hawthorns Halt
Spon Lane
Handsworth + Smethwick
Soho + Winson Green
Hockley
Great Barr
HAMSTEAD
PERRY BARR
WITTON
ASTON
Streetly
BLAKE STREET
BUTLERS LANE
FOUR OAKS
Sutton Park
SUTTON COLDFIELD
WYLDE GREEN
CHESTER ROAD
ERDINGTON
GRAVELLY HILL
Penns
WATER ORTON
Coleshill
Castle Bromwich
Bromford Bridge
STECHFORD for Yardley
LEA HALL
MARSTON GREEN
BIRMINGHAM INTERNATIONAL
ADDERLEY PARK
SNOW HILL
NEW STREET
MOOR STREET
BORDESLEY
Monument Lane
FIVE WAYS
Harborne
UNIVERSITY
SELLY OAK
BOURNVILLE
KINGS NORTON
SMALL HEATH + Sparkbrook
TYSELEY
ACOCKS GREEN
OLTON
SOLIHULL
SPRING ROAD
HALL GREEN
YARDLEY WOOD

60

LICHFIELD, BIRMINGHAM + BANBURY

RAILWAYS

No.	Company
0	BRITISH RAIL new lines
1	LONDON + NORTH EASTERN (LNE)
2	LONDON MIDLAND + SCOTTISH (LMS)
23	LMS + GW JOINT
3	GREAT WESTERN (GW)
4	BATTLEFIELD STEAM (preserved)

STATIONS

Name	Opened/Closed	Ry Ref
ACOCKS GREEN + South Yardley	68	3 P18
ADDERLEY PARK		2 P18
Alcester	† 62	2 P05
Aldridge	* 65	2 K00
Alrewas	* 65	2 K11
ALVECHURCH		2 P07
Arley + Fillongley	60	2 P28
Armitage	60	2 K01
Ashby-de-la-Zouch	* 64	2 K31
ASTON		2 P08
ATHERSTONE		2 P39
Bagworth + Ellistown	* 64	2 K40
BANBURY General	61	3 P44
Banbury Merton Street	61	2 P44
Bardon Hill	52	2 K41
BARNT GREEN		2 P07
Barton + Walton	58	2 K21
BEARLEY Halt	65 68	3 P16
BEDWORTH	* 65 88	2 P38
Bengeworth	53	2 P04
BERKSWELL		2 P27
BESCOT STADIUM	91	2 P09
Bidford-on-Avon	49	2 P15
Binton	1 49	2 P15
Birdingbury	59	2 P46
BIRMINGHAM		P08
MOOR STREET		3 P08
NEW STREET		2 P08
SNOW HILL	72 87	3 P08
BIRMINGHAM INTERNATIONAL	76	2 P18
BLAKE STREET		2 K10
BLOXWICH	* 65 89	2 K00
BORDESLEY		3 P08
BOURNVILLE	2 78	2 P08
Brandon + Wolston	60	2 P47
Brinklow	75	2 P48
Bromford Bridge	65	2 P18
Broom Junction	† 62	2 P05
Brownhills	* 65	2 K00
BUTLERS LANE	57 91 92	2 P19
Campden	A § 52	3 P14
CANLEY Halt	?	2 P37
Castle Bromwich	68	2 P19
Chalacombe Road Halt	56	1 P44
CHESTER ROAD		2 P19
Chilvers Coton	* 65	2 P38
Chipping Camden	A § 52 66	3 P14
CLAVERDON		3 P26
Coalville Town	* 64	2 K41
Coleshill	68	2 P19
Coughton	52	2 P05
Coundon Road	* 65	2 P37
COVENTRY		2 P37
Cropredy	56	3 P44
Daimler Halt	* 65	2 P37
DANZEY		3 P16
Desford	* 64	2 K40
DORRIDGE, Knowle +	74	3 P17
DUDDESTON, Vauxhall +	74	2 P18
Dunchurch	59	2 P47
EARLSWOOD Lakes	74	3 P17
Elford	52	2 K10
Elmesthorpe	* 68	2 P49
ERDINGTON		2 P19
Ettington	52	2 P25
Evesham	63	2 P04
EVESHAM		3 P04
Fenny Compton	* 64	3 P45
Fenny Compton West	52	2 P45
FIVE WAYS	50 78	2 P08
Flecknoe	52	2 P46
Foleshill	* 65	2 P38
FOUR OAKS		2 P19
GRAVELLY HILL		2 P19
GREAT BARR	B § 74	2 P09
Gresley	* 64	2 K21
Grimes Hill + WYTHALL	74	3 P07
HALL GREEN		3 P18
Hammerwich	* 65	2 K00
HAMPTON-IN-ARDEN		2 P28
HAMSTEAD	B § 74	2 P09
Handsworth + Smethwick	3 68 72	3 P08
Harvington	† 62	2 P04
HATTON		3 P26
Hawkesbury Lane	* 65	2 P38
Hawthorns Halt, The	3 68	3 P08
HENLEY-IN-ARDEN		3 P16
HINCKLEY		2 P49
Hinton	† 63	2 P04
Hockley	3 72	3 P08
HONEYBOURNE	69 85	3 P14
Kenilworth	* 65	2 P27
Kineton	52	2 P35
Kingsbury	68	2 P29
KINGS NORTON		2 P07
Knowle + DORRIDGE	4 68 72	3 P17
LANGLEY GREEN, Oldbury +	68	3 P08
LAPWORTH		3 P16
LEA HALL		2 P18
Leamington Spa Avenue	* 51 65	2 P36
LEAMINGTON SPA General	50 68	3 P36
Leamington Spa Milverton	* C § 52 65	2 P36
LICHFIELD CITY		2 K10
LICHFIELD TRENT VALLEY	5 *	2 K10
High Level	5 * 65 88	2 K10
Low Level	5	2 K10
Littleton + Badsey	* 66	3 P04
Longford + Exhall	49	2 P38
Longbridge	6	23 P07
LONGBRIDGE	6 78	2 P07
Long Marston	* 66	3 P14
(MARKET BOSWORTH)	?	4 K30
MARSTON GREEN		2 P18
Marton	59	2 P46
Milcote	* 66	3 P15
Moira	* 64	2 K31
Monument Lane	58	2 P08
MOOR STREET	8	3 P08
Napton + Stockton	58	2 P46
NEW STREET		2 P08
NORTHFIELD		2 P07
Nuneaton Abbey Street	68	2 P39
NUNEATON Trent Valley	69	2 P39
Oldbury + LANGLEY GREEN	68	3 P08
OLTON		3 P18
Pebworth Halt	* 66	3 P14
Pelsall	* 65	2 K00
Penns for Walmley	* 65	2 P19
PERRY BARR		2 P09
Pleck	58	2 P09
POLESWORTH		2 K20
REDDITCH	7	2 P06
Rugeley Town	* 65	2 K01
RUGELEY Trent Valley	68	2 K01
Salford Priors	† 62	2 P05
Saltley	68	2 P08
SELLY OAK	78	2 P08
(SHACKERSTONE)	?	4 K30
(SHENTON)	?	4 K30
SHENSTONE		2 K10
Shilton	57	2 P48
SHIRLEY		3 P17
Shustoke	68	2 P29
SMALL HEATH + Sparkbrook	68	3 P18
SMETHWICK ROLFE STREET	63	2 P08
SMETHWICK Junction WEST	56	3 P08
SNOW HILL	72 87	3 P08
Soho	49	2 P08
Soho + Winson Green	3 D § 65	3 P08
SOLIHULL		3 P17
Southam + Long Itchington	58	2 P46
Southam Road + Harbury	* 64	3 P35
Spon Lane	* 64	2 P08
SPRING ROAD		3 P18
STECHFORD		2 P18
Stockingford	68	2 P39
Stoke Golding	9 56	4 P39
Stratford-on-Avon	52	2 P25
STRATFORD-UPON-AVON	51	3 P15
Stratford Racecourse Halt	10 68	3 P15
Streetly	* 65	2 P09
Studley + Astwood Bank	† 62	2 P06
SUTTON COLDFIELD		2 P19
Sutton Park	* 65	2 P19
Swadlincote	62	2 K21
Swannington	51	2 K41
TAME BRIDGE	90	2 P09
TAMWORTH High Level	71	2 K20
TAMWORTH Low Level	71	2 K20
The Hawthorns Halt	3 68	3 P08
THE LAKES Halt	68	3 P17
TILE HILL		2 P27
TYSELEY		3 P18
UNIVERSITY	78	2 P08
Vauxhall + DUDDESTON	74	2 P08
WALSALL		2 P09
WARWICK		3 P26
Warwick Milverton	C § 52	2 P36
WATER ORTON		2 P19
West Bromwich	72	3 P09
Weston-sub-Edge	60	3 P14
Whitacre	68	2 P29
WHITLOCK END Halt	68	3 P17
WIDNEY MANOR		3 P17
Willersey Halt	64	3 P14
WILMCOTE		3 P15
WILNECOTE		2 K20
Winson Green	57	2 P08
Winson Green	D § 65	3 P08
WITTON		2 P09
Wixford	50	2 P05
WOOD END		3 P17
Woodville	11 62	2 K31
WOOTTON WAWEN Platform	74	3 P16
WYLDE GREEN		2 P19
WYTHALL, Grimes Hill +	74	3 P07
YARDLEY WOOD		3 P18

15 Additional Station: Brindley Heath 59 2 K01

GOODS

No	Name/Location	Closed	Ry Ref
1	Overseal	59	2 K22
2	Brownhills	12 30	2 K00
3	Bell Green	65	2 P38
4	Cosford Green	65	2 P37
5	Henley-in-Arden	62	3 P16
6	Shipston-on-Stour	60	3 P24
7	BESCOT YARD	0	0 P09

ENGINE SHEDS 13

No	Name/Location	Closed	Ry Ref
E1	Coventry	58	2 P37
2	Nuneaton	66	2 P37
3	Warwick Milverton	58	2 P36
4	Overseal	64	2 K31
5	Coalville	65	2 K41
6	Redditch	64	2 P06
7	Stratford-on-Avon	57	2 P15
8	Leamington Spa	65	3 P36
9	Evesham	61	3 P04
10	Stratford-on-Avon	62	3 P15
11	Honeybourne	65	3 P14
12	TYSELEY	66	3 P18
13	SALTLEY	67	2 P18
14	Bournville	60	2 P08
15	Aston	65	2 P08
16	Monument Lane	62	2 P08
17	Walsall	14 58	2 P09
18	SOHO	0	0 P08

TUNNELS

No	Name/Location	Length	Ry Ref
1	Wood End	176	3 P17
2	Campden	887	3 P14

NOTES:

- Ref: All in SK or SP, initial S omitted.
- § Old name, $ New name } Change of name
- Identical letters give other name
- † Last train pre-nationalisation.
- * Closed
- 1 Re-opening of station closed 1946
- 2 Re-opening of station closed 1946
- 3 Station to be part of proposed Metro; see fuller details on 59
- 4 became Knowle in 68. Then became DORRIDGE in 72.
- 5 High + Low Level dropped although stations at both levels remained open.
- 6 Two different stations.
- 7 Rebuilt on adjoining site in 73.
- 8 With re-opening of SNOW HILL had through platforms added.
- 9 Regular services ended in 31.
- 10 Open only on Race days.
- 11 Last passenger train was in 47.
- 12 Date staff lost but remained in use into the 60's.
- 13 Closure is for steam. Sheds shown in CAPITALS are still open.
- 14 On closure to steam became a DMU depot but abandoned quite soon due to inconvenient location.

The line Gresley to Desford is proposed for re-opening.

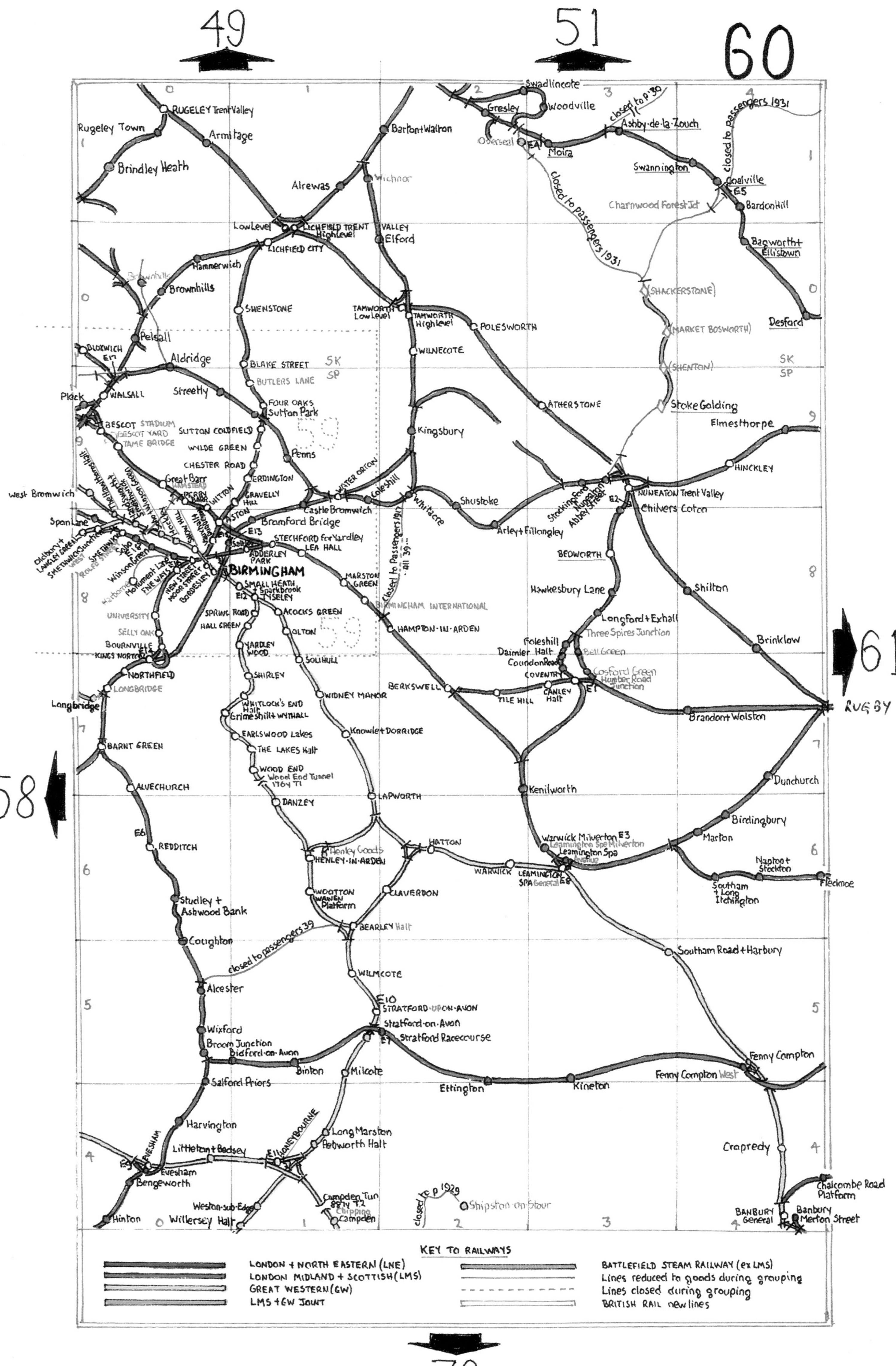

49
51
60
61
58
76
RUGELEY Trent Valley
Rugeley Town
Armitage
Brindley Heath
Barton+Walton
Wichnor
Alrewas
Swadlincote
Gresley
Woodville
Overseal
Moira
closed to p '30
Ashby-de-la-Zouch
closed to passengers 1931
Swannington
Coalville
Bardon Hill
Bagworth+ Ellistown
Charnwood Forest Jct
Low Level
LICHFIELD TRENT VALLEY High Level
Elford
LICHFIELD CITY
Hammerwich
Brownhills
SHENSTONE
TAMWORTH Low Level
TAMWORTH High Level
POLESWORTH
(SHACKERSTONE)
(MARKET BOSWORTH)
(SHENTON)
Stoke Golding
Desford
Pelsall
BLOXWICH
Aldridge
WALSALL
Streetly
BLAKE STREET
BUTLERS LANE
WILNECOTE
FOUR OAKS
Sutton Park
SUTTON COLDFIELD
WYLDE GREEN
CHESTER ROAD
ERDINGTON
GRAVELLY HILL
ATHERSTONE
Elmesthorpe
HINCKLEY
Kingsbury
Pleck
BESCOT STADIUM
BESCOT YARD
TAME BRIDGE
Penns
Great Barr
West Bromwich
Spon Lane
WATER ORTON
Coleshill
Whitacre
Shustoke
Arley+Fillongley
NUNEATON Trent Valley
Chilvers Coton
Castle Bromwich
Bromford Bridge
STECHFORD for Yardley
LEA HALL
ADDERLEY PARK
BIRMINGHAM
SMALL HEATH
Sparkbrook
TYSELEY
MARSTON GREEN
closed to passengers 1917
BIRMINGHAM INTERNATIONAL
HAMPTON-IN-ARDEN
BEDWORTH
Hawkesbury Lane
Shilton
Longford+Exhall
Three Spires Junction
Brinklow
SPRING ROAD
HALL GREEN
ACOCKS GREEN
OLTON
UNIVERSITY
SELLY OAK
BOURNVILLE
KINGS NORTON
NORTHFIELD
LONGBRIDGE
Longbridge
YARDLEY WOOD
SHIRLEY
SOLIHULL
Foleshill
Daimler Halt
Coundon Road
COVENTRY
Bell Green
Gosford Green
Humber Road Junction
BERKSWELL
TILE HILL
CANLEY Halt
WIDNEY MANOR
WHITLOCK'S END Halt
Grimes Hill+WYTHALL
EARLSWOOD Lakes
THE LAKES Halt
Knowle+Dorridge
RUGBY
Brandon+Wolston
BARNT GREEN
WOOD END
Wood End Tunnel
DANZEY
LAPWORTH
ALVECHURCH
Kenilworth
Dunchurch
Birdingbury
REDDITCH
HATTON
Henley Goods
HENLEY-IN-ARDEN
Warwick Milverton
Leamington Spa
WARWICK
LEAMINGTON SPA General
Marton
Napton+Stockton
Southam+Long Itchington
Flecknoe
Studley+Ashwood Bank
WOOTTON WAWEN Platform
CLAVERDON
BEARLEY Halt
closed to passengers 39
Coughton
Southam Road+Harbury
WILMCOTE
Alcester
STRATFORD-UPON-AVON
Stratford-on-Avon
Stratford Racecourse
Wixford
Broom Junction
Bidford-on-Avon
Binton
Milcote
Salford Priors
Ettington
Kineton
Fenny Compton
Fenny Compton West
Harvington
Long Marston
Pebworth Halt
EVESHAM
Littleton+Badsey
HONEYBOURNE
Evesham
Bengeworth
Cropredy
Campden Tun
Weston-sub-Edge
Chipping Campden
closed to p 1929
Shipston-on-Stour
Chalcombe Road Platform
Banbury General
Banbury Merton Street
Hinton
Willersey Halt
SK
SP
KEY TO RAILWAYS
LONDON + NORTH EASTERN (LNE)
LONDON MIDLAND + SCOTTISH (LMS)
GREAT WESTERN (GW)
LMS + GW JOINT
BATTLEFIELD STEAM RAILWAY (ex LMS)
Lines reduced to goods during grouping
Lines closed during grouping
BRITISH RAIL new lines

LEICESTER + NORTHAMPTON

RAILWAYS

No	Company
1	LONDON + NORTH EASTERN (LNE)
2	LONDON MIDLAND + SCOTTISH (LMS)
3	LNE + LMS JOINT
4	GREAT CENTRAL (ex LNE)

STATIONS

Station	Opened / Closed	Ry	Ref
Althorpe Park	60	2	P66
Asfordby	51	2	K71
Ashby Magna	* 69	1	P59
Ashley + Weston	52	2	P79
Ashwell	* 66	2	K81
Barrow-on-Soar + Quorn	4 * 68	2	K51
BEDE ISLAND	3	2	K50
Belgrave + Birstall	A § 1 † 63 91	4	K50
Billing	52	2	P86
Blaby	* 68	2	P59
Blakesley	52	2	P64
Blisworth	60	2	P75
Bradwell	* 64	2	P84
Braunston London Road	50 58	2	P56
Braunston + Willoughby	57	1	P56
Brixworth	60	2	P77
Brooksby	61	2	K61
Broughton Astley	62	2	P59
Burton Latimer for Isham	50	2	P87
Byfield	52	2	P55
Castle Ashby + Earl's Barton	* 64	2	P86
Castlethorpe	* 64	2	P74
Chalcombe Road Halt	56	1	P54
Charwelton	† 63	1	P55
Clifton Mill	62	2	P57
Clipstone + Oxendon	60	2	P78
Corby + Weldon	* 2 57 66	2	P88
Corby	87 90	2	P88
Countesthorpe	62	2	P59
Cranford	56	2	P97
Croft	* 68	2	P59
Culworth	58	1	P54
Daventry	58	2	P56
Desborough + Rothwell	* 68	2	P88
Ditchford	52	2	P96
East Langton	* 64	2	P79
East Norton	57	3	K70
Edmondthorpe + Wymondham	59	2	K81
Eydon Road Halt	56	1	P54
Farthinghoe	52	2	P54
Flecknoe	52	2	P56
Frisby	61	2	K61
Geddington	48	2	P88
Glendon + Rushton	60	2	P88
Great Dalby	53	3	K71
Great Glen	51	2	P69
Great Linford	* 64	2	P84
Gretton	* 66	2	P99
Hallaton	59	3	P79
Harringworth	48	2	P99
Helmdon Village	50 51	2	P54
Helmdon for Sulgrave	† 63	1	P54
Higham Ferrers	59	2	P96
Humberstone	† 62	1	K60
Humberstone Road	* 68	2	K60
Ingarsby	62	1	P70
Irchester	60	2	P96
Irthlingborough	* 64	2	P97
John o' Gaunt	57	3	K70
Kelmarsh	60	2	P78
KETTERING for (4) Corby	5 70 78	2	P87
Ketton + Collyweston	* 66	2	P90
Kibworth	* 68	2	P69
Kilsby + Crick	70	2	P57
Kirby Muxloe	4 * 64	2	K50
Lamport	60	2	P77
LEICESTER			
Belgrave Road	† 62	1	K60
Central	* 69	1	K50
Humberstone	† 62	1	K60
Humberstone Road	* 68	2	K60
LEICESTER London Road	69	2	K60
(NORTH)	A § 91 91	4	K50
LEICESTER FOREST EAST	3	2	K50
Leire Halt	62	2	P59
Lilbourne	* 66	2	P57
LONG BUCKBY		2	P66
Loughborough Central	* 69 74	4	K51
Lowesby	62	1	K70
Lubenham	* 66	2	P78
Luffenham	* 66	2	K90
Lutterworth	* 69	1	P58
Manton	* 66	2	K80
MARKET HARBOROUGH		2	P78
Melton Mowbray North	13 † 53	3	K71
MELTON MOWBRAY South Midland	B § 50 57	2	K71
MELTON MOWBRAY Town	* B § 57 65	2	K71
Marcott	* 66	2	K90
Morton Pinkey	52	2	P55
NARBOROUGH	* 68 70	2	P59
Newport Pagnell	* 64	2	P84
Northampton Bridge Street	* 64	2	P75
NORTHAMPTON Castle	66	2	P76
OAKHAM	*	2	K80
Olney	62	2	P85
PARK RISE	3		K50
Piddington	62	2	P85
Pitsford + Brampton	6 52	2	P76
Quorn + Woodhouse	† 63	4	K51
RANCLIFFE CRESCENT	3	2	K50
Rearsby	51	2	K61
Ringstead + Addington	* 64	2	P97
Roade	* 64	2	P75
Rockingham	* 66	2	P89
Rothley	† 63 67	4	K51
RUGBY Midland	52 70	2	P57
Rugby Central	* 69	1	P57
Rushden	59	2	P96
Saxby	61	2	K81
Seaton	* 66	2	P99
Sharnbrook	60	2	P96
Sileby	4 * 68	2	K61
South Witham	59	2	K91
SOUTH WIGSTON	86	2	P59
Spratton	49	2	P77
Syston	* 68 94	2	K61
Theddingworth	* 66	2	P68
Thrapston Bridge Street	* 64	2	P97
Thrapston Midland Road	59	2	P97
Thurnby + Scraptoft	† 62	1	K60
Tilton	53	3	K70
Towcester	52	2	P64
Turvey	62	2	P95
Twywell	51	2	P97
Ullesthorpe	62	2	P58
Uppingham	7 64	2	K80
Wakerley + Barrowden	* 66	2	P99
Wappenham	51	2	P64
Weedon	58	2	P65
Welford + Kilworth	* 66	2	P68
Wellingborough London Road	* 64	2	P86
WELLINGBOROUGH Midland Road		2	P96
Welton	58	2	P56
Whetstone	† 63	1	P59
Whissendine	53	2	K81
WIGSTON			
(Glen Parva)	* 68	2	P59
		2	P59
Wigston Magna	* 68	2	P69
Wigston South	62	2	P59
Woodford + Hinton	C § 48	1	P55
Woodford Halse	* C § 48 66	1	P55
WOLVERTON		2	P84
Yelvertoft + Stanford Park	* 66	2	P57

GOODS

No	Name/Location	Closed	Ry	Ref
G1	Derby Road Loughborough	55	2	K51
2	Holwell	58	2	K71
3	Leicester West Bridge	66	2	K50
4	Enderby	?	2	P59
5	Stoke Bruern	62	2	P75
6	Wolverton	70	2	P84

ENGINE SHEDS

No	Name/Location	Closed (10)	Ry	Ref
E1	Kettering	65	2	P87
2	Leicester Central	63	1	K50
3	LEICESTER	8 66	2	K60
4	Market Harborough	65	2	P78
5	Newport Pagnell	55	2	P84
6	Northampton	65	2	P76
7	Rugby	12 65	2	P57
8	Seaton	61	2	P99
9	Wellingborough	9 66	2	P96
10	Wigston	11 55	2	K50

TUNNELS

No	Name/Location	Length	Ry	Ref
T1	Knighton	104	2	K50
2	Glenfield	1796	2	K50
3	Ingersby		1	K60
4	Gill's Corner	95	2	P58
5	Catesby	2997	1	P55
6	Kilsby	2426	1	P56
7	Crick	595	2	P57
8	Watford Lodge	115	2	P66
9	Ashby Magna		1	P58
10	Asfordby	419	2	K71
11	Manton	749	2	K80
12	Glaston	1849	2	K90
13	Marcott		2	K90
14	Wing	353	2	K80
15	Corby	1926	2	P89
16	Oxenden		2	P78
17	Kelmarsh		2	P77
18	Stowe Hill	491	2	P65
19	Seaton	206	2	P99
20	East Norton		3	P79
21	Hunsbury Hill	1152	2	P75

JUNCTIONS

No	Name/Location	Ry	Ref
J1	Trent Valley	2	P57
2	Dunston North (Northampton)	2	P76
3	Dunston East (Northampton)	2	P75
4	Dunston South (Northampton)	2	P75
5	Ravenstone Wood	2	P85
6	Cransley Branch – Kettering	2	P87
7	Drayton	23	P87
8	Welham	23	P77
9	Marefield North	13	K70
10	Marefield South	13	K70
11	Knighton North (Leicester)	2	K50
12	Knighton South (Leicester)	2	K50
13	Saffron Lane	2	K50

NOTES:

REF All in SK or SP, therefore initial S omitted.

§ Old version(s) } Change of name

§ Newer version } Change of name

Identical letters indicate other version

1 Re-opened by 4 with name change as indicated.

2 The new Corby was on a different site.

3 Proposed new station.

4 Proposed to re-open.

5 Name changes as follows:

Start	Name	Finish
70	For CORBY	75
75	+ CORBY	77
77	For CORBY	78

6 Regular services ended 50.

7 Regular services ended 60.

8 Still open closure is for steam.

9 Continued in use for diesels for a period after the shed had closed for steam.

10 Closure dates are for steam.

11 Stabling only after nationalisation.

12 Works here, also closed 65.

13 Shown in Beeching but closed in 53!

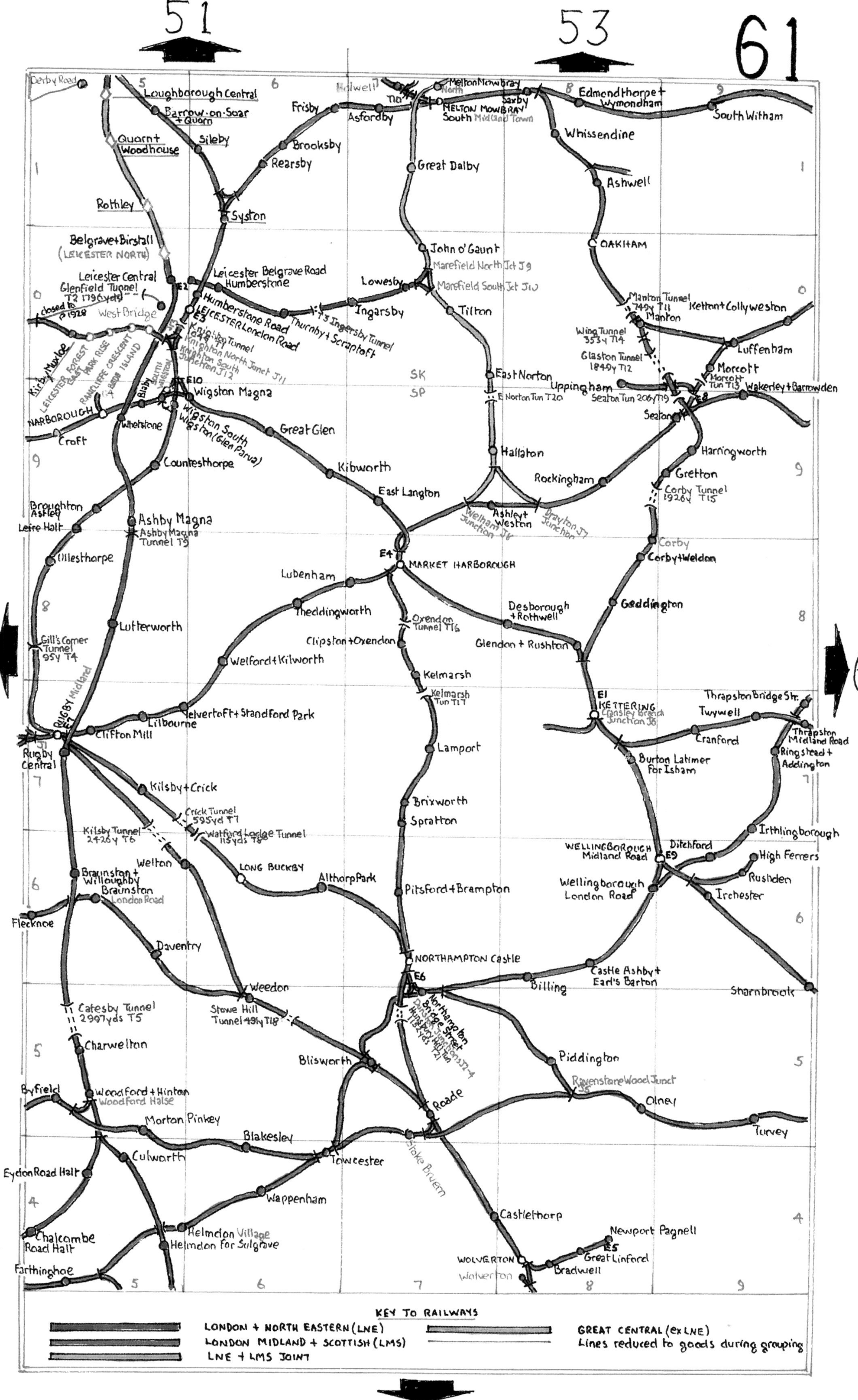

Derby Road
Loughborough Central
Barrow-on-Soar + Quorn
Quorn + Woodhouse
Sileby
Rothley
Syston
Frisby
Brooksby
Rearsby
Holwell
Asfordby
Melton Mowbray North
MELTON MOWBRAY South
Midland Town
Saxby
Edmondthorpe + Wymondham
South Witham
Whissendine
Ashwell
Great Dalby
Belgrave + Birstall
(LEICESTER NORTH)
Leicester Central
Glenfield Tunnel T2 1796 yds
closed to P 1928
West Bridge
E2
Leicester Belgrave Road
Humberstone
Humberstone Road
E3
LEICESTER London Road
Thurnby + Scraptoft
T3 Ingersby Tunnel
Ingarsby
Lowesby
John o' Gaunt
Marefield North Jct J9
Marefield South Jct J10
Tilton
OAKHAM
Manton Tunnel 749y T11
Manton
Ketton + Collyweston
Wing Tunnel 353y T14
Glaston Tunnel 1849y T12
Luffenham
Morcott
Morcott Tun T13
Wakerley + Barrowden
Uppingham
Seaton Tun 206y T19
Seaton
E8
Kirby Muxloe
LEICESTER FOREST EAST
PARK RISE
RANCLIFFE CRESCENT
BIRDS ISLAND
Knighton Tunnel 104y T1
Knighton North Junct J11
Knighton South Junction J12
E10
Wigston Magna
Blaby
NARBOROUGH
Whetstone
Wigston South
Wigston (Glen Parva)
Croft
Great Glen
SK
SP
East Norton
E Norton Tun T20
Hallaton
Countesthorpe
Kibworth
East Langton
Rockingham
Harringworth
Gretton
Corby Tunnel 1926y T15
Ashley + Weston
Welham Junction J8
Drayton Junction J7
Broughton Astley
Leire Halt
Ashby Magna
Ashby Magna Tunnel T3
Ullesthorpe
E4
MARKET HARBOROUGH
Lubenham
Corby
Corby + Weldon
Theddingworth
Oxendon Tunnel T16
Desborough + Rothwell
Geddington
Lutterworth
Clipston + Oxendon
Glendon + Rushton
Gill's Corner Tunnel 95y T4
Welford + Kilworth
Kelmarsh
Kelmarsh Tun T17
E1
KETTERING
Cransley Branch Junction J6
Thrapston Bridge St.
Twywell
RUGBY Midland
J1
Rugby Central
Clifton Mill
Lilbourne
Yelvertoft + Stanford Park
Cranford
Thrapston Midland Road
Ringstead + Addington
Burton Latimer For Isham
Lamport
Kilsby + Crick
Crick Tunnel 595yd T7
Watford Lodge Tunnel 115yds T8
Kilsby Tunnel 2426y T6
Welton
Brixworth
Spratton
Irthlingborough
WELLINGBOROUGH Midland Road
Ditchford
E9
High Ferrers
Rushden
Wellingborough London Road
Irchester
LONG BUCKBY
Althorp Park
Braunston + Willoughby
Braunston London Road
Pitsford + Brampton
Flecknoe
Daventry
NORTHAMPTON Castle
E6
Castle Ashby + Earl's Barton
Billing
Sharnbrook
Weedon
Stowe Hill Tunnel 491y T18
Catesby Tunnel 2997yds T5
Northampton Bridge Street
Hunsbury Hill Tun 1155yds T21
Charwelton
Blisworth
Piddington
Ravenstone Wood Junct J5
Byfield
Woodford + Hinton
Woodford Halse
Roade
Olney
Morton Pinkey
Blakesley
Turvey
Culworth
Towcester
Stoke Bruern
Eydon Road Halt
Wappenham
Castlethorp
Newport Pagnell
E5
Great Linford
Chalcombe Road Halt
Helmdon Village
Helmdon For Sulgrave
WOLVERTON
Wolverton
Bradwell
Farthinghoe
KEY TO RAILWAYS
LONDON + NORTH EASTERN (LNE)
LONDON MIDLAND + SCOTTISH (LMS)
LNE + LMS JOINT
GREAT CENTRAL (ex LNE)
Lines reduced to goods during grouping

51
53
60
62
77

PETERBOROUGH, BEDFORD + CAMBRIDGE

Railways

No	Company
1	LONDON + NORTH EASTERN (LNER)
2	LONDON MIDLAND + SCOTTISH (LMS)
3	MIDLAND + GREAT NORTHERN JOINT (LNER+LMS)
4	NENE VALLEY (ex LMS)

STATIONS

Station	Opened/Closed	Ry Ref
Abbots Ripton	58	1L27
Barnwell	* 64	2L08
Barnwell Junction	62	1L45
BEDFORD Midland Road	4 78 88	2L05
BEDFORD ST JOHNS Halt	84 89	2L04
BIGGLESWADE		1L14
Blunham	68	2L15
Bourne	59	1F01
Bracewell Spa Halt	51	1F01
Buckden	59	2L27
CAMBRIDGE		1L45
Cardington	2 62	2L04
Castle Bytham	59	2F01
Castor	3	2L19
Chatteris	* 67	1L38
Coldham	66	1F40
Cowbit	61	1F21
Deeping, St James	61	1F11
Elton	53	2L09
Emneth	68	1F40
Essendine	59	1F01
Eye Green	57	3F20
Fen Ditton Halt	62	1L46
(FERRY MEADOWS)	A § 77 77	4L19
Ferry	59	3F41
FOXTON		1L44
French Drove + Gedney Hill	61	1F30
Gamlingay	68	2L25
Godmanchester	59	1L27
Grafham	59	2L16
GREAT CHESTERFORD		1L44
Guyhirne	53	1F30
Haddenham	5 56	1L47
Harston	† 63	1L45
Helpston	* 66	2F10
Histon	* 70	1L46
Holme	59	1L18
Huntingdon East	1 65	12L27
HUNTINGDON North	64	1L27
KEMPSTON HARDWICK Halt	*	2L04
Kimbolton	59	2L07
Kings Cliffe	* 66	2L09
Little Bytham	59	1F01
Littleworth	61	1F21
Long Stanton	* 70	1L36
Lord's Bridge	68	2L35
MANEA		1L49
MARCH		1L49
MELDRETH + Melbourn	71	1L34
MILLBROOK		2L04
Murrow East	48 59	3F30
Murrow West	48 53	1F30
Nassington	57	2L09
Oakley	58	2L05
Oaklington	* 70	1L46
Offord + Buckden	59	1L26
Old North Road	68	2L35
(ORTON MERE)	77	4L19
Orton Waterville	A § 52 77	2L19
Oundle	6 * 64	2L08
Peakirk	61	1F10
Peterborough East	66	2L19
PETERBOROUGH North	66	1F10
(PETERBOROUGH TOWN)	86	4L19
Postland	61	1F21
Potton	68	2L24
Raunds	59	2L07
ROYSTON		1L34
Ryhall + Belmisthorpe	59	1F01
St Ives	* 70	1L37
St James Deeping	61	1F10
ST NEOTS		1L16
SANDY		12L14
Sharnbrook	60	2L06
SHELFORD		1L45
SHEPRETH		1L34
Somersham	* 67	1L37
Southill	62	2L14
Stamford East	57	1F00
STAMFORD Town	* 50 60	2F00
STEWARTBY	*	2L04
Stonea	66	1L49
Sutton	5 56	1L47
Swavesey	* 70	1L36
Tallington	59	1F00
Tempsford	56	1L15
Thorney	57	3F20
Thorpe	* 64	2L08
Thurlby	51	1F01
Twenty	59	3F11
Tydd	59	3F41
Uffington + Barnack	52	2F00
Walton	53	2F10
Wansford	57 77	4L09
WATERBEACH		1L46
WHITTLESEA		1L29
WHITTLESFORD		1L44
Wilburton	5 56	1L47
Willington	68	2L15
Wilsthorpe Crossing Halt	51	1F01
Wimblington	* 67	1L49
Wisbech East	48 68	1F40
Wisbech North	48 59	3F41
Wisbech St Mary	59	3F40
Wootton Broadmead	7 52	2L04
Wryde	57	3F30
Yaxley + Farcet	59	1L19

GOODS

No	Name/Location	Closed	Ry Ref
G1	Benwick	64	1L39
2	Bedford	70	2L05
3	Cambridge Mill Road Wharf	71	2L45
4	Cambridge Tenison Road	65	1L45
5	Cambridge Upper Yard Hills Road	66	1L45
6	Chatteris Dock	55	1L38
7	Fletton Peterborough	72	1L19
8	Ramsey East	66	1L28
9	Ramsey North	73	1L28
10	Sutton	64	1L47
11	Wisbech Harbour East	66	1F41
12	Long Stow	53	2L17
13	Guyhirne	64	1F30

ENGINE SHEDS

No	Name/Location	Closed steam	Ry Ref
E1	Bedford	63	2L05
2	Bourne	53	3F01
3	PETERBOROUGH New England	63	1F10
4	Peterborough Spital	60	2F10
5	Huntingdon	59	1L27
6	Stamford	59	1F00

TUNNELS

No	Name/Location	Length	Ry Ref
T	Yarwell	616	4L09

JUNCTIONS

No	Name/Location	Ry	Ref
J1	Westwood Peterborough	13	F10
2	Crescent Peterborough	12	L19
3	Yarwell	24	L09
4	Needingworth	1	L37
5	Chesterton Cambridge	1	L46
6	Hills Road Cambridge	1	L45

NOTES:

REF All in TF or TL. Initial T omitted

§ Old Name, § New Name } Change of name

Letter gives alternative name indication

1 Two stations in theory. But in practice just different platforms. Reg service only to 59.

2 Closure date is for regular services - continued in use for service personel.

3 On preserved line but this station not yet brought back into use

4 Midland Road to 78 then Midland until 88 then became simply BEDFORD

5 Regular service ended in 1931 but used for excursion traffic until date shown for closure

6 Excursion traffic for a year after closure.

7 Regular service to 64. Then for staff and wives until closure date shown.

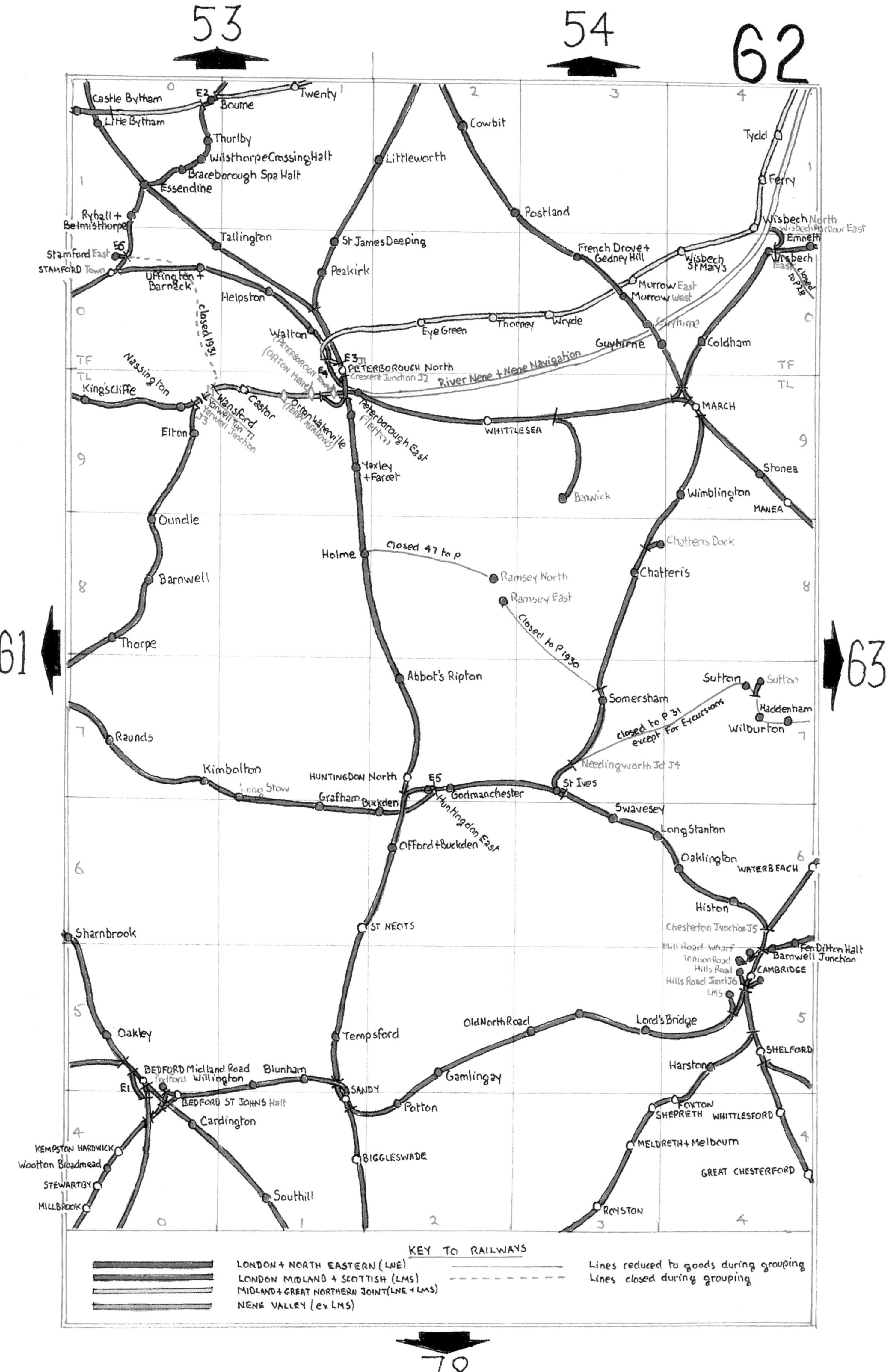

53
54
62
61
63
78
Castle Bytham
Little Bytham
Bourne
Twenty
Thurlby
Wilsthorpe Crossing Halt
Braceborough Spa Halt
Essendine
Ryhall + Belmisthorpe
Stamford East
STAMFORD Town
Uffington + Barnack
Tallington
Helpston
closed 1931
Walton
Littleworth
St James Deeping
Peakirk
Cowbit
Postland
French Drove + Gedney Hill
Tydd
Ferry
Wisbech North
Wisbech Harbour East
Emneth
Wisbech St Mary's
Wisbech East
closed to P 38
Murrow East
Murrow West
Eye Green
Thorney
Wryde
Guyhirne
Coldham
PETERBOROUGH North
Crescent Junction J2
River Nene + Nene Navigation
Nassington
King's Cliffe
Wansford
Castor
Orton Waterville
Peterborough East
Fletton
Elton
Yaxley + Farcet
WHITTLESEA
MARCH
Stonea
Benwick
Wimblington
MANEA
Chatteris Dock
Chatteris
Oundle
Holme
closed 47 to P
Ramsey North
Ramsey East
closed to P 1930
Barnwell
Thorpe
Abbot's Ripton
Somersham
Sutton
Haddenham
Wilburton
closed to P 31 except for Excursions
Needingworth Jct J4
Raunds
Kimbolton
Long Stow
Grafham
Buckden
HUNTINGDON North
Huntingdon East
Godmanchester
St Ives
Swavesey
Long Stanton
Oakington
WATERBEACH
Offord + Buckden
Histon
Chesterton Junction J5
Mill Road Wharf
Fen Ditton Halt
Barnwell Junction
CAMBRIDGE
Hills Road
Hills Road Junct J6
LMS
ST NEOTS
Sharnbrook
Oakley
Tempsford
Old North Road
Lord's Bridge
SHELFORD
Harston
BEDFORD Midland Road
Willington
Blunham
SANDY
Gamlingay
Potton
BEDFORD ST JOHNS Halt
Cardington
FOXTON
SHEPRETH
WHITTLESFORD
MELDRETH + Melbourn
KEMPSTON HARDWICK
Wootton Broadmead
STEWARTBY
MILLBROOK
Southill
BIGGLESWADE
GREAT CHESTERFORD
ROYSTON
KEY TO RAILWAYS
LONDON + NORTH EASTERN (LNE)
LONDON MIDLAND + SCOTTISH (LMS)
MIDLAND + GREAT NORTHERN JOINT (LNE + LMS)
NENE VALLEY (ex LMS)
Lines reduced to goods during grouping
Lines closed during grouping

DEREHAM, ELY + NEWMARKET

Railways

No	Company
1	LONDON + NORTH EASTERN (LNE)
3	MIDLAND + GREAT NORTHERN JOINT (LNE + LMS)

Stations

Name	Opened/Closed	Ry	Ref
Ashdon Halt	* 64	1	L54
Barnham	53	1	L87
Bartlow	* 67	1	L54
Birdbrook	62	1	L74
Black Bank	† 63	1	L58
Bottisham + Lode	62	1	L56
BRANDON		1	L78
Burwell	62	1	L56
BURY ST EDMUNDS		1	L86
Cavendish	* 67	1	L84
Chettisham	60	1	L58
Clare	* 67	1	L74
Clenchwarton	59	3	F51
Cockfield	61	1	L85
Dereham	69	1	F91
DOWNHAM MARKET	81	1	F60
DULLINGHAM		1	L65
Dunham	68	1	F81
East Winch	68	1	F61
ECCLES ROAD		1	M08
ELMSWELL		1	L96
ELY		1	L57
Exning Road Halt	62	1	L66
Fordham	65	1	L66
Fransham	68	1	F81
Fulbourne	67	1	L55
Gayton Road	59	3	F61
Glemsford	* 67	1	L84
GREAT CHESTERFORD		1	L54
Hadleigh	5 52	1	M04
Hardingham	69	1	G00
HARLING ROAD		1	L98
Haughley	67	2	M06
Haverhill North	* 67 52	1	L64
Higham	67	1	L76
Hilgay	63	1	L59
Holme Hale	* 64	1	F80
Ingham	53	1	L87
Isleham	62	1	L67
KENNETT		1	L66
LAKENHEATH		1	L78
Lavenham	61	1	L95
Linton	* 67	1	L54
LITTLEPORT		1	L58
Long Melford	* 67	1	L84
MAGDALEN ROAD	A § 68 75 89	1	F61
Middle Drove	68	1	F50
Middleton Towers	68	1	F61
Mildenhall	62	1	L67
Narborough + Petney	* 68	1	F71
NEWMARKET		1	L66
North Elmham	* 64	1	F91
Pampisford	* 67	1	L54
Quy	62	1	L56
Roundham Junction	2 64	1	L98
Saxham + Risby	67	1	L76
Seven Hills Halt	53	1	L87
SHIPPEA HILL		1	L68
Six Mile Bottom	67	1	L55
Smeeth Road	68	1	F50
Soham	65	1	L57
South Lynn	59	3	F61
Stoke	* 67	1	L74
Stow Bardolph	63	1	F60
Stow Bedon	* 64	1	L99
STOWMARKET		1	M06
Stretham	1 56	1	L57
Sturmer	* 67	1	L64
SUDBURY	*	1	L84
Swaffham	68	1	F80
Swaffhamprior	62	1	L56
Terrington	59	3	F51
THETFORD		1	L88
Thetford Bridge	53	1	L88
THURSTON		1	L96
Thuxton	69	1	G00
Walpole	59	3	F51
WATERBEACH		1	L56
Watton	* 64	1	F90
WATLINGTON	A § 89	1	F61
Welnetham	61	1	L85
Wendling	68	1	F91
Warlington Golf Links Halt	62	1	L67
Wretham + Hockham	* 64	1	L99
Yaxham	69	1	F90

Goods

No	Name/Location	Closed	Ry	Ref
G 1	Hardwick Road South Lynn	65	3	F61
2	Haverhill South	65	1	L64
3	Stoke Ferry	65	1	L69
4	Sudbury	66	1	L84
5	Upwell	66	1	F50

Engine Sheds

No	Name/Location	Closed Steam	Ry	Ref
E 1	Bury St Edmunds	59	1	L86
3	Dereham	4 55	1	F91
4	Ely	3 62	1	L57
5	Sudbury	59	1	L84
6	Swaffham	59	1	F80

Tunnels

No	Name	Length	Ry	Ref
T 1	Warren Hill	1100	1	L66

Junctions

No	Name/Location	Ry	Ref
J 1	Warren Hill Newmarket	1	L66
2	Chippenham Newmarket	1	L66
3	Snailwell Newmarket	1	L66

Notes:

REF In TF, TG, TL or TM. Initial T omitted.

§ MAGDALEN ROAD became § WATLINGTON

1 Regular services ended in '31.

2 Excursion traffic only after '31.

3 Stabling only

4 Diesels to '68

5 Station was closed to passengers in '32. The date shown covers excursions? But line as shown is goods only.

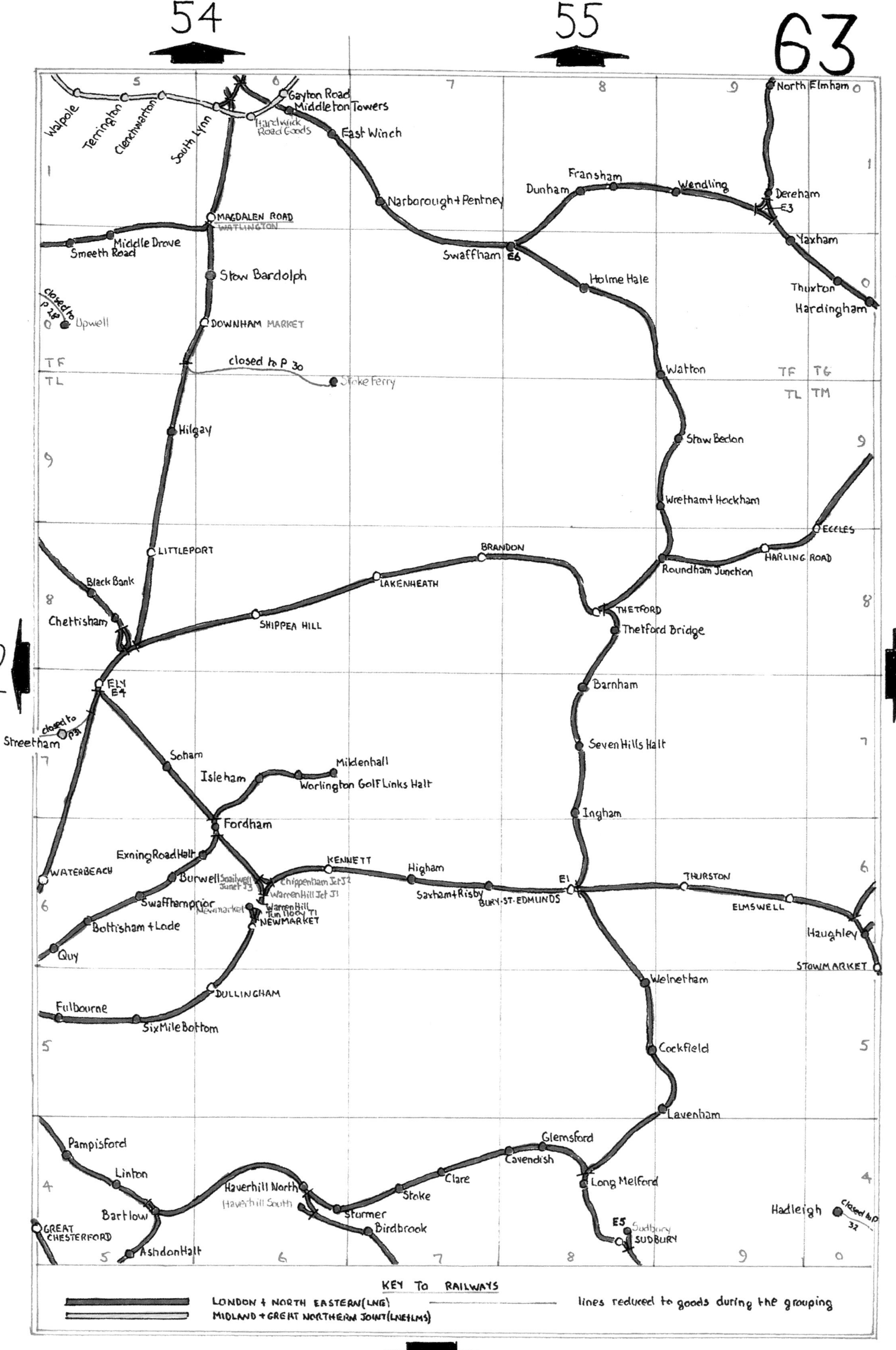
54
55
64
85
Walpole
Terrington
Clenchwarton
South Lynn
Gayton Road
Middleton Towers
Hardwick Road Goods
East Winch
Narborough + Pentney
Swaffham E6
Dunham
Fransham
Wendling
Dereham
E3
North Elmham
Yaxham
Thuxton
Hardingham
Holme Hale
MAGDALEN ROAD
WATLINGTON
Middle Drove
Smeeth Road
Stow Bardolph
closed to P 28
Upwell
DOWNHAM MARKET
closed to P 30
Stoke Ferry
Watton
TF
TL
TG
TM
Hilgay
Stow Bedon
Wretham + Hockham
ECCLES
HARLING ROAD
Roundham Junction
LITTLEPORT
BRANDON
LAKENHEATH
Black Bank
Chettisham
SHIPPEA HILL
THETFORD
Thetford Bridge
ELY E4
Barnham
closed to P 31
Streetham
Soham
Seven Hills Halt
Isleham
Mildenhall
Worlington Golf Links Halt
Fordham
Ingham
Exning Road Halt
WATERBEACH
Burwell
Snailwell Junct J3
Chippenham Jct J2
Warren Hill Jct J1
Warren Hill Tun Noey T1
KENNETT
Higham
Saxham + Risby
BURY ST EDMUNDS
E1
THURSTON
ELMSWELL
Haughley
STOWMARKET
Swaffham prior
Newmarket
NEWMARKET
Bottisham + Lode
Quy
DULLINGHAM
Welnetham
Fulbourne
Six Mile Bottom
Cockfield
Lavenham
Pampisford
Glemsford
Cavendish
Linton
Haverhill North
Haverhill South
Clare
Stoke
Sturmer
Birdbrook
Long Melford
Bartlow
GREAT CHESTERFORD
Ashdon Halt
E5
Sudbury
SUDBURY
Hadleigh
closed to P 32
KEY TO RAILWAYS
LONDON + NORTH EASTERN (LNE)
MIDLAND + GREAT NORTHERN JOINT (LNE + LMS)
lines reduced to goods during the grouping

NORWICH, LOWESTOFT + IPSWICH

RAILWAYS

No	Company
1	LONDON + NORTH EASTERN (LNE)
3	MIDLAND + GREAT NORTHERN JOINT (LNE + LMS)
12	Other LNE + LMS JOINT lines
4	BURE VALLEY (Site of ex LNE) 1'8" gauge

STATIONS

Station	Opened Closed	Ry	Ref
ACLE		1	G31
Aldeburgh	* 66	1	M46
Aldeby	59	1	M49
Aspall + Thorndon	52	1	M16
ATTLEBOROUGH		1	M09
Attlebridge	59	1	G11
Bealings	56	1	M24
BECCLES	*	1	M49
Belton + Burgh	59	1	G40
BERNEY ARMS		1	G40
Bramford	55	1	M14
BRAMPTON	*	1	M48
Brockford + Wetheringsett	52	1	M16
BRUNDALL		1	G30
BRUNDALL GARDENS Halt	68	1	G30
BUCKENHAM		1	G30
Bungay	53	1	M39
Burston	66	1	M18
Caister Camp Halt	1 59	3	G51
Caister-on-Sea	59	3	G51
California Halt	1 59	3	G51
CANTLEY		1	G30
Claydon	† 63	1	M15
Coltishall	52 ?	4	G21
Corton	* 70	12	M59
DARSHAM	*	1	M37
DERBY ROAD		1	M14
DISS		1	M17
Ditchingham	53	1	M39
Drayton for Costessy	59	1	G11
Earsham	53	1	M38
Ellingham	53	1	M39
Finningham	66	1	M06
Flordon	66	1	M19
Forncett	66	1	M19
Framlingham	2 66	1	M26
Geldeston	53	1	M39
Gorleston Links Halt	* 70	12	G50
Gorleston-on-Sea	* 70	1	G50
Great Ormesby	59	3	G41
GREAT YARMOUTH	2 89	1	G50
Hacheston Halt	52	1	M35
Haddiscoe High Level	59	1	M49
HADDISCOE Low Level	60	1	M49
HALESWORTH	*	1	M37
Harleston	53	1	M28
Hellesdon	52	1	G11
Hemsby	59	3	G41
Hethersett	66	1	G10
Homersfield	53	1	M28
Hopton-on-Sea	* 70	12	M59
Horham	52	1	M27
HOVETON + WROXHAM	66	1	G21
(HOVETON)	?	4	G21
IPSWICH		1	M14
Kenton	52	1	M16
Kimberley Park	69	1	G00
Laxfield	52	1	M27
Leiston	* 66	1	M46
Lenwade	59	1	G01
LINGWOOD		1	G30
LOWESTOFT Central	73	1	M59
Lowestoft North	* 70	12	M59
Marlesford	52	1	M35
Martham for Rollesby		3	G41
Mellis	66	1	M07
MELTON	55 84	1	M25
Mendlesham	52	1	M06
NEEDHAM MARKET	71	1	M05
Newtown Halt	59	3	G51
NORWICH			G20
City	59	1	G20
NORWICH Thorpe	69	1	G20
Orwell	59	1	M24
OULTON BROAD NORTH		1	M59
OULTON BROAD SOUTH	*	1	M59
Parham	52	1	M36
Potter Heigham	59	3	G41
Potter Heigham Bridge Halt	1 59	3	G41
Pulham Market	53	1	M18
Pulham St Mary	53	1	M28
REEDHAM		1	G40
St Olaves	59	1	G40
SALHOUSE		1	G21
SAXMUNDHAM	*	1	M36
Scratby Halt	1 59	3	G41
SOMERLEYTON		1	M49
SPOONER ROW		1	M69
Stradbroke	52	1	M27
Swainsthorpe	54	1	G20
Thorpeness Halt	* 65	1	M46
Tivetshall	66	1	M18
WESTERFIELD		1	M14
Whitlingham	55	1	G20
WICKHAM MARKET	*	1	M35
Wilby	52	1	M27
WOODBRIDGE	*	1	M24
Worlingworth	52	1	M26
WROXHAM, HOVETON	66	1	G21
WYMONDHAM		1	G10
YARMOUTH			G50
Beach	59	3	G50
GREAT YARMOUTH	2 89	1	G50
South Town	* 70	112	G50

GOODS

No	Location	Closed	Ry	Ref
G 1	Eye	64	1	M17
2	IPSWICH LOWER YARD		1	M14
3	Lowestoft Kirtley	66	1	M59
4	Lowestoft South Side	67	1	M59
5	Snape	60	1	M35

ENGINE SHEDS

No	Name/Location	Closed Steam	Ry	Ref
E 1	Aldeburgh	55	1	M45
2	Framlingham	52	1	M26
3	IPSWICH	3 60	1	M14
4	Lowestoft	62	1	M59
5	NORWICH	3 62	1	G20
6	Yarmouth Beach	?	3	G50
7	Yarmouth South Town	59	1	G50
8	Yarmouth Vauxhall	59	1	G50

JUNCTIONS

No	Name	Ry	Ref
J 1	Fleet Haddiscoe	1	M49
2	Swing Bridge Norwich	1	G20
3	Caister Road Yarmouth	1	G50
4	Coke Ovens Lowestoft	1	M59

NOTES:

REF All in TG or TM therefore initial T omitted.
1 Seasonal Halts only, last train called in '58.
2 GREAT added in 89.
3 Still open at atlas terminal date.

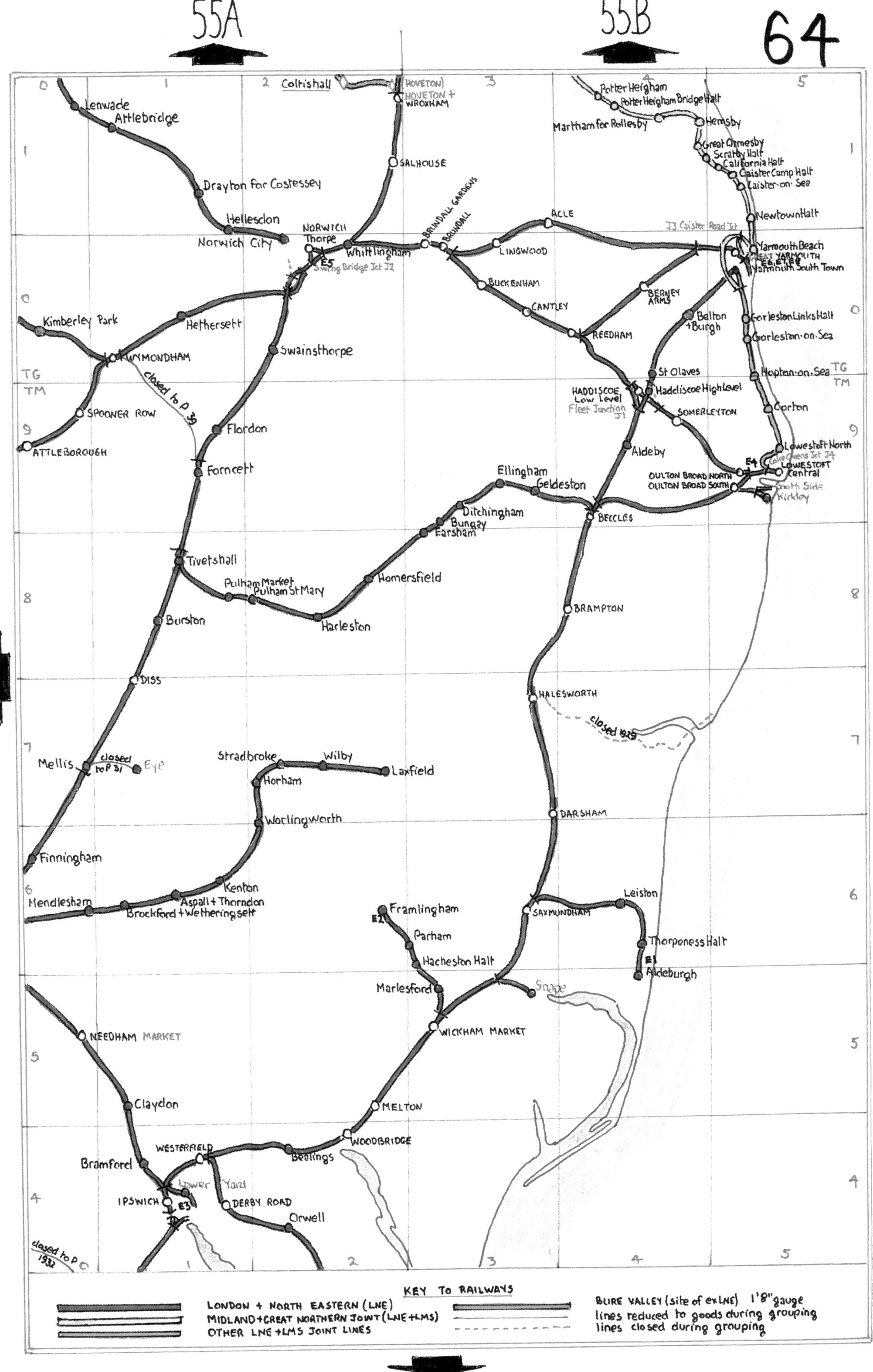
55A
55B
63
86
Coltishall
HOVETON
HOVETON + WROXHAM
SALHOUSE
Lenwade
Attlebridge
Drayton for Costessey
Hellesdon
Norwich City
NORWICH Thorpe
Whittlingham
Swing Bridge Jct J2
E5
BRUNDALL GARDENS
BRUNDALL
LINGWOOD
ACLE
BUCKENHAM
CANTLEY
REEDHAM
BERNEY ARMS
Potter Heigham
Potter Heigham Bridge Halt
Martham for Rollesby
Hemsby
Great Ormesby
Scratby Halt
California Halt
Caister Camp Halt
Caister-on-Sea
Newtown Halt
J3 Caister Road Jct
Yarmouth Beach
GREAT YARMOUTH
Yarmouth South Town
Gorleston Links Halt
Gorleston-on-Sea
Hopton-on-Sea
Corton
Lowestoft North
Coke Ovens Jct J4
LOWESTOFT Central
South Side
Kirkley
E4
OULTON BROAD NORTH
OULTON BROAD SOUTH
Belton + Burgh
St Olaves
HADDISCOE Low Level
Haddiscoe High Level
Fleet Junction J1
SOMERLEYTON
Aldeby
BECCLES
Ellingham
Geldeston
Ditchingham
Bungay
Earsham
Homersfield
Harleston
Pulham Market
Pulham St Mary
Tivetshall
Burston
DISS
Kimberley Park
Hethersett
WYMONDHAM
closed to P 39
SPOONER ROW
ATTLEBOROUGH
Swainsthorpe
Flordon
Forncett
BRAMPTON
HALESWORTH
closed 1929
Mellis
closed to P 31
Eye
Stradbroke
Wilby
Laxfield
Horham
Worlingworth
Finningham
Mendlesham
Brockford + Wetheringsett
Aspall + Thorndon
Kenton
DARSHAM
Leiston
SAXMUNDHAM
Thorpeness Halt
E1
Aldeburgh
Framlingham
E2
Parham
Hacheston Halt
Marlesford
Snape
WICKHAM MARKET
NEEDHAM MARKET
Claydon
MELTON
WOODBRIDGE
Bealings
WESTERFIELD
Bramford
Lower Yard
IPSWICH
E3
DERBY ROAD
Orwell
closed to P 1932
TG
TM
KEY TO RAILWAYS
LONDON + NORTH EASTERN (LNE)
MIDLAND + GREAT NORTHERN JOINT (LNE + LMS)
OTHER LNE + LMS JOINT LINES
BURE VALLEY (site of ex LNE) 1'8" gauge
lines reduced to goods during grouping
lines closed during grouping

65 FISHGUARD, CARMARTHEN + PEMBROKE

RAILWAYS

No.	Company
0	BRITISH RAIL new lines
2	LONDON MIDLAND + SCOTTISH (LMS)
3	GREAT WESTERN (GW)
4	GWILI (ex GW)
5	VALE OF TEIFI (on site of ex GW) 2'0" gauge

STATIONS

Station	Opened / Closed	Ry Ref
Abergwili	† 63	2N42
Beaver's Hill Halt	* 64	3N00
Boncath	† 62	3N24
Bronwydd Arms	* 65?	4N42
Cardigan	† 65	3N14
CARMARTHEN		3N42
CLARBESTON ROAD	*	3N02
CLUNDERWEN	§ A 80	3N12
CLYNDERWEN Halt	A § * 65 69 80	3N12
Conwil	1 * 65	4N32
Crymmych Arms	† 62	3N13
(CWMDWYFRAN)	?	4N42
FERRYSIDE	*	3N31
Fishguard + Goodwick	2 * 64	3M94
FISHGUARD HARBOUR		3M94
Glogue	† 62	3N23
HAVERFORDWEST		3M91
Henllan	52	5N34
JOHNSTON		3M91
Jordanston Halt	* 64	3M93
KIDWELLY	*	3N40
Kidwelly Flats Halt	57	3N40
KILGETTY	*	3N10
Kilgerran Halt	† 56 62	3N24
LAMPHEY	*	3N00
Llandyssul	52	3N44
Llanfalteg	† 62	3N12
Llanfyrnach	† 62	3N23
Llanglydwen	† 65	3N12
Llanpumpsaint	* 65	3N43
(LLWYFAN CERRIG)	?	4N32
Login	3 † 62	3N12
MANORBIER	*	3N00
Mathry Road	* 64	3M93
MILFORD HAVEN		3M90
NARBERTH		3N11
Newcastle Emlyn	52	3N34
Neyland	64	3M90
PEMBROKE		3M90
PEMBROKE DOCK		3M90
PENALLY	4 * 64 72	3N10
Pentrecourt Platform	52	3N34
Rhydowen	† 62	3N23
St Clears	* 64	3N21
Sarnau	* 64	3N32
SAUNDERSFOOT	*	3N10
Templeton	* 64	3N11
TENBY		3N10
Welsh Hook Halt	* 64	3M93
WHITLAND		3N21
Wolf's Castle Halt	* 64	3M92

GOODS

Name	Location	5 Ry	Ref
Esso Oil	Milford Haven	0	M90
Gulf Oil	Milford Haven	0	M90

ENGINE SHEDS

No	Name / Location	Closed steam	Ry Ref
E1	Cardigan	62	3N14
2	Carmarthen	64	3N42
3	Fishguard (Goodwick)	63	3M94
4	Milford Haven	62	3M90
5	Newcastle Emlyn	52	3N34
6	Neyland	63	3M90
7	Pembroke Dock	63	3M90
8	Whitland	66	3N21

TUNNELS

No	Name / Location	Length yards	Ry Ref
T1	Maenclochog	180	3N02
2	Spittal	243	3M92
3	Golden Hill	460	3M90
4	Narberth	273	3N11
5	Whitland	189	3N21
6	Pencader	988	3N43
7	Alltycefn	167	3N34

JUNCTIONS

No	Name / Location	Ry	Ref
J1	Letterston	3	M93
2	Trecwn	3	M93
3	Old Milford Branch	3	M91
4	Gulf Oil Branch	30	M91
5	Herbrandston	30	M91
6	Clarbeston	3	N02
7	Narberth Road	3	N12
8	Cardigan	3	N12
9	P+T Loop	3	N42
10	Carmarthen Bridge	3	N42
11	Myrtle Hill	3	N42

NOTES:

Ref All locations in SM or SN. Initial S omitted.

§ Old version } Change of name.
§ New version }

1 Due to re-open GWILI

2 Some irregular services continued to use the station until 67

3 Shown as halt in Beeching

4 Open seasonally 70 + 71 before re-opening on a permanent basis in 72.

5 These are new BR locations.

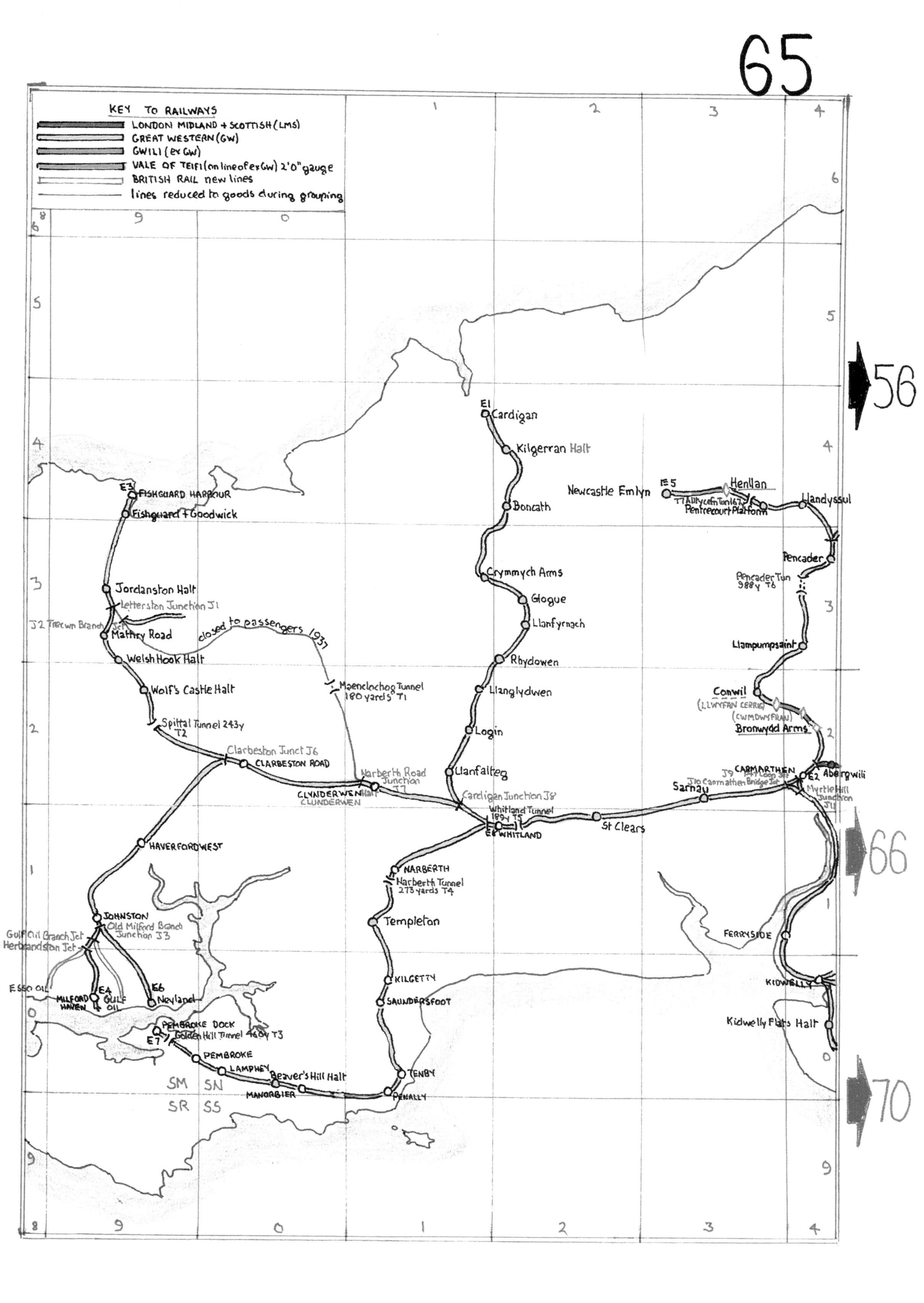
KEY TO RAILWAYS
LONDON MIDLAND + SCOTTISH (LMS)
GREAT WESTERN (GW)
GWILI (ex GW)
VALE OF TEIFI (on line of ex GW) 2'0" gauge
BRITISH RAIL new lines
lines reduced to goods during grouping
56
66
70
E1 Cardigan
Kilgerran Halt
Boncath
Crymmych Arms
Glogue
Llanfyrnach
Rhydowen
Llanglydwen
Login
Llanfalteg
Cardigan Junction J8
Newcastle Emlyn
E5
Henllan
Pentrecourt Platform
Llandyssul
Pencader
Pencader Tun 988y T6
Llampumpsaint
Conwil
Bronwydd Arms
CARMARTHEN
E2
Abergwili
Myrtle Hill Junction
Sarnau
St Clears
Whitland Tunnel
E8 WHITLAND
E3 FISHGUARD HARBOUR
Fishguard + Goodwick
Jordanston Halt
Letterston Junction J1
J2 Trecwn Branch Jct
Mathry Road
closed to passengers 1937
Welsh Hook Halt
Wolf's Castle Halt
Maenclochog Tunnel 180 yards T1
Spittal Tunnel 243y T2
Clarbeston Junct J6
CLARBESTON ROAD
Narberth Road Junction
CLYNDERWEN Halt
CLUNDERWEN
HAVERFORDWEST
NARBERTH
Narberth Tunnel 273 yards T4
Templeton
KILGETTY
SAUNDERSFOOT
TENBY
PENALLY
MANORBIER
Beaver's Hill Halt
LAMPHEY
PEMBROKE
PEMBROKE DOCK
Golden Hill Tunnel
E7
JOHNSTON
Old Milford Branch Junction J3
Gulf Oil Branch Jct
Herbrandston Jct
ESSO OIL
MILFORD HAVEN
E4
GULF OIL
E6
Neyland
FERRYSIDE
KIDWELLY
Kidwelly Flats Halt
SM
SN
SR
SS

LLANGADOCK + PANTYFFYNON

RAILWAYS

No	Company
2	LONDON MIDLAND + SCOTTISH (LMS)
23	LMS + GW JOINT
3	GREAT WESTERN (GW)

STATIONS

Station		Opened closed	Ry Ref
Abergwili	†	63	2 42
Ammanford		58	3 61
AMMANFORD + Tirydail Halt (65-69) A§	†	60 73	3 61
Ammanford Colliery Halt		58	3 61
Brynamman East		50 50	2 71
Brynamman West		50 58	3 71
Cwmllynfell		50	2 71
Cwmmawr		53	3 51
Derwydd Road		54	3 61
Drysllwyn	†	63	2 51
FFAIRFACH Halt	†	61 69	3 62
Garnant		58	3 61
Glanamman		58	3 61
Glanrhyd Halt		55	23 62
Golden Grove	†	63	2 52
Gwys		50	2 71
Llanarthney Halt	†	54 63	2 51
Llandebie LLANDYBIE	†	71	3 61
Llandilo Bridge	†		2 62
Llandilo LLANDEILO	†	71	3 62
Llangadock LLANGADOG Halt	†	65 69	23 62
Nantgaredig	†	63	2 42
PANTYFFYNON	†		3 61
Parcyrhun Halt		55	3 61
Pont Henry		53	3 40
Pontyberem		53	3 41
Tally Road		55	23 62
TIRYDAIL	A§	60	3 61
Ystalyfera		50	2 70

GOODS

No	Name/Location	Closed	Ry Ref
G 1	Cross Hands (East)	50	3 51
2	Cross Hands (West)	63	3 51
3	Cwm Blawd	59	3 40
4	Tumble	?	3 51

ENGINE SHEDS

No	Name/Location	Closed	Ry Ref
E 1	Pantyffynon	64	3 61

TUNNELS

No	Name	Length	Ry Ref
T 1	Abergwili		2 42
2	Pontamman	37	3 61

JUNCTIONS

No	Name/Location	Ry	Ref
J 1	Carmarthen Valley	23	62
2	Mountain Branch	3	61
3	Amman Valley	3	61
4	Raven	3	61
5	Cwmgorse Branch	3	61
6	Caelliau Colliery Branch	2	71
7	Gurnos	2	70

NOTES

REF All in therefore letters omitted.

§ Older version } Change of name
§ Newer version }

Other changes are Welsh alterations, often alteration is of a single letter. The later version is shown in red.

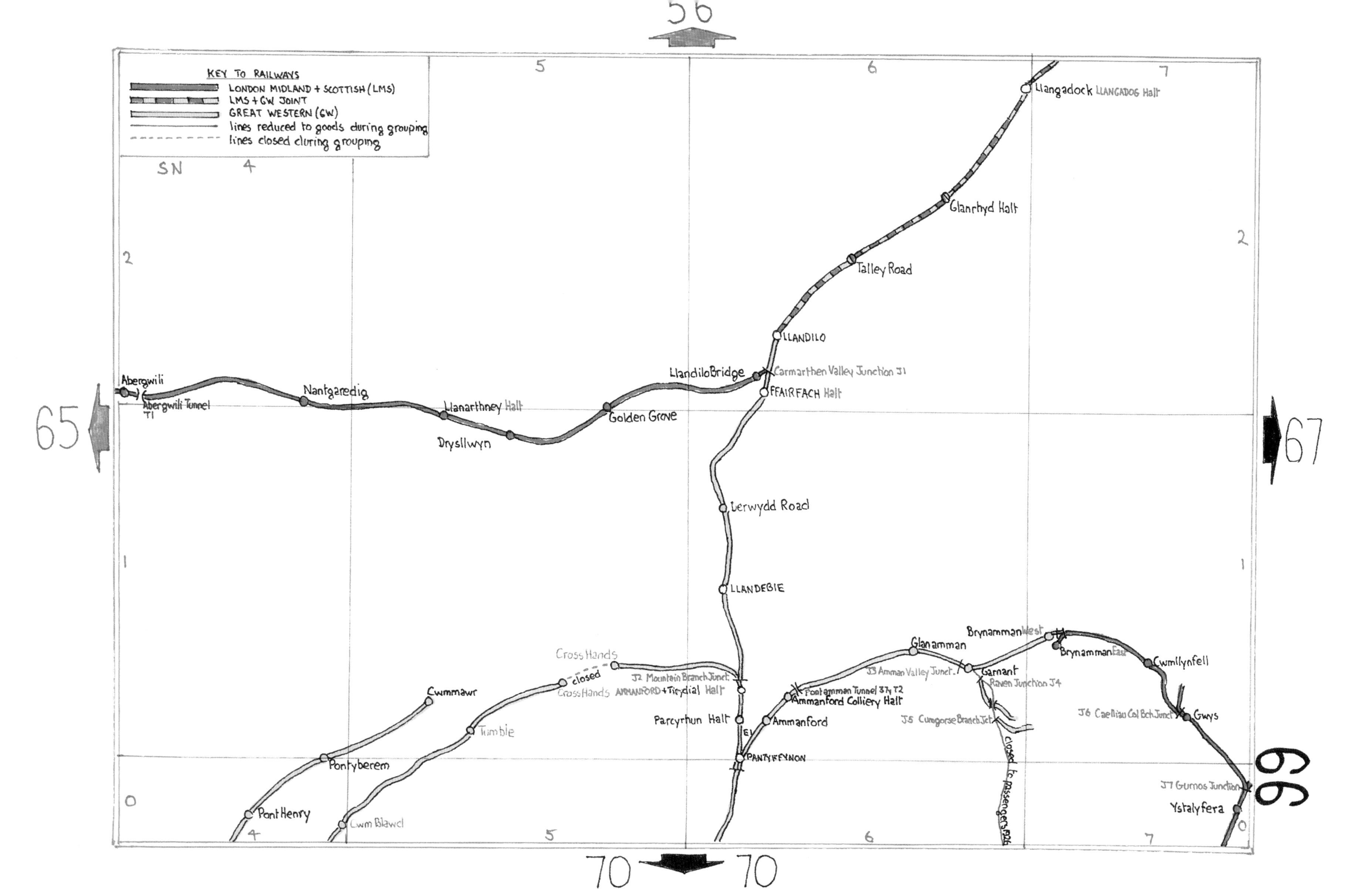
KEY TO RAILWAYS
LONDON MIDLAND + SCOTTISH (LMS)
LMS + GW JOINT
GREAT WESTERN (GW)
lines reduced to goods during grouping
lines closed during grouping
SN
56
65
67
70
70
Llangadock LLANGADOG Halt
Glanrhyd Halt
Talley Road
LLANDILO
Carmarthen Valley Junction J1
LlandiloBridge
FFAIRFACH Halt
Abergwili
Abergwili Tunnel T1
Nantgaredig
Llanarthney Halt
Dryslwyn
Golden Grove
Derwydd Road
LLANDEBIE
Cross Hands
closed
Cross Hands
J2 Mountain Branch Junct.
AMMANFORD + Tirydial Halt
Parcyrhun Halt
PANTYFFYNON
Cwmmawr
Pontyberem
Pont Henry
Tumble
Cwm Blawd
Ammanford
Pontamman Tunnel 3¾ T2
Ammanford Colliery Halt
J3 Amman Valley Junct.
Glanamman
Garnant
Raven Junction J4
J5 Cwmgorse Branch Jct.
closed to passengers 1926
Brynamman West
Brynamman East
Cwmllynfell
J6 Caelliau Col Bch Junct
Gwys
J7 Gurnos Junction
Ystalyfera

BRECON

RAILWAYS

No	Company
2	LONDON MIDLAND + SCOTTISH (LMS)
23	LMS + GW JOINT
3	GREAT WESTERN (GW)
4	BRECON MOUNTAIN (ex GW) now 1' 11¾" gauge

TUNNELS

No	Name	Length	Ry	Ref
T1	Morlais	1040	2	000
2	Torpantau	667	3	001

NOTES:

Ref All in SN or SO therefore initial S omitted

STATIONS

Station	Opened	Closed	Ry	Ref
Aberbran	†	62	3	N92
Abercamlais Halt	†	62	3	N92
Brecon	†	62	3	002
Colbren Junction	†	62	3	N81
Cradoc	†	62	3	082
Craig-y-Nos	†	62	3	N81
Cray	†	62	3	N82
Devynock + Sennybridge	†	62	3	N92
Dolygaer	†	62 80	4	001
Groesffordd Halt	†	62	3	002
Onllwyn	†	62	3	N80
Pant	†	62 80	4	000
Pantyffordd Halt	†	62	3	N80
Penpont Halt	†	62	3	N92
Pentir Rhiw Halt	†	62	3	001
Pont Sarn for Vaynor Halt	53 58	61	23	000
Pontsticill	†	62 80	4	001
Torpantau	†	62 80	4	001

GOODS

No	Name/Location	Closed	Ry	Ref
G1	Brecon Mount Street	62	3	002
2	Brecon Watton	64	3	002

ENGINE SHED

No	Name/Location	Closed	Ry	Ref
E	Brecon	62	3	002

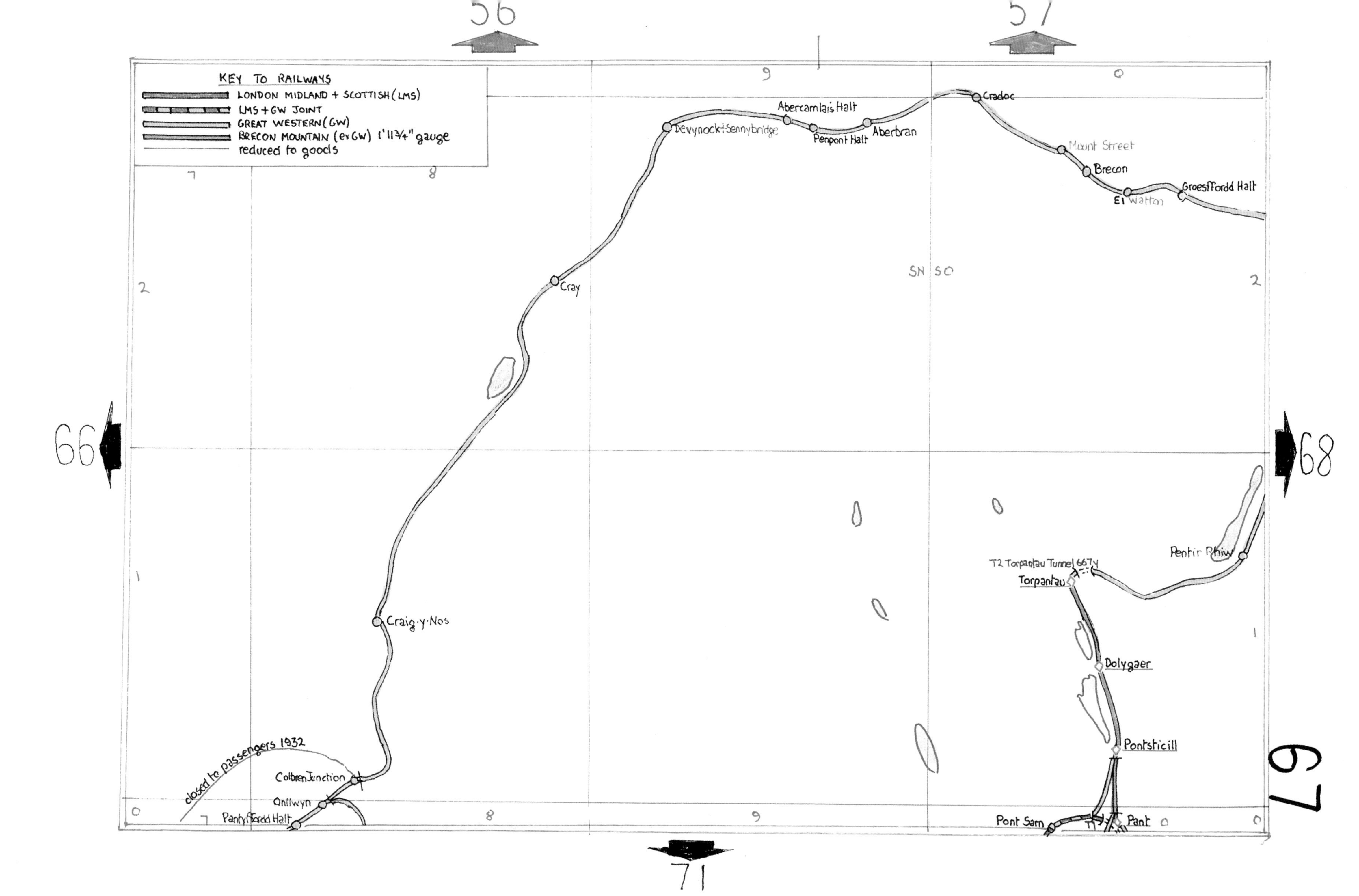
KEY TO RAILWAYS
LONDON MIDLAND + SCOTTISH (LMS)
LMS + GW JOINT
GREAT WESTERN (GW)
BRECON MOUNTAIN (ex GW) 1'11¾" gauge
reduced to goods
Devynock + Sennybridge
Abercamlais Halt
Penpont Halt
Aberbran
Cradoc
Mount Street
Brecon
El Watton
Groesffordd Halt
SN SO
Cray
Craig-y-Nos
Colbren Junction
Onllwyn
Pantyffordd Halt
closed to passengers 1932
Pentir Rhiw
T2 Torpantau Tunnel 667y
Torpantau
Dolygaer
Pontsticill
Pont Sarn
Pant

RHYMNEY, EBBW VALE + PONTYPRIDD

RAILWAYS

No	Company
2	LONDON MIDLAND + SCOTTISH (LMS)
23	LMS + GW JOINT
3	GREAT WESTERN (GW)

STATIONS

Station		Opened closed	Ry	Ref
Aberbargoed	†	62	3	010
Aberbeeg		62	3	020
Abergavenney Brecon Road		58	2	021
Abersychan Low Level		62	3	020
Abertillery		62	3	020
Argoed		60	2	T19
BARGOED			3	T19
Bargoed Colliery Halt	†	62	3	T19
Beaufort		58	2	011
Beaufort		61	3	011
Bedwellty Pits		60	2	010
Blackwood		60	2	T19
Blaenavon Low Level		50 62	3	020
Blaendare Road Halt, Pontypool		62	3	T29
Blaina		62	3	010
Bournville Halt		62	3	020
Brecon Road		58	2	021
BRITHDIR			3	010
Brynmawr		62	2	011
Celynen North Halt		62	3	T29
Clydach		58	2	021
Crumlin High Level	†	64	2	T29
Crumlin Low Level		62	3	T29
Crumlin Valleys Colliery Platform		61	3	T29
Cwm		62	3	010
Cwmavon Halt		53 62	3	020
Cwmffrwd		62	3	020
Cwmsyfiog	†	62	3	010
Cwmsyfiog Colliery Halt	†	62	3	010
Darran + Deri	†	62	3	010
Ebbw Vale High Level		49 51	2	010
Ebbw Vale Low Level		50 62	3	010
Elliot Pit Colliery Halt	†	62	3	010
Fleur-de-Lis	†	62	3	T19
Fochriw	†	62	3	010
Gelli Felen Halt		58	2	020
GILFACH FARGOED Halt		70	3	T19
Gilwern Halt		58	2	021
Govilon		58	2	021
Groesfaen Colliery Platform	†	62	3	010
Hafodyrynys Platform	†	64	3	T29
Holly Bush		60	2	010
Llangorse Lake Halt	†	62	3	012
Llanhilleth		62	3	020
Marine Colliery Platform		61	3	010
Markham Village Halt		60	2	010
Nantybwch		60	2	011
Nantyglo		62	3	010
Newbridge		62	3	T29
New Tredegar	†	62	3	010
Ogilvie Colliery Halt	†	62	3	010
Ogilvie Village Halt	†	62	3	010
Panteg + Griffithstown		62	3	T29
PENGAM (Glam)			3	T19
Pengam (Mon)	†	62	3	T19
Pentir Rhiw Halt	†	62	3	011
Ponchin Pits		60	2	010
PONTLOTTYN			3	010
Pontlottyn Colliery Halt		?	3	010
Pontnewynydd		62	3	020
Pontrhydyrun		62	3	T29
PONTYPOOL				
Blaendare Road Halt		62	3	T29
Clarence Street	†	64	3	020
Crane Street		62	3	020
PONTYPOOL	A §	72	3	T29
Road	A §	72	3	T29
RHYMNEY			3	010
Rhymney Bridge		58	2	010
Sebastapol		62	3	T29
Sirhowy		60	2	010
Six Bells Halt		62	3	020
Snatchwood Halt		53	3	020
Taff Merthyr Colliery Halt	†	64	3	T19
Talybont-on-Usk	†	62	3	012
Talyllyn Junction	†	62	3	021
TIR-PHIL TIR PHIL	1	80	3	010
Tredegar		60	2	010
Trefeinon	†	62	3	021
Trelewis Halt	†	64	3	T19
Trelewis Platform	†	64	3	T19
Treowen Halt		60	3	T29
Trevil		58	2	011
Tyllwyn Halt		62	3	010
Victoria		62	3	010

GOODS

No	Name/Location	Closed	Ry	Ref
G1	Blaendare	65	3	T29
2	Brynmawr	63	2	011

ENGINE SHEDS

No	Name/Location	Closed	Ry	Ref
E1	Aberbeeg	64	3	020
2	Abergavenny, Brecon Road	58	2	021
3	Branches Fork	52	3	020
4	Pontypool Road	65	3	T29
5	Rhymney	65	3	010
6	Tredegar	60	2	010

TUNNELS

No	Name	Length	Ry	Ref
T1	Clydach	330	2	021
2	Gelli Felen	352	2	021
3	Bryn	398	3	T29
4	Talyllyn	674	3	012

BRIDGES + VIADUCTS

No	Name/Location	Ry	Ref
V1	Crumlin Viaduct	3	T29
2	Cwmnantddu	3	020

JUNCTIONS

No	Name	Ry	Ref
J1	Cwmtillery Branch	3	020
2	Varteg Colliery Branch	2	020
3	Colynos	23	020
4	Garndiffaith	223	020
5	Talywain	323	020
6	Branches Fork	3	020
7	Trevithin	3	020
8	Crumlin	3	T29
9	Llanhilleth	3	T29
10	Panteg	3	T29
11	Western Valleys	223	011
12	Joint Line	223	011
13	Junction with Joint	323	010
14	Talyllyn North	3	012
15	Talyllyn East	3	012
16	Talyllyn West	3	012

NOTES:

REF All in SO or ST therefore initial S omitted.

§ Old Name } Change of name
§ New Name }

1 Hyphen dropped from name 80.

2 PONTYPOOL Road became PONTYPOOL in 72 became PONTYPOOL + NEW INN in 94.

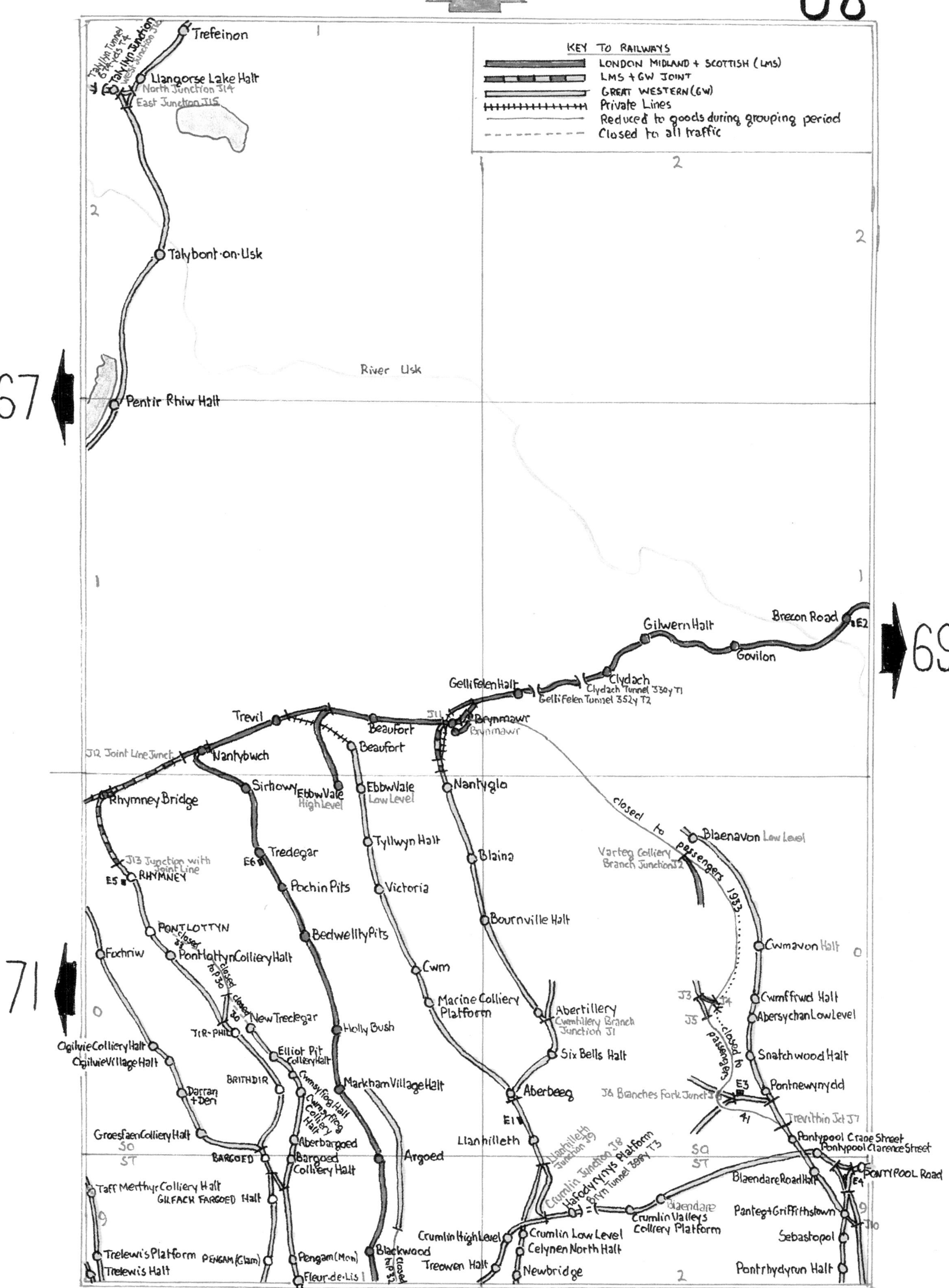
57
KEY TO RAILWAYS
LONDON MIDLAND + SCOTTISH (LMS)
LMS + GW JOINT
GREAT WESTERN (GW)
Private Lines
Reduced to goods during grouping period
Closed to all traffic
Trefeinon
Talyllyn Tunnel 674yds T4
Talyllyn Junction
West Junction J6
Llangorse Lake Halt
North Junction J14
East Junction J15
Talybont-on-Usk
River Usk
Pentir Rhiw Halt
67
69
71
Brecon Road
E2
Gilwern Halt
Govilon
Clydach
Clydach Tunnel 330y T1
Gellifelen Halt
Gellifelen Tunnel 352y T2
Trevil
Beaufort
Beaufort
J11
Brynmawr
Brynmawr
J12 Joint Line Junct
Nantybwch
Rhymney Bridge
Sirhowy
Ebbw Vale High Level
Ebbw Vale Low Level
Nantyglo
closed to passengers 1933
Blaenavon Low Level
Varteg Colliery Branch Junction J2
J13 Junction with Joint Line
E5
RHYMNEY
Tredegar
E6
Tyllwyn Halt
Blaina
Pochin Pits
Victoria
Bournville Halt
PONTLOTTYN
Fochriw
Pontlottyn Colliery Halt
Bedwellty Pits
Cwm
Cwmavon Halt
Marine Colliery Platform
Cwmffrwd Halt
Abersychan Low Level
Abertillery
Cwmtillery Branch Junction J1
J3
J4
J5
closed to passengers
New Tredegar
TIR-PHIL
Holly Bush
Ogilvie Colliery Halt
Ogilvie Village Halt
Elliot Pit Colliery Halt
Six Bells Halt
Snatchwood Halt
BRITHDIR
Darran + Deri
Cwmsyfiog Halt
Cwmsyfiog Colliery Halt
Markham Village Halt
Aberbeeg
J6 Branches Fork Junct
E3
Pontnewynydd
E1
Trevithin Jct J7
Groesfaen Colliery Halt
Aberbargoed
Llanhilleth
Llanhilleth Junction J9
Pontypool Crane Street
Pontypool Clarence Street
SO
ST
BARGOED
Bargoed Colliery Halt
Argoed
Crumlin Junction J8
Hafodyrynys Platform
Glyn Tunnel 398y T3
PONTYPOOL Road
E4
Blaendare Road Halt
Taff Merthyr Colliery Halt
GILFACH FARGOED Halt
Blaendare
Crumlin Valleys Colliery Platform
Panteg + Griffithstown
J10
Crumlin High Level
Crumlin Low Level
Sebastopol
Trelewis Platform
PENGAM (Glam)
Pengam (Mon)
Blackwood
Celynen North Halt
Treowen Halt
Trelewis Halt
Fleur-de-Lis
Newbridge
Pontrhydyrun Halt

73

PONTRILAS + ABERGAVENNY

RAILWAYS

No	Company
2	LONDON MIDLAND + SCOTTISH (LMS)
3	GREAT WESTERN (GW)

ENGINE SHEDS

No	Name/Location	Closed	Ry	Ref
E1	Pontrilas	53	3	032
2	Pontypool Road	65	3	T29

STATIONS

Station		Opened Closed	Ry	Ref
ABERGAVENNY Monmouth Road		50 68	3	031
Abergavenny Junction		58	3	031
Cefn Tilla Halt		54 55	3	040
Dingestow		55	3	041
East Access Halt	A §	49 54	3	030
Elms Bridge Halt		55	3	040
Glascoed	]	57	3	030
Glascoed Crossing Halt		55	3	030
Glascoed Factory East Access Halt	A §	49	3	030
Glascoed ROF		61	3	030
Little Mill Junction		55	3	030
Llandenny		65	3	040
Llanvihangel		58	3	031
Nantderry		58	3	030
Pandy		58	3	032
Penpergwm		58	3	030
Pontrilas		58	3	032
PONTYPOOL Road		72	3	T29
Raglan		55	3	040
Raglan Road Crossing Halt		55	3	040
St Devereux		58	3	042
Usk		55	3	030
Wern Hir		55	3	030

TUNNELS

No	Name/Location	Length	Ry	Ref
T1	Usk	256	3	030
2	Pontrilas	37	3	032

VIADUCTS + BRIDGES

No	Name/Location	Ry	Ref
V1	Penpergwm River Bridge	3	030
2	Usk Viaduct	3	030

JUNCTIONS

No	Name	Ry	Ref
J1	Golden Valley	3	032

NOTES:

REF In SO or ST therefore initial S omitted.

§ Old name } Change of name
§ New name

Change was in 49 and new name is shown on map.

] Regular service ended in 1955

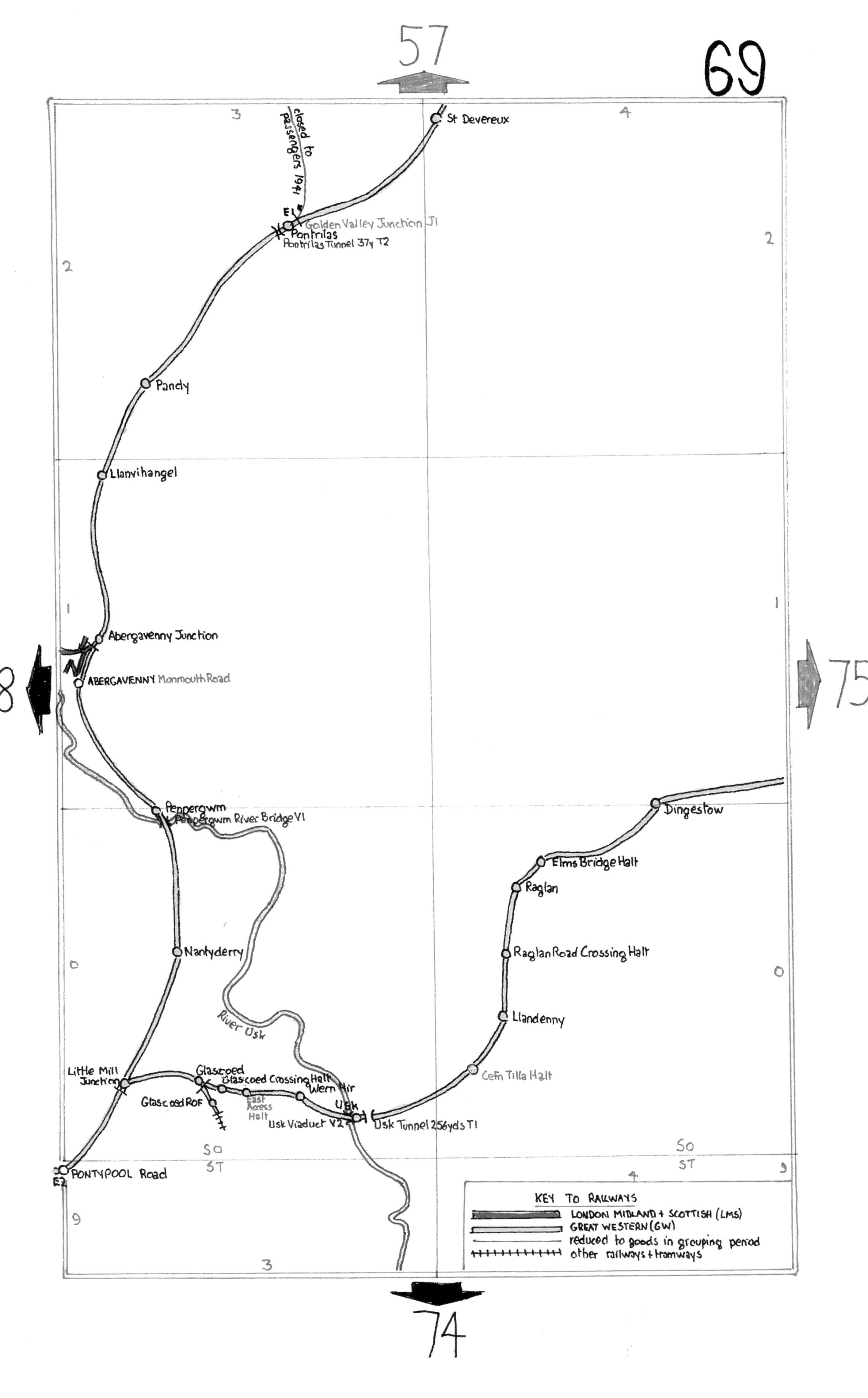
57
68
75
74
St Devereux
closed to passengers 1941
E1
Golden Valley Junction J1
Pontrilas
Pontrilas Tunnel 37y T2
Pandy
Llanvihangel
Abergavenny Junction
ABERGAVENNY Monmouth Road
Penpergwm
Penpergwm River Bridge V1
Nantyderry
River Usk
Little Mill Junction
Glascoed
Glascoed Crossing Halt
Glascoed ROF
East Access Halt
Wern Hir
Usk
Usk Viaduct V2
Usk Tunnel 256yds T1
Cefn Tilla Halt
Llandenny
Raglan Road Crossing Halt
Raglan
Elms Bridge Halt
Dingestow
PONTYPOOL Road
E2
SO
ST
KEY TO RAILWAYS
LONDON MIDLAND + SCOTTISH (LMS)
GREAT WESTERN (GW)
reduced to goods in grouping period
other railways + tramways

LLANELLY + SWANSEA

RAILWAYS

No	Company
2	LONDON MIDLAND + SCOTTISH (LMS)
23	LMS + GW JOINT
3	GREAT WESTERN
4	SWANSEA + MUMBLES

Note 1

STATIONS

Name	Opened Closed	Ry	Ref
Aberavon Seaside	† 62	3	SS78
Aberavon Town	† 62	3	SS70
Briton Ferry	✳ 64 94	3	SS79
Bryn Mill	60	4	SS69
Burry Port	53	3	SS49
BYNEA Halt	† 59 69	3	SS59
Cadoxton Terrace Halt	† 62	3	SS79
Clydach-on-Tawe South	50 50	2	SS69
Cockett	✳ 64	3	SS69
Copper Pit Halt	56	3	SS69
Craiglon Bridge Halt	53	3	SN40
Dunvant	† 64	2	SS59
Felin Fran Halt	56	3	SS69
Glais	50	2	SN60
Glyn Abbey Halt	53	3	SN40
Gorseinon	† 64	2	SS59
GOWERTON North	✳ 50 68	3	SS59
Gowerton South	† 50 64	2	SS59
Killay	† 64	2	SS59
Lando Platform	64	3	SN40
Landore	✳ 64	3	SS69
Landore Low Level	54	3	SS69
LLANELLY LLANELLI	60	3	SS59
LLANGENNECH Halt	† 59 69	3	SN50
Llansamlet North	✳ 4 50 64 94	3	SS69
Loughor	60	3	SS59
Morriston East	50 50	2	SS69
Morriston West	50 56	3	SS69
Mumbles	60	4	SS68
Mumbles Road	† 64	2	SS69
NEATH General	68	3	SS79
Neath Riverside	† 64	3	SS79
Oystermouth	60	4	SS68
PEMBREY + BURY PORT	✳	3	SS49
Pembrey Halt	53	3	SN40
Pentrefelin Halt	56	3	SS69
Pinged Halt	53	3	SN40
Plas Marl	56	3	SS69
Pontardawe	50	2	SN70
PONTARDULAIS Halt (65-69)	† 80	3	SN50
Pontyates	53	3	SN40
PORT TALBOT General PARKWAY	84	3	SS78
Rutland Street	60	4	SS69
St Gabriel's	60	4	SS69
St Helen's	60	4	SS69
St Thomas	50	2	SS69
Skewen	✳ 64 94	3	SS79
Southend	60	4	SS68
SWANSEA		5	S69
High Street	A § 68	3	SS69
Rutland Street	60	4	SS69
St Thomas	50	2	SS69
SWANSEA	A § 68	3	SS69
Victoria	† 64	2	SS69
Swansea Bay	† 64	2	SS69
Trimsaran Road	53	3	SN40
Upper Bank	50	2	SS69
Victoria	† 64	2	SS69
West Cross	60	2	SS68

GOODS

No	Location	(Note 5) Closed	Ry	Ref
G 1	Clydach-on-Tawe	65	3	SN60
2	Cockett	65	3	SS69
3	Cynheidre	65	3	SN40
4	Dafen	63	3	SS59
5	Felinfoel	63	3	SN50
6	Felin Fran	81	3	SS69
7	High Street Swansea (Hafod)	81	3	SS69
8	Horeb	59	3	SN40
9	Llangyfelach	65	3	SS69
10	Llanelly Albert Road	65	3	SS59
11	Llanelly Docks	65	3	SS59
12	Llanmorlais	57	2	SS59
13	Llansamlet South	4 64	2	SS69
14	Neath	81	3	SS79
15	Neath Canalside	65	3	SS79
16	Port Talbot Docks	81	3	SS78
17	Swansea Dock	64	2	SS69
18	Trimsaran	57	3	SN40
19	Pont Lliw	65	3	SN60

ENGINE SHEDS

No	Name/Location	Steam Closed	Ry	Ref
E 1	Burry Port	62	3	SS49
2	Dan-y-graig	64	3	SS69
3	Landore (Swansea)	2 61	3	SS69
4	Llanelly	65	3	SS59
5	Neath Cadoxton	64	3	SS79
6	Neath Court Sart	65	3	SS79
7	Swansea East Dock	3 64	3	SS69
8	Swansea Victoria	59	2	SS69
9	Upper Bank	63	2	SS69

TUNNELS

No	Name/Location	Length	Ry	Ref
T 1	Penllergaer	286	3	SS69
2	Llangyfellach	1952	3	SS69
3	Peniel Green	924	3	SS79
4	Cockett	788	3	SS69

BRIDGES + VIADUCT

No	Name/Location	Ry	Ref
V 1	Neath River Viaduct	3	SS79
2	Landore Viaduct	3	SS69

JUNCTIONS

No	Name	Ry	Ref
J 1	Kidwelly Branch	3	SN40
2	Kidwelly Loop West	3	SN40
3	Kidwelly Loop South	3	SN40
4	Trimsaran	3	SN40
5	Dock	3	SS49
6	Sandygate	3	SS49
7	St Davids Crossing	3	SS59
8	Morfa	3	SS59
9	Llandilo	3	SS59
10	Morlais South	3	SN50
11	Morlais	3	SN50
12	Hendy	3	SN50
13	Wind Street	3	SS69
14	Hafod	3	SS69
15	Swansea Valley	3	SS69
16	Six Pit	3	SS69
17	Lonla		

NOTES:

1 Swansea + Mumbles was not nationalised being regarded as a tramway. However it was distinguish by the RCH and carried some goods to date of closure
2 Still open
3 Still in use for stabling
4 The South station is North of the North station!
5 There is an open goods location: BURROWS in the region of E2

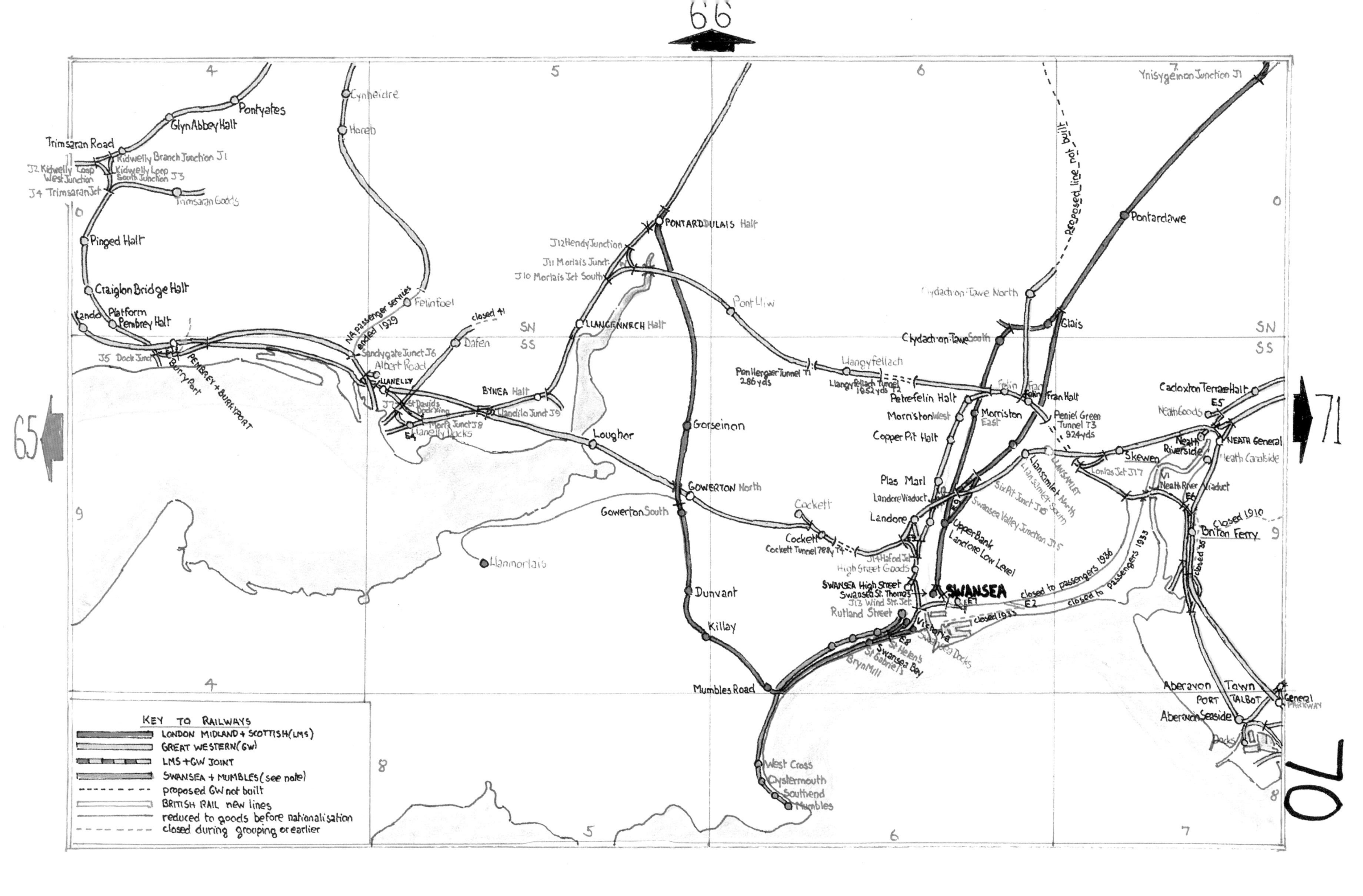
66
65
71
Pontyates
Glyn Abbey Halt
Trimsaran Road
Kidwelly Branch Junction J1
J2 Kidwelly Loop West Junction
Kidwelly Loop South Junction J3
J4 Trimsaran Jct
Trimsaran Goods
Pinged Halt
Craiglon Bridge Halt
Platform
Pembrey Halt
J5 Dock Junct
Burry Port
PEMBREY + BURRYPORT
Cynheidre
Horeb
Felinfoel
NA passenger services ended 1929
closed 41
Dafen
Sandygate Junct J6
Albert Road
LLANELLY
St Davids Dock Xing
Morfa Junct J8
Llanelly Docks
BYNEA Halt
Llandilo Junct J9
Loughor
PONTARDDULAIS Halt
J12 Hendy Junction
J11 Morlais Junct
J10 Morlais Jct South
LLANGENNECH Halt
Pont Lliw
Gorseinon
GOWERTON North
Gowerton South
Llanmorlais
Dunvant
Killay
Mumbles Road
West Cross
Oystermouth
Southend
Mumbles
Penllergaer Tunnel T1 286 yds
Llangyfelach
Llangyfelach Tunnel T2 1652 yds
Cockett
Cockett Tunnel 788 yds T4
J14 Hafod Jct
High Street Goods
SWANSEA High Street
Swansea St. Thomas
J13 Wind St. Jct.
Rutland Street
Victoria
Swansea Docks
St Helens
Swansea Bay
St Gabriel's
Brynmill
SWANSEA
closed 1933
closed to passengers 1936
closed to passengers 1933
Landore
Landore Viaduct
Plas Marl
Copper Pit Halt
Morriston West
Morriston East
Petrefelin Halt
Felin Fran
Felin Fran Halt
Peniel Green Tunnel T3 924 yds
Upper Bank
Landore Low Level
Swansea Valley Junction J15
Six Pit Junct J16
Llansamlet North
Llansamlet South
LLANSAMLET
Clydach-on-Tawe South
Clydach-on-Tawe North
Glais
Proposed line not built
Pontardawe
Ynisygeinon Junction J1
Cadoxton Terrace Halt
Neath Goods
NEATH General
Neath Riverside
Neath Canalside
Skewen
Lonlas Jct J17
Neath River Viaduct
Briton Ferry
closed 1910
closed 35
Aberavon Town
PORT TALBOT
General
PARKWAY
Aberavon Seaside
Docks
SN
SS
KEY TO RAILWAYS
LONDON MIDLAND + SCOTTISH (LMS)
GREAT WESTERN (GW)
LMS + GW JOINT
SWANSEA + MUMBLES (see note)
proposed GW not built
BRITISH RAIL new lines
reduced to goods before nationalisation
closed during grouping or earlier

71 ABERDARE, CYMMER, DOWLAIS, MERTHYR + PONTYPRIDD

RAILWAYS

No	Company
2	LONDON MIDLAND + SCOTTISH (LMS)
23	LMS + GW JOINT
3	GREAT WESTERN (GW)
X	DOWLAIS TRAMWAY

STATIONS

Station	Opened Closed	Ry	Ref
Aberaman	✱ 64	3	000
Aberavon Town	† 62	3	S78
Abercanaid	51	3	000
Abercwmboi Halt	1 56	3	T09
ABERCYNON NORTH	88	3	T09
ABERCYNON SOUTH	88	3	T09
Aberdare Gadlys Road Platform	48	3	N90
ABERDARE High Level	2 † 64 88	3	000
Aberdare Low Level	✱ 64	3	000
Aberdylais Halt	† 54 64	3	S79
Aberfan	51	3	000
Abergwynfi	60	3	S89
Abernant	† 62	3	000
Bedlinog	† 64	3	000
Bedlinog Colliers Platform	54	3	000
Blaengarw	53	3	S89
Blaengwynfi	✱ 70	3	S89
Blaenrhondda	3 ✱ 70	3	S99
Cae Harris	† 64	3	000
Caerau	✱ 70	3	S89
Cefn Coed	61	23	000
Cefn Coed Colliery Halt	† 62	3	N70
Cilfrew Halt	† 57 62	3	S79
Clydach Court Halt	52	3	T09
Clyne Halt	† 64	3	N70
Crynant	† 62	3	N70
Crynant New Colliery Halt	54	3	N70
Cwmavon	† 62	3	S79
CWMBACH Halt	† 64 88	3	000
Cwmbargoed	† 64	3	000
Cymmer Afan	✱ 70	3	S89
Cymmer Corrwg	64	3	S89
Cymmer General	50	3	S89
Cynonville Halt	56	3	S89
Dillwyn + Brynteg Halt	A § 54	3	N70
Dillwyn Platform	† A § 54 62	3	N70
DINAS Rhondda		3	T09
DOWLAIS			000
Cae Harris	† 64	3	000
Central	60	3	000
High Street	58	2	000
Pant	† 62 80	4	000
Pantysgallog Halt High Level	50 60	3	000
Pantysgallog Halt Low Level	50 58	2	000
Top	† 62	3	000
Duffryn Rhondda Halt	✱ 66	3	S89
Ferndale	✱ 64	3	S99
FERNHILL	1 88	3	T09
Fochriw	† 62	3	000
Gadlys Road Platform	48	3	N90
GARTH	4 92	3	S88
Gilfach Goch Colliers Platform	54	3	S99
Glyncorrwg	64	3	S89
Glyn Neath	† 64	3	N80
Heolgerrig	61	23	000
Hirwaun	† 64	3	N90
Hirwaun Pond Halt	† 64	3	N90
Llwydcoed	† 62	3	N90
Llwynypia LLWYNPIA	80	3	S99
Maerdy	✱ 64	3	S99
MAESTEG Castle Street	✱ 68 70 92	3	S89
MAESTEG EWENNY ROAD	92	3	S89
Matthewstown Halt	✱ 63	3	T09
Melyncourt Halt	† 64	3	N80
MERTHYR High Street TYDFIL	6 80	3	000
MERTHYR VALE		3	T09
Mountain Ash Cardiff Road	† 64	3	T09
MOUNTAIN ASH Oxford Street	✱ 80 88	3	T09
Nantewlaeth Colliery Halt	54	3	S89
Nantmelyn Platform	48	3	N90
Nantyffyllon	✱ 70	3	S89
Nantymoel	58	3	S99
North Rhondda Colliery Halt	64	3	S89
Ogmore Vale	58	3	S99
Old Ynysybwl Halt	52	3	T09
Pant	† 62 80	4	000
Pantyffordd	† 62	3	N80
Pantysgallog Halt High Level	50 60	3	000
Pantysgallog Halt Low Level	50 58	2	000
Pantywaun Halt	† 62	3	000
Penrhiwceiber High Level	† 64	3	T09
PENRHIWCEIBER Low Level	✱ 5 80 88	3	T09
Penscynor Halt	† 62	3	S79
PENTREBACH PENTRE BACH		3	000
Penydarren Platform	54	3	000
Penygraig	58	3	S99
Pontcynon Bridge Halt	✱ 53 64	3	T09
Pontrhydyfen	† 62	3	S79
Pont Sarn for Vaynor Halt	7 53 61	23	000
Pontwalby Halt	† 64	3	N80
Pontycymmer	53	3	S89
Pontygwaith Halt	51	3	T09
PONTYPRIDD		3	T08
PORTH		3	T09
Quakers Yard High Level	† 64	3	T09
QUAKERS YARD Low Level	68	3	T09
Resolven	† 64	3	N80
Rhigos Halt	† 64	3	N90
Robertstown Halt	52	3	T09
Seven Sisters	† 62	3	N80
South Pit Halt	64	3	S89
TON PENTRE	B § 86	3	S99
TONYPANDY + Trealaw		3	S99
Trecynon Halt	† 64	3	N90
Treforest Halt	56	3	T08
TREHAFOD		3	T09
Treharris	† 64	3	T09
TREHERBERT		3	S99
TREORCHY		3	S99
TROEDY RHIW TROED-Y-RHIW	80	3	000
Troedyrhiew GARTH	✱ 4 70 93	3	S88
Tylorstown	✱ 64	3	T09
Wyndham Halt	58	3	S99
Ynyshir	✱ 64	3	T09
YNYSWEN	86	3	S99
Ynysybwl	52	3	T09
Ynysybwl New Road Halt	52	3	T09
Ystalyfera	50	2	N70
Ystrad Rhondda	B § 86	3	S99
YSTRAD (RHONDDA)	86	3	S99

GOODS

No	Name/Location	Closed	Ry	Ref
G1	Caerau	56	3	S89
2	Clapham Wharf	?	2	N70
3	Duffryn Rhondda	65	3	S89
4	Maesteg Neath Road	64	3	S89
5	Maesycoed	56	3	T08
6	Middle Duffryn	?	3	T09
7	Plymouth Street, Merthyr	67	3	000
8	Wattstown	63	3	T09
9	Ystradgynlais	57	3	N70

ENGINE SHEDS

No	Name/Location	Closed	Ry	Ref
E1	Abercynon	64	3	T09
2	Aberdare	65	3	000
3	Cae Harris	64	3	000
4	Dowlais Central	60	3	000
5	Ferndale	64	3	S99
6	Glyn Neath	64	3	N80
7	Gurnos	62	2	N70
8	Merthyr	64	3	000
9	Treherbert	65	3	S99

TUNNELS

No	Name	Length	Ry	Ref
T1	Gyfylcha	1109	3	S79
2	Cwm Cerwyn	1010	3	S89
3	Cymmer	1595	3	S89
4	Rhondda	3443	3	S89
5	Pontypridd	1323	3	T08
6	Pencaedrain	526	3	N90
7	Merthyr	2497	3	000
8	Quakers Yard	703	3	T09
9	Merlais	1040	2	000
10	Gelli	167	3	S89

JUNCTIONS

No	Name	Ry	Ref
J1	Gelli Taw West	3	N90
2	Zig Zag Lines	3	000
3	Fochriw	3	000
4	Pont Shon Norton	3	T09
5	Tonmawr	3	S79
6	Tonygroes West	3	S78

NOTES:

REF In SN, SO, SS or ST. Initial S omitted.

1 Abercwmboi closed 56 replaced by FERNHILL in 88 on adjoining site.

2 Regular service ended 64 but excursion traffic continued on a fairly regular basis until 80.

3 Last train was in 68.

4 Troedyrhiew GARTH closed in 70. Reopened as GARTH in 93

5 Regular services finished in 64.

6 High Street dropped TYDFIL added in 80.

7 For Vaynor dropped Halt added in 53.

§ Older name } Change of name.
§ Later name } corresponding letter refers to other name.

Some spelling changes noted as part of same entry.

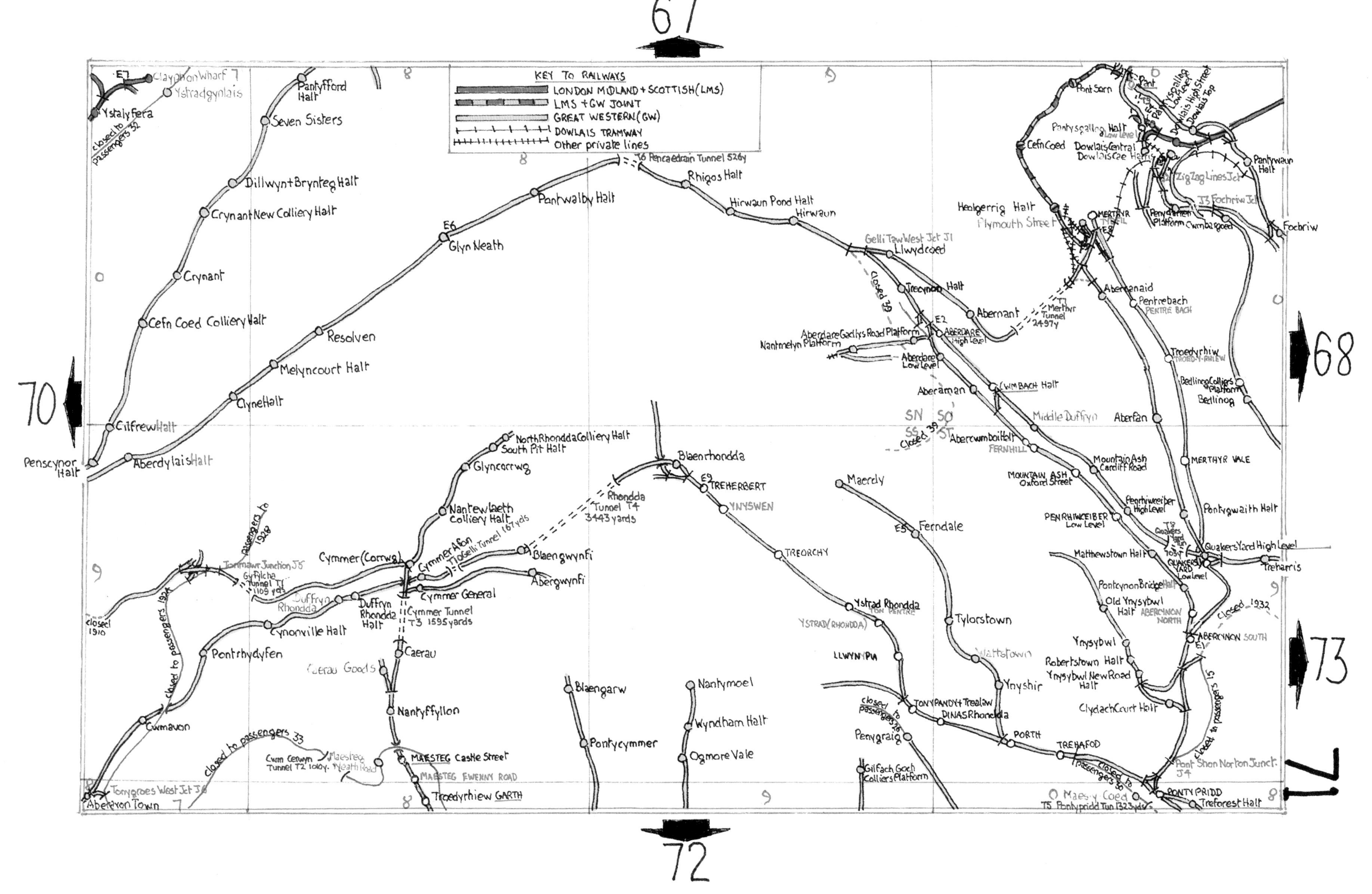

67
68
70
71
72
73
KEY TO RAILWAYS
LONDON MIDLAND + SCOTTISH (LMS)
LMS + GW JOINT
GREAT WESTERN (GW)
DOWLAIS TRAMWAY
Other private lines
Claypon Wharf
Ystradgynlais
Ystalyfera
closed to passengers 32
Pantyffordd Halt
Seven Sisters
Dillwyn+Brynteg Halt
Crynant New Colliery Halt
Crynant
Cefn Coed Colliery Halt
Cilfrew Halt
Penscynor Halt
Aberdylais Halt
Clyne Halt
Melyncourt Halt
Resolven
Glyn Neath
Pantwalby Halt
T6 Pencaedrain Tunnel 526y
Rhigos Halt
Hirwaun Pond Halt
Hirwaun
Gelli Taw West Jct J1
Llwydcoed
closed 39
Trecynon Halt
Abernant
T7 Merthyr Tunnel 2497y
Aberdare Gadlys Road Platform
Nantmelyn Platform
ABERDARE High Level
Aberdare Low Level
Aberaman
CWMBACH Halt
Middle Duffryn
Abercwmboi Halt
FERNHILL
closed 39
Mountain Ash Cardiff Road
MOUNTAIN ASH Oxford Street
Penrhiwceiber High Level
PENRHIWCEIBER Low Level
Matthewstown Halt
Pontcynon Bridge Halt
Old Ynysybwl Halt
ABERCYNON NORTH
Ynysybwl
Robertstown Halt
Ynysybwl New Road Halt
Clydach Court Halt
ABERCYNON SOUTH
closed 1932
closed to passengers 15
Pont Shon Norton Junct. J4
PONTYPRIDD
Treforest Halt
Maesy Coed
T5 Pontypridd Tun 1323yds
closed to passengers 56
TREHAFOD
PORTH
DINAS Rhondda
TONYPANDY+Trealaw
closed to passengers 56
Penygraig
Gilfach Goch Colliers Platform
LLWYNYPIA
YSTRAD (RHONDDA)
Ystrad Rhondda
TON PENTRE
Ynyshir
Wattstown
Tylorstown
Ferndale
Maerdy
TREORCHY
YNYSWEN
TREHERBERT
Blaenrhondda
Rhondda Tunnel T4 3443 yards
Blaengwynfi
Abergwynfi
T10 Gelli Tunnel 167yds
Cymmer Afon
Cymmer (Corrwg)
Cymmer General
Cymmer Tunnel T3 1595 yards
Duffryn Rhondda Halt
Duffryn Rhondda
Nantewlaeth Colliery Halt
Glyncorrwg
North Rhondda Colliery Halt
South Pit Halt
Tonmawr Junction J5
Gyfylcha Tunnel T1 1109 yds
closed to passengers 1928
closed 1910
closed to passengers 1924
Cynonville Halt
Pontrhydyfen
Cwmavon
Tonygroes West Jct J6
Aberavon Town
closed to passengers 33
Cwm Cerwyn Tunnel T2 1010y.
Maesteg Neath Road
Caerau
Caerau Goods
Nantyffyllon
MAESTEG Castle Street
MAESTEG EWENNY ROAD
Troedyrhiew GARTH
Blaengarw
Pontycymmer
Nantymoel
Wyndham Halt
Ogmore Vale
Pont Sarn
Pant
Pantysgallog Halt Low Level
Pantysgallog
Dowlais High Street
Dowlais Top
Cefn Coed
Dowlais Central
Dowlais Cae Harris
Pantywaun Halt
Zig Zag Lines Jct
J3 Fochriw Jct
Fochriw
Pengarnddu Platform
Cwmbargoed
Heolgerrig Halt
Plymouth Street
MERTHYR
Abercanaid
Pentrebach
PENTRE BACH
Troedyrhiw
TROED-Y-RHIEW
Bedlinog Colliers Platform
Bedlinog
Aberfan
MERTHYR VALE
Pontygwaith Halt
Quakers Yard High Level
QUAKERS YARD Low Level
Treharris
SN SO
SS ST

PORT TALBOT, BRIDGEND, PETERSTON + ABERTHAW

RAILWAYS

No	Company
3	GREAT WESTERN (GW)

STATIONS

Name	Opened Closed	Ry	Ref
Aberthaw	* 64	3	T06
Beddau Halt	52	3	T08
Blackmill	58	3	S98
BRIDGEND		3	S98
Brynmenyn	58	3	S98
Church Village Halt	52	3	T08
Coed Ely	58	3	T08
Cowbridge	51	3	S97
Creigiau	† 62	3	T08
Cross Inn	52	3	T08
Dynea Halt	56	3	T08
Efail Isaf	† 62	3	T08
Gileston	* 64	3	T06
Kenfig Hill	58	3	S88
Lewistown Halt	51	3	S98
Llandow Halt	* 64	3	S97
Llandow Wick Road Halt	* 64	3	S97
Llangeinor	53	3	S98
Llangynwyd	* 70	3	S88
Llanharan	* 64	3	S98
Llanharry	51	3	T08
Llantrisant	3 * 64 92	3	T08
Llantwit Fadre	52	3	T08
Llantwit Major	* 64	3	S96
Margam	48 64	3	S78
Nottage Halt	† 63	3	S87
PENCOED	* 64 92	3	S98
Peterston	* 64	3	T07
PONTYCLUN	3 92	3	T08
Pontyrhyll	53	3	S98
Porthcawl	† 63	3	S87
PORT TALBOT PARKWAY	84	3	S78
Pyle	2 * 64 94	3	S88
Rhoose	* 64	3	T06
Rhydfelin Halt High Level	53	3	T08
St Athan	* 64	3	S96
SARN	92	3	S88
Southerndown Road	61	3	S97
TONDU	* 70 92	3	S88
Tonteg Halt	† 1 62	3	T08
Tonyrefail	58	3	T08
TREFOREST TREFFOREST	80	3	T08
Treforest Halt	56	3	T08
Tremains Halt	63	3	S98
Trerhyngyll + Maendy	51	3	T07
WILDMILL	92	3	S98
Ystradowen	61	3	T07

GOODS

No	Name/Location	Closed	Ry	Ref
G 1	Bridgend + Coity	65	3	S98
2	Cowbridge	65	3	S97
3	Margam	65	3	S78
4	Port Talbot Central	60	3	S78

TUNNELS

No	Name	Length	Ry	Ref
T 1	Pontypridd	13 23	3	T09
2	Nottrage	63	3	S87
3	Porthkerry No.2	71	3	T06
4	Porthkerry No.1	545	3	T06

ENGINE SHEDS

No	Name/Location	Closed	Ry	Ref
E 1	Bridgend	50	3	S98
2	Tondu	64	3	S88
3	Llantrisant	64	3	T08

BRIDGES + VIADUCTS

No	Name/Location	Ry	Ref
V 1	Porthkerry Viaduct	3	T06

JUNCTIONS

No	Name	Ry	Ref
J 1	Waterfall	3	S88
2	Cefn	3	S88
3	Heol-y-Sheet	3	S88
4	Cornelly	3	S88
5	Ynysawre	3	S88
6	Ogmore	3	S88
7	Tyncoed	3	S98
8	Coity	3	S98
9	Bryncethin	3	S98
10	Ogmore Valley	3	S98
11	Gilfach	3	S98
12	Branch	3	T08
13	Mwyndy	3	T08
14	Gelynog Colliery	3	T08
15	Common Branch	3	T08
16	Llantrisant Common	3	T08
17	Gellyrhaidd	3	T08
18	Treferig	3	T08

NOTES:

REF All in SS o ST therefore initial S omitted

1 Partly closed (one platform) in 52.

2 Closed at terminal date but scheduled to re-open. Actually opened in 94.

3 Re-opened 92 PONTYCLUN was previously Llantrisant.

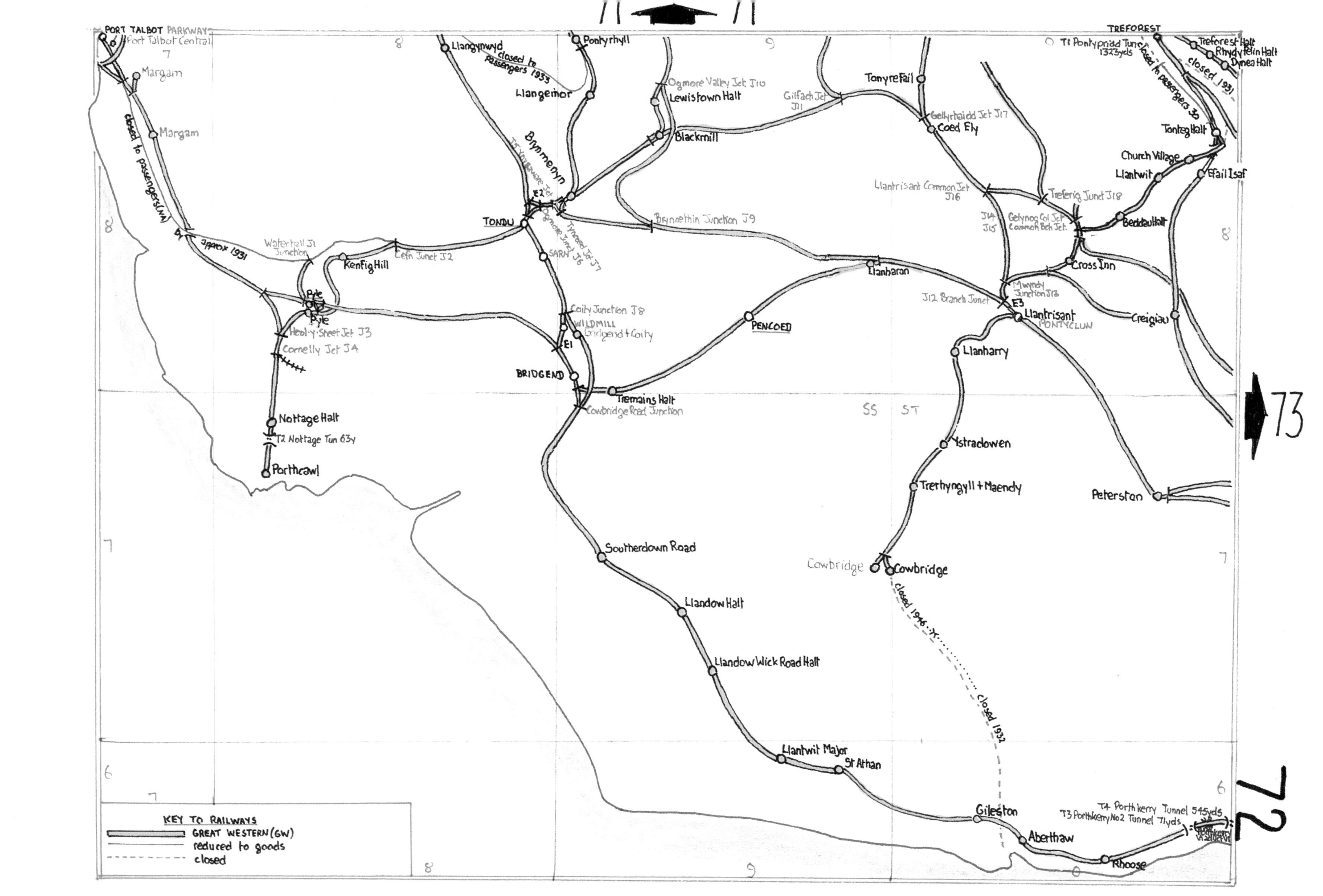
71
73
PORT TALBOT PARKWAY
Port Talbot Central
Margam
Margam
closed to passengers (NA)
approx 1931
Llangynwyd
closed to passengers 1933
Pontyrhyll
Llangeinor
Brynmenyn
TONDU
E2
Ogmore Valley Jct J10
Lewistown Halt
Blackmill
Gilfach Jct J11
Tonyrefail
Gellyrhaidd Jct J17
Coed Ely
Llantrisant Common Jct J16
Treferig Junct J18
TREFOREST
Tt Pontypridd Tun 1323yds
closed to passengers 30
Treforest Halt
Rhydyfelin Halt
Dynea Halt
closed 1931
Tonteg Halt
Church Village
Llantwit
Efail Isaf
Beddau Halt
J14
J15
Gelynog Col Jct
Common Bch Jct.
Cross Inn
Mwyndy Junction J13
J12 Branch Junct
E3
Llantrisant
PONTYCLUN
Creigiau
Llanharan
Brynethin Junction J9
Ogmore Junct J6
Tynewydd Jct J7
SARN
Waterhall Jt Junction
Cefn Junct J2
Kenfig Hill
Pyle
Pyle
Heol-y-Sheet Jct J3
Cornelly Jct J4
Coity Junction J8
WILDMILL
Bridgend & Coity
E1
BRIDGEND
PENCOED
Tremains Halt
Cowbridge Road Junction
Llanharry
SS
ST
Ystradowen
Trerhyngyll & Maendy
Peterston
Nottage Halt
T2 Nottage Tun 634
Porthcawl
Southerdown Road
Cowbridge
Cowbridge
closed 1946
closed 1932
Llandow Halt
Llandow Wick Road Halt
Llantwit Major
St Athan
Gileston
Aberthaw
Rhoose
T4 Porthkerry Tunnel 545yds
T3 Porthkerry No2 Tunnel 71yds
KEY TO RAILWAYS
GREAT WESTERN (GW)
reduced to goods
closed

HENGOED, CAERPHILLY, CARDIFF + BARRY

RAILWAYS

No	Company
2	LONDON MIDLAND + SCOTTISH (LMS)
3	GREAT WESTERN (GW)

STATIONS

Station	Opened/Closed	Ry Ref
Abercarn	62	3 29
ABER Junction Halt	68	3 18
Abertridwr	* 64	3 18
Alberta Place Halt	68	3 17
BARRY		3 16
BARRY DOCKS		3 16
BARRY ISLAND		3 16
Barry Pier	71	3 16
Bassaleg	† 62	3 28
Bassaleg Junction	62	3 28
Bedwas	† 62	3 18
BIRCHGROVE Halt	* 69	3 18
BUTE ROAD (Cardiff)		3 17
CADOXTON		3 16
CAERPHILLY		3 18
Caerphilly Locomotive Works		3 18
CARDIFF		17
BUTE ROAD		3 17
CENTRAL	A § 73	3 17
Clarence Road	* 64	3 17
General	A § 73	3 17
QUEEN STREET		3 17
Riverside	1 40	3 17
Cathays Woodville Road Halt	B § 52	3 17
CATHAYS	83	3 17
Cefn-Onn	80 86	3 18
Celynen South Halt	62	3 29
Church Road	57	3 28
Clarence Road	* 64	3 17
COGAN		3 17
CORYTON Halt	* 69	3 18
Cross Keys	62	3 29
Cwmbran	3 62	3 29
CWMBRAN	3 86	3 29
Cwmcarn	62	3 29
DANESCOURT		3 17
DINAS POWIS POWYS	2 80	3 17
DINGLE ROAD Halt	69	3 17
EASTBROOK	87	3 17
Ely Main Line	† 62	3 17
FAIRWATER	87	3 17
Fleur-de-Lis	† 62	3 19
Fountainbridge Halt	56	3 18
GRANGETOWN		3 17
Groeswen Halt	56	3 18
Gwernydomen Halt	56	3 18
HEATH Halt HIGH LEVEL	69	3 18
HEATH Halt LOW LEVEL	* 69	3 18
Hengoed High Level	†	3 19
HENGOED Low Level	68	3 19
Lavernock	68	3 16
LISVANE + THORNHILL	85	3 18
LLANBRADACH		3 18
Llanbradach Colliery Halt	54	3 19
LLANDAFF for Whitchurch	80	3 17
LLANISHEN		3 18
Lower Penarth Halt	54	3 16
Lower Pontnewydd	58	3 29
Machen	† 63	2 28
Maesycwmmer	† 62	3 19
Maindy North Road Halt	4 52 58	3 17
Marshfield	59	3 28
Nant Garw Halt High Level	56	3 18
Nelson + Llancaiach	† 64	3 19
Newbridge	62	3 29
Nine Mile Point	59	2 29
NINIAN PARK Halt	69 75 79	3 17
Penarth Dock	62	3 17
PENARTH Town	63	3 17
Pentwynmawr	† 64	3 19
Penyrheol	* 64	3 18
Pont Lawrence Halt	57	2 19
Pontllanfraith Low Level	† 50 64	3 19
Pont llanfraith High Level	49 60	2 19
Pontnewydd, Lower	58	3 29
Pontnewydd, Upper	62	3 29
Pontrhydyrun Halt	62	3 29
QUEEN STREET (Cardiff)		3 17
RADYR		3 18
RHIWBINA Halt	* 69	3 18
Rhiwderin	54	3 28
Risca	62	3 28
Riverside		3 17
Rogerstone	62	3 28
St Fagan's	† 62	3 17
Senghenydd	* 64	3 19
Sully	68	3 16
Swanbridge Halt	68	3 16
TAFFS WELL		3 18
TREFOREST ESTATE		3 18
Trelewis Halt	† 64	3 19
Treowen Halt	60	3 28
Trethomas	† 62	3 18
TY GLAS		3 18
Tynycwm Halt	62	3 28
Upper Boat Halt	56	3 18
Upper Pontnewydd	62	3 28
Waterloo Halt	56	3 18
WAUN-GRON PARK	87	3 17
Wenvoe	† 62	3 17
WHITCHURCH	*	3 18
White Hart Halt	52	3 18
Windsor Colliery Halt	64	3 18
Woodville Road Halt	B § 52 58	3 17
Wyllie Halt	60	2 19
Ynysddu	60	2 19
YSTRAD MYNACH		3 19

GOODS

No	Name/Location	Closed	Ry Ref
G1	RADY YARD	O	3 18
2	TIDAL YARD	O	3 27
3	BARRY DOCKS	O	3 16
4	Penmaen	64	3 19
5	Penrhiwfelin	58	3 19
6	Ystrad Mynach	65	3 19
7	Ynysddu	60	2 19
8	Cwmbran	65	3 29
9	Adam Street Cardiff	66	3 17
10	Newtown + Tyndall Field	81	3 17
11	Nine Mile Point	59	2 19

WORKS

No	Name	Closed	Ry Ref
W1	Caerphilly	63	3 18

ENGINE SHEDS

No	Name/Location	Closed steam	Ry Ref
E1	Barry	64	3 16
2	Cardiff CANTON	5 62	3 17
3	Cardiff Cathays	64	3 17
4	Cardiff East Dock	65	3 17
5	Radyr Penarth Junction	65	3 17

TUNNELS

No	Name/Location	Length	Ry Ref
T1	Caerphilly	1933	3 18
2	Walnut Tree	490	3 18
3	Wenvoe	1867	3 17
4	Cogan	222	3 17
5	Porthkerry No.1	595	3 16
6	Bryn	398	3 19
7	Penar	239	3 19
8	Pier (Barry)	280	3 16

BRIDGES + VIADUCTS

No	Name/Location	Ry	Ref
V1	Walnut Tree Viaduct	3	18
2	Pen-y-rheol Viaduct (disused)	3	18
3	Pwll-y-Pant (disused)	3	18
4	St Fagan's Viaduct	3	17
5	Drope Viaduct	3	17

JUNCTIONS

No	Name	Ry	Ref
J1	Gelligoes	2	19
2	Bird-in-Hand	3	19
3	Tredegar	23	19
4	Penar	3	19
5	Barry	3	18
6	Halls Road	3	29
7	Llantarnum	3	29
8	Watford Crossing	3	18
9	Penrhos Lower	3	18
10	Roath Branch	3	17
11	Pengam	3	27
12	Penarth	3	18
13	Crockherbertstown	3	17

NOTES:

Ref All in ST therefore letters omitted.

§ Older version } Name change
§ Newer version }

Some other changes shown as part of entry but others ignored.

1 Merged into General in 1940
2 Change to Welsh spelling 1980
3 Stations on different sites and even on different lines
4 North Road dropped from title 52
5 Still in use as modern depot.

68

72

74

ST 1 2

Trelewis Halt
Nelson + Llancaiach
closed 1932
Penrhiwfelin
Ystrad Mynach
YSTRAD MYNACH
Fleur-de-Lis
Pontllanfraith High Level
Birdin Hand J2
Pontllanfraith Low Level
T6
Tredegar Jct J3
Gelligoes Junction J1
Hengoed Low Level
Hengoed High Level
Maesycwmmer
Wyllie Halt
Ynysddu
Ynysddu
Treowen Halt
Penmaen
J4
Pentwynmawr
T7
Newbridge
Celynen South Halt
Abercarn
Cwmcarn
Cross Keys
Halls Road Junction J6
Pontrhydyrun Halt
Upper Pontnewynydd
Lower Pontnewynydd
CWMBRAN
Cwmbran
Cwmbran
J7
9

Senghenydd
LLANBRADACH
Llanbraddach Colliery Halt
Barry Jct
Windsor Colliery Halt
Abertridwr
V3
Bedwas
Trethomas
Nine Mile Point
Nine Mile Point
Pontllanwrene Halt
Machen
Risca
Tynycwm Halt
Rogerstone
Fountain Bridge Halt
White Hart Halt
Waterloo Halt
Gwernydomen Halt
Church Road
Rhiwderin
Bassaleg
Bassaleg Junction
Upper Boat Halt
closed 31
Penyrheol
V2
closed 1931
ABER Junction Halt
W1
Caerphilly Loco Works
Groeswen Halt
Nantgarw Halt High Level
TREFOREST ESTATE
CAERPHILLY
Watford Crossing Jct J8
Penrhos Lower Junction J9
T1 Caerphilly Tunnel 1993y
8
TAFFS WELL
Cefn-Onn
LISVANE + THORNHILL
LLANISHEN
Walnut Tree Tun T2 490yds
closed to passengers 1931
WHITCHURCH (S Glam)
CORYTON Halt
RHIWBINA Halt
BIRCHGROVE Halt
TY GLAS Halt
HEATH LOW LEVEL
HEATH HIGH LEVEL
Marshfield
RADYR
Penarth Jct J12
RADYR YARD
E5
LLANDAFF
Roath Branch Jct J10
DANESCOURT
Mainly North Road Halt
Woodville Road Halt
E3
CATHAYS
FAIRWATER
V3
WAUN-GRON PARK
J13 Crockherbtown Jct
QUEEN STR.
General
CENTRAL
Adam Str
Pengam Jct J11
TIDAL YARD
EV4
St Fagan's
Ely Main Line
NINIAN PARK Halt
E4
T3 Wenvoe Tunnel 1867yds
7
GRANGETOWN
CARDIFF
Riverside
BUTE ROAD
Clarence Road
Wenvoe
COGAN
T4 Cogan Tun 222yds
EASTBROOK
Penarth Dock
DINGLE ROAD Halt
PENARTH Town
DINAS Powis Powys
Alberta Place Halt
Lower Penarth Halt
CADOXTON
Sully
BARRY DOCKS
Lavernock
Swanbridge Halt
BARRY
T5
Barry Pier
BARRY ISLAND
6
2

KEY TO RAILWAYS
LONDON MIDLAND + SCOTTISH (LMS)
GREAT WESTERN (GW)
Private lines
Reduced to goods during grouping
Closed early 20th century.

NEWPORT + WESTON·SUPER·MARE

RAILWAYS

No	Company
3	GREAT WESTERN (GW)

STATIONS

Name	Opened / Closed	Ry	Ref
Caerleon	62	3	39
CALDICOT Halt	* 69	3	48
Clevedon	* 66	3	47
Congesbury	† 63	3	47
Llantarnum	62	3	39
Llanwern	60	3	38
Magor	* 64	3	48
NAILSEA + BACKWELL	1	3	46
NEWPORT High Street	?	3	38
Ponthir	62	3	39
Portbury	62	3	47
Portishead	2 * 64	3	47
Puxton + Worle	* 64	3	36
Sandford + Banwell	† 63	3	46
SEVERN TUNNEL JUNCTION		3	48
Undy Halt	* 64	3	48
WESTON MILTON Halt	69	3	36
WESTON·SUPER·MARE General	64	3	36
Weston·Super·Mare Locking Road	64	3	36
WORLE	90	3	36
YATTON		3	46

GOODS

No	Name/Location	Closed	Ry	Ref
G1	Newport Mill Street	66	3	38
2	Newport Dock Street	?	3	38
3	EAST USK YARD	O	3	38
4	Severn Tunnel	65	3	48
5	Burrington	50	3	46
6	Portishead Dock	?	3	48

JUNCTIONS

No	Name	Ry	Ref
J1	Cheddar Valley	3	46
2	Wrington	3	46
3	Maindee North	3	38
4	Maindee East	3	38
5	Maindee West	3	38
6	Gaer	3	38
7	Ebbw	3	38

ENGINE SHEDS

No	Name/Location	Closed	Ry	Ref
E1	Newport Ebbw	65	3	
2	Newport Pill	65	3	
3	Severn Tunnel	65	3	
4	Weston·super·Mare	60	3	
5	Yatton	60	3	

TUNNELS

No	Name/Location	Length	Ry	Ref
T1	Newport Old	742	3	38
	Newport New	762	3	38
2	Caer	403	3	38
3	Severn	7669	3	48

BRIDGES + VIADUCTS

No	Name	Ry	Ref
V	Usk Viaduct	3	38

NOTES:

Ref Allin ST so letters omitted.

1 Backwell omitted from title for a period then restored.

2 Rebuilt on changed site in 54.

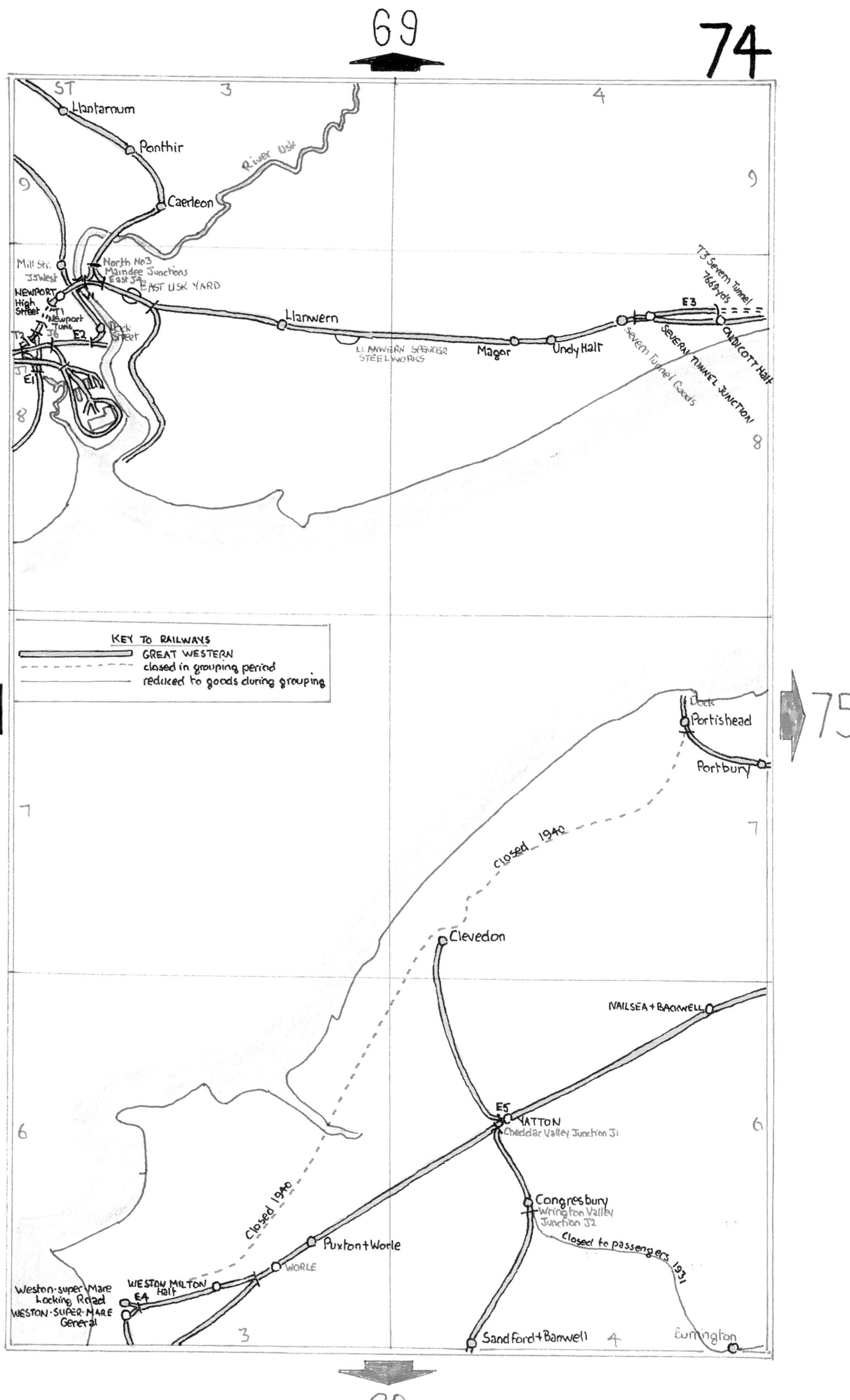
69
74
ST
3
4
9
Llantarnum
Ponthir
Caerleon
River Usk
Mill Str. Jn West
North No3
Maindee Junctions
East Jn
EAST USK YARD
NEWPORT High Street
T1 Newport Tuns
J6
E2
Dock Street
T2
J7
E1
8
Llanwern
LLANWERN SPENCER STEELWORKS
Magor
Undy Halt
T3 Severn Tunnel 7669yds
E3
Severn Tunnel Goods
SEVERN TUNNEL JUNCTION
CALDICOTT Halt
KEY TO RAILWAYS
GREAT WESTERN
closed in grouping period
reduced to goods during grouping
73
75
Dock
Portishead
Portbury
7
Closed 1940
Clevedon
NAILSEA + BACKWELL
6
E5
YATTON
Cheddar Valley Junction J1
Congresbury
Wrington Valley Junction J2
Closed to passengers 1931
Closed 1940
Puxton + Worle
WORLE
WESTON MILTON Halt
Weston-super-Mare Locking Road
E4
WESTON-SUPER-MARE General
Sandford + Banwell
Burrington
89

CHELTENHAM, GLOUCESTER + BRISTOL

RAILWAYS

No	Company
2	LONDON MIDLAND + SCOTTISH (LMS)
3	GREAT WESTERN (GW)
5	SEVERN + WYE (LMS + GW)
23	other LMS + GW JOINT Lines
24	SOMERSET + DORSET (LMS + Southern)
6	DEAN FOREST (ex Severn + Wye)
7	AVON VALLEY (ex LMS)

STATIONS

Station	Opened / Closed	Ry Ref
Aschurch	15 71	293
Ashley Hill	* 64	367
Ashton Gate Halt	* 62 64 70 81	357
Ashton-under-Hill	† 63	293
AVONCLIFF Halt	* 69	386
AVONMOUTH Dock	* 66	2357
Avonmouth ST ANDREWS RD.	*	358
Awre	59	360
Backney Halt	62	352
Badminton	68	388
Ballingham	* 64	353
Barber's Bridge	59	372
Bathampton	* 66	376
Bathford Halt	* 65	376
Bath Green Park	* 51 66	276
BATH SPA	49	376
Beanacre Halt	55	386
Beckford	† 63	293
BEDMINSTER		357
Berkeley	* 64	2360
Berkeley Road	* 65	2370
Bishops Cleeve	60	392
Bitton	* 66	767
Black Dog Siding Halt	* 53 65	397
Blaisdon Halt	* 64	371
Bowbridge Crossing Halt	† 64	380
Box	* 65	386
Box Mill Lane Halt	* 65	386
BRADFORD-ON-AVON		386
Bredon	* 65	293
Brimscombe	* 64	380
Brimscombe Bridge Halt	† 64	380
Brislington	59	367
BRISTOL		
Ashley Hill	64	367
Ashton Gate Halt	* 62 64 70 81	357
BEDMINSTER		357
Brislington	59	367
Clifton Bridge	* 64	357
CLIFTON DOWN	*	2357
LAWRENCE HILL		367
MONTPELIER	*	2357
PARSON STREET		357
REDLAND		2357
St Annes Park	70	367
St Philips	53	257
STAPLETON ROAD		367
TEMPLE MEADS		357
BRISTOL PARKWAY	72	368
Brockweir Halt	59	350
Bromham + Rowde Halt	* 66	396
Broughton Gifford Halt	55	386
Bullo Cross Halt	64	361
Calne	* 65	397
Cam	† 62	270
Cashes Green Halt	† 64	380
Chalford	* 64	380
Charfield for Wootton-under-Edge	* 65	279
Charlton Kings	† 62	391
CHELTENHAM		92
Leckhampton	† A § 52 62	392
Race Course	13 68 71 76	392
South + Leckhampton	A § 52	392
SPA Lansdown	?	292
Spa Malvern Road	* 66	392
Spa St James	64	392
CHEPSTOW		359
CHIPPENHAM		397
Chipping Sodbury	61	378
Chittening Platform	* 48 64	358
Christian Malford Halt	* 65	397
Churchdown	* 64	2382
Church's Hill Halt	* 59 64	399
Cinderford	58	561
Cleeve	50	292
Clifton Bridge	* 64	357
CLIFTON DOWN	*	2357
Clutton	59	366
Coaley	* 65	270
Coalpit Heath	61	368
Corsham	* 65	386
Cross Hands Halt	* 64	358
Culkerton Halt	* 1 59 64	399
Dauntsey	* 65	398
Devizes	* 66	396
Downfield Crossing Halt	† 64	380
Dudbridge	2 49	280
Dursley	† 62	279
Dymock	59	363
Ebley Crossing Halt	† 64	380
Fawley	* 64	352
FILTON Junction	68	367
Filton Platform, North	3 86	368
Fishponds	* 66	267
Flax Bourton	* 63	357
Four Oaks Halt	59	362
FRESHFORD	*	376
Frocester	61	270
GLOUCESTER Central	51 75	381
Gloucester Eastgate	51 75	281
Gotherington	55	392
Grange Court	* 64	371
Greenway Halt	59	363
Gretton Halt	60	392
Hadnock Halt	51 59	351
Ham Green Halt	* 64	357
Ham Mill Crossing Halt	† † 57 64	380
Haresfield	* 65	281
Henbury	* 64	258
Holme Lacy	* 64	353
Holt Junction	* 66	386
Horfield	* 64	367
Hullavington	61	388
Jackments Bridge Halt	48	399
Kelston for Saltford	49	266
KEMBLE		399
Kerne Bridge	59	351
KEYNSHAM + Somerdale	74	366
Lacock Halt	* 66	386
Lansdown, Cheltenham	?	292
LAWRENCE HILL		367
LEDBURY		373
Ledbury Town Halt	61	363
Limpley Stoke	* 66	376
Little Sommerford	61	398
Llandogo Halt	59	350
Longhope	* 64	361
Lydbrook Junction	59	2551
LYDNEY Junction	68	360
Lydney Junction	60	560
LYDNEY LAKESIDE		660
Lydney Town	* 60	560
Malmesbury	51	398
Malswick Halt	59	372
Malvern Road Cheltenham	* 66	392
Mangotsfield	* 66	267
MELKSHAM	* 66 85	386
Midford	* 66	2476
Mitcheldean Road	* 64	362
Monmouth May Hill	59	351
Monmouth Troy	59	351
MONTPELIER	*	2357
Nailsworth	49	289
Netherhope Halt	49	359
Newent	59	372
Newnham	* 64	361
New Passage Halt	* 64	358
NORCHARD		660
North Filton Halt	* 3 86	368
Oakle Street	* 64	371
OLDFIELD PARK		376
Oldland Common Halt	* 64 66	767
PARSON STREET		357
PATCHWAY		368
Penallt Halt	59	350
Pensford	59	366
Pill	* 64	357
PILNING High Level	68	358
Pilning Low Level	* 64	358
Portskewett	* 64	358
Redbrook-on-Wye	59	350
REDLAND	*	2357
Ripple	61	283
Rodmarton Platform	* 64	399
Ross-on-Wye	* 64	352
Ruspidge Halt	58	361
Ryeford	49	280
ST ANDREWS ROAD	*	358
St Annes Park	70	367
St Briavels	59	350
St James, Cheltenham	64	392
St Marys Crossing Halt	† 64	380
St Philips, Bristol	53	257
Saltford	70	366
SEA MILLS	*	2357
Seend	* 66	396
Semington Halt	* 66	396
SEVERN BEACH	*	358
Severn Bridge	* 60	560
Sharpness	* 64	560
SHIREHAMPTON	*	2357
Stanley Bridge Halt	* 58	397
Staple Hill	* 66	267
STAPLETON ROAD		367
Staverton Halt	* 66	386
Stonehouse Bristol Road	* 51 65	270
STONEHOUSE Burdett Road	51 68	380
STROUD		380
Stroud	49	280
Symond's Yat	59	351
TEMPLE MEADS		2357
Tetbury	* 64	399
Tewkesbury	61	283
Tidenham	59	359
Tintern	59	359
Tintern Quarry Halt	54	359
Trouble House Halt	* 64	399
Tutshill for Beachley Halt	59	359
Upper Soudley Halt	58	361
Walford	59	352
Warmley	* 64	267
Westbury-on-Severn Halt	59	371
Weston	53	276
Weston-under-Penyard	* 64	362
Whitchurch Halt	62	366
Whitebrook Halt	59	350
Wickwar	* 65	278
Winterbourne	61	368
Woodchester	5 49	280
Woolaston	54	369
Wyesham Halt	59	351
YATE	* 65 89	268

GOODS

No	Name/Location	Closed	Ry Ref
1	Avonmouth Dock	66	2357
2	Blakeney	49	360
3	Bullo Pill	63	361
4	Canons Marsh	65	357
5	Coleford	67	551
6	Coleford	67	351
7	Drybrook	49	361
8	Lydney Harbour	63	560
9	Parkend	67	560
10	Sharpness Dock	64	560
11	Thornbury	64	268
12	Tetbury Road (Coates)	63	399

ENGINE SHEDS

No	Name/Location	Closed Steam	Ry Ref
E1	Bath	61	376
2	Bath Green Park	8 66	2476
3	Brimscombe	63	380
4	Bristol Barrow Road	65	2357
5	BRISTOL BATH ROAD	7 60	357
6	BRISTOL ST PHILIPS MARSH	9 64	357
7	Chalford	51	380
8	Cheltenham	63	392
9	Chippenham	64	397
11	Dursley	62	279
12	Gloucester	65	381
13	Gloucester	64	281
14	HEREFORD	10 0	053
15	Ledbury	64	373
16	Lydney Junction	64	560
17	Malmesbury	51	398
18	Ross	63	362
19	Tetbury	64	389
20	Tewkesbury	62	283

TUNNELS 12

No	Name/Location	Length	Ry Ref
T1	Dinedor	110	353
2	Ledbury	1318	373
3	Tewkesbury	418	283
4	Ballingham	1206	353
5	Fawley	537	353
6	Mitcheldean	782	362
7	Monmouth	148	351
10	Symonds Yat	433	351
11	Lydbrook	630	351
12	Mierystock	242	561
13	Coles Rock	30	561
14	Drybrook	90	361
15	Blue Rock	109	361
16	Newnham	232	361
17	Bradley Hill	299	361
19	Whitecliffe	55	351
20	Tintern	182	350
21	Moseley Green	503	560
22	Bullo	1065	361
23	Severn Bridge	503	560
24	Tidenham	1190	359
25	Sapperton Long	1864	390
26	Sapperton Short	352	390
27	Kemble	415	399
28	Hunting Butts	97	392
29			
30	Clifton Bridge No.1	59	357
31	Clifton Bridge No.2	232	357
32	Sandstone	88	357
33	Pill	665	357
34	Clifton Down	1751	2357
35	Redcliffe	299	357
36	Flax Bourton	110	357
37	Charlton	302	358
38	Ableton Lane	97	358
39	Severn	7669	358
40	St Annes No.2 11	154	367
41	St Annes No 3 11	1017	367
42	Montpelier	288	2357
43	Patchway New	1760	358
44	Patchway Long	1264	358
45	Patchway Short	62	358
46	Grovesend	167	268
47	Tytherington	224	268
48	Combe Hay	66	376
49	Combe Down	1829	2476
50	Devonshire	447	2476
51	Twerton Short	45	376
52	Twerton Long	264	376
53	Spring Gardens West	99	376
54	Spring Gardens East	77	376
55	Chipping Sodbury	4444	386
56	Wickwar	1397	288
57	Alderton	506	388
58			
59	Malmesbury	105	398
60	Middle Hill	198	386
61	Box	3212	386
62	Bradford	159	386
63	Devizes	140	396

BRIDGES + VIADUCTS

No	Name	Ry	Ref
V1	Severn Bridge	5	60
2	Kerne Bridge Viaduct	3	51
3	Lydbrook Viaduct	5	51
4	Midford Viaduct	24	76
5	St James Viaduct Bath	3	76

JUNCTIONS

No	Name	Ry	Ref
J1	Rotherwas	23	53
2	Red Hill	23	53
3	Serridge	5	61
4	Coleford	35	51
5	Tufts	5	60
6	Otters Pool	53	60
7	Forest of Dean	3	61
8	Oldminster	5	60
9	Wye Valley	3	59
10	Drybrook Road	5	61
11	Bilson Loop	3	61
12	Quay Branch	2	83
13	Gloucester Loop	3	92
14	Hatherley Curve	23	92
15	Engine Shed	23	81
16	Standish	23	80
17	Over	3	81
18	Tramway	23	81
19	Dr Days Bridge	3	67
20	Bedminster	3	57
21	South Liberty	3	57
22	Westerleigh North	3	68
23	Westerleigh East	3	78
24	Westerleigh West	3	68
25	Thingley	3	87
26	Air Ministry Loop	3	87
27	New Malmesbury	3	98
28	Stoke Gifford	3	6
29	Kingswood	2	6
30	Cammerton Branch	3	7

NOTES:

Ref In SO or ST but letters omitted due to lack of space

§ Old name } Change of
§ New name } name

1. The Halt addition was for only part of '59
2. Closure date is as shown, but last train for passengers was the pre-nationalisation era.
3. Regular traffic finished in '64
4. Crossing dropped from title in 1957
5. Last train (passengers) 1947
6. Staple Edge Halt Closed 58 (GW) ref 61 omitted from this gazetteer.
7. Replaced by modern depot. This continued in use until the atlas terminal date but is now closed
8. Also LMS shed but main use was SOMERSET + DORSET
9. Replaced by modern depot, still in use.
10. New modern depot, still in use
11. St Annes No.1 opened out.
12. Missing numbers allocated to tunnels closed or on adjoining map.
13. The Gloucestershire Warwickshire is proposing to extend to this station
14. Proposed reopening on nearby site as CAM + DURSLEY. Actually re-opend late '94.
15. Proposed for re-opening as: ASHCHURCH for TEWKESBURY

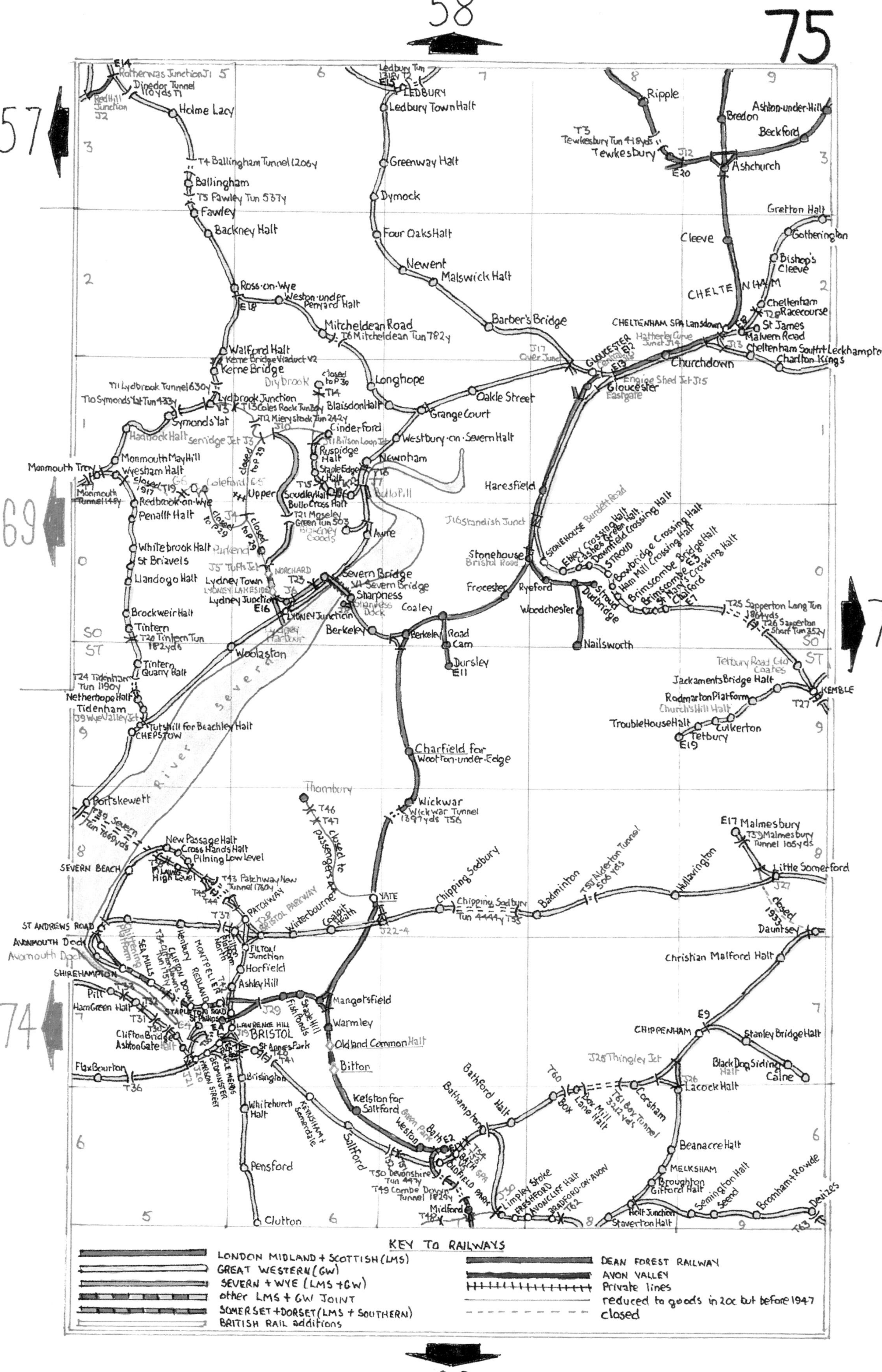
75
58
57
69
74
76
90
Rotherwas Junction J1
Dinedor Tunnel 1110yds T1
Redhill Junction J2
Holme Lacy
T4 Ballingham Tunnel 1206y
Ballingham
T5 Fawley Tun 537y
Fawley
Backney Halt
Ross-on-Wye
E18
Weston-under-Penyard Halt
Mitcheldean Road
T6 Mitcheldean Tun 782y
Walford Halt
Kerne Bridge Viaduct V2
Kerne Bridge
T11 Lydbrook Tunnel 630y
T10 Symonds Yat Tun 433y
Lydbrook Junction
T13 Coles Rock Tun 30y
Symonds Yat
Hadnock Halt
Monmouth Troy
Monmouth May Hill
Wyesham Halt
Monmouth Tunnel 148y
Redbrook-on-Wye
Penallt Halt
Whitebrook Halt
St Briavels
Llandogo Halt
Brockweir Halt
Tintern
T20 Tintern Tun 182yds
Tintern Quarry Halt
T24 Tidenham Tun 1190y
Netherhope Halt
Tidenham
J9 Wye Valley Jct
Tutshill for Beachley Halt
CHEPSTOW
Portskewett
T39 Severn Tun 7669yds
Ledbury Tun 1318y T2
E15
LEDBURY
Ledbury Town Halt
Greenway Halt
Dymock
Four Oaks Halt
Newent
Malswick Halt
Barber's Bridge
Longhope
Blaisdon Halt
Grange Court
Oakle Street
Westbury-on-Severn Halt
Cinderford
Ruspidge Halt
Staple Edge Halt
Newnham
Bullo Pill
Upper
Soudley Halt
Bullo Cross Halt
T21 Moseley Green Tun 503
Awre
Parkend
J5 Tufts Jct
NORCHARD
Lydney Town
LYDNEY LAKESIDE
Lydney Junction
E16
LYDNEY Junction
Lydney Harbour
Severn Bridge
V1 Severn Bridge
Sharpness
Coaley
Berkeley
Berkeley Road
Cam
Dursley
E11
Woolaston
River Severn
Ripple
T3 Tewkesbury Tun 418yds
Tewkesbury
E20
J12
Bredon
Ashton-under-Hill
Beckford
Ashchurch
Gretton Halt
Gotherington
Cleeve
Bishop's Cleeve
CHELTENHAM
Cheltenham Racecourse
CHELTENHAM SPA Lansdown
Malvern Road
St James
Hatherley Curve Junct J14
Cheltenham South + Leckhampton
Charlton Kings
Churchdown
GLOUCESTER
Gloucester Eastgate
Engine Shed Jct J15
J17 Over Junct
Haresfield
J16 Standish Junct
Stonehouse
Bristol Road
Frocester
Ryeford
Woodchester
Nailsworth
Dudbridge
Stroud
Brimscombe
Chalford
T25 Sapperton Long Tun 1864yds
T26 Sapperton Short Tun 352y
Tetbury Road Goods Coates
KEMBLE
T27
Jackaments Bridge Halt
Rodmarton Platform
Church's Hill Halt
Trouble House Halt
Culkerton
Tetbury
E19
Charfield for Wootton-under-Edge
Wickwar
Wickwar Tunnel 1397yds T56
Thornbury
T46
T47
closed to passengers
YATE
J22-4
Chipping Sodbury
Chipping Sodbury Tun 4444y T55
Badminton
T57 Alderton Tunnel 506 yds
Hullavington
E17 Malmesbury
T59 Malmesbury Tunnel 105yds
Little Somerford
J27
closed 1933
Dauntsey
Christian Malford Halt
E9
CHIPPENHAM
Stanley Bridge Halt
Black Dog Siding Halt
Calne
J25 Thingley Jct
J26
Lacock Halt
Corsham
T61 Box Tunnel 3212yds
Box
Box Mill Lane Halt
T60
Beanacre Halt
MELKSHAM
Broughton Gifford Halt
Holt Junction
Staverton Halt
Semington Halt
Seend
Bromham + Rowde
Devizes
T63
New Passage Halt
Cross Hands Halt
Pilning Low Level
Pilning High Level
T43 Patchway New Tunnel 1760y
SEVERN BEACH
PATCHWAY
BRISTOL PARKWAY
Winterbourne
Coalpit Heath
ST ANDREWS ROAD
AVONMOUTH Dock
Avonmouth Docks
SHIREHAMPTON
SEA MILLS
Henbury
CLIFTON DOWN
REDLAND
MONTPELIER
FILTON Junction
Horfield
Ashley Hill
J29
Fishponds
Staple Hill
Mangotsfield
Warmley
Oldland Common Halt
Bitton
Pill
Ham Green Halt
T31
T32
Clifton Bridge
Ashton Gate Halt
Flax Bourton
T36
LAWRENCE HILL
BRISTOL
St Philips
St Annes Park
Brislington
Whitchurch Halt
Pensford
Clutton
KEYNSHAM + Somerdale
Saltford
Kelston for Saltford
Weston
Bath
E2
BATH SPA
OLDFIELD PARK
T50 Devonshire Tun 447y
T49 Combe Down Tunnel 1829y
Midford
Bathampton
Bathford Halt
Limpley Stoke
FRESHFORD
AVONCLIFF Halt
BRADFORD-ON-AVON
T62
J30
KEY TO RAILWAYS
LONDON MIDLAND + SCOTTISH (LMS)
GREAT WESTERN (GW)
SEVERN + WYE (LMS + GW)
other LMS + GW JOINT
SOMERSET + DORSET (LMS + SOUTHERN)
BRITISH RAIL additions
DEAN FOREST RAILWAY
AVON VALLEY
Private lines
reduced to goods in 20c but before 1947
closed

BANBURY, SWINDON + NEWBURY

RAILWAYS

No	Company
2	LONDON MIDLAND + SCOTTISH (LMS)
3	GREAT WESTERN (GW)
4	SWINDON + CRICKLADE (ex GW)
5	GLOUCESTERSHIRE + WARWICKSHIRE (ex GW)

STATIONS

Station	Opened Closed	Ry	Ref
Abingdon	† 63	3	U49
Adderbury	51	3	P43
Addlestrop	* 64	3	P22
Alvescot	62	3	P20
Andoversford Junction	† 62	3	P02
ASCOTT·UNDER·WYCHWOOD Halt	* 65 69	3	P31
Aynho for Deddington	* 64	3	P43
Aynho Park	† 63	3	P53
BANBURY General	61	3	P43
Banbury Merton Street	61	2	P44
BEDWYN Halt	* 64 69	3	U26
Blenheim + Woodstock	54	3	P41
Bletchington	* 64	3	P41
Blockley	* 64	3	P13
Bloxham	51	3	P43
(BLUNSDON)	1	4	U18
Bourton·on·the·Water	† 62	3	P12
Boxford	60	3	U47
Brinkworth	61	3	U08
Brize Norton + Bampton	62	3	P30
Broadway	60	3	P03
Campden	A §	3	P13
Carterton	62	3	P20
Cassington Halt	62	3	P41
Challow	* 64	3	U39
CHARLBURY	*	3	P31
Chedworth	61	3	P01
Chesterton Lane Halt	* 59 64	3	P00
Chipping Campden	A § * 52 66	3	P13
Chipping Norton	† 62	3	P32
Chiseldon	61	3	U17
Chiseldon Camp Halt	61	3	U17
Cirencester Town	* 64	3	P00
Cirencester Watermoor	61	3	P00
COMBE	*	3	P41
Cricklade	61	4	U09
Dauntsey	* 65	3	U08
Eastbury Halt	60	3	U37
East Garston	60	3	U37
Eynsham	62	3	P40
Fairford	62	3	P10
Faringdon	51	3	U29
FINSTOCK Halt	* 69	3	P31
Foss Cross	61	3	P00
Fritwell + Somerton	* 64	3	P42
Grafton + Burbage	61	3	U26
Great Shefford	60	3	U37
(GRETTON MEADOW)		5	P03
(HAILES ABBEY)	2	5	P03
HANDBOROUGH HANBOROUGH	* 92	3	P41
Hannington	53	3	U19
Hayles Abbey Halt	2 60	3	P03
HEYFORD	*	3	P42
Highclere	60	3	U46
Highworth	3 62	3	U19
Hook Norton	51	3	P33
HUNGERFORD Halt	64 69	3	U36
Kelmscott + Langford Halt	62	3	P20
Kidlington for Blenheim	* 64	3	P41
KINGHAM		3	P22
KING'S SUTTON Halt	64 68	3	P43
KINTBURY Halt	* 64 69	3	U36
Lambourn	60	3	U37
Laverton Halt	60	3	P03
Lechlade	62	3	P20
Manningford Halt	* 66	3	U16
Marlborough Low Level	61	3	U26
Milton Halt	51	3	P43
Minety + Ashton Keynes	* 64	3	U09
MORETON·IN·MARSH		3	P23
NEWBURY		3	U46
NEWBURY RACECOURSE		3	U46
Newbury West Fields Halt	57	3	U46
Notgrove	† 62	3	P02
Oaksey Halt	* 64	3	U09
Ogbourne	61	3	U27
Park Leaze Halt	* 64	3	U09
PEWSEY	*	3	U16
Purton	* 64	3	U08
Rollright Halt	51	3	P33
Sarsden Halt	† 62	3	P22
Savernake High Level	58	3	U26
Savernake Low Level for Marlborough	* 61 66	3	U26
SHIPTON Halt	* 66 69	3	P21
Shipton·on·Cherwell Halt	54	3	P41
Shrivenham	* 64	3	U28
South Cerney	61	3	U09
South Leigh	62	3	P30
Speen	60	3	U46
Stanton	53	3	U19
Steventon	* 64	3	U49
Stockcross + Bagnor Halt	60	3	U47
Stow·on·the·Wold	† 62	3	P12
Stratton	53	3	U18
Stratton Park Halt	* 64	3	U18
SWINDON		3	U18
(SWINDON MOREDON)	4	4	U18
Swindon Town	61	3	U18
TACKLEY Halt	* 69	3	P42
Toddington	60 84	5	P03
Uffington	* 64	3	U39
Wantage Road	* 64	3	U49
Welford Park	60	3	U47
Winchcombe	60 86	5	P03
Withington	61	3	P01
Witney	62	3	P30
Woodborough	* 66	3	U16
Woodhay	60	3	U46
Wootton Bassett Junction	* 65	3	U08
Wootton Rivers Halt	* 66	3	U16
Yarnton	62	3	P41

GOODS

No	Name/Location	Closed	Ry	Ref
G 1	Savernake	64	3	U26
2	Marlborough High Level	64	3	U16
3	Witney	70	3	P31

SUMMITS

No	Location	Ht Ft	Ry	Ref
S 1	Savernake		3	U26
2	Notgrove	760	3	P02

WORKS

No	Name	Closed	Ry	Ref
W 1	Swindon	86	3	U18

ENGINE SHEDS

No	Name/Location	Closed to steam	Ry	Ref
E 1	Abingdon	54	3	U49
2	Banbury	66	3	P43
3	Cirencester	64	3	P00
4	Fairford	62	3	P10
5	Faringdon	51	3	U29
6	Kingham	62	3	P22
7	SWINDON	5 64	3	U18

TUNNELS

No	Name/Location	Length	Ry	Ref
T 1	Chedworth	498	3	P01
2	Greet	693	3	P03
3	Chipping Norton	685	3	P32
4	Hook Norton	418	3	P33
5	Marlborough	684	3	U26
6	Ardley	1147	3	P54

JUNCTIONS

No	Name	Ry	Ref
J 1	Wolfhall	3	U26
2	Rushey Platt	3	U18
3	Gloucester	3	U18
4	Flyover (Aynho)	3	P53
5	Cheltenham	3	P43
6	Chipping Norton	3	P22
7	Tramway	3	P23
8	Oxford Road	3	P41
9	Witney	3	P41
10	Blenheim Branch	3	P41

NOTES:

REF All in SP or SU therefore initial S omitted.

§ Older version } Change of name
§ Newer version }

1 On site of station closed during grouping (24).
2 Re-opened 'preserved' line.
3 Regular services ended '53.
4 Proposed re-opening on site of halt closed 24.
5 Modern depot still in use.

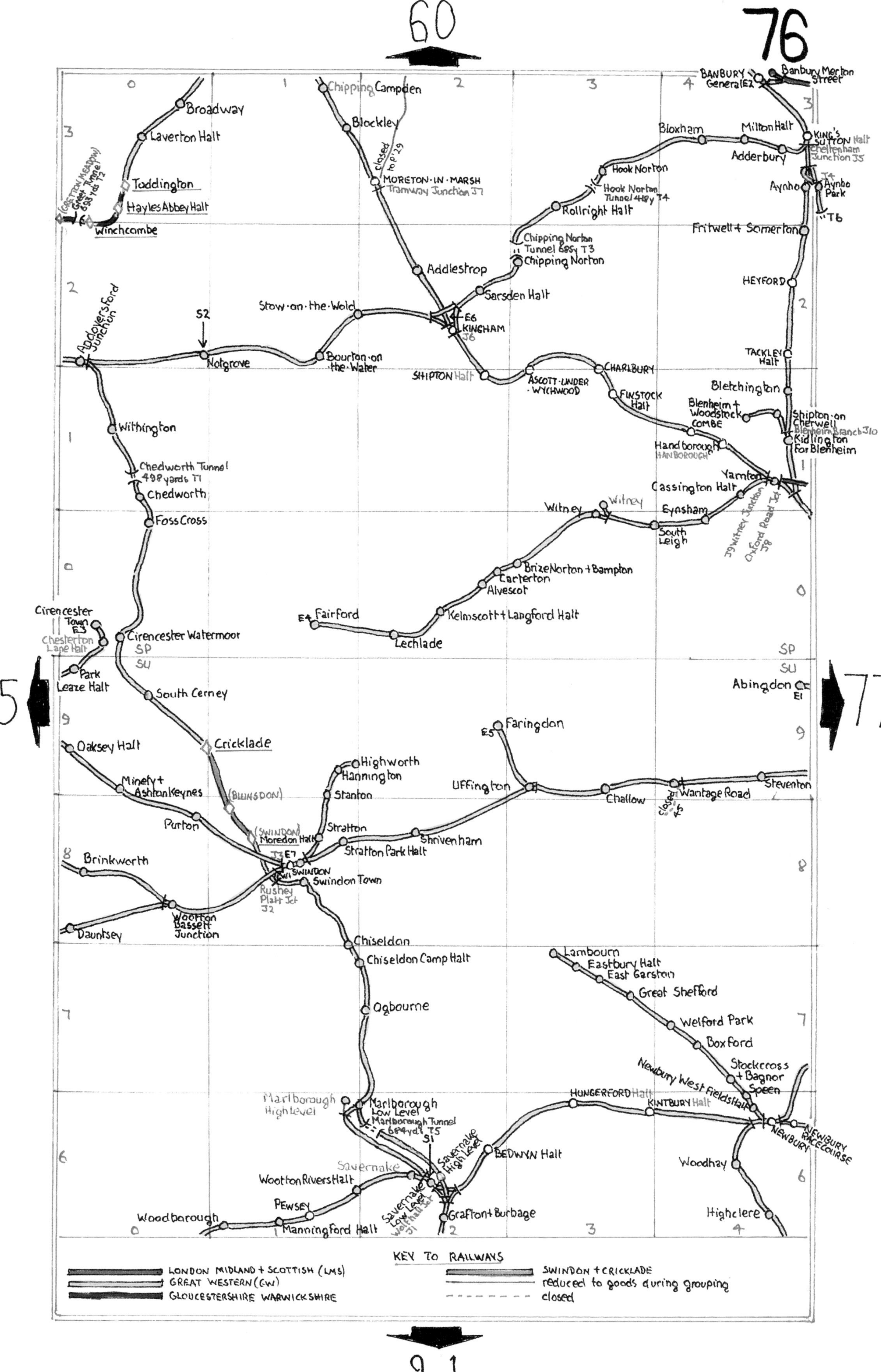

60
76
75
77
91
Chipping Campden
Blockley
closed to P '29
MORETON-IN-MARSH
Tramway Junction J7
Broadway
Laverton Halt
Toddington
Hayles Abbey Halt
Winchcombe
Addlestrop
Stow-on-the-Wold
Notgrove
Bourton-on-the-Water
Andoversford Junction
KINGHAM
SHIPTON Halt
Sarsden Halt
Chipping Norton
Chipping Norton Tunnel 685y T3
Rollright Halt
Hook Norton
Hook Norton Tunnel 418y T4
Bloxham
Milton Halt
Adderbury
BANBURY General E7
Banbury Merton Street
KING'S SUTTON Halt
Cheltenham Junction J5
Aynho
Aynho Park
Fritwell + Somerton
HEYFORD
TACKLEY Halt
Bletchington
Shipton-on-Cherwell
Blenheim Branch J10
Kidlington for Blenheim
Blenheim + Woodstock
COMBE
Handborough
HANBOROUGH
Yarnton
Cassington Halt
Eynsham
South Leigh
Witney
CHARLBURY
FINSTOCK Halt
ASCOTT-UNDER-WYCHWOOD
Withington
Chedworth Tunnel 498 yards T1
Chedworth
Foss Cross
Cirencester Town
Chesterton Lane Halt
Park Leaze Halt
Cirencester Watermoor
South Cerney
Cricklade
(BLUNSDON)
(SWINDON)
Moredon Halt
Brize Norton + Bampton
Carterton
Alvescot
Kelmscott + Langford Halt
Lechlade
Fairford
Abingdon
Faringdon
Uffington
Challow
Wantage Road
Steventon
Oaksey Halt
Minety + Ashton Keynes
Purton
Highworth
Hannington
Stanton
Stratton
Stratton Park Halt
Shrivenham
SWINDON
Swindon Town
Rushey Platt Jct J2
Brinkworth
Dauntsey
Wootton Bassett Junction
Chiseldon
Chiseldon Camp Halt
Ogbourne
Marlborough High Level
Marlborough Low Level
Marlborough Tunnel 684yd T5
Savernake
Savernake High Level
Savernake Low Level
Wolfhall Jct J1
Wootton Rivers Halt
Pewsey
Manningford Halt
Woodborough
Grafton + Burbage
BEDWYN Halt
HUNGERFORD Halt
KINTBURY Halt
Lambourn
Eastbury Halt
East Garston
Great Shefford
Welford Park
Boxford
Stockcross + Bagnor
Speen
Newbury West Fields Halt
NEWBURY
NEWBURY RACECOURSE
Woodhay
Highclere
KEY TO RAILWAYS
LONDON MIDLAND + SCOTTISH (LMS)
GREAT WESTERN (GW)
GLOUCESTERSHIRE WARWICKSHIRE
SWINDON + CRICKLADE
reduced to goods during grouping
closed

VERNEY JUNCTION, DIDCOT + READING

RAILWAYS

No	Company
1	LONDON + NORTH EASTERN (LNE)
13	LNE + GW JOINT
135	LNE, GW + LPTB JOINT
15	LNE + LPTB JOINT
2	LONDON MIDLAND + SCOTTISH (LMS)
3	GREAT WESTERN (GW)
4	SOUTHERN
5	LONDON PASSENGER TRANSPORT BOARD (LPTB)
6	CHOLSEY + WALLINGFORD (ex GW)

STATIONS

Station	Opened / Closed	Ry	Ref
Abingdon	† 63	3	U49
ALDERMASTON Halt	* 64 69	3	U66
AMERSHAM		15	U99
APPLEFORD Halt	69	3	U59
Ardley Halt	† 55 63	3	P52
ASCOT		4	U96
ASPLEY GUISE	*	2	P93
Aston Rowant		3	U79
Aylesbury High Street	50 53	2	P81
AYLESBURY Joint	50	135	P81
Aynho for Deddington	* 64	3	P53
Aynho Park	† 63	3	P43
BAGSHOT		4	U96
BEACONSFIELD		13	U99
BERKHAMSTED		2	P90
BICESTER London Road 1A §	68 68	2	P52
BICESTER TOWN 1A §	87 87	2	P52
BICESTER NORTH 2	49 68 87	3	P52
Blackthorn	53	3	P61
BLACKWATER		4	U86
Bledlow	† 63	3	P70
Bledlow Bridge Halt	57	3	P70
BLETCHLEY		2	P83
BOURNE END		3	U88
BOW BRICKHILL	*	2	P93
Brackley	61	2	P53
Brackley Central	* 66	1	P53
BRACKNELL		4	U86
Brill + Ludgershall	† 63	3	P61
Buckingham	* 64	2	P63
BURNHAM (Bucks)	75	3	U98
Calvert	† 63	1	P62
CAMBERLEY		4	U86
CHALFONT + LATIMER		15	U99
CHEDDINGTON		2	P91
CHESHAM		15	P90
Chinnor	57	3	P70
CHOLSEY + Moulsford	3 ?	3	U58
Churn	† 62	3	U58
Claydon	* 68	2	P72
Compton	† 62	3	U58
COOKHAM		3	U88
CROWTHORNE		4	U86
CULHAM		3	U59
DATCHETT		4	U97
DIDCOT PARKWAY	85	3	U59
Dorton Halt	† 63	3	P61
EARLEY		4	U77
Farthinghoe	52	2	P53
FENNY STRATFORD	*	2	P83
Finmere	† 63	1	P63
Fulwell + Westbury	61	2	P63
FURZE PLATT		3	U88
GERARD'S CROSS		13	U98
GORING + STREATLEY		3	U68
GREAT MISSENDEN		15	P80
HADDENHAM/THAME PARKWAY	† 63 87	13	P70
Hampstead Norris	† 62	3	U57
HENLEY-ON-THAMES		3	U78
Hermitage	† 62	3	U57
HIGH WYCOMBE		13	U89
Horspath Halt	† 63	3	P50
Ilmer Halt	† 63	13	P70
ISLIP	68 89	2	P51
KING'S SUTTON Halt	* 64 68	3	P53
Kingston Crossing Halt	57	3	U79
Launton	* 68	2	P62
LEIGHTON BUZZARD		2	P92
Lewknor Bridge Halt	57	3	U79
LIDLINGTON	*	2	P93
LITTLE KIMBLE		13	P80
Littlemore	† 63	3	P50
LONGCROSS Halt	69	4	U96
Loudwater	70	3	U89
MAIDENHEAD		3	U88
MARLOW	4	3	U88
Marsh Gibbon + Poundon	* 68	2	P62
Marston Gate	53	2	P81
MARTINS HERON	88	4	U86
MIDGHAM Halt	* 64 69	3	U56
MILTON KEYNES CENTRAL	82	2	P83
MONKS RISBOROUGH + Whiteleaf Halt	5 69 74 86 86	13	P80
Morris Cowley	† 63	2	P50
MORTIMER		3	U66
OXFORD General	48 55	3	P50
Oxford Rewley Road	51	2	P50
Padbury	* 64	2	P73
PANGBOURNE		3	U67
Pinewood Halt	† 62	3	U57
PRINCES RISBOROUGH		3	P70
QUAINTON ROAD	6 † 63	15	P71
Radclive Halt	56 61	2	P63
RADLEY		3	U59
READING General	49 66	3	U77
Reading South Southern	7 49 65	4	U77
READING WEST		3	U67
RIDGEMONT	*	2	P93
SANDHURST Halt	69	4	U86
SAUNDERTON		13	U89
SEER GREEN + Jordans	50 74	13	U99
SHIPLAKE		3	U77
SLOUGH		3	U98
Slough Estate	56	3	U98
South Aylesbury Halt	67	13	P81
Stanbridgeford	62	2	P92
STOKE MANDEVILLE		15	P81
SUNNINGDALE		4	U96
SUNNYMEADS		4	U97
Swanbourne	* 68	2	P82
TAPLOW		3	U98
Thame	† 63	3	P70
THAME PARKWAY, HADDENHAM +	63 87	13	P70
THATCHAM Halt	64 69	3	U56
THEALE Halt	64 69	3	U67
Tiddington	† 63	3	P60
TILEHURST		3	U67
Towersey Halt	† 63	3	P70
TRING		2	P91
TWYFORD		3	U77
Upton + Blewbury	† 62	3	U58
Verney Junction	* 68	215	P72
VIRGINIA WATER		4	U96
Wainhill Halt	57	3	P70
Wallingford	59 67 68	6	U58
WARGRAVE		3	U77
Water Stratford Halt	56 61	2	P63
Watlington	57	3	U69
WENDOVER		15	P80
West Wycombe	58	13	U89
Wheatley	† 63	3	P50
WINDSOR + ETON CENTRAL	49	3	U97
WINDSOR + ETON RIVERSIDE	49	4	U97
WINNERSH Halt	69	4	U77
WINNERSH TRIANGLE	86	4	U77
Winslow	* 68	2	P72
WOBURN SANDS	*	2	P93
WOKINGHAM		4	U86
Wooburn Green	70	3	U98
Wotton	53	1	P71

ENGINE SHEDS

No	Name/Location	Closed Steam	Ry	Ref
E 1	Abingdon	54	3	U49
2	AYLESBURY	8 62	3	P81
3	BLETCHLEY	8 62	2	P83
4	Didcot	65	3	U59
5	Henley-on-Thames	58	3	U78
6	Leighton Buzzard	62	2	P92
7	Marlow	62	3	U88
8	Oxford	67	3	P50
9	Oxford	50	2	P50
10	Reading	65	3	U67
11	Reading	65	4	U77
12	Wallingford	56	3	U58
13	Watlington	57	3	U69

TUNNELS

No	Name	Length	Ry	Ref
T 1	Bagshot	121	4	U96
2	Northchurch	349	2	P90
3	Whitehouse	352	3	U99
4	Wheatley	524	3	P50
5	Ardley	1147	3	P52
6	Saunderton	88	3	P80
7	Brill	191	3	P61
8	Wolvercot	145	2	P51

SUMMITS

No	Name	Height	Ry	Ref
S 1	Dutchlands		15	P80
2	Tring		2	P91

JUNCTIONS

No	Name	Ry	Ref
J 1	Flyover (Aynho)	3	P53
2	Cheltenham	3	P53
3	Bedford Line	2	P83
4	Oxford Line	2	P83
5	Dunstable Branch	2	P92
6	Aylesbury Branch	2	P91
7	Ashendon	21	P61
8	Grendon Underwood	1	P72
9	Buckingham Branch	2	P72
10	Aylesbury Line	152	P72
11	Oxford Road	2	P51
12	Chalfont	15	U99
13	Marlow Branch	3	U88
14	Bath Road	3	U97
15	Windsor Branch	3	U98
16	Oxford Road	3	U67
17	Basingstoke Line	3	U77
18	Foxhall	3	U59
19	Kennington	3	P50
20	Henley Branch	3	U77
21	Shepherd's Furze	1	P62
22	Abingdon Branch	3	U59

NOTES:

REF In SP or SU. Initial S omitted

§ Older version } Change of name
§ Modern version

The double blue underline shows stations still in use and both of main line status AND Underground. Single underline shows station once part of both systems but at 12/93 only part of one system. ie: CHESHAM only Underground — AYLESBURY only main line.

1. Closed as London Road in 68. Re-opened as Town 87.
2. NORTH added 49, dropped 68, then again re-added 87
3. Date Moulsford dropped unclear. Preserved line extended to here but after 12/93.
4. Rebuilt in 67 on altered alignment.
5. Halt dropped from title 69. Whiteleaf dropped from title 74. Station closed for a short time in 86.
6. Closed for regular services as is shown. But continues in use for excursions.
7. South added to title in 1949. changed to Southern in 1961.
8. Modern depot still in use.

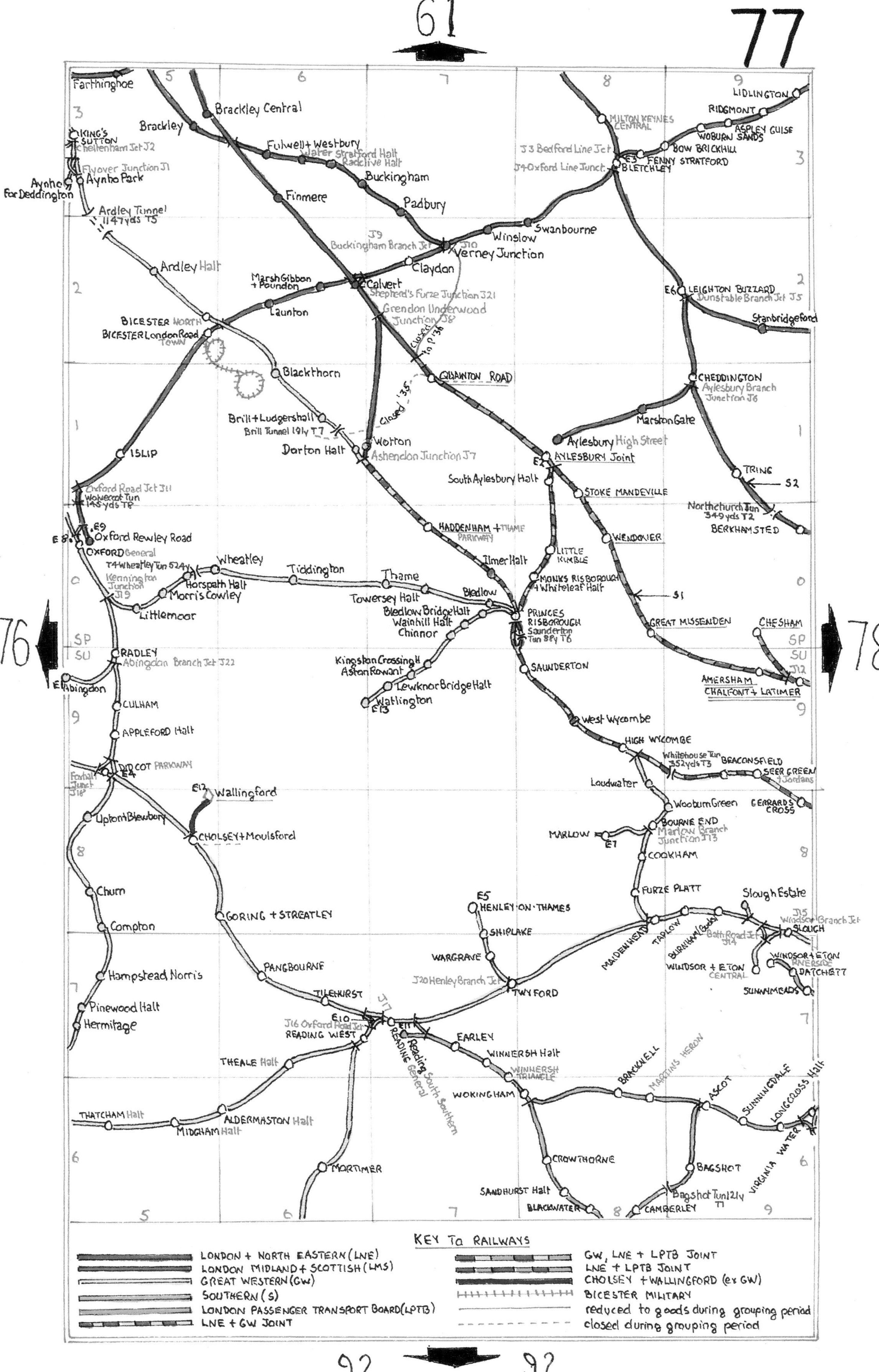
61
76
78
92
Farthinghoe
Brackley
Brackley Central
Fulwell + Westbury
Water Stratford Halt
Radclive Halt
Buckingham
Padbury
Finmere
KING'S SUTTON
Cheltenham Jct J2
Flyover Junction J1
Aynho Park
Aynho For Deddington
Ardley Tunnel 1147yds T5
Ardley Halt
Buckingham Branch Jct J9
J10
Verney Junction
Winslow
Swanbourne
Claydon
Marsh Gibbon + Poundon
Calvert
Shepherd's Furze Junction J21
Grendon Underwood Junction J8
Launton
BICESTER NORTH
BICESTER London Road TOWN
Blackthorn
QUAINTON ROAD
Brill + Ludgershall
Brill Tunnel 191y T7
Dorton Halt
Wotton
Ashendon Junction J7
ISLIP
Oxford Road Jct J11
Wolvercot Tun 145yds T8
Oxford Rewley Road
OXFORD General
T4 Wheatley Tun 524y
Kennington Junction J19
Wheatley
Horspath Halt
Morris Cowley
Littlemore
Tiddington
Thame
Towersey Halt
Bledlow
Bledlow Bridge Halt
Wainhill Halt
Chinnor
Kingston Crossing H
Aston Rowant
Lewknor Bridge Halt
Watlington
HADDENHAM + THAME PARKWAY
Ilmer Halt
LITTLE KIMBLE
MONKS RISBOROUGH + Whiteleaf Halt
PRINCES RISBOROUGH
Saunderton Tun 88y T6
SAUNDERTON
South Aylesbury Halt
Aylesbury High Street
AYLESBURY Joint
STOKE MANDEVILLE
WENDOVER
GREAT MISSENDEN
MILTON KEYNES CENTRAL
J3 Bedford Line Jct
J4 Oxford Line Junct
BLETCHLEY
FENNY STRATFORD
BOW BRICKHILL
WOBURN SANDS
ASPLEY GUISE
RIDGMONT
LIDLINGTON
LEIGHTON BUZZARD
Dunstable Branch Jct J5
Stanbridgeford
CHEDDINGTON
Aylesbury Branch Junction J6
Marston Gate
TRING
Northchurch Tun 349yds T2
BERKHAMSTED
CHESHAM
AMERSHAM
CHALFONT + LATIMER
RADLEY
Abingdon Branch Jct J22
Abingdon
CULHAM
APPLEFORD Halt
DIDCOT PARKWAY
Foxhall Junct J18
Upton + Blewbury
Wallingford
CHOLSEY + Moulsford
Churn
Compton
Hampstead Norris
Pinewood Halt
Hermitage
GORING + STREATLEY
PANGBOURNE
TILEHURST
J16 Oxford Road Jct
READING WEST
Reading General
Reading South Southern
THEALE Halt
THATCHAM Halt
MIDGHAM Halt
ALDERMASTON Halt
MORTIMER
West Wycombe
HIGH WYCOMBE
Whitehouse Tun 352yds T3
BEACONSFIELD
SEER GREEN + Jordans
GERRARDS CROSS
Loudwater
Wooburn Green
BOURNE END
Marlow Branch Junction J13
MARLOW
COOKHAM
FURZE PLATT
MAIDENHEAD
TAPLOW
BURNHAM (Bucks)
Bath Road Jct J14
Slough Estate
Windsor Branch Jct J15
SLOUGH
WINDSOR + ETON CENTRAL
WINDSOR + ETON RIVERSIDE
DATCHET
SUNNYMEADS
HENLEY ON THAMES
SHIPLAKE
WARGRAVE
J20 Henley Branch Jct
TWYFORD
EARLEY
WINNERSH Halt
WINNERSH TRIANGLE
WOKINGHAM
BRACKNELL
MARTINS HERON
ASCOT
SUNNINGDALE
LONGCROSS Halt
VIRGINIA WATER
CROWTHORNE
SANDHURST Halt
BLACKWATER
BAGSHOT
Bagshot Tun 121y T1
CAMBERLEY
Closed '35
Closed '35 to P
KEY TO RAILWAYS
LONDON + NORTH EASTERN (LNE)
LONDON MIDLAND + SCOTTISH (LMS)
GREAT WESTERN (GW)
SOUTHERN (S)
LONDON PASSENGER TRANSPORT BOARD (LPTB)
LNE + GW JOINT
GW, LNE + LPTB JOINT
LNE + LPTB JOINT
CHOLSEY + WALLINGFORD (ex GW)
BICESTER MILITARY
reduced to goods during grouping period
closed during grouping period

HITCHIN, ST ALBANS + LONDON

RAILWAYS

No.	Company
1	LONDON + NORTH EASTERN (LNE)
2	LONDON MIDLAND + SCOTTISH (LMS)
3	GREAT WESTERN (GW)
4	SOUTHERN (S)
5	LONDON PASSENGER TRANSPORT BOARD (LPTB) + successors
13	LNE + GW
135	LNE, GW + LONDON TRANSPORT
15	LNE + LPTB
25	LMS + LPTB
35	GW + LONDON TRANSPORT

STATIONS

Station	Opened Closed	Ry	Ref
ABBEY WOOD		4	Q47
ADDISCOMBE (Croydon)	55	4	Q36
ADDLESTONE		4	Q06
ALBANY PARK		4	Q47
Ampthill	59	2	L03
ANGEL ROAD		1	Q39
APSLEY		2	L00
ARLESEY + Henlow	59 88	1	L13
ARNOS GROVE		5	Q39
ASHFORD		4	Q07
ASHWELL + MORDEN		1	L33
Ayot	48	1	L21
BALDOCK		1	L12
BANSTEAD		4	Q26
BARNEHURST		4	Q47
BAYFORD		1	L30
BECONTREE		5	Q48
BEDLINGTON LANE Halt	69	4	Q36
BELMONT		4	Q26
BELVEDERE		4	Q47
BEXLEY		4	Q47
BEXLEYHEATH		4	Q47
Bingham Road	83	4	Q36
BISHOPS STORTFORD		1	L42
BOUNDS GREEN		5	Q39
BOWES PARK		1	Q39
Braughing	*64	1	L32
BRICKET WOOD	*	2	L10
BRIMSDOWN		1	Q39
BROOKMANS PARK		1	L20
BROXBOURNE		1	L30
BUCKHURST HILL		5	Q49
Buntingford	*64	1	L32
Burnt Mill	A § 60	1	L41
BUSHEY + Oxhey		2	Q19
BUSH HILL PARK		1	Q39
BYFLEET + NEW HAW	B § 62	4	Q06
CANONS PARK		5	Q19
Carpenders Park	]52	2	Q19
CARPENDERS PARK	]52	2	Q19
CARSHALTON		4	Q26
CARSHALTON BEECHES		4	Q26
CASTLE BAR PARK Halt	69	3	Q18
CHALFONT + LATIMER		15	Q09
CHADWELL HEATH		1	Q48
CHEAM		4	Q26
CHELSFIELD		4	Q46
CHERTSEY		4	Q06
CHESHUNT		1	L30
CHESSINGTON NORTH		4	Q16
CHESSINGTON SOUTH		4	Q16
CHIGWELL		5	Q49
Chigwell Lane	C § 49	5	Q49
Chiltern Green For Luton Hoo	52	2	L11
CHINGFORD		1	Q39
CHORLEY WOOD + Chenies		15	Q09
CLAYGATE		4	Q16
COCKFOSTERS		5	Q29
Cole Green	51	1	L21
Colnbrook	*65	3	Q07
Colnbrook Estate Halt	* 61 65	3	Q07
Coombe Road	† 83	4	Q36
Coulsdon North	83	4	Q36
Cowley	† 62	3	Q08
CREWS HILL		1	L30
CROXLEY Green	49	5	Q09
CROXLEY GREEN	*	2	Q09
CUFFLEY + Goff's Oak	71	1	L30
DAGENHAM DOCK		2	Q48
DAGENHAM HEATHWAY		5	Q48
(DEBDEN)	C § 49	5	Q49
DENHAM		13	Q08
DENHAM GOLF CLUB Platform	54	13	Q08
DRAYTON GREEN Halt	69	3	Q18
Dunstable North	* 50 65	2	L02
Dunstable Town	* 65	1	L02
EASTCOTE		5	Q18
EAST CROYDON		4	Q36
EDGWARE		5	Q29
EDMONTON GREEN	D § 92	1	Q39
EGHAM		4	Q07
ELSTREE + Boreham Wood	53 74	2	Q19
ENFIELD CHASE		1	Q39
ENFIELD LOCK		1	Q39
ENFIELD TOWN		1	Q39
EPPING		5	L40
EPSOM		4	Q26
ESHER		4	Q16
EWELL EAST		4	Q26
EWELL WEST		4	Q26
FELTHAM		4	Q17
FLITWICK		2	L03
FULWELL		4	Q17
GARSTON	66	2	L10
GERRARD'S CROSS		13	Q08
GORDON HILL		1	Q39
GRANGE HILL		5	Q49
GRANGE PARK		1	Q39
Greenford	71	135	Q18
HACKBRIDGE		4	Q26
Hadham	*64	1	L41
HADLEY WOOD		1	Q29
HAINAULT		5	Q49
HAMPTON		4	Q17
HAMPTON COURT		4	Q16
HANWELL + Elthorne	74	3	Q18
HARLINGTON		2	L03
HARLOW MILL	60	1	L41
HARLOW TOWN	A § 60	1	L41
HARPENDEN Central	50 66	2	L11
Harpenden East	* 50 65	1	L11
HARROW + WEALDSTONE		25	Q18
HARROW-ON-THE-HILL		25	Q18
HATCH END		3	Q19
HATFIELD		1	L20
(HATTON CROSS)	75	5	Q07
HAYES		4	Q46
HAYES + HARLINGTON		3	Q18
HEADSTONE LANE		2	Q19
HEATHROW TERMINALS 1, 2 + 3	77	5	Q08
HEATHROW TERMINAL 4	86	5	Q08
HEMEL HEMPSTEAD + Boxmoor		2	L00
Henlow Camp	62	2	L13
HERSHAM		4	Q16
HERTFORD EAST		1	L31
HERTFORD NORTH		1	L31
Hertingfordbury	51	1	L31
HIGHAMS PARK + Hale End		1	Q39
HIGH BARNET		5	Q29
Hill End	51	5	L10
HILLINGDON		5	Q08
HINCHLEY WOOD		4	Q16
HITCHIN		1	L12
HOUNSLOW		4	Q17
HOUNSLOW CENTRAL		5	Q17
HOUNSLOW EAST		5	Q17
HOUNSLOW WEST		5	Q17
How Wood	88	2	L10
ICKENHAM		5	Q08
ISLEWORTH for Spring Grove		4	Q17
IVER		3	Q08
KEMPTON PARK		4	Q17
KENLEY		4	Q36
KINGS LANGLEY + Abbot's Langley		2	L00
KNEBWORTH		1	L22
KNOCKHOLT		4	Q46
LANGLEY		3	Q08
LEAGRAVE		2	L02
LETCHWORTH		1	L23
LOUGHTON		5	Q49
Lower Edmonton	D § 92	1	Q39
Luton Bute Street	* 56 65	1	L02
LUTON Midland Road	50 65	2	L02
Luton Hoo	* 65	1	L11
MALDEN MANOR		4	Q26
Mardock	* 64	1	L31
MILLBROOK	*	2	L03
MILL HILL BROADWAY	50	2	Q29
MOOR PARK + Sandy Lodge		15	Q09
Napsbury	59	2	L10
Nast Hyde Halt	51	1	L20
NEW BARNET		1	Q29
NEW SOUTHGATE + Friern Barnet	71	1	Q29
NORTH HARROW		5	Q18
(NORTHOLT)	48	5	Q18
NORTHOLT PARK Village	55	1	Q18
NORTH WEALD		5	L40
Northwood	61	15	Q09
Northwood Hills	61	15	Q19
OAKLEIGH PARK		1	Q29
OAKWOOD		5	Q39
ORPINGTON		4	Q46
OSTERLEY		5	Q17
OXSHOTT + Fairmile		4	Q16
PALMERS GREEN		1	Q39
PARK STREET + Frogmore	* 74	2	L10
PETTS WOOD		4	Q46
PINNER		5	Q18
PONDERS END		1	Q39
POTTERS BAR + South Mimms	74	2	L20
Poyle Estate Halt	* 54 65	3	Q07
Poyle For Stanwell Moor Halt	* 65	3	Q07
PURLEY		4	Q36
PURLEY OAKS		4	Q36
RADLETT		2	L10
RAYNERS LANE		5	Q18
REEDHAM		4	Q36
RICKMANSWORTH		15	Q09
Rickmansworth Church Street	50 52	2	Q09
RIDDLESDOWN		4	Q36
RODING VALLEY		5	Q47
ROYDON		1	L41
RUISLIP		5	Q08
(Ruislip Gardens)	2 58 48	135	Q18
RUISLIP MANOR		5	Q18
RYE HOUSE		1	L31
ST ALBANS ABBEY	*	2	L10
ST ALBANS City	68	2	L10
St Albans London Road	51	1	L10
ST HELIER		4	Q26
ST MARGARET'S		1	L31
SANDERSTEAD		4	Q36
SAWBRIDGEWORTH		1	L41
Selsdon	† 83	4	Q36
Shefford	62	2	L13
SHEPPERTON		4	Q06
SILVER STREET		1	Q39
Smallford	51	1	L10
SMITHAM		4	Q36
SOUTHGATE		5	Q39
SOUTHALL		3	Q18
SOUTHBURY	60	1	Q39
SOUTH CROYDON		4	Q36
SOUTH GREENFORD Halt	69	3	Q18
SOUTH HARROW		5	Q18
SOUTH RUISLIP	3	135	Q18
Staines West	* 49 65	3	Q07
STAINES Junction Central	4 49 66	4	Q07
Standon	* 64	1	L32
STANMORE		5	Q19
Stanmore Village	52	2	Q19
Stevenage	5 73	1	L22
STEVENAGE	5 73	1	L22
STONELEIGH		4	Q26
STRAWBERRY HILL		4	Q17
SUDBURY HILL		5	Q18
SUDBURY HILL + HARROW		1	Q18
SUNBURY		4	Q17
SUNNYMEADS		4	Q07
SUTTON		4	Q26
SUTTON COMMON		4	Q26
THAMES DITTON		4	Q16
THEOBALD'S GROVE	60	1	L30
THEYDON BOIS		5	Q49
Three Counties	59	1	L13
TOLWORTH		4	Q16
TOTTERIDGE + WHETSTONE		5	Q29
TURKEY STREET	60	1	Q39
UPPER HALLIFORD Halt	69	4	Q06
UXBRIDGE		5	Q08
Uxbridge Vine Street	† 62	3	Q08
VIRGINIA WATER		4	Q06
WADDON		4	Q36
WADDON MARSH Halt	69	4	Q36
WALLINGTON		4	Q26
WALTHAM CROSS + Abbey	69	1	L30
WALTON-ON-THAMES		4	Q06
WARE		1	L31
WATFORD		5	Q19
WATFORD HIGH STREET		2	Q19
WATFORD JUNCTION		2	Q19
WATFORD NORTH	*	2	Q19
WATFORD STADIUM	82	2	Q19
WATFORD WEST	*	2	Q19
WATTON-AT-STONE	82	1	L31
WELHAM GREEN	86	1	L20
WELWYN GARDEN CITY		1	L21
WELWYN NORTH		1	L21
WEST BYFLEET		4	Q06
WEST CROYDON		4	Q36
WEST DRAYTON + Yiewsley		3	Q08
WEST EALING		3	Q18
WEST FINCHLEY		5	Q29
WEST HARROW		5	Q18
West Mill	* 64	1	L32
WEST RUISLIP		135	Q08
WEST SUTTON		4	Q26
West Weybridge	B § 62	4	Q06
WEST WICKHAM		4	Q36
WEYBRIDGE		4	Q06
Wheathampstead	* 65	1	L11
WHITTON		4	Q17
Widford	* 64	1	L31
WINCHMORE HILL		1	Q39
WOODFORD		5	Q49
WOODSIDE		4	Q36
WOODSIDE PARK		5	Q29
WORCESTER PARK		4	Q26
WRAYSBURY		4	Q07
Yeoveney Halt	62	3	Q07

GOODS

No	Name/Location	Closed	Ry	Ref
G1	Heath Park	59	2	L00
2	Dunstable	67	2	L02
3	Hitchin	64	2	L13
4	Langford	64	1	L13
5	Uxbridge High Street	64	3	Q08
6	Edgware	64	1	Q19

ENGINE SHEDS

No	Name/Location	Closed	Ry	Ref
E1	Bishops Stortford	60	1	L42
2	Enfield	60	1	Q30
3	Epping	57	1	L40
4	Feltham	67	4	Q17
5	Hatfield	61	1	L20
6	Hertford	60	1	L31
7	Hitchin	61	1	L13
8	St Albans	60	2	L10
9	Southall	65	3	Q18
10	Watford	65	2	Q19

TUNNELS 6

No	Name/Location	Length	Ry	Ref
T1	Ampthill	716	2	L03
2	Welwyn North	1047	1	L21
3	Welwyn South	447	1	L21
4	Ponsbourne	2684	1	L30
5	Watford Fast	1815	2	L00
6	Watford Slow	1990	2	L00
7	Potters Bar	1214	1	L20
8	Molewood	364	1	L31
9	Elstree Old (Fast)	1050	2	Q19
10	Elstree New (Slow)	1058	2	Q19
11	Hadley Wood North	232	1	Q29
12	Hadley Wood South	384	1	Q29
13	Barnet	605	1	Q29
14	Chelsfield	597	4	Q46
15	Polhill	2611	4	Q46
16	Riddlesdown	837	4	Q36

BRIDGES + VIADUCTS

No	Name	Ry	Ref
V1	Digswell (Welwyn)	1	L21

JUNCTIONS

No	Name		Ry	Ref
J1	Buntingford Branch		1	L31
2	Stockley Bridge	7	30	Q08
3	Bury Street		1	Q39

NOTES:

Ref: In TL or TQ so initial T omitted

§ Old name } Change of name
§ New name }

identical letters indicate alternative name

] Later station is on adjoining site

1. Main line station closed 58 'Underground' opened in 48
2. Main line station closed 58 'Underground' opened in 48
3. 'Underground' opened in 48
4. Junction became Central in 49 but suffix dropped in 66
5. Station site changed in 73
6. Tunnels on 'Underground' are ignored.
7. Proposed Junction for new line planned to Heathrow Terminals, line is showned ---- on map.

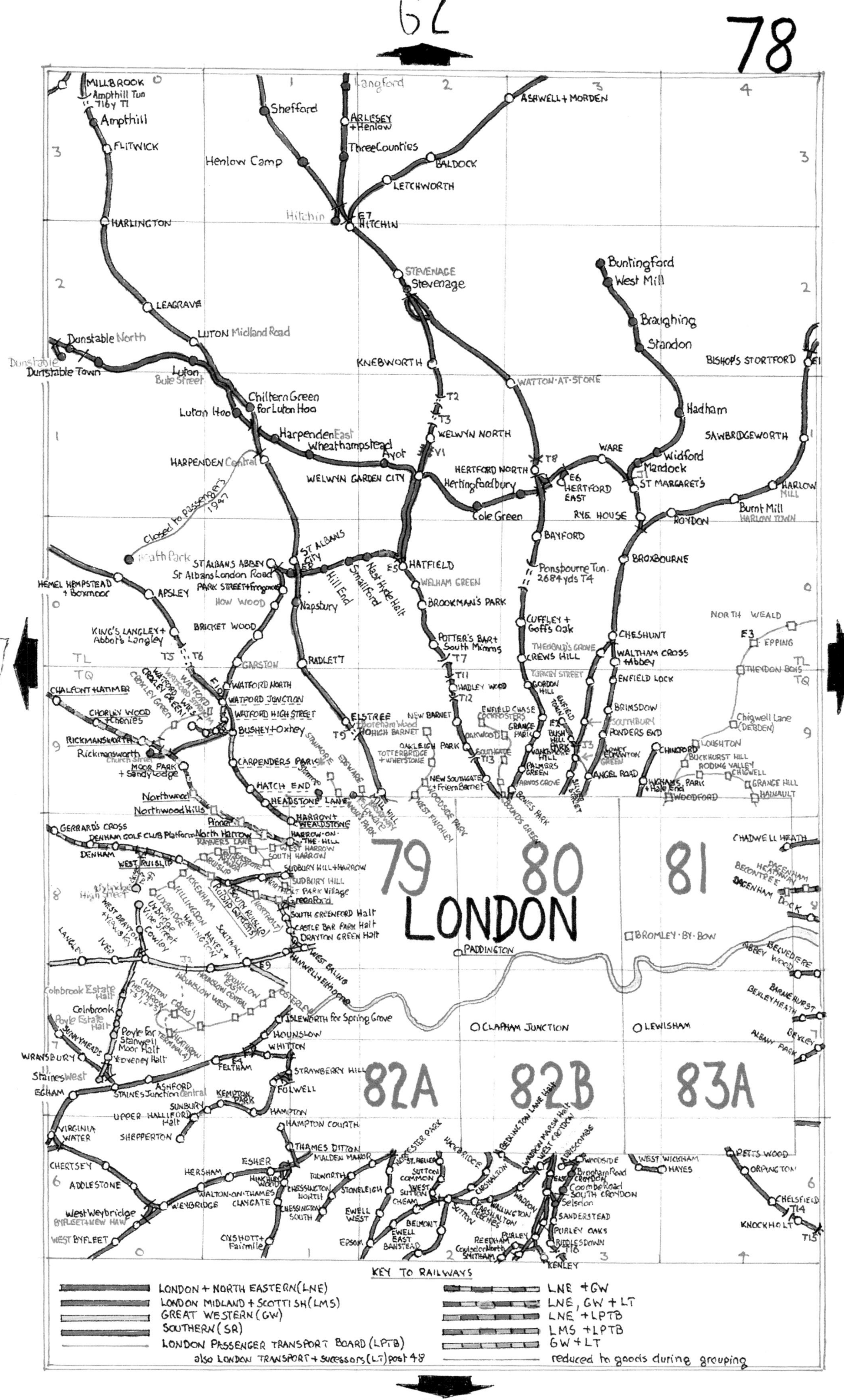

62
77
85
93
79
80
81
82A
82B
83A
LONDON
TL
TQ
MILLBROOK
Ampthill Tun 716y T1
Ampthill
FLITWICK
HARLINGTON
LEAGRAVE
LUTON Midland Road
Dunstable North
Dunstable
Dunstable Town
Luton
Bute Street
Chiltern Green for Luton Hoo
Luton Hoo
Harpenden East
Wheathampstead
HARPENDEN Central
Closed to passengers 1947
Heath Park
Shefford
Langford
ARLESEY + Henlow
Three Counties
Henlow Camp
Hitchin
E7
HITCHIN
ASHWELL + MORDEN
BALDOCK
LETCHWORTH
STEVENAGE
Stevenage
KNEBWORTH
T2
T3
WELWYN NORTH
V1
Ayot
WELWYN GARDEN CITY
WATTON-AT-STONE
HERTFORD NORTH
Hertingfordbury
Cole Green
T8
E6
HERTFORD EAST
Buntingford
West Mill
Braughing
Standon
Hadham
Widford
Mardock
WARE
ST MARGARET'S
RYE HOUSE
BISHOP'S STORTFORD
SAWBRIDGEWORTH
HARLOW MILL
Burnt Mill
HARLOW TOWN
ROYDON
BROXBOURNE
BAYFORD
Ponsbourne Tun. 2684 yds T4
CUFFLEY + Goff's Oak
THEOBALD'S GROVE
CREWS HILL
CHESHUNT
WALTHAM CROSS + Abbey
ENFIELD LOCK
BRIMSDOWN
PONDERS END
NORTH WEALD
E3
EPPING
THEYDON BOIS
Chigwell Lane (DEBDEN)
LOUGHTON
BUCKHURST HILL
RODING VALLEY
CHIGWELL
GRANGE HILL
HAINAULT
CHINGFORD
WOODFORD
ANGEL ROAD
ST ALBANS ABBEY
St Albans London Road
ST ALBANS CITY
PARK STREET + Frogmore
HOW WOOD
Hill End
Smallford
Nast Hyde Halt
Napsbury
HATFIELD
E5
WELHAM GREEN
BROOKMAN'S PARK
POTTER'S BAR + South Mimms
T7
T11
HADLEY WOOD
T12
HEMEL HEMPSTEAD + Boxmoor
APSLEY
KING'S LANGLEY + Abbot's Langley
T5
T6
BRICKET WOOD
GARSTON
RADLETT
WATFORD NORTH
WATFORD JUNCTION
WATFORD HIGH STREET
BUSHEY + Oxhey
ELSTREE
T9
Boreham Wood
HIGH BARNET
NEW BARNET
ENFIELD CHASE
COCKFOSTERS
OAKWOOD
GRANGE PARK
OAKLEIGH PARK
TOTTERIDGE + WHETSTONE
SOUTHGATE
T13
NEW SOUTHGATE + Friern Barnet
PALMERS GREEN
ARNOS GROVE
BOWES PARK
BOUNDS GREEN
WOODSIDE PARK
WEST FINCHLEY
GORDON HILL
TURKEY STREET
ENFIELD TOWN
BUSH HILL PARK
SOUTHBURY
WINCHMORE HILL
CHALFONT + LATIMER
CHORLEY WOOD + Chenies
CROXLEY GREEN
RICKMANSWORTH
Rickmansworth Church Street
MOOR PARK + Sandy Lodge
CARPENDERS PARK
HATCH END
HEADSTONE LANE
STANMORE
EDGWARE
Northwood
Northwood Hills
Pinner
North Harrow
HARROW + WEALDSTONE
HARROW-ON-THE-HILL
WEST HARROW
SOUTH HARROW
RAYNERS LANE
SUDBURY HILL + HARROW
SUDBURY HILL
NORTHOLT PARK
GREENFORD
SOUTH GREENFORD Halt
CASTLE BAR PARK Halt
DRAYTON GREEN Halt
WEST EALING
HANWELL + ELTHORNE
GERRARD'S CROSS
DENHAM GOLF CLUB Platform
DENHAM
WEST RUISLIP
RUISLIP
ICKENHAM
HILLINGDON
UXBRIDGE
High Street
Vine Street
Cowley
WEST DRAYTON + Yiewsley
HAYES + HARLINGTON
SOUTHALL
LANGLEY
IVER
T2
E9
HOUNSLOW EAST
HOUNSLOW CENTRAL
HOUNSLOW WEST
OSTERLEY
Colnbrook Estate Halt
Colnbrook
Poyle Estate Halt
Poyle for Stanwell Moor Halt
Yeoveney Halt
SUNNYMEADS
WRAYSBURY
Staines West
EGHAM
ISLEWORTH for Spring Grove
HOUNSLOW
WHITTON
FELTHAM
ASHFORD
STAINES Junction Central
STRAWBERRY HILL
FULWELL
KEMPTON PARK
SUNBURY
UPPER HALLIFORD Halt
HAMPTON
SHEPPERTON
VIRGINIA WATER
HAMPTON COURT
THAMES DITTON
MALDEN MANOR
CHERTSEY
ADDLESTONE
HERSHAM
ESHER
WALTON-ON-THAMES
WEYBRIDGE
West Weybridge
BYFLEET + NEW HAW
WEST BYFLEET
CLAYGATE
OXSHOTT + Fairmile
TOLWORTH
CHESSINGTON NORTH
CHESSINGTON SOUTH
STONELEIGH
EWELL WEST
EPSOM
WORCESTER PARK
ST. HELIER
SUTTON COMMON
WEST SUTTON
CHEAM
BELMONT
EWELL EAST
BANSTEAD
SUTTON
HACKBRIDGE
CARSHALTON
CARSHALTON BEECHES
WALLINGTON
WADDON
BEDDINGTON LANE Halt
WADDON MARSH Halt
WEST CROYDON
EAST CROYDON
LOUGHBOROUGH JUNCTION
ADDISCOMBE
WOODSIDE
Bingham Road
Coombe Road
SOUTH CROYDON
Selsdon
SANDERSTEAD
PURLEY OAKS
PURLEY
RIDDLESDOWN
KENLEY
REEDHAM
Coulsdon North
SMITHAM
T16
WEST WICKHAM
HAYES
PETTS WOOD
ORPINGTON
CHELSFIELD
T14
KNOCKHOLT
T15
CHADWELL HEATH
DAGENHAM HEATHWAY
BECONTREE
DAGENHAM DOCK
BROMLEY-BY-BOW
PADDINGTON
BELVEDERE
ABBEY WOOD
BARNEHURST
BEXLEYHEATH
BEXLEY
ALBANY PARK
CLAPHAM JUNCTION
LEWISHAM
KEY TO RAILWAYS
LONDON + NORTH EASTERN (LNE)
LONDON MIDLAND + SCOTTISH (LMS)
GREAT WESTERN (GW)
SOUTHERN (SR)
LONDON PASSENGER TRANSPORT BOARD (LPTB)
also LONDON TRANSPORT + successors (LT) post 48
LNE + GW
LNE, GW + LT
LNE + LPTB
LMS + LPTB
GW + LT
reduced to goods during grouping

LONDON NORTH WEST

KEY TO RAILWAYS

No	Railway
1	LONDON + NORTH EASTERN (LNE)
2	LONDON MIDLAND + SCOTTISH (LMS)
3	GREAT WESTERN (GW)
4	SOUTHERN (S)
5	LONDON PASSENGER TRANSPORT BOARD (LPTB) SEE NOTE (JOINT LINE with main line company)
5	LPTB (underground only lines) SEE NOTES
15	LNER + LPTB JOINT
23	LMS + GW JOINT (WEST LONDON)
234	LMS, GW + S JOINT (WEST LONDON EXTENSION)
25	LMS + LPTB JOINT
35	GW + LPTB JOINT
45	S + LPTB JOINT
	lines reduced to goods before nationalisation.

NOTE: LINES shown as joint LPTB and main line are not always true joint lines. Some cases are true joint lines with both services using the same tracks but more often the 'underground' lines use separately dedicated tracks. With joint underground lines where two lines use the same route they too can use the same or different lines and in some cases lines will be at different levels For example Piccadilly runs under the District at Earls Court.

STATIONS

Station	Opened Closed	Ry	Ref
ACTON CENTRAL	*	2	28
ACTON MAIN LINE	49	3	28
ACTON TOWN		5	17
ACTON see also under N,S,E+W			
ALPERTON		5	18
BARNES		4	27
BARNES BRIDGE		4	27
BARONS COURT		5	27
BAYSWATER		5	28
Belmont	* 64	2	19
BOSTON MANOR		5	17
BRENT (CROSS)	76	5	28
BRENTFORD Central	50 84	4	17
BRONDESBURY	*	2	28
BRONDESBURY PARK	*	2	28
BURNT OAK		5	29
CANONS PARK		5	19
CASTLE BAR PARK Halt	69	3	18
CHISWICK		4	27
CHISWICK PARK		5	27
COLINDALE		5	29
CRICKLEWOOD		2	28
DOLLIS HILL		5	28
DRAYTON GREEN Halt	69	3	18
EALING BROADWAY		35	18
EALING COMMON		5	18
EARLS COURT		5	27
EAST ACTON		5	28
EAST PUTNEY		5	27
FINCHLEY CENTRAL		5	28
FINCHLEY ROAD		5	28
FINCHLEY ROAD + FROGNAL	*	2	28
FULHAM BROADWAY		5	27
GLOUCESTER ROAD		5	27
GOLDERS GREEN		5	28
GOLDHAWK ROAD		5	28
GUNNERSBURY		45	27
HAMMERSMITH		5	27
HAMMERSMITH Broadway		5	27
HAMPSTEAD		5	28
HANGER LANE		5	18
HARLESDEN		25	28
HARROW + WEALDSTONE		25	19
HENDON		2	28
HENDON CENTRAL		5	28
HIGH STREET, KENSINGTON		5	27
HOLLAND PARK		5	28
KENSAL GREEN		25	28
KENSAL RISE	*	2	28
KENSINGTON HIGH STREET		5	28
KENSINGTON OLYMPIA		2345	27
KENTON		25	18
KEW BRIDGE		4	17
KEW GARDENS		45	17
KILBURN + Brondesbury	50	5	28
KILBURN HIGH ROAD		2	28
KILBURN PARK		5	28
KINGSBURY		5	19
LADBROKE GROVE		5	28
LANCASTER GATE		5	28
LATIMER ROAD		5	28
MAIDA VALE		5	28
MILL HILL BROADWAY		5	29
MILL HILL EAST		5	29
MORTLAKE		4	27
NEASDEN		5	28
NORTH ACTON		5	28
NORTH EALING		5	18
NORTHFIELDS		5	17
NORTH SHEEN		4	17
NORTH WEMBLEY		25	18
NORTHWICK PARK		5	18
NOTTING HILL GATE		5	28
PADDINGTON	1 §	35	28
Praed Street	1 § 48	5	28
PARK ROYAL		5	18
PARSONS GREEN		5	27
PERIVALE		5	18
PRESTON ROAD		5	18
PUTNEY		4	27
PUTNEY BRIDGE		5	27
QUEENSBURY		5	19
QUEENS PARK		25	28
QUEENSWAY		5	28
RAVENSCOURT PARK		5	27
RICHMOND		45	17
ROYAL OAK		5	28
SHEPHERDS BUSH		5	28
SHEPHERDS BUSH		5	28
SOUTH ACTON	*	2	27
SOUTH EALING		5	17
SOUTH GREENFORD		3	18
SOUTH HAMPSTEAD		2	28
SOUTH KENSINGTON		5	27
SOUTH KENTON		25	18
STAMFORD BROOK		5	27
STONEBRIDGE PARK		25	18
SUDBURY + HARROW ROAD		1	18
SUDBURY TOWN		5	18
SWISS COTTAGE		5	28
SYON LANE		4	17
TURNHAM GREEN		5	27
WANDSWORTH TOWN		4	27
WARWICK AVENUE		5	28
WEMBLEY for Sudbury	48		
CENTRAL	48	25	18
WEMBLEY Hill Complex	?		
STADIUM	?	1	18
WEMBLEY PARK		5	28
Wembley Stadium	69	1	28
WEST ACTON		5	18
Westbourne Park	92	35	28
WEST BROMPTON		5	27
WEST EALING		3	18
West End Lane	* A § 75	2	28
WEST HAMPSTEAD	A § 75	2	28
WEST HAMPSTEAD			
THAMES LINK	88	2	28
WEST HAMPSTEAD		5	28
WEST KENSINGTON		5	27
WHITE CITY		5	28
WILLESDEN GREEN		5	28
WILLESDEN JUNCTION		25	28
Low Level * High Level 2			

GOODS

No	Name/Location	Closed	Ry	Ref
G1	Brentford Town	64	3	17
2	Brentford Dock	65	3	17
3	Hammersmith + Chiswick	65	2	27

ENGINE SHEDS

No	Name/Location	Closed	Ry	Ref
E1	Cricklewood	3 64	2	28
2	OLD OAK COMMON	O	3	28
3	WILLESDEN	O	2	28
4	NEASDEN	O	5	28
5	Neasden	?	1	28
6	WEMBLEY PARK	O	5	18
7	EALING COMMON	O	5	18
8	ACTON WORKS	O	5	27
9	HAMMERSMITH	O	5	27
10	WHITE CITY	O	5	28
11	NORTHFIELDS	O	5	17

TUNNELS

No	Name	Length	Ry	Ref
T1	Drayton Green	506	3	18
2	Honeypot Hill 4	317	2	28
3	Honeypot Hill New 4	317	2	28
4	Hampstead Heath	1166	2	28
5	Belsize Slow	1867	2	28
6	Belsize Fast	1771	2	28
7	St Johns Wood	1606	1	28
8	Hampstead	694	1	28

VIADUCTS + BRIDGES

No	Name	Ry	Ref
V1	Richmond Bridge	4	17
2	Strand Green Bridge	45	17
3	Barnes Bridge	4	27
4	Fulham Bridge	5	27
5	Cremorne Viaduct	234	27

JUNCTIONS

No	Name/Location	Ry	Ref
J1	Brent Curve	2	28
2	Cricklewood Curve	2	28
3	Dudding Hill	2	28
4	Greenford East	335	18
5	Hanwell East	3	18
6	Stanmore Branch	2	19
7	Mitre Bridge	2	28
8	Acton Wells	2	28
9	North Acton	355	28
10	North Pole	2323	28
11	Hampstead	2	28
12	West London Line	2	28
13	Junction for High Wycombe	3	28
14	Old Oak Junctions	2	28
15	Kensal Rise	2	28
16	Hanger Lane	5	18
17	Hammersmith Branch	2	27
18	Acton Lane	45	27
19	Brentford Road	45	27
20	Addison Road	223	27

NOTES:

REF All in TQ therefore letters omitted.

§ Old Version, § New Version } Change of name

A Name Change

1 Praed Street became part of PADDINGTON in 1948 just after nationalisation

2 There were various suffixes at WILLESDEN Low Level and High Level being the ones lasting longest. The current station has platform at both levels.

3 Continued for use by diesels for a short while after closure for steam which is the date shown.

4 Tunnels were usually known as Kensal Green after the new tunnel was built.

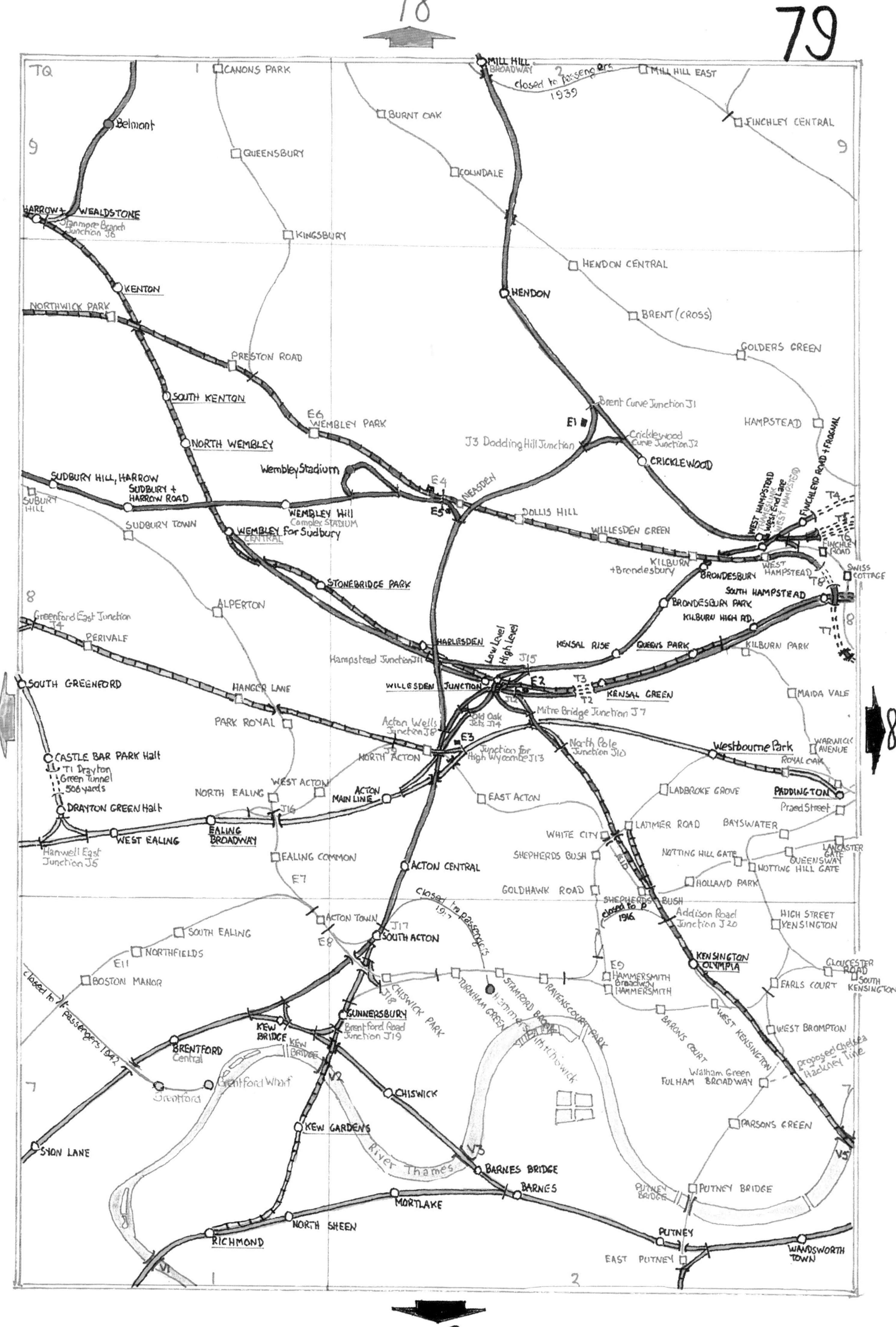
78
TQ
MILL HILL BROADWAY
CANONS PARK
closed to passengers 1939
MILL HILL EAST
BURNT OAK
FINCHLEY CENTRAL
Belmont
QUEENSBURY
COLINDALE
HARROW + WEALDSTONE
Stanmore Branch Junction J6
KINGSBURY
HENDON CENTRAL
KENTON
HENDON
NORTHWICK PARK
BRENT (CROSS)
PRESTON ROAD
GOLDERS GREEN
SOUTH KENTON
Brent Curve Junction J1
E6
WEMBLEY PARK
HAMPSTEAD
E1
Cricklewood Curve Junction J2
J3 Dodding Hill Junction
NORTH WEMBLEY
CRICKLEWOOD
FINCHLEY ROAD + FROGNAL
Wembley Stadium
SUDBURY HILL, HARROW
E4
NEASDEN
SUDBURY + HARROW ROAD
WEMBLEY Hill
Complex STADIUM
E5
DOLLIS HILL
SUDBURY HILL
SUDBURY TOWN
WEMBLEY for Sudbury
CENTRAL
WILLESDEN GREEN
WEST HAMPSTEAD
T4
T5
T6
FINCHLEY ROAD
KILBURN + Brondesbury
BRONDESBURY
WEST HAMPSTEAD
SWISS COTTAGE
STONEBRIDGE PARK
SOUTH HAMPSTEAD
T8
ALPERTON
BRONDESBURY PARK
KILBURN HIGH RD.
Greenford East Junction
T4
PERIVALE
HARLESDEN
Low Level
High Level
KENSAL RISE
QUEENS PARK
KILBURN PARK
T7
Hampstead Junction J11
J15
SOUTH GREENFORD
HANGER LANE
WILLESDEN JUNCTION
E2
T3
T2
KENSAL GREEN
MAIDA VALE
J12
PARK ROYAL
Acton Wells Junction J8
Old Oak Jcts J14
Mitre Bridge Junction J7
80
E3
North Pole Junction J10
Westbourne Park
WARWICK AVENUE
CASTLE BAR PARK Halt
T1 Drayton Green Tunnel 506 yards
J9
NORTH ACTON
Junction for High Wycombe J13
ROYAL OAK
WEST ACTON
ACTON MAIN LINE
LADBROKE GROVE
PADDINGTON
NORTH EALING
EAST ACTON
Praed Street
DRAYTON GREEN Halt
J16
LATIMER ROAD
BAYSWATER
WEST EALING
EALING BROADWAY
WHITE CITY
Hanwell East Junction J5
EALING COMMON
SHEPHERDS BUSH
NOTTING HILL GATE
LANCASTER GATE
QUEENSWAY
NOTTING HILL GATE
ACTON CENTRAL
E7
GOLDHAWK ROAD
HOLLAND PARK
Closed to passengers 1917
SHEPHERDS BUSH
closed to P 1916
HIGH STREET KENSINGTON
Addison Road Junction J20
ACTON TOWN
J17
SOUTH EALING
SOUTH ACTON
E8
NORTHFIELDS
KENSINGTON OLYMPIA
GLOUCESTER ROAD
E11
E9
HAMMERSMITH Broadway
HAMMERSMITH
BOSTON MANOR
EARLS COURT
SOUTH KENSINGTON
closed to passengers 1942
J18
CHISWICK PARK
TURNHAM GREEN
STAMFORD BROOK
RAVENSCOURT PARK
GUNNERSBURY
Brentford Road Junction J19
BARONS COURT
WEST KENSINGTON
WEST BROMPTON
KEW BRIDGE
BRENTFORD Central
proposed Chelsea Hackney line
Walham Green
FULHAM BROADWAY
V2
Brentford
Brentford Wharf
CHISWICK
KEW GARDENS
PARSONS GREEN
SYON LANE
River Thames
V3
BARNES BRIDGE
V5
BARNES
PUTNEY BRIDGE
MORTLAKE
NORTH SHEEN
RICHMOND
PUTNEY
EAST PUTNEY
WANDSWORTH TOWN
V1
82

LONDON NORTH CENTRAL

KEY TO RAILWAYS

No	Company
1	LONDON + NORTH EASTERN (LNE)
2	LONDON MIDLAND + SCOTTISH (LMS)
3	GREAT WESTERN (GW)
4	SOUTHERN (S)
M	METROPOLITAN (MAIN LINE SECTION)
5	UNDERGROUND lines
X	WATERLOO + CITY (S)
12	LNE + LMS JOINT
234	WEST LONDON EXTENSION (LMS, GW + S)
O	proposed new lines
	reduced to goods only pre 1948
	closed pre 1948

NOTE: Lines shown as JOINT LPTB and main line are not always true joint lines. More often than not there are separately dedicated tracks although sometimes both using the same track. With joint underground lines the same situation can occur, and in addition of the 'joint lines' may in fact be at a different level. For example the two lines shown at South Kensington are in fact at different levels.

STATIONS

Station	Opened/Closed	Ry	Ref
Aldersgate + BARBICAN	68	M5	38
ALDGATE		5	38
ALDGATE EAST		5	38
ALDWYCH	94	5	38
ALEXANDRA PALACE	A § 82	1	39
Alexandra Palace	1 54	1	29
ANGEL		5	38
ARCHWAY		5	28
ARSENAL		5	38
BAKER STREET		5	28
BANK		5	38
BARBICAN, Aldersgate +		M5	38
BATTERSEA PARK		4	27
BELSIZE PARK		5	28
BETHNAL GREEN		1	38
BETHNAL GREEN		5	38
BLACKFRIARS		45	38
BLACKHORSE ROAD	2 * 81	25	39
BOND STREET		5	28
BOROUGH		5	38
BOUNDS GREEN		5	29
Bow Road	49	1	38
BOW ROAD		5	38
BRIXTON		45	37
BROCKLEY		4	37
Broad Street	86	2	38
BRUCE GROVE		1	39
CALEDONIAN ROAD		5	38
CALEDONIAN ROAD + BARNSBURY		2	38
CAMBRIDGE HEATH	3	1	38
CAMDEN Town ROAD	50	2	28
CAMDEN TOWN		5	28
(CANARY WHARF)	91	5	38
CANNON STREET		45	38
CANONBURY		2	38
CHALK FARM		5	28
CHANCERY LANE		5	38
CHARING CROSS		45	38
CHARING CROSS (EMBANKMENT)	B § 76	5	38
CITY		X	38
CITY THAMESLINK	C §	4	38
CLAPHAM COMMON		5	27
CLAPHAM HIGH STREET		4	27
CLAPHAM JUNCTION		234	27
CLAPHAM NORTH		5	37
CLAPHAM SOUTH		5	27
CLAPTON		1	38
COVENT GARDEN		5	38
Cranley Gardens	4 54	1	29
CROFTON PARK		4	37
Crouch End	4 54	1	28
CROUCH HILL	*	2	38
Dalston Junction	86	2	38
DALSTON KINGSLAND	83	2	38
DENMARK HILL		4	37
DEPTFORD		4	37
(DEVONS ROAD)	87	5	38
DRAYTON PARK	5	5	38
East Brixton	76	4	37
EAST DULWICH		4	37
EAST FINCHLEY		5	29
EDGWARE ROAD	6	5	28
ELEPHANT + CASTLE		45	37
EMBANKMENT	B § 76	5	38
ESSEX ROAD	5	5	38
EUSTON		25	28
EUSTON SQUARE		5	28
FARRINGDON		M5	38
FENCHURCH STREET		1	38
FINSBURY PARK	5	15	38
GOODGE STREET		5	28
GOSPEL OAK	*	2	28
GREAT PORTLAND STREET		5	28
GREEN PARK		5	28
HACKNEY CENTRAL	80	1	38
HACKNEY DOWNS		1	38
HACKNEY WICK	80	12	38
HAMPSTEAD HEATH	*	2	28
HARRINGAY West	51 71	1	38
HARRINGAY Park GREEN LANES	6 *	2	38
HERNE HILL		4	37
(HERON QUAYS)	87	5	38
HIGHBURY + ISLINGTON		15	38
Highgate	4 (54)	25	28
HOLBORN		5	38
Holborn Viaduct	7 90	5	38
HOLLOWAY ROAD		5	38
HOMERTON	85	1	38
HORNSEY		1	39
HYDE PARK CORNER		5	28
Junction Road	8 49	12	28
KENNINGTON		5	37
KENTISH TOWN		25	28
KENTISH TOWN WEST	* 9 76 86	2	28
KINGS CROSS		15	38
KINGS CROSS + St Pancras			38
THAMESLINK	88	1M5	38
KNIGHTSBRIDGE		5	27
LAMBETH NORTH		5	37
LANCASTER GATE		5	28
Lea Bridge	85	1	38
LEICESTER SQUARE		5	28
LIMEHOUSE	10 D § 87	15	38
LIVERPOOL STREET		15	38
LONDON BRIDGE		45	38
LONDON FIELDS	81 86	1	38
LOUGHBOROUGH JUNCTION		4	37
MANOR HOUSE		5	38
MANSION HOUSE		5	38
MARBLE ARCH		5	28
MARYLEBONE		15	28
MILE END		5	38
MONUMENT		5	38
MOORGATE		M5	38
MORNINGTON CRESCENT		5	28
Muswell Hill	4 54	1	29
NEW CROSS		45	37
NEW CROSS GATE		45	37
Noel Park	† 63	1	39
NORTH DULWICH		4	37
NORTHUMBERLAND PARK		1	39
NUNHEAD		4	37
OLD STREET		5	38
OVAL		5	37
OXFORD CIRCUS		5	28
PADDINGTON		35	28
Palace Gates	† 63	1	39
PECKHAM RYE		4	37
PICCADILLY CIRCUS		5	28
PIMLICO		5	27
(POPLAR)	87	5	38
Praed Street	11 § 48	5	28
Primrose Hill	92	2	28
QUEENS ROAD PECKHAM		4	37
QUEENSTOWN ROAD		4	27
RECTORY ROAD		1	38
REGENTS PARK		5	28
ROTHERHITHE		5	38
RUSSELL SQUARE		5	38
ST JAMES PARK		5	28
ST JAMES STREET		1	38
ST JOHNS		4	37
ST JOHNS WOOD		5	28
ST PANCRAS		2	28
ST PAULS		5	38
St Pauls Thameslink	C § 90 91	5	38
SEVEN SISTERS		15	39
(SHADWELL)	87	5	38
SHOREDITCH		5	38
SLOANE SQUARE		5	27
SOUTH BERMONDSEY		4	37
SOUTH KENSINGTON		5	27
(SOUTH QUAY)	87	5	38
SOUTH TOTTENHAM	*	2	38
STAMFORD HILL		1	38
Stepney East	D § 87	5	38
STEPNEY GREEN		5	38
STOCKWELL		5	37
STOKE NEWINGTON		1	38
Strand	12 73	5	38
Stroud Green	4 54	1	38
SURREY Docks (QUAYS)	89	5	37
SWISS COTTAGE		5	28
TEMPLE		5	38
TOTTENHAM COURT ROAD		5	28
TOTTENHAM HALE	68	1	39
(TOWER GATEWAY)	87	5	38
TOWER HILL		5	38
Trafalgar Square	13 76	5	38
TUFNELL PARK		5	28
TURNPIKE LANE		5	39
UPPER HOLLOWAY	*	12	28
VICTORIA		45	27
WALTHAMSTOW Hoe Street CENTRAL	68	1	39
WALTHAMSTOW QUEENS ROAD	* 68	2	38
WANDSWORTH ROAD		4	27
WAPPING		5	38
WARREN STREET		5	28
WATERLOO		45X	38
WATERLOO EAST		4	38
(WEST FERRY)	87	5	38
West Green	† 63	1	39
(WEST INDIA QUAY)	87	5	38
WESTMINSTER		5	37
WHITECHAPEL		5	38
WHITE HART LANE		1	39
WOOD GREEN		5	39
Wood Green (Alexandra Park)	A §	1	39
York Road	77	1	38

PROPOSED STATIONS 14

Station	Ry	Ref
BERMONDSEY	5	37
CANADA WATER	5	37
SOUTHWARK	5	38

GOODS

No	Name	Closed	Ry	Ref
G1	St Pancras	75	2	28
2	Bricklayers Arms	77	4	37
3	Deptford Wharf	64	4	37

WORKS

No	Location	Closed	Ry	Ref
C1	Bow	60	2	38

ENGINE SHEDS 15

No	Name/Location	Closed	Ry	Ref
E1	Palace Gates	54	1	39
2	Camden	62 66	2	28
3	Kentish Town	63	2	28
4	HORNSEY	67 71	1	38
5	Kings Cross Top	63	1	28
6	Kings Cross Bottom	65 80	1	28
7	LONDON ROAD		5	38
8	HIGHGATE		5	29
9	NORTHUMBERLAND PARK		5	39
10	NEW CROSS		5	37
11	Devons Road Bow	58 64	2	38
12	STEWARTS LANE	63 67	4	27
13	Bricklayers Arms	62	4	37
14	New Cross Gate	49	4	37
15	Nine Elms	57	4	37

BRIDGES + VIADUCTS

No	Name/Location	Ry	Ref
V1	Grosvenor Bridge	4	27
2	Cannon Street Bridge	4	38
3	St Pauls Bridge	4	38

TUNNELS

No	Name/Location	Length	Ry	Ref
T1	Wood Green	706	1	39
2	Highgate		1	28
3	Clapton	284	1	38
4	Queens Road	445	1	38
5	Dalston		2	38
6	Canonbury	545	1	38
7	Copenhagen	594	1	38
8	Gasworks	528	1	38
9	Tottenham N Curve No1	160	2	28
10	Tottenham N Curve No2	70	2	28
11	Tottenham N Curve No3	103	2	28
12	Camden Road	315	2	28
13	Park Street	162	2	28
14	Snow Hill	770	4	38
15	Hampstead	1166	2	28
16	Belsize Slow	1867	2	28
17	Belsize Fast	1771	2	28
18	Primrose Hill	1182	2	28
19	Denmark Hill	63	4	37
20	Grove	132	4	37

JUNCTIONS

No	Name/Location	Ry	Ref
J1	Park	15	28
2	Bowes Park	1	39
3	Carlton Road	2	28
4	Highgate Road	112	28
5	St Pauls Road	2	28
6	Kentish Town	2	28
7	Navarino Road	12	38
8	Graham Road Curve	12	38
9	Victoria Park	12	38
10	Hall Farm North	1	38
11	Hall Farm South	1	38
12	Copper Mill North	1	38
13	Copper Mill South	1	38
14	Blackfriars	4	38
15	Stoney Street	4	38
16	Salmons Lane	1	38
17	Stepney	1	38
18	Tilbury	2	38
19	Canterbury Road	4	37
20	Cambria	4	37
21	Old Kent Road	4	37
22	North Kent	4	37
23	Latchmere	234	27
24	Stewarts Lane	4	27
25	Battersea Pier	4	27

NOTES:

REF All in TQ

§ Older version } Name change. letter

§ New version } shows other name

1 Closed 10/51 to 1/52

2 Rebuilt 81 on nearby site to assist interchange facilities

3 Closed 86 for rebuild.

4 Closed 51, Reopened 52 before final closure as shown

5 Closed 75, Re-opened 76 (Moorgate Crash)

6 Rebuilt 90-2

7 Temp Closure in 86

8 Last passenger train 43.

9 Last passenger train 71 although official closure as shown.

10 Docklands station opened 87.

11 Became part of Paddington

12 Became part of Charing Cross

13 Became part of Charing Cross

14 Only totally new stations shown

15 Where two dates - First is steam

78

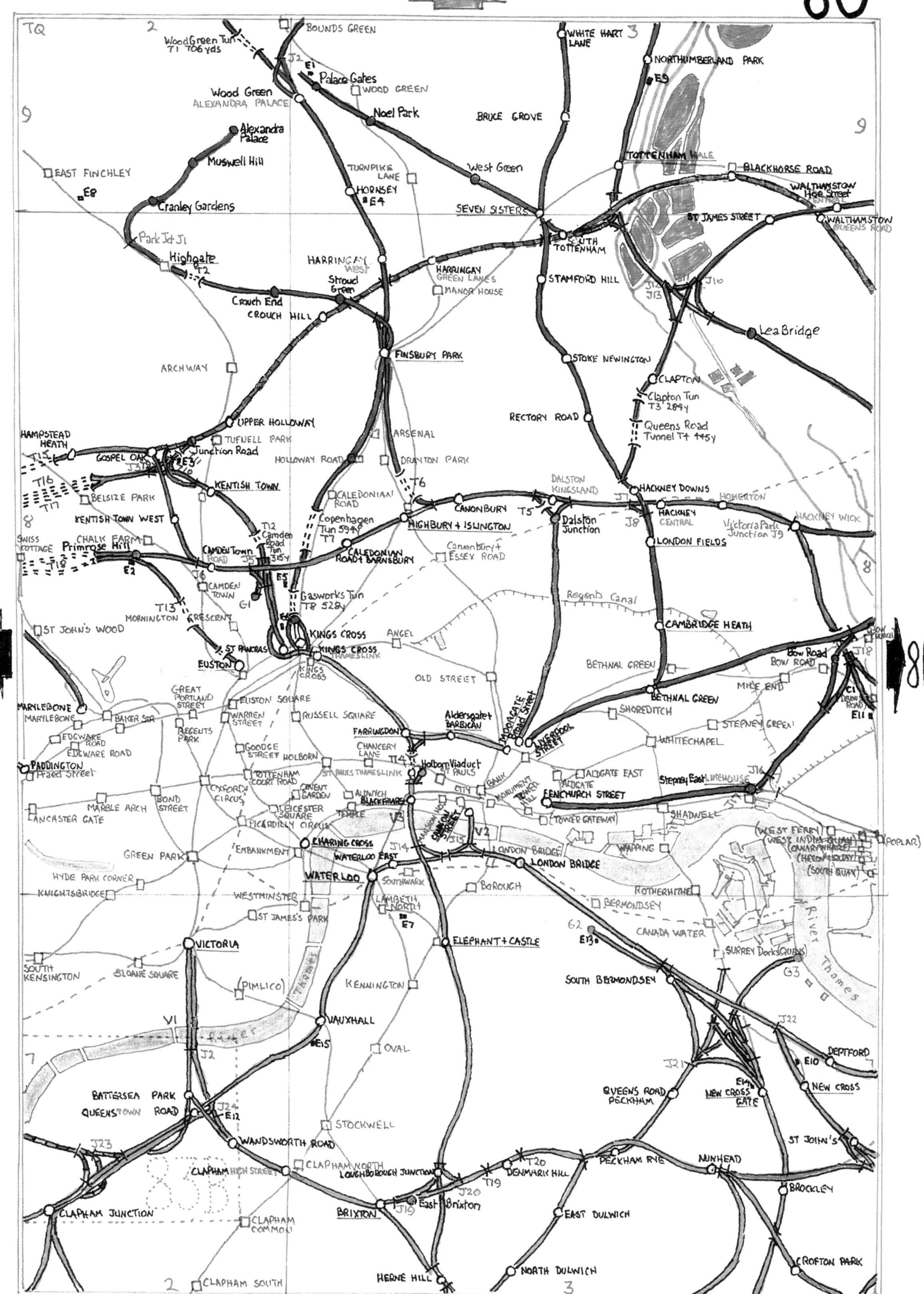
TQ
2
3
9
8
7
Bounds Green
Wood Green Tun
T1 706yds
J2
E1
Palace Gates
Wood Green
Wood Green
Alexandra Palace
Noel Park
Alexandra Palace
Muswell Hill
Cranley Gardens
East Finchley
E8
Turnpike Lane
Hornsey
E4
Bruce Grove
West Green
Seven Sisters
White Hart Lane
Northumberland Park
E9
Tottenham Hale
Blackhorse Road
Walthamstow Hoe Street
Walthamstow Queens Road
St James Street
South Tottenham
Park Jct J1
Highgate
T2
Harringay West
Harringay Green Lanes
Manor House
Stroud Green
Crouch End
Crouch Hill
Stamford Hill
J12
J13
J10
Lea Bridge
Archway
Finsbury Park
Stoke Newington
Clapton
Clapton Tun
T3 284y
Queens Road Tunnel T4 445y
Rectory Road
Upper Holloway
Hampstead Heath
T15
Gospel Oak
Tufnell Park
Junction Road
E3
Holloway Road
Arsenal
Drayton Park
T6
T16
T17
Belsize Park
Kentish Town
Caledonian Road
Hackney Downs
Homerton
Dalston Kingsland
T5
Canonbury
Hackney Central
J8
Dalston Junction
Victoria Park Junction J9
Hackney Wick
London Fields
Kentish Town West
T12
Camden Road Tun 315y
Copenhagen Tun 594y
T7
Highbury + Islington
Swiss Cottage
Chalk Farm
Primrose Hill
T18
E2
Camden Town
Camden Road
J5
J6
Caledonian Road + Barnsbury
Canonbury + Essex Road
E5
Gasworks Tun
T8 522y
G1
Regents Canal
Camden Town
T13
Mornington Crescent
E6
Cambridge Heath
St John's Wood
St Pancras
Kings Cross
Kings Cross Thameslink
Angel
Euston
Kings Cross
Bethnal Green
Bow Road
Bow Road
J18
Old Street
Mile End
Marylebone
Marylebone
Baker Str
Great Portland Street
Euston Square
Warren Street
Russell Square
Aldersgate + Barbican
Moorgate
Broad Street
Bethnal Green
Shoreditch
Stepney Green
Edgware Road
Edgware Road
Regents Park
Goodge Street
Holborn
Farringdon
Chancery Lane
Liverpool Street
Whitechapel
Paddington
Praed Street
Tottenham Court Road
St Pauls Thameslink
T14
Holborn Viaduct
St Pauls
Bank
Aldgate East
Aldgate
Stepney East
Limehouse
J16
Marble Arch
Bond Street
Oxford Circus
Covent Garden
Aldwych
Blackfriars
City
Monument
Tower Hill
Fenchurch Street
Lancaster Gate
Leicester Square
Temple
V3
Cannon Street
V2
Tower Gateway
Shadwell
Piccadilly Circus
Charing Cross
J15
Wapping
West Ferry
West India Quay
Poplar
Green Park
Embankment
J14
Waterloo East
London Bridge
London Bridge
South Quay
Hyde Park Corner
Waterloo
Southwark
Borough
Rotherhithe
Knightsbridge
Westminster
Lambeth North
Bermondsey
St James's Park
E7
G2
E13
Canada Water
Victoria
Elephant + Castle
Surrey Docks Quays
River Thames
South Kensington
Sloane Square
(Pimlico)
Kennington
South Bermondsey
G3
Vauxhall
V1
River Thames
E15
Oval
J22
Deptford
J2
J21
E10
New Cross
Battersea Park
Queens Road Peckham
New Cross Gate
Queenstown Road
J24
E12
Stockwell
Wandsworth Road
J23
St John's
Clapham High Street
Clapham North
Loughborough Junction
T20
Denmark Hill
Peckham Rye
Nunhead
J20
T19
Brockley
Clapham Junction
Brixton
J19
East Brixton
East Dulwich
Clapham Common
Herne Hill
North Dulwich
Crofton Park
Clapham South
79
81

82

LONDON NORTH EAST

KEY TO RAILWAYS

No		Company
1	(line)	LONDON + NORTH EASTERN (LNE)
2	(line)	LONDON MIDLAND + SCOTTISH (LMS)
4	(line)	SOUTHERN (S)
5	(line)	Underground lines

No		Company
	(line)	reduced to goods pre-nationalisation
	(dashed line)	closed pre-nationalisation
P	(dashed line)	proposed new lines

Note: Lines shown as joint underground + main line railway normally have separately dedicated tracks, sometimes at different levels.

STATIONS	Opened Closed	Ry	Ref
ABBEY WOOD		4	47
(ALL SAINTS)	87	5	38
BARKING		25	48
BARKINGSIDE		5	49
BECKTON	94	5	48
BECKTON PARK	94	5	48
BECONTREE	D	(2)5	48
BEXLEYHEATH		4	47
BLACKHEATH		4	47
BLACKWALL	94	5	38
(BOW CHURCH)	87	5	38
BROMLEY (·BY·BOW)	D 67	(2)5	38
BRUNSWICK WHARF	94	15	38
(CANARY WHARF)	91	5	38
CANNING TOWN	A (94)	15	48
CHADWELL HEATH		1	48
CHARLTON		4	47
CONNAUGHT		P	48
(CROSSHARBOUR)	87	5	37
CUSTOM HOUSE	B 94 94	1P	48
CUTTY SARK		P	37
CYPRUS	94	5	48
DEPTFORD CREEK/BRIDGE	C	P	37
(DEVONS ROAD)	87	5	37
EAST HAM	D	5(2)	48
ELVERSTON ROAD		P	37
ELTHAM	E 85	4	47
Eltham Park	85	4	47
Eltham Well Hall	85	4	47
FAIRLOP		5	49
FALCONWOOD		4	47
FOREST GATE		1	48
GALLIONS REACH	94	5	48
GANTS HILL		5	48
GOODMAYES		1	48
GREENWICH		4	37
GREENWICH		P	37
(HERON QUAYS)	87	5	38
HITHER GREEN		4	37
ILFORD		1	48
(ISLAND GARDENS)	87	5	37
KIDBROOKE		4	47
LADYWELL		4	37
LEWISHAM		4	37
LEWISHAM		P	37
LEYTON		5	38
LEYTON MIDLAND ROAD	*49	2	38
LEYTONSTONE		5	48
LEYTONSTONE HIGH ROAD	*49	2	48
MANOR PARK		1	48
MARYLAND		1	38
MAZE HILL for National Maritime Museum		4	47
(MUDCHUTE)		5	37
NEWBURY PARK		5	48
NORTH GREENWICH		P	38
NORTH WOOLWICH	F 94	1	47
PLAISTOW	D	5(2)	48
PLUMSTEAD		4	47
(POPLAR)	87	5	38
PRINCE REGENT		P	48
PUDDING MILL LANE		P	38
REBBRIDGE		5	48
ROYAL ALBERT	94	5	48
ROYAL VICTORIA	E	15	48
ST JOHN'S		4	37
SEVEN KINGS		1	48
SILVERTOWN + LONDON CITY AIRPORT	F 84 94	1	48
SNARESBROOK		5	49
(SOUTH QUAY)	87	5	37
SOUTH WOODFORD		5	49
STRATFORD	G	15	38
STRATFORD	H	P	38
Stratford Market	57	1	38
UPNEY	D	(2)5	48
UPTON PARK	D	(2)5	48
WANSTEAD		5	48
WANSTEAD PARK	*	2	48
WELLING		4	47
WESTCOMBE PARK		4	47
WEST HAM		1	38
WEST HAM	DJ	(2)5	48
WEST HAM	J	P	48
(WEST INDIA QUAY)	87	5	38
WOODGRANGE PARK	*	2	48
WOOD STREET Walthamstow	71	1	39
WOOLWICH ARSENAL		4	47
WOOLWICH DOCKYARD		4	47

GOODS

No	Name/Location	Closed	Ry	Ref
G1	Blackwall	67	1	38
2	Thames Wharf	65	1	48
3	Angerstein Wharf	56	4	47
4	TEMPLE MILLS	O	1	38

COMPANY WORKS

No	Name/Location	Closed	Ry	Ref
C1	Stratford	K 62	1	38
2	Temple Mills	L 84	1	38

ENGINE SHEDS

No	Name/Location	Closed	Ry	Ref
E1	Wood Street	60	1	39
2	Plaistow	62	2	38
3	Stratford	63	1	38
4	Devons Road (Bow)	M 58	2	38
5	HITHER GREEN	N O	4	37
6	ILFORD	P O	1	48

TUNNELS

No	Name	Length	Ry	Ref
T1	Silvertown	600	1	48
2	Charlton	154	4	47
3	Mount Street	121	4	47
4	Dock Street	121	4	47
5	Coleman Street	89	4	47
6	George IV	238	4	47
7	Calderwood Street	58	4	47
8	Cross Street	134	4	47
9	Blackheath	1681	4	47
10	Kidbrooke	437	4	47
11	Greenwich College	450	4	37

JUNCTIONS

No	Name	Ry	Ref
J1	Tilbury Line	2	48
2	Carpenters Road	1	38
3	Channelsea North	1	38
4	High Meads	1	38
5	Lea	1	38
6	Forest Gate	12	48
7	Angerstein	4	47
8	Parks Bridge	4	37
9	Courthill Loop North	4	37
10	Courthill Loop South	4	37

NOTES:

REF: All in TQ so letters omitted.

A Docklands line did not open until after the atlas termination date in 1994

B Main line closed when Docklands line opened but proposed to re-open

C Alternative names

D Ex LMS platforms closed prior to nationalisation.

E Opened midway between two other stations which were closed at this time – viz Park and Well Hall

F Closed past terminal date.

G Main open station is at two levels as shown. The level designation has now been dropped. Underground platforms also within station

H This was planned as seperate station but whether it will materialise as such is not known.

J See Note D. It is planned to open the main line platform.

K Carriage works closed in 63

L Wagon Works

M Closure date is for steam. The shed closed for diesels in 64.

N Closure for steam was in 61.

P Closure for steam was pre-war, in 39.

This is a most unusual railway area in so many different ways. In the first place there is only three stations closed, and two of those were in fact replaced by the single station at Eltham.

The second unusual feature is only one station proposed for closure in the Beeching Report.

There were a few closures but these all took place before nationalisation, and were mainly LNE lines. My map shows although some of these lines continued in use for goods they, in fact, not used by LNE but by the Port of London Authority!

In addition the area has no less than 4 new lines proposed with the area or just outside it – Docklands extension, Jubilee Line Extension, Chelsea-Hackney line and just outside the area the extension of the East London. There also proposed openings and re-openings of main line stations and/or platforms.

78

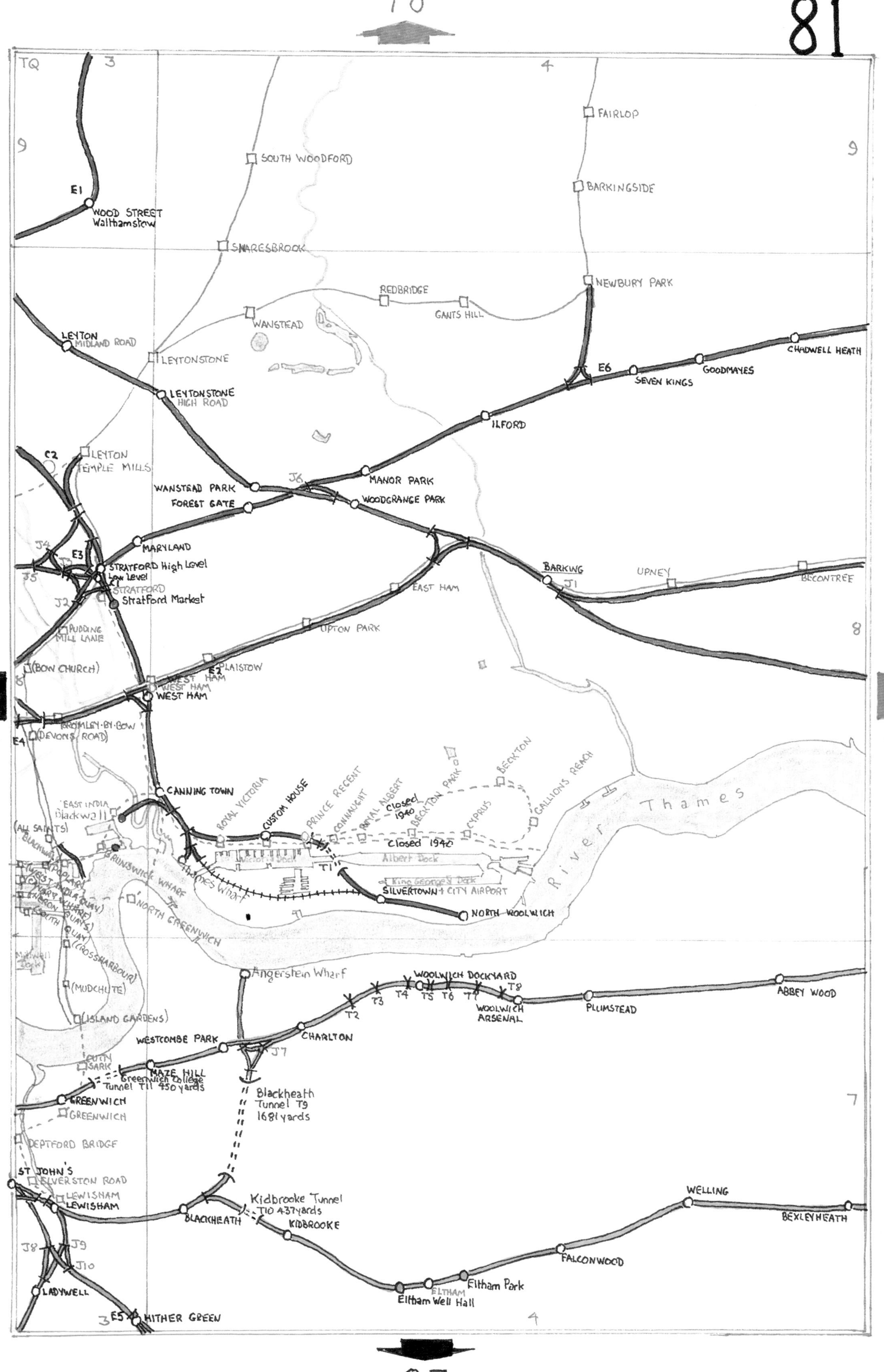
TQ
3
4
9
E1
WOOD STREET Walthamstow
SOUTH WOODFORD
FAIRLOP
BARKINGSIDE
SNARESBROOK
NEWBURY PARK
REDBRIDGE
GANTS HILL
WANSTEAD
LEYTON MIDLAND ROAD
LEYTONSTONE
LEYTONSTONE HIGH ROAD
E6
SEVEN KINGS
GOODMAYES
CHADWELL HEATH
ILFORD
C2
LEYTON TEMPLE MILLS
J6
MANOR PARK
WANSTEAD PARK
FOREST GATE
WOODGRANGE PARK
MARYLAND
J4
E3
J3
J5
STRATFORD High Level
Low Level
STRATFORD
Stratford Market
J2
BARKING
J1
UPNEY
BECONTREE
EAST HAM
PUDDING MILL LANE
UPTON PARK
8
(BOW CHURCH)
PLAISTOW
E2
WEST HAM
WEST HAM
BROMLEY-BY-BOW
E4
(DEVONS ROAD)
BECKTON
GALLIONS REACH
CANNING TOWN
ROYAL VICTORIA
CUSTOM HOUSE
PRINCE REGENT
CONNAUGHT
ROYAL ALBERT
BECKTON PARK
CYPRUS
Closed 1940
Closed 1940
EAST INDIA
Blackwall
(ALL SAINTS)
Albert Dock
King George V Dock
T1
SILVERTOWN + CITY AIRPORT
NORTH WOOLWICH
Thames Wharf
BRUNSWICK WHARF
NORTH GREENWICH
River Thames
(CROSSHARBOUR)
(MUDCHUTE)
(ISLAND GARDENS)
Angerstein Wharf
WOOLWICH DOCKYARD
T2
T3
T4
T5
T6
T7
T8
WOOLWICH ARSENAL
PLUMSTEAD
ABBEY WOOD
WESTCOMBE PARK
CHARLTON
J7
CUTTY SARK
MAZE HILL
Greenwich College Tunnel T11 450 yards
Blackheath Tunnel T9 1681 yards
GREENWICH
GREENWICH
7
DEPTFORD BRIDGE
ST JOHN'S
ELVERSTON ROAD
LEWISHAM
LEWISHAM
Kidbrooke Tunnel T10 437 yards
BLACKHEATH
KIDBROOKE
WELLING
BEXLEYHEATH
FALCONWOOD
J8
J9
J10
Eltham Park
ELTHAM
Eltham Well Hall
LADYWELL
E5
HITHER GREEN
4

83

82 LONDON SOUTH WEST + LONDON SOUTH CENTRAL

KEY TO RAILWAYS

No		Company	No		Company
4	▬▬▬	SOUTHERN		────	Reduced to goods – prenationalisation
45	┼┼┼┼┼	SOUTHERN + DISTRICT LINE		- - - -	Closed pre-nationalisation
5	────	UNDERGROUND			

Note: All in TQ therefore those letters omitted, but A or B indicates map on which gazetteer item appears

STATIONS

Station	Opened Closed	Ry	Ref
ANERLEY		4	B37
BALHAM		5	B27
BALHAM + Upper Tooting		4	B27
BECKENHAM JUNCTION		4	B36
BEDDINGTON LANE		4	B26
BERRYLANDS		4	A26
BIRBECK		4	B36
CATFORD		4	B37
CATFORD BRIDGE		4	B37
CLAPHAM SOUTH		5	B27
CLOCK HOUSE		4	B36
COLLIERS WOOD		5	A27
CROFTON PARK		4	B37
CRYSTAL PALACE Low Level	55	4	B37
Crystal Palace High Level	54	4	B37
EARLSFIELD		4	A27
EDEN PARK		4	B36
ELMERS END		4	B36
FOREST HILL		4	B37
GIPSEY HILL For Upper Norwood		4	B37
HAMPTON WICK		4	A17
HAYDON'S ROAD		4	A27
HERNE HILL		4	B37
Honor Oak	54	4	B37
HONOR OAK PARK		4	B37
KENT HOUSE		4	B37
KINGSTON		4	A16
Lordship Lane	54	4	B37
LOWER SYDENHAM		4	B37
Malden For Coombe	1 A §55 57	4	A26
MERTON PARK		4	A26
MITCHAM		4	B26
MITCHAM JUNCTION		4	B26
MORDEN		5	A26
MORDEN ROAD		4	A26
MORDEN SOUTH		4	A26
MOTSPUR PARK		4	A26
NEW BECKENHAM		4	B37
NEW MALDEN	A§	4	A26
NORBITON		4	A16
NORBURY		4	B36
NORTH DULWICH		4	B37
NORWOOD JUNCTION		4	B36
PENGE EAST		4	B37
PENGE WEST		4	B37
RAYNES PARK		4	A26
ST HELIER		4	A26
ST MARGARET'S		4	A17
SELHURST		4	B36
SOUTHFIELDS	4	45	A27
SOUTH MERTON		4	A26
SOUTH WIMBLEDON		5	A27
STRAWBERRY HILL		4	A17
STREATHAM		4	B27
STREATHAM COMMON		4	B27
STREATHAM HILL		4	B27
SURBITON For Bushey Park		4	A16
SYDENHAM		4	B37
SYDENHAM HILL		4	B37
TEDDINGTON		4	A17
THORNTON HEATH		4	B36
TOOTING		4	B27
TOOTING BEC	2 50	5	B27
TOOTING BROADWAY		5	B27
Trinity Road (Tooting Bec)	2 50	5	B27
TULSE HILL		5	B37
TWICKENHAM		5	A17
Upper Sydenham	54	4	B37
WANDSWORTH COMMON		4	B27
WEST DULWICH		4	B37
WEST NORWOOD		4	B37
WIMBLEDON	4	45	A27
WIMBLEDON CHASE		4	A26
WIMBLEDON PARK	4	45	A27
Wimbledon Staff Halt	3	4	A27
WOODSIDE		4	B36

1 for Coombe dropped from title 55. Changed to NEW MALDEN 57
2 Trinity Road dropped from title 50
3 Not a public station.
4 Line north from Wimbledon is District (underground) only for passengers but is also used for goods traffic.
5 All continuations see 78

ENGINE SHEDS

No	Name/Location	Closed steam	Ry	Ref
E1	Wimbledon		4	A27
2	Morden		5	A26

TUNNELS

No	Name/Location	Length	Ry	Ref
T1	Leigham Court	443	4	B37
2	Streatham	220	4	B37
3	Leigham	302	4	B37
4	Penge/Sydenham	2141	4	B37
5	Crystal Palace	745	4	B37
6	Knights Hill	331	4	B37
7	Upper Norwood		4	B37
8	Upper Sydenham		4	B37

BRIDGES + VIADUCTS

No	Name/Location	Ry	Ref
V1	Kingston Bridge	4	A16

JUNCTIONS

No	Name	Ry	Ref
J1	Wimbledon A	445	A27
2	Wimbledon B	4	A27
3	Wimbledon C	4	A27
4	Shacklegate	4	A17
5	Leigham	4	B37
6	Leigham Spur	4	B37
7	Crystal Palace Tunnel	4	B37
8	Norwood Flyover	4	B36
9	Bromley	4	B36
10	Spur	4	B36
11	Hayes Branch	4	B36

NOTES

§ Old Name } Change of name
§ New Name }
letter indicates other name

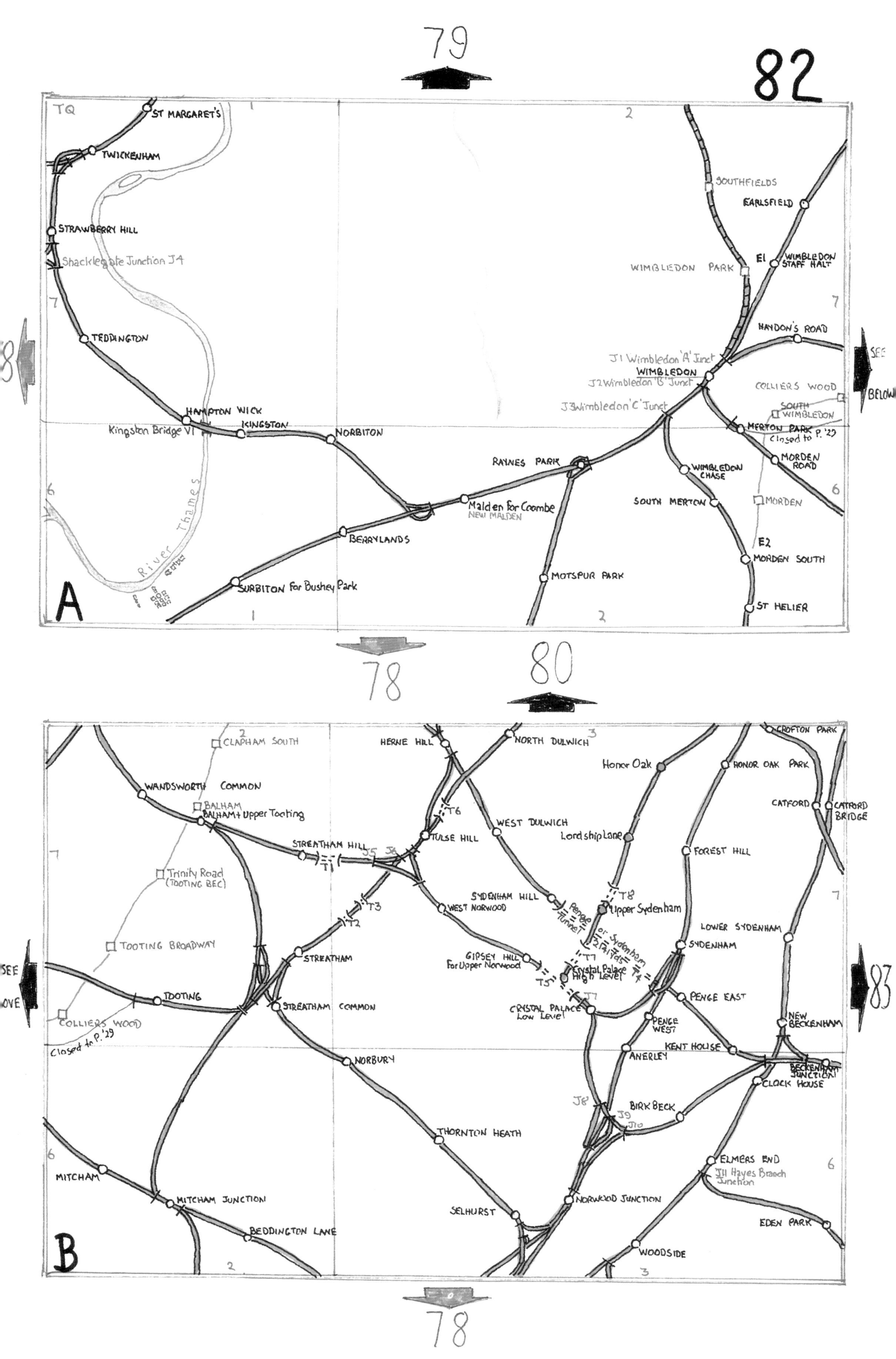

79
TQ
ST MARGARET'S
TWICKENHAM
STRAWBERRY HILL
Shacklegate Junction J4
TEDDINGTON
HAMPTON WICK
Kingston Bridge V1
KINGSTON
NORBITON
River Thames
SURBITON for Bushey Park
BERRYLANDS
Malden for Coombe
NEW MALDEN
RAYNES PARK
MOTSPUR PARK
SOUTHFIELDS
EARLSFIELD
WIMBLEDON PARK
E1
WIMBLEDON STAFF HALT
HAYDON'S ROAD
J1 Wimbledon 'A' Junct
WIMBLEDON
J2 Wimbledon 'B' Junct
J3 Wimbledon 'C' Junct
COLLIERS WOOD
SOUTH WIMBLEDON
MERTON PARK
Closed to P. '29
MORDEN ROAD
WIMBLEDON CHASE
SOUTH MERTON
MORDEN
E2
MORDEN SOUTH
ST HELIER
SEE BELOW
A
78
80
CLAPHAM SOUTH
HERNE HILL
NORTH DULWICH
Honor Oak
HONOR OAK PARK
CROFTON PARK
WANDSWORTH COMMON
BALHAM
BALHAM + Upper Tooting
STREATHAM HILL
T1
J5
J6
T6
TULSE HILL
WEST DULWICH
Lordship Lane
FOREST HILL
CATFORD
CATFORD BRIDGE
Trinity Road (TOOTING BEC)
T3
T2
WEST NORWOOD
SYDENHAM HILL
Penge Tunnel
T8
Upper Sydenham
LOWER SYDENHAM
SYDENHAM
TOOTING BROADWAY
STREATHAM
GIPSEY HILL For Upper Norwood
T5
Crystal Palace High Level
T7
J7
T4
PENGE EAST
SEE ABOVE
TOOTING
COLLIERS WOOD
Closed to P. '29
STREATHAM COMMON
CRYSTAL PALACE Low Level
PENGE WEST
NEW BECKENHAM
83
KENT HOUSE
ANERLEY
BECKENHAM JUNCTION
NORBURY
CLOCK HOUSE
J8
BIRK BECK
J9
J10
THORNTON HEATH
ELMERS END
J11 Hayes Branch Junction
MITCHAM
MITCHAM JUNCTION
NORWOOD JUNCTION
SELHURST
BEDDINGTON LANE
EDEN PARK
WOODSIDE
B
78

83 LONDON SOUTH EAST + CLAPHAM JUNCTION

KEY TO RAILWAYS

No	Company	No	Company
2	LONDON MIDLAND + SCOTTISH (LMS)	234	WEST LONDON EXTENSION (LMS, GW + S)
3	GREAT WESTERN (GW)	0	NEW LINES
23	WEST LONDON (LMS + GW)	5	VICTORIA LINE (underground)
4	SOUTHERN (S)		

STATIONS

Station	Opened Closed	Ry	Ref
ALBANY PARK		4	A47
BATTERSEA PARK		4	B27
BECKENHAM HILL		4	A37
BELLINGHAM		4	A37
BICKLEY		4	A46
BROMLEY NORTH		4	A46
BROMLEY SOUTH		4	A46
CATFORD		4	A37
CATFORD BRIDGE		4	A37
CHISLEHURST		4	A46
CLAPHAM JUNCTION		4	B27
EDEN PARK		4	A36
ELMSTEAD WOODS		4	A47
GROVE PARK		4	A47
LEE for Burnt Ash		4	A47
MOTTINGHAM		4	A47
NEW ELTHAM		4	A47
PETTS WOOD		4	A46
QUEENSTOWN ROAD		4	B27
RAVENSBOURNE		4	A37
ST MARY CRAY		4	A46
SHORTLANDS		4	A46
SIDCUP		4	A47
SUNDRIDGE PARK		4	A47
VAUXHALL		45	B37
WANDSWORTH ROAD		4	B27

GOODS

No	Name/Location	Closed	Ry	Ref
G1	Chelsea Basin		23	B27
2	Clapham Goods + Coal Wharf		2	B27
3	Stewarts Lane	70	4	B27
4	Battersea	70	4	B27
5	South Lambeth		3	B27
6	LMS Coal Depot		2	B27
7	Nine Elms		4	B27

ENGINE SHEDS

No	Name/Location	Notes	Steam Closure	Ry	Ref
E1	Nine Elms		57	4	B27
2	STEWARTS LANE	1	63	4	B27

VIADUCTS + BRIDGES

No	Name	Ry	Ref
V1	Cremorne Viaduct	234	B27
2	Grosvenor Bridge	4	B27

TUNNELS

No	Name/Location	Length	Ry	Ref
T1	Chislehurst Slow (North)	649	4	A47
2	Chislehurst Fast (South)	591	4	A47

JUNCTIONS

No	Name	Notes	Ry	Ref
J1	Lee Loop		4	A47
2	Lee Spur		4	A47
3	Bromley Branch		4	A47
4	Chatham Loop North		4	A46
5	Chatham Loop East		4	A46
6	Bickley		4	A46
11	Falcon		4	B27
12	Ludgate		4	B27
13	Pouparts		4	B27
14	West London		4	B27
15	Latchmere No 2		234	B27
16	Latchmere No 1		234	B27
17	Latchmere No 3		234	B27
18	Longhedge Junctions		234/4	B27
19	Factory		4	B27
20	Stewarts Lane			B27
21	Battersea Pier		4	B27
22	Nine Elms		40	B27
23	Linford Street		40	B27
24	Battersea Park		4	B27
25	Lavender Hill	2	4	B27

NOTES:

Ref All in TQ. Letter A + B used to distinguish map.

1 Shed extended to include maintenance + Carriage Depot. Still in use at end of period

2 End-on Junction ceased to be important at start of grouping period.

84 LONDON UNDERGROUND

The map of the underground system which follows has no gazetteer and to avoid needless clutter a few notes relating to this map are included here.

The map shows the underground system as at the end of 1993 and also includes the WATERLOO + CITY and the GREAT NORTHERN + CITY as these two lines although not part of the London Underground Limited have always effectively been part of the system. Although the proposed Docklands line (opened 1994) and the Jubilee extension are shown later proposals are omitted but are referred to in connection with Map 81.

The principal alterations to the system in addition to those which are obvious from the map were as follows:

1. The GREAT NORTHERN + CITY line had been purchased by the METROPOLITAN and was part of the system until the Moorgate crash. But when it was re-opened it was by BRITISH RAIL as the map shows.
2. The line from Baker Street to Stanmore was part of the BAKERLOO line but became JUBILEE when Baker Street was rebuilt and to improve traffic flows.
3. North Weald and Ongar were closed in 1994.
4. Mudchute and Island Gardens are to be rebuilt when the Docklands line is extended to south of the river.
5. The Bakerloo line to Watford Junction was for a time terminated at Stonebridge Park but later re-opened as far as Harrow + Wealdstone.

81

A

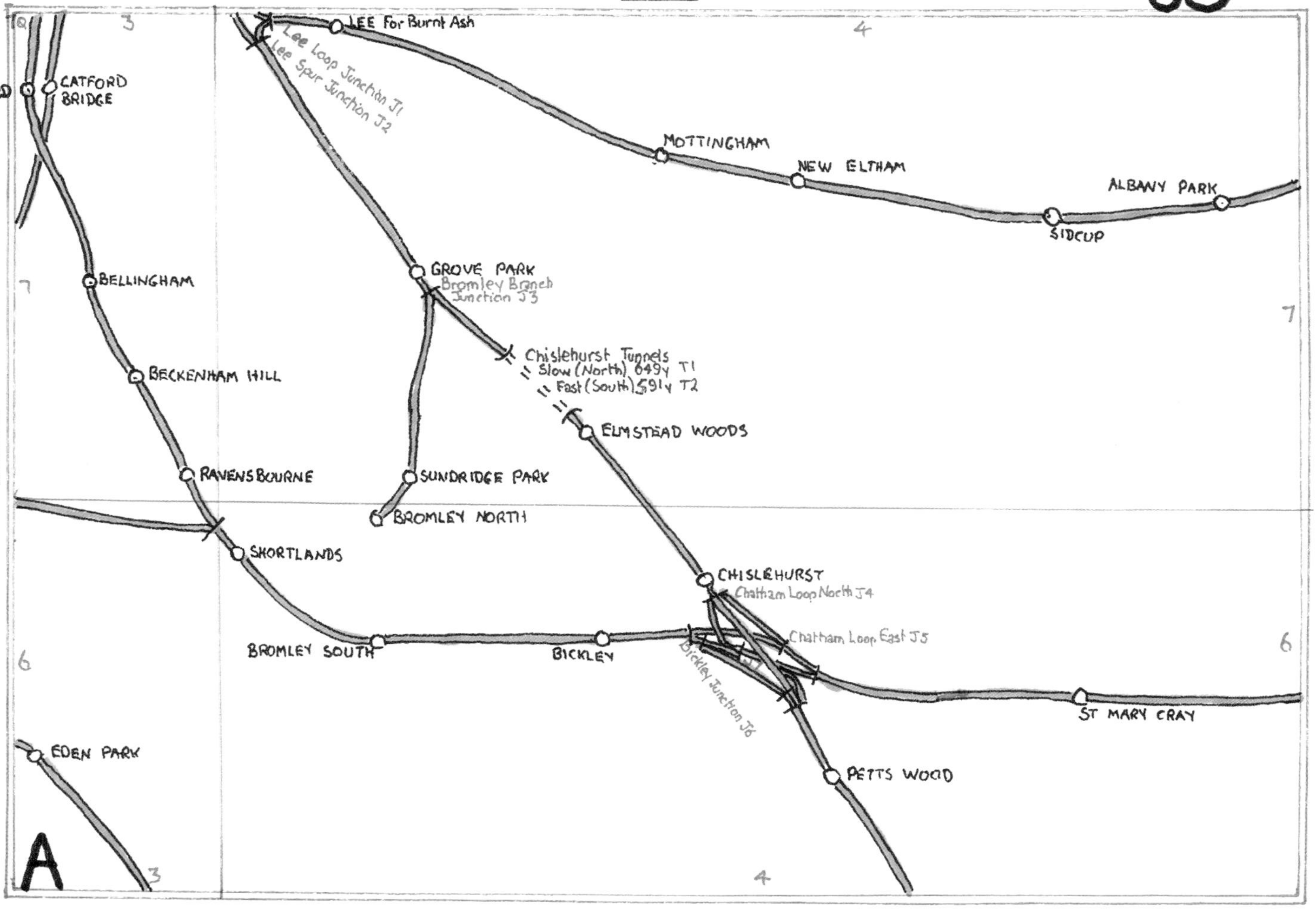

LEE For Burnt Ash
Lee Loop Junction J1
Lee Spur Junction J2
CATFORD
CATFORD BRIDGE
MOTTINGHAM
NEW ELTHAM
ALBANY PARK
SIDCUP
BELLINGHAM
GROVE PARK
Bromley Branch Junction J3
Chislehurst Tunnels
Slow (North) 649y T1
Fast (South) 591y T2
BECKENHAM HILL
ELMSTEAD WOODS
RAVENSBOURNE
SUNDRIDGE PARK
BROMLEY NORTH
SHORTLANDS
CHISLEHURST
Chatham Loop North J4
Chatham Loop East J5
BROMLEY SOUTH
BICKLEY
Bickley Junction J6
ST MARY CRAY
EDEN PARK
PETTS WOOD

82
78
78
78

B

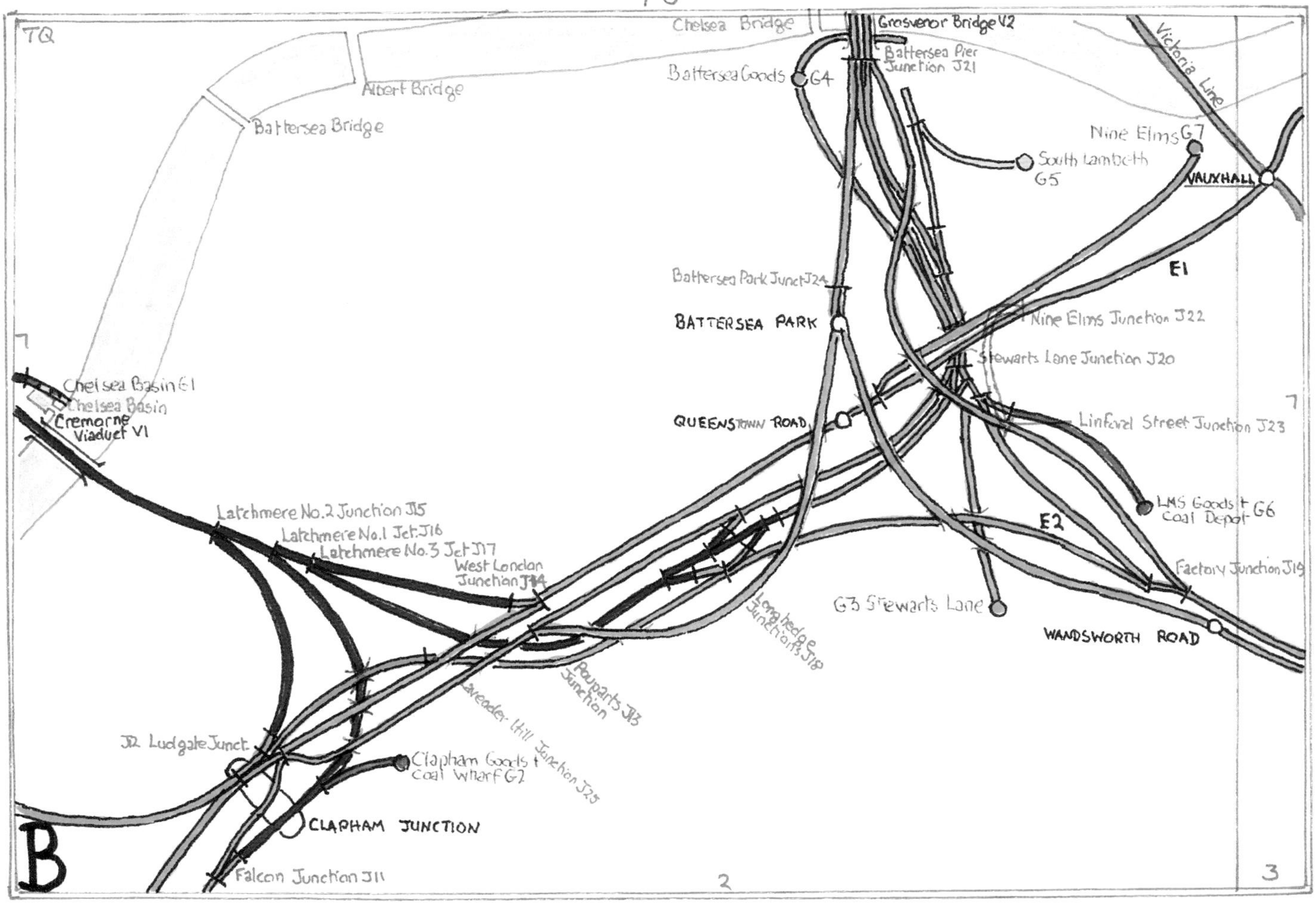

TQ
Chelsea Bridge
Grosvenor Bridge V2
Battersea Pier Junction J21
Albert Bridge
Battersea Goods G4
Victoria Line
Battersea Bridge
Nine Elms G7
South Lambeth G5
VAUXHALL
E1
Battersea Park Junct J24
BATTERSEA PARK
Nine Elms Junction J22
Stewarts Lane Junction J20
Chelsea Basin G1
Chelsea Basin
Cremorne Viaduct V1
QUEENSTOWN ROAD
Linford Street Junction J23
LMS Goods & Coal Depot G6
E2
Latchmere No.2 Junction J15
Latchmere No.1 Jct. J16
Latchmere No.3 Jct J17
West London Junction J14
Factory Junction J19
G3 Stewarts Lane
Longhedge Junction J18
WANDSWORTH ROAD
Pouparts Junction J13
Lavender Hill Junction J25
J12 Ludgate Junct.
Clapham Goods & Coal Wharf G2
CLAPHAM JUNCTION
Falcon Junction J11

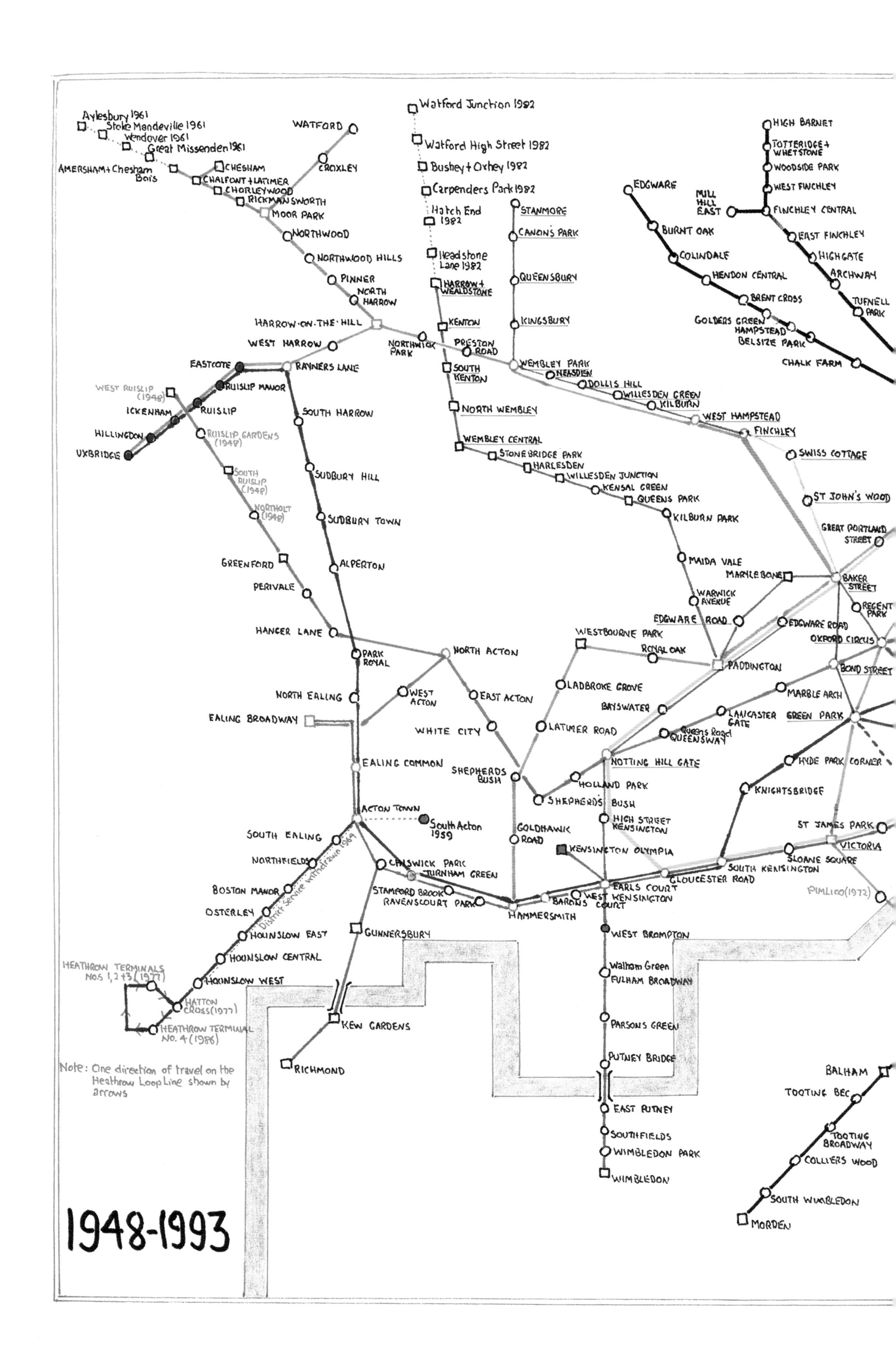

Aylesbury 1961
Stoke Mandeville 1961
Wendover 1961
Great Missenden 1961
AMERSHAM + Chesham Bois
CHESHAM
CHALFONT + LATIMER
CHORLEYWOOD
RICKMANSWORTH
MOOR PARK
WATFORD
CROXLEY
NORTHWOOD
NORTHWOOD HILLS
PINNER
NORTH HARROW
HARROW-ON-THE-HILL
WEST HARROW
NORTHWICK PARK
PRESTON ROAD
EASTCOTE
RAYNERS LANE
RUISLIP MANOR
WEST RUISLIP (1948)
ICKENHAM
RUISLIP
HILLINGDON
UXBRIDGE
RUISLIP GARDENS (1948)
SOUTH RUISLIP (1948)
NORTHOLT (1948)
SOUTH HARROW
SUDBURY HILL
SUDBURY TOWN
ALPERTON
GREENFORD
PERIVALE
HANGER LANE
PARK ROYAL
NORTH ACTON
NORTH EALING
WEST ACTON
EAST ACTON
EALING BROADWAY
WHITE CITY
EALING COMMON
SHEPHERDS BUSH
ACTON TOWN
South Acton 1959
SOUTH EALING
NORTHFIELDS
District service withdrawn 1964
CHISWICK PARK
TURNHAM GREEN
BOSTON MANOR
STAMFORD BROOK
RAVENSCOURT PARK
OSTERLEY
HOUNSLOW EAST
GUNNERSBURY
HOUNSLOW CENTRAL
HEATHROW TERMINALS NOS 1,2+3 (1977)
HOUNSLOW WEST
HATTON CROSS (1977)
HEATHROW TERMINAL NO. 4 (1986)
KEW GARDENS
RICHMOND
Note: One direction of travel on the Heathrow Loop Line shown by arrows
1948-1993
Watford Junction 1982
Watford High Street 1982
Bushey + Oxhey 1982
Carpenders Park 1982
Hatch End 1982
Headstone Lane 1982
HARROW + WEALDSTONE
KENTON
SOUTH KENTON
NORTH WEMBLEY
WEMBLEY CENTRAL
STONEBRIDGE PARK
HARLESDEN
WILLESDEN JUNCTION
KENSAL GREEN
QUEENS PARK
KILBURN PARK
MAIDA VALE
WARWICK AVENUE
STANMORE
CANONS PARK
QUEENSBURY
KINGSBURY
WEMBLEY PARK
NEASDEN
DOLLIS HILL
WILLESDEN GREEN
KILBURN
WEST HAMPSTEAD
FINCHLEY
SWISS COTTAGE
ST JOHN'S WOOD
EDGWARE
BURNT OAK
COLINDALE
HENDON CENTRAL
BRENT CROSS
GOLDERS GREEN
HAMPSTEAD
BELSIZE PARK
CHALK FARM
HIGH BARNET
TOTTERIDGE + WHETSTONE
WOODSIDE PARK
WEST FINCHLEY
MILL HILL EAST
FINCHLEY CENTRAL
EAST FINCHLEY
HIGHGATE
ARCHWAY
TUFNELL PARK
GREAT PORTLAND STREET
MARYLEBONE
BAKER STREET
REGENT PARK
EDGWARE ROAD
EDGWARE ROAD
OXFORD CIRCUS
WESTBOURNE PARK
ROYAL OAK
PADDINGTON
BOND STREET
LADBROKE GROVE
MARBLE ARCH
BAYSWATER
LANCASTER GATE
GREEN PARK
LATIMER ROAD
Queens Road QUEENSWAY
NOTTING HILL GATE
HYDE PARK CORNER
HOLLAND PARK
KNIGHTSBRIDGE
SHEPHERDS BUSH
GOLDHAWK ROAD
HIGH STREET KENSINGTON
ST JAMES PARK
VICTORIA
KENSINGTON OLYMPIA
SLOANE SQUARE
SOUTH KENSINGTON
GLOUCESTER ROAD
EARLS COURT
BARONS COURT
WEST KENSINGTON
HAMMERSMITH
PIMLICO (1972)
WEST BROMPTON
Walham Green
FULHAM BROADWAY
PARSONS GREEN
PUTNEY BRIDGE
EAST PUTNEY
SOUTHFIELDS
WIMBLEDON PARK
WIMBLEDON
BALHAM
TOOTING BEC
TOOTING BROADWAY
COLLIERS WOOD
SOUTH WIMBLEDON
MORDEN

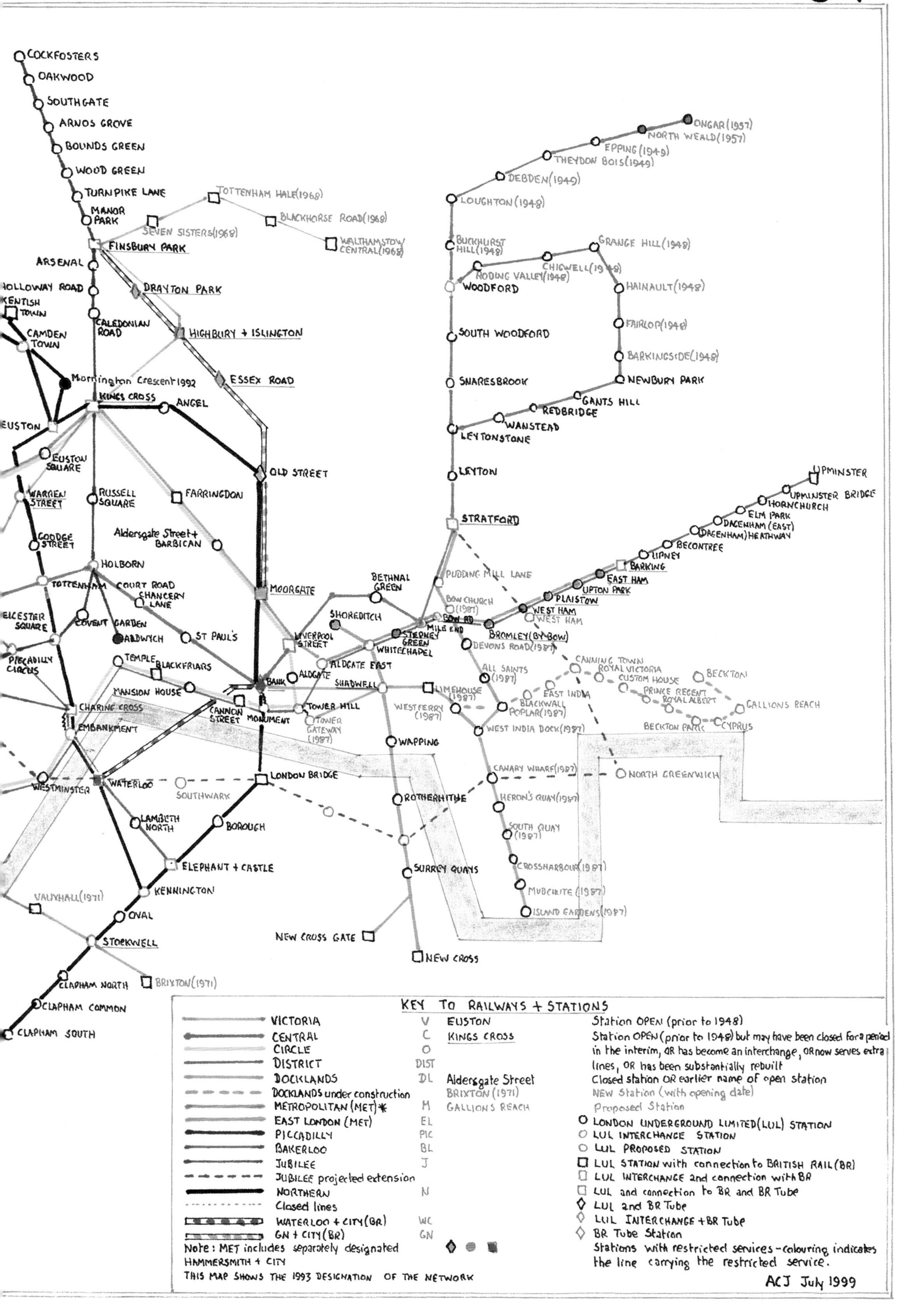

COCKFOSTERS
OAKWOOD
SOUTHGATE
ARNOS GROVE
BOUNDS GREEN
WOOD GREEN
TURNPIKE LANE
MANOR PARK
TOTTENHAM HALE(1968)
SEVEN SISTERS(1968)
BLACKHORSE ROAD(1968)
WALTHAMSTOW CENTRAL(1968)
FINSBURY PARK
ARSENAL
HOLLOWAY ROAD
KENTISH TOWN
DRAYTON PARK
CALEDONIAN ROAD
CAMDEN TOWN
HIGHBURY + ISLINGTON
Mornington Crescent 1992
ESSEX ROAD
KINGS CROSS
ANGEL
EUSTON
EUSTON SQUARE
OLD STREET
WARREN STREET
RUSSELL SQUARE
FARRINGDON
GOODGE STREET
Aldersgate Street + BARBICAN
HOLBORN
TOTTENHAM COURT ROAD
CHANCERY LANE
MOORGATE
LEICESTER SQUARE
COVENT GARDEN
ALDWYCH
ST PAUL'S
LIVERPOOL STREET
PICCADILLY CIRCUS
TEMPLE
BLACKFRIARS
BANK
ALDGATE
ALDGATE EAST
MANSION HOUSE
CHARING CROSS
CANNON STREET
MONUMENT
TOWER HILL
TOWER GATEWAY (1987)
EMBANKMENT
WESTMINSTER
WATERLOO
SOUTHWARK
LONDON BRIDGE
LAMBETH NORTH
BOROUGH
ELEPHANT + CASTLE
KENNINGTON
VAUXHALL(1971)
OVAL
STOCKWELL
CLAPHAM NORTH
BRIXTON(1971)
CLAPHAM COMMON
CLAPHAM SOUTH
ONGAR(1957)
NORTH WEALD(1957)
EPPING(1949)
THEYDON BOIS(1949)
DEBDEN(1949)
LOUGHTON(1948)
BUCKHURST HILL(1948)
GRANGE HILL(1948)
CHIGWELL(1948)
RODING VALLEY(1948)
WOODFORD
HAINAULT(1948)
FAIRLOP(1948)
SOUTH WOODFORD
BARKINGSIDE(1948)
SNARESBROOK
NEWBURY PARK
GANTS HILL
REDBRIDGE
WANSTEAD
LEYTONSTONE
LEYTON
STRATFORD
UPMINSTER
UPMINSTER BRIDGE
HORNCHURCH
ELM PARK
DAGENHAM (EAST)
DAGENHAM) HEATHWAY
BECONTREE
UPNEY
BARKING
EAST HAM
UPTON PARK
PLAISTOW
WEST HAM
PUDDING MILL LANE
BETHNAL GREEN
BOW CHURCH (1987)
BOW RD
MILE END
BROMLEY(BY-BOW)
SHOREDITCH
STEPNEY GREEN
WHITECHAPEL
DEVONS ROAD(1987)
ALL SAINTS (1987)
CANNING TOWN
ROYAL VICTORIA
CUSTOM HOUSE
BECKTON
SHADWELL
LIMEHOUSE (1987)
EAST INDIA
BLACKWALL
POPLAR(1987)
PRINCE REGENT
ROYAL ALBERT
GALLIONS REACH
WESTFERRY (1987)
WEST INDIA DOCK(1987)
BECKTON PARK
CYPRUS
WAPPING
CANARY WHARF(1987)
NORTH GREENWICH
ROTHERHITHE
HERON'S QUAY(1987)
SOUTH QUAY (1987)
CROSSHARBOUR(1987)
SURREY QUAYS
MUDCHUTE (1987)
ISLAND GARDENS(1987)
NEW CROSS GATE
NEW CROSS
KEY TO RAILWAYS + STATIONS
VICTORIA V
CENTRAL C
CIRCLE O
DISTRICT DIST
DOCKLANDS DL
DOCKLANDS under construction
METROPOLITAN (MET) * M
EAST LONDON (MET) EL
PICCADILLY PIC
BAKERLOO BL
JUBILEE J
JUBILEE projected extension
NORTHERN N
Closed lines
WATERLOO + CITY (BR) WC
GN + CITY (BR) GN
Note: MET includes separately designated HAMMERSMITH + CITY
THIS MAP SHOWS THE 1993 DESIGNATION OF THE NETWORK
EUSTON Station OPEN (prior to 1948)
KINGS CROSS Station OPEN (prior to 1948) but may have been closed for a period in the interim, OR has become an interchange, OR now serves extra lines, OR has been substantially rebuilt
Aldersgate Street Closed station OR earlier name of open station
BRIXTON (1971) New Station (with opening date)
GALLIONS REACH Proposed Station
LONDON UNDERGROUND LIMITED (LUL) STATION
LUL INTERCHANGE STATION
LUL PROPOSED STATION
LUL STATION with connection to BRITISH RAIL (BR)
LUL INTERCHANGE and connection with BR
LUL and connection to BR and BR Tube
LUL and BR Tube
LUL INTERCHANGE + BR Tube
BR Tube Station
Stations with restricted services - colouring indicates the line carrying the restricted service.
ACJ July 1999

CHELMSFORD + ROCHESTER

RAILWAYS

No	Company
1	LONDON + NORTH EASTERN (LNE)
2	LONDON MIDLAND + SCOTTISH (LMS)
4	SOUTHERN (S)
5	Underground lines
0	BRITISH RAIL (new lines)
X	SITTINGBOURNE + KEMSLEY 2'6" gauge

STATIONS

Station	Opened/Closed	Ry Ref
Acrow Halt	* 57 64	1 L53
All-Hallows-on-Sea	61	4 Q87
ALTHORNE		1 Q89
AUDLEY END		1 L53
Bannister Green Halt	52	1 L62
BARNEHURST		4 Q47
BASILDON		2 Q68
BATTLESBRIDGE		1 Q79
Beluncle Halt	61	4 Q77
BELVEDERE		4 Q47
BENFLEET (For Canvey Island)	84	2 Q78
BILLERICAY		1 Q69
Blake Hall	81	5 L50
BRAINTREE + Bocking	*	1 L72
Brambledown Hall	50	4 Q97
BRENTWOOD + Warley	69	1 Q59
BURES	*	1 L83
BURNHAM-ON-CROUCH		1 Q99
CHAFFORD HUNDRED		P Q57
CHALKWELL		2 Q88
CHAPPEL + WAKES COLNE	*	1 L82
CHATHAM		4 Q76
CHELMSFORD		1 L60
Cliffe	61	4 Q77
COLCHESTER		1 L92
COLCHESTER TOWN	A § 91	1 M02
CRAYFORD		4 Q57
CRESSING	*	1 L72
Cutlers Green Halt	52	1 L52
CUXTON		4 Q76
DAGENHAM EAST		5 Q58
DARTFORD		4 Q57
Denton Halt	61	4 Q67
Dunmow	1 61	1 L62
Earles Colne	62	1 L82
Eastchurch	50	4 Q97
East Minster-on-Sea	50	4 Q97
Easton Lodge	52	4 L52
EAST TILBURY Halt	49	2 Q67
ELM PARK		5 Q58
ELSENHAM		1 L52
Elsenham	52	1 L52
EMERSON PARK Halt	* 70	2 Q58
ERITH		4 Q57
EYNSFORD		4 Q56
FAMBRIDGE		1 Q89
FARNINGHAM ROAD + Sutton-at-Hone	80	4 Q56
Fawkham For Hartley + Longfield	B § 61	4 Q56
Feering Halt	51	1 L81
Felstead	C § 50	1 L61
Felsted	C § 50 61	1 L61
GIDEA PARK + Squirrels Heath	69	1 Q58
GILLINGHAM		4 Q76
Grain (Crossing Halt)	2 51 61	4 Q87
GRAVESEND Central	65	4 Q67
Gravesend West Street	49 53	4 Q67
GRAYS		2 Q57
GREENHITHE		4 Q57
HALLING		4 Q76
Halstead	62	1 L83
HAROLD WOOD		2 Q59
Harty Road Halt	50	4 R06
HATFIELD PEVEREL		1 L71
Henham Halt	52	1 L52
HIGHAM		4 Q77
High Halstow Halt	61	4 Q77
Hockerill Halt	52	1 L52
HOCKLEY		1 Q89
HOO STAFF HALT	56	4 Q67
HORNCHURCH		5 Q58
HYTHE		1 M02
INGATESTOW		1 Q69
Inworth	50	1 L81
KELVEDON		1 L81
KEMSLEY Halt	69	4 Q96
(KEMSLEY MILL/DOWN)	70	X Q96
LAINDON		2 Q68
Langford + Ulting	* 64	1 L80
LEIGH-ON-SEA		2 Q88
Leysdown	50	4 R06
LONGFIELD for FAWKHAM + HARTLEY	B § 61	4 Q56
Longfield Halt for Pinden + Westwood	53	4 Q56
Low Street	67	2 Q67
Maldon East + Heybridge	* 64	1 L80
MARKS TEY		1 L92
MEOPHAM		4 Q66
Middle Stoke Halt	61	4 Q87
Mill Road Halt	52	1 L52
Milton Range Halt	3 56	4 Q67
Minster-on-Sea	50	4 Q97
NEWINGTON		4 Q86
NEWPORT		1 L53
NORTHFLEET		4 Q67
NORTH WEALD	94	5 L50
OCKENDEN		2 Q58
ONGAR	94	5 L50
PITSEA for Vange		2 Q78
Port Victoria	51	4 Q87
PRITTLEWELL		1 Q88
PURFLEET		2 Q57
QUEENSBOROUGH		4 Q97
RAINHAM Essex		2 Q58
RAINHAM Kent		4 Q86
RAYLEIGH		1 Q79
Rayne	1 61	1 L72
Rifle Range Halt	48	2 Q57
ROCHESTER		4 Q76
ROCHFORD		1 Q88
ROMFORD		1 Q58
St Botolphs	A § 91	1 M02
Saffron Walden	* 64	1 L53
Sharnal Street	61	4 Q77
Shell Haven Halt	50 56	2 Q78
Sheerness East	50	4 Q97
SHEERNESS-ON-SEA		4 Q97
SHENFIELD + Hutton Junction	69	1 Q69
SHOEBURYNESS		2 Q98
SHOREHAM		4 Q56
Sible + Castle Hedingham	52	1 L73
Sibley's For Chickney + Broxted		1 L52
(SITTINGBOURNE)	90	X Q96
SITTINGBOURNE + Milton Regis	70	4 Q96
SLADES GREEN	4	4 Q57
SNODLAND		4 Q76
SOLE STREET		4 Q66
SOUTHEND-on-Sea CENTRAL	5 49 69	2 Q88
SOUTHEND-on-Sea EAST	5 49 69	2 Q88
SOUTHEND-on-Sea VICTORIA	5 49 69	1 Q88
Southfield	53	4 Q67
SOUTHMINSTER		1 Q99
Stane Street Halt	52	1 L52
STANFORD-LE-HOPE		2 Q68
STANSTED AIRPORT	91	0 L52
STANSTED MOUNTFITCHET	90	1 L52
Stoke Junction Halt	61	4 Q87
STONE CROSSING Halt	69	4 Q57
STROOD		4 Q76
SWALE	6 60	4 Q96
SWANLEY		4 Q56
SWANSCOMBE		4 Q57
Takeley	1	1 L52
TEYNHAM		4 Q96
Thames Haven	7 55	2 Q78
Thaxted	52	1 L62
THORPE BAY		2 Q98
Tilbury Riverside	92	2 Q67
TILBURY TOWN		2 Q67
Tiptree	51	1 L81
Tollesbury	51	1 L90
Tolleshunt d'Arcy	51	1 L91
Tolleshunt Knights	51	1 L81
UPMINSTER		25 Q58
UPMINSTER BRIDGE		5 Q58
Uralite Halt	61	4 Q67
WESTCLIFF-on-Sea	69	2 Q88
WEST HORDON	8 § 49	2 Q68
White Colne	62	1 L82
WHITE NOTLEY	*	1 L71
WICKFORD		1 Q79
Wickham Bishops	* 64	1 L81
WITHAM		1 L81
WIVENHOE		1 M02
WOODHAM FERRERS		1 Q79
Yeldham	62	1 L73

GOODS [9]

No	Name/Location	Closed	Ry Ref
G1	Braintree	10	1 L72
2	Tollesbury Pier	51	1 L90
3	Malden	60	1 L80
4	Chelmsford	10	1 L60
5	Romford	70	2 Q58
6	Erith Wharf		4 Q57
7	Sheerness Dockyard	63	4 Q97
8	Dockyard Gates	60	4 Q97
9	Chatham Dockyard		4 Q76
10	Graveney	71	4 R06
11	Faversham Coal	71	4 R06

ENGINE SHEDS

No	Name/Location	Closed	Ry Ref
E1	Colchester	59	1 L92
2	Brentwood	49	1 Q59
3	Gillingham	60	4 Q76
4	Shoeburyness	62	2 Q98
5	Tilbury	62	2 Q67
6	Upminster	56	2 Q58
7	Southminster	57	1 Q99
9	Southend Victoria	57	1 Q88
10	SLADE GREEN	0	4 Q57
11	Kelvedon	51	1 L81
12	Saffron Walden	58	1 L53
13	Maldon	60	1 L08
14	Braintree	59	1 L72
15	Thaxted	52	1 L52

TUNNELS

No	Name/Location	Length	Ry Ref
T1	Littlebury	407	1 L53
2	Audley End	456	1 L53
3	Coopers Lane	1944	0 L52
4	Strood	2329	4 Q77
5	Ford Pit	428	4 Q76
6	Chatham	297	4 Q76
7	Gillingham	897	4 Q76
8	Eynsford	828	4 Q56
9	Greenhithe	253	4 Q57
10	Higham	1531	4 Q77

BRIDGES + VIADUCTS

No	Name	Ry	Ref
V1	Queens Bridge	4	Q96

JUNCTIONS

No	Name	Ry	Ref
J1	Crayford Creek	4	Q57
2	Perry Street Fork	4	Q57
3	Rosherville Line	4	Q56
4	Sheppey	4	Q97
5	Woodham	4	Q89
6	Colne Valley	4	L82
7	Tollesbury Line	1	L81

NOTES:

REF All in TL, TM, TQ or TR. Therefore initial T omitted in the reference.

§ Older version } Name changes
§ Newer version }
Corresponding letter indicates the other name

1 Regular services ended in 52
2 Site changed in 51 when halt dropped from title. Site of new station close to old.
3 Regular services ended in 32.
4 s of Slades dropped in 53
5 Distinguishing designations added in 49. 'on-Sea' dropped in 69.
6 New site in 60. Halt may have been dropped at this time.
7 Regular passenger services had ended earlier.
8 East Hordon until '49
9 Closing dates only if known.
10 Previously passenger station.

63

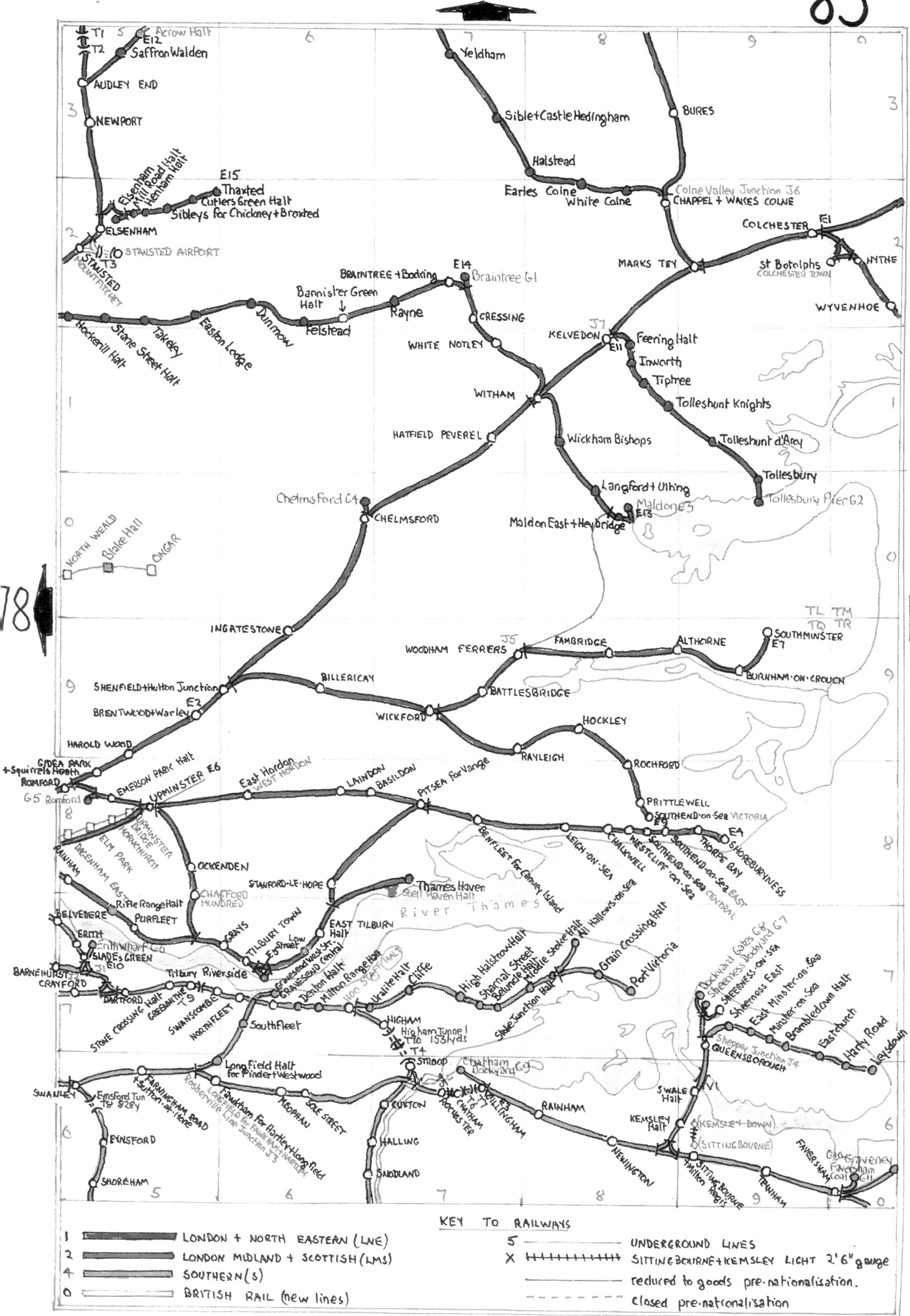

78
86
Acrow Halt
E12
Saffron Walden
T1
T2
AUDLEY END
NEWPORT
Elsenham
Mill Road Halt
Henham Halt
E15
Thaxted
Cutlers Green Halt
Sibleys for Chickney + Broxted
ELSENHAM
STANSTED MOUNTFITCHET
T3
STANSTED AIRPORT
Yeldham
Sible + Castle Hedingham
Halstead
Earles Colne
White Colne
BURES
Colne Valley Junction J6
CHAPPEL + WAKES COLNE
COLCHESTER
E1
MARKS TEY
St Botolphs
COLCHESTER TOWN
HYTHE
WYVENHOE
BRAINTREE + Bocking
E14
Braintree G1
Bannister Green Halt
Rayne
Felstead
Dunmow
Easton Lodge
Takeley
Stane Street Halt
Hockerill Halt
CRESSING
WHITE NOTLEY
KELVEDON
J7
E11
Feering Halt
Inworth
Tiptree
Tolleshunt Knights
Tolleshunt d'Arcy
Tollesbury
Tollesbury Pier G2
WITHAM
HATFIELD PEVEREL
Wickham Bishops
Langford + Ulting
Maldon G3
E13
Maldon East + Heybridge
Chelmsford G4
CHELMSFORD
NORTH WEALD
Blake Hall
ONGAR
INGATESTONE
TL TM
TQ TR
SOUTHMINSTER
E7
J5
WOODHAM FERRERS
FAMBRIDGE
ALTHORNE
BURNHAM-ON-CROUCH
SHENFIELD + Hutton Junction
BILLERICAY
BATTLESBRIDGE
E2
BRENTWOOD + Warley
WICKFORD
HOCKLEY
HAROLD WOOD
RAYLEIGH
ROCHFORD
GIDEA PARK + Squirrels Heath
ROMFORD
G5 Romford
EMERSON PARK Halt
UPMINSTER E6
East Horndon
WEST HORNDON
LAINDON
BASILDON
PITSEA for Vange
PRITTLEWELL
SOUTHEND-on-Sea VICTORIA
E8
E4
UPMINSTER BRIDGE
HORNCHURCH
ELM PARK
DAGENHAM EAST
RAINHAM
BENFLEET for Canvey Island
LEIGH-ON-SEA
CHALKWELL
WESTCLIFF-on-Sea
SOUTHEND-on-Sea CENTRAL
SOUTHEND-on-Sea EAST
THORPE BAY
SHOEBURYNESS
OCKENDEN
CHAFFORD HUNDRED
STANFORD-LE-HOPE
Thames Haven
Shell Haven Halt
River Thames
Rifle Range Halt
PURFLEET
BELVEDERE
ERITH
Erith Wharf G6
SLADES GREEN
E10
J1
BARNEHURST
CRAYFORD
GRAYS
TILBURY TOWN
EAST TILBURY
Low Street
E5
Gravesend West Str.
Gravesend Central
Tilbury Riverside
DARTFORD
Stone Crossing Halt
GREENHITHE
T9
SWANSCOMBE
NORTHFLEET
Denton Halt
Milton Range Halt
Hoo Staff Halt
Uralite Halt
Cliffe
High Halstow Halt
Sharnal Street
Beluncle Halt
Middle Stoke Halt
All Hallows-on-Sea
Grain Crossing Halt
Port Victoria
Stoke Junction Halt
Southfleet
HIGHAM
Higham Tunnel T10 1531yds
T4
STROOD
Chatham Dockyard G9
Dockyard Gates G8
Sheerness Dockyard G7
SHEERNESS-ON-SEA
Sheerness East
East Minster-on-Sea
Minster-on-Sea
Brambledown Halt
Eastchurch
Harty Road
Leysdown
Sheppey Junction J4
QUEENSBOROUGH
Swale Halt
V1
Kemsley Halt
KEMSLEY DOWN
SITTINGBOURNE
SWANLEY
Eynsford Tun T8 328y
FARNINGHAM ROAD + Sutton-at-Hone
Longfield Halt for Pinden + Westwood
Fawkham for Hartley + Longfield
Longfield for Fawkham + Hartley
Rosherville Line Junction J3
MEOPHAM
SOLE STREET
CUXTON
HALLING
SNODLAND
ROCHESTER
CHATHAM
GILLINGHAM
E3
RAINHAM
NEWINGTON
SITTINGBOURNE + Milton Regis
TEYNHAM
FAVERSHAM
Graveney
Faversham Coal G11
EYNSFORD
SHOREHAM
KEY TO RAILWAYS
1 LONDON + NORTH EASTERN (LNE)
2 LONDON MIDLAND + SCOTTISH (LMS)
4 SOUTHERN (S)
0 BRITISH RAIL (new lines)
5 UNDERGROUND LINES
X SITTINGBOURNE + KEMSLEY LIGHT 2'6" gauge
reduced to goods pre-nationalisation
closed pre-nationalisation

94

86A MANNINGTREE + HARWICH

RAILWAYS

No	Company
1	LONDON + NORTH EASTERN

STATIONS

Name	Opened / Closed	Ry	Ref
ALRESFORD		1	02
Ardleigh	67	1	02
Bentley	66	1	13
Bradfield	56	1	13
Brightlingsea	1* 64	1	01
CLACTON-on-Sea + Holland-on-Sea	69	1	11
DOVERCOURT Bay	72	1	23
Felixstowe Beach	*59 60 67	1	23
Felixstowe Pier	51	1	23
FELIXSTOWE Town	69	1	33
FRINTON-on-Sea	69	1	22
GREAT BENTLEY		1	12
HARWICH PARKESTON QUAY		1	23
HARWICH TOWN		1	23
KIRBY CROSS		1	22
MANNINGTREE		1	03
MISTLEY		1	13
Priory Halt	2 65	1	13
Thorington	57	1	02
THORPE-LE-SOKEN		1	12
TRIMLEY		1	23
WALTON-ON-NAZE		1	22
WEELEY		1	12
WRABNESS		1	13
WIVENHOE		1	02

ENGINE SHEDS

No	Name/Location	Closed	Ry	Ref
E1	Clacton	59	1	11
2	Parkeston Quay	67	1	23
3	Walton	60	1	22
4	Felixstowe	3 52	2	23

NOTES:

REF All in TM So letters omitted

1 Closed in 53 but re-opened later in year.

2 Staff unadvertised Halt

3 Exact closure date unclear.

86B MARGATE, ASHFORD + DOVER

RAILWAYS

No	Company
4	SOUTHERN
5	EAST KENT
6	ROMNEY HYTHE + DYMCHURCH 1'3" gauge

STATIONS

Name	Opened / Closed	Ry	Ref
ADISHAM		4	25
ASHFORD		4	04
Ash Town	48	5	25
AYLESHAM		4	25
BEKESBOURNE		4	15
BIRCHINGTON-ON-SEA		4	26
BROADSTAIRS		4	36
BURMARSH ROAD HALT		6	13
CANTERBURY EAST		4	15
Canterbury Road Wingham	48	5	25
CANTERBURY WEST		4	15
CHARTHAM		4	15
CHERITON SHUTTLE TERMINAL	94	0	13
CHESTFIELD + SWALECLIFFE		4	16
CHILHAM		4	05
Chislet Colliery Halt	69 71	4	26
DEAL		4	35
DOVER Marine WESTERN DOCKS	79 94	4	33
DOVER PRIORY		4	34
DUMPTON PARK		4	36
DUNGENESS		6	01
DYMCHURCH		6	02
Eastry Junction	48	5	25
Eastry South	48	5	25
Elvington	48	5	25
Eythorne	1 48 P	5	24
FAVERSHAM		4	06
FOLKESTONE CENTRAL		4	23
FOLKESTONE HARBOUR		4	23
FOLKESTONE Junction EAST	62 65	4	23
Folkestone Warren Halt	71	4	23
FOLKESTONE WEST	A § 62	4	23
(Golden Sands)	51 77	6	02
Greatstone-on-Sea Halt	* 54 67	4	02
Greatstone (Halt)	80 83	6	02
Grove Ferry + Upstreet	54 66	4	26
HAM STREET + Orleston	* 76	4	03
Harty Road	50	4	06
HERNE BAY + Hampton-on-Sea	51	4	16
Hythe	51	4	13
HYTHE		6	13
(JEFFERSON LANE)	B § 81	6	02
KEARNSEY		4	24
Knowlton	48	5	25
LADE HALT		6	01
Leysdown	50	4	06
Lydd-on-Sea	* 67	4	01
Lydd Town	* 67	4	02
Margate East	53	4	36
MARGATE West		4	36
MARTIN MILL		4	34
MINSTER		4	26
NEW ROMNEY		6	02
New Romney + Littlestone-on-Sea	* 67	4	02
Pilot Halt, The	83	6	01
PRIORY, DOVER		4	34
RAMSGATE		4	36
ROMNEY SANDS	6 '67	6	02
St Mary's Bay	B § 81	6	02
SANDLING Junction For Hythe	51 80	4	13
SANDWICH		4	35
SELLING		4	05
SHAKESPEARE STAFF HALT		4	23
SHEPHERD'S WELL		4	24
Shepherd's Well	48	5	24
Shorncliffe	A § 62	4	23
Smeeth	54	4	03
SNOWDOWN + Nonington (Halt)	(69) 80	4	25
Staple	48	5	25
Stonehall + Lydden Halt	54	4	24
STURRY		4	15
TILMANSTONE	2 P	5	25
WALMER		4	35
WESTENHANGER		4	13
WESTGATE-ON-SEA		4	36
WHITSTABLE + Tankerton		4	16
Wingham	48	5	25
Wingham Canterbury Road	48	5	25
Wingham Town	48	5	25
Woodnesborough	48	5	25
WYE		4	04

GOODS

No	Name/Location	Closed	Ry	Ref
G1	Graveney	62	4	06
2	Whitstable Harbour	53	4	16
3	Sandwich Road	50	5	35
4	Dungeness	52	4	02

WORKS

No	Location	Closed	Ry	Ref
C1	Ashford	62	4	04

ENGINE SHEDS

No	Name/Location	Closed	Ry	Ref
E1	Ashford	3 63	4	04
2	Canterbury West	55	4	15
3	Dover	61	4	34
4	Faversham	4 59	4	06
5	Folkestone	61	4	23
6	Ramsgate	60	4	36

TUNNELS

No	Name	Length	Ry	Ref
T1	Golgotha	5 460	3	24
2	Hackington or Tyler Hill	1012	4	15
3	Shakespeare	1387	4	33
4	Abbotscliffe	1942	4	23
5	Lydden	2369	4	24
6	Martello	532	4	23
7	Dover Harbour	684	4	34
8	Priory	158	4	34
9	Charlton	264	4	34
10	Guston	1412	4	34
11	Saltwood	954	4	13
12	Sandling	100	4	13
13	Selling	405	4	05

JUNCTIONS

No	Name		Ry	Ref
J1	Archcliffe		4	34
2	Hawkesbury Street		4	34
3	Pier		4	34
4	Buckland		4	34
5	Kearnsey Loop		4	34
6	Deal		4	34
7	Harbledown	closed	4	15
8	Whitstable Line		4	15
9	Guildford Colliery Branch		3	24

NOTES:

REF All in TR therefore letters are omitted.

§ Old name } Change of name
§ New name
corresponding letter shows other variation

1 Proposed preserved railway. The location of station unclear.

2 Proposed station exact position not known.

3 Diesels to 66

4 Continued for some further period as a diesel depot

5 Exact length not known.

6 This station had been reopened in 1947 as Littlestone Holiday Camp it later became Maddieson's Camp before taking its current name in '67.

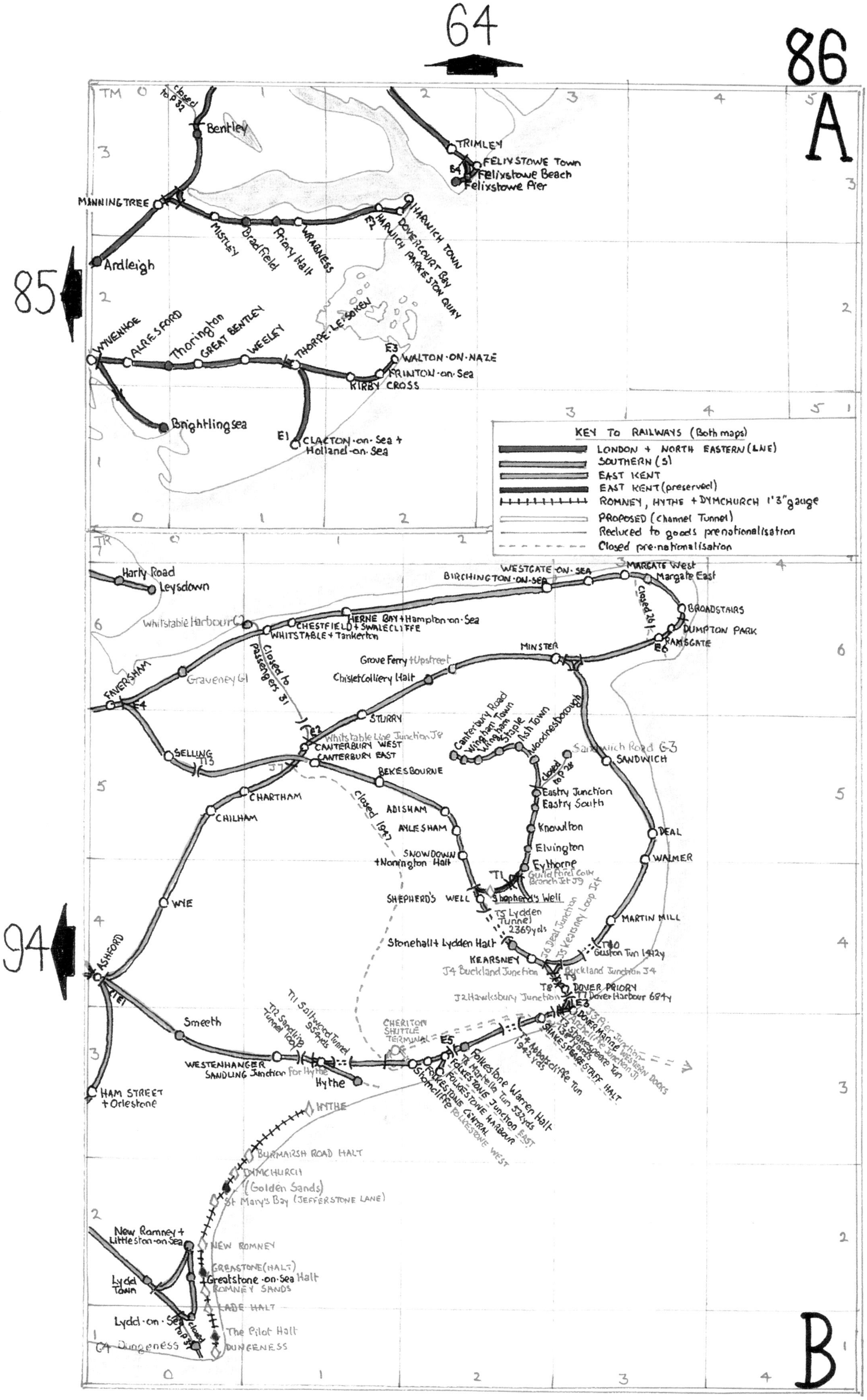

64

A

85

TM

closed to p 32

Bentley

TRIMLEY

FELIXSTOWE Town

Felixstowe Beach

Felixstowe Pier

E4

MANNINGTREE

MISTLEY

Bradfield

Priory Halt

WRABNESS

E2

HARWICH TOWN

DOVERCOURT Bay

HARWICH PARKESTON QUAY

Ardleigh

WIVENHOE

ALRESFORD

Thorington

GREAT BENTLEY

WEELEY

THORPE-LE-SOKEN

E3

WALTON-ON-NAZE

FRINTON-on-Sea

KIRBY CROSS

Brightlingsea

E1

CLACTON-on-Sea + Holland-on-Sea

KEY TO RAILWAYS (Both maps)

- LONDON + NORTH EASTERN (LNE)
- SOUTHERN (S)
- EAST KENT
- EAST KENT (preserved)
- ROMNEY, HYTHE + DYMCHURCH 1'3" gauge
- PROPOSED (Channel Tunnel)
- Reduced to goods prenationalisation
- Closed pre-nationalisation

TR

Harty Road

Leysdown

WESTGATE-ON-SEA

MARGATE West

Margate East

BIRCHINGTON-ON-SEA

Closed 26

BROADSTAIRS

DUMPTON PARK

E6

RAMSGATE

Whitstable Harbour C2

CHESTFIELD + SWALECLIFFE

WHITSTABLE + Tankerton

HERNE BAY + Hampton-on-Sea

MINSTER

Grove Ferry + Upstreet

Chislet Colliery Halt

FAVERSHAM

E4

Graveney G1

Closed to passengers 31

STURRY

E2

Whitstable Line Junction J8

CANTERBURY WEST

CANTERBURY EAST

J7

SELLING

T13

Canterbury Road

Wingham Town

Wingham

Staple

Ash Town

Woodnesborough

Sandwich Road G3

SANDWICH

closed to p 28

Eastry Junction

Eastry South

BEKESBOURNE

CHARTHAM

CHILHAM

closed 1947

ADISHAM

AYLESHAM

SNOWDOWN + Nonington Halt

Knowlton

Elvington

Eythorne

Guilford Colly Branch Jct J9

T1

SHEPHERD'S WELL

Shepherd's Well

DEAL

WALMER

WYE

T5 Lydden Tunnel 2369yds

J6 Deal Junction

J5 Kearsney Loop Jct

MARTIN MILL

T10 Guston Tun 1412y

Stonehall + Lydden Halt

KEARSNEY

J4 Buckland Junction

Buckland Junction J4

ASHFORD

T9

T8

DOVER PRIORY

T7 Dover Harbour 684y

J2 Hawksbury Junction

E3

DOVER MARINE

J3 Pier Junction

WESTERN DOCKS

E1

T6 Shakespeare Tun

Archcliffe Junction J1

SHAKESPEARE STAFF HALT

Smeeth

T11 Saltwood Tunnel 954yds

T12 Sandling Tunnel 1061y

CHERITON SHUTTLE TERMINAL

E5

Folkestone Warren Halt

T3 Martello Tun 532yds

T4 Abbotscliffe Tun 1942yds

WESTENHANGER

SANDLING Junction for Hythe

Hythe

Shorncliffe

FOLKESTONE CENTRAL

FOLKESTONE HARBOUR

FOLKESTONE Junction

EAST

FOLKESTONE WEST

HAM STREET + Orlestone

HYTHE

BURMARSH ROAD HALT

DYMCHURCH

(Golden Sands)

St Mary's Bay (JEFFERSTONE LANE)

New Romney + Littlestone-on-Sea

NEW ROMNEY

Lydd Town

GREATSTONE (HALT)

Greatstone-on-Sea Halt

ROMNEY SANDS

LADE HALT

Lydd-on-Sea

closed to p 37

The Pilot Halt

G4 Dungeness

DUNGENESS

94

B

LAUNCESTON, HALWILL + BIDEFORD

RAILWAYS

No.	Company
3	GREAT WESTERN (GW)
4	SOUTHERN (S)

STATIONS

Name		Closed	Ry	Ref
Ashbury for North Lew		* 66	4	X49
Ashwater		* 66	4	X39
Bideford	1	* 65	4	S42
Braunton		* 70	4	S43
Brentor		* 68	4	X48
Bude		* 66	4	S20
Camelford		* 66	4	X08
Coryton		† 62	3	X48
Delabole		* 66	4	X08
Dunsbear Halt		* 65	4	S41
Dunsland Cross		* 66	4	S40
Egloskerry		* 66	4	X28
Halwill		* 66	4	X49
Hole		* 65	4	S40
Holsworthy		* 66	4	S30
Instow	1	* 65	4	S42
Launceston North	2	51 52	3	X38
Launceston South	2	* 51 66	4	X38
Liddaton Halt		† 62	3	X48
Lifton		† 62	3	X38
Lydford		62	3	X48
Lydford		* 68	4	X48
Mortehoe + Woolacombe		* 50 70	4	S44
Otterham		* 66	4	X18
Torrington		* 65	4	S41
Tower Hill		* 66	4	X39
Tresmeer		* 66	4	X28
Watergate Halt		* 65	4	S41
Whitstone + Bridgerule		* 66	4	S20
Wrafton		* 70	4	S43
Yarde Halt		* 65	4	S41

GOODS

Name	Closed	Ry	Ref
Bideford	65	4	S42
Bude Quay	64	4	S20

ENGINE SHEDS

No	Name			Closed	Ry	Ref
E1	Launceston	4	3	66	4	X38
2	Bude		3	64	4	S20
3	Torrington			59	4	S41
4	Launceston			62	3	X38

TUNNELS

No	Name	Length	Ry	Ref
T1	Lancast	196	4	S42

NOTES:

REF All in SS or SX therefore initial S omitted.

1 Re-opend for two weeks in 1/68

2 After closure of ex GW station, trains continued to run on ex GW line from Lifton and via crossover into ex S station

3 Transferred to W region in 62.

4 Launceston Steam Railway 1'11½" gauge opened for a mile. Being extended.

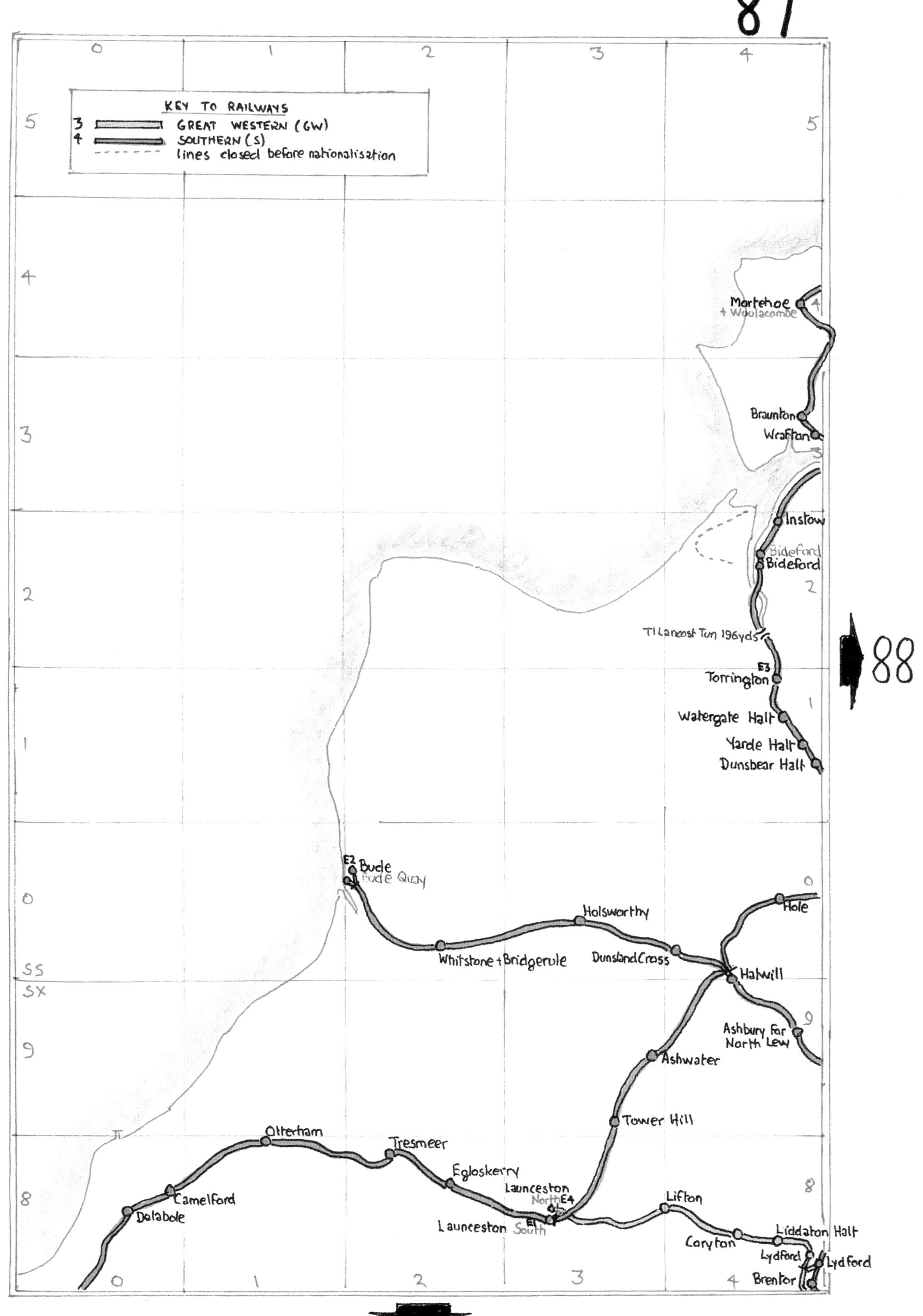
KEY TO RAILWAYS
3 GREAT WESTERN (GW)
4 SOUTHERN (S)
lines closed before nationalisation
Mortehoe + Woolacombe
Braunton
Wrafton
Instow
Bideford
Bideford
Tl Lancast Tun 196yds
E3
Torrington
Watergate Halt
Yarde Halt
Dunsbear Halt
E2 Bude
Bude Quay
Holsworthy
Whitstone + Bridgerule
Dunsland Cross
Hole
Halwill
Ashbury for North Lew
Ashwater
Tower Hill
Otterham
Tresmeer
Egloskerry
Launceston North
E4
Launceston South
E1
Camelford
Delabole
Lifton
Coryton
Liddaton Halt
Lydford
Lydford
Brentor
SS
SX

88

96

BARNSTAPLE + EXETER

RAILWAYS

No	Company
3	GREAT WESTERN (GW)
4	SOUTHERN (S)
5	WEST SOMERSET (preserved ex GW)

STATIONS

Name	Opened Closed	Ry	Ref
Alphington Halt	58	3	X99
Ashton	58	3	X88
Bampton	† 63	3	S92
Barnstaple Victoria Road	49 60	3	S53
BARNSTAPLE Junction	70	4	S53
Barnstaple Town	* 70	4	S53
Bishops Nympton + Molland	* 66	3	S72
Bolham Halt	† 63	3	S91
Bow	* 72	4	S70
Brampford Speke Halt	† 63	3	X99
Brentor	* 68	4	X58
Bridestowe	* 68	4	X58
Broad Clyst	* 66	4	X99
Burn (for Butterleigh) Halt	† 63	3	S90
Cadeleigh	† 63	3	S90
CHAPELTON	*	4	S52
Christow	58	3	X88
Clyst St Mary + Digby Halt	3 48	4	X99
COPPLESTONE	*	4	S70
Cove Halt	† 63	3	S91
CREDITON		4	X89
Dulverton	* 66	3	S92
Dunsbear Halt	* 65	4	S51
Dunsford Halt	58	3	X89
Dunster	* 71 76	5	S94
East Anstey	* 66	3	S82
EGGESFORD		4	S61
EXETER			X99
CENTRAL		4	X99
ST DAVIDS		3	X99
ST JAMES PARK	*	4	X99
ST THOMAS	*	3	X90
Exminster	* 64	3	X98
EXMOUTH	*	4	X98
EXTON Halt 65-69	* A § 58	4	X98
Filleigh	* 66	3	S62
Fremington	1 * 65	4	S53
Halberton Halt	* 64	3	S91
Hatherleigh	* 65	4	S50
Hawkmoor Halt	B § 55	3	X78
Hele + Bradninch	* 64	3	S90
Ide Halt	58	3	X89
Ilfracombe	* 70	4	S54
KINGS NYMPTON	* C § 51	4	S61
LAPFORD		4	S70
Longdown	58	3	X89
Lustleigh	59	3	X78
Lydford	* 68	4	X58
Lydford	62	3	X58
LYMPSTONE Halt 65-9 VILLAGE	* 91	4	X98
LYMPSTONE COMMANDO	76	4	X98
Maddaford Moor Halt	* 66	4	X59
Meeth Halt	* 65	4	S51
Meldon Quarry Staff Halt	2 68	4	X59
Minehead	* 71 76	5	S94
MORCHARD ROAD Halt 65-69	*	4	S70
Morebath	* 66	3	S92
Morebath Junction Halt	* 66	3	S92
Moretonhampstead	59	3	X78
Mortehoe + Woolacombe	* 50 70	4	S44
NEWTON ST CYRES	*	4	X89
North Tawton	* 72	4	X69
OKEHAMPTON	72	4	X59
Petrockstow	* 65	4	S51
PINHOE	* 66 83	4	X99
POLSLOE BRIDGE Halt	* 69	4	X99
PORTSMOUTH ARMS	*	4	S61
Pullabrook Halt	B § 55 59	3	X78
ST DAVIDS		3	X99
ST JAMES PARK	*	4	X99
ST THOMAS	*	3	X99
Sampford Courtenay Halt 65-69	* 72	4	X69
Silverton	* 64	3	S90
South Molton	* 66	3	S72
South Molton Road	C § 51	4	S61
STARCROSS	*	3	X98
Stoke Canon	60	3	X99
Swimbridge	* 66	3	S62
Thorverton	† 63	3	S90
Tiverton	* 64	3	S91
TOPSHAM	*	4	X98
Trusham	58	3	X88
UMBERLEIGH	*	4	S62
Up Exe Halt	† 63	3	S90
West Exe Halt	† 63	3	S91
Woodbury Road	A § 58	4	X98
YEOFORD	*	4	X79
Yeo Mill Halt	* 66	3	S82

ENGINE SHEDS

No	Name/Location	Closed	Ry	Ref
E1	Barnstaple Junction	64	4	S53
2	Ilfracombe	64	4	S54
3	Exmouth	63	4	X98
4	Exmouth Junction	65	4	X99
5	Okehampton	64	4	X59
6	Minehead	56	3	S94
7	Barnstaple	51	3	S53
8	Exeter	63	3	X99

TUNNELS

No	Name	Length	Ry	Ref
T1	Castle Hill	319	3	S62
2	Nightcote	44	3	S86
3	Perridge	836	3	X89
4	St Davids	184	4	X99

VIADUCTS + BRIDGES

No	Name	Ry	Ref
V1	Meldon Viaduct	4	X59

JUNCTIONS

No	Name	Ry	Ref
J1	Heathfield Branch	3	X99
2	Cowley Bridge	34	X99
3	Exmouth Branch	4	X99
4	Coleford	4	X79
5	Tiverton + North Devon	3	S91
6	Ilfracombe	4	S53
7	Loop West	34	S53
8	South Loop	3	S53
9	East Loop	3	S53
10	Loop	3	S53
11	Meldon	4	X59

NOTES:

REF All in SS or SX therefore initial S omitted.

§ Older version } Change of name
§ Newer version }

Corresponding letters indicate alternative version.

1 Re-opened for two weeks 1/68

2 Unadvertised workers halt.

3 Re-opened post privatisation as DIGBY + SOWTON

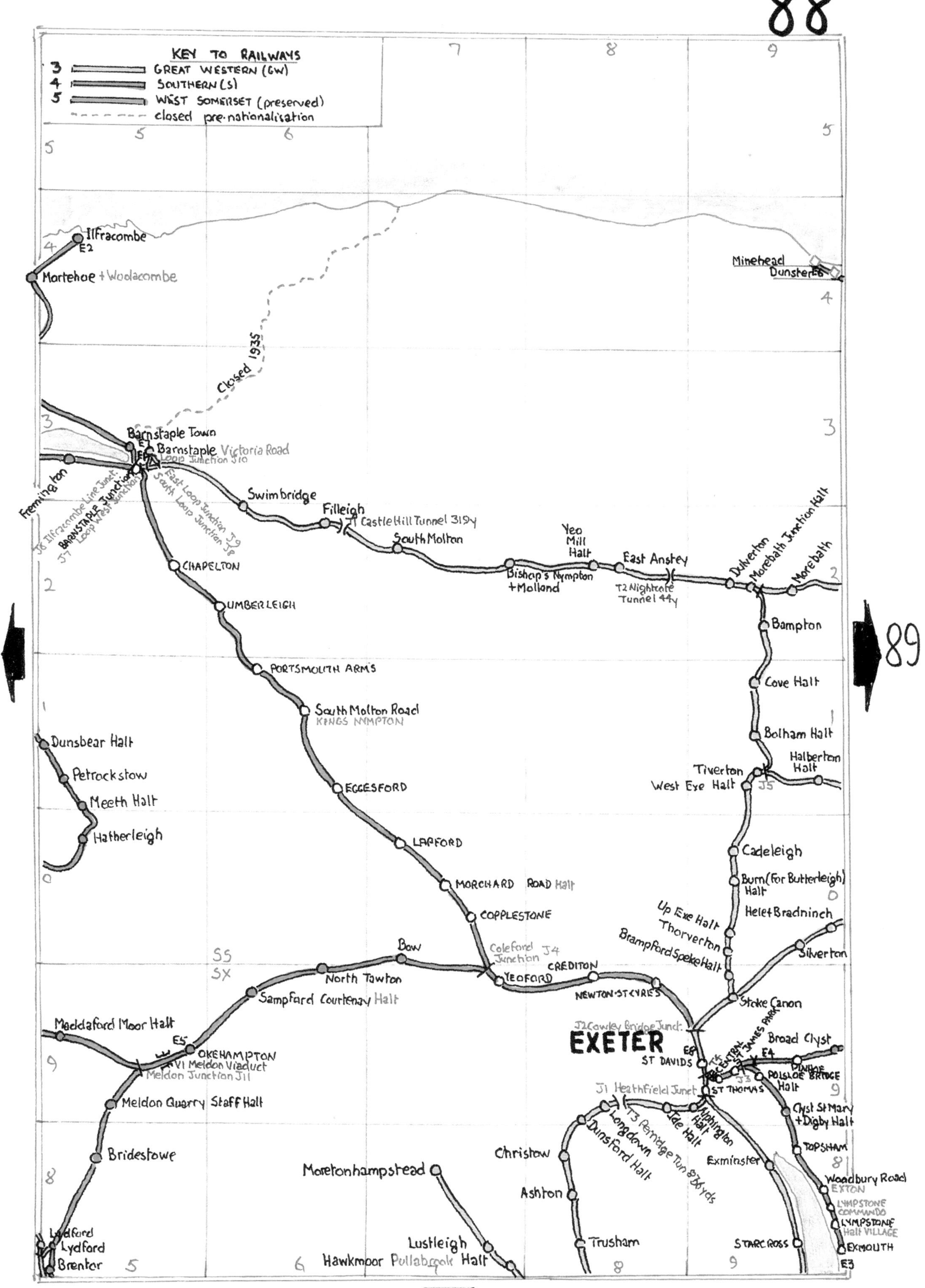
KEY TO RAILWAYS
3 GREAT WESTERN (GW)
4 SOUTHERN (S)
5 WEST SOMERSET (preserved)
closed pre-nationalisation
Ilfracombe
E2
Mortehoe + Woolacombe
Closed 1935
Minehead
Dunster
E6
Barnstaple Town
Barnstaple Victoria Road
Loop Junction J10
Fremington
J6 Ilfracombe Line Junct.
BARNSTAPLE Junction
J7 Loop West Junction
East Loop Junction J9
South Loop Junction J8
Swimbridge
Filleigh
Castle Hill Tunnel 319y
South Molton
Yeo Mill Halt
Bishop's Nympton + Molland
East Anstey
T2 Nightcote Tunnel 44y
Dulverton
Morebath Junction Halt
Morebath
Bampton
Cove Halt
Bolham Halt
Tiverton
Halberton Halt
West Exe Halt
J5
Cadeleigh
Burn (for Butterleigh) Halt
Hele & Bradninch
Up Exe Halt
Thorverton
Brampford Speke Halt
Silverton
Stoke Canon
CHAPELTON
UMBERLEIGH
PORTSMOUTH ARMS
South Molton Road
KINGS NYMPTON
EGGESFORD
LAPFORD
MORCHARD ROAD Halt
COPPLESTONE
Coleford Junction J4
YEOFORD
CREDITON
NEWTON ST CYRES
Bow
North Tawton
Sampford Courtenay Halt
SS
SX
Dunsbear Halt
Petrockstow
Meeth Halt
Hatherleigh
Maddaford Moor Halt
E5
OKEHAMPTON
V1 Meldon Viaduct
Meldon Junction J11
Meldon Quarry Staff Halt
Bridestowe
Lydford
Lydford
Brentor
J2 Cowley Bridge Junct.
EXETER
E8
ST DAVIDS
Broad Clyst
E4
ST JAMES PARK
CENTRAL
J3
POLSLOE BRIDGE Halt
ST THOMAS
J1 Heathfield Junct.
Clyst St Mary + Digby Halt
TOPSHAM
Christow
Longdown
Dunsford Halt
T3 Perridge Tun 836yds
Ide Halt
Alphington Halt
Exminster
Ashton
Trusham
Moretonhampstead
Lustleigh
Hawkmoor Pullabrook Halt
STARCROSS
Woodbury Road EXTON
LYMPSTONE COMMANDO
LYMPSTONE Halt VILLAGE
EXMOUTH
E3
87
89
96

HIGHBRIDGE, TAUNTON + EXMOUTH

RAILWAYS

No	Company
24	SOMERSET + DORSET (LMS + S)
3	GREAT WESTERN (GW)
34	CHARD JOINT STATION (GW + S)
4	SOUTHERN (S)
5	WEST SOMERSET PRESERVED (ex GW)
6	SEATON TRAMWAY (ex S route) 2' 9" gauge

STATIONS

Station	Opened Closed	Ry	Ref
Ashcott	* 66	24	T43
Athelney	* 64	3	T32
Axbridge	† 63	3	T45
AXMINSTER		4	Y29
Bason Bridge	* 66	24	T34
Bawdrip Halt	52	24	T33
Bishops Lydeard	* 71 76	5	T12
Bleadon + Uphill	* 64	3	T35
Blue Anchor	* 71 78	5	T04
Brean Road Halt	55	3	T35
Brent Knoll	* 71	3	T35
BRIDGWATER Central	49 52	3	T33
Bridgwater North	49 52	24	T33
Bridport	* 75	3	Y49
Budleigh Salterton	* 67	4	Y08
Burlescombe	* 64	3	T01
Burnham-on-Sea	1 62	24	T22
Chard Central	† 62	34	T30
Chard Junction	* 66	4	T30
Cheddar	† 63	3	T45
Coldharbour Halt	† 63	3	T01
Coly Ford	* 66	6	Y29
Colyton	* 66	6	Y29
Combpyne	* 65	4	Y39
Cossington	52	24	T34
(COWNHAYNE)		6	Y29
Creech St Michael Halt	* 64	3	T22
CREWKERNE		4	T40
Crowcombe	* 71 79	5	T13
Cullompton	* 64	3	T00
Culmstock	† 63	3	T01
(DONIFORD BEACH HALT)	87	5	T04
Donyatt Halt	† 62	3	T31
Draycott	† 63	3	T45
Dunball Halt	* 61 64	3	T34
Dunster	* 71 76	5	T04
Durston	* 64	3	T32
East Budleigh	* 67	4	Y08
Edington Junction Burtle	* 53 66	24	T34
EXMOUTH	*	4	Y08
FENITON	A § 67	4	Y09
Glastonbury + Street	* 66	24	T43
Hatch	† 62	3	T32
Hemyock	† 63	3	T11
Highbridge East	* 49 66	24	T34
HIGHBRIDGE West	49 52	3	T34
HONITON		4	T10
Ilminster	† 62	3	T31
Ilton Halt	† 62	3	T31
Langport East	† 62	3	T42
Langport West	* 64	3	T42
Littleham	* 67	4	Y08
Lodge Hill	† 63	3	T44
Long Sutton + Pitney Halt	† 62	3	T42
Lyme Regis	* 65	4	Y39
Lyng Halt	* 64	3	T32
Martock	* 64	3	T42
Milverton	* 66	3	T12
Montacute	* 64	3	T41
Newton Poppleford	* 67	4	Y09
Norton Fitzwarren	61	3	T12
Ottery St Mary	* 67	4	Y09
Sampford Peverell	2 B § * 64 86	3	T01
Sandford + Barnwell	† 63	3	T45
Seaton	* 66	6	Y29
Seaton Junction	* 66	4	Y29
Shapwick	* 66	24	T44
Sidmouth	* 67	4	Y18
Sidmouth Junction	* A § 64 71	4	Y09
Somerton	† 62	3	T42
Stogumber	* 71 78	5	T13
TAUNTON		3	T22
Thorney + Kingsbury Halt	* 64	3	T42
Thornfalcon	† 62	3	T22
Tipton St Johns	* 67	4	Y09
Tiverton Junction	2 * 86	3	T01
TIVERTON PARKWAY	B § 86	3	T01
Uffculme	† 63	3	T01
Venn Cross	* 66	3	T02
Washford	* 71 76	5	T04
Watchet	* 71 76	5	T04
Wellington	* 64	3	T12
WHIMPLE	*	4	Y09
Whitehall Halt	† 63	3	T11
Williton	* 71 76	5	T04
Winscombe	† 63	3	T45
Wiveliscombe	* 66	3	T02

GOODS

No	Name	Closed	Ry	Ref
G 1	Bridport West Bay	62	3	Y49

ENGINE SHEDS

No	Name	Closed	Ry	Ref
E 1	Bridgwater	60	3	T33
2	Bridport	59	3	Y49
3	Exmouth	63	4	Y08
4	Highbridge	59	24	T34
5	Lyme Regis	63	4	Y39
6	Seaton	63	4	Y29
7	Taunton	64	3	T22
8	Tiverton Junction	64	3	T01

SUMMITS

No	Name	Height	Ry	Ref
S 1	Whiteball		3	T01
2	Hewish		4	T40
3	Honiton		4	T10

TUNNELS

No	Name/Location	Length	Ry	Ref
T 1	Shuteshelf	198	3	T45
2	Venn Cross	246	3	T02
3	Bathealton	445	3	T02
4	Whiteball	1088	3	T01
5	Hatch	152	3	T32
6	Somerton	1053	3	T42
7	Honiton	1345	4	T10
8	Crewkerne	205	4	T40

JUNCTIONS

No	Name	Ry	Ref
J 1	Budleigh Salterton	4	Y08
2	Sidmouth	4	Y09
3	Culm Valley Branch	3	T01
4	Tiverton Branch	3	T01
5	Barnstaple Branch	3	T12
6	Minehead Branch	3	T12
7	Creech	3	T22
8	Cogload	3	T22
9	Uphill	3	T35
10	Curry Rivell	3	T42
11	Wells Branch	24	T43
12	Wharf	324	T34

NOTES:

REF All in ST or SY and initial S omitted

§ Old Version, § New Version } Change of name

Corresponding letter indicates the other version.

1 Regular services ended in '51.

2 Sampford Peverell closed in '64 but reopened in 86 as a replacement for Tiverton Junction.

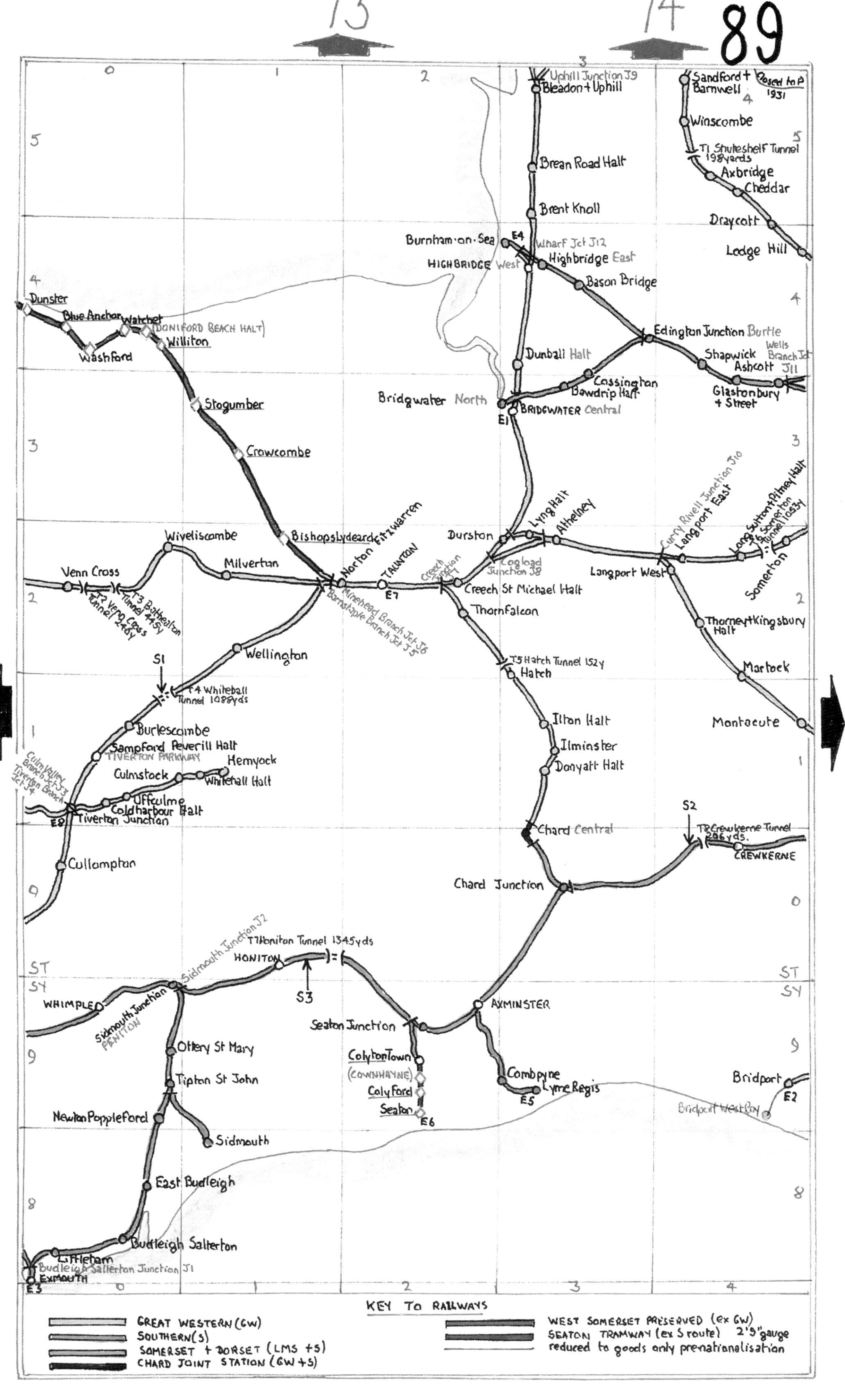

73
74
88
90
Uphill Junction J9
Bleadon + Uphill
Sandford + Barnwell
Closed to P 1931
Winscombe
T1 Shuteshelf Tunnel 198yards
Axbridge
Cheddar
Draycott
Lodge Hill
Brean Road Halt
Brent Knoll
Burnham-on-Sea
Wharf Jct J12
HIGHBRIDGE West
Highbridge East
Bason Bridge
Edington Junction Burtle
Shapwick
Wells Branch Jct J11
Ashcott
Glastonbury + Street
Dunball Halt
Cossington
Bawdrip Halt
Bridgwater North
BRIDGWATER Central
Dunster
Blue Anchor
Watchet
(DONIFORD BEACH HALT)
Washford
Williton
Stogumber
Crowcombe
Bishops Lydeard
Fitzwarren
Norton
TAUNTON
Creech Junction J7
Durston
Lyng Halt
Athelney
Cogload Junction J8
Curry Rivell Junction J10
Langport East
Long Sutton + Pitney Halt
T6 Somerton Tunnel 1053y
Somerton
Langport West
Wiveliscombe
Milverton
Venn Cross
T3 Bathealton Tunnel 445y
T2 Venn Cross Tunnel 246y
Creech St Michael Halt
Thornfalcon
Minehead Branch Jct J6
Barnstaple Branch Jct J5
Wellington
Thorney + Kingsbury Halt
Martock
Montacute
T5 Hatch Tunnel 152y
Hatch
S1
T4 Whiteball Tunnel 1088yds
Burlescombe
Sampford Peverill Halt
TIVERTON PARKWAY
Hemyock
Culmstock
Whitehall Halt
Culm Valley Branch Jct J3
Tiverton Branch Jct J4
Uffculme
Coldharbour Halt
Tiverton Junction
Cullompton
Ilton Halt
Ilminster
Donyatt Halt
Chard Central
S2
T8 Crewkerne Tunnel 206yds.
CREWKERNE
Chard Junction
Sidmouth Junction J2
T7 Honiton Tunnel 1345yds
HONITON
S3
WHIMPLE
Sidmouth Junction
FENITON
Seaton Junction
AXMINSTER
Ottery St Mary
Tipton St John
Colyton Town
(COWNHAYNE)
Coly Ford
Seaton
Combpyne
Lyme Regis
Bridport
Bridport West Bay
Newton Poppleford
Sidmouth
East Budleigh
Budleigh Salterton
Littleham
Budleigh Salterton Junction J1
EXMOUTH
KEY TO RAILWAYS
GREAT WESTERN (GW)
SOUTHERN (S)
SOMERSET + DORSET (LMS + S)
CHARD JOINT STATION (GW + S)
WEST SOMERSET PRESERVED (ex GW)
SEATON TRAMWAY (ex S route) 2'9" gauge
reduced to goods only pre-nationalisation

WESTBURY + WEYMOUTH

RAILWAYS

No	Company
24	SOMERSET + DORSET (LMS+S)
3	GREAT WESTERN (GW)
34	WEYMOUTH + PORTLAND (GW+S)
4	SOUTHERN (S)
5	EASTON + CHURCH HOPE (GW+S)
6	EAST SOMERSET (ex GW)
7	SWANAGE (ex S)

STATIONS

Name	Closed / Opened	Ry	Ref
Abbotsbury	52	3	Y58
Alford Halt	† 62	3	T63
Bailey Gate	* 66	24	Y99
Binegar	* 66	24	T64
Blandford Forum	* 53 66	24	T80
Bradford Peverell + Stratton Halt	* 66	3	Y69
BRUTON	*	3	T63
CASTLE CARY		3	T63
Cattistock Halt	* 66	3	T50
Charlton Mackrell	† 62	3	T52
Charlton Marshall	56	24	T99
CHETNOLE Halt	* 69	3	T60
Chilcompton	* 66	24	T65
Clutton	59	3	T65
Codford	55	3	T93
Cole	* 66	24	T63
Corfe Castle	72 Ro	7	Y98
Coryates Halt	52	3	Y68
Cranmore	† 63 Ro	6	T64
(CRANMORE WEST)	O	6	T64
DILTON MARSH Halt	69	3	T85
DORCHESTER SOUTH	49	4	Y69
DORCHESTER WEST	* 49	3	Y69
Easton	52	5	Y67
Edington + Bratton	52	3	T95
Evercreech Junction	* 66	24	T63
Evercreech New	* 66	24	T63
Evershot	* 66	3	T50
Farrington + Guerney Halt	59	3	T65
FROME		3	T74
GILLINGHAM		4	T82
Grimstone + Frampton	* 66	3	Y69
Hallatrow	59	3	T65
HAMWORTHY Junction	72	4	Y99
Hendford Halt	* 64	3	T51
Henstridge	* 66	24	T71
Heytesbury	55	3	T84
HOLTON HEATH		4	Y99
Keinton Mandeville	† 62	3	T53
Lavington	* 66	3	T95
Lodge Hill	† 63	3	T54
MAIDEN NEWTON	*	3	Y59
Marston Magna	* 56	3	T62
Masbury	* 66	24	T64
Melcombe Regis	1 59	34	Y68
Mells Road Halt	56 59	3	T75
(MERRYFIELD LANE)		6	T64
Midford	* 66	24	Y76
Midsomer Norton + Welton	59	3	T65
Midsomer Norton + Welton Upper	* 49 66	24	T65
Milborne Port Halt	* 61 66	4	T62
Monkton + Came Golf Links Halt	57	3	Y68
Montacute	* 64	3	T51
MORETON		4	Y78
Polsham Halt	51	24	T54
Portesham	52	3	Y68
Portland		34	Y67
Powerstock	* 75	3	Y59
Pylle Halt	* 57 66	24	T63
Radipole Halt	69 84	3	Y68
Radstock North	* 49 66	24	T65
Radstock West	49 59	3	T65
Rodwell	52	34	Y67
Sandsfoot Castle Halt	52	34	Y67
Semley	* 66	4	T82
Shepton Mallet Charlton Road	* 66	24	T64
Shepton Mallet High Street	† 49 63	3	T64
SHERBORNE		4	T61
Shillingstone	* 64	24	T81
Shoscombe + Single Hill Halt	* 66	24	T75
Sparkford	* 66	3	T62
Spetisbury	56	24	T90
Stalbridge	* 66	24	T71
Staverton Halt	* 66	3	T86
Stourpaine + Durweston Halt	56	24	T80
Strap Lane Halt	50	3	T74
Sturminster Newton	* 66	24	T71
Sutton Bingham	62	4	T51
TEMPLECOMBE	* 66	4	T72
Templecombe	* 66	24	T72
THORNFORD Bridge 74 Halt 69	*	3	T51
TISBURY	*	4	T92
Toller	* 75	3	Y59
TROWBRIDGE		3	T85
Upwey	52	3	Y68
UPWEY Junction [52] + Broadway [52-80]	52 80	3	Y68
Upwey Wishing Well Halt	57	3	Y68
Wanstrow	† 63	3	T74
WAREHAM		4	Y98
WARMINSTER		3	T84
Wellow	* 66	24	T75
Wells Priory Road	51	24	T54
Wells Tucker Street	† 50 63	3	T54
WESTBURY		3	T85
Westham Halt	52	34	Y67
West Pennard Halt	* 62 66	24	T54
WEYMOUTH		3	Y67
Wincanton	* 64	24	T72
Witham	* 66	3	T74
Wookey	† 63	3	T54
WOOL		4	Y88
Wyke Regis Halt	52	34	Y67
YEOVIL JUNCTION		4	T51
YEOVIL PEN MILL	*	3	T51
Yeovil Town	* 67	34	T51
YETMINSTER	*	3	T61

GOODS

No	Name/Location	Closed	Ry	Ref
G 1	Hendford	67	3	T51
2	Portland	65	34	Y67
3	Hamworthy	65	4	Y99
4	Templecombe	50	24	T72

ENGINE SHEDS

No	Name/Location	Closed	Ry	Ref
E 1	Radstock	66	24	
2	Templecombe	66	24	
3	Templecombe Upper	51	4	
4	Wells	51	24	
5	Wells	63	3	
6	Weymouth	67	3	

TUNNELS

No	Name/Location		Length	Ry	Ref
T1	Combe Hey		66	3	T75
2	Chilcompton		66	24	T65
3	Winsor Hill Old	2	230	24	T64
4	Windsor Hill North	2	126	24	T64
5	Murdercombe		55	3	T74
6	Buckhorn Weston		742	4	T72
7	Evershot		348	3	T60
8	Frampton		660	3	Y69
9	Roundbury		264	3	Y69
10	Dinscombe North		814	3	Y68
11	Dinscombe South		48	3	Y68

BRIDGES + VIADUCTS

No	Name	Ry	Ref
V 1	Midford Viaduct	24	T75

JUNCTIONS

No	Name	Ry	Ref
J 1	Camerton Branch	3	T65
2	Bradford North	3	T85
3	Bradford South	3	T85
4	Bradford West	3	T85
5	Heywood Road	3	T85
6	Loop	3	T85
7	Hawkeridge	3	T85
8	Salisbury Branch	3	T85
9	Fairwood	3	T85
10	Clink Road	3	T74
11	Blatchbridge	3	T74
12	Radstock Branch	3	T74
13	Mineral Loop	3	T74
14	Vobster	3	T75
15	Yeovil South	34	T51
16	Templecombe No 3	24	T72
17	Templecombe No. 2	24	T72
18	Portland	334	Y68
19	Worgret	4	Y98
20	Holes Bay Curve	4	Y99

NOTES:

REF All in ST or SY, therefore initial S is omitted.

1 Regular services ended in 52

2 Old Tunnel is to South, New is to North.

75

89

91

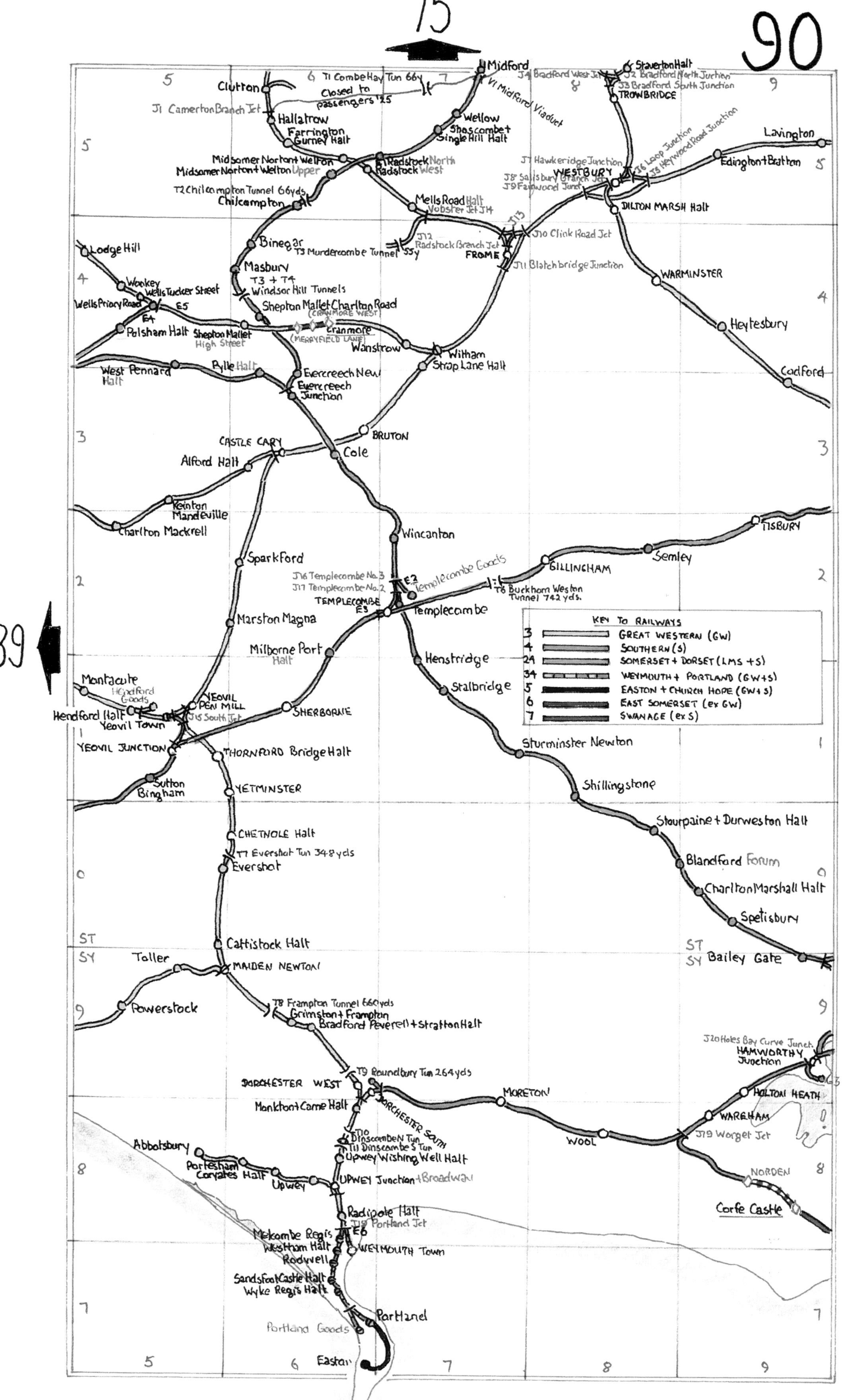
Midford
T1 Combe Hay Tun 66y
V1 Midford Viaduct
Clutton
Closed to passengers '25
J1 Camerton Branch Jct
Hallatrow
Farrington Gurney Halt
Wellow
Shoscombe Single Hill Halt
Midsomer Norton Welton
Midsomer Norton Welton Upper
Radstock North
Radstock West
T2 Chilcompton Tunnel 66yds
Chilcompton
Mells Road Halt
Vobster Jct J14
J12 Radstock Branch Jct
Binegar
T3 Murdercombe Tunnel 55y
FROME
J10 Clink Road Jct
J11 Blatchbridge Junction
J13
Masbury
T3 + T4 Windsor Hill Tunnels
Shepton Mallet Charlton Road
(CRANMORE WEST)
Cranmore
(MERRYFIELD LANE)
Wanstrow
Witham
Strap Lane Halt
Lodge Hill
Wookey
Wells Tucker Street
Wells Priory Road
E4
E5
Polsham Halt
Shepton Mallet High Street
West Pennard Halt
Pylle Halt
Evercreech New
Evercreech Junction
BRUTON
CASTLE CARY
Cole
Alford Halt
Keinton Mandeville
Charlton Mackrell
Wincanton
Sparkford
J16 Templecombe No.3
J17 Templecombe No.2
E2
Templecombe Goods
TEMPLECOMBE
E3
Templecombe
Marston Magna
Milborne Port Halt
Henstridge
Stalbridge
Montacute
Hendford Goods
Hendford Halt
Yeovil Town
YEOVIL PEN MILL
J15 South Jct
SHERBORNE
YEOVIL JUNCTION
THORNFORD Bridge Halt
Sutton Bingham
YETMINSTER
CHETNOLE Halt
T7 Evershot Tun 348 yds
Evershot
Cattistock Halt
Toller
MAIDEN NEWTON
Powerstock
T8 Frampton Tunnel 660yds
Grimston + Frampton
Bradford Peverell + Stratton Halt
T9 Poundbury Tun 264yds
DORCHESTER WEST
DORCHESTER SOUTH
Monkton + Came Halt
T10 Dinscombe N Tun
T11 Dinscombe S Tun
Upwey Wishing Well Halt
Abbotsbury
Portesham
Coryates Halt
Upwey
UPWEY Junction + Broadway
Radipole Halt
J18 Portland Jct
E6
Melcombe Regis
Westham Halt
Rodwell
WEYMOUTH Town
Sandsfoot Castle Halt
Wyke Regis Halt
Portland
Portland Goods
Easton
Staverton Halt
J4 Bradford West Jct
J2 Bradford North Junction
J3 Bradford South Junction
TROWBRIDGE
J7 Hawkeridge Junction
J6 Loop Junction
J5 Heywood Road Junction
J8 Salisbury Branch Jct
J9 Fairwood Junct
WESTBURY
DILTON MARSH Halt
Lavington
Edington + Bratton
WARMINSTER
Heytesbury
Codford
TISBURY
Semley
GILLINGHAM
T6 Buckhorn Weston Tunnel 742 yds.
KEY TO RAILWAYS
3 GREAT WESTERN (GW)
4 SOUTHERN (S)
24 SOMERSET + DORSET (LMS + S)
34 WEYMOUTH + PORTLAND (GW + S)
5 EASTON + CHURCH HOPE (GW + S)
6 EAST SOMERSET (ex GW)
7 SWANAGE (ex S)
Sturminster Newton
Shillingstone
Stourpaine + Durweston Halt
Blandford Forum
Charlton Marshall Halt
Spetisbury
Bailey Gate
ST
SY
J20 Holes Bay Curve Junct.
HAMWORTHY Junction
MORETON
HOLTON HEATH
WAREHAM
WOOL
J19 Worgret Jct
NORDEN
Corfe Castle

ANDOVER + SOUTHAMPTON

RAILWAYS

No	Company
24	SOMERSET + DORSET (LMS + S)
3	GREAT WESTERN (GW)
4	SOUTHERN (S)
5	SWANAGE (ex S)

STATIONS

Name	Opened Closed	Ry	Ref
Amesbury	52	4	U14
Ampress Works Halt	56 90	4	Z39
ANDOVER Junction	64	4	U34
Andover Town	* 64	4	U34
Ashley Heath Halt	* 64	4	U10
BEAULIEU ROAD		4	U30
BITTERNE		4	U41
Boscombe	65	4	Z19
BOURNEMOUTH Central	66	4	Z19
Bournemouth West	65	4	Z09
BRANKSOME		4	Z09
Breamore	* 66	4	U11
Broadstone	* 66	4	Z09
BROCKENHURST		4	U30
Bulford	52	4	U14
Bulford Camp	52	4	U24
Burghclere	60	3	U45
BURSLEDON		4	U41
Calbourne + Shalfleet	53	4	Z48
Carisbrooke Halt	53	4	Z48
Cement Mills Halt	66	4	Z49
Chandlers Ford	* 69	4	U42
CHRISTCHURCH		4	Z19
Clatford	* 64	4	U34
Collingbourne	61	3	U25
Collingbourne + Kingston Halt	61	3	U25
Corfe Mullen (East End) Halt	56	24	Z09
Cowes	* 66	4	Z49
Creekmore Halt	* 66	4	Z09
Daggons Road	* 64	4	U11
DEAN		4	U22
Dinton	* 66	4	U03
Downton	* 64	4	U12
Dunbridge	A § 88	4	U32
EASTLEIGH		4	U41
Fawley	66	4	U40
Fordingbridge	* 64	4	U11
Freshwater	53	4	Z38
Fullerton	* 64	4	U34
Grafton + Burbage	61	3	U25
GRATELEY	*	4	U24
HAMBLE Halt	69	4	U40
Hardley Halt	58 65	4	U40
(HARMANS CROSS)	88	5	Z08
HEDGE END	90	4	U41
(HERSTON HALT)		5	Z08
HINTON ADMIRAL		4	Z29
Holmsley	* 64	4	U20
Horsebridge	* 64	4	U33
Hurstbourne	* 64	4	U44
Hythe	66	4	U40
Idmiston Halt	* 68	4	U23
Kings Worthy	60	4	U43
Litchfield	60	3	U45
Ludgershall	1 61	3	U25
LYMINGTON PIER		4	Z39
LYMINGTON TOWN		4	Z39
LYNDHURST ROAD		4	U31
Manningford Halt	* 66	3	U15
Marchwood	66	4	U30
MILLBROOK	B § 80	4	U31
Mill Hill	* 66	4	Z49
Mottisfont	* 64	4	U32
MOTTISFONT DUNBRIDGE	A § 88	4	U32
NETLEY		4	U40
NEW MILTON		4	Z29
Newport	* 66	4	Z48
Newton Tony	52	4	U24
Ningwood	53	4	Z38
Northam	66	4	U41
Nursling	57	4	U31
Pans Lane Halt	* 66	3	U05
PARKSTONE		4	Z09
Patney + Chirton	* 66	3	U05
PEWSEY		3	U15
POKESDOWN		4	Z19
POOLE		4	Z09
Porton	* 68	4	U13
REDBRIDGE		4	U31
Ringwood	* 64	4	U10
ROMSEY		4	U32
ST DENYS		4	U41
SALISBURY		4	U13
SHAWFORD		4	U42
SHOLING		4	U41
Southampton EASTERN DOCKS	66	4	U41
SOUTHAMPTON Central CENTRAL	67 94	4	U41
SOUTHAMPTON Airport PARKWAY	86 94	4	U41
Southampton MILLBROOK	B § 80	4	U31
SOUTHAMPTON WESTERN DOCKS		4	U41
Southampton Terminus	66	4	U41
Stockbridge	* 64	4	U33
Sutton Scotney	60	3	U44
Swanage	72 89	5	Z07
SWAY		4	Z29
SWAYTHLING		4	U41
Tidworth	2 55	3	U25
TOTTON		4	U31
Verwood	* 64	4	U00
Watchingwell Halt	48 53	4	Z48
West Moors for Ferndown	* 64	4	U00
Weyhill	61	3	U34
WHITCHURCH North	* 49 72	4	U44
Whitchurch Town	49 60	3	U44
Wilton North	49 55	3	U13
Wilton South	* 49 66	4	U13
Wimborne	* 64	4	U00
WINCHESTER City	49 67	4	U43
Winchester Cheesehill Chesil	49 61	3	U43
Wishford	55	3	U03
Woodborough	* 66	3	U15
WOOLSTON		4	U41
Worthy Down Platform Halt	51 60	3	U43
Wylye	65	3	U03
Yarmouth	53	4	Z38

GOODS

No	Name/Location	Closed	Ry	Ref
G1	Medina Wharf	?	4	Z49
2	Milford Salisbury	67	4	U13
3	Bulford	63	4	U14
4	Fisherton Yard Salisbury	?	3	U13

COMPANY WORKS

No	Name	Closed	Ry	Ref
C1	EASTLEIGH	3 0	4	U41

ENGINE SHEDS

No	Name/Location	Closed	Ry	Ref
E1	Andover Junction	58	3	U34
2	Andover Junction	62	4	U34
3	Salisbury	67	4	U13
4	Salisbury	50	3	U13
5	Winchester City	4 63	4	U43
6	Winchester	53	3	U43
7	EASTLEIGH	5 67	4	U41
8	Southampton	66	4	U41
9	Swanage	66	4	Z08
10	Lymington	66	4	Z39
11	Newport	57	4	Z59

TUNNELS

No	Name	Length	Ry	Ref
T1	Downton		4	U12
2	Fisherton	443	4	U13
3	Winchester	441	3	U43
4	Southampton	528	4	U41

JUNCTIONS

No	Name	Ry	Ref
J1	Patney	3	U05
2	Laverstock North	4	U13
3	Laverstock South	4	U13
4	Milford	4	U13
5	Alderbury	4	U12
6	Fisherton	4	U13
7	Eastleigh East	4	U42
8	Eastleigh West	4	U41
9	North Loop	3	U43
10	Red Posts	34	U34
11	Town	4	U34
12	Viaduct	4	U44
13	Holes Bay	4	Z09
14	Quay	4	Z09
15	Kimbridge	4	U32

NOTES:

1 Open for excursions
2 Military use continued after BR Closure
3 Also carriage works
4 Used for diesels until '69
5 Closure date is for steam. Remains in use
§ Change of name, letter shows alternative.

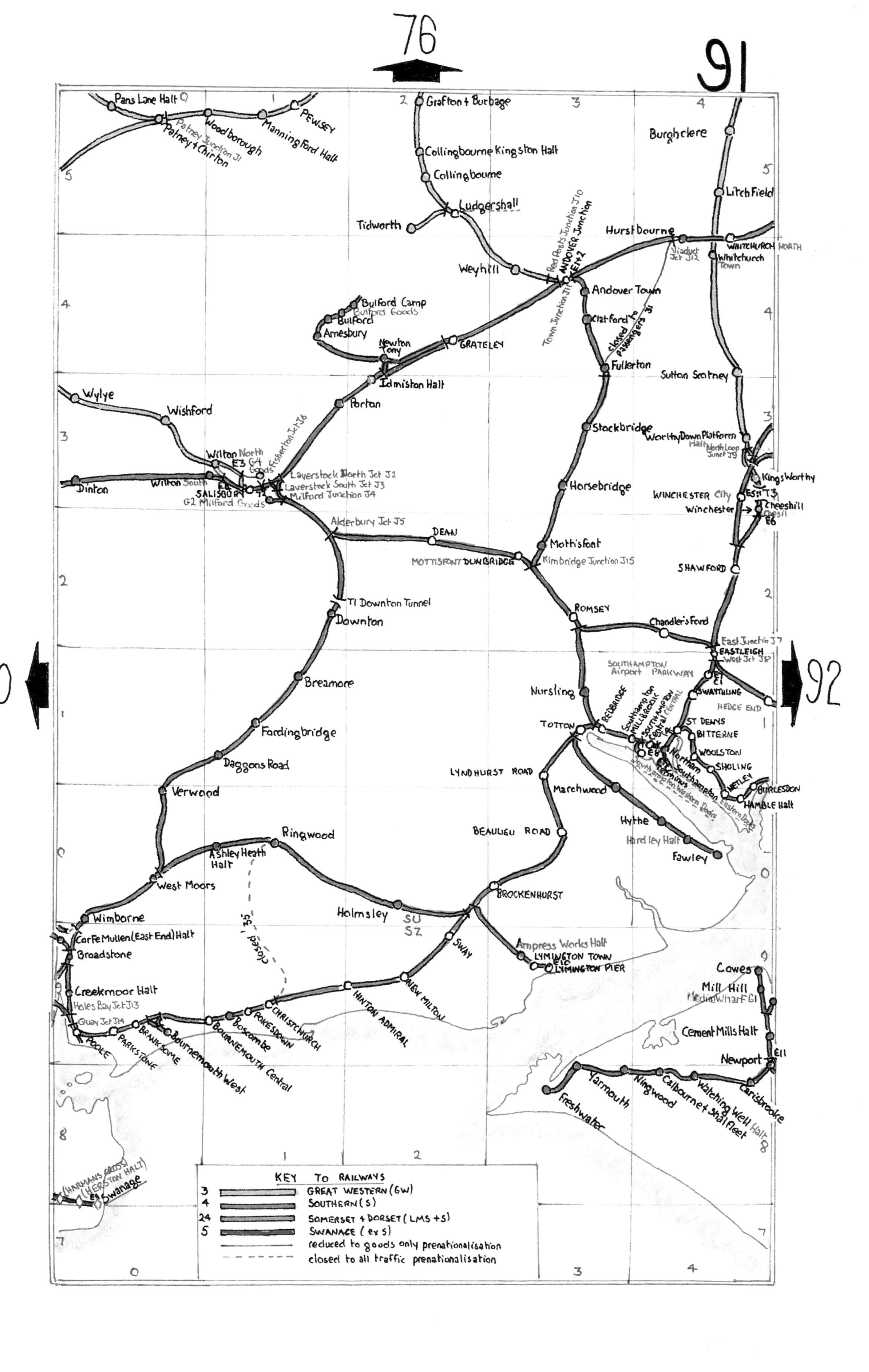

76
91
90
92
Pans Lane Halt
Pewsey
Woodborough
Manning Ford Halt
Patney Junction J1
Patney + Chirton
Grafton + Burbage
Collingbourne Kingston Halt
Collingbourne
Ludgershall
Tidworth
Burghclere
Litch Field
Hurst Bourne
Whitchurch North
Whitchurch Town
Weyhill
Andover Junction
Andover Town
Clatford
Fullerton
Bulford Camp
Bulford Goods
Bulford
Amesbury
Newton Tony
Grateley
Idmiston Halt
Porton
Sutton Scotney
Wylye
Wishford
Wilton North
Wilton South
Dinton
Salisbury
Laverstock North Jct J2
Laverstock South Jct J3
Milford Junction J4
G2 Milford Goods
Stockbridge
Worthy Down Platform Halt
Kings Worthy
Horsebridge
Winchester City
Winchester
Cheeshill
Alderbury Jct J5
Dean
Mottisfont
Mottisfont Dunbridge
Kimbridge Junction J15
Shawford
T1 Downton Tunnel
Downton
Romsey
Chandler's Ford
East Junction J7
Eastleigh
West Jct J8
Southampton Airport Parkway
Swaythling
Hedge End
Breamore
Nursling
Fordingbridge
Totton
Redbridge
St Denys
Bitterne
Woolston
Sholing
Netley
Bursledon
Hamble Halt
Daggons Road
Verwood
Lyndhurst Road
Marchwood
Hythe
Hardley Halt
Fawley
Ringwood
Ashley Heath Halt
Beaulieu Road
West Moors
Brockenhurst
Wimborne
Holmsley
SU
SZ
Corfe Mullen (East End) Halt
Broadstone
Sway
Ampress Works Halt
Lymington Town
Lymington Pier
Cowes
Mill Hill
Creekmoor Halt
Holes Bay Jct J13
Hinton Admiral
New Milton
Cement Mills Halt
Quay Jct J14
Poole
Parkstone
Branksome
Bournemouth West
Bournemouth Central
Boscombe
Pokesdown
Christchurch
closed '35
Newport
Yarmouth
Ningwood
Calbourne + Shalfleet
Watching Well Halt
Carisbrooke
Freshwater
Swanage
KEY TO RAILWAYS
3 GREAT WESTERN (GW)
4 SOUTHERN (S)
24 SOMERSET + DORSET (LMS + S)
5 SWANAGE (ex S)
reduced to goods only prenationalisation
closed to all traffic prenationalisation

GUILDFORD + PORTSMOUTH

RAILWAYS

No	Company
3	GREAT WESTERN (GW)
4	SOUTHERN (S)
5	MID HANTS (ex S)
6	ISLE OF WIGHT STEAM (ex S)
X	LONGMOOR MILITARY

STATIONS

Station	Opened/Closed	Ry Ref
ALDERSHOT		4 U18
Alresford	* 73 77	5 U53
ALTON		45 U73
Alverstone	56	4 Z58
ASH		4 U85
Ashey	* 66 93	6 Z58
ASH VALE		4 U85
BARNHAM		4 U90
BASINGSTOKE	1	(3)4 U65
BEDHAMPTON Halt	69	4 U60
Bembridge	53	4 Z68
BENTLEY		4 U74
Blackwater (IoW)	56	4 Z58
BLACKWATER		4 U85
BOGNOR REGIS		4 U90
Bordon	57	4 U73
BOSHAM		4 U80
BOTLEY	*	4 U51
BRADING	2 *	4 Z68
BRAMLEY		3 U65
BROOKWOOD		4 U95
CHICHESTER		4 U80
COSHAM		4 U60
Cowes	* 64	4 Z59
Droxford	55	4 U61
Elsted	55	4 U81
EMSWORTH		4 U70
FAREHAM		4 U50
FARNBOROUGH MAIN	86	4 U85
FARNBOROUGH NORTH		4 U85
FARNCOMBE		4 U94
FARNHAM		4 U84
Farringdon	55	4 U63
FISHBOURNE Halt	69	4 U80
FLEET		4 U85
FORD		4 U90
Fort Brockhurst	53	4 U50
FRATTON		4 U60
FRIMLEY		4 U85
GODALMING		4 U94
Godshill Halt for Sandford	52	4 Z58
Gosport	53	4 U60
GUILDFORD		4 U94
GUILDFORD, LONDON ROAD		4 U95
HASLEMERE		4 U83
HAVANT		4 U70
Haven Street	* 66 71	6 Z59
Hayling Island	† 63	4 U70
HEDGE END	90	4 U51
HILSEA Halt	69	4 U60
HOOK		4 U75
Horringford	56	4 Z58
Itchen Abbas	* 73	4 U53
Kingsley Halt	57	4 U73
Knowle Halt	64	4 U50
LAKE	87	4 Z58
Langston	† 63	4 U70
Lavant	3 54	4 U80
LIPHOOK		4 U83
LISS		4 U72
LONDON ROAD GUILDFORD		4 U95
Medina Wharf Platform	66	4 Z39
Medstead + Four Marks	* 73 85	5 U63
Merstone	56	4 Z58
MICHELDEVER		4 U54
Midhurst	55	4 U81
MIDFORD		4 U94
Mill Hill	* 66	4 Z59
Newchurch	56	4 Z58
Newport	* 66	4 Z58
NORTH CAMP		4 U85
North Hayling	† 63	4 U70
NUTBOURNE Halt	69	4 U70
Oakley	* 63	4 U55
OVERTON	*	4 U55
PETERSFIELD		4 U72
Petworth	55	4 U91
PORTCHESTER		4 U60
PORTSMOUTH + SOUTHSEA		4 U60
PORTSMOUTH HARBOUR		4 U60
Privett	55	4 U62
Rogate	55	4 U72
Ropley	* 73 77	4 U63
ROWLANDS CASTLE		4 U71
RYDE ESPLANADE		4 Z59
RYDE PIER HEAD		4 Z69
RYDE ST JOHN'S ROAD	*	4 Z59
St Helens	53	4 Z68
St Lawrence for Blackgang	52	4 Z57
SANDOWN	*	4 Z58
Selham	55	4 U91
SHALFORD	*	4 U94
SHANKLIN	*	4 Z58
Shide	56	4 Z58
SMALLBROOK	91	46 Z59
SOUTHBOURNE Halt	69	4 U70
SWANWICK		4 U50
Tisted	65	4 U63
Ventnor	* 66	4 Z57
Ventnor West	52	4 Z57
WANBOROUGH		4 U95
WARBLINGTON Halt	69	4 U70
West Meon	55	4 U62
Whippingham	53	4 Z59
Whitwell Halt	52	4 Z57
Wickham	55	4 U51
WINCHFIELD		4 U75
WITLEY		4 U93
WOKING		4 U95
Wootton	53 71	6 Z59
WORPLESDON		4 U95
Wroxhall	* 66	4 U58

GOODS

No	Name/Location	Closed	Ry Ref
G 1	Bishops Waltham	62	4 U51
2	Mislingford	62	4 U51
3	St Helen's Quay	53	4 U51

ENGINE SHEDS

No	Name/Location	Closed	Ry Ref
E 1	Bognor	53	4 U90
2	Bordon	51	4 U73
3	Fratton	59	4 U60
4	Guildford	67	4 U94
5	Newport	57	4 Z59
6	St John's Road Ryde	67	4 Z69
7	Basingstoke	67	4 U65
8	Basingstoke	50	3 U65
9	Gosport	4 62	4 Z69

SUMMITS

No	Name/Location	Height	Ry Ref
S 1	Buriton		4 U71
2	Litchfield		4 U54

TUNNELS

No	Name/Location	Length	Ry Ref
T 1	Popham No.1	265	4 U54
2	Popham No.2	199	4 U54
3	Litchfield	198	4 U54
4	Wallers Ash	501	4 U53
5	West Meon	539	4 U62
6	Privett	1058	4 U62
7	Fareham No.1	56	4 U50
8	Fareham No.2	553	4 U50
9	Boniface Down	5 1300	4 Z57
10	Buriton	485	4 U71
11	Corking	740	4 U81
12	Singleton	744	4 U81
13	West Dean	443	4 U81
14	Tapnage	122	4 U51
15	Midhurst	276	4 U81
16	Ryde Esplanade	391	4 Z59

BRIDGES + VIADUCTS

No	Name	Ry	Ref
V 1	Langston (Swing Bridge)	4	U70

JUNCTIONS

No	Name	Ry	Ref
J 1	Meon Valley	4	U50
2	Butts	4	U63
3	Battledown	4	U55
4	Sturt	4	U85
5	Sturt North	4	U85
6	Sturt West	4	U85
7	Loop	4	U85
8	Peasmarsh	4	U94
9	Aldershot South	4	U85
10	Aldershot North	4	U85
11	Pirbright	4	U95
12	Bordon Line	4	U74
13	Farlington	4	U60

NOTES:

REF All in SU or SZ therefore initial S omitted.

1 Used by GW

2 Closed for short periods in 67 and 92.

3 Regular service ended 35.

4 Became disused earlier.

5 Tunnel length estimated.

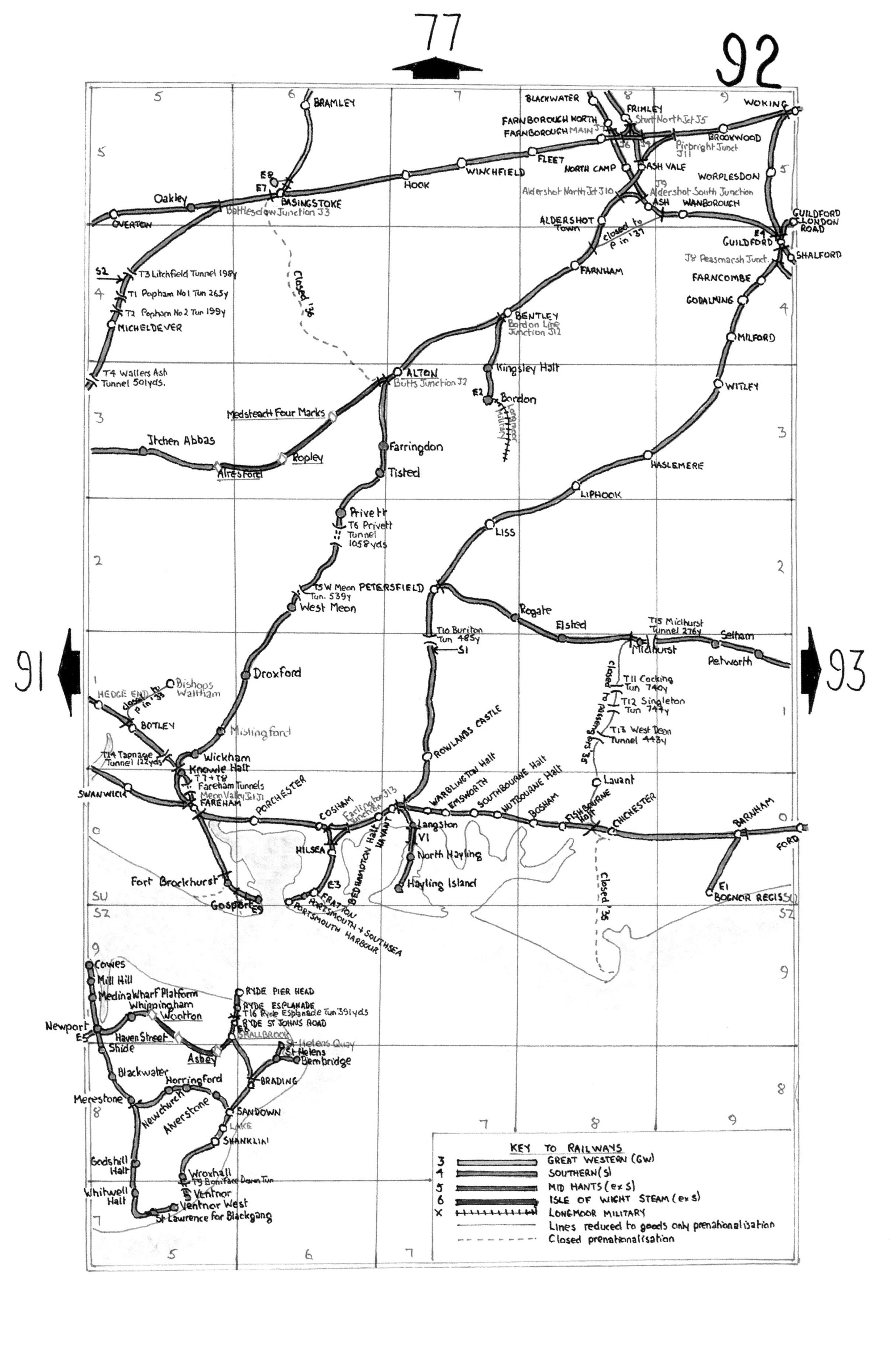
77
91
93
BRAMLEY
BLACKWATER
FRIMLEY
Sturt North Jct J5
FARNBOROUGH NORTH
FARNBOROUGH MAIN
WOKING
BROOKWOOD
Pirbright Junct J11
FLEET
WINCHFIELD
HOOK
NORTH CAMP
ASH VALE
WORPLESDON
Aldershot North Jct J10
J9 Aldershot South Junction
ASH
WANBOROUGH
ALDERSHOT Town
closed to p in '37
GUILDFORD LONDON ROAD
GUILDFORD
E4
SHALFORD
J8 Peasmarsh Junct.
FARNHAM
FARNCOMBE
GODALMING
BASINGSTOKE
Bottlesdow Junction J3
Oakley
OVERTON
E8
E7
Closed '36
S2
T3 Litchfield Tunnel 198y
T1 Popham No1 Tun 265y
T2 Popham No2 Tun 199y
MICHELDEVER
T4 Wallers Ash Tunnel 501yds.
BENTLEY
Bordon Line Junction J12
ALTON
Butts Junction J2
Kingsley Halt
E2
Bordon
Longmoor Military
MILFORD
WITLEY
Medstead & Four Marks
Itchen Abbas
Alresford
Ropley
Farringdon
Tisted
HASLEMERE
LIPHOOK
LISS
Privett
T6 Privett Tunnel 1058yds
T5 W Meon Tun. 539y
PETERSFIELD
West Meon
Rogate
Elsted
T15 Midhurst Tunnel 276y
Selham
Midhurst
Petworth
T10 Buriton Tun 485y
S1
Droxford
Bishops Waltham
HEDGE END
closed to p in '33
BOTLEY
Mislingford
T11 Cocking Tun 740y
T12 Singleton Tun 744y
T13 West Dean Tunnel 443y
closed to passengers '35
T14 Tapnage Tunnel 122yds
Wickham
Knowle Halt
T7+T8 Fareham Tunnels
Meon Valley Jct J1
SWANWICK
FAREHAM
PORCHESTER
ROWLANDS CASTLE
WARBLINGTON Halt
EMSWORTH
SOUTHBOURNE Halt
NUTBOURNE Halt
BOSHAM
FISHBOURNE Halt
Lavant
CHICHESTER
BARNHAM
FORD
COSHAM
Farlington Junction J13
HAVANT
BEDHAMPTON Halt
Langston
V1
North Hayling
Hayling Island
HILSEA
E3
Fort Brockhurst
Gosport
E5
FRATTON
PORTSMOUTH + SOUTHSEA
PORTSMOUTH HARBOUR
Closed '35
E1
BOGNOR REGIS
SU
SZ
Cowes
Mill Hill
Medina Wharf Platform
Whippingham
Wootton
Newport
E5
Haven Street
Shide
Ashey
RYDE PIER HEAD
RYDE ESPLANADE
T16 Ryde Esplanade Tun 391yds
RYDE ST JOHNS ROAD
E6
SMALLBROOK
St Helens Quay
St Helens
Bembridge
BRADING
Blackwater
Horringford
Merestone
Newchurch
Alverstone
SANDOWN
LAKE
SHANKLIN
Godshill Halt
Wroxhall
T9 Boniface Down Tun
Ventnor
Ventnor West
Whitwell Halt
St Lawrence for Blackgang
KEY TO RAILWAYS
3 GREAT WESTERN (GW)
4 SOUTHERN (S)
5 MID HANTS (ex S)
6 ISLE OF WIGHT STEAM (ex S)
X LONGMOOR MILITARY
Lines reduced to goods only prenationalisation
Closed prenationalisation

DORKING + BRIGHTON

RAILWAYS

No	Company
4	SOUTHERN (S)
5	BLUEBELL (ex S)
6	LAVENDER (ex S)
7	VOLKS ELECTRIC (2' 8½" gauge)

STATIONS

Name	Opened Closed	Ry	Ref
ALDRINGTON Halt	69	4	20
AMBERLEY		4	01
ANGMERING		4	00
Ardingley	† 63	4	32
AQUARIUM		7	30
ARUNDEL		4	00
ASHTEAD		4	15
BALCOMBE		4	32
Barcombe	55	4	41
Barcombe Mills	* 69	4	41
Baynards	* 65	4	03
BETCHWORTH	*	4	25
BILLINGSHURST		4	02
BISHOPSTONE	*	4	49†
BOOKHAM		4	15
Box Hill + Burford Bridge	A§ 58	4	15
BOX HILL + WESTHUMBLE	A§ 58	4	15
Bramber	* 66	4	10
Bramley + Wonersh	* 65	4	04
Brasted Halt	55 61	4	45
BRIGHTON		4	30
BRIGHTON LONDON ROAD		4	30
BURGESS HILL		4	31
CATERHAM		4	35
Chevening Halt	61	4	45
CHILWORTH + Albury	* 80	4	04
CHIPSTEAD		4	25
CHRIST'S HOSPITAL		4	12
CLANDON		4	05
COBHAM + STOKE D'ABERNON	51	4	15
COOKSBRIDGE	*	4	31
Coulsden North	83	4	35
COULSDEN SOUTH		4	35
COWDEN		4	44
Cranleigh	* 65	4	03
CRAWLEY	1	4	23
DEEPDENE	* B§ 87	4	15
DORKING DEEPDENE	B§ 87	4	15
DORKING North	67	4	15
DORKING Town WEST	* 87	4	14
DORMANS		4	44
DURRINGTON-ON-SEA		4	10
EARLSWOOD		4	24
East Grinstead High Level	67	4	33
EAST GRINSTEAD Low Level	67	45	33
EAST WORTHING Halt	C§ 49 69	4	10
EDENBRIDGE	*	4	44
EDENBRIDGE TOWN		4	44
EFFINGHAM JUNCTION		4	15
EPSOM DOWNS		4	25
FALMER		4	30
FAY GATE	2 53	4	23
FISHERSGATE		4	20
Fittleworth	55	4	01
FORD		4	00
Forest Row	* 67	4	43
(Freshfield Halt)	D§ 60 89	5	32
Galwick Airport	58	4	24
GATWICK AIRPORT	58	4	24
GLYNDE	*	4	40
GODSTONE	*	4	34
GOMSHALL + Sheire	* 80	4	04
GORING-BY-SEA		4	00
Grange Road for Crawley Down + Turner's Hill	*	4	33
GUILDFORD LONDON ROAD		4	05
Ham Bridge Halt	C§ 49	4	10
Hartfield	* 67	4	43
HASSOCKS		4	31
HAYWARDS HEATH		4	32
Henfield	* 64	4	11
HEVER		4	44
Holland Road Halt	56	4	30
HOLMWOOD		4	14
HORLEY		4	24
HORSHAM		4	13
HORLEY		4	24
Horsted Keynes	† 62 62	5	32
HOVE		4	20
HURST GREEN Halt	61	4	45
IFIELD		4	23
Isfield	* 69 RO	6	41
(KETCHES FARM HALT)	D§ 89	5	32
Kingscote for Turner's Hill	58 94	5	33
KINGSWOOD + Burgh Heath	68	4	25
LANCING		4	10
Lancing Works Platform	64	4	10
LEATHERHEAD		4	15
LEWES		4	40
LINGFIELD		4	34
LITTLEHAMPTON		4	00
LITTLEHAVEN Halt	69	4	13
LONDON ROAD BRIGHTON		4	30
LONDON ROAD GUILDFORD		4	05
MARINA (BLACK ROCK)		7	30
MERSTHAM		4	25
MOULSCOOMB	80	4	30
NEWHAVEN Boat Station MARINE	84	4	49†
NEWHAVEN HARBOUR		4	40
NEWHAVEN TOWN		4	40
Newick + Chailey	55 56 58	4	32
NUTFIELD	*	4	34
OCKLEY + Capel	52 80	4	14
OXTED		4	35
Partridge Green	* 66	4	11
PASTON PLACE		7	30
PLUMPTON	*	4	31
PORTSLADE West Hove	80	4	20
PRESTON PARK		4	30
PULBOROUGH		4	01
REDHILL		4	25
REIGATE		4	25
Row Fant	* 67	4	33
Rudgwick	* 65	4	03
SALFORDS		4	24
SEAFORD		4	49†
SHALFORD		4	04
Sheffield Park	58 60	5	42
SHOREHAM-BY-SEA		4	20
Slinfold	* 65	4	13
SMITHAM		4	25
SOUTHEASE + Rodmell Halt	* 80 69	4	40
Southwater	* 66	4	12
SOUTHWICK		4	20
Steyning	* 66	4	11
TADWORTH + Walton-on-Hill	68	4	25
TATTENHAM CORNER		4	25
THREE BRIDGES for East Crawley		4	23
UCKFIELD	*	4	41
UPPER WARLINGHAM		4	35
Warlingham + Cane Hill	E§ 56	4	35
WARNHAM		4	13
Westerham	61	4	45
West Grinstead	* 64	4	12
West Hoathley	58 RO	5	33
WEST WORTHING		4	10
WHYTELEAFE		4	35
WHYTELEAFE SOUTH	E§ 56	4	35
Withyham	* 67	4	53
WIVELSFIELD		4	31
WOKING		4	05
WOLDINGHAM		4	35
WOODMANSTERNE		4	25
WORTHING Central	68	4	10

GOODS

No	Name/Location	Closed	Ry	Ref
G1	Brighton Lewes Road	71	4	30
2	Brighton Kemp Town	71	4	30
3	Holland Road Hove	71	4	20
4	Brighton	71	4	30

COMPANY WORKS

No	Name	Closed	Ry	Ref
C1	Brighton	64	4	20
2	Lancing	62	4	10

ENGINE SHEDS

No	Name/Location	Closed	Ry	Ref
E1	Brighton	64	4	30
2	Horsham	64	4	13
3	Newhaven	63	4	40
4	Three Bridges	64	4	23
5	EFFINGHAM JUNCTION	3 O	4	15
6	Redhill	65	4	24

TUNNELS

No	Name	Length	Ry	Ref
T1	Clayton	2259	4	21 31
2	Cliftonville	536	4	20
3	Hove	231	4	30
4	Kemp Town	1024	4	30
5	Patcham	488	4	20
6	Haywards Heath	250	4	32
7	Falmer	495	4	30
8	Kingston	103	4	40
9	Balacombe	1133	4	23
10	Sharpthorpe	730	4	33
11	Rudgwick	330	4	03
12	East Grinstead No.1	78	4	43
13	East Grinstead No 2	48	4	43
14	Lywood	218	4	32
15	Lewes	397	4	41
16	North Stoke	84	4	01
17	Cinder Hill	63	4	32
18	Bookham	91	4	15
19	Mickleham	524	4	15
20	Merstham New or Quarry	2113	4	35
21	Merstham Old	1831	4	25
22	Kingswood	310	4	25
23	Hoppity	37	4	25
24	Woldingham or Oxted	2266	4	35
25	Limpsfield	550	4	35
26	Edenbridge	319	4	44
27	Bletchingley	1327	4	34
28	Redhill	502	4	24
29	Betchworth	385	4	14
30	Mark Beech	1338	4	44

JUNCTIONS

No	Name	Ry	Ref
J1	Kemp Town	4	30
2	Montpelier	4	30
3	Crowhurst North	4	44
4	Crowhurst South	4	44
5	Dyke	4	20
6	Shoreham	4	20
7	Southerham	4	40
8	Culver	4	41
9	Hardham	4	01
10	Arundel North	4	00
11	Arundel South	4	00
12	Keymer	4	31
13	Copyhold	4	32
14	Stammerham	4	12
15	Itchingfield	4	12
16	St Margarets	4	33

NOTES

REF All in TQ except for three stations in TV marked † in Ref column.

§ Older version } Change of name
§ New version }

Identical letters refer to other version.

1 Rebuilt in 68 on adjoining site.

2 Name change in 53 became one word FAYGATE.

3 Shed opened in 20's for storage of multiple electric units.

78

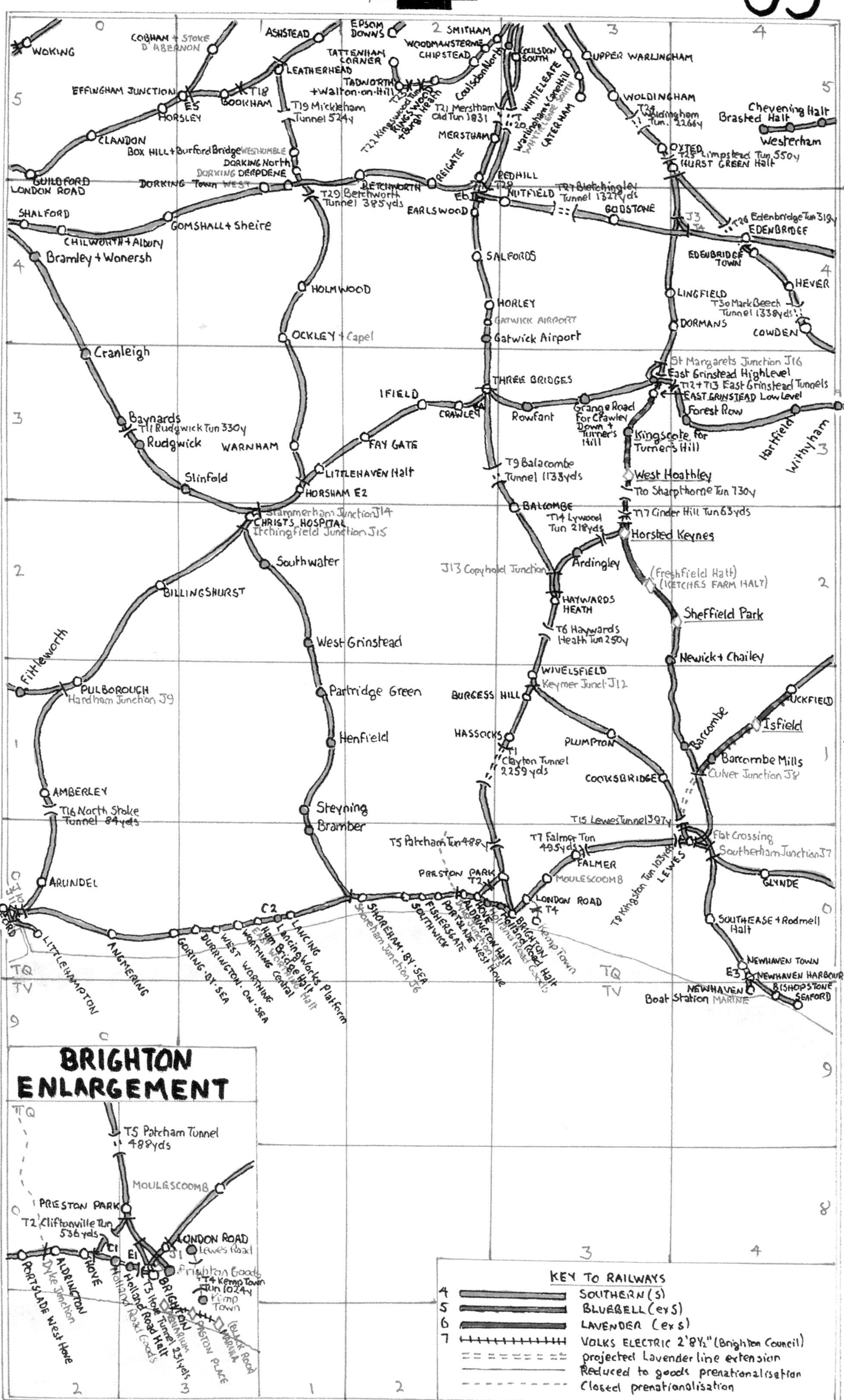
WOKING
COBHAM + STOKE D'ABERNON
ASHSTEAD
EPSOM DOWNS
SMITHAM
WOODMANSTERNE
CHIPSTEAD
TATTENHAM CORNER
LEATHERHEAD
TADWORTH + Walton-on-Hill
EFFINGHAM JUNCTION
BOOKHAM
HORSLEY
T19 Mickleham Tunnel 524y
T21 Merstham Old Tun 1831
COULSDON SOUTH
Coulsdon North
WHYTELEAFE
UPPER WARLINGHAM
WOLDINGHAM
Woldingham Tun. 2266y
Chevening Halt
Brasted Halt
Westerham
CLANDON
BOX HILL + Burford Bridge WESTHUMBLE
DORKING North
DORKING DEEPDENE
DORKING Town WEST
MERSTHAM
REIGATE
BETCHWORTH
T29 Betchworth Tunnel 385yds
REDHILL
NUTFIELD
EARLSWOOD
T27 Bletchingley Tunnel 1327yds
GODSTONE
OXTED
T25 Limpstead Tun 550y
HURST GREEN Halt
CATERHAM
GUILDFORD LONDON ROAD
SHALFORD
CHILWORTH + Albury
GOMSHALL + Sheire
Bramley + Wonersh
T26 Edenbridge Tun 319y
EDENBRIDGE
EDENBRIDGE TOWN
HEVER
T30 Mark Beech Tunnel 1338yds
COWDEN
SALFORDS
HORLEY
GATWICK AIRPORT
Gatwick Airport
HOLMWOOD
OCKLEY + Capel
LINGFIELD
DORMANS
Cranleigh
St Margarets Junction J16
East Grinstead High Level
T12 + T13 East Grinstead Tunnels
EAST GRINSTEAD Low Level
Forest Row
THREE BRIDGES
IFIELD
CRAWLEY
Rowfant
Grange Road for Crawley Down + Turner's Hill
Kingscote for Turner's Hill
Hartfield
Withyham
Baynards
T11 Rudgwick Tun 330y
Rudgwick
WARNHAM
FAY GATE
LITTLEHAVEN Halt
HORSHAM
T9 Balcombe Tunnel 1133yds
West Hoathley
T10 Sharpthorne Tun 730y
Slinfold
Stammerham Junction J14
CHRIST'S HOSPITAL
Itchingfield Junction J15
BALCOMBE
T14 Lywood Tun 218yds
T17 Cinder Hill Tun 63yds
Horsted Keynes
Southwater
J13 Copyhold Junction
Ardingley
(Freshfield Halt)
(KETCHES FARM HALT)
BILLINGSHURST
HAYWARDS HEATH
T6 Haywards Heath Tun 250y
Sheffield Park
West Grinstead
Fittleworth
PULBOROUGH
Hardham Junction J9
WIVELSFIELD
Keymer Junct J12
Newick + Chailey
Partridge Green
BURGESS HILL
Uckfield
Isfield
Henfield
HASSOCKS
T1 Clayton Tunnel 2259yds
PLUMPTON
Barcombe
Barcombe Mills
Culver Junction J8
AMBERLEY
T16 North Stoke Tunnel 84yds
COOKSBRIDGE
Steyning
Bramber
T15 Lewes Tunnel 397y
T5 Patcham Tun 488y
T7 Falmer Tun 495yds
Flat Crossing
Southerham Junction J7
LEWES
FALMER
PRESTON PARK
MOULESCOOMB
ARUNDEL
T8 Kingston Tun 103yds
GLYNDE
LONDON ROAD
T4
LITTLEHAMPTON
ANGMERING
GORING-BY-SEA
DURRINGTON-ON-SEA
WEST WORTHING
WORTHING Central
EAST WORTHING Halt
Ham Bridge Halt
LANCING
Lancing Works Platform
SHOREHAM-BY-SEA
Shoreham Junction J6
SOUTHWICK
FISHERSGATE
PORTSLADE West Hove
ALDRINGTON Halt
HOVE
BRIGHTON
Holland Road Halt
Kemp Town
SOUTHEASE + Rodmell Halt
NEWHAVEN TOWN
NEWHAVEN HARBOUR
NEWHAVEN
Boat Station MARINE
BISHOPSTONE
SEAFORD
TQ
TV
BRIGHTON ENLARGEMENT
T5 Patcham Tunnel 488yds
MOULESCOOMB
PRESTON PARK
T2 Cliftonville Tun 536yds
LONDON ROAD
Lewes Road
Brighton Goods
T4 Kemp Town Tun 1024y
Kemp Town
ALDRINGTON
Dyke Junction
PORTSLADE West Hove
HOVE
Holland Road Goods
T3 Hove Tunnel 23yds
Holland Road Halt
BRIGHTON
AQUARIUM
PASTON PLACE
MARINA
(BLACK ROCK)
KEY TO RAILWAYS
4 SOUTHERN (S)
5 BLUEBELL (ex S)
6 LAVENDER (ex S)
7 VOLKS ELECTRIC 2'8½" (Brighton Council)
projected Lavender line extension
Reduced to goods prenationalisation
Closed prenationalisation

92

94

MAIDSTONE, TUNBRIDGE + HASTINGS

RAILWAYS

No	Company
4	SOUTHERN (S)
3	KENT + EAST SUSSEX (Light)
3X	KENT + EAST SUSSEX (Preserved)
3X	KENT + EAST SUSSEX (Preserved - proposed)

STATIONS

Station	Closed / Opened	Ry Ref
APPLEDORE	*	4 93
ASHURST		4 53
AYLESFORD		4 75
BARMING		4 75
BAT + BALL	A § 50	4 55
BATTLE		4 71
BEARSTED + Thurnham	80	4 75
BELTRING + Banbridges (Halt 69)	80	4 64
BERWICK	*	4 50
BEXHILL Central	70	4 70
Bexhill West	* 64	4 70
Biddenden	54	3 83
Bodiham	58 80	3X 72
BOROUGH GREEN + WROXAM	B § 62	4 65
Brookland Halt	* 67	4 92
BUXTED	*	4 52
CHARING		4 94
COLLINGTON Halt	69	4 70
COODEN BEACH		4 70
Cranbrook	61	4 73
CROWBOROUGH + Jarvis Brook	80	4 52
CROWHURST	*	4 71
DOLEHAM Halt	* 69	4 81
DUNTON GREEN		4 55
EASTBOURNE		4 60
EAST FARLEIGH		4 75
EAST MALLING Halt	69	4 75
ERIDGE		4 53
ETCHINGHAM		4 72
FRANT	*	4 63
Frittenden Road	54	3 84
Goudhurst	61	4 73
Groombridge	* 85	4 53
Hailsham	* 68	4 50
HAMPDEN PARK		4 60
HAM STREET + Orleston	* 76	4 93
HARRIETSHAM		4 85
HASTINGS		4 81
Hawkhurst	61	4 73
Headcorn	54	3 84
HEADCORN		4 84
Heathfield	* 65	4 52
Hellingley	* 65	4 51
(Hexden Bridge)	1 83?	3X 82
HIGH BROOMS		4 54
High Halden Road		3 83
High Rocks Halt	52	4 53
HILDENBOROUGH		4 54
HOLLINGBOURNE		4 85
Horam	D § * 53 65	4 51
Horsmorden	61	4 74
Hothfield Halt	59	4 94
Junction Road	2 57	3X 72
KEMSING		4 55
LEIGH	* C § 60	4 54
LENHAM		4 85
Lyghe Halt	C § 60	4 54
MAIDSTONE BARRACKS		4 75
MAIDSTONE EAST		4 75
MAIDSTONE WEST		4 75
MALLING, WEST	49	4 65
MARDEN		4 74
Mayfield	* 65	4 52
Mountfield Halt	* 69	4 72
NEW HYTHE		4 75
NORMANS BAY Halt	69	4 60
Northiam	54 90	3X 82
ORE		4 81
OTFORD		4 55
PADDOCK WOOD		4 64
PENSHURST	*	4 54
PEVENSEY + WESTHAM		4 60
PEVENSEY BAY Halt	69	4 60
PLUCKLEY		4 94
POLEGATE	3	4 50
ROBERTSBRIDGE	4	4(3X) 72
Rolvenden	54 74	3X 83
Rotherfield + Mark Cross	* 65	4 53
RYE	*	4 92
ST LEONARDS WARRIOR SQUARE		4 81
ST LEONARDS, WEST		4 71
St Leonards West Marina		4 70
Salehurst	2 54	3X 72
Sevenoaks BAT + BALL	A § 50	4 85
SEVENOAKS + Tub Hill	50	4 85
Sidley	* 64	4 70
Snailham Halt	59	4 81
STAPLEHURST		4 74
STONEGATE	*	4 62
Tenterden St Michaels	54	3 83
Tenterden Town	54 74	3X 83
Teston Crossing Halt	59	4 75
THREE OAKS + Guestling (Halt 69)	* 80	4 81
TONBRIDGE		4 54
TUNBRIDGE WELLS Central	85	4 54
Tunbridge Wells West	* 85	4 53
WADHURST	*	4 63
Waldron + Horam	D § 53	4 51
WATERINGBURY		4 65
WEST MALLING	49	4 65
WEST ST LEONARDS		4 71
WINCHELSEA Halt	* 61 69	4 81
Withyham	* 67	4 53
Wittersham Road	54 77	3X 82
Wrotham + Borough Green	B § 62	4 65
YALDING		4 65

GOODS

No	Location	Closed	Ry Ref
G1	Torvil	77	4 75

ENGINE SHEDS

No	Name/Location	Closed	Ry Ref
E1	Eastbourne	52	4 60
2	ST LEONARDS	5 0	4 71
3	Tonbridge	64	4 54
4	Tunbridge Wells	63	4 54

TUNNELS

No	Name	Length	Ry Ref
T1	Grove	190	4 53
2	Grove Hill	287	4 54
3	Wells	823	4 54
4	Strawberry Hill	286	4 53
5	Wheeler Street	358	4 75
6	Bo-Peep	1318	4 71
7	Hastings	788	4 81
8	Heathfield	266	4 55
9	Somerhill	410	4 54
10	Best Beech Hill	1205	4 63
11	Sevenoaks	3453	4 55
12	Polhill	2612	4 55
13	Hawkhurst		4 73
14	London Road	63	4 75
15	Mountfield	526	4 72
16	Ore	1402	4 81
17	Mount Pleasant	230	4 81
18	Crowborough	1022	4 52

JUNCTIONS

No	Name	Ry	Ref
J1	Grove	4	53
2	Willingdon	4	60
3	Redgate Mill	4	53
4	Birchenden	4	53
5	Vestry North	4	55
6	Vestry South	4	55
7	Vestry East	4	55
8	Westerham Branch	4	55
9	Stone Cross	4	60
10	Bo-Peep	4	70
11	Lydd	4	92

NOTES:

REF All gazetteer entries within TQ, therefore letters in reference omitted.

§ Older version } Change of name
§ Newer version

Identical letters refer to other version

1 Temporary station pending further extension of preserved line
2 Proposed extension of preserved line
3 Rebuilt on adjoining site in '86.
4 Proposed to also accomodate extension of preserved line
5 Closed for steam in '58.

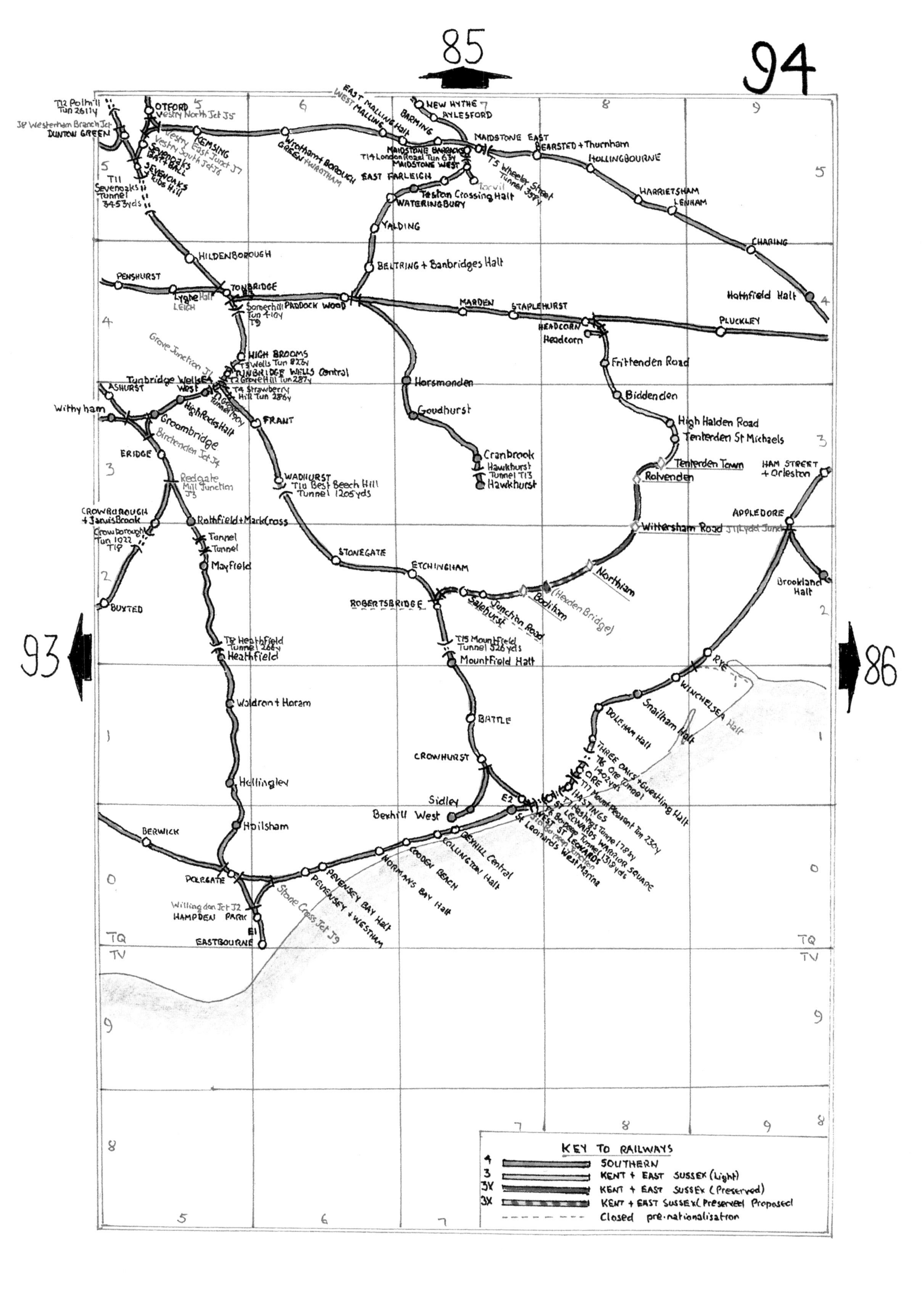
85
93
86
OTFORD
Vestry North Jct J5
DUNTON GREEN
KEMSING
Vestry East Junct J7
Vestry South Jct J6
SEVENOAKS
Tubs Hill
T11 Sevenoaks Tunnel 3453yds
HILDENBOROUGH
PENSHURST
TONBRIDGE
Somerhill Tun 410y
T9
PADDOCK WOOD
HIGH BROOMS
T3 Wells Tun 823y
TUNBRIDGE WELLS Central
T2 Grove Hill Tun 287y
T4 Strawberry Hill Tun 286y
Grove Junction J1
Tunbridge Wells West
ASHURST
Withyham
Groombridge
High Rocks Halt
ERIDGE
Birchenden Jct J4
Redgate Mill Junction J3
FRANT
WADHURST
T10 Best Beech Hill Tunnel 1205yds
CROWBOROUGH + Jarvis Brook
Crowborough Tun 1022 T18
Rotherfield + Mark Cross
Tunnel
Mayfield
BUXTED
T8 Heathfield Tunnel 266y
Heathfield
Waldron + Horam
Hellingly
Hailsham
BERWICK
POLEGATE
Willingdon Jct J2
HAMPDEN PARK
E1
EASTBOURNE
Stone Cross Jct J9
PEVENSEY + WESTHAM
PEVENSEY BAY Halt
NORMANS BAY Halt
COODEN BEACH
COLLINGTON Halt
BEXHILL Central
Bexhill West
Sidley
CROWHURST
BATTLE
Mountfield Halt
T15 Mountfield Tunnel 526 yds
ROBERTSBRIDGE
Salehurst
Junction Road
Bodiam
(Hexden Bridge)
Northiam
ETCHINGHAM
STONEGATE
E2
WEST ST LEONARDS
St Leonards West Marina
WARRIOR SQUARE
HASTINGS
ORE
T17 Mount Pleasant Tun 230y
T16 Ore Tunnel 1402yds
THREE OAKS + Guestling Halt
DOLEHAM Halt
Snailham Halt
WINCHELSEA Halt
RYE
APPLEDORE
J11 Lydd Junct
Brookland Halt
HAM STREET + Orleston
Wittersham Road
Rolvenden
Tenterden Town
Tenterden St Michaels
High Halden Road
Biddenden
Frittenden Road
HEADCORN
Headcorn
PLUCKLEY
STAPLEHURST
MARDEN
Horsmonden
Goudhurst
Cranbrook
Hawkhurst Tunnel T13
Hawkhurst
BELTRING + Banbridges Halt
YALDING
WATERINGBURY
Teston Crossing Halt
EAST FARLEIGH
MAIDSTONE WEST
MAIDSTONE BARRACKS
T14 London Road Tun 631
MAIDSTONE EAST
T5 Wheeler Street Tunnel 357y
BEARSTED + Thurnham
HOLLINGBOURNE
HARRIETSHAM
LENHAM
CHARING
Hothfield Halt
BARMING
EAST MALLING Halt
WEST MALLING
NEW HYTHE
AYLESFORD
Wrotham + BOROUGH GREEN
Lyghe Halt
LEIGH
TQ
TV
KEY TO RAILWAYS
4 SOUTHERN
3 KENT + EAST SUSSEX (Light)
3X KENT + EAST SUSSEX (Preserved)
3X KENT + EAST SUSSEX (Preserved Proposed)
Closed pre-nationalisation

REDRUTH, TRURO + PENZANCE

RAILWAYS

No	Company
3	GREAT WESTERN (GW)
4	SOUTHERN (S)

GOODS

No	Name	Closed	Ry Ref
1	Hayle Wharves	67	3 53
2	Padstow Quay	64	4 97
3	Wadebridge Quay	73	4 97
12	Treamble Branch		3 85
13	Newham Branch		3 84
14	Roskear		3 63
15	Padstow Quay Branch		4 97

STATIONS

Name	Opened closed	Ry Ref
CAMBORNE		3 63
CARBIS BAY	*	3 53
Carn Brea	61	3 64
Chacewater	* 64	3 74
FALMOUTH DOCKS	89	3 83
FALMOUTH TOWN	I § 70 75 89	3 83
Goonbell Halt	† 63	3 75
Goonhaven Halt	† 63	3 75
Grampound Road	* 64	3 94
Gwinear Road	* 64	3 53
HAYLE	*	3 53
Helston	† 62	3 62
LELANT Halt	* 59 69	3 53
LELANT SALTINGS	90	3 53
Marazion	* 64	3 53
Mitchell + Newlyn Halt	† 63	3 85
Mithian Halt	† 63	3 75
Mount Hawke Halt	† 63	3 74
Nancegollan	† 62	3 63
NEWQUAY		3 84
Padstow	* 67	4 97
PENMERE Platform	69	3 73
PENRYN		3 73
PENZANCE		3 43
Perranporth	† 63	3 75
Perranporth Beach Halt	† 63	3 75
PERRANWELL		3 73
Praze	† 62	3 63
Probus + Ladock Platform	57	3 84
QUINTREL DOWNS Platform	* 56	3 86
REDRUTH		3 74
ROCHE	*	3 96
St Agnes	† 63	3 74
ST COLOMB ROAD	*	3 95
ST ERTH		3 53
ST IVES	*	3 53
Scorrier	* 64	3 74
Shepherds	† 63	3 85
The Dell	I A § 75 89	3 83
Trewerry + Trerice Halt	† 63	3 85
TRURO		3 84
Truthall Platform	† 62	3 62
Wadebridge	* 67	4 97

ENGINE SHEDS

No	Name/Location	Closed	Ry Ref
E1	Helston	63	3 62
2	PENZANCE	2	43
3	St Ives	61	3 53
4	Truro	2 65	3 84
5	Wadebridge	3 65	4 97

TUNNELS

No	Name/Location	Length	Ry Ref
T1	Coswath	31	3 86
2	Higher Town, Truro	70	3 84
3	Buckshead	320	3 84
4	Polperro	581	3 84
5	Sparnick	491	3 74
6	Perran	374	3 73

VIADUCTS + BRIDGES

No	Name/Location	Ry	Ref
V1	Carron Viaduct	3	74
2	Tregarne Viaduct	3	84
3	Coombe St Stephen Viaduct	3	95
4	Guildford Viaduct	3	53
5	Angarrack Viaduct	3	53
6	Chacewater Viaduct (Blackwater)	3	74
7	Perran Viaduct	3	73
8	Ponsanooth Viaduct	3	73
9	Collegewood Viaduct	3	73
10	Cober Viaduct	3	62

JUNCTIONS

No	Name	Ry	Ref
J1	St Ives Branch	3	53
2	Wharves Branch	3	53
3	Helston Branch	3	63
4	Chacewater East	3	74
5	Tolcarn	3	86
6	Treloggan	3	86
7	Lane	3	86
8	St Denis	3	96
9	Burngullow	3	95
10	Dinnick Mill	3	95
11	Penwithers	3	84

NOTES:

REF All in SW so letters omitted.

§ Older version } Change of name
§ Newer version

1 Name changes and dates of change are as follows

START DATE	NAME	END DATE
70	FALMOUTH TOWN	75
75	The Dell	89
89	FALMOUTH TOWN	

2 Closed to steam '62

3 Closure for steam continued for stabling of diesels.

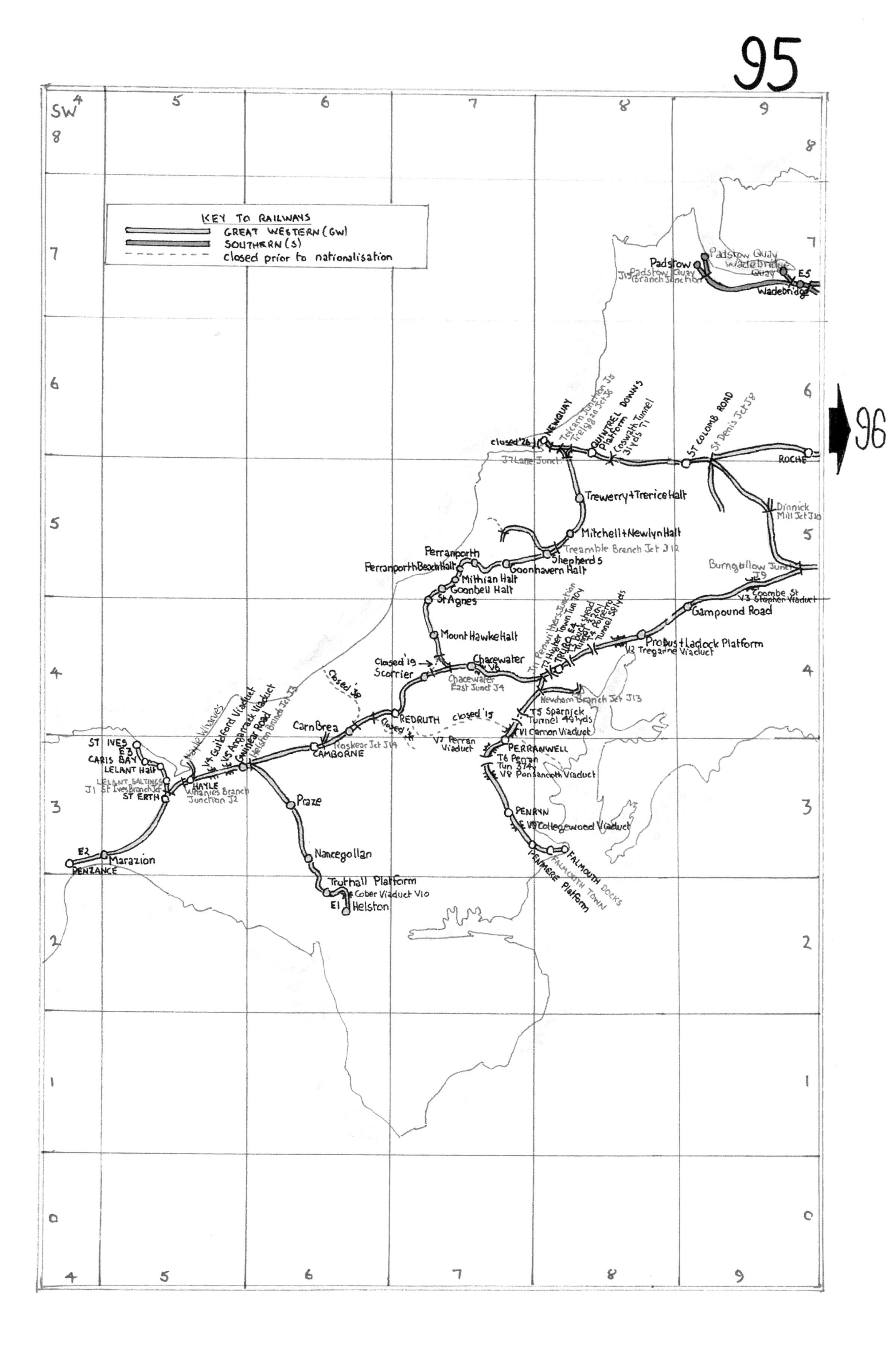

SW
KEY TO RAILWAYS
GREAT WESTERN (GW)
SOUTHERN (S)
closed prior to nationalisation
Padstow
Padstow Quay
Wadebridge Quay
Wadebridge
E5
NEWQUAY
QUINTREL DOWNS Platform
Coswarth Tunnel 31yds T1
ST COLOMB ROAD
St Dennis Jct J8
ROCHE
Trewerry+Trerice Halt
Mitchell+Newlyn Halt
Treamble Branch Jct J12
Dinnick Mill Jct J10
Burngullow Junct J9
Coombe St Stephen Viaduct
Grampound Road
Probus+Ladock Platform
V2 Tregarne Viaduct
Perranporth
Perranporth Beach Halt
Shepherds
Goonhavern Halt
Mithian Halt
Goonbell Halt
St Agnes
Mount Hawke Halt
Chacewater
Chacewater East Junct J4
Scorrier
closed '19
closed '38
REDRUTH
closed '15
Carn Brea
CAMBORNE
Roskear Jct J14
V7 Perran Viaduct
TRURO
Newham Branch Jct J13
T5 Sparnick Tunnel 491yds
V1 Carnon Viaduct
PERRANWELL
T6 Penryn Tun 374y
V8 Ponsanooth Viaduct
PENRYN
V9 Collegewood Viaduct
FALMOUTH DOCKS
FALMOUTH TOWN
PENMERE Platform
ST IVES
E3
CARIS BAY
LELANT Halt
LELANT SALTINGS
J1 St Ives Branch Jct
ST ERTH
HAYLE
Hayle Wharves
Wharves Branch Junction J2
V4 Guildford Viaduct
V5 Angarrack Viaduct
Gwinear Road
Helston Branch Jct J3
Praze
Nancegollan
Truthall Platform
Cober Viaduct V10
E1
Helston
E2
Marazion
PENZANCE
96

BODMIN, PLYMOUTH, TOTNES + NEWTON ABBOT

RAILWAYS

No	Company
1	PAIGNTON + DARTMOUTH (ex GW)
2	BODMIN + WENFORD (ex GW and to be partly ex S)
3	GREAT WESTERN (GW)
4	SOUTHERN (S)
5	SOUTH DEVON (ex GW)

STATIONS

Name	Opened / closed	Ry	Ref
Ashburton	1 58 69 71	5	77
Avonwick	† 63	3	75
BERE ALSTON	*	4	46
BERE FERRERS	*	4	46
Bickleigh	† 62	3	56
Bittaford Platform	59	3	65
Bodmin General	* 49 67 RO	2	06
Bodmin North	* 49 67	4	06
BODMIN Road PARKWAY	2 84	32	16
Boscarne Exchange Platform	3 64	234	06
Bovey	59	3	87
Brent	* 64	3	76
Brimley Halt	59	3	87
Britannia Halt	4 72 72	1	85
Brixham	† 63	3	95
Buckfastleigh	58 69	5	76
BUGLE	*	3	05
Burrator Halt	56	3	56
Callington for Stoke Climsland	* 49 66	4	37
CALSTOCK	*	4	46
CAUSELAND	*	3	25
Chilsworthy	* 66	4	47
Chudleigh	58	3	87
Chudleigh Knighton Halt	58	3	87
Churston Junction	4 * 72 72	1	85
Clearbrook Halt	† 62	3	56
(COLESLOGGET HALT)	0	2	06
COOMBE	*	3	26
Cornwood	59	3	55
(DARTMOUTH FERRY †) Kingswear	A§ 4 72 72	1	85
DAWLISH		3	97
DAWLISH WARREN		3	97
DEVONPORT Albert Road	49 68	3	45
Devonport Kings Road	* 49 64	4	45
Devonport Barracks	54	3	45
DOCKYARD Halt	69	3	45
Doublebois	* 64	3	26
Dousland	56	3	56
Dunmere Halt	* 67	4	06
Ford	* 64	4	45
Fowey	5 * 65	3	15
Gara Bridge	† 63	4	75
Golant Halt	* 65	3	15
Goodrington Sands	4 72 72	1	85
Grogley Halt	* 67	4	06
GUNNISLAKE	*	4	47
Heathfield	59	3	87
Horrabridge	† 62	3	56
Ingra Tor Halt	56	3	57
Ivy Bridge	59 94	3	65
KEYHAM		3	45
Kingsbridge	† 63	3	74
Kingskerswell	* 64	3	86
Kingswear	4 A§ 72 72 77	1	85
King Tor Halt	56	3	57
Latchley Halt	* 66	4	47
LISKEARD		3	26
Loddiswell Halt	† 61 63	3	74
LOOE	*	3	25
LOSTWITHIEL	*	3	16
Lucas Terrace Halt	51	4	45
Luckett	* 66	4	37
LUXULYAN	*	3	05
Marsh Mills	† 62	3	55
Marytavy + Blackdown	† 62	3	47
MENHENIOT	*	3	26
Millbay SEE PLYMOUTH G		3	45
Nanstallon Halt	* 67	4	06
NEWTON ABBOT		3	87
North Road SEE PLYMOUTH		3	45
Oreston	51	4	55
PAIGNTON		3	86
(PAIGNTON QUEENS PARK)	74	1	86
PAR		3	05
Plym Bridge Platform	† 62	3	56
PLYMOUTH			45
DOCKYARD Halt		3	45
Friary	58	4	45
North Road, PLYMOUTH	6 58	3	45
Plympton	59	3	55
Plymstock	51	4	55
Port Isaac Road	* 66	4	07
Princetown	56	3	57
(RIVERSIDE, TOTNES)	69	5	76
ST AUSTELL		3	05
ST BUDEAUX Platform FERRY ROAD	49	3	45
ST BUDEAUX VICTORIA ROAD	* 49	4	45
ST GERMANS Halt	65 69	3	35
St Kew Highway	* 66	4	07
ST KEYNE	*	3	26
SALTASH		3	45
SANDPLACE Halt	* 53 69	3	25
Shaugh Bridge Platform	† 62	3	56
Staverton (Bridge)	58 69	5	76
Tamerton Foliot	62	4	46
Tavistock North	* 68	4	47
Tavistock South	† 62	3	47
Teigngrace	59	3	87
TEIGNMOUTH		3	97
TORQUAY		3	96
TORRE		3	96
TOTNES		3	76
(TOTNES RIVERSIDE)	69	5	76
Turnchapel	51	4	45
Whitchurch Down Platform	† 62	3	47
Wrangaton	59	3	65
Yelverton	† 62	3	56

GOODS

No	Name/Location	Closed	Ry	Ref
G1	Steer Point	60	3	55
2	Yealampton	60	3	55
3	Totnes Quay	65	3	86
4	Wenford	67	4	07
5	Plymouth Millbay Docks	71	3	45

SUMMITS

No	Name	Height	Ry	Ref
S1	Rattery (Wrangaton)		3	65
2	Dainton		3	86

ENGINE SHEDS

No	Name/Location	Closed	Ry	Ref
E1	Ashburton	58	3	77
2	Bodmin	62	3	06
3	Callington	64	4	37
4	Kingsbridge	61	3	74
5	Moorswater	60	3	26
6	Newton Abbot	62	3	87
7	Plymouth Dock	55	3	45
8	Plymouth Friary	63	4	45
9	PLYMOUTH Laira (Steam 64)	0	3	45
10	Princetown	56	3	57
11	ST BLAZEY (Steam 62)	0	3	05

TUNNELS

No	Name/Location	Length	Ry	Ref
T1	Devonport Tunnels No1 + No2		4	45
2	Mutley	183	3	45
3	Phillot	49	3	97
4	Coryton	227	3	97
5	Kennaway	205	3	97
6	Greenaway	495	3	85
7	Marley	869	3	76
8	Dainton	264	3	86
9	Sorley	638	3	74
10	Shaugh	367	3	56
11	Yelverton	641	3	56
12	Greenopen	374	3	44
13	Shillingham	451	3	35
14	Brownqueen	88	3	16
15	Treverrin	565	3	05
16	Pinnock	1173	3	05
17	Bridges	50	3	05
18	Gulwell	47	3	76
19	Wrangaton	47	3	65
20	Parsons	513	3	97
21	Clerks	58	3	97

VIADUCTS + BRIDGES

No	Name	Ry	Ref
V1	Royal Albert Bridge	3	45
2	Slade Viaduct	3	55
3	Blachford Viaduct	3	65
4	St German's Viaduct	3	35
5	Notter Viaduct	3	35
6	Coldrennick Viaduct	3	26
7	Tresulgan Viaduct	3	26
8	Penadlike Viaduct	3	16
9	Derrycombe Viaduct	3	16
10	Largin Viaduct	3	16
11	St Pinnox Viaduct	3	16

JUNCTIONS

No	Name	Ry	Ref
J1	Ruthern	4	06
2	Boscarne	234	06
3	Wenford Branch	24	06
4	Carbis	3	06
5	Fowey Branch	3	15
6	Goonbarrow	3	05
7	Trenance	3	05
8	Looe Branch	3	26
9	Friary West	4	45
10	Aller	3	86
11	Teign Valley	3	87
12	Totnes Quay Branch	3	86
13	Ashburton	35	86
14	Brixham Branch	13	85
15	Kingsbridge Branch	3	66
16	Princetown Branch	3	56
17	Laira	3	55

NOTES

REF All in SX therefore letters omitted

§ Older version } Change of name
§ New version

1 Reopened before closing due to motorway.
2 Also re-opened for BODMIN + WENFORD trains
3 Due to re-open for BODMIN + WENFORD
4 Did not actually close, BR ran for local authority pending formalisation of purchase by SOUTH DEVON
5 Opened during summer '94 for excursions
6 Became just PLYMOUTH in '58.

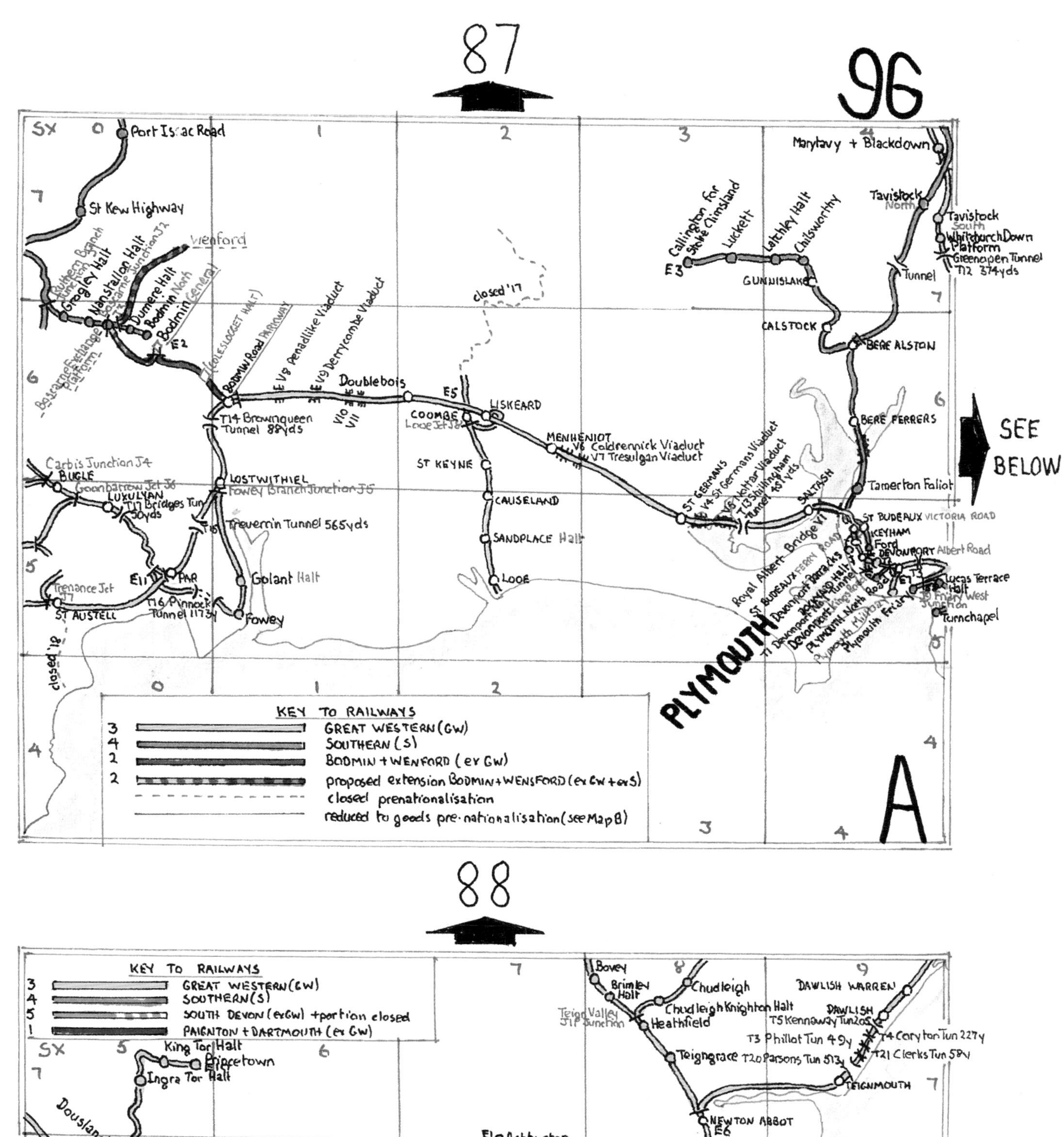
87
96
SX
Port Isaac Road
St Kew Highway
Wenford
Grogley Halt
Nanstallon Halt
Dunmere Halt
Bodmin North
Bodmin General
E2
Bodmin Road
T14 Brownqueen Tunnel 88yds
V8 Penadlake Viaduct
V9 Derrycombe Viaduct
Doublebois
V10
V11
E5
COOMBE
Looe Jct
LISKEARD
closed '17
MENHENIOT
V6 Coldrennick Viaduct
V7 Tresulgan Viaduct
ST KEYNE
CAUSELAND
SANDPLACE Halt
LOOE
Carbis Junction J4
BUGLE
Goonbarrow Jct
LUXULYAN
T17 Bridges Tun 30yds
LOSTWITHIEL
Fowey Branch Junction J5
Treverrin Tunnel 565yds
E11
PAR
Golant Halt
Trenance Jct
ST AUSTELL
T16 Pinnock Tunnel 1173y
Fowey
closed '18
Callington for Stoke Climsland
E3
Luckett
Latchley Halt
Chilsworthy
GUNNISLAKE
CALSTOCK
Marytavy + Blackdown
Tavistock North
Tavistock South
Whitchurch Down Platform
Grenofen Tunnel T12 374yds
Tunnel
BERE ALSTON
BERE FERRERS
Tamerton Foliot
ST GERMANS
SALTASH
Royal Albert Bridge
ST BUDEAUX VICTORIA ROAD
KEYHAM
Ford
DEVONPORT
Albert Road
Lucas Terrace Halt
Turnchapel
PLYMOUTH
SEE BELOW
KEY TO RAILWAYS
3 GREAT WESTERN (GW)
4 SOUTHERN (S)
2 BODMIN + WENFORD (ex GW)
2 proposed extension BODMIN + WENSFORD (ex GW + ex S)
closed prenationalisation
reduced to goods pre-nationalisation (see Map B)
A

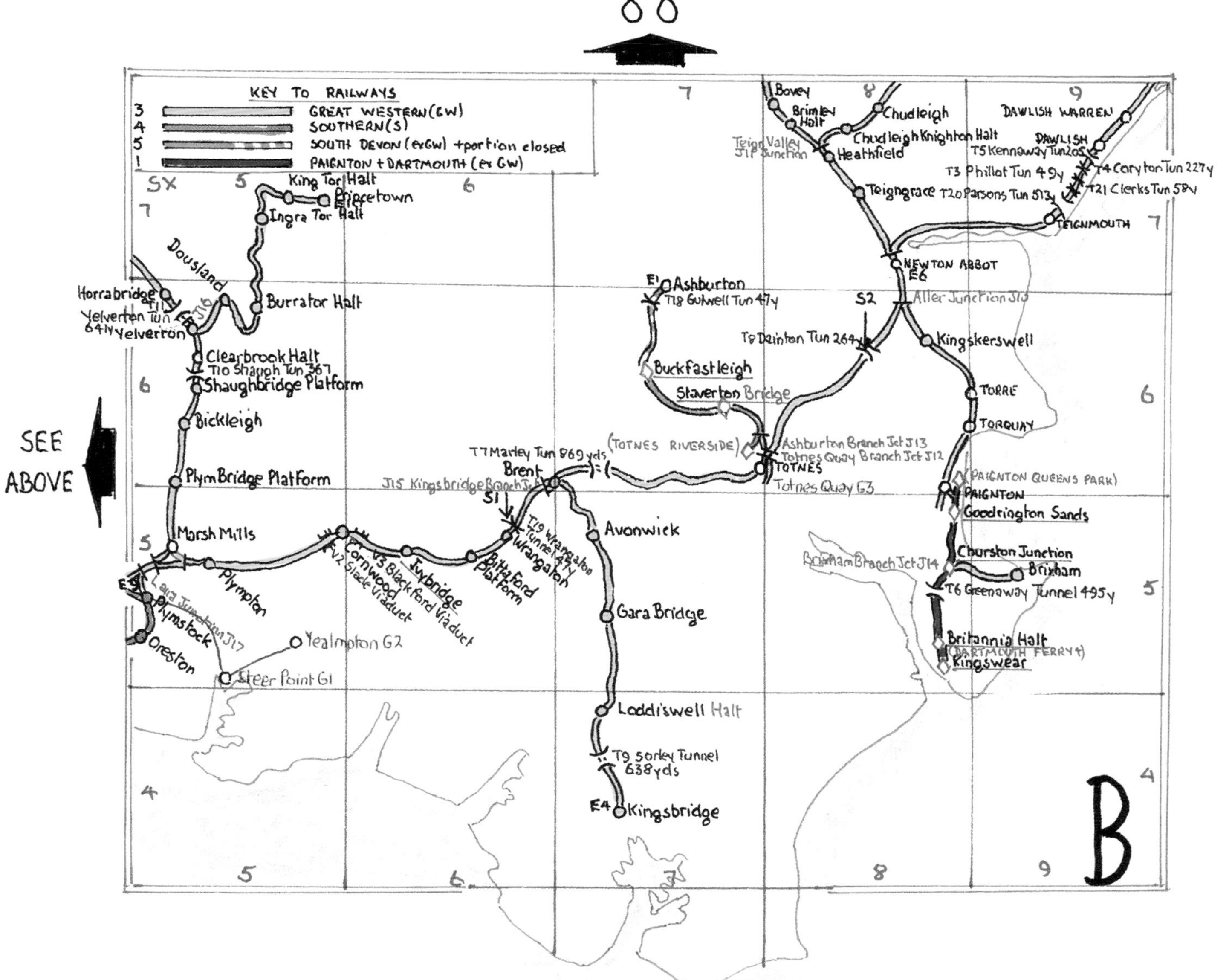
88
KEY TO RAILWAYS
3 GREAT WESTERN (GW)
4 SOUTHERN (S)
5 SOUTH DEVON (ex GW) + portion closed
1 PAIGNTON + DARTMOUTH (ex GW)
SX
King Tor Halt
Princetown
Ingra Tor Halt
Dousland
Burrator Halt
Horrabridge
Yelverton Tun 641y
Yelverton
Clearbrook Halt
T10 Shaugh Tun 367
Shaughbridge Platform
Bickleigh
Plym Bridge Platform
Marsh Mills
Plympton
Plymstock
Oreston
Yealmpton G2
Steer Point G1
Cornwood
V3 Blackford Viaduct
Ivybridge
Bittaford Platform
Wrangaton
T7 Marley Tun 869 yds
Brent
S1
Avonwick
Gara Bridge
Loddiswell Halt
T9 Sorley Tunnel 638yds
E4
Kingsbridge
SEE ABOVE
Bovey
Brimley Halt
Chudleigh
Chudleigh Knighton Halt
Heathfield
Teign Valley Junction
Teigngrace
DAWLISH WARREN
DAWLISH
T5 Kennaway Tun
T3 Phillot Tun 49y
T4 Coryton Tun 227y
T20 Parsons Tun 513y
T21 Clerks Tun 58y
TEIGNMOUTH
NEWTON ABBOT
E6
Aller Junction
S2
E1
Ashburton
T18 Gulwell Tun 47y
T8 Dainton Tun 264y
Kingskerswell
Buckfastleigh
Staverton Bridge
(TOTNES RIVERSIDE)
Ashburton Branch Jct J13
Totnes Quay Branch Jct J12
TOTNES
Totnes Quay G3
TORRE
TORQUAY
(PAIGNTON QUEENS PARK)
PAIGNTON
Goodrington Sands
Churston Junction
Brixham Branch Jct J14
Brixham
T6 Greenaway Tunnel 495y
Britannia Halt
(DARTMOUTH FERRY)
Kingswear
B

BIBLIOGRAPHY

A RAILWAY CLEARING HOUSE PUBLICATIONS

(i) Country Maps

	Map Date
IRELAND	1912
IRELAND	1927
SCOTLAND	1927
SCOTLAND	1960
ENGLAND + WALES	1940
ENGLAND + WALES	1947
ENGLAND + WALES	1950

(ii) District Maps

Edinburgh + Glasgow	1920
Cumberland + Westmorland	1912
Durham + District	1914
Lancashire + Cheshire District	1901
Manchester District	1911
Yorkshire District North	1921
Yorkshire District South	1923
Derby + Nottingham District	1889
South Wales	1926
Gloucestershire + Oxfordshire District	1911
East of England	1917
West of England	1924
London + Environs	1927
South of England	1924

(iii) Other Publications

Railway Junction Diagrams	1928
Handbook of Stations	1938
Handbook of Stations	1956

B OTHER MAP + GAZETTEER SOURCES

(i) Maps + Atlases

Rail Atlas of Great Britain (+ Ireland) Baker OPC — 1977
1st Edition, 7th Edition, 8th Edition — 1992, 1996

Railway Track Diagrams Quail Map Company

Vol		
1	Scotland and the Isle of Man	1993
2	England: East (ex Eastern + Anglia)	1998
3	Western Region	1992
4	London Midland Region	1990
5	England South + London Underground	1994
6	Ireland	1995

Midland Railway System Maps Peter Kay

Vol	
1	Settle + Carlisle (Cumbrian Railways Ass)
2	Leeds-Leicester, Derby-Manchester, Cheshire Lines
3	Leicester-London, Mid + GN, London Tilbury + Southend
4	Birmingham-Bristol, South Wales, Somerset + Dorset
5	Introduction, Location Index, Scotland + Canals
6	Gradient Diagrams

Pre-Grouping Railway Atlas of the British Isles with the up to date situation as at 1989. Alan Jowett

Complete British Railways Maps + Gazetteer 1825-1985 C J Wignall OPC

Atlas of the Great Western Railway RA Cooke WSP

A Railway Atlas of Ireland S M Hajducki D+C

(ii) Chronologies, Timetables, Gazetteer Sources

Opening dates of Public Passenger Stations ME Quick

The Midland Railway - A Chronology John Gough

Chronology of London Railways HV Borley

Directory of Railway Stations RVJ Butt PSL

The Re-shaping of British Railways - The Beeching Report

Private and Untimetabled Railway Stations - Croughton, Kidner + Young - Oakwood Press.

Clinker's Register 1830-1980 CR Clinker - Avon-Anglia

A-Z of Rail Reopenings - Railway Development Society

GWR Timetables October 1947 - OPC Reprint

Bradshaws in particular July 1938, December 1947

BR Timetables in particular 5-10/1993, 9.94 - 5.95.

C OTHER RAILWAY BOOKS

(i) Regional History of the Railways of Great Britain D+C

Vol	Title	Author
1	The West Country	D StJ Thomas
2	Southern England	H P White
3	Greater London	H P White
4	The North East	K Hoole
5	Eastern Counties	DI Gordon
6	Scotland - The Lowlands + Borders	J Thomas
7	The West Midlands	R Christiansen
8	South + West Yorkshire	D Joy
9	The East Midlands	R Lelux
10	The North West	GO Holt
11	North + Mid Wales	PE Baughan
12	South Wales	DSM Barrie
13	Thames + Severn	R Christiansen
14	The Lake Counties	D Joy
15	Scotland - The Highlands	AJS Patterson
16	Ireland	JWP Rowledge

(ii) Forgotten Railways D+C

Vol	Title	Author
	Forgotten Railways Introductory Volume	HP White
1	North East England	K Hoole
2	East Midlands	PH Anderson
3	Chilterns + Cotswolds	Davies + Grant
4	North + Mid Wales	R Christiansen
5	Scotland	J Thomas
6	South East England	H P White
7	East Anglia	RS Joby
8	South Wales	J Page
9	North West England	J Marshall
10	West Midlands	R Christiansen
11	Severn Valley + Welsh Border	R Christiansen

(iii) Engine Sheds

Vol	Title	Author	Publisher
	GW Engine Sheds London Division	Hawkins + Reeve	OPC
	Historical Survey GW Sheds 1947	Lyons	OPC
	1837-1947	Lyons + Mountford	OPC
	Southern Sheds Historical Survey	Hawkins + Reeve	OPC
	LMS Engine Sheds	Hawkins + Reeve	
1	London + North Western		OPC
2	Midland		OPC
3	Lancashire + Yorkshire		OPC
4	Other Smaller English		OPC
5	Caledonian		OPC
6	Highland		Irwell
7	Glasgow + South Western		Irwell
	Great Northern Engine Sheds	Griffiths + Hooper	
1	Southern Area		Irwell
2	Lincolnshire Loop, Notts + Derbys		Challenger
	Great Eastern Engine Sheds Part I	Hawkins + Reeve	WSP
	Great Eastern Engine Sheds Part II	Hawkins + Reeve	WSP
	North Eastern Locomotive Sheds	K Hoole	D+C
	BR Steam Depots Scottish Region	Bolger	IA
	BR Steam Depots ME Region	Bolger	IA

(iv) Others

Encyclopaedia of British Railway Companies	C Awdry	PSL
Encyclopaedia of Narrow Gauge Railways	T Middelmass	PSL
British Railway Workshops	E Larkin	OPC
Over the Summit	C Awdry	SLP
Regional Railway Reviews 4 volumes: Western, Southern + Eastern (2 volumes)	G Body	PSL
History of Great Western Railway 3 vols	McDermott + Nock	IA
History of Southern Railway	Marshall	IA
Great Central 3 vols	Dow	IA
Lancashire + Yorkshire Railway 3 vols	Marshall	D+C

INDEX OF STATIONS

This index includes passenger stations only. The following points should be noted:

(1) Where a place has two or more closely adjoining stations, there will often be only one entry in this index, under the place name.
(2) Where a station is shown on two or more maps at differing scales, this index will normally direct to the map at the "smallest" scale.
(3) Only the map number is shown. Further information will be shown on the facing page gazetteer.
(4) Some unusual station names – where the station is known by its designation alone – are included, for example: CITADEL (Carlisle), TEMPLE MEADS (Bristol) and the London Main Line Termini.
(5) Name changes are usually indexed under old and new names – unless the change consists of dropping part of the title.
(6) Some stations consisting of two elements may be indexed under each element. Inclusion depends upon a period name change or the name consisting of the two elements still in use at the end of the period.

INDEX OF RAILWAYS

In the index which follows, railways open at the terminal date are shown in CAPITAL LETTERS. Closed railways, or those which became part of the nationalised network are shown in lower case lettering. Railways which came into existence after 1·1·1948 are bracketed.

The index is not fully comprehensive. In the case of the older companies these can be excluded if they were short in length and this would particularly be the case if they did not carry passenger traffic, even though they may be shown in the atlas. Also it should be noted that joint lines usually known by the names of the owning partners are excluded. However where a joint line had its own name it will be included, for example: Cheshire Lines Committee or Somerset + Dorset.

With regard to lines still open, there are two types of exclusion here: First, those ex BR lines which whilst using the old track bed have been replaced by a minature railway. Secondly some of the modern Metro systems and others which can be classed as trams or super-trams.